Spiritan Life and Mission since Vatican II

Spiritan Life and Mission since Vatican II

William Cleary

Foreword by
John Fogarty

WIPF & STOCK · Eugene, Oregon

SPIRITAN LIFE AND MISSION SINCE VATICAN II

Copyright © 2018 William Cleary All rights reserved. Except for brief quotations in critical publications or reviews, no part of this book may be reproduced in any manner without prior written permission from the publisher. Write: Permissions, Wipf and Stock Publishers, 199 W. 8th Ave., Suite 3, Eugene, OR 97401.

Wipf & Stock
An Imprint of Wipf and Stock Publishers
199 W. 8th Ave., Suite 3
Eugene, OR 97401

www.wipfandstock.com

PAPERBACK ISBN: 978-1-5326-3469-7
HARDCOVER ISBN: 978-1-5326-3471-0
EBOOK ISBN: 978-1-5326-3470-3

Manufactured in the U.S.A.

Dedication

This work is dedicated to the Young Spiritans with whom I was privileged to share community and mission at Silveira House and Des Places House, Tafara, Harare, Zimbabwe, and to all who live the Spiritan Mission today.

Contents

Foreword by John Fogarty | xi
Acknowledgments | xv
Abbreviations | xvii
Introduction | xxi

Chapter 1. The Spiritan Charism | 1

1. Understanding Charism
2. The Founding Spiritan Charism
3. The Lived Spiritan Charism

Chapter 2. The Spiritan Congregation, Change, and Vatican II | 31

1. The Phenomenon of Change
2. The "French" Congregation of the Holy Spirit
3. A Changing Church and an Unchanging Mgr. Lefebvre
4. The Mgr. Lefebvre Mandate (1962–1968)

Chapter 3. The General Chapter of Renewal | 68

1. A Council Ends and a Chapter Begins
2. The Congregation's *Aggiornamento* Takes Off
3. Understanding the Experience
4. Finding a Way Forward with CDD

Chapter 4. Continuing the Journey of Renewal | 101

1. Apostolic Religious Life in a Vatican II Church
2. A New Missionary Epoch
3. Animation for Spiritan Renewal and Collaboration
4. GC XIV: *Guidelines for Animation*
5. GC XV: "Mission Today"—Justice and Peace
6. The Spiritan Brother and Lay Spiritan

Chapter 5. Writing a Rule | 132

1. A Changed Ecclesial Context
2. Writing and Approving a Text
3. The *Spiritan Rule of Life* (*SRL*)
4. New Beginnings

Chapter 6. From *SRL* to GC XIX (1968–2004) | 168

1. The Superiors General Reports (1992–2004)
2. General Chapters following *SRL* (GC XVII–GC XIX)
3. Enlarged General Council Meetings following *SRL*

Chapter 7. Spiritan Mission | 186

1. The Ecclesial Context for Spiritan Mission since *SRL*
2. Organization for Spiritan Mission
3. Dialogue and Inculturation in Spiritan Mission
4. Spiritan Mission: Justice, Peace, and the Integrity of Creation (JPIC)
5. Education as Spiritan Mission
6. Formation for Mission

Chapter 8. Spiritan Community | 213

1. The Importance of Community Life
2. Diversity of Membership

Chapter 9. Spiritan Religious Life | 228

    1. Different Religious Identities in the Catholic Church

    2. Spiritan Religious Life since *SRL*

Chapter 10. The Rediscovery of the Spiritan Charism | 238

    1. In the Power of the Holy Spirit

    2. Interpreting the Spiritan Journey of Renewal in 2018

    3. The Journey Continues

Bibliography | 251

Foreword

IN A RECENT ADDRESS to the Union of Superiors General in Rome, Fr. Arturo Sosa, SJ, stressed the dynamic and evolutionary nature of the charism of a religious congregation:

> The call of Vatican II to go back to our sources is not an attempt to freeze the charism of an intangible "culture" that is passed on unchanged from generation to generation. On the contrary, it is a call to creative fidelity to the dynamics of incarnation shown by Jesus and to openness to present-day challenges to the mission of consecrated life as part of the church, whose raison d'être lies in evangelizing history.[1]

It is precisely in terms of creative fidelity to the charism of its founders that William Cleary interprets the lengthy and often turbulent process of renewal of the Congregation of the Holy Spirit in the years that followed the Second Vatican Council. His detailed analysis of the principal events in the life of the congregation that engaged the call to renewal and structured its evolving response from the end of the council to the general chapter of 2004 makes fascinating reading and highlights key moments, people, decisions and processes that were essential to its successful outcome. Many members of the congregation who lived through these challenging years and struggled to understand the issues involved, as well as the changing face of the religious-missionary congregation they had joined, will appreciate the author's clear, chronological presentation of the gradual but radical evolution in the self-understanding of the congregation and its mission in parallel with that of the church itself over the years in question.

In the midst of this period, I recall Fr. Damien Byrne, OP, former master general of the Dominican order, addressing an Irish Spiritan provincial chapter and sharing his experience of the difficulty of effecting institutional

---

1. *Interculturality, Catholicity and Consecrated Life*, Union of Superiors General Assembly, May 24–26, 2017.

change. He added, however, that if those entrusted with leadership maintained a clear focus and a commitment to renewal, while change may not be evident on a year-to-year basis, significant transformation can be brought about in the long term. Cleary's research shows the veracity of this claim as well as the various factors which, in addition to good leadership, are important if the end is to be achieved: a desire to be faithful to the church; an ability to live with ambiguity; a confidence in the guidance of the Holy Spirit; a self-confidence within the group in its capacity to overcome internal tension, rooted in its memory of surmounting past adversity; a consistent and continuous process of animation and widespread consultation of the membership by those in leadership through the different means of communication at their disposal.

Of particular interest to many will be the author's detailed historical presentation of the role of the schismatic Mgr. Marcel Lefebvre, superior general of the congregation at the time of Vatican II, and of the ultimate rejection by the congregation as a whole of his intransigence to change. The unprecedented challenge of the 1968 general chapter to Lefebvre's authority represented a defining moment in the process of renewal and shaped the subsequent movement of the congregation from a highly centralized and hierarchical organization to one based on the principle of subsidiarity and respect for the Holy Spirit working in the life of each individual member. In the words of the author, it was "a metamorphosis: from law to Spirit; from missions to Mission; from institutions to Community; from an aggregation of provinces to an International Congregation."

The story of the renewal of the Spiritan congregation in the post-Vatican era reflects a fundamental intuition of its cofounder, Francis Libermann. A convert Jew, he lived, as Martin Buber expressed it, "in the consciousness that the proper place for his encounter with God lies in the ever-changing situation of life." Libermann distrusted preestablished systems, rules and regulations that were not open to the presence and action of the Holy Spirit in the concrete reality of life. He insisted that the Provisional Rule for his newly founded Society of the Holy Heart of Mary must be open to experience and he had no problem in changing some central elements of its content as soon as he heard "God's voice in a different way in the language spoken by unforeseen situations" (Buber, *Der Glaube, der Profeten*, 104). Implicit in this conviction is the fact that the process of conversion and renewal is always ongoing and that one can never succumb to the temptation to believe that one has finally arrived at the destination. This realization is enshrined in the *Spiritan Rule of Life* itself which calls for regular review of the reasons that underlie the congregation's present commitments and a readiness to disengage from existing works in order to respond creatively to the needs of evangelization of our time (*SRL* 2 and 25).

Written, on the author's own admission, from the limited viewpoint of an Irish member of the Holy Spirit Congregation drawing on his experience and study of the Anglophone world, I have no doubt that this extensive and well-researched work will appeal to a much wider audience, both in Spiritan circles and beyond. It captures the perennial challenge faced by all religious and missionary congregations who in fidelity to their founding charism and tradition, continuously seek to read and respond to the signs of the times in order to "keep up with God's mission."

V. Rev. Fr. John Fogarty, CSSp
Superior General, Congregation of the Holy Spirit

Acknowledgments

SPIRITAN LIFE AND MISSION *since Vatican II* is the product of a year's research conducted at Duquesne University of the Holy Spirit, Pittsburgh, Pennsylvania. The author was invited as Spiritan Scholar in Residence 2016–17 to research the congregation's program of renewal following the Second Vatican Council. The Scholar program is an initiative of the Center for Spiritan Studies jointly supported by Duquesne University and the Congregation of the Holy Spirit. Its purpose is the development of scholarship in different areas of Spiritan life and mission.

My profound thanks to Fr. James Chukwuma Okoye, CSSp, director of the Center for Spiritan Studies. The work would not have progressed into its present form without his scholarly exactitude bringing order to the author's ramblings and cohesion to fragmented thoughts. Fr. Okoye's copy editing of the work made for an easy passage from typed script to printed word. His assistant, Judith O'Brien, provided a warm "Irish" welcome to the university and ongoing secretarial support that lightened the load. Fr. Brian Cronin, CSSp, not only accompanied the work but also introduced the author to downtown Pittsburgh.

My thanks to the university for this opportunity and for providing an unrivaled ambience for such research. The gracious welcome and continuing interest received from Duquesne University president, Dr. Ken Gormley, and the dean of the College of Liberal Arts, Dr. James Swindal, gave much encouragement. The unfailing courtesy and expertise of the Gumberg Library staff, particularly, Dr. Sara Baron, library director; and the life-saving assistance provided by the university's computer technical services staff, made for a research "without tears." I am grateful to Malachy O'Higgins, Spiritan Mission volunteer, for his translation of Fr. Libermann's 1846 *Memorandum to Propaganda Fide*.

Participation in Duquesne's Division of Mission and Identity and Spiritan Campus Ministry events provided insight into Spiritan mission in action. My thanks to Fr. Raymond French, CSSp, university vice president for mission and identity; Dr. Darlene Weaver, director, Center for Catholic Faith and Culture; and Fr. Dan Walsh, CSSp, campus ministry director, and their colleagues. The invitation to participate in the Theology Department's World Issues for Theology (WIFT) lectures provided a much-valued sounding board for this research. My thanks to the coordinator, Dr. Devassikutty Madathummuriyil, and its members for their insights and good humor. My gratitude also goes to Dr. Anne Marie Hansen and the Spiritan Lay Associates for engagement and discussion on their experience of the lay Spiritan vocation.

I was privileged to share in the life and prayer of the intercultural Spiritan community at the university's Trinity Hall. My sincere thanks to its members and particularly Fr. Seán Hogan, CSSp, the community leader, for his constant solicitude. Eva Bosetti and all the staff at Trinity Hall provided me with a "home away from home."

Any research requires widespread collaboration, particularly one that covers the life and work of an international group of people over a significant period of time. While this work has one author, it benefited from many sources of inspiration, direction and insight. I wish to express my thanks to those members of the worldwide Spiritan community invited to contribute in a variety of ways. Some rendered valuable assistance in accessing materials: Frs. Huy Dinh, CSSp, USA province archives; Roger Tabard, CSSp, the congregation archives at Chevilly-Larue, Paris; Brian O'Toole, CSSp, and staff of the Irish province Mission Resource and Heritage Center; Jean-Pascal Lombart, CSSp, for putting me in the right direction on one occasion; Anthony Gittins, CSSp, for his timely correspondence. Others provided guidance in the interpretation of the texts studied: Frs. Christopher Burke, CSSp, Brian Cronin, CSSp, Jean Michel Gelmetti, CSSp, Bernard Kelly, CSSp, Don Nesti, CSSp, and Vincent O'Grady, CSSp.

Valuable feedback on different chapters of the work was provided by Lay Spiritan Dr. Anne Marie Hansen and Frs. Paul Coulon, CSSp, Seán de Léis, CSSp, Michael Kilkenny, CSSp, Don Nesti, CSSp, Jude Nnorom, CSSp, Vincent O'Grady, CSSp, Brian O'Toole, CSSp, Patrick J. Ryan, CSSp, Elochukwu Uzukwu, CSSp, and Marc Whelan, CSSp. To these and the many others who shared a memory, gave an opinion, or told a favorite story, my acknowledgment and gratitude.

The publishers, Wipf & Stock, are to be thanked for offering to publish this work. Their assistance and unfailing courtesy throughout the publication process have made it a relatively painless and, indeed, joyful experience. Finally, my appreciation to Very Rev. Fr. John Fogarty, CSSp, Superior General, who, with many demands on his time, graciously and generously agreed to provide the foreword for this work.

List of Abbreviations

AA	*Apostolicam actuositatem.* Vatican II Decree on the Apostolate of the Laity.
AAS	*Acta Apostolicae Sedis.* Official Acts of the Holy See.
AG	*Ad gentes.* Vatican II Decree on the Mission Activity of the Church.
CBQ	*Catholic Biblical Quarterly*
CCC	*Catechism of the Catholic Church*
CDD	*Chapter Directives and Decisions* of GC XIII
CSSp	Congregation of the Holy Spirit
EGC	Enlarged General Council
EG	*Evangelii gaudium.* Apostolic Exhortation of Pope Francis, The Gospel of Joy (2013).
EN	*Evangelii nuntiandi.* Aposotlic Exhortation of Pope Paul VI on Evangelization in the Modern World (1975).
ES	*Écrits Spirituels.* Spiritual writings of Venerable Francis Libermann.
ET	*Evangelica testificatio.* Apostolic Exhortation on the Renewal of Religious Life.
GA	*Guidelines for Animation.* Document of GC XIV.
GB	*General Bulletin of the Congregation of the Holy Spirit.*
GC X	General Chapter 10. Paris 1926.
GC XI	General Chapter 11. Paris, 1950.

GC XII	General Chapter 12. Paris, 1962.
GC XIII	General Chapter 13. Rome/Paris, 1968–69.
GC XIV	General Chapter 14. Paris, 1974.
GC XV	General Chapter 15. Paris, 1980.
GC XVI	General Chapter 16. Paris, 1986.
GC XVII	General Chapter 17. Itaici, Brazil, 1992.
GC XVIII	General Chapter 18. Maynooth, Ireland, 1998.
GC XIX	General Chapter 19. Torre d'Aguilha, Portugal, 2004.
GS	*Gaudium et spes.* Vatican II Pastoral Constitution on the Church in the Modern World.
I/D	*Information/Documentation*
ITC	The International Theological Commission
JPIC	Justice, Peace, and the Integrity of Creation
LG	*Lumen gentium.* Vatican II Dogmatic Constitution on the Church.
N.D.	*Notes et Documents relatifs à la vie et à l'Oeuvre du Vénérable François Marie-Paul Libermann.* 16 volumes of the writings of the Congregation's cofounder, Venerable François-Marie-Paul Libermann.
OMI	Oblates of Mary Immaculate
PC	*Perfectae caritatis.* Vatican II Decree on the Adaptation and Renewal of Religious Life.
RD	*Redemptionis donum.* Pope John Paul II's Apostolic exhortation to Men and Women Religious on their Consecration in the Light of the Mystery of the Redemption (1984).
RM	*Redemptoris missio.* Pope John Paul II's Encyclical on the Church's Missionary Mandate (1990).
SCAF	South Central African Foundation
SECAM	Symposium of Episcopal Conferences of Africa and Madagascar
SEDOS	Service of Documentation and Study on Global Mission, Rome

SIST	Spiritan International School of Theology, Enugu, Nigeria
SJ	Society of Jesus
SL	*Spiritan Life*. Document of GC XV.
SM	Society of Mary
SRL	*Spiritan Rule of Life*
TA	Torre d'Aguilha. GC XIX document *Faithful to the Gift Entrusted to Us*.
TS	*Theological Studies*
UR	*Unitatis redintegratio*. Vatican II Decree on Ecumenism.
VC	*Vita consecrata*. Post-synodal Apostolic Exhortation of Pope John Paul II on the Consecrated life and its Mission in the Church and in the World (1996).
WAF	West African Foundation

Introduction

THE HISTORY OF ANY organization has pivotal moments when fundamental choices are made that give shape to its development. Spiritans have known many such moments at local, regional, and congregational level. Times of crisis are part of the Spiritan story providing opportunity for greater fidelity to the Spiritan missionary vocation. The beginning of the Congregation of the Holy Spirit (CSSp) in Paris, France, as a community of poor students in 1703 with Claude Poullart des Places, a seminarian, as its founder is an extraordinary story of faith and courage. Its transition in 1734 from an informal residence and school for poor seminarians to a recognized seminary preparing priests for the French colonies put it on the national stage and gave it legal status. Providentially, it survived the French Revolution.

In 1848, Francis Libermann brought his youthful missionary society, the Immaculate Heart of Mary, into the Spiritan fold. His leadership rescued the Spiritan congregation from possible extinction and widened the boundaries of Spiritan mission to embrace the poorest and most abandoned in the world: the freed slaves of the colonies and the peoples of Africa. That missionary thrust propelled the congregation beyond France to many European countries, beginning with Ireland in 1859, in quest of vocations for its missionary work in Africa.

In the 1960s the congregation had reached the pinnacle of its success with some five thousand members, a strong central authority and juridical organization operating within a fixed understanding of religious life and mission. It was strong in numbers and structures, confident of its mission. It was part of a "perfect" church with divine mandate and infallible doctrine. But all that was about to change.

A growing secularization in Western countries and the "wind of change" blowing through Africa were "signs of the times" with which the church and the congregation had to contend. Pope St. John XXIII's agenda of *aggiornamento* for the church required a response. Openness to change and engagement with renewal in the church was at first resisted. The election of Archbishop Marcel Lefebvre as superior general in 1962 and the general chapter decisions of that year suggest a congregation ill-prepared for the renewal and adaptation that the Second Vatican Council would require from all religious institutes.

Spiritan Life and Mission since Vatican II is a narrative of the congregation's journey from its pre-Vatican II existence to a congregation renewed in life and mission in the spirit of Vatican II. The story is told from an Irish perspective drawing particularly from the Anglophone experience of the congregation. The ecclesial context is developed through a commentary on Vatican II and subsequent church documents addressing issues of mission and religious life. The research material on which this account is based consists of general chapter documents of the time, deliberations of general councils and the views shared by many Spiritans who made the journey through change to the *Spiritan Rule of Life* (henceforth *SRL*) agreed in 1986.

The journey continued beyond 1986 with a consolidation of *SRL* as it was reflected upon and lived by those for whom it was intended. The congregation's leadership since 1986 and its general chapters of 1992, 1998 and 2004 are interpreted as milestones in the development of Spiritan life and mission as set out in *SRL*. They translate into practice how *SRL* understood Spiritan mission, community living, and religious life. Through living by its rule of life the congregation remains faithful within the church to its founding intention as a missionary religious community dedicated to the evangelization of the poor.

The year 2018 marks the fiftieth anniversary of the beginning of that journey of renewal with the extraordinary chapter of 1968 (GC XIII) and offers an opportunity to revisit an important moment in the history of the congregation. With all its inevitable faults and failings, the Spiritan journey of Vatican II fashioned the thinking and language Spiritans use today in their efforts to remain true to the founding vision and charism of their ancestors, particularly Claude Poullart des Places, and Francis Libermann.

Spiritan Life and Mission since Vatican II is a story of the changes involved in leaving aside "old ways" to take up the "new ways" required by the Catholic Church. New understandings of Christian holiness and mission grounded in Scripture and in Vatican II's ecclesiology of communion called for a new way to fulfill the Spiritan missionary vocation. Finding that way was not easy.

Chapter 1—"The Spiritan Charism." The rediscovery of the charismatic dimension of the church at Vatican II and of the religious vocation as charism formed the basis for the congregation's understanding of itself as a Spirit-led community with a charism to be lived in service of the church.

INTRODUCTION xxiii

Chapter 1 tells the story of the congregation as "led by the Spirit" from its beginning with Poullart des Places and its consolidation with Francis Libermann. It was that same Spirit which accompanied the congregation through its three hundred years of service celebrated in the Spiritan Year of Jubilee, from 2 February 2002 to Pentecost Sunday 2003. That celebration occasioned an awakening of new energy and enthusiasm in the Spiritan vocation as a gift from God for the church. What the Pharisee, Gamaliel, said of the first Christian community can be applied to the congregation. If it was not of God it would not have survived (Acts 5:34–39). But, as it is of God, it has survived.

A rediscovery of the Spiritan charism sustained the journey of renewal. This was made possible through study of the congregation's founding purpose, its founders, and its history; a reimagining of Spiritan life lived in apostolic community; and engagement with church teaching on religious life and mission.

Chapter 2—"The Spiritan Congregation, Change, and Vatican II." The "root and branch" renewal required by the council involved a "paradigm shift" in lifestyle and mission that did not happen automatically or without opposition. As in all organizations, there were those who recognized the need for change more quickly than others. It was a difficult time with more questions than answers. It was a time of risk and letting go of much that was cherished in the old to embrace the new. The choice of Mgr. Marcel Lefebvre as superior general in the very year of the first session of Vatican II seems an incredible decision.

Chapter 2 documents the general chapter that elected him and the different currents of thought operative in a congregation confident of its past, but fearful of its future. Like the proverbial ostrich, it resolved to bury its head in the sand and reject the need for radical change. As the council program of renewal progressed it became increasingly evident that change within the congregation was required. Lefebvre was opposed to this and, as congregational leader, offered only a piecemeal approach to its renewal. This was not enough for a growing number of his French confreres who saw the need to replace him as superior general.

The general chapter held in 1968 was, at first, designated as "administrative" with the task of updating the congregation's Rules and Constitutions in the light of Vatican II. Lefebvre's term of office and that of his council would run until 1974 and he would preside as general at the chapter and oversee the implementation of its decisions.

Chapter 3—"The General Chapter of Renewal." Chapter 3 tells of the growing popular movement to make the chapter elective and to ensure a "root and branch" review of the congregation's life and mission. A head-on collision with Lefebvre was unavoidable, resulting in his walking away from the congregation that in turn rejected his authoritarian style of leadership and the semi-monastic practices associated with him. The election of Fr. Joseph Lécuyer, CSSp, to succeed him calmed nerves and steadied the chapter which concluded with a strong affirmation of first evangelization as the congregation's primary purpose.

The general malaise in religious life and ambiguity about missionary work adversely affected the new leadership's efforts at renewal in the congregation. Different interpretations of Vatican II and of the congregation's purpose caused divisions and undermined morale. Radical changes in lifestyle and missionary orientation confused some and alienated others, putting the unity of the congregation at risk.

Chapter 4—"Continuing the Journey of Renewal." Chapter 4 traces the journey the congregation took in drawing back from the abyss of extinction following the initial period after the 1968 general chapter (GC XIII). This was a confusing, uncertain, and painful time for all concerned. The varying interpretations of Vatican II generated different approaches to the application of its teaching. The general chapter of 1974 (GC XIV) set out to restore unity among the membership through a more inclusive definition of Spiritan mission.

Fr. Frans Timmermans, CSSp, was elected general, and, with his council, engaged in an animation of the membership to facilitate renewal and increased collaboration between provinces. There was a growing appreciation of the international nature of the congregation as it established foundations in its mission districts and sent international teams on mission to new countries. The antidote for the confusion and divisions of the time was new structures of collaboration; new tools of communication among the membership, and serious research into the founders, traditions, and history of the congregation.

GC XV in 1980 reelected Timmermans as superior general and called on all Spiritans to work for justice and peace wherever they were. While acknowledging many obstacles along the path of renewal, the chapter also recognized "a great desire to strengthen unity" as witnessed by the renewal of community life in many places and a growth in solidarity within the congregation.

Chapter 5—"Writing a Rule." The renewal process involved the rewriting of the congregation's rules and constitutions. This required a congregation-wide consultation which acted as an effective way to engage members in appreciating their life and mission as Spiritans in the light of Vatican II. Chapter 5 charts the process that brought the *"ad experimentum"* period to a conclusion. It was a time of consolidation with new confidence engendered by increasing membership and the strengthening of the congregation's presence in Africa and South America.

The work of consultation concluded with GC XVI and the final text of the *Spiritan Rule of Life* (*SRL*) in 1986. It resolved the old polarities between the missionary and religious life dimensions of the Spiritan vocation by uniting them in the one reality of the "apostolic life" (*SRL* 3). The congregation now had a rule to guide it in its mission and way of life. GC XVI also elected Fr. Pierre Haas, CSSp, and a general council to lead the congregation for the next six years.

Chapter 6—"From *SRL* to GC XIX (1968–2004)." Decision-making in the congregation was radically changed in 1968. Before that a more hierarchical, "top-down" system was in place. The central role of general chapters in the organization and life of religious institutes was rediscovered. Spiritan chapters are key moments in the life of the congregation when the membership gathers through representation and acts as the "supreme authority in the congregation."

Spiritan general chapters have traditionally started with a "state of the congregation" report given by the superior general. That report usually sets the chapter's agenda and, since GC XVI in 1986, has included an overview of world affairs as seen through Spiritan eyes. Chapter 6 gives a summary of how the world was viewed from the Spiritan perspective as reported in 1992, 1998, and 2004. This provides the changing geopolitical and social contexts for the deliberations of GC XVII, XVIII and XIX. The modalities of each general chapter since *SRL* (GC XVI–XIX) are recounted to demonstrate the importance of these important milestones in the congregation's journey through time. An outline of their "satellite" enlarged general council meetings completes the narrative.

Chapter 7—"Spiritan Mission." Chapter 7 considers the impact of "new evangelization" and Pope St. John Paul II's *Redemptoris missio* on the congregation's interpretation of its mission. The tensions associated with dialogue were experienced and shared at GC XVII by confreres working with the Coptic Church in Ethiopia. GC XVII also elected Fr. Pierre Schouver, CSSp, who would go on to serve two terms as superior general (1992–2004).

GC XVIII interpreted mission as going to people "to be with them, live with them, walk beside them, listen to them and share our faith with them." Spiritan mission also included peace building, conflict resolution, reconciliation, advocacy for the poor and marginalized of society. GC XIX incorporated the aspect of care for the earth and protection of the environment into the justice, peace, and integrity of creation (JPIC) activities of the congregation. Education as part of Spiritan mission and formation for Spiritan mission are also considered.

Chapter 8—"Spiritan Community." Spiritan community is defined by the mission it undertakes. "It is a privileged means of practicing the evangelical counsels in the service of the Good News" (*SRL* 28). Spiritans exercise "evangelical availability" through living in community and committing themselves to its mission. Chapter 8 examines how GC XVIII and GC XIX addressed the challenges associated with living in international and multicultural communities. GC XIX elected Fr. Jean-Paul Hoch, CSSp, as superior general following the new regulation of one nonrenewable term of eight years (2004–2012).

The classification of the congregation as a clerical religious institute is examined. The clerical status of most members was judged an obstacle to community renewal, as it contributed to a two-tiered status of membership. GC XVII and XIX called for the elimination of clericalism and welcomed the lessening of divisions between brothers and priests in the congregation. The Lay Spiritan Associate form of membership has long been acknowledged in the congregation and was recognized as "a branch of the Spiritan tree." For that branch to grow it is important to recognize that the Spiritan charism is not the exclusive preserve of professed members.

Chapter 9—"Spiritan Religious Life." Chapter 9 locates the Spiritan vocation within the context of a variety of religious vocations. It highlights the distinctive way in which Spiritans live the evangelical counsels in generous self-giving for the sake of the poor they are called to serve. The congregation's leadership reflected on the Spiritan way of living the vows "for the Kingdom" as elaborated in *SRL*. These reflections are summarized in chapter 9.

Chapter 10—"The Rediscovery of the Spiritan Charism." The fiftieth anniversary of Vatican II occasioned much debate on how to interpret its significance in the history of the church. Chapter 10 draws parallels between the Spiritan journey of renewal and the interpretation and implementation of the council from its conclusion in 1965 to 2015. A hermeneutic of continuity confirms the council as a moment in the journey of a pilgrim church remaining true to its New Testament beginnings. The Spiritan congregation can similarly interpret the history of its renewal since Vatican II as a journey of radical change made in creative fidelity to its founding charism. GC XIII was the first step taken in that journey of renewal which, arguably, constitutes a third founding event (after Des Places in the eighteenth century and Libermann in the nineteenth century) when the Spiritan identity was rediscovered; the congregation as a worldwide community was realized; and its mission widened to encompass the *oikoumene*, the whole wide world.

Spiritan Life and Mission since Vatican II can act as an *aide memoire* for those who have lived through this time of change. For young Spiritans, this account of their recent past tells of the congregation's transition from its pre-Vatican II form to its current identity, structure, and purpose. For old and young, this history can be read as a narrative of fidelity to divine providence at work among us.

In a letter to a confrere, angry with him because of changes he had made, Fr. Libermann wrote, "Until now we have stayed in the path of providence and God alone has been our guide. I was never able to bring to fulfillment a plan that I had conceived on my own. Nonetheless, I have consistently succeeded—as if by magic, though surrounded by problems and annoyances—in every enterprise that was thrust upon us by providence."[2] May the worldwide congregation of the Holy Spirit continue along the path of providence in service of the *missio Dei*.

---

2. Congregation of the Holy Spirit, *Spiritan Anthology*, 308.

Chapter 1

The Spiritan Charism

1. Understanding Charism

THE SPIRITAN VOCATION IN its many dimensions—religious and missionary, cleric and lay—was recognized at the time of the congregation's renewal since Vatican II as a gift to the church given through Fr. Claude François Poullart des Places (1679–1709) and Fr. Francis Libermann (1802–1852) and lived in creative fidelity by generations of Spiritans of different times and circumstances. The Holy Spirit is the giver and sustainer of this gift and it is through discernment of the Spirit that the life and mission of the congregation unfolds.

A scriptural basis for the appreciation of spiritual gifts, *charismata*, is explored through reference to St. Paul's conceptualization of *charismata* in the life of the *ekklēsia* particularly in 1 Corinthians 12. This is our starting point as the debate at Vatican II on the mystery of the church and its charismatic nature followed Paul's ordering of the charismatic and hierarchical dimensions of the church.

The subsequent development of church doctrine and law gave direction to religious communities for their renewal. It was within this development that the rediscovery of the Spiritan charism became the catalyst for a new interpretation of Spiritan life and mission.

Charism in St. Paul

Charis (χάρις), translated from Greek to Latin as *gratia* and in English as "grace," has a multivalent use in Christian theology to render several

Hebrew concepts about God summarized by three main ideas: condescending love, conciliatory compassion, and absolute fidelity.[1] Grace is a new life and a new way of existence given by God in Jesus Christ and made accessible in history through Christ and the church he founded (Heb 10:20; John 14:6). The church is not an abstraction but part of history as a "grace-filled" communion of believers and the "sacrament" of God's grace at work in the world. "Every and all grace is given to the church and for the benefit of the church, to benefit both the individual receiving it and the community."[2]

Charis (χάρις) is a key concept for St. Paul and occurs 101 times in his writings, twice as frequently as in all the rest of the Christian Scriptures. Paul speaks of *charis* in an undefined way, to denote the whole range of God's self-communication understood as totally gratuitous, unmerited, and undeserved. When speaking of grace, and a life lived by grace, he sought to convey a new way of being alive, "a new creation," given by God in Jesus Christ through which the Christian becomes one with Jesus as Son, and, as such, is united to the Father, through the Spirit. "Grace is the new order ushered in by God's uncontainable generosity made manifest in the death-resurrection of Jesus Christ."[3]

Charisma (χάρισμα) in Paul, is an effect of *charis*, a concrete materialization of God's grace. The word *charisma* denotes a divine gift (a "favor bestowed" by God). Paul relates them to stress that the *charismata* he writes about to the young Christian communities are gifts of grace given freely and generously by God through the working of the Holy Spirit (*pneuma*).[4] It is one category of the *pneumatika* (manifestations of the Spirit), the others being *diakoniai* (services) and *energēmata* (works).[5]

Paul uses the word *charisma* fourteen times in his letters to the Corinthians: 1 Cor 1:7; 7:7; 12:4, 9, 28, 30, 31; 2 Cor 1:11; and in his letter to the Romans 1:11; 5:15–16; 6:23; 11:29; 12:6.[6] *Charisma* is also found in

---

1. Haight, *Experience and Language of Grace*, 6.
2. Fransen, *New Life of Grace*, 90.
3. Duffy, *Dynamics of Grace*, 35.
4. Ibid., 37.
5. 1 Cor 12:4–6. "Now there are varieties of gifts, but the same Spirit; and there are varieties of service, but the same Lord; and there are varieties of working, but it is the same God who inspires them all in everyone."
6. St. Jerome in the Vulgate only once transcribes "*charisma*," in 1 Cor 12:31. "*Aemulamini autem charismata meliora*" ("Earnestly desire the higher gifts"). He offers the translation "*gratia*" to the other instances listed above. In Greek, the suffix *-ma* expresses the result of the action indicated by the verb; in this instance, a gift bestowed. It is important to distinguish the Greek understanding of "*charisma*" (a gift bestowed to perform a task in service of the *ecclesia*) from the Latin "*gratia*" with a broader interpretation to denote personal sanctification.

1 Tim 4:14; 2 Tim 1:6; 1 Pet 4:10 and used to denote the Spirit's dynamic engagement through individual gifts that combine to build up the Christian community.[7] The grace of Christ animates and sustains the *ekklēsia*, the assembly of God's people. There are a variety of gifts by which the *ekklēsia* (1 Cor 1:2; 4:17; 6:4; 7:17; 10:32; 11:16, 18, 22) is animated and sustained in its life in Christ, but it is the same Spirit (1 Cor 12:4). It is God's Spirit, promised by Jesus, which guides the Christian community (Acts 1:4–5).[8]

> Now, concerning spiritual gifts, brethren, I do not want you to be uninformed. To each is given the manifestation of the Spirit for the common good. To one is given through the Spirit the utterance of wisdom, and to another the utterance of knowledge according to the same Spirit, to another faith by the same Spirit, to another gifts of healing by the one Spirit, to another the working of miracles, to another prophecy, to another the ability to distinguish between spirits, to another various kinds of tongues, to another the interpretation of tongues. (1 Cor 12:1, 7–10)

There are a variety of services and common graces, but it is always the same Lord. Paul spoke of these gifts as given by the Spirit "for the common good" (1 Cor 12:7) and ordered toward the building up of the community (1 Cor 14:12). The *ekklēsia* is, by its very nature, a charismatic community. It is "defined by the Spirit, and cannot look to itself for its goals, but must look outward to the plan of God."[9]

Paul recognized his gift as that of apostle (Rom 1:1). It was for him to encourage and give strength to the community sustained by the power of salvation expressed in specific gifts. He exhorted the individual members, each "gifted" differently by God, to prophesy, serve, teach, exhort, contribute, give aid, do acts of mercy. He also recognizing himself as a prophet, (1 Cor 14:6, 37). In a ranking of roles in the community, he placed prophets after apostles, then teachers and then the workers of miracles, healers, helpers, administrators, speakers in tongues (1 Cor 12:28). This regulation of the gifts was given so that "all things should be done decently and in order" (1 Cor 14:40). Paul included office holders as also having a charism to exercise their functions in service of the community. "Paul used the word to include the whole gamut of gifts existing in the community, from pneumatic

---

7. Fitzmyer, *First Corinthians*, 464.

8. Brown, *Jerome Biblical Commentary*, 80.30.

9. "The church of the New Testament must be seen as dependent upon the Holy Spirit in its mission to carry out the plan of God. It must act upon the initiating, directing, and moulding action of the Spirit. It is the people of God who are fashioned according to the will of the Spirit, in order that the plan of God may be brought about." Koupal, "Charism," 541.

phenomena to authority."[10] All members of the *ekklēsia* were subject to the law of love, to the life of God given to empower love, one for another (1 Cor 13:13). The regulation of the gifts is itself a gift given to build up the *ekklēsia*. Antipathy between charismatics and office bearers had no place in a community when it is recognized that it is the Spirit that posits the law and enables the keeping of the law.[11]

Charism at Vatican II

A decisive debate took place at Vatican II about whether the church still needed the charismatic gifts, or whether they were intended solely for its beginning to help with its establishment. Giving direction to this debate, Blessed Pope Paul VI[12] welcomed the "self-awareness" of the church emerging at the council. "The church is a mystery. It is a reality imbued with the hidden presence of God. It lies, then, within the very nature of the church to be always open to new and greater exploration."[13] It was in this context that Cardinal Leo-Jozef Suenens addressed the Vatican Council on "The Charismatic Dimension of the Church."[14] Commenting on contributions to the debate, he said, "The remarks made about the charisms of the Christian people are so few that one could get the impression that charisms are nothing more than a peripheral and unessential phenomenon in the life of the church."[15]

Suenens spoke of the church as the dwelling of God in the world; an *oikos pneumatikos* (a "spiritual dwelling") and drawing deeply and extensively from St. Paul, particularly 1 Corinthians 12 and Ephesians 4:11, demonstrated the wonderful activity of the Holy Spirit in New Testament times. As charisms were needed then, so also, they are needed in all times, "she needs them today as well and needs them in her ordinary everyday life."[16]

---

10. Nardoni, "Charism," 80.
11. Bromley, *Dictionary of the New Testament*, 1306.
12. Pope Paul VI was beatified by Pope Francis on October 19, 2014.
13. See Küng et al., *Speeches of Vatican II*, 26.
14. Cardinal Leo-Jozef Suenens (1904–1996) was archbishop of Mechelen-Brussel, Belgium, and a close confidant of Pope John XXIII. Pope Paul VI appointed him as one of the four moderators of the council and he can be numbered among the chief architects of the *Dogmatic Constitution on the Church* (*Lumen gentium*) and the *Pastoral Constitution on the Church in the Modern World* (*Gaudium et spes*).
15. Küng et al., *Speeches of Vatican II*, 29.
16. Ibid., 32.

In support of Suenens, Hans Küng, writing in a Catholic journal in 1965, asserted that as Vatican I was sometimes interpreted as "the Council for the pope" (confirming papal authority), so Vatican II could be interpreted as "the Council for bishops" (asserting episcopal authority). But it needed to be more than that, as "no member of the community possesses all the charismata in their fullness."[17] Looking to the New Testament church and quoting 1 Thessalonians 5:19 ("Do not quench the Spirit") he argued that it was impossible to limit *charismata* in the church to its officeholders. "The administrative gifts do in no way lead to a kind of 'leading class' that stands apart from the community and rises above it to dominate it."[18]

Küng pointed out that the New Testament spoke of "service" (*diakonia*) and avoided secular terms such as *archē*, *timē*, *telos* as they connote domination of one over another. Paul preferred to speak of *charismata* with which all Christians are gifted (1 Cor 7:7). They are "the manifestation, the concrete and individual expression of the *charis* (love), of God's grace-giving power, that seizes us in order to lead us in service and so to give us our individual share in Christ's power."[19]

The council followed Paul's use of *charisma*, influencing the vocabulary which gives the Vatican II documents their distinctive style. Instead of a vocabulary of pessimism and rejection of people outside the institutional church, the documents are filled with words like "brothers/sisters, friendship. Cooperation, collaboration, partnership. Freedom, dialogue, pilgrim, servant . . . evolution charism, dignity. . . . Collegiality, people of God, priesthood of believers."[20] In this, Vatican II proclaimed that the church was more than an institution; it was also a charismatic community. The Holy Spirit inspired both the institutional and charismatic dimensions of the church which were in dynamic relation with one another. A brief review of the council documents on the nature of the church, its missionary activity, and religious life will help us better understand the dynamic reinterpretation since Vatican II of the place and role of active religious congregations in the life and mission of the church.

Lumen gentium, Vatican II's dogmatic constitution on the church, gave the primary understanding of the church as the *People of God* who share in Christ's prophetic office and who, "anointed as they are by the Holy One, cannot err in matters of belief" (*LG* 12). It gave new recognition to the primacy of baptism and the Spirit at work among all the baptized both

17. Küng, "Charismatic Structure of the Church," 304.
18. Ibid.
19. Ibid., 306.
20. O'Malley, *Vatican II*, 306.

individually and collectively in the building up of the church. The charismatic gifts are an important accompaniment to the health of the internal life of the church and the preaching of the gospel. The council fathers voted overwhelmingly to affirm this truth and formulated the key paragraph in *Lumen gentium* articulating this understanding.

> It is not only through the sacraments and the ministries of the church that the Holy Spirit sanctifies and leads the people of God and enriches it with virtues, but, "allotting his gifts to everyone according as he wills," (1 Cor 12:11) he distributes special graces among the faithful of every rank. By these gifts he makes them fit and ready to undertake the various tasks and offices which contribute toward the renewal and building up of the church, according to the words of the apostle: "The manifestation of the Spirit is given to everyone for profit." (1 Thess 5:12, 19–21) These charisms, whether they be the more outstanding or the more simple and widely diffused, are to be received with thanksgiving and consolation for they are perfectly suited to and useful for the needs of the church.[21]

This conciliar recognition of the church's charismatic dimension affirmed a dynamic vision of lay participation in the life of the church expressed in terms of the council's "universal call to holiness" and its "universal call to mission."[22] The place and role of religious within the church is best located within this affirmation. Rather than speak of charism in relation to religious life, *Lumen gentium* (LG) used terms signifying the evangelical counsels as "divine gift" (*donum divinum*, LG 43); and referred to the spirit of the founders (*spiritus fundatorum*, LG 45) and the religious calling as a vocation given by God (*vocatio in quam a Deo vocatus est*, LG 47). Vatican II recognized the guidance of the Holy Spirit at work both in the "outstanding men and women" (founders) who presented their new constitutions for approval and in the authority that approved them and continued to guide their foundations "in order that these same institutes may grow and flourish according to the spirit of the founders" (*LG 45*).

---

21. *LG* 12.

22. In an address to Ecclesial Movements and New Communities on the eve of Pentecost, 30 May 1998, Pope St. John Paul II, who attended the council as a bishop, remembered the important rediscovery of the charismatic dimension of the church at Vatican II. Quoting *Lumen gentium* 12, he said, "Whenever the Spirit intervenes, he leaves people astonished. He brings about events of amazing newness; he radically changes persons and history. This was the unforgettable experience of the Second Vatican Ecumenical Council during which, under the guidance of the same Spirit, the church rediscovered the charismatic dimension as one of her constitutive elements."

Consecrated religious are bound to the church in a special way. "The church itself, by the authority given to it by God, accepts the vows of the newly professed" (*LG* 45). The professed then dedicate themselves to "the welfare of the whole church" in accordance with their contemplative or apostolic calling. The church was therefore obliged to preserve and foster "the special character of her various religious institutes" (*LG* 44). Because of that obligation the church directed that each institute conduct its renewal and adaptation according to its own character and work.

Ad gentes, Vatican II's decree on the mission activity of the church, proclaimed that "the pilgrim church is missionary by its very nature" (*AG* 2). It followed an ecclesiology of mission grounded in the mystery of the Blessed Trinity. For "it is from the mission of the Son and the mission of the Holy Spirit that it takes its origin, in accordance with the decree of God the Father" (*AG* 2). Christians "have welcomed the news of salvation which is meant for every human being" (*GS* 1) and it is "the Holy Spirit, who distributes the charismata as he wills for the common good (1 Cor 12:11). He inspires the missionary vocation in the hearts of individuals, and at the same time he raises up in the church certain institutes which take as their own special task the duty of preaching the gospel, a duty belonging to the whole church."[23] This specific missionary charism entrusted to some is best understood and achieves greatest effect through assisting the Christian community to realize its missionary nature and so be a "sign of God's presence in the world" (*AG* 15). Christian communities realize their nature as *imago Dei* through living in imitation of the communion of love that is the Blessed Trinity and so partake in the *missio Dei*. "It is in the witness of true holiness, which is ultimately authentic, vibrant humanity found in individuals and pulsating in a community, that women and men will be attracted to ask the questions that can lead them to faith in Christ."[24]

Perfectae caritatis, Vatican II's decree on the adaptation and renewal of religious life, recognized the evangelical counsels as a gift for the good of the church. Religious life is God's gift to the church expressed in a variety of ways. The primary relationship of vowed religious is to the church. Consecrated through the practice of the evangelical counsels, they were to take the gospel as their fundamental rule so that they "bind themselves to the Lord in a special way" (*PC* 1). As there was debate on the charismatic dimension of the people of God, so there was significant debate between two different understandings of religious life: one static, emphasizing religious life as a state of perfection; and the other, dynamic, seeing the need for religious

---

23. *AG* 23.
24. Bevans, "Revisiting Mission at Vatican II," 281.

to be apostolically engaged in the world. Cardinal Suenens, an advocate for the dynamic understanding, promoted a spirituality of the active life for religious to replace "the traditions and mentality of the cloister."[25] In contrast, Cardinal Francis Spellman of New York called for the protection of the contemplative life of religious. He did not want it to be "submerged beneath the onrushing waves of modern apostolic activism."[26] Suenens, on the other hand, wanted the "anachronisms in religious life that damage its worth in the church" removed to enable greater involvement of religious in the church's apostolate.[27]

Perfectae caritatis, generally evaluated as one of the weaker documents of the council, gave both a static and dynamic understanding of religious life.[28] On the one hand, it presented religious consecration as "the pursuit of perfect charity through the evangelical counsels" by which religious were "joined to Christ by a total life-long gift of themselves" (*PC* 1). On the other, it also urged active religious to adjust their way of life to meet modern needs

---

25. Confoy, "Religious Life," 324. Suenens "recognized that with the numbers of religious in that period [1962–65]—300,000 men and 1,200,000 women—new ways of serving church and world that addressed the cultural needs of the time could be generated." Ibid., 326. One commentator writing twenty-five years after *Perfectae caritatis* urged understanding of the task that faced the council when addressing religious life. "We must not forget that for the first time in history, the theme of religious life as a particular state in the church was being systematically treated in a council." See Jurado, "Consecrated Life," 6.

26. Alberigo et al., *History of Vatican II*, 4:366.

27. Ibid., 367. Commenting on *Perfectae caritatis*, Friedrich Wulf pointed out that active religious institutes were not simply derived from monasticism in a straight line of development. But rather, "from time to time there have been original and independent creations arising from some illumination and impulse of grace, which are bound to have stamped them with a special charism, and given them an idiosyncrasy that is expressed in their concrete life." Wulf added that monastic traditions were often obstacles in the way of achieving a unity between the demands of a monastic style religious life and apostolic work. "There has been and still is a standard of institution and custom that has generally been accepted as essential to genuine religious life, and hardly anyone has been able to opt out of this standard." Wulf, "Declaration," 352.

28. Wulf commented that there was little unity in the document, or in the commission that produced it. He also pointed out that the theological foundation for religious life in the church was already worked out in *Lumen gentium*, ch. 6. *LG* is considered the central document from which *PC*, a relatively short document, and all the other conciliar decrees must be referred. *LG* was structured to convey the universal call to holiness, the roles of the hierarchy and the laity and the special call of religious "to forward the saving mission of the church." The theological significance of *LG* for ecclesiological debate was profound. George Lindbeck evaluated it from a Protestant perspective as "much the fullest dogmatic statement on the nature of the church which has ever been formulated by any Christian body." See Lindbeck, "Protestant Point of View," conference address (March 20–26, 1966).

and so better "devote themselves to various apostolic tasks" (*PC* 8). *Perfectae caritatis* related religious life to the general state of Christians in the world by recognizing many different gifts by which different apostolic religious institutes were graced by God, and which, in turn were to serve the church's mission in the world.[29]

> There are in the church very many communities, both clerical and lay, which devote themselves to various apostolic tasks. The gifts which these communities possess differ according to the grace which is allotted to them. Administrators have the gift of administration, teachers that of teaching, the gift of stirring speech is given to preachers, liberality to those who exercise charity and cheerfulness to those who help others in distress (cf. Rom. 12:5–8). "The gifts are varied, but the Spirit is the same" (1 Cor. 12:4). (*PC* 8)

This text distinguished between the gift possessed and the grace by which the gift is realized. The gift is possessed and developed through the grace of God. The term "charism" was studiously avoided in relation to religious life. In this there was a consistency in the Vatican II documents when using the term "gift" in relation to religious life where the meaning of charism as used in *LG* 12 was intended.[30]

Each apostolic religious institute was founded to achieve a particular apostolate. It is this chosen apostolate that constitutes the institute and it was not to be understood as peripheral to the religious life lived by its members.[31] The fulfillment of each institute's apostolate is God's gift to the church and the council called on institutes to make the adaptations necessary to fulfill their God-given apostolate to better serve God's church in a changed world. It is through fidelity to their apostolate that religious "transfigure the world and present God only in the spirit of the beatitudes" which they make visible and tangible as they rediscover their founding intention.[32]

---

29. Confoy, "Religious Life," 329.

30. The relationship between the charismatic nature of religious life and the church's magisterium was developed following the council, particularly in *Ecclesiae sanctae II* (1966) and *Mutuae relationes* (1978).

31. There was a "parallelism" between religious observance and apostolic work inherited from monastic tradition and practices by the active institutes which needed to be resolved. Religious life and apostolic work ought to form an indissoluble unity. The council came to accept through significant input from the superior generals of active religious institutes that "the starting point and plumb-line of every consideration must always be the apostolate to which they are dedicated, and for the sake of which the community was founded." Wulf, "Declaration," 352.

32 Ibid.

"Therefore, let their founders' spirit and special aims they set before them as well as their sound traditions—all of which make up the patrimony of each institute—be faithfully held in honor" (PC 2b).

Charism and Religious Life in the Post-Vatican II Church

Fr. Anthony J. Gittins, CSSp, writing on Spiritan charism in 2006, contrasted the sparing use of "charism" in the Vatican II documents[33] with its frequent usage by the magisterium when speaking of religious life since Vatican II. He wrote, "Since then, charism has been attributed to at least the following: founders of religious institutes, religious life itself, communities, and even individuals. It is also understood both as gift and as call."[34] The first mention of charism by the magisterium in relation to the founders of religious institutes since Vatican II was made in Blessed Pope Paul VI's *Evangelica testificatio* (*ET*), 1971, where religious were told that without the combination of a contemplative life with apostolic love they would be unable "to reawaken hearts to truth and to divine love in accordance with the charisms of your founders who were raised up by God within his church" (*ET* 11).

The document spoke of the "charism of religious life," the "charisms of the founders," and the "charisms of the various institutes," each with its own distinctive character (*ET* 32). This character was recognized and safeguarded by the hierarchy as it emanated from "an experience of the Spirit." The church, as Paul pointed out, is the Body of Christ animated by his Spirit. The publication in 1978 of directives for mutual relations between bishops and religious in the church, *Mutuae relationes*, took this for its operating principle.

> Every authentic charism implies a certain element of genuine originality and of special initiative for the spiritual life of the church. . . . The specific charismatic note of any institute demands, both of the founder and his disciples, a continual examination regarding fidelity to the Lord; docility to his Spirit; intelligent attention to circumstances and an outlook cautiously directed to the signs of the times; the will to be part of the

---

33. The word *charism* appears 11 times in the Vatican II documents. There are four references to the charisms of infallibility in *Lumen gentium* (*LG* 25) the pope (twice), the bishops and the church. It is used twice in relation to the apostolate of the laity in (*AA* 3 and 30); twice in relation to the missionary work of the church (*AG* 23 and 28); twice referring to the church as gifted with "charismatic gifts" (*LG* 4 and 7) and once in the decree on the priesthood (*PO* 9) with reference to the charisms of the laity. Deretz and Nocent, *Dictionary of the Council*.

34. Gittins, "Root, Shoot and Fruit," 32.

church; the awareness of subordination to the sacred hierarchy; boldness of initiatives; constancy in the giving of self; humility in bearing with adversities.[35]

A pneumatological-ecclesiological dynamic shaped the development of thinking around the relationship between religious founders and church authority. Both are gifted to the church through God's bountiful grace and interact for the building up of the church and its mission in the world. There are a variety of gifts, but the same Spirit at work in them all (1 Cor 12:4). Each member of the church is called to "hate what is evil, hold fast to what is good" (Rom 12: 9). As in Paul's time, so also for the postconciliar church: maintaining unity through coordination of the Spirit's gifts was of paramount importance. A balance between freedom of the Spirit and order in the church was achievable when it was understood that "the Holy Spirit guides the church, in order to achieve through it his work of transforming humanity to Christ. By means of his inspirations and charisms, the Holy Spirit empowers the church to carry "out its mission of being an instrument of sanctification and of testifying to Christ throughout the whole world. The numerous vocations to various forms of consecrated life in the church are due to this activity of the Holy Spirit."[36]

The new Code of Canon Law (1983) enshrined the theology of Vatican II on consecrated life in its juridical norms for *The People of God* (book 2 of the Code). References were made to the presence of the Holy Spirit in the church, but mostly in relation to the functioning of the institution (e.g., the sacrament of confirmation Can. 879; in relation to apostolic succession of bishops Can. 375 §1; and the church's universal teaching office Can. 747 §1). The Code's "Norms Common to All Institutes of Consecrated Life" (Can. 573–606) considered religious life as a choice made by some faithful to totally dedicate themselves to God. The language of "special gift" (*peculiaris donum*) was used which has all the characteristics of a charism and was previously expressed as charism by Blessed Pope Paul VI.[37] The institutional

---

35. *Mutuae relationes* 12. This document gave guidelines for discerning the authenticity of new foundations recognized the importance of a discernible charism, a gift of the Holy Spirit: "A credible presence of the Holy Spirit, both to receive His gifts 'with thanksgiving and consolation' (*LG* 12) and also to avoid the possibility that 'institutes may be imprudently brought into being which are useless or lacking in sufficient resources' (*PC* 19). In fact, when judgment regarding the establishment of an institute is formulated only in view of its usefulness and suitability in the field of action, or simply on the basis of the comportment of some person who experiences devotional phenomena, in themselves ambiguous, then indeed it becomes evident that the genuine concept of religious life in the church is in a certain manner distorted" (*Mutuae relationes* 51).

36. Jurado, "Consecrated Life," 19.

37. A similar vocabulary of "gifts of the Holy Spirit" was used by the Code to speak

approach was adopted when the Code in its norms for all institutes and societies required religious institutes to faithfully observe their founders' intentions and their "sound traditions" as approved by competent ecclesiastical authority. "All must observe faithfully the mind and designs of the founders regarding the nature, purpose, spirit, and character of an institute, which have been sanctioned by competent ecclesiastical authority, and its sound traditions, all of which constitute the patrimony of the same institute" (Can. 578).[38]

Pope St. John Paul II, writing in 1984 (apostolic exhortation, *Redemptionis donum*), described religious consecration as a call which is a gift of God (*RD* 6), and a gift of reciprocal love, a gift of "spousal covenant" (*RD* 8). It is a Trinitarian act (*RD* 8): a gift to Christ that is a gift of self to the Father (*RD* 14), and an act of love lived out in the Holy Spirit (*RD* 10). It is a consecration in which apostolate and witness are rooted (*RD* 15). The pope affirmed the nature of the relationship between the consecrated religious, their institute and the church's mission.

> This consecration determines your place in the vast community of the church, the People of God. And at the same time this consecration introduces into the universal mission of this people a special source of spiritual and supernatural energy: a particular style of life, witness and apostolate, in fidelity to the mission of your institute and to its identity and spiritual heritage. (*RD* 7)

An institute's spiritual heritage is a living spiritual energy giving direction to its life, witness, and apostolate. As institutes redefine their heritage in contemporary terms they keep alive the gift that their institute is for the whole church. In this way, what was recognized as a charism of the founder, inspires the living charism of the institute.[39]

---

of the institutes of consecrated life, in preference to "charisms" (as used in the 1982 schema). Although subsequent church documents did speak of "charisms" in relation to religious life, the Vatican II documents themselves did not. Perhaps this is the reason for the substitution made in 1983. In this an institutional approach prevailed over a pneumatological one. Corecco suggested that "the Code yielded to the repeated objection that no juridical value can be assigned to charisms and did not have the courage to penetrate to the heart of the church's constitutional structure by tackling the ontological essence of the faithful in all its aspects." Corecco, "Reception of Vatican II," 266.

38. Part 3 of the *Code of Canon Law* (1983) is entitled "Institutes of Consecrated Life and Societies of Apostolic Life." It consists of two subsections: the first, "Norms Common to All Institutes of Consecrated Life" (Can. 573–606), and the second, "Religious Institutes" (Can. 607–709). The second gives the essential features and regulations for religious life in the Catholic Church.

39 See Beyer, "Evangelical Counsels," 64–89.

> This apostolate is always born from that particular gift of your founders, which, received from God and approved by the church, has become a charism for the whole community. That gift corresponds to the different needs of the church and the world at particular moments of history, and in its turn, it is extended and strengthened in the life of the religious communities as one of the enduring elements of the church's life and apostolate. (*RD* 15)

For the pope, the mission of the church was the greater reality in which the religious institute's mission finds its purpose.

The post-Vatican II *Catechism of the Catholic Church* affirmed that "the state of life constituted by the profession of the evangelical counsels belongs to the church's life and holiness rather than its hierarchical structure" (*CCC* 914). It spoke of the different kinds of religious consecration in religious families and gave the image of one great tree with many branches, depicting the diversity and the unity of the religious calling. "Different religious families have come into existence in which spiritual resources are multiplied for the progress in holiness of their members and for the good of the entire Body of Christ" (*CCC* 917).

The *Catechism* gave attention to the eschatological witness of religious life. "In the consecrated life, Christ's faithful, moved by the Holy Spirit, propose to follow Christ more nearly, to give themselves to God who is loved above all and, pursuing the perfection of charity in the service of the Kingdom, to signify and proclaim in the church the glory of the world to come" (*CCC* 916). The church called on religious women and men to bear witness to God's love in the world. "Religious life derives from the mystery of the church. It is a gift she has received from her Lord, a gift she offers as a stable way of life to the faithful called by God to profess the counsels. Thus, the church can both show forth Christ and acknowledge herself to be the Savior's bride. Religious life in its various forms is called to signify the very charity of God in the language of our time" (*CCC* 926).

The 1994 Synod of Bishops took as its theme "The Consecrated Life and Its Mission in the Church and in the World." It was grateful to God's Holy Spirit for the many different forms of consecrated life that existed in the church. In his introduction to the post-synodal apostolic exhortation, Pope St. John Paul II spoke of "the many charisms" by which the Holy Spirit had blessed the church.

> In every age there have been men and women who, obedient to the Father's call and to the prompting of the Spirit, have chosen this special way of following Christ, in order to devote

themselves to him with an "undivided" heart (cf. 1 Cor 7:34). Like the apostles, they too have left everything behind in order to be with Christ and to put themselves, as he did, at the service of God and their brothers and sisters. In this way, through the many charisms of spiritual and apostolic life bestowed on them by the Holy Spirit, they have helped to make the mystery and mission of the church shine forth, and in doing so have contributed to the renewal of society.[40]

2. The Founding Spiritan Charism

The new understanding of the Spiritan charism that came with its Vatican II renewal was grounded in an appreciation of the lives of cofounders, Claude Poullart des Places and Francis Libermann. Continuous research and discussion on Spiritan identity and mission in a postconciliar spirit from 1968 (GC XIII, the extraordinary general chapter of renewal) to 1986 (GC XVI, the general chapter of the *Spiritan Rule of Life*) led to a rediscovery of the Spiritan vocation: life in religious community for the evangelization of the poor (*SRL* 2, 4). "What would Poullart des Places do today?" "What would Libermann do today?" Are these valid questions to ask? Yes, in the sense that, as following their inspiration, those who walk in their footsteps in the distinctive character of their foundation seek to do as they did in their time responsive as they were to the Spirit at work in them in the context of their times. They are not to be copied in the details of lifestyle and time-conditioned thinking but in terms of the charism which God had bestowed on the church through them. That gift, "which the Holy Spirt gave them and continues to give to their followers," needs to be "constantly deepened and clarified."[41]

Founders are best appreciated when they are considered in terms of their time and place. It is not the particularities of their lives that their followers ought to imitate. The working of the Holy Spirit in their lives can be understood in two respects. First, as they sought to do God's will and experienced divine providence at work in them in the everyday events of their lives. Second, as founders and progenitors of a story that continues to be told and unfolds in new places and times keeping the thread that began with them and connects the present with its past from which strength and inspiration is drawn. The thread can be identified as the spirituality and mission constantly reexpressed in new language that speaks to different

40. *Vita consecrata* (25 March 1996), 1.
41. Gilbert and Fay, "Spiritan Vocation," 17.

times and places. J. M. R. Tillard, OP, distinguished between a founder's charism and the foundation's charism.

> Someone has the inspiration of a "foundation" and receives from the Spirit the graces needed to realize it. But this inspiration does not necessarily come from a private spiritual vision, from a great mystical perception one wishes others to share. Very often, on the contrary, it is simply a question of noting a need to be met, the discovery of a void nothing is filling. And, in the light of the gospel, one feels compelled to incarnate the precept of charity into that situation. Then one gathers men or women inflamed with love of the gospel and gives them a rule. ... As for the more properly spiritual or mystical vision nourishing the evangelical form of existence that one gives the group, it is often drawn from a prominent spiritual current or devotion of the time. The "foundation" shines forth more than the person who gave rise to it. . . . The grace of this "inspired" person, "his charism," will have been to allow a group to appear that the church or society needed.[42]

The metanarrative or "deep story" of Spiritan life and mission told in the time of change occasioned by Vatican II needs to be told anew and its language understood so that the rich heritage that the experience produced, the new rule of life (*SRL*), and how it was subsequently implemented, is more completely appreciated. Spiritan Casimer Eke, writing in *Spiritan Horizons*,[43] reflected on the work of the Marist, Bernard J. Lee's *The Beating of Great Wings*, who distinguished between a religious family's charism and what he terms its "deep story" and defined as "the narrative structure of a community's life deeply embedded in its reflected and un-reflected instincts."[44] Storytelling is therapeutic and life-giving. It is the product of interpersonal or social interactions and enables new understandings and possibilities for its participants. It generates a language of reflection and

---

42. Gobeil, "Life-Experience," 47–48.

43. *Spiritan Horizons* was first published in 2006 and has continued publication with one issue each year. It is a research journal, produced only in the English language, involving academics, particularly from Duquesne University, as well as Spiritans, lay and religious. Articles are grouped under the headings of "Wellsprings," which refer to the Spiritan charism, heritage, and history; "Soundings," which widens reflection to include topical missiological and ecclesiological questions as they relate to Spiritan mission and life; "Education," with articles on different aspects of the Spiritan education apostolate. A forum on "Lived Experience" includes a wide range of reflections from Spiritans on their mission and life experience.

44. Eke, "Re-inventing the Spiritan Charism," 41.

partnership and provides opportunities to locate present concerns within a bigger context in which deeper meanings are found.[45]

Claude Poullart des Places

Irish Spiritan historian Fr. Seán Farragher, CSSp, chose *Led by the Spirit* as the title for his book on the life and work of Claude Poullart des Places. This title was applied not only to Claude but to the movement which began with him and continued long after him. Farragher found the source for Claude's devotion to the Holy Spirit in his growing up in Brittany at a time of religious renewal. That renewal was influenced by the spiritual doctrine of Jesuit Fr. Louis Lallemant (1588–1635) who taught the importance of purity of heart and the guidance of the Holy Spirit, with the first enabling the second. One quotation from Lallemant demonstrates that influence.

> When a soul has given itself up to the leading of the Holy Spirit, he raises it little by little, and directs it. At the first it knows not whither it is going, but gradually the interior light illuminates it, and enables it to behold all its own actions, and the governance of God therein, so that it has scarcely aught else to do than to let God work in it and by it whatever he pleases; thus, it makes wonderful progress.[46]

Other formative influences that influenced Claude was his education at Collège Saint-Thomas, a Jesuit school where Lallement's doctrine was well-known. Claude's friendship there with St. Louis Grignon de Montfort brought him into contact with Fr. Julien Bellier, a young priest working at Rennes cathedral animating youth to visit and care for the poor.[47]

Farragher connected this early spiritual development to Claude's choice of Pentecost Sunday (27 May 1703) for the beginning of his community of poor scholars. "Claude had chosen that feast because he had for his own reasons decided to dedicate his community in a particular way to the Holy Spirit under the patronage of Mary Immaculate."[48] The first words

---

45. See Kwok, "Narrative Therapy," 201–12. Kwok advocates the incorporation of spirituality in the counseling process which provides clients the opportunity to appreciate God and reality through a narrative perspective. Narrative therapy meets the need to reflect on experience, particularly traumatic experiences, and in recognizing a providential aspect to them, meaning is given to them and new energy acquired through their appreciation.

46. Farragher, *Led by the Spirit*, 126.

47. See Michel, *Poullart des Places*, 12–16.

48. Ibid.

of Claude's rule for his community confirmed this. The students "will have a great devotion to the Holy Spirit, to whom they are consecrated in a special way." This starting point comes from deep within his own experience of God's personal love for him. God could not be outdone in generosity. "In exchange for a small act of love of God, I experienced interiorly God's reciprocal gifts which words cannot fittingly describe." And again, in his *Reflections on the Past* he wrote, "Whenever I made some effort to approach the Lord, that merciful Master immediately carried me for many leagues on his shoulders. Finally, I was able to do without effort what formerly I considered impossible for a man like me."[49]

In 1979, Fr. Jean Savoie, CSSp, gave a conference in Rome to celebrate the birthday of Claude Poullart des Places (26 February). This was one of many conferences and research papers given about him in the years of renewal connecting Spiritans with their first founder.

> He was a spiritual man who abandoned himself to the Holy Spirit in the circumstances which life presented. He heard the Spirit call him through the people he met. He imitated Christ his Master first of all. . . . Poullart did not spin theories,—he lived. He is a witness more than a teacher. He is a spiritual man who allowed himself to be conquered and led by God little by little.[50]

In 1985, Fr. Gobeil published his research on the continuity of the Spiritan identity from the eighteenth to the twentieth century. He recognized the influence of Lallemant both on Fr. Claude Poullart des Places and on Fr. Francis Libermann who "spoke of purification, self-denial, mortification in order to reach the point where one is led by the Holy Spirit, through surrender and leading to union."[51] Gobeil noted that Libermann wrote from Rennes to a seminarian recommending that he read Lallemant. He also pointed out that Libermann and Lallemant used the same image of a boat in full sail to describe a soul being led by the Spirit (*N.D.* XI.87).

Fr. Amadeu Martins reflected on the beginnings of the congregation and the significance of a retreat given by Poullart des Places to the group of twelve he had chosen to form community with him at Gros Chapelet in Rue des Cordiers in 1703.[52] The retreat was entitled "He Has Sent Me to Preach the Gospel to the Poor." That, for Martins, is the inspiration that continued to sustain the congregation through its long history. He discovered a similar

---

49. Koren, *Spiritual Writings*, 133.
50. Savoie, "Spiritual Personality," 23.
51. Gobeil, "Breath of the Spirit," 31.
52. Martins, "When the Spirit Inspires," 3–25.

text also inspired by Luke 4:18, at the Seminary at Rue Lhomond. It read, "*Pauperes evangelizantur ad revelationem gentium et gloriam plebis suae*," and he concluded that "the words give good expression to the purpose and spirit of the congregation and summarize its activity during the almost three hundred years of its existence."[53] This motto was borne out by the students formed in the seminary. Martins quoted from letters written by Fr. Louis Bouic, des Places's successor, to confirm this.[54]

> Thanks to God's mercy, we have already trained a good number (of priests) who are working zealously and giving a good example. Every day we receive good reports about most of them to the effect that they are very edifying and are doing fruitful work for the salvation of souls. Several of them, in less than three years, have re-established many parishes, restoring faith and piety and the frequentation of the sacraments. They learned here the importance of these things; now they are communicating it to others.[55]

The des Places formula, "to train the poor to evangelize the poor," continued in his followers. His care for seminarians was also continued. Martins quoted from another of Bouic's letters.

> The preoccupation with the health of the students was enshrined in the rules the founder wrote for the seminary: "the food was to be simple but solid." The food is simple, but nourishing: a little meat at dinner and at supper on non-fast days; almost always vegetables on fast days, half a pint of wine per day. The bread is excellent, the meat and the wine are fair, and hunger makes it all taste good.[56]

The Holy Ghost Seminary survived the French Revolution; changing political fortunes; continuous attacks from a Gallican hierarchy and a Jansenist clergy; a skeleton staff and, at times, low morale both in the seminary and in the colonies. But time and adverse conditions had taken their toll. A

---

53. Ibid. This text was placed on the cornerstone of the foundations of the chapel of the Congregation at 30 rue Lhomond in Paris on October 3, 1777. "The poor are being evangelized, the nations enlightened, and the people give him glory."

54. Koren, *Spiritans*, 19. Fr. Jacques Hyacinthe Garnier succeeded des Places but died in March 1710. Fr. Louis Bouic (1684–1763) followed and had the ability and support of his confreres (he was approved as superior seventeen times) "to consolidate the young society firmly and to build up its defenses against a variety of hostile forces that soon began to threaten its very existence."

55. Martins, "When the Spirit Inspires," 20.

56. Ibid., 7.

report in 1847, quoted by Martins, spoke disparagingly of the colonial clergy at that time, many of which had been trained at the Holy Ghost Seminary.

> There is no way to defend the present-day colonial clergy. With few exceptions, they are an ignorant lot of priests, insolent and sometimes dissolute. There are several reasons for this: . . . They look upon themselves as the clergy of the white people exclusively. . . . —For some time now, a different outlook is beginning to appear: some attempts are being made, but they are weak, irregular, and without much fruit.[57]

The same correspondent saw where the problem was and suggested a solution. "The Congregation of the Holy Ghost needs new blood and new life; but such an undertaking is beyond human power."[58] Martins saw divine intervention at work in *Propaganda Fide*'s strategy of bringing together the descendants of des Places and the followers of Libermann.

> True enough, the "undertaking" was beyond human power, but God did not want to let perish that admirable work which for a century and a half had done so much good. To give it that new blood it needed, God raised up Libermann and his Work for the Blacks. Since 1841, some of his disciples were already at work among the black slaves in the colonies and were drawing the same kind of praise as the missionaries trained at Holy Ghost Seminary for more than a century.[59]

The "rediscovery" at the beginning of the twentieth century of Claude Poullart des Places as the congregation's founder in 1703 enriched its mission.[60] Archbishop Le Roy, superior general at the time, recognized the

---

57. Ibid., 23.

58. Ibid.

59. Ibid., 23–24.

60. Following the death of Libermann, his successor, Schwindenhammer, considered Libermann as the first superior general of the congregation. The collection of Libermann's spiritual writings, Écrits Spirituels, published in 1891 when Fr. Ambroise Emonet was superior general, for example, recognized Libermann on the title page as the "Premier Supérieur Général de la Congrégation du S. Esprit et du S. Coeur de Marie." This practice continued into the generalate of Mgr. Le Roy. An American publication, *Spiritual Letters of the Venerable Francis Mary Paul Libermann* (vol. 1), translated by Fr. Charles L. Grunewald, gave Fr. Libermann the title "First Superior General of the Congregation of the Holy Ghost and the Immaculate Heart of Mary." The publication received the "approbation" of Alexandre Le Roy. This book was originally published by John Bornman & Son (Detroit, 1901), and republished by Forgotten Books (Delaware, 2012). Another biography of Libermann by Helen Walker Homan, entitled *Star of Jacob: The Story of Venerable Francis Libermann* and published in 1953, referred to Libermann as "Founder of the Congregation of the Holy Ghost and of the Immaculate

fortuitousness of this discovery, not only ensuring the legal status of the congregation but also strengthening its charism.[61] The founding charisms of the congregation are those of des Places and Libermann and continues from them in paths they could not have anticipated and services to the church in the world they could not have imagined. Writing in 1985, Gobeil recognized the "lasting imprint" Poullart des Places made that remained largely unacknowledged in the nineteenth and early twentieth centuries. He interpreted the development of the congregation in fidelity to the charism given it at its beginning in Poullart des Places and interpreted it as "a re-foundation" (I/D 36, 2–4). "As well as the rich witness of his life, Claude Poullart implanted a spirit in his seminary which marked with lasting imprint several generations of apostolic workers. And many treasures of our Spiritan tradition in expressions like '*one heart and one soul*' (Letter of Fr. Lanoe, 6 November 1784), availability '*parati ad omnia*' (Rules and Constitutions of 1734), '*towards the abandoned posts*' (Patent Letters of 1726) might surprise some people by the date of their origin."[62]

Francis Libermann

Farragher considered it "a remarkable coincidence" that des Places's home town of Rennes was also the location of the Eudist Novitiate (Antrain, north of Rennes) where Libermann was novice director. He wrote that led by the Spirit,

> both Claude Francis Poullart des Places and Francis Mary Paul Libermann had set out from almost the same spot in Rennes, though at an interval of one hundred and thirty years, leaving a life of security behind them and putting their trust only in God as they went in search of their vocation. Claude, instead of opting for the diocesan priesthood and entering the major seminary conducted by the Eudists, had, all unknown to himself at the time, sown the seeds of his real vocation through involvement with Fr. Bellier in training poor students for the priesthood. In 1839 Libermann was to walk away from the material

---

Heart of Mary."

61. The challenge to the legal status of the congregation in France in 1901 occasioned the fortuitous rediscovery of the congregation's origin with des Places in 1703. Subsequently the general chapter in 1919 under Archbishop Le Roy affirmed Poullart des Places as the first founder of the congregation and Francis Libermann as its second founder and spiritual father. See "A Merger, an Attempted Takeover," by Michael Kilkenny, CSSp, in *Spiritan Horizons* 5 (2010) 19–33.

62. Gobeil, "Life Experience," 48.

security of the Eudist novitiate in Rennes to throw in his lot with a group of students fired with zeal for the pastoral care of the black slaves being liberated at the time.[63]

It was not difficult for Farragher to attribute the coming together of the two congregations to divine providence. Libermann saw it that way. "The union of our two societies has always appeared to me to be in accord with the designs and the will of God; they undertake the same work and are travelling along the same path. Now it is not according to the designs of providence to raise up two societies to do one special work if one can do the work alone."[64]

Libermann agreed to the dissolution of his Holy Heart of Mary congregation for its members to join the Holy Ghost congregation in 1848. At first, his decision met with resistance from his members who could remember that only six years earlier Libermann had rejected a merger with another congregation, Fr. Moreau's Congregation of the Holy Cross. In a letter to his collaborator Fr. Eugene Tisserant, he doubted that the proposed union was for the glory of God and the well-being of "our poor blacks." He urged that the question be approached calmly, as the works of God did not demand swift replies. He noted that Moreau's congregation of the Holy Cross was founded in 1837, and was stronger than the Holy Heart of Mary congregation. Consequently, he feared that the charism of his congregation, dedication to the evangelization of the poor, particularly its *l'oeuvre des noirs*, would suffer as the result of a merger. Although assurances would be given at the time that this would not be the case, what would happen when Moreau, Tisserant, himself and others that agreed the merger, had died? What would happen to the work for the blacks then?[65]

Martins asked the question, "When Poullart des Places founded the seminary for poor students, could he have foreseen the future development of his project?" He did not think so and quoted the memorable words Libermann wrote to Tisserant. "It is true that when the Holy Spirit inspires a work, he almost never gives advance notice of its full development, but only gradually as the occasion presents itself. However, the entire development is contained in the initial impulse he gives to the one he inspires to begin it.

63. Farragher, *Led by the Spirit*, 272.
64. N.D. X.339.
65. N.D. III.153–59. Blessed Basile Moreau (1799–1873) was a priest of the diocese of Le Mans and founded his congregation, Sainte-Croix, on 1 March 1837 initially from the clergy of Le Mans. Like Libermann he studied at Saint Sulpice. The charism of the Holy Cross Congregation was "to educate in the faith" as Moreau saw education to be the key to evangelization. He sought to battle the secularization of society in postrevolutionary France through education. The Holy Cross congregation included priests, brothers and a congregation of sisters founded in 1841.

There is a certain unity in all the diversity of its history."[66] Martins argued that Libermann's "fusion" with the Holy Ghost congregation was strategic as through it his mission to "the poor blacks" would be advanced as both were founded to serve the poor. "Neither one of the two congregations changed; neither one took the place of the other; they completed one another. Libermann did not take the place of Poullart des Places; he represents rather the full development of his spirit and his work. All that was implicit in Poullart des Places becomes explicit in Libermann."[67]

> We have always placed our confidence and our happiness in the Heart of Mary filled with the superabundance of the Holy Spirit, and, if we did not express that plenitude of the Holy Spirit in the Heart of Mary, nevertheless it formed the essence of our devotion to the Most Holy Heart of Mary. We are not making a change! What was understood and pre-supposed before, we now make explicit.[68]

In 1998, the Year of the Holy Spirit, Fr. Francis Malinowski, CSSp, presented Libermann's doctrine of the Holy Spirit in a series of "in-house" publications for use in the USA province. He compared Pope St. John Paul II's thoughts on the Holy Spirit with those of Libermann. Malinowski recognized in Libermann's writings an evolution

> from the cocoon life behind the monastic structures to the wide-open savanna of experience and horrible deprivation of the Black People in mission territory. In the complexity of coming to the aid of the poor, weak and oppressed, the poverty of means and the powerlessness of human endeavor called for continued and greater reliance on the Holy Spirit. The Spirit was now called upon to be a light to the missionary path and a consoling presence in the missionary's labor and fatigue.[69]

Malinowski presented Libermann's thinking on the Holy Spirit through study of his letters. Letter writing was Libermann's chief form of communication with his missionaries and one to which he fully dedicated himself. They brought light and consolation. He often counseled calmness and patience, as can be seen in his letter to his colleague Fr. Frederic Le Vavasseur in 1846. "The work of God has need of force, constancy, and a calm prudence. I plead with you for the love of God to think no longer of

---

66. Ibid., 158.
67. Martins, "When the Spirit Inspires," 25.
68 *N.D.* XII.133.
69. Malinowski, "Holy Spirit in Francis Libermann," 5.

yourself and what regards you. Do the work of God and act with calm according to the divine Spirit. Otherwise the demon will destroy this work of God as one burns straw."[70] Libermann, the wise respecter of persons, appreciated that the Spirit works in accordance with human nature. Malinowski summarized Libermann's understanding of the relationship between grace and nature. "Holiness, like human maturation, does not happen without our cooperation, without our sustained intention to be united with God in all we do and experience . . . divine grace, sown in the soul as a seed of life, does not develop without our fidelity and cooperation."[71]

In a letter to the community at La Neuville written from Rome in 1846, Libermann listed the signs of the Spirit. "Preserve my dear confreres, the spirit that animates you; preserve and fortify yourselves in that without ceasing and yet more. Oh, yes, it is a good spirit, it is the Spirit of God. The most infallible marks of the presence of God among us, is when this spirit is a spirit of peace, sweetness, mutual charity, simplicity, humility, obedience, and regularity."[72] The absence of this spirit prevents the Holy Spirit from doing "great things" in his missionaries. Communities in Africa looked to Libermann for advice and encouragement. He wasn't found lacking in either. The community of Dakar and Gabon, needed to see beyond their first impressions of the place and people they were called to serve and rely on the love of God.

> Listen to everything and be peaceful within you; examine the things in the Spirit of Jesus Christ, with independence of every impression, every bias whatever, and filled, animated, with the charity of God and with the pure zeal that his Spirit gives you. I am sure you will judge very differently our poor Blacks that all these men speak of.[73]

Libermann, who never traveled to Africa, was sensitive to the frustrations associated with being on mission in a tropical climate and encountering a new culture very different to what the pioneer missionaries were accustomed. He wrote to Bishop Truffet in 1847.

> You will learn in the spirit of prayer . . . to unite sweetness, patience, and apostolic moderation with the energy of nature and power of the action of the Spirit of God. . . . The difficulties are great and the pains strong . . . but Jesus wishes that his

---

70. Ibid., 71.
71. Malinowski, "Holy Spirit in the Writings," 13.
72. Ibid., *N.D.* VIII.190.
73. *N.D.* IX.330.

work remains pure and exempt from the faults of your nature whose very strengths are real weaknesses, whose grandeurs are pettiness and whose beauties are flaws when they come to be mixed in the so pure and so delicate action of the Spirit of Jesus. ... [May] Jesus and his divine Spirit animate you, illumine you, and give you life and force. ... You will know how to preserve, with all the energy and power of the Spirit of Jesus in you, sweetness, moderation, patience, humility, modesty, and the wisdom of Jesus.[74]

Libermann's advice to Truffet continued to guide Spiritans as they responded to Vatican II's call to adaptation and renewal. The Spiritan story of that time tells of a dynamic continuity through great change. The survival of the Spiritan congregation and its mission in the post Vatican II church can be attributed to the guidance of the Holy Spirit, loyalty to the church, and creative fidelity to its founding charism.

3. The Lived Spiritan Charism

The Spiritan Year (2 February 2002 to Pentecost Sunday 2003) provided a graced opportunity to celebrate the Spiritan charism and spirituality following the writing of the *Spiritan Rule of Life* (*SRL*) in 1986.[75] The superior general, Fr. Pierre Schouver, CSSp, in his letter on behalf of the general council, welcomed it as an "attempt to rediscover the inspiration of our beginnings by responding creatively to the challenges of our own day." He referred to the Spiritan year logo which consisted of a boat (in blue) like a *currach* (an Irish boat with a wooden frame and canvas) expressive of an invitation to get on board for a voyage and above it, the sail (in red embossed with the dove representing the Holy Spirit) fully extended, stretched, and filled by the breath of the Spirit. The year's events were about looking back to the past to set out once again with new energy into the future.

This energy would come from "the strength of the Spirit of Christ in the lived experience of those who have made our history up to the present day." By remembering the humble trust of Poullart des Places and Libermann's confidence in the Lord the congregation was sustained in its mission and life. From des Places, we read:

---

74. N.D. IX.351–52.

75. The Second of February 2002 marked 150 years since the death of Libermann; Pentecost Sunday 2003 marked 300 years since Poullart des Places founded his community of poor scholars.

> Let others say what they please about me; let them approve of me or make fun of me, treat me as a visionary, a hypocrite, or a righteous man! All this henceforth must leave me indifferent. He has given me life only that I may use it to serve him faithfully.... God alone loves me sincerely and wants what is good for me. If I can please him, I shall be exceedingly happy. If I displease him, I am the most wretched man in the world. I have won everything if I live in grace. Losing it, I lose everything.[76]

Libermann wrote in 1844 to his community at Cape Palmas on the West African coast:

> Don't be frightened by the difficulties you meet; never let them discourage you. You have not come in your own name; you are not the ones who are doing the work: it is he who sent you. You are not alone; he is always with you if you remain faithful. So, don't be faint-hearted or weak in your faith. An apostle of Jesus Christ can never be put off by obstacles. Put up with them with patience and in peace, but always persevere with your plans when they are truly for the glory of God and the salvation of souls. Wait a bit when you meet difficulties that you can't overcome for the moment; just wait confidently for God's moment to arrive. It will come if you don't lose faith.[77]

Schouver's letter pointed to an understanding of the Spiritan charism as a lived reality. Its progenitors, des Places and Libermann, provide the standard and Spiritans both past, present and to come, follow that standard with personal commitment and community solidarity in the evangelization of the poor. Each Spiritan responds to the call to follow Jesus and to announce the good news of God's kingdom in the world through creative fidelity to the Spiritan way marked out by its rule. The Spiritan vocation "challenges us to discernment, to reproduce the spirit of the founders in the conditions of our time."[78] The congregation made its *aggiornamento* after Vatican II with many meetings and the writing of *SRL*, but "the challenge of the contemporary world is an on-going thing." The congregation would not be found wanting as "many confreres are giving an example of calm strength, perseverance, new initiatives despite obstacles and disappointments, a simple

---

76. From Claude Poullart des Places, "Reflection on the Truth of Religion," quoted in *A Message to All Confreres for the Spiritan Year* 1/D 60 (2003).

77. N.D. VI.3–8.

78. *Handbook for the Spiritan Rule of Life*, 12.

presence amongst the people, of fraternal life amongst different cultures, of a sense of responsibility and a deep concern for spiritual renewal."[79]

In 1982 Henry Koren, CSSp, defined the Spiritan charism as "an evangelical availability which remains attentive to the Holy Spirit manifesting himself in the concrete situations of life."[80] For des Places, and Libermann after him, there was a double availability at work: to the Lord and to others. For des Places, the Savoyard chimney sweeps, and poor seminarians; for Libermann, it was the poor and abandoned people wherever they were to be found and most particularly, the peoples of Africa. The apostolic and the religious dimensions are intertwined in the one Spiritan vocation. Evangelical availability implied a simple lifestyle unencumbered by material things or the desire for them and an openness to the experience of life allowing oneself to be led by the Spirit discerning what comes from God rather than any fixed way of thinking determined by one's own limited understanding.[81] Koren highlighted the openness of des Places and Libermann to life experience. He recognized their generous self-giving in service of others and the establishment of God's kingdom. They did not speak in absolutist terms but encouraged their followers to be ever responsive to human need as it became known to them. Libermann entitled his 1840 Rule "provisional" as it would be perfected through experience in subsequent years.

Libermann's evangelical availability knew no bounds. He wanted the members of the Holy Heart of Mary to take on the task of meeting the needs of the poor that older societies in France had left undone. He planned to begin in Bordeaux and extend an apostolate to the poor of France from there. "The old religious institutes do not undertake this task because originally their societies did not concern themselves with it." Although dedicated to missionary work in Africa he would expend energy closer to home in responding to the call of the poor.[82] Like the boy Samuel in the Old Testament, Libermann was ever attentive to the voice of God (1 Sam 3:1–14). Koren suggested that Libermann's Jewish background made him sensitive to God's action in every day events.[83]

---

79. Ibid.

80. Koren, "Our Spiritan Charism," 15.

81. Bishop Jean Gay summarized Libermann's spirituality as "listening calmly to what the Holy Spirit has to tell us and living intensely the love of Christ so as to be close to the poor—this is the essence of the teaching of Père Libermann, the summary of his spirituality." Quoted in *Spiritan Anniversaries Diary*, 8.

82. Referring to work among the poor in Bordeaux, Libermann wrote that he would try "to give this work the greatest extension possible according to the resources in personnel and funds which divine Providence will place at my disposal" (*N.D.* IX.275).

83. Koren, *Essays*, 26. Koren's insight into the influence of Libermann's Jewishness

> He does not silence God under the pretext that He has already spoken before and in a different way. He does not try to hide from this voice behind a model of life and works which he had undertaken before in obedience to that voice, but he always remains in an attitude of unconditional availability before God. He abstains from assigning to God a place fixed by himself in a system of serving God based on the religious past.[84]

Koren's own thinking on Libermann was shaped by the postconciliar engagement of the church with the world. Vatican II understood that "apostolic and charitable activity belongs to the very nature of the religious life, seeing that it is a holy service and a work characteristic of love, entrusted to them by the church to be carried out in its name" (*PC* 8). It was hoped that the renewal and adaptation of the apostolic religious institutes would enable the taking up of "tasks for which the church has difficulty in finding workers" (*SRL* 4).

Telling the Spiritan Story

A story about storytelling from the Rabbi Israel Baal Shem Tov collection of Hasidic stories illustrates the importance of storytelling for a people in their relationship with one another, others, and God.[85]

> Whenever the Jews were threatened with disaster, the Baal Shem Tov would go to a certain place in the forest, light a fire, and say a special prayer. Always a miracle would occur, and the disaster would be averted.
>
> In later times when disaster threatened, his disciple, the Maggid of Mezritch, would go to the same place in the forest and say, "Master of the Universe, I do not know how to light the fire, but I can say the prayer." And again, the disaster would be averted.

---

on his sensitivity to God's involvement in the present moment was substantiated by reference to the writing of Jewish philosopher Martin Buber, who wrote, "The believing Jew lives in the consciousness that the proper place for his encounter with God lies in the ever-changing situations of life. . . . Again and again, the believing Jew hears God's voice in a different way in the language spoken by unforeseen and changed situations." Quotation from *Der Glaube, der Profeten* (Zürich: Manesse Verlag, 1950), 104.

84. Koren, *Essays*, 26.

85. Hasidic Judaism is a branch of Orthodox Judaism that promotes spirituality through the popularization and internalization of Jewish mysticism as the fundamental aspect of the faith. It was founded in eighteenth century Eastern Europe by Rabbi Israel Baal Shem Tov in reaction to the overly legalistic Judaism of his time.

> Still later, his disciple, Moshe Leib of Sasov, would go to the same place in the forest and say, "Lord of the World, I do not know how to light the fire or say the prayer, but I know the place and that must suffice." And it always did.
>
> When Israel of Rizhyn needed intervention from heaven, he would say to God, "I no longer know the place, nor how to light the fire, nor to say the prayer, but I can tell the story and that must suffice." . . . And it did.[86]

Hasidic wisdom tells us that remembering stories gives life. It is not so much that we possess the story, but more, that the story possesses us. As the novelist Chinua Achebe put it,

> It is only the story that can continue beyond the war and the warrior. It is the story that outlives the sound of war-drums and the exploits of brave fighters. It is the story . . . that saves our progeny from blundering like blind beggars into the spikes of the cactus fence. The story is our escort; without it, we are blind. Does the blind man own his escort? No, neither do we the story; rather it is the story that owns us and directs us.[87]

Each individual story is part of a bigger story and it is that bigger story which validates the individual stories. It is the common story that unites a group through expression of a common culture, heritage, and destiny.

Every religious family has a deep story which preserves unity, confirms identity, and sustains purpose. While on the surface much changes, yet at the deeper level of the common story, the group's identity abides. Since Vatican II many religious congregations were traumatized by dramatic change and unable to maintain unity of membership and integrity of purpose. Some disappeared altogether, unable to reconnect with their founding charism in changed circumstances. A community's charism needed expression, or like earth deprived of moisture it becomes a wasteland.

> To live religious life without signs and symbols is impossible. We are sign-makers and live in a world of signs. Of course, it is possible to have signs without signification, as one might see in a dying monastery. What happened in the past forty years or so is not the abolition of signs but the dissolution of common signs. Often in the name of apostolic service or availability, common signs were rejected. Work, for example, would always excuse a religious from prayer, Mass, or a meal. The result was not an absence of signs but a new set of signs that separated or divided

---

86. Frankel, *Classic Tales*, 551.
87. Achebe, *Anthills of the Savannah*, 114.

rather than unified. A community without common signs often lost the meaning that those signs were meant to express.[88]

The rediscovery of the life-giving Spiritan story in the congregation's journey since Vatican II has sustained its life and mission. In the turmoil of change a "deep story" was discovered and retold. It was the gathering together and the telling of this story that replaced so much of what formerly maintained unity through lives defined by work, uniformity of lifestyle and a submissive obedience.

The Spiritan Story

The Spiritan story, as with any human story, is a complex one. Conflicts on different levels of the individual, the community and mission once dealt with through rules and obedience were, since Vatican II, addressed through dialogue and discernment. There were many challenges in transitioning from a directive to a participative model of authority with tensions between individual freedom and the common good; demands of the apostolate and the requirements of religious life; congregation building at home and missionary work abroad; all construed in binary opposition to each another.

At the personal and human level, the dominant pre-Vatican II understanding of religious obedience as self-abasement and personal mortification was at odds with the fast-growing personal psychology advocating autonomy and human fulfillment. A comparison of "Rodriguez," the prescribed spiritual text for novitiates in religious institutes before Vatican II, with the language of modern psychologists such as Abraham Maslow, is instructive.

Alphonsus Rodriguez, SJ, in his *Practice of Perfection and Christian Virtues* (1929), gave examples and practices for the development of the Christian virtues. One example given was that of the Abbot Agatho who for three years carried a pebble below his tongue to gain the virtue of silence. Another was taken from St. Jerome who, when visiting a monastery in the desert, noticed a monk dragging a large stone uphill some three miles. This he had been doing each day for eight years so that through this act of

---

88. Lienhard, "Signs of the Times," 99–100. Gribble recognized the importance of signs and symbols for religious life post Vatican II. "The almost wholesale and unprecedented abandonment of accepted signs after Vatican II has helped send the consecrated life into its present malaise and tailspin. In some cases, when old signs were abandoned new ones were taken on, but these new signs often conflicted with the old, leading to a turn to secularity, conflict, and disunity." Gribble, *Religious Life*, 13.

obedience to his superior he could mortify his judgment.[89] In contrast, the new psychology offered a more holistic appreciation of the human person. Abraham Maslow, for example, in *Motivation and Personality* advocated self-actualization achieved through the satisfaction of physical, social, and personal/spiritual needs. A positive Christian anthropology, developed since Vatican II, corresponds well with contemporary personality theories. The assertion of St. Irenaeus in the second century that "the glory of God is humanity fully alive"[90] is in tune with Maslow's psychology of the twentieth century when it states that "a musician must make music, an artist must paint, a poet must write, if he is to be at ultimate peace with himself. What a man *can* be, he *must* be. He must be true to his own nature."[91]

The quest for personal growth and the need to give meaning to the religious and missionary Spiritan vocation gave rise to many conflicting viewpoints in the congregation. These conflicts dominated the sixties and percolated through the seventies to be addressed through the emergence of a growing respect for each individual member and a reimagining of Spiritan community as the primary locus to satisfy the personal belonging needs and growth of its members. Congregational leadership promoted widespread animation that sought to build respect among members, one for another; the reconciliation of differences and the promotion of unity among an increasingly diverse membership. The renewal process located contemporary challenges within the bigger Spiritan story and its charism which brought much-needed stability to the congregation enabling it to seek new members in former mission territories and engage in a wider range of ministries.

---

89 "Rodriguez" was remembered by Irish Spiritans as "a rather strange mixture of ascetical teaching, illustrated with a host of pious myths and legends which novices read walking around what was called the 'Rodriguez Walk'. Its pious legends provided much light relief for most novices, who had enough common sense not to take them seriously." Ryan, *Kimmage Manor*, 31. The humor associated with reading Rodriguez can be explained by the fact that the cultural experience of the novices had changed but the novitiate program had not.

90. *Adversus Haereses* [Against heresies] 4.34.7. *"Gloria enim Dei vivens homo, vita autem hominus visio Dei"* [For the glory of God is a living man, and the life of man consists in beholding God.]

91. Maslow, *Motivation*, 48.

Chapter 2

The Spiritan Congregation, Change, and Vatican II

1. The Phenomenon of Change

MILLENNIALS MAY HAVE DIFFICULTY in imagining a time when change was gradual with predictable outcomes. The American writer and futurist Alvin Toffler wrote a best seller in 1970 analyzing the psychological state of stress and disorientation suffered by people and entire societies experiencing too much change in too short a time. He labelled the phenomenon as "future shock," the title of his book. Since the 1970s there have been many studies on the human condition affected by societal change with the move from industrial to super-industrial societies. The reality was that "change is not merely necessary for life. It is life." Toffler spoke of the need for individuals and societies to protect themselves from such trauma. One way for doing this was to create oases of security in their lives in which they could find refuge from the fast current of change.[1]

The Catholic Church, prior to Vatican II, represented such an oasis for many. It was a confident and fixed institution which preserved its traditions and institutions through a worldwide conformity to ritual, teaching, and law. Bismarck's *Kulturkampf* in Germany and Italy's *Risorgimento* in the late nineteenth century threatened the Catholic Church. The response was a strengthening of papal powers in the wake of its reduced temporal authority

---

1. Hugh McLeod has provided an authoritative study on the religious crisis of the 1960s. He provides a detailed, comparative and in many respects nuanced account of what happened to Christianity in Europe, North America and Australasia in his book *Religious Crisis of the 1960s*. He characterized the "long sixties" from 1958 to 1975 as "the final crisis of Christendom."

throughout Europe and particularly in Italy. Pope Pius IX, who surrendered the Papal States to the new nation of Italy, became "the prisoner of the Vatican" from which he governed the Catholic Church. His papacy culminated in the First Vatican Council (1870) at which the spiritual authority of the papacy was confirmed and papal infallibility declared before the assembled bishops of the world. This exaltation of spiritual power acted as an antidote to shrinking temporal power.

The Lateran Treaty of 1929 between the fascist prime minister of Italy, Benito Mussolini, and Pope Pius XI settled the "Roman Question" by creating the Vatican state and regulated church/state relations in Italy. One of the chief negotiators for the Vatican in arriving at that treaty was its secretary of state, the brilliant Cardinal Eugenio Pacelli, who would succeed Pius XI in March 1939.

Pope Pius XII

Pope Pius XII (1876–1958) was a noted statesman and scholar. He not only steered the Catholic Church through a time of great political upheaval and change but also introduced gradual changes in thinking and church practices. For most Catholics living in the first fifty to sixty years of the twentieth century these changes were not immediately obvious as they were mostly at the level of leadership and scholarship in their church. His was a papacy of gradual adaptation in response to increasingly rapid change in the world. The breadth of Pius's learning and understanding was applied to maintaining the teachings of his predecessors on the one hand and addressing the demands for change put on the Catholic Church as part of a rapidly changing world.

There was a sense that, in Pius XII, the Catholic Church had reached the apogee of perfection enshrined in law and sacrament.[2] All that could be said had been said. Following the Second World War (1939–45) Catholics around the world looked to the bishop of Rome for intellectual guidance and moral strength. Authority in the Catholic Church was centralized in Rome with diocesan bishops functioning as vicars of the Vicar of Christ. The uniformity of language and custom, of belief and practice, was valued as a formidable strength of an invincible global institution. This was the perfect society that had survived the totalitarian regimes of the past and was equal to the challenges posed by the social change and secular thought of the twentieth century.

2. For those traditionalists who would come to consider the teachings of Vatican II as invalid he was "the last real pope."

In the early 1950s Pope Pius XII gave religious significance to the growing political divisions in the world. Speaking of the missionary work of the church he held up the specter of a world divided between those who were for Christ and those who were opposed.[3] A new impetus was given to the church's mission after the Second World War resulting in the strengthening of missionary societies and congregations through an increase in vocations.

Papal encyclicals represented the highest teaching authority of the church, and were accepted by Catholics without question.[4] The tension to sustain the old and introduce the new can be seen in them. Writing on the church (*Mystici corporis Christi*, 1943) he spoke of its mystical nature while also maintaining its juridical reality. He welcomed new departures in scripture scholarship (*Divino afflante Spiritu*, 1943) while also affirming the authority of the magisterium in the interpretation of scripture. In church liturgy (*Mediator Dei*, 1947) he distinguished between the divine and the human elements of the liturgy. While its human element was characterized by a certain relativity and, as such, subject to modification; the divine element remained immutable. He also set limits to theological research (*Humani generis*, 1950).[5]

In his encyclical on the missions, *Evangelii praecones* (1951), Pius XII demonstrated political astuteness in directing missionaries to introduce social reforms in mission territories. The preaching of the gospel required not only charity, but justice. He also recognized that non-Christian philosophies and cultures could be perfected and asserted that "Christian principles fit into any culture."[6]

A Pre-Vatican II Missiology

The salvation of souls and extending the borders of the Catholic Church continued to be the prevailing approach to missionary activity for the first

---

3. "Venerable Brethren, you are well aware that almost the whole human race is today allowing itself to be driven into two opposing camps, for Christ or against Christ. The human race is involved today in a supreme crisis, which will issue in its salvation by Christ, or in its dire destruction." Pius XII, encyclical letter, *Evangelii praecones* (1951) 70.

4. Pollard, *Papacy*, 415. "If the Supreme Pontiffs in their official documents purposely pass judgment on a matter up to that time under dispute, it is obvious that the matter, according to the mind and will of the same pontiff, cannot any longer be discussed among theologians" (*Humani generis*, 20).

5. The teaching of Pius XII is generally evaluated as enlightened and nuanced indicating knowledge of the "new thinking" on topics covered by his encyclicals which would prevail at Vatican II.

6. Pollard, *Papacy*, 426–27.

half of the twentieth century. Bevans and Schroeder have elaborated on the theological underpinnings of this approach under six headings.

First, the christological perspective highlights the divine satisfaction for sin and victory over the devil achieved through the cross. This objective act of redemption needed to be appropriated by each individual person "and this could only take place if one heard the message of Jesus, and explicitly confessed Jesus as Lord and Savior."[7]

Second, the dominant ecclesiology took literally the dictum attributed to St. Cyprian, the third-century bishop of Carthage, that there is no salvation outside the church, *extra ecclesiam nulla salus*. The Roman Catholic Church was the institution that mediated the salvation won by Christ to the world with emphasis on the hierarchy "as those who minister the sacraments that provide the means of salvation and who enforce the laws by which Christians can live out their lives in loyalty to God's law."[8] The goal of missionary activity was the extension of this church, which was identified with the European church as it was known at the time.

Third, the eschatological understanding of the time was a powerful motivation for missionary activity. Apart from general judgment at the end of time, there was particular judgment for each individual soul after death. "Those judged worthy of eternal life go immediately to their reward, those judged unworthy go immediately to their eternal punishment in the fires of hell. Those who are still in need of purification spend some time of cleansing and 'temporal punishment' in purgatory, a time that can be shortened by the prayers and good deeds of Christians on earth."[9] Future missionaries were encouraged in their vocation by vivid imagery of hell's torments awaiting the unbaptized millions in "pagan lands."

Fourth, the theological understanding of salvation was the single most important motivation for missionary work. Human beings were "enmeshed in sin, and so, if left on their own, doomed to eternal punishment and damnation. It is through Christ's satisfactory, redeeming work that people become 'disentangled' and so are able to live in ways that will ensure eternal life."[10]

Fifth, a negative anthropology understood the human being primarily as "fallen from grace" and in need of salvation. The sin of Adam had the devastating effect of alienating the human race and all of creation from God. The result of original sin was an enduring conflict between soul and body.

---

7. Bevans and Schroeder, *Constants in Context*, 39.
8. Ibid., 41.
9. Ibid., 43.
10. Ibid., 44.

St. Augustine (354–430) following Plato's philosophical distinction between body and soul, spoke of the soul as imprisoned in the body and in conflict with it. This dualism cast a long shadow over natural activity that was only alleviated through spiritual healing affected by God's grace. Human effort, unaided by grace was futile. "Full humanity, it was believed, was to be achieved by a denial of the body and a flight from the material world."[11]

Sixth, the negative anthropology led to the dismissal of all cultures outside of Christendom as lacking any value. The Christian culture of the West was, in Bernard Lonergan's terminology, normative, universal, and permanent. Other cultures were valued according to it. The gospel message was brought to other parts of the world packaged in the many layers of culture-bound European theologies that were impervious to change. "What was Christian was implicitly assumed to be Western, and what was Western, in the same way, was assumed to be Christian."[12] The churches established in mission territories were modeled on the European church with its many practices translated "lock, stock, and barrel."

Bevans and Schroeder concluded that it was such thinking that motivated "millions of Christians in the two thousand–year span of Christianity to suffer incredible hardships and to risk their lives so that the world might believe and so be saved."[13]

The Catholic Church, unlike its Protestant counterparts, was for the most part little affected by the enlightenment. The "fortress church" maintained its identity and place in a fractious and hostile world through the unerring central institution of the papacy.[14] A hierarchical, clerical, and juridical church culture was firmly in place since the Council of Trent (1545–1563) which codified the liturgy, revised canon law and established

---

11. Ibid., 46.

12. Ibid., 48.

13. Ibid., 49. The hardships and tragedies for missionaries on the West Coast of Africa in the nineteenth century are well documented beginning with the loss of most of Libermann's first band of twelve missionaries in the early 1840s. The first to die was Père Léopold de Régnier who wrote in his journal with fevered hand, on the night that he died: "I am going to bed. Bessieux has the African fever. . . . Gregory is half dead. . . . If I had the choice, I would do it again, a thousand times over, for the love of Jesus and Mary." De Régnier died on 30 December 1843 at Cape Palmas (in modern-day Liberia) after only three months in Africa. He was the first Catholic missionary of the nineteenth century to give his life in service of the African mission (Koren, *To the Ends of the Earth*, 186).

14. Conflicts between the center and the periphery were infrequent but significant. For example, the Gallican movement within the French church emphasized its independence over Rome with those loyal to Rome dubbed as *"ultramontane"* (beyond the mountain, i.e., looking to Rome and the supreme authority of the pope).

seminaries, And what of the Catholic Church in France, the headquarters for the missionary Congregation of the Holy Spirit?

France: Pays de Mission?

To what extent could France be declared a Catholic country? Apart from the big cities, about one-tenth of the population regularly practiced the faith.[15] There were many areas of society where "the institutions are pagan, the moral atmosphere is pagan, the people individually are pagans."[16] The shift from Catholic to "pagan" was measured generationally. At the time of the First World War the forty-year-old soldiers gave proof of Christian faith on the battlefield. The eighteen-year-old ones much less so, and those born after 1919 constituted a growing "pagan proletariat."[17] The root cause of this situation was the separation in France of religion from life. Since the Second World War, the church in France had embarked on a mission to secular society through initiatives such as the Young Catholic Workers movement, liturgical reform, and the worker priests. But was this too little, too late?

Postwar France was a society in ferment with a church in crisis. In response to this a new way of doing theology and engaging with society was emerging when Archbishop Angelo Roncalli, the future Pope John XXIII, was appointed papal nuncio in 1945.[18] He would later maintain that the calling of the Second Vatican Council resulted from an inspiration of the Holy Spirit received after becoming pope. It can be surmised that the Holy Spirit was at work much earlier in his life preparing the way for that inspiration, particularly during his seven years in Paris. Roncalli was familiar with the debates taking place at the time and troubled by the lack of the practice of religion in an increasingly secular state. He said in 1947, "I am concerned about the practice of religion, the unresolved question of the schools, the lack of clergy and the spread of socialism and communism."[19]

---

15. Ward, *France Pagan?*, 67. Regular church practice was much less in the cities.

16. Ibid., 79.

17. Ibid.

18. A theological revival was underway in France since the mid-1930s. This was a new approach to theology with attention given to religious experience and historical hermeneutics rather than the neo-Thomist method of syllogistic analysis. The group of revivalist Thomists was led principally by the Jesuits of the Lyons province and the Dominicans of Le Saulchoir, categorized by their opponents as the *"nouvelle théologie."* Some of the great names of twentieth-century Catholic scholarship are associated with the revival. These included Henri de Lubac, Jean Daniélou, Hans Urs von Balthasar, Yves Congar, Marie-Dominique Chenu, and Louis Bouyer.

19. Pollard, *Papacy*, 390.

We can get a flavor of the public debate on the church in France through the journal *Esprit*, which ran articles entitled "L'Église va-t-elle émigrer?" and "L'agonie du christianisme?" (May 1946) by M. Dupouey and E. Mounier (*Esprit*'s founder), respectively. The French Dominican theologian Fr. Yves Congar commented that "Dupouey was critical of the externals of the church, its sociological condition, its excessive 'prudence', and the advanced age of its leaders as well as the mediocrity and the impotence to which Christians seemed to resign themselves within the church."[20]

Congar noted that an exposé on "The Modern World and the Christian World" in the August–September edition (1946) of *Esprit* made clear that "the pastoral activities of the church no longer had much meaning for most people, especially the more radical and dynamic among them." He confirmed this to be the case as "people, both priests and lay faithful, received the things of Christ in forms inherited from an honorable but culturally obsolete past, in acts and formulas that were scarcely more than rituals, lacking the power to invite others to life or to express their life."[21]

2. The "French" Congregation of the Holy Spirit

The French province was the oldest and largest in the congregation. The mother house in Paris (the former Holy Ghost Seminary) served not only as headquarters for the province but also for a worldwide congregation and network of missions in Africa staffed by over a thousand Spiritans. This network covered an area of approximately two million square miles with a population of some twenty-five million people.[22]

The superior general at the time of Archbishop Roncalli's arrival in Paris was the former vicar apostolic of Senegambia, Archbishop Louis Le Hunsec, CSSp. He was elected at the General Chapter (GC IX) in 1926 at the age of forty-eight and remained in office until 1950 when GC XI chose his assistant, Fr. Francis Griffin from Ireland, to succeed him and continue with the model of a strong centralized authority for the congregation.[23]

---

20. Congar, *True and False Reform*, 23. A second print and translation into other languages was forbidden by the Holy Office and Congar was silenced. The translator notes that it was read by Archbishop Roncalli when he was living in Paris. After calling for the council, Pope John appointed Congar to the council's preparatory theological commission (see translator's introduction xi–xii).

21. Ibid., 24.

22. Koren, *To the Ends of the Earth*, 411.

23 Ibid., 396. The practice of "chapter" in religious congregations comes from the ancient Benedictine custom of monks gathering at regular intervals, usually weekly, to read and discuss a chapter from St. Benedict's rule. The place of meeting in the

Like all other institutes within the church, the Congregation of the Holy Spirit was part of the "fortress church" culture of the time. Koren's history of the Spiritan congregation describes the time span between GC X held in 1926 and GC XII, held in 1962 as "an era of astonishing growth and development." This period can be divided in two with the first half, during the mandate of Le Hunsec, dominated by events leading up to the Second World War and the war itself. Koren wrote that "despite these agonies, the congregation shared joyfully in the general enthusiasm of the era for the church's work of evangelization and saw its roster increase from about 2,100 members and 2,000 aspirants around 1926 to more than 5,000 members and 3,000 aspirants by 1962."[24]

According to Koren, Le Hunsec "begged" the general chapter of 1950 to relieve him of his responsibility as general. He made this request to the eighty-two capitulants gathered "around the tomb of the Venerable Father" at Chevilly-Larue, Paris, from 20 July to 5 August 1950. The composition of the chapter was significant. There were thirteen bishops and archbishops; nine *ex officio* members of the general council; thirty-nine *ex officio* as major superiors and twenty-one elected delegates. In his address Le Hunsec warned of difficult times ahead. He said,

> We are inevitable witnesses of the rapid changes that are taking place all around us. Events outrun our best imaginings. Society

---

monastery came to be known as the "chapter room" where the monks gathered for "chapter." This practice goes back to the sixth century beginning with Benedict himself. The chapter was how every member, even the most junior, had the opportunity to discuss and give advice concerning the affairs of the monastery and to elect the abbot. With the increase of Benedictine monasteries connections were maintained between them through representatives gathering regularly in chapter to review together their fidelity to the rule of St. Benedict. The church recognized the importance of this practice in the early thirteenth century when it was made obligatory for all religious congregations. The mendicant orders, particularly the Dominicans incorporated the practice into the general administration of their order and it became part of the centralized governance of many of the new congregations that emerged since the sixteenth century. The first Spiritan general chapter (GC) was held after the death of Fr. Libermann in 1853 and confirmed his chosen successor, Fr. Ignatius Schwindenhammer, as superior general. Schwindenhammer called the second GC (GC II) in 1875. Following his death in 1881, GC III elected Fr. Frederick Le Vavasseur. Le Vavasseur died in 1883 and Fr. Ambrose Emonet was the unanimous choice to succeed him (GC IV). Emonet called a general chapter in 1884 (GC V). Mgr. Le Roy succeeded Emonet who was in ill health at GC VI in 1896. Mgr. Le Roy conducted two chapters in his period, GC VII in 1906 and GC VIII in 1919.

24. Koren, *To the Ends of the Earth*, 395. Le Hunsec succeeded Archbishop Le Roy who had been the first bishop elected general and the first not to have known Fr. Libermann personally. Le Roy had been vicar apostolic of Gabon and superior general for thirty years (1896–1926).

is being transformed at an accelerated pace. It is even impossible for us to predict what the morrow will bring. . . . Everything around us, in Europe, America, Africa, may undergo radical changes. Even amidst the upheavals of the world, we must remain loyal to these two points: obedience to bishops and the rules of our religious life.[25]

Change was perhaps, the "elephant in the room" at GC XI which was best tackled by greater obedience to the rule. Fr. Griffin's first address to the congregation as Le Hunsec's successor, addressed the phenomenon of change in supernatural terms of service of souls and personal sanctification.

> Our Venerable Father recalls on every page of his letters and spiritual writings that our missionary life is one that must belong to the supernatural order, and that the obligations of our religious life must form an integral part of our ministry. If then we want our apostolic activity to produce substantial and lasting fruit, we must not merely spend ourselves and be spent in the service of the souls confided to our care, but we must work for our personal sanctification and remain faithful, at all costs, to the obligations imposed upon us by our Constitutions and freely assumed by us.[26]

GC XI responded to changes in the world, as Le Hunsec suggested, by "obedience to bishops and the rules of our religious life" and as Griffin added, by lives "that must belong to the supernatural order." It was in that spirit that its deliberations continued under six headings: general organization, the religious life, houses of formation, the provinces, the missions, and temporal affairs. There is no evidence of changes in the world impacting on the congregation and its mission. Consequently, the congregation was

---

25. *GB* 41 (1950) 443–46. The General Bulletin, *Bulletin de la Congrégation*, provided the official record of the congregation covering such matters as the erection of dioceses, appointments of bishops, candidates for vows and ordination, and a listing of deceased members. It was first published in 1857 in French and Latin (the official documents from the Holy See were in Latin) with the subtitle, *Actes Officiels, Avis et Recommendations Nouvelles Générales de l'Institut*. Many provinces had their own newsletters, journals, and promotion magazines. The *General Bulletin* was sent to the superiors of circumscriptions and seen by few, particularly non-francophone Spiritans. English was introduced in the 1960s. The statutes of the general chapter of 1962 were given both in French and English. See *GB* 47, supplement (1962). An English translation was not provided for the 1950 Chapter Report. See *GB* 41 (1950) 461. It was during Archbishop Lefebvre's mandate that the bulletin was first provided in English as well as in French.

26. *GB* 41 (1950) 425–27.

curiously out of contact with the era of change which would greatly affect the congregation and its mission.[27]

GC XI did speak of decisions being made in the light of experience.[28] The experience referred to was not of the world the congregation was called to serve but its own history and traditions. In preparation for the celebration of the centenary of Venerable Libermann's death, the chapter referred to the "other founder," Poullart des Places, and directed that his feast should also be celebrated. It also called for specialists on the congregation's founders to research the congregation's beginnings. The message from GC XI was "steady as she goes."

The many congratulations offered in 1952 at the celebrations of the centenary of Fr. Libermann's death included a message from Pope Pius XII. He wrote:

> You recall first of all the ardent figure of Father Libermann, this convert illuminated by grace like Saul on the road to Damascus; the man tragically struck by an illness that prevented his approach to the altar to which he aspired; this simple cleric, without ecclesiastical position but not without authority, already undertaking the direction of souls.

The pope also acknowledged the growth of the congregation with charge of thirty ecclesiastical jurisdictions and nearly one thousand members buried in Africa. He added: "In 1852, there were already 88 religious who wept at the premature death of their Father. But in one century, the plant that was tender and fragile, has grown and has sunk its roots deep. Today it is not without emotion that the 4,500 members of your congregation spread over three continents, render thanks to God for spiritual fecundity of this life of an apostle."[29]

Fr. Griffin's leadership was exercised at a time of general optimism for the expansion of the Catholic Church in mission territories.[30] The growth of

---

27. Ten years later, in 1960, British Prime Minister Harold Mc Millan would speak of "a wind of change" in an address to the South African parliament. This was hardly a startling remark as the movement from colonial rule in Africa had been underway for some time and in that same year Nigeria and Tanzania with fifteen other African countries were admitted to the United Nations. The signs of change were indeed the signs of the times which some could see, but others did not.

28. *GB* 41 (1950) 467–89.

29. *GB* 42 (1952) 245–47. Koren gave the number of members in the congregation at the death of Libermann as 89. There were 56 priests and 33 brothers. Of these 33 priests and 22 brothers were on mission *ad extra*. Koren, *Spiritans*, 200.

30. Only a year earlier, the pope wrote that "the Catholic missionary movement both in Christian and pagan lands has gained such force and momentum and is of such

the church in mission lands was remarkable. The number of Catholic missions had increased from 400 in 1926 to about 600 in 1951 with an increase of Catholics from 15,000,000 to 20,800,000. The number of indigenous and foreign priests increased to 26,800 in 1952 compared with 14,800 in 1926. Membership of the congregation also rose from 2,645 priests and 790 brothers in 1950 to 3,382 priests and 824 brothers in 1962. Another statistic, the number of seminarians in the congregation, suggested a different trajectory with ominous portent for the future. In 1962, the number of Spiritan scholastics dropped to 837 worldwide compared with 952 in 1950. The statistics in 1968 would show a further fall to 619 scholastics.

It was in the context of an imminent church council that Fr. Griffin looked for a strong and sure pair of hands to succeed him in the leadership of the congregation. There was significant suspicion that he orchestrated the election of his successor pointing to Archbishop Lefebvre as "the official candidate." At least Lefebvre was of this opinion. Prior to GC XII in 1962, in conversation with Cardinal Agagianian, prefect of the Propagation of the Faith, he confided that his congregation might have need of his services.[31]

GC XII (1962)

There is little evidence that the general chapter called in 1962, like its predecessor in 1950, gave much attention to the currents of change abroad in the world and increasingly in the church. An Irish Spiritan, Fr. William Jenkinson, CSSp, remembered the preparations for GC XII. "Theological, political, and social developments were becoming evident in the closing years of the nineteen fifties. Were Irish Spiritans aware of the rumblings even within their own congregation in the lead up to the general chapter of 1962?" Jenkinson did not think so and went on to acknowledge that "theological and ecclesiastical developments were challenging the understanding of mission and the evolution of the churches where Spiritans were deeply involved. The [Irish] province was legitimately proud of its missionary outreach, but perhaps it was not sufficiently aware of the temptation to triumphalism and to the profound changes that would soon call in question many of its certainties."[32]

GC XII was the last of the pre-Vatican II chapters. It followed the pattern of previous chapters with propositions submitted by individual

---

proportions as perhaps was never witnessed before in the annals of Catholic missions." *Evangelii praecones* (1951) 1.

31. Perrin, "Mgr. Lefebvre," 153.
32. Jenkinson, "Mission Outreach of the Irish Province," 153.

confreres, collated, and vetted by provincial administrations and forwarded to the general council. The gathering of forty-five *de jure* members (major superiors, members of the general council and administration) and thirty elected delegates (representing the membership by provinces and mission areas) was held in the same location as previous chapters, the major seminary of the French province, at Chevilly-Larue, a commune in the southern suburbs of Paris. It began with three days of retreat led by one of the general councilors, Fr. Nicholas Moysan, CSSp, on 21 July. A decision had then to be made about when the election of the new general would happen. The constitutions required it to take place when the chapter assembled immediately following reports on the general state of the congregation (Rules and Constitutions 82–83). In submissions made before the chapter a delay in the election was proposed to allow time for capitulants coming from all over the world to get to know each other.[33]

Despite the submission made and the permission given, the proposal for an immediate election was made and quickly passed with 57 votes. The election for a new superior general at a critical time in world history and the life of the church, took place on 26 July, only five days after the start of the chapter. The suspicion that Fr. Griffin had a chosen successor in mind, in the person of Archbishop Lefebvre, was confirmed for some when he advised the chapter that the Vatican would not object to the election of a bishop as superior general provided he secured two-thirds majority of the vote as required by canon law.[34]

The first straw vote gave 41 votes to Lefebvre, 10 to Fr. Vernon Gallagher (American provincial), 3 to Fr. Louis Ledit, superior of Chevilly and 2 to Fr. Joseph Lécuyer. On the first official ballot held on 26 July, Archbishop Marcel Lefebvre secured the needed two-thirds majority and was elected eighteenth superior general with 53 votes out of 75 votes. The election of general councilors followed in the evening. These represented different provinces with the elections of Frs. Heinrich Hack (first assistant) from Germany; Joseph Hirtz (second assistant), France; Lambertus Vogel,

---

33. Statutes of the General Chapter 1962 *GB* 47, supplement, 67*, 77*–78*. Fr. Griffin had petitioned the Sacred Congregation of Religious to table this motion and so allow the change which would require a two thirds majority.

34. Fr. Griffin in a letter of 17 May 1962 asked Fr. Daniel Murphy, CSSp, the congregation's Procurator general to the Holy See to "sound out" the Congregations for Propaganda and Religious and the secretariat of state on the possibility of the chapter electing Archbishop Lefebvre as superior general. He wrote that it was "almost certain" that he would be elected. Perrin, "Mgr. Lefebvre," 153.

Holland; William Higgins, Ireland; Charles Connors, USA; and Avelino Costa, Portugal.[35]

The confirmation of Lefebvre's election by Pope John XXIII communicated by telegram from Rome was received by the chapter at 10:35 a.m. on Saturday, 28 July. That evening at 6:30 p.m., the capitulants with all the members of the Chevilly community assembled in the seminary chapel. All professed members made their act of obedience to the newly elected superior general. Gallagher reported to his American confreres that an outstanding superior general had been elected with a "broad spectrum" council. He was confident that the congregation would enjoy effective leadership for the next twelve years.[36]

Archbishop Lefebvre went on to preside over the chapter which included work in commissions addressing six broad discussion areas around which the nearly seven hundred propositions submitted for consideration were organized. Each of the six commissions was chaired by one of the general councilors. Their conclusions were arranged by the topics discussed and decided upon. They were: religious life, organization of the congregation, superiors and functionaries, houses of formation, brothers, missions, temporal affairs, and the secretariat.

Many proposals coming from the membership calling for changes of lifestyle in keeping with the world around them were resisted and existing rules confirmed. GC XII responded with a request for greater fervor among the membership. The capitulants, well-schooled in the old discipline of "keep the rule, and the rule will keep you," saw themselves perhaps as sentries vigilant against a relaxation of the rule and the infiltration of modern and secular ways into the congregation. They voted to keep the "great silence" in all communities; confreres were not allowed radios in their rooms, and superiors were reminded of the "grave obligation in conscience" concerning the use of television.[37] In missionary matters, GC XII similarly endorsed the status quo when, for example, it was not considered desirable to establish the principle of internationalizing communities. Pragmatism was the basis for that decision and the approval given for greater involvement of lay staff in Spiritan schools.[38]

---

35. Fr. Hirtz spoke in later years of the difficulties he faced in serving on Lefebvre's general council. He had been elected by those who sought a counterweight to Mgr. Lefebvre. But Hirtz had little opportunity to influence the direction of the council as Lefebvre dominated it. From an interview with Fr. Jean-Michel Gelmetti, CSSp.

36. Gallagher, *Our Province*, 31 (1962) 5.

37. Statutes of GC XII 1962, *GB* 47, supplement, 17*.

38. Ibid., 51*, 53*.

Two propositions were approved concerning the "Ends of the Congregation," a topic that would dominate the first session of the extraordinary general chapter to be held in 1968. GC XII accepted the Latin Rule (Rules and Constitutions) without change and praised it for being "very broad in its statement of the choice of the difficult works for which the congregation has been founded." It left open the possibility of accepting "good vocations" although "they may not have a pronounced taste for the missionary life."[39] The chapter also approved the transfer of the congregation's headquarters from Paris to Rome. This was a strategy with a double objective: to free the French province from the direct supervision of the superior general, and to establish the congregation as a worldwide organization.[40]

GC XII concluded with statutes approved on 13 August just two months before the first session of the Second Vatican Council began. With fervor renewed by their meeting the capitulants made a request to Mgr. Lefebvre.

> The chapter earnestly requests the Most Reverend Father General and his Council to address a Circular Letter to all the confreres on the occasion of the Ecumenical Council, inviting them to practice with greater fervor their religious vows, particularly in the interests of the African missions and for the salvation of souls.[41]

Luc Perrin of the University of Strasbourg researched GC XII and described it as "*un chapitre verrouillé*," that is, a chapter locked into predetermined outcomes. There were three keys.[42] The first was the configuration of capitulants with forty-five of them attending *de jure* as members of the general administration or provincial and district superiors, all of whom were appointed by the superior general. There were only thirty elected as representatives of confreres from different circumscriptions. This, Perrin suggested, put the ball in the court of the presiding authority.

Perrin commented that the organization of the congregation's leadership was something like "*de chaises musicales*," musical chairs, with those already in positions of authority swapping one superior-ship for another. Fr.

---

39. Ibid., 19*.

40. The transfer of the general administration from Paris to Rome had implications for the legal status of the congregation in France. Negotiations with the French government took eight years to complete with the agreement that the congregation's legal status could be transferred to the French province. See Koren, *To the Ends of the Earth*, 476.

41. Statutes of GC XII (1962). *GB* 47, supplement.

42. Perrin, "Mgr. Lefebvre."

Moysan, for example, who preached the chapter retreat as general counsellor, was, following the chapter, appointed provincial of France.

Second, there was the juridical bind by which any change to the constitutions required a two-thirds majority. A third block to change was the mentality of profound obedience that was pervasive in the congregation. This was more pronounced, Perrin suggested, than among either Jesuits or Dominicans. "The debates of the capitulants were placed under the entire control of the moral authority of the superior general."[43] An example of this was the proposal for the voting rights of brothers in the congregation which, rejected at the 1950 chapter, was proposed again in 1962 and recommended for approval by the central commission. It was rejected as Mgr. Lefebvre said the proposal contravened Canon Law.

Perrin concludes that the GC XII program was adequate for the 1950s and for a pre-Vatican II chapter, but not for the 1960s, and for a chapter held in the same year as Vatican II's first session. The cracks evident then became wide open gaps in 1968.[44] The Spiritans would have to wait another six years for the wind of change to have full effect in their congregation.

The positive and unifying experience of GC XII[45] gave way to a growing malaise that would fester up to and beyond the General Chapter of Renewal. This was due, in great part to the leadership of Mgr. Lefebvre who the congregation came to realize was out of step with changing times and a changing church. Koren recognized that although Lefebvre was elected with

---

43. Ibid., 148. What could be described as a sluggish engagement with changes in the world and new thinking in the church, was adopted by the Spiritans in the 1950s and 1960s. This approach can be contrasted with other congregations engaging inquisitively and positively with new thinking in the church, particularly in relation to religious life. Take, for example, a paper entitled "The Constitutions of Religious Institutes and Modern Trends" given by Claretian Canon Lawyer, Basil Frison in 1958 to the Reverend Mothers General meeting at the Dominican College in San Rafael, California, as an outline and guide for a series of conferences on the constitutions of religious institutes. Published in the *Jurist* 18 (1958) 149–76.

44. Perrin, "Mgr. Lefebvre," 172.

45. The American Provincial Fr. Vernon Gallagher wrote to his American confreres of this positive and affirming atmosphere. "Recreation periods, reminiscent of Ferndale, [Formation House of the American Province] began at the door of the chapel where confreres grouped together by three, to 'walk around the woods'. As a result, there were very few people you had not met by the time the retreat ended. They were wonderful people too. Perhaps you stumbled around rather awkwardly in their language and they made a highly tentative stab at yours, but the spirit of camaraderie and solid unity caused linguistic barriers to shrink rapidly. It made one prouder than ever of belonging to a world-wide organisation that kept the characteristics of a close-knit family in spite of its gigantic size." Gallagher, *Our Province*, 31 (1962) 4.

more than two-thirds of the votes there were "strong misgivings among certain delegates."[46]

3. A Changing Church and an Unchanging Mgr. Lefebvre

The pre-Vatican II theology underpinning Christian mission was in sharp contrast to what came to be understood and decreed by the twenty-first ecumenical Council of the Catholic Church. Pope John XXIII, elected to succeed Pius XII in October 1958, called the council while on a visit to the Basilica of St. Paul without the Walls to celebrate the conclusion of the week of Prayer for Church Unity. It was the feast of the Conversion of St. Paul (25 January 1959) and at a meeting with cardinals and members of the curia in the chapter-house of the abbey, announced his intention to summon an ecumenical council that would gather bishops from all over the world to the Vatican. It was less than three months since his election and this holy and elderly man, chosen as a caretaker pope to provide a breathing space before the next conclave, took everyone by surprise. The surprise was due in part to the feeling that "no obvious crisis troubled the Catholic Church. In fact, except in those parts of the world where Christianity was undergoing overt persecution, mainly in countries under communist domination, the church in the decade and a half since the end of World War II projected an image of vigor and self-confidence."[47]

As the conclave elected Roncalli pope, the Spiritans elected Lefebvre superior general. Roncalli would call the council that Lefebvre would resist, and ultimately reject. The congregation was destined to be caught up in a conflict between the council's call to renewal and resistance to that renewal. To understand this period in the history of the congregation we need to familiarize ourselves with both the Second Vatican Council and the congregation's eighteenth superior general.

Vatican II

Pope St. John XXIII not only called the council but he set out a course for it to follow. He outlined three tasks: the better ordering of the church; the promotion of world peace; and unity among Christians. And more than

---

46. Koren, *To the Ends of the Earth*, 476.

47. O'Malley, *Vatican II*, 17. Pope St. John XXIII also called a synod for the diocese of Rome and commissioned a revision of the Code of Canon Law.

that, his very presence encouraged a way of thinking that was new. He did not have in mind the continuation of the First Vatican Council which had been suspended on 20 October 1870 due to the Franco-Prussian War. His predecessor, Pope Pius XII, had considered calling a council to complete its work and further strengthen church doctrine and papal authority.

The agenda prepared by the preparatory commission and the curia required, in their estimation, perhaps only one session. This would be due to their excellent preparation—like the teacher who not only asks the questions but provides the answers as well. It turned out that the council would require four sessions (from 1962 to 1965) to conclude its business. Once the bishops were gathered they wanted to be heard, and together with the pope, produced sixteen documents addressing many aspects of the complex reality of a church sensitive to its own vocation and the signs of the times.

Over 2,500 bishops gathered around the successor of Peter in Rome for the Second Vatican Council. As Karl Rahner pointed out some time afterwards, this was the first truly ecumenical or "world council" since ancient times. And since those times, the Western church had increasingly centralized its authority in the See of Rome culminating with the definitions of papal primacy and infallibility in 1870. He commented that Vatican II was "the first major official event in which the church actualized itself precisely as a *world* church."[48]

Vatican II's primary conception of the church was as "The People of God." This put emphasis on the authority of the *sensus fidelium* in matters of faith and morals.[49] The criterion for true faith is what has been accepted "always, everywhere, and by everyone" (*semper, ubique, et ab omnibus*).[50] The process of *ressourcement* at work in this council would restore an ancient practice going back to the Acts of the Apostles and the first council of the Church at Jerusalem (ca. AD 50). It would be a collective responsibility for the church, the people of God with debate going beyond the old struggles between bishops and the pope and the conciliarism condemned by popes in the past, to an understanding of the collegiality of the episcopacy, by which

---

48. Rahner, "Fundamental Theological Interpretation," 717. Of the 2,676 bishops who attended the council, about 1,040 were Europeans, 956 came from the Americas, 380 from Africa and 300 were from Asia.

49. See the document of the ITC (2014) "*Sensus Fidei* in the Life of the Church."

50. This axiom is attributed to Vincent of Lerins, a fifth-century monk of southern France and is widely cited. He was refuting the heresies of his time—Arianism, Donatism, Pelagianism. To recognize sound doctrine one traces what is now being said with what was said in the past. The present develops out of the past and is in continuity with it.

the "local churches" in communion with the successor of Peter exercise responsibility for the universal church.[51]

This is what Pope Pius XII had relied on when asking bishops of established churches to come to the assistance of the new churches with *fidei donum* priests. It was a core theological understanding of church with practical implications for church governance. "Collegiality was the supreme instance in the council of the effort to moderate the centralizing tendencies of the ecclesiastical institution, of the effort to give those from the periphery a more authoritative voice not only back home but also in the center."[52]

Perfectae caritatis applied this theme of collective responsibility for the life of the church to the cooperation required from all the members of religious congregations to ensure the effective renewal and adaptation of religious life (*PC* 4). This was reiterated in the norms for renewal which called on religious congregations to convoke meetings of their members (chapters) with all cooperating to "prepare the spirit of the chapters, to carry out the works of the chapters, to observe faithfully the law and norms enacted by the chapters" (*Ecclesiae sanctae*).[53] The new relationship between the center (superiors) and the periphery (members) advanced at Vatican II would take a considerable amount of time and effort to work out. The clash of theologies and world views experienced at the council would, once again, be evident as religious institutes began to figure out the implications for them of belonging to a church in a time of transition. If the church was understood as "*ecclesia semper reformanda*" (the church must always be reformed), or to use the council's preferred formula, "*ecclesia semper purificanda*" (the church must always be purified), then religious congregations which are "of the church" should similarly understand themselves as being always *in via*, or, on the way to being what they should be. Institutes would

---

51. Mgr. Lefebvre, with like-minded council fathers, saw the new emphasis on collegiality as undermining papal authority and persuaded Pope Paul to add a *nota explicativa praevia* (preliminary note of explanation) to accompany *Lumen gentium* (16 November 1964). This was included as an appendix at the end of the final text. In paragraph 3 it states that "there is no such thing as the college without its head: it is '*The subject of supreme and entire power over the whole church.*' This much must be acknowledged lest the fullness of the Pope's power be jeopardized." See Flannery, *Vatican Council II*, 425.

52. O'Malley, *Vatican II*, 303.

53 The *motu proprio* of Blessed Pope Paul VI *Ecclesia sanctae* (1966) gave deadlines for the revision of the Constitutions of the Institutes of Consecrated Life. Period 1: The Period of the Special Chapters to be held between 1967 and 1971; Period 2: The Period of the Intermediate Chapters to be held between 1972 and 1976; and, Period 3: The Period of the Constituent Chapters which would submit the revised constitutions for definitive approval by the Holy See.

each experience and respond in similar and different ways to the call to reform and purification.

Pope St. John XXIII in his opening address to the council on 11 October 1962 said that the church should act by "making use of the medicine of mercy rather than severity . . . and by showing herself to be the loving mother of all, benign, patient, full of mercy and goodness." The council responded to this invitation with a language that spoke with respect and affection to modern society troubled in many ways. Probably the most quoted passage from the council documents, the opening sentences of *Gaudium et spes* come quickly to mind: "The joy and hope, the grief and anguish of the men and women of our times, especially those who are poor or afflicted in any way are the joy and hope, the grief and affliction of the followers of Christ as well. Nothing that is genuinely human fails to find an echo in their hearts." The council positioned the church as walking with the peoples of the world rather than walking ahead of them and talking at them. To use a spatial image, the council fathers came to see the church in horizontal relationship with other churches, other religions, and those of no religion rather than a vertical relationship that laid claim to superior knowledge and rights.[54]

There is coherence to the sixteen council documents that present a unified sense of the Catholic Church's self-understanding at the middle of the twentieth century. The scope of these documents seemed all-encompassing as they addressed the issues of the time, both within and without the church. The council spoke authoritatively on the adaptation of the liturgy, the understanding of sacred Scripture as God's Word, the mystery of the church, the mission of the church and leadership within the church, the training of priests and the renewal of religious life, respect for other Christian churches, other religions, and human dignity. It also spoke a message of joy and hope to the world. This comprehensive body of doctrine set a trajectory for the Catholic Church in the third millennium. It constituted a true "paradigm shift" from a hierarchical, juridical, and triumphalist church to a pilgrim, pastoral, and servant church, heralding the kingdom of God for all peoples in all places. This is what is referred to as "the spirit of the council." For the first time in history, a council has taken care to infuse its documents

---

54 "Error has no rights" is an ultra-traditionalist point of view which ruled out dialogue as a form of mission. This is the thinking of another time, a pre-Vatican II thinking. "The Catholic Church, as we have already said, is a perfect society and has as its foundation the truth of faith infallibly revealed by God. For this reason, that which is opposed to this truth is, necessarily, an error, and the same rights which are objectively recognized for truth cannot be afforded to error. In this manner, liberty of thought and liberty of conscience have their essential limits in the truthfulness of God in Revelation." Pope Pius XII, *Ecco che gia un anno*, 6 October 1946.

with a vocabulary and themes common to them all. In that sense, it can be said that Vatican II communicated a "spirit."⁵⁵

Mgr. Marcel Lefebvre

Mgr. Marcel Lefebvre, one of the 2,500 bishops attending Vatican II, was born in 1905. He was the third of eight children born into a wealthy family in Tourcoing, near the city of Lille in northeastern France. His father, René, was the owner of a textile factory and with his wife, Gabrielle, were devout Catholics and monarchists. Their hope had been that through the restoration of the French monarchy the wrongs of the 1789 revolution could be put right and the former honor and glory of France would be restored. René, a political activist, operated a spy ring for the British in the First World War when the Germans occupied Tourcoing. He was also active in the French Underground during World War II until he was captured and incarcerated in the Sonnenburg concentration camp where he died in 1944. This family upbringing and the political views of his father shaped the mind and heart of young Marcel who became a seminarian for the diocese of Lille in 1923. It was at the insistence of his father that the bishop of Lille sent him to the French Seminary in Rome.

Marcel's decision to join the Spiritans was due, in no small measure, to the influence of Fr. Henri le Floch, CSSp, rector of the French Seminary in Rome from 1904 to 1927. Le Floch provided Action Française with a doctrinal justification for its fight against the principles of the French Revolution.⁵⁶ He found in Le Floch a frame of mind that was, like his father René, monarchist and ultramontane.⁵⁷ With his fellow seminarians at the French Seminary, he was immersed in an ideology presented as loyalty to

---

55. O'Malley, *Vatican II*, 310.

56. Action Française was founded as a nationalist movement in 1899 by Charles Maurras (1868–1952) in reaction to the combined forces of Freemasonry and liberalism seen as intent on anarchy. Pius X supported the movement. The relationship of the church to Action Française changed with Benedict XV, but World War I delayed any action. His successor, Pius XI, issued a condemnation of Maurras and Action Française in 1926. Archbishop Le Hunsec was directed by Pope Pius XI to immediately remove Le Floch from the French Seminary because of his support for Action Française. Following the intervention of the secretary of state, Cardinal Gasparri, Le Floch was allowed to resign and left the seminary with Archbishop Le Hunsec on 18 July 1927. See Koren, *To the Ends of the Earth*, 396–401, and Prévotat, "La Condemnation."

57. Lefebvre's father wrote to Le Floch following his dismissal from the French Seminary. "My two sons, René and Marcel, are very appreciative of your direction and the wisdom of your counsel." Letter dated 17 October 1927. Prévotat, "La Condamnation," 90.

the Catholic Church and generating a perspective that detested any form of liberalism as an evil originating with the French Revolution and resulting in the exclusion of Christ the King from public life. From Le Floch's perspective, the final goal of the liberal agenda was the elimination of the Mass and the supernatural life of Christ, the sovereign high priest, from society. The only way out of the current social morass in Europe was the return of monarchy and the reenthronement of God in society. A former seminarian remembered the readings at meals carefully chosen by Fr. Le Floch for them to consider how "the mystical Body of Christ transformed the pagan society of imperial Rome and prepared the growing movement that recognized the plans for a society of Our Lord Jesus Christ, Priest and King."[58]

Le Floch's influence extended far beyond the confines of the French Seminary in Rome. He was a confidant of many in the Vatican Curia with ready access to Pope Pius XI before the condemnation of Action Française in 1926. His writings, while controversial, won him many disciples both within the congregation and without. Lefebvre, with many others, was greatly influenced by Le Floch. In 1979, he wrote of him:

> He was the one who taught us what the popes were to the world and the church, what they had taught for a century and a half against liberalism, modernism and communism, and the whole doctrine of the church on these topics. He really made us understand and share in this battle of the popes to preserve the world and the church from these scourges which plague us today.[59]

Following his ordination in 1929, Marcel continued his studies in Rome and received a doctorate in divinity the following year. He made known to the bishop of Lille his desire to pursue a missionary vocation and after a brief period in parish ministry was released from the diocese to join the Spiritan novitiate in Orly where, at the end of the novitiate year, he made temporary profession in the congregation on 8 September 1932. His first mission appointment was to Gabon where he worked as theology professor at the seminary in Libreville. Two years later he became its rector and took permanent vows in the congregation. He remained in Gabon as district superior until the end of the war when he was recalled to France to teach in the Spiritan seminary at Mortain in Normandy.

In 1947 Pope Pius XII appointed Fr. Lefebvre, CSSp, as vicar apostolic of Dakar, Senegal, and the following year as apostolic delegate to all French Africa. He was consecrated bishop on 18 September 1947 in his home parish church of Tourcoing by Cardinal Liénart, the bishop of Lille. On this

58. Tissier de Mallerais, *Marcel Lefebvre*, 37.
59. Ibid., 36.

occasion, at the reception following his consecration, the new bishop acknowledged a debt of gratitude to Le Floch, saying, "I thank him sincerely from the bottom of my heart because he showed us the path to truth."[60]

In 1955 Dakar became an archdiocese with Lefebvre as its first archbishop. He was the thirteenth Spiritan to serve as bishop in Dakar since 1863. In June 1960 Senegal declared independence from France and Léopold Sédar Senghor became its first president in September 1960. He advocated African socialism for the governance of Senegal. A devout Catholic, Senghor spoke of his brand of socialism as adapted to the challenges facing Africa at the time. He claimed that his policies were compatible with Christian principles.[61]

Lefebvre thought differently and recognized in them the language of socialism. He decided, against the advice of his vicar general, to publish his criticism in a pastoral letter, entitled "On the Duty of Living according to Truth and Avoiding Ambiguity," in March 1961. He based his criticism on Pope Pius XI's encyclical *Quadragesimo anno* (1931), which rejected socialism. As predicted, the archbishop was called before President Senghor to explain his opposition. He reiterated what he had written and could not change it as it was the teaching of the Catholic Church.[62]

Lefebvre knew that his days in Senegal were numbered. Apart from the political tension between president and archbishop, Rome had encouraged the resignation of missionary bishops in Lomé and Yaoundé and appointed local clergy to succeed them. While welcoming this for Dakar, Lefebvre sought a delay by petitioning Rome for a co-adjutor. No reply was received. He therefore submitted his resignation and traveled to Rome. Before he

60. Mgr. Lefebvre's biographer Tissier de Mallerais noted that Cardinal Liénart promptly reported this to the nuncio in Paris, Archbishop Roncalli. See *Marcel Lefebvre*, 155.

61. Senghor wrote the preface to Coulon and Brasseur, *Libermann 1802–1852*. He acknowledged the importance of Libermann's life experience as a Jew in forming his missionary principle of inculturation. Senghor quoted from his "famous letter of 19 November 1847 to missionaries in Dakar and Gabon." In that letter Libermann called on his missionaries to allow the mystery of the incarnation to be realized in them. For God in Jesus not only became human but also became a servant (Phil 2:6–8). Senghor suggested that Jesus, as a Jew, belonged to those who were colonized. So Libermann "demanded from his missionaries who travel to the colonies of black Africa, to become colonized with the colonized, more concretely, 'to be negro with the negro.' But Libermann did not intend to be pejorative in the use of the term. He precisely intended, in effect, that the missionaries become used to their teachers, to their practices and customs, to their 'negritude,' as we say today. . . . Libermann advised a 'making perfect,' a 'sanctifying,' and an 'elevation,' of the negro-African civilisation." Coulon, *Libermann*, 11.

62. Tissier de Mallerais, *Marcel Lefebvre*, 247.

arrived, the decision was made to appoint him to a diocese in France. He was well-received, and, with resignation accepted, "sidelined" to one of the smallest dioceses in France.[63]

Mgr. Lefebvre, as archbishop of Dakar, was appointed to the Central Preparatory Commission for the council in June 1960, and would play an important role in the council closely aligned with a group nicknamed the "Romans" (identified as "traditionalists").[64] These included prominent ecclesiastics such as Cardinal Alfredo Ottaviani, head of the Holy Office (renamed "The Congregation for the Doctrine of the Faith") whose episcopal motto was *"semper idem"* (always the same); Cardinal Ernesto Ruffini, archbishop of Palermo; Cardinal Giuseppe Siri, archbishop of Genoa; Cardinal Michael Browne, past student of an Irish Spiritan school and former master general of the Dominicans.

The theological outlook of these ecclesiastics was well-known. Ottaviani took a "metahistorical approach to issues and problems, one of the most telling characteristics setting him and most of the minority off from those whom they opposed."[65] Ruffini favored a literal reading of the Genesis creation account in a book on evolution he wrote in 1948. Siri was rumored to have been Pius XII's preference to succeed him as pope. Browne was vice president of the Doctrinal Commission, whose task was, as he understood it, to safeguard papal primacy. Lefebvre was, in Jesuit church historian John O'Malley's estimation, more extreme than any of these. He was at the heart of this group within the council that continually lobbied against any change inconsistent with the teachings of previous popes from Leo XIII to Pius XII. For them, the role of the council was to reaffirm those teachings.[66]

---

63. The Diocese of Tulle, in the ecclesiastical province of Poitiers. He had already anticipated his succession by appointing a local priest as his second vicar general, Fr. Hyacinthe Thiandoum, who would succeed him and serve in Dakar from 1962 to 2000, first as archbishop and later, as cardinal.

64. The *Coetus Internationalis Patrum* (the "International Group of Fathers") was formed principally by Archbishop Geraldo de Proença Sigaud, SVD, of Brazil. Archbishop Lefebvre was one of his chief collaborators. The group sought to ensure that the conservatism of the members could find a voice in all topics under deliberation at the council. See Alberigo, *History of Vatican II*, 195.

65. O'Malley, *Vatican II*, 110.

66. Faggioli noted that Lefebvre was one of the seventy council fathers (representing about 3 percent of the total) who voted against the council's "Declaration on Religious Liberty" (*Dignitatis humanae*) on 7 December 1965. See Faggioli, *Battle for Meaning*, 31.

4. The Mgr. Lefebvre Mandate (1962–68)

There had been some unease within the French province at the election of Mgr. Lefebvre as superior general.[67] The strident and archaic language and content of his first letter to the congregation suggests a reason for that opposition. He wrote of firmly maintaining what was "fundamental and absolute" to the congregation as well as relating to the changed conditions in which "incarnate souls" exist.

> We must, with firmness, maintain the fundamental and absolute principles which make up the very life of the congregation, that is to say, our faith in Our Lord, in Peter, in the church, in the works of our founders approved by the church, and we must resolutely behold the present and the future to keep up and develop the vital relations with the incarnate souls in circumstances of time, of place, of family life, social, political, which are not those of yesterday.[68]

This message firmed up the resolve of those intent on maintaining the status quo while allowing for the incremental changes demanded by the exigencies of the time.

One of the important principles for Lefebvre was the distinctiveness of the religious and priestly vocation. In a directive to all confreres he called for the wearing of religious dress pointing out that "the priest is in the world without being of the world; he is distinct from it while living in it." He advocated the wearing of the soutane not primarily as a matter of propriety but more to distinguish the cleric or religious from others. It also acted as a witness to the gospel. "By his soutane, by his faith, the priest is a living sermon. The apparent absence of all priests, especially in the city, is a serious set-back to the preaching of the gospel."[69] Lefebvre likened the priest wearing clerical dress to a soldier wearing a uniform. Underlying this directive was his opposition to all forms of secularism which sought to alienate the Catholic

---

67. Perrin, "Mgr. Lefebvre," 151. Fr. Henri Littner at Chevilly wrote an indictment denouncing the movement by certain members of the mother house "in favor of one of our archbishops as future superior general."

68. *GB* 47 (1962) 167.

69. *GB* 48 (1963) 337. Fr. Brian Cronin, CSSp, recalled receiving an individual copy of Lefebvre's instruction on wearing the habit, as did all the other seminarians in Kimmage. They, like him, wondered at the superior general attaching so much importance to this issue. French Spiritans recall a humorous account of Fr. Georges Thibault (who would be one of the moderators at GC XIII and future French provincial), dressed in a suit, arriving at Chevilly-Larue and meeting Archbishop Lefebvre with some confreres all dressed in soutanes. Lefebvre greeted him, *"Bonjour, monsieur,"* to which Thibault replied, *"Bonjour, madame."*

THE SPIRITAN CONGREGATION, CHANGE, AND VATICAN II 55

Church from the life of the state. For Lefebvre secularism was an insidious atheism that penetrated little by little into every aspect of society and was to be resisted at all costs. The antidote to the deadly virus which, for Lefebvre, had its origins in the French Revolution and the liberalization of society emanating from it, was a robust external demonstration of religious loyalty.

Lefebvre understood that church liturgy and the papacy were the chief weapons to be used in the war against secularism. In remarks at the end of the first session of the Vatican Council which dealt mostly with the renewal of the liturgy, he exalted the liturgical role of the pope to the mystical heights of "perfect minister of the liturgy . . . who bridges the gap between earthly realities and eternal life." Following the line of Pius XII in *Mediator Dei* (1947) rather than the unfolding themes of the council's Constitution on the Sacred Liturgy, he spoke of the divine and human character of the liturgy asserting that the liturgy is always an action of the church as such, that is, the church universal, and therefore it is entirely appropriate that it is celebrated in a universal language. "God is the proper object of prayer, not the understanding of texts."[70]

Lefebvre looked for a return of the *ancien régime*. He wanted the ways of the church before the council restored, and a pope in the style of Pius XII on the "throne of Peter." In this he was not alone. Other council fathers were similarly nostalgic for the "model pope," that iconic figure who personified a papacy, and a brand of Catholicism which belonged to the past.[71] Would the newly elected Pope Paul VI return the Catholic Church to a steadier and more traditionalist course? He met with Lefebvre at the end of the first session of the council (6 December 1963). Lefebvre came away from the audience with confidence restored as he had found in Paul a worthy successor to Pius XII. "It was clear to me that God has given us the pilot the church needs and that he is in firm control of his ship. Our Lord's promises to Peter are still operative today."[72] Alas, this impression was not to last. At the end of the second session of the council he expressed alarm at the proliferation of what he called "private experiments" in liturgy which, he hoped, would cease with the soon to be published instructions of the Holy See on the liturgy.[73] He also asserted the primacy of Peter, with bishops only exercising power in their dioceses through the authority of the pope. This was the line

---

70. *GB* 48 (1963) 708.
71. Pollard, *Papacy in the Age of Totalitarianism*, 446.
72. *GB* 48 (1963) 667.
73. *GB* 48 (1964) 755.

Lefebvre expected Pope Paul VI to take and so prove himself a worthy successor to Pope Pius XII.[74]

In his *Avis du Mois* given in the May–June *General Bulletin* (1964), Lefebvre spoke of the importance of formation as perhaps a sergeant-major may speak to the privates under his command. "All the years of our formation are directed to strengthen our will: to provide the means, natural and supernatural, necessary to maintain it in the pursuit of good, of duty, of the will of God."[75] He clearly articulated a traditionally hierarchical and static, pre-Vatican II ecclesiology in all that he wrote. This is well-illustrated in his reflection on the conciliar proclamation of Mary as Mother of the Church. He joyfully stated that "no other truth affirmed in this council will in fact be as important as that one." For him a truth that he always held dearly was now proclaimed by a council with which he was becoming increasingly uncomfortable. He read the proclamation to mean that "we cannot go to Jesus, except through Mary, we can only go to Mary through the church, the Roman and Catholic Church in union with the Pope."[76] In this, Lefebvre saw what he wanted to see. He only accepted what would fit with his logic of grace at work in the world, a hierarchical grace channeled through the Catholic Church in the person of the pope, to the world. *Extra ecclesiam non est salus* was his conviction. The logic was as simple as it was of another time. He wrote in 1965, "As Mary is mother of only one son, Jesus, so she is mother of only one church, one mystical body: The Roman Church and all the member churches in communion with her."[77]

Lefebvre opposed three general and fundamental orientations of the council: (1) the need for change in the church; (2) relationships in the church between the center and the periphery (specifically, collegiality) and, (3) how the church would relate to the world.[78] The council's resolution of these issues constituted a paradigm shift in every aspect of church teaching, governance, and ministry. A new way of being church evolved as the council progressed. It was a way rejected by Lefebvre. This rejection led to

---

74. The prohibition of the Tridentine Latin Mass represented for "traditionalists" a break with the past and prompted what would ultimately result in schism, with Archbishop Lefebvre its leader. With the benefit of hindsight, the telltale signs for this outcome can be detected in his leadership of the congregation.

75. *GB* 48 (1964) 901.

76. Ibid.

77. *GB* 49 (1965) 95.

78. O'Malley, *Vatican II*, 299–313. O'Malley understood the council through a hermeneutic of change that brought about a new way of being church with, specifically, a new relationship between its centre and periphery. The church, at Vatican II, also adopted a new language for dialogue with the world.

his departure from the congregation, the founding of his own seminary and society in opposition to Vatican II, and ultimately, his excommunication. The society was "the French-based St. Pius X Society, the followers of Mgr. Marcel Lefebvre, who broke allegiance to Rome because he believed that the Second Vatican Council had been hijacked by 'freemasons, Jews, and modernists,' and perhaps the Devil himself. Lefebvre founded what is in effect a schismatic, traditionalist church which still has a small but devoted band of faithful in many countries."[79]

Mgr. Lefebvre's Understanding of Renewal

As Mgr. Lefebvre was superior general, the Spiritans were in a more difficult position to other religious institutes responding to the council's call to change. Some members sided with him in preferring a controlled and orderly development to the uncertainties associated with adaptation and renewal. We have seen that GC XII maintained the style of operation of previous general chapters. The pace of change in the congregation was slow and reluctant.

The other forty Spiritan missionary bishops at the council were ill at ease with the ultra-traditionalist position taken by their superior general in relation to many of the council's discussions. Mgr. Jean Gay, bishop of Guadeloupe, acted as a spokesman for the group and arranged a meeting with Lefebvre. The bishops made known their disquiet and concerns. He listened respectfully, acknowledging that they were free to follow their own lights and consciences as he would follow his. "You have your way of thinking, I have mine. I would never force any of you to vote the same way as myself, even less to think the same way as I do. We all have a conscience: everyone must follow his own."[80] His biographer maintains that "the Archbishop did not care" and consoled himself with support he received from individual members of the congregation.[81]

The congregation's seminary at Chevilly-Larue, where Lefebvre had been elected superior general, received his unwanted attention. The seminary superior, Fr. Louis Ledit, CSSp, had expected this at the time of GC XII and warned that if Lefebvre were elected, Chevilly would be targeted by him.

---

79. Pollard, *Papacy in the Age of Totalitarianism*, 446.
80. Congregation of the Holy Spirit, *2000 Years of Evangelization*, 51.
81. Tissier de Mallerais, *Lefebvre*, 316–17, referred to a letter Lefebvre received from M'bour, Senegal, in which one of his confreres wrote: "At least one Holy Ghost Father is proud of your attitude, because you have had the courage to express your ideas before the entire church for its greater good."

Anticipating this, he asked that there would be an appreciation of the youth culture in which the seminary was operating. "The youth today despise the old-fashioned ways; and it is that attitude one would like to stop. It is there without doubt that the tension between young and old is situated. . . . There is in today's youth a great generosity full of engagement with their fellow man. This is a danger but it is also an opportunity."[82] Ledit's prediction was proved correct as Lefebvre thought that "too much emphasis was put on the personal research of students, and there was a general craze for acquiring expertise in scriptural studies or patristics, without making this learning subject to the system of the Angelic Doctor."[83] Resistance to change was Lefebvre's response to the youthful energy and experimentation at Chevilly. As his father before him had played his part in the resistance in the German occupation during the war so now, Lefebvre, fighting the cosmic struggle of good against evil, took up the weapon of papal authority and church tradition (as he understood it) in holy warfare against the secularism of the age.

Lefebvre set about a root and branch reform of Chevilly by demanding that the *nouvelle théologie* be discouraged. Books written by theologians such as Frs. Congar and Chenu, were to be withdrawn from the library. These theologians, once silenced by Pius XII, had been restored to favor by John XXIII and were present as *periti* (theological experts) to the council. He also transferred some professors, including Frs. Fourmand and Béguerie.[84] The seminary formation in the Portuguese province was more to Lefebvre's liking and his wish to transfer the Chevilly seminarians to the seminary at Carcavelos was only forestalled by opposition from his own councilors who did not go along with him on that proposal or on following the rigors of

---

82. Perrin, "Mgr. Lefebvre," 146.

83. Tisssier de Mallerais, *Marcel Lefebvre*, 339–40. The title "angelic doctor" refers to St. Thomas Aquinas.

84. Fr. Béguerie, professor of liturgy, was subsequently incardinated into the Archdiocese of Paris and continued teaching liturgy. He responded to what he termed the "hagiography" of Lefebvre written by Mgr. Bernard Tissier de Mallerais, a bishop of the Pius X Society, with a book entitled *Vers Écône*. He asserted that de Mallerais's account of Lefebvre's relationship with the congregation was flawed as he did not have access to the Spiritan archives at Chevilly-Larue. Béguerie's access provided 54 new documents on Lefebvre's relationship with the Spiritan congregation. While Béguerie's work brought new documentation to light his approach to the subject is polemical as he engaged once again with his nemesis who had fired him from his professorship at Chevilly-Larue. He dedicated the book to Fr. Louis Ledit, CSSp, superior of Chevilly-Larue at the time and arch rival to Lefebvre. Ledit was instrumental in deposing him in 1968, and was subsequently elected to the general council that replaced him. It was acknowledged in Florian Michel's "afterword" to *Vers Écône* that the testimony of Fr. Béguerie was not neutral as he was one of the main opponents to Lefebvre. See Béguerie, *Vers Écône*, 471.

Pope St. Pius X's encyclical *Sacrorum antistitum* (1910), requiring all seminary staff to take the oath against modernism.[85] Lefebvre's desire to restore the old formation model for the preparation of future missionaries was all the more astonishing as the need for change was keenly felt in many mission seminaries. Those responsible for the seminary at Chevilly-Larue knew that the era of colonialism and imperialism for which the old model of formation prepared future missionaries, had ended.[86]

Lefebvre's evaluation of the formation in the Irish province was positive. Fr. Charles Connors, CSSp, a general councilor, made an official visitation to the Kimmage scholasticate in October 1963. This was followed in 1965 by the visit of Fr. Gerald FitzGerald, the prefect general of studies in the congregation. Many recommendations resulted from that visit including the need to update the library and to introduce new courses in missiology, anthropology, and pastoral psychology. Ryan, in his review of this updating of studies at Kimmage, recognized the irony involved. "One of the ironies of this whole process of renewal and upgrading of studies was that it was initiated by Archbishop Lefebvre, who would soon show himself so opposed to many aspects of the renewal being promoted by Vatican II."[87] Lefebvre, perhaps, took solace in the traditional view of Ireland as *"semper fidelis"* unlike France, whose loyalty and devotion as elder daughter of the Catholic Church had long grown cold.

Mgr. Lefebvre understood renewal in terms of a return to the founding principles of the congregation which, for him, was the observance of religious life and attention to the needs of "incarnate souls" which it served. He spoke of fidelity as loyalty to unchanging truths and of "a perfect church" which, as it was perfect (of a higher order), did not require change. For a growing number in the congregation, Lefebvre was seen to be speaking of a higher order than the reality they experienced. As Cardinal Newman put it, "In a higher world it is otherwise, but here below to live is to change, and to be perfect is to have changed often" (from *An Essay on the Development of Christian Doctrine*, ch. 1).

At a meeting with the general council and nine provincials and three vice-provincials in Paris from 15 to 22 May 1966, Mgr. Lefebvre spoke of three necessary conditions for a successful renewal of the congregation. First, acceptance of sacrifice and the reality of the cross as central to religious life; second, union with God; and third, commitment to the theological

---

85. Tisssier de Mallerais, *Marcel Lefebvre*, 344. Perrin referred to Lefebvre's *"rêve du Dakar"* in which he desired to establish an international Spiritan seminary in Dakar. He had previously proposed this to GC XII in 1962. Perrin, "Mgr. Lefebvre," 172.

86. O'Malley, *Vatican II*, 268.

87. Ryan, *Kimmage Manor*, 116.

principles underpinning the reason for the Spiritan apostolate, especially the need for salvation, the repentance of sinners, and the necessity of baptism.[88] His priority was fidelity to the old ways of thinking and acting.[89] In this he was out of step with the general renewal going on in the Catholic Church as described by Blessed Pope Paul VI in *Ecclesiam suam* (1964).

> The church will rediscover its youthful vitality not so much by changing its external legislation, as by submitting to the obedience of Christ and observing the laws which the church lays upon itself with the intention of following in Christ's footsteps. Herein lies the secret of the church's renewal, its *metanoia*, to use the Greek term, its practice of perfection.[90]

The language of this encyclical suggested that fidelity was about openness to the new, with the old adapted and reinterpreted in the light of what was new. The exigencies of the time heralded by Pope St. John XXIII called for a fundamental change, an *aggiornamento*, that would require *a metanoia* (change of heart), a creative response, if fidelity to the past was to be maintained.

For Lefebvre ideas did not change. He only admitted to organizational change implemented in an orderly and measured manner. In this, he misread the situation by overestimating his support within the congregation and underestimating the effect of Vatican II and its call to *metanoia* on the membership. Fr. Anthony Geoghegan, CSSp, an Irish Spiritan, shared an insightful remembrance of the tension of those days before GC XIII.

> To those used to seeing changelessness and uniformity as good and innovation as a threat to stability and security, talk of updating and renewal and inculturation seemed destructive. To those pained by the tension between their spiritual and religious life

---

88. *Cor Unum* 3 (1966) 27. This was the last time for such a meeting at the Generalate in Rue des Pyrénées, Paris, as it was due to transfer to its new location at Clivo di Cinna, Rome.

89. Gerald O'Collins made an incisive observation about Mgr. Lefebvre and his rejection of the Vatican Council. "In support of his position, Lefebvre invoked 'the tradition' (understood in the sense of what came from the sixteenth-century Council of Trent) and 'the church' (understood in the sense of French Catholics who longed for the restoration of the monarchy), and avoided appealing to the gospels or invoking Jesus himself and the guidance of the Holy Spirit." He also studied an interview given by Lefebvre to *Newsweek* (19 December 1977). In it, O'Collins noted, Lefebvre spoke about the "church 13 times, 3 times about tradition(s) and twice about 'God', but there was not a mention of Jesus or the gospels." See O'Collins, *Living Vatican II*, 149–50.

90. *Ecclesiam suam* (1964), 51.

on the one hand and life in the world all around them, on the other, this new openness to the world was a liberation.[91]

The Changing Spiritan *Habitus*

The engagement with change was threatening for some and liberating for others. For all Spiritans, the time immediately following the council involved a reevaluation of past practices and a development of new lifestyles in keeping with their Spiritan identity and appropriate to their time. It can be remembered that Fr. Libermann acknowledged social change in his time and advocated creative adaptation to change. Fr. Adrian van Kaam, CSSp, a psychologist and founder of the School of Formative Spirituality at Duquesne University, when writing a biography on Libermann noted his flexibility in matters of formation. He translated into English a telling quotation from Libermann justifying changes to the Constitutions of 1848 concerning formation. "These days, the education of seminarians must be totally different from the methods in vogue before the Revolution of '93. Experience shows that the old approach is now no longer applicable."[92] Following on from this advice, the General Customary of the Congregation directed novice masters to "have at heart the initiating of the novices very specifically into the spirituality of Our Venerable Father in order to help them to live in the spirit of the Congregation."[93] This directive suggests that a spirit of flexibility and adaptation in the spirit of Fr. Libermann should be applied in the congregation's novitiates, to better facilitate the personal, moral, spiritual and missionary development of the novices. Ryan, reflecting on the pre-Vatican II Irish novitiate experience, suggests that a more rigid approach prevailed. The novitiate year "involved total immersion into a system that was highly structured and regulated and animated by an intensive program in spirituality."[94] It was as if an assembly line model of formation operated from novitiate, through philosophy, working in one of the Spiritan colleges ("prefecting") for a period of one or two years, and theology. Kimmage was for the Irish province a hothouse of piety by acting as a *"seminarium"*—a seed plot or nursery where young plants were nur-

91. Geoghegan, "Mission of the Irish Province," 222.

92. "Le mode d'éducation pour les jeunes ecclésiastiques, à l'époque où nous vivons, doit être tout à fait différent de celui qui a été mis en usage avant la Révolution de 93. Il est reconnu par l'expérience que les méthodes anciennes sont maintenant inapplicables." N.D. XII.524–25. See van Kaam, *Light to the Gentiles*, 55.

93. General Customary of the Congregation. Mother House, Paris, 1959, no. 171.

94. Ryan, *Kimmage Manor*, 89.

tured. Ryan suggests that "in terms of human and spiritual development many found this period of formation a very negative experience. A negative view of self, of the human body, and of God-given gifts pervaded formation. The world was looked upon with mistrust."[95]

Spiritan formation, as outlined above, resembled a military training inculcating a lifelong *esprit de corps*. One of the formation maxims stated, "As you are in the novitiate so you will be for the rest of your life." Constancy and dedicated single-mindedness were valued qualities in the personality and character of future missionaries. Obedience was highly prized and any sign of independent thinking was suspect. Conformity to the rule was all important. As another formation maxim went, "Keep the rule, and the rule will keep you." Formation was about forming habits in candidates so that they could fulfill the end of the congregation they aspired to join. Spiritans not only dressed in religious habit, but were formed into a lifestyle, or "*habitus*" appropriate to their way of life.

The French sociologist and anthropologist, Pierre Bourdieu, interpreted the Aristotelian notion of *habitus* (how individuals acquire virtue) as "a strategy-generating principle enabling agents to cope with unforeseen and ever-changing situations."[96] This, he said, happened through a socialization process whereby the individual acquired the way of thinking and acting approved by a group. It can be appreciated through the analogy of learning how to play a game. When learning to play a new game, the rules are learned and through practice the skills of the game are acquired. The skilled player interprets the flow of the game and responds to the changing circumstances of the game to good effect.

> We get a "sense of the game," not just by reading the rulebook but by actually playing. . . . Players have ingrained dispositions, propensities, and instincts of just what to do and when to do it. . . . These ingrained dispositions are what enable the player/actor/agent to improvise, and over time these improvisations can become routinized and eventually change the game itself.[97]

An analogy can be made with religious life. Through formation and the early years of living one's vocation, the young religious acquires the dispositions and skill to function in a way that is in keeping with his or her religious community. But the religious community functions within a context. When that context changes dramatically then a change in the way the

---

95. Ibid., 95.
96. Sacks, "Church That Can and Cannot Change," 307.
97. Ibid., 308.

members of the community live together and are on mission is demanded. Such a time of change causes inevitable tension.

Given what was in place and the transformation required to aspire to the ideals of the council it is not surprising that there was much confusion and turmoil among Spiritans exacerbated surely by the dramatic hemorrhaging of membership and drop in vocations. The rules of the game had changed and players were clumsily finding out what the new rules were and how to implement them. Old certainties had quickly given way to a *laissez-faire* approach to religious observance. Along with this, for missionaries, the changing political landscape in mission territories added to an anxiety that, in many instances, weakened religious observance. Describing what he saw in the district of Pointe-Noire, Congo, an official visitor reported to Lefebvre:

> One cannot say that the prayer life has been abandoned, but there is some slackness. The priests are first to recognize it and want to do something about it. Thus, in many parishes, they recite the office with the sisters. They know that the sisters are more regular than themselves, which is a good incentive. Besides, it is a good example for the Christian community.[98]

Old certainties were set aside without adequate replacement. It would take time for the new skins to develop to hold the new wine of Vatican II! Old traditions no longer went unquestioned. And, once questioned, they were seen to be outdated and of little use in a new context. There was a trauma associated with this hiatus between the "no longer" and the "not yet." The 1960s were difficult and challenging years, what we might call a "threshold time," when one had let go of the old but did not yet know the new. This was a time of few certainties. It seemed that change was the only certainty. This was the time in Europe and the United States of America of "flower power," hippies, student riots, and a bewildering number of lifestyles from which to choose.

A Jesuit Perspective

It is instructive to consider another Catholic religious institute and how it coped with change in the second half of the 1960s. The thirty-first Jesuit General Congregation was held in Rome during the final session of Vatican II in 1965.[99] Patrick Howell, SJ, painted a picture of Jesuit life not unlike

---

98. Pannier, *L'Église de Pointe-Noire*, 231.
99. The Jesuit general congregation was held in two sessions. The first was held from

that experienced by Spiritans at the time. He wrote, "By 1965 a certain stagnation had settled into Jesuit life. Jesuit spirituality was rote, loaded with rules, and laden with monasticism." He went on to recall that efforts made in 1957 at the previous General Congregation to carry out some updating of the society were preempted by Pope Pius XII when he "delivered an address that in great measure closed off any discussion of possible changes that the delegates might have wished to consider."[100]

The Jesuit General Congregation, unlike GC XII of the Spiritans in 1962, took place toward the end of the council and had the benefit of the council's direction to religious institutes for their adaptation and renewal. It made changes to its rules and regulations. The external changes were the most obvious. Howell documented those changes.

> Cassocks gave way to clerical shirts, and pants and for some the formality of shirt and tie. Jesuit superiors allowed for increased personal initiative and creativity. Many monastic practices, such as silence during meals, strictures on family visits, tight restrictions on travel, gave way to more humane religious practices. The transformation of the Latin liturgy into the vernacular also shook the pillars of tradition. The change in an "unchanging" liturgy led many to assume that almost anything could change.[101]

The Jesuits recognized that fidelity to tradition required change. They chose quite a different candidate to Archbishop Lefebvre when electing their superior general. Fr. Pedro Arrupe, SJ, was, like St. Ignatius, a Basque born in Bilbao in 1907, two years after Lefebvre. Two days after his election on 24 May 1965, Arrupe addressed the assembly that had elected him. He summarized his approach to the daunting challenges that lay ahead by proposing the question, "What would Ignatius have done today?" He looked to the Jesuit founder for inspiration and guidance in all the decisions that were to be made. He would ask himself what to do, following Ignatius's thinking and attitudes. This was a question he often repeated as superior general.

Arrupe was a man for the time, well equipped to lead the Jesuits through creative fidelity to the Ignatian charism. Fifty years later, Howell reflecting on Arrupe at that time wrote that "he embodied a view of religious leadership rooted in collegiality, discernment, and service. He led

---

7 May to 15 July 1965; the second from 8 September to 17 November 1967. See Padberg, *Together as a Companionship*.

100. Howell, "'New' Jesuits," 7. According to Howell this included asking the society to ban smoking among its members. As a result, he concluded that "much energy was misdirected to enforcing this healthy, but ill-conceived, mandate."

101. Ibid., 8.

the Society in responding to Vatican II and urgent needs of the world with courage, generosity, and remarkable optimism."[102] It is interesting here to note that Arrupe encountered opposition from within Jesuit ranks for wholeheartedly following the lead of the council. He had to face the threat of a division of the society in Spain as well as resistance from many university Jesuits, particularly those at the Gregorian University in Rome. He also had to contend with a fraught relationship with Pope St. John Paul II, which culminated in the removal of his assistant as interim general (Fr. Arrupe had suffered a stroke in August 1981).[103]

A Time of Conflict

The 1960s was a decade of controversy where old ways of living religious life and being on mission were strongly debated. A critique of traditional missionary methods was underway among Spiritans following the council. An article by Maryknoll Missionary Fr. Albert J. Nevins, MM, on the new missiology of *Ad gentes*, was published in the congregation's journal, *Cor Unum*, in 1966.[104] Nevins maintained that the era of missionary activity allied with colonial administration was at an end. The social, political, and economic evolution taking place in "mission territories" required a new form of missionary presence. The old attitudes devaluing local cultures and imposing European and North American values were anachronistic and no longer acceptable. He criticized missionary activity in the past as the product of paternalism and cultural imperialism that only subjugated people to a foreign way of thinking and behaving. This old way of being missionary was dead. Nevins did acknowledge that mission was still needed, but a new way for being on mission was needed. This new way was given in Vatican II's teaching that all members of the church were missionary; that mission was no longer defined geographically, but as the bringing to reality the "fullness of the mystical body of Christ."[105]

---

102. Howell, "'New' Jesuits," 9.

103. Ibid.

104. *Cor Unum* was a quarterly journal first published by the Generalate in January 1964. All confreres were invited to express their ideas, make suggestions, express their hopes. The journal also contained news from the different circumscriptions of the congregation and acted as a forum for the general administration to give reports on their work and on meetings of the congregation.

105. *Cor Unum* 3 (1966) 12–16. See de Jong, *Challenge of Vatican II*, 17–26, for a discussion on missionary adaptation by Dutch missionaries in East Africa in the late nineteen-fifties and the beginning of the sixties before Vatican II. Four differing forms of adaptation were considered by de Jong: translation, substitution, assimilation and

Irish Spiritan Fr. Seán Byron, CSSp, writing from Onitsha, Nigeria, took issue with Nevins's generalizations about former missionary methods. Nowhere in the council documents was such a critique as that of Nevins to be found. The attitudes and methods of the past were good for that time, and often the only ones possible. Nevins's call for new methods was "preaching to the converted," for Spiritans recognized the changes taking place around them and were evolving in accordance with sound missionary principles. The debate should not be about principles, Byron wrote, but how to apply the principles to concrete problems.

While Lefebvre allowed such debate, dissatisfaction with his leadership and the pace of change in the congregation was mounting. For some, his continuing support for Action Française did not sit well. In 1968, a young, newly ordained Irish Spiritan took the unprecedented step of writing a letter to a national newspaper spelling out his disquiet over the leadership of his superior general. The editor captioned the letter "Priest who disagrees with his superior"—a novel thought for that time.

> The Archbishop's concept of authority amounts to little more than an ecclesiastical dictatorship, and is hardly compatible with the evangelical ideal of service, as taken up, at least in part, by the recent council.... Inevitably, the new spirit of freedom that, thank God, is blowing through the Catholic Church has brought with it certain difficulties, dangers, and even excesses, but the gains in Christian understanding, commitment, and maturity far outweigh these. It does little service to the church or to the world to generalize gloomily about catastrophes to come. Like the early Christians, we are living in a time of challenge and the air is bracing, not deadly.[106]

The wind of change was, perhaps, experienced differently in France than in Ireland. For some French Spiritans the existential "life or death"

Christianization.

106. Fr. Brian Hearne, CSSp, *Sunday Independent*, 18 August 1968. Hearne was responding to an article by Lefebvre published on 7 March 1968 in *Rivarol*, which Hearne identified as "the organ of the reactionary right-wing in France on ecclesiastical and political levels." Lefebvre wrote that the church had resisted heresies and errors at the time of Vatican II, that was "severely upsetting for not only the traditional enemies of the church inspired by the prince of the world . . . when one knows the vision of those who seek to dominate the world, the communists and the international financial technocrats, the only true obstacle to the subservience of the Catholic Church is the church, Catholic and Roman, one would not be surprised of the efforts conjured up by communists and free-masons to change the magisterium and the hierarchical structure of the church." Bégeurie, *Vers Écône*, 395. Bégeurie pointed out that the *Rivarol* article caused a media storm and was deeply troubling for many French Spiritans.

question needed to be asked of the congregation. The question was put in the context of the council's decree, *Ad gentes*, which asserted that the church of its very nature was missionary and that mission was the responsibility of all church members. A logical development of this idea in *Lumen gentium*, that the local church was the primary agent for mission, challenged the rationale for missionary institutes.

In a special edition of the French journal *Spiritus*, preparing for GC XIII, the editor, Fr. Athanase Bouchard, CSSp, feared that, given the changed circumstances since the general chapter of 1962, "it is very clear that a failure of this present chapter would have altogether more radical consequences for the congregation than that of 1962." Bouchard urged the capitulants to the forthcoming chapter to have the courage to "see things as they are: it is certain that there is among us—especially among the young—an easy resignation to the eventuality of a dissolution of the Spiritans; they see no other future apart from this."[107] He painted an "end game" scenario for the congregation giving GC XIII the ominous title of "*le chapitre de la dernière chance.*"

---

107. Athanase Bouchard, CSSp, in *Spiritus, Supplément Spécial / Chapitre 1968*, 5.

Chapter 3

The General Chapter of Renewal

1. A Council Ends and a Chapter Begins

VATICAN II ENDED ON 8 December 1965. In a circular letter of 6 January 1966, Mgr. Lefebvre asked superiors of provinces and districts to ensure that members receive and study the conciliar decrees already promulgated especially those on religious life, the missions, priestly life, and seminary training. The letter made no mention of the spirit of the council that set out a new understanding of the church, its mission, and place in the world.[1] Study groups were recommended and individual members could make suggestions. All members were to be involved in the most widespread and inclusive consultation process to take place in the history of the congregation. Each circumscription was asked to arrange four commissions to gather submissions from communities, groups, and individuals with each covering one of the general areas of concern: (1) legislation; (2) religious life and the apostolate; (3) formation; (4) the brothers. Once the commissions had completed their work, an enlarged provincial/district council would synthesize the submissions and write a report for the general council. Lefebvre emphasized that superiors were to give full freedom to confreres in making submissions.[2] A time span of twelve months was allowed for this process after which elections for capitulants to a general administrative chapter could begin.

Feedback came first from the Dutch Enlarged Provincial Council which had "discussed and approved" its legislative commission's report

---

1. Perrin, "Mgr. Lefebvre," 166.

2. Lefebvre's official letter in French said, "Les supérieurs veilleront aussi a préserver la liberté d'expression des confrères" (6 January 1966).

as early as 22 March 1966. This report was also circulated to the general council and to all provincials and major superiors in the congregation. The Dutch proposed that the direction given to the enlarged councils be applied to the process at general administration level of "arranging and recording *only*" and "arranging and recording *everything*" that was submitted to them. They also proposed that a preparatory commission be established by the general council to complete this work of collation; and added, "It exceeds the competence of this committee to make an arbitrary selection of subjects, views, and proposals, let alone to omit them altogether."[3]

The Dutch raised several other issues. Could "a presiding superior general reject a proposal to the general chapter merely on his own authority or after consulting his council, either before or during the chapter?" An answer was sought from a renowned canon lawyer, Fr. J. P. Gallen, SJ, who replied that it depended on the institute's constitutions which may give that authority before the chapter. However, this was rare and "never after the chapter is in session."[4] The Dutch commission also proposed that the chapter should be held in two sessions. The first would agree basic principles and be followed by the second to provide "detailed elaborations" on them. It cautioned against delay causing a vacuum in which innovations would be made at local level. The following spring was proposed. The first session should appoint an international central commission to oversee the business of the chapter (as at the Vatican Council).

The commission proposed the principle that all members of the congregation ought to be present at the chapter as fundamental matters were

---

3. *In Preparation of the General Chapter CSSp*, paper of the Legislatio Commission, Dutch Province, 22 March 1966, 3.

4. The journal, *Review for Religious*, published a series of articles by Fr. Joseph Gallen, SJ, professor of canon law at Woodstock College, Maryland, in 1958 on General Chapters in a question and answer format. The Dutch *Legislatio* Commission quoted from these articles to substantiate its opinions. The answer to the above question was: "It is possible that your constitutions give this authority to the superior general before the opening of the chapter. However, this is found most rarely and never after the chapter is in session. It is to be remembered that the chapter is the supreme authority within the institute. The superior general, even though he presides, is merely a member of the chapter. He does not act as superior in the chapter. Evidently, he is to be given the customary respect and reverence, and his proposals and comments merit greater attention and consideration. He should submit all proposals to the chapter committee or committees on proposals. This does not prevent a committee from stating that a proposal should be rejected or referred to the superior general as a matter of ordinary government. To the degree that a committee fails to do this, the chapter, fatigued, frustrated, and irritated by extraneous details, will be rendered less efficient and less effective. When a committee has made its report, the chapter, not the superior general alone, is the judge as to whether a proposal should be accepted or rejected." *Review for Religious* 17 (1958) 286.

to be decided. Presence could be achieved through representation. It referred to Constitution 75 of the Rules and Constitutions which required the attendance of major superiors as ex-officio members of the chapter. This arrangement came from another time and mentality, that of the "superior—inferior" relationship, which needed rethinking in accordance with the council which placed the tract on the people of God before the one on the church's hierarchy in its constitution on the church, *Lumen gentium*. A new thinking of service and brotherhood prevailed and the composition of membership of the general chapter should reflect that. While it would be impractical "to abandon, immediately and radically, the statute of the *ex-officio* members," a new ratio of two elected members for every one ex-officio member was proposed. This was at variance with Constitution 75 which determined that delegated members should be "not less than half nor more than two thirds of the *ex-officio* members." It also took issue with Constitution 76 which restricted those with active and passive vote for the general chapter to "the fathers with perpetual vows." The commission asked, "Aught we not to say that the general chapter is a matter which concerns the whole *congregation* and is therefore the concern of *all* the members, not of the fathers only?"[5]

Lefebvre and the general council accepted the principle of greater representation at the general chapter, and sought a dispensation from the Holy See to increase the number of elected delegates to equal the number of ex-officio delegates. But that was as far as Lefebvre was prepared to go and he remarked that some members were "substituting themselves for the general council" and that no one had a mandate to "influence the thinking of other provinces, districts or confreres."[6] He assured the members that the chapter would be so well prepared that capitulants would be able "to make a genuinely conscientious and enlightened choice of possible alternatives."[7]

Four preparatory commissions were set up to analyze the feedback from the provinces and districts, and report to the general council. These four commissions were organized by the topics (1) the brothers; (2) religious life and the apostolate; (3) formation; and (4) legislation. They were composed of members invited from different provinces (France, Ireland, Trinidad, Germany, Portugal, USA, Belgium, Holland, England, Canada, and Switzerland). A member of the Generalate community joined the brothers commission and two members sat on each of the other commissions.

---

5. *In Preparation of the General Chapter CSSp*, paper of the Legislatio Commission, Dutch Province, 22 March 1966, 9.

6. *GB* 729 (1966) 205.

7. Ibid., 207.

Subcommissions were also set up to expedite the work and provide summaries of the documents that had been studied. If necessary, commissions could seek expert advice on complex questions. The council agreed to appoint a central pre-capitular commission that would be representative of the worldwide membership. It consisted of Frs. J. Lécuyer, J. Troupeau, F. Mulcahy, J. Walsh, J. Bondallaz, P. Walsh, M. van der Drift and T. Murray, who worked together from 15 January to Easter 1968 preparing documentation for the final consultation of the membership before the chapter.[8]

A growing impatience was evident from members at the slow pace of adaptation to Vatican II in the congregation. One confrere, Fr. P. J. des Grottes, in his submission to the pre-capitular commission, which he entitled "Reflections on My Family," wrote six pages "of vitriol" complaining that the conditions of life lived in the congregation belonged to another age and another mentality. He asked for attention to be given to the malaise among the young members. He abhorred the way brothers were treated in the congregation and asked, "Are we aristocrats?"[9] An event that brought the gap between modern thinking and the preparatory work for the chapter to the surface was the refusal of Dutch novices to take public vows. They would only take private vows for a year. This was but the beginning. More would come resulting in the recognition that a change of leadership was needed in the congregation.

Lefebvre and his council had been elected in 1962 for twelve years, that is, until GC XIII which was scheduled for 1974. GC XIII, however, would be brought forward; it would be non-elective and termed an "extraordinary" and "administrative" chapter. This was how Lefebvre understood the situation and as the Holy See had agreed it.[10] Consequently, the general council communicated to the membership in July 1966 that the chapter would be administrative, dealing with the necessary adaptations to be made to the Rules and Constitutions resulting from the directives of Vatican II. But a growing dissatisfaction among the membership was discerned by the general council. A questionnaire conducted in France, for example, returned the result that of 312 replies, 226 wanted two-thirds of the capitulants to

---

8 Ibid., 164.

9. Ibid., 143.

10. Cardinal Antoniutti, prefect of the Congregation for Religious, wrote on 5 May 1966 to Archbishop Lefebvre that the chapter may be held "not in view of new elections but only to take decisions necessary to the *aggiornamento* by the application of the Conciliar Decree on Religious and the Post-Conciliar Instruction." *GB* 727 (1966). GC XIII was entitled "extraordinary," as Constitution 77 required a chapter only to be held "every time it is necessary to elect a superior general, that is, at least every twelve years." It also stipulated that "for exceptional reasons" the superior general could call a general chapter with the approval of his council and permission of the Holy See.

be elected. And although the question was not put, 59 replies requested an elective chapter.

In October 1967, Mgr. Lefebvre formally convoked the "special extraordinary chapter" with the term "administrative" dropped from the title. His communication outlined details of time and place, details about ex-officio members and the organization of electoral circumscriptions for the nomination and election of capitulants. It was decided that the chapter would be held in Rome at Domus Mariae, with delegates arriving on 1 September 1968 and the work to start the following week (8 September).[11] Lefebvre wrote, "In all sincerity we can say that the Holy Spirit, our protector, is guiding the congregation in these preparatory steps which are proceeding in a spirit of deep fraternal charity, true liberty, and sincere desire to give the congregation a new impetus of interior and of apostolic life."[12]

The number of elected capitulants would equal ex-officio members. The final number of capitulants would be 110 (55 ex-officio and 55 elected), with a representation of approximately 1 delegate to 77 voting members.[13] The result of the first "worldwide" ballot was announced on 2 February 1968, with 9 capitulants elected by absolute majority to represent their provinces/districts. The remaining 46 were elected by second ballot before the deadline of 15 April. The final list was given after the second ballot and published in the May–June *General Bulletin*. The preparations having been made, all that remained was for those concerned to make their way to *Domus Mariae* in Rome.

The Superior General and the Chapter

Fr. Jean P. Le Gall, CSSp, the chronicler for the chapter, stated in preliminary remarks to his report on the first session, that "since the death of Venerable Father Libermann, no other chapter in the history of our congregation has been as important as this one or has lasted as long, and we are still only at

---

11. Domus Mariae was a conference center run by the Italian Feminine Action group and situated on Via Aurelia.

12. *GB* 50 (1967) 303.

13. The Irish capitulants included Frs. Higgins and Farrelly from the Generalate, and the provincial Fr. Vincent Dinan. Other Irish Spiritans present, either *de jure* or as elected members, included: Patrick Joseph Walsh, Michael O'Carroll, William Jenkinson, Des Kenny, Bernard Kelly, Tom Farrelly, Andrew O'Toole, Donal O'Sullivan (Fr. O'Sullivan and Bishop Okoye were unable to attend the beginning of the first session of GC XIII due to the Biafra War); Niall Macauley, John Byrne (Trinidad), Gearoid McCarthy and Francis Griffin (Superior General Emeritus).

the first session."[14] The agenda was vast as every aspect of Spiritan life, both missionary and religious, had to be addressed and brought up to date.

Le Gall noted that there was an uneven level of preparation among participants; with some more prepared than others. The documentation was presented under nine topics: (1) the specific aim of the congregation; (2) the members of the congregation; (3) apostolic and religious life; (4) organization of the congregation; (5) formation; (6) clerical status of the congregation; (7) brothers; (8) temporal goods; (9) the nature of the congregation. It is clear from Le Gall's report that taking control of the chapter from Lefebvre was paramount for some well-prepared delegates.[15]

Mgr. Lefebvre, concluding his report at the beginning of the chapter, reiterated the announcement made earlier in the year that he and his council offered their resignations which would become effective following the election of a new superior general and council. But until then he would preside over the chapter. Some capitulants were vehemently opposed to this as the chapter was the legislative body of the congregation and not subject to the executive. If the chapter was independent and acting as the supreme authority of the congregation, then, a central commission elected by the capitulants to coordinate the work of the chapter was required. Should the superior general act as chair of the central commission, and so preside over the chapter? There was division over this crucial issue and it needed to be resolved. Following two days of discussion in plenary session a vote was taken on whether Archbishop Lefebvre, as superior general, should chair the central commission. There were 40 votes in favor, and 63 votes against.

This was a critical moment in the life of the chapter and in the history of the congregation. We have seen the role Lefebvre played at the Vatican Council, his unstinting resistance to change; his assertion of centralized authority and commitment to the "old ways." He clearly advocated a pre-Vatican II theology and, during his mandate as superior general, a return to a pre-Vatican II model of church.[16] But this was only fully appreciated by

14. *GB* 51 (1968) 313.

15. Lefebvre's biographer wrote that Lefebvre had confided to close friends that he intended to resign as superior general as he was no longer listened to or wanted by the congregation. Tissier de Mallerais, *Lefebvre*, 368.

16. Those who followed Lefebvre's *Avis du Mois* in the *General Bulletin* would have recognized a recalcitrant approach to the teaching of Vatican II. The first topic he chose to focus on after the council was the Decree on the Ministry and Life of Priests. See *GB* 50 (1966). Lefebvre used the language of *sacerdos*, of one who administers the sacraments and offers sacrifice, rather than *presbyter*, a term taken from the New Testament and early Christian sources, which, as O'Malley puts it, suggested "a broadening of definition beyond administering the sacraments and offering sacrifice, which priest as *sacerdos* implied and which, since the Middle Ages, had been the standard understanding

some of the capitulants who were adamant that the general chapter should act independently of him. Following this vote, Lefebvre absented himself from the assembly.

One can only begin to imagine the tension that filled the aula of *Domus Mariae* on that fateful Wednesday of 11 September. Writing forty years later, Fr. Frans Timmermans, CSSp, who would become superior general in 1974, recalled the scene.

> I will never forget the crisis which exploded in the general chapter in what could be called the "failed coup" of Mgr. Lefebvre. He was profoundly unhappy with the preparations for the chapter and the way that events were unfolding, so he tried to force the hands of the capitulants by insisting on taking over the presidency of the central commission. In this way, he could control and direct the way the chapter would go. But the chapter rejected this by vote, so he left the assembly, but not before accusing the capitulants of infidelity to the doctrine of the church and the charism of the congregation.[17]

It is important to remember the magnetic personality of Mgr. Lefebvre who, not only commanded the respect of many confreres, but held an important place in the history of the church in West Africa. Had the chapter acted correctly? How was it to proceed without him? It can be assumed that there were those who regretted his leaving. His biographer records that on the following day Lefebvre wrote to the Sacred Congregation for Religious informing it of what had happened. He contested that the vote removing his authority over the chapter was unconstitutional.[18]

The chapter continued in the absence of the superior general according to an agreed method and program. The central commission consisted of a secretary general with Fr. Matt Farrelly, general secretary of the congregation, elected to that position. Three moderators would also sit on the commission and Frs. Patrick Walsh (Ireland), Georges Thibault (France) and Gerard Roy (Canada) were elected. The regulation also required two coordinators and Frs. Van Der Drift (Holland) and Jorge Sanchez (Portugal) were elected. Each working group or commission chose a representative to complete the central commission.

The chapter approached the substantive issues to be decided, beginning with the specific aim of the congregation. This was approached in the context of two talks given by Fr. Ageneau, CSSp, on Libermann's understanding

---

of it." O'Malley, *Vatican II*, 273.

17. Timmermans, "New Spring," 57.

18. Tissier de Mallerais, *Marcel Lefebvre*, 371–72.

of unity in the congregation and the relationship between the two founders. Ageneau placed the work of the general chapter within the context of its long history. He suggested that a sense of history would help the capitulants distinguish what was essential to Spiritan identity from what had been accumulated over the years. Ageneau outlined Libermann's approach to living religious life in community and the demands of the apostolate. The relationship between religious life and the apostolate was a key issue for GC XIII.[19]

Fr. Eugene Hillman, CSSp, an American Spiritan in Tanzania, gave a talk to the capitulants on the meaning of missionary activity. He pointed out the significance of the titles of the Vatican II documents on the church and on its mission: *Lumen gentium* and *Ad gentes*. The church was the light of the world that must be brought to all the peoples of the world. This was the work entrusted to each missionary and to missionary institutes (*AG* 23). Hillman, referring to the challenge put by *Ad gentes* (*AG* 40), defined missionary activity in terms of preaching the gospel to those who had not yet heard it. This was the specific missionary purpose of the congregation for which all its members abroad and at home (in necessary tasks ordered toward first evangelization, such as vocations fostering, formation and fundraising) should be engaged. This being so, were Spiritans to continue with assistance to the young developing churches or were they to concentrate on those peoples not yet evangelized and among whom the church was not yet established?[20]

The capitulants had this and many other new and challenging questions to consider. Not unlike the steep learning curve for the bishops attending the Second Vatican Council, so also for the capitulants in *Domus Mariae*. There were indications that minds were opening to a new way of

---

19. For a summary of Ageneau's two talks see *Cor Unum* 5 (1968) 7–24. He referred to Libermann's 1846 *Memorandum to Propaganda Fide* which argued for the establishment of local churches in Africa and warned of the need to regulate the apostolate and religious life of the missionaries. "As for the mode of local government, if nothing is decided in this regard, serious disorder and significant obstacles to the success of the missions will often arise. The source of the trouble usually stems from two principles. The first is the double interest that exists in the missions. This double interest is represented by two authorities, that of the bishop, head of the missionaries in their quality as missionaries, and that of the religious superiors, head of the missionaries in their role as members of the community. If unity exists between these two representatives, the two interests powerfully reinforce each other; if not, they tend to mutually destroy one another, and great damage can be the result. Regulations will thus have to be put in place to reconcile these two interests, by maintaining in all its integrity the power of the bishop in his mission, and yet giving the community sufficient guarantees for the preservation of its rules and its spirit." N.D. VIII.249–50.

20. Hillman's talk "The Meaning of Missionary Activity" is summarized in *Cor Unum* 5 (1968) 1–6.

seeing things. The commissions reported back to the plenary session of 19 September on their work. Progress was made in identifying the specific mission of the congregation and a sense of its spirit, *cor unum et anima una*, was becoming more evident among capitulants as they addressed the common task the church has set before them.

It was in such a context that Archbishop Lefebvre returned. Convinced that a minority of capitulants was manipulating the chapter, he gave an address (28 September) to reassert his position as superior.[21] He explained that he went on retreat to Assisi to reflect on the writings of Fr. Libermann and had arrived at some conclusions which he wanted to share with the chapter. He presented the links between religious life, community life, and missionary activity that were the hallmark of Libermann's teaching. And then, about half way through his speech, he threw down the gauntlet to those who opposed him. "The realization, in practice of this community life and religious life, is the observance of the Rule under the vigilance of the superior." He went on to say, "We must recognize in all humility that this religious life and this community life, such as they are essentially known by our Venerable Father, are no longer wanted by many of us. Why hide it? Already for a certain number of years, slowly, progressively, but irremediably a good many confreres have lost the esteem and the practice of true religious life and community life."[22] His words indicate that he was well informed about the progress of the chapter and the emphasis being placed on the missionary activity of the congregation in general and first evangelization, in particular. He had read Libermann's writings and interpreted them in the light of his own convictions.

Lefebvre confronted those who opposed him for the last time.

> Let those who feel they can no longer accept these two foundation stones of our society, as our Venerable Father defines them, look elsewhere for another society that may suit them or let them found a new one; otherwise that spiritual renewal so desirable and expected will be illusory. Our extraordinary chapter will only be confirming false tendencies of individualism, of liberty, and our society will be in effect a caricature of a religious congregation, with non-religious members, and a caricature of community life where anarchy, disorder, and individual initiative have free reign.[23]

---

21 Timmermans, "New Spring," 57.
22. *GB* 51 (1968) 175.
23. Ibid., 179.

What response did Lefebvre expect to his words? He was elected with more than a two-thirds majority only six years earlier. As superior general, he had been welcomed to many provinces and districts. Where were those who welcomed him then? What of his own general council? We saw that Fr. Matt Farrelly, his secretary general and trusted colleague, accepted the position of general secretary to the chapter. Another Irish man and general councilor, Fr. Bill Higgins, spoke many years later in Kenya of his affection for Lefebvre and his sadness at his departure. But neither he, nor anybody else left the chapter to follow the superior general. He was on his own.[24]

The Work of the Chapter Continued

The work of the chapter continued with a parliamentary process in place to agree propositions. A consensus quickly formed around the principles of subsidiarity, solidarity, and unity for governance of the congregation which would proceed from "the bottom up." That is, from the individual, to the local community, to the district/provincial community, to the general council. Subsidiarity, the chapter realized, only had meaning when people were in solidarity with one another and united by a common purpose toward a common end.

Le Gall's report covered 102 sittings in general assembly and he noted a restiveness among some of the capitulants caused perhaps by the difficulty in finding ways to translate these principles into organizational practice. "Clear lines had to be drawn, establishing the principles of decentralization, of adaptation and of co-ordination of the various layers, in the structure of the congregation."[25] The chapter did succeed in articulating a common vision of the Spiritan vocation as an "indissoluble unity of life, viewed as a

---

24. One intervention at the first session of the general chapter was from a confrere working in Brazil, Cristovao Arnaud Freire, who said that the chapter was about adaptation and not the destruction of the congregation. He was surprised to hear criticism of the pope, bishops, and superiors from fellow capitulants. He said that from the beginning the chapter had been dominated by a group who carried personal slights from Archbishop Lefebvre and were incapable of distinguishing between those hurts and the superior general. Because of this, he decided to return to his mission and would continue to pray to Our Lady of Fatima for the authors of all the trouble. Perrin "Mgr. Lefebvre," 170.

25. *GB* 51 (1968) 340. The Jesuits required a similar need for patience at their congregation. "When a topic of great importance or delicacy was the subject for plenary discussion, the air of seriousness in the aula was palpable. Almost always the discussion was both frank and respectful, but tensions could and did arise, as was only to be expected, especially as the congregation dragged on." Padberg, *Together as a Companionship*, 55.

whole, and in all its aspects, Spiritan and ecclesial, humanitarian and christianizing, active and prayerful, missionary, and religious, which we call the apostolic Spiritan life."[26] A definition of the relationship between missionary activity and religious life could not be agreed. The commission researching this had the difficulty of, on the one hand, appeasing those eager to forge a new missionary path, and, on the other hand, those committed to retaining its religious nature. Le Gall pointed out that "much weariness of mind" probably stymied the debate as the end of the first session was in sight and some capitulants were already finalizing their travel plans.

The commission's text, referring to Libermann's *Règle Provisoire* of 1841 and the *Règlements* of 1849, advanced the proposition: "The congregation is a missionary society, living the religious life, but in the course of its history, it was led, by an inexact interpretation of religious law, to enshrine its religious life in a more or less monastic framework, which is not its own, since it considers itself to be primarily apostolic."[27] While this formulation was recognized by some to reflect postconciliar thinking, others thought it too extreme. Le Gall reported one capitulant as saying, "We had to be careful, in blazing a trail, not to set fire to our principles."[28] There were clearly different understandings of religious life at work among capitulants. The commission suggested a way forward by replacing "religious life" with "community" and proposed that the congregation is "a missionary community, modelled on that of Jesus Christ and the apostles, which gives itself to the evangelization of the poor while living the evangelical counsels in an official consecration." Not surprisingly perhaps, this formulation did not get the support required with 26 voting for, 25 voting against and 43 undecided. The moderators recognized that more research and discussion was needed on the nature of the congregation if agreement was to be reached and so, to the disappointment of some, further discussion was deferred to the second session of the chapter, the following year.

The mode of election for a new superior general and council was agreed and an exploratory vote for general was held on 26 October. Fr. Joseph Lécuyer was elected on the third scrutiny by 75 votes out of 105.[29]

26. GB 51 (1968) 363. The vote accepting the document summarized by this formula was 85 for and 7 against.

27. Ibid., 366.

28. Ibid., 339.

29. Fr. Lécuyer was born in 1912. His great uncle, Mgr. Pierre-Marie Le Berre (1819–1891), was received into the Society of the Holy Heart of Mary by Fr. Libermann and completed his novitiate at La Neuville. He succeeded Bishop Bessieux as second bishop of Gabon. Lécuyer studied philosophy and theology at the Gregorian University while in the French Seminary in Rome. A distinguished academic career followed

He had given a talk at the beginning of the chapter, entitled "The Place of the Congregation in the Church." The prophetic dimension of his words, in light of subsequent events at the chapter, made a deep impression on capitulants who recognized in him the theologian attuned to the signs of the times, who could lead the congregation in its task of adaptation and renewal. Frans Timmermans, a capitulant and Lécuyer's successor in 1974, praised him for stepping into the breach and saving the day.

> It was at this time that we had Fr. Lécuyer, an academic, a very wise and profound man, a man of God, and one who was devoted with all his heart to the congregation.... I can say that Fr. Lécuyer saved the congregation because ultimately his presence inspired confidence among confreres. Everybody recognized his loyalty to the church and to the Spiritan charism and, in the end, Mgr. Lefebvre wasn't followed in his movement, except by a few.[30]

The following evening an exploratory vote for members of the general council was held. They were Frs. Donal O'Sullivan (Ireland), subsequently elected first assistant; Louis Ledit (France) subsequently elected second assistant; George Sanches (Portugal); Joseph Stocker (Germany); Quirinus J. Houdijk (Holland); and Robert J. Eberhardt (USA). Significantly, Frs. O'Sullivan and Sanches received the two-thirds majority on the first ballot with Ledit, Stocker and Houdijk on the second. Eberhardt was elected on the third round. A consensus and unanimity was growing among the capitulants not only with a shared vision for the future, but also in electing an administration to achieve that vision.

The first session of the chapter concluded on Friday, 15 November, with Lécuyer's promulgation, *ad experimentum*, of the decisions concerning decentralization that were voted on and contained in the document on the organization of the congregation. Lécuyer inspired hope in the capitulants in his concluding remarks saying that "congregations spring from the will of the members to live together and that their place is that which the societies themselves decide upon, first by the choice of their founder and then by the renewed choice of their members." He recognized the challenges facing the congregation as (1) a return to gospel simplicity; (2) fidelity to its

---

culminating in his appointment to preconciliar commissions and then as a member of the Theological Commission, the Commission on Clergy, and the Commission for Seminaries at the council.

30. From an interview with Frans Timmermans in Rome, June 2016, by Baba Gaston Temgoua and published in the Generalate's quarterly bulletin.

own vocation; (3) participation in the life of the church; (4) openness to the world of today; (5) spiritual renewal.[31]

Some days before the conclusion of the first session in 1968, the capitulants met in audience with Pope Paul VI and two other religious congregations also meeting in chapter (11 November). The pope exhorted them to be authentic religious in the midst of vast change overtaking contemporary society. He said,

> It is more important than ever to ask yourselves what is essential and cannot be replaced in the type of life you have embraced and also ask what can be and what should be changed according to time and place. . . . Each congregation has its own spirit, its style; this has to be kept, but it needs to be adapted in a way that fits in with what is possible and what is imposed by specific activities in the ecclesial community.[32]

Addressing the Spiritans specifically, Pope Paul VI thanked them on behalf of the church "for the admirable work you are doing, particularly in Africa. . . . May the necessary adaptations be aimed at rendering more efficacious and more ardent your missionary impetus."[33] This affirmation by the Successor of Peter brought relief to the capitulants as they had come to recognize that fidelity to the founding charism of the congregation in the context of the times demanded a creative and radical renewal which some have referred to as a "re-foundation."[34]

---

31. *GB* 51 (1968) 315–16. An inter-sessionary committee comprising Frs. Van der Drift, Walsh and Hirtz, with chapter secretaries Frs. Bouchaud and Moore, was tasked with preparations for the second part of GC XIII to be held the following year. *GB* 51 (1968) 385.

32. Ibid., 381–82.

33. Ibid.

34. *Refoundation* has been critiqued as an inaccurate expression of what Vatican II had in mind for the renewal of religious institutes. The term suggests that there is something wrong with the original foundation and hence the congregation's charism. Peter Hans-Kolvenbach, SJ, superior general of the Society of Jesus, proposed "creative fidelity" as more accurately expressing what the renewal of Vatican II means in relating the present to the past. He suggested that Jesuit renewal constituted "a fidelity to the experience of Ignatius which is at the same time creative." To speak of "refoundation" is to suggest that "there is a disconnect between the desire to follow Christ and the way in which the spiritual legacy of the founder is actually lived out." See "Creative Fidelity in Mission," an address by Kolvenbach to the Worldwide Gathering of Provincials of the Society of Jesus, Loyola, Spain (September 2000), http:www.onlineministries.creighton.edu/CollaborativeMinistry/kolvenbach_spain.html.

2. The Congregation's *Aggiornamento* Takes Off

Fr. Lécuyer, in his first letter to the congregation as superior general, called on all members and communities to take time to reflect on the documents drawn up by the general chapter. Although they had not reached their final stage (the finalization and approval would come in the second session) and some were but rough drafts prepared by commissions, still they warranted attention as "it is only with the participation of all of you that we shall be able to finalize the work we have undertaken." Lécuyer went on to set a high expectation for the *agggiornamento* then underway in the congregation. "All this work of adaptation should give the whole congregation a new impetus to that fervor and dynamism which animated our founders and our society at the beginning."[35]

The new general council set to work implementing the chapter decision on the devolution of powers to provincial and principal superiors. They were empowered, following due consultation, to appoint directors of formation and members to their councils and community superiors. The general council also set about establishing a secretariat for information and planning, with Le Gall, the chapter chronicler, appointed as its acting director. It discontinued the review *Cor Unum* with the expectation that the *General Bulletin* would include more information from the membership and act to unite the congregation.[36]

Fr. Lécuyer wrote in February 1969 to the bishops and superiors of all mission districts communicating the chapter decision that the congregation "should be absolutely faithful to its proper vocation, namely, the evangelization of non-Christians in those groups of mankind which are the poorest materially and spiritually." He asked for their cooperation in planning a withdrawal of the congregation from those areas of work in Africa which were well advanced and from certain works in Europe and America. This would make personnel available to engage in works "more completely in conformity with the specific aim of the congregation" as defined by the chapter.[37] In this Lécuyer anticipated the landmark address of Blessed Pope Paul VI in Kampala, Uganda, heralding a new mission era for Africa when he recognized that the church in Africa had come of age and that Africans were missionaries to themselves. The time had come for an "African Christianity" but the missionary was still needed for collaboration and support. In language, reminiscent of Libermann, the pope acknowledged that Africans

---

35. *GB* 51 (1968) 195–96.

36. Shortly after Le Gall's appointment, he was seconded to the Vatican secretariat of state.

37. *GB* 51 (1969) 445–49.

"possess human values and characteristic forms of culture which can rise up to perfection such as to find in Christianity, and for Christianity, a true superior fullness, and prove to be capable of a richness of expression all its own, and genuinely African."[38]

Preparing for the second session of the chapter, Lécuyer could note with satisfaction that a diligent study of the chapter documents was underway. He saw this as a sign of the vitality of the congregation and was full of hope for the future. He also noted a confusion in some quarters about the future of the congregation's missionary vocation. He concluded his letter with an impassioned plea: "May Spiritans give to the world an ever-increasing witness of their faith under the action of the Spirit of God; it is thus we shall be strong, it is thus we shall be victorious."[39]

The Second Session of the Chapter 1969

Each province and district had been invited to respond to the documents already prepared by GC XIII at its first session and to report on the actual situation of the congregation's life and mission. Fr. Michael O'Carroll, CSSp, chronicler for the second session, pointed out that these circumscription reports took a lot of time but "if there was a loss of time, there was a gain in realism and a call to seek the essential basis not only of improvement but survival."[40]

O'Carroll depicted the second session of the chapter which was held at Chevilly-Larue as focusing on the congregation's renewal which required both a return to the sources and an adaptation to the conditions of the times. It was important to preserve the unity between these if progress was to be made. And, as the reports made clear, progress was needed. The reports, while in general affirming the direction taken by the chapter, voiced apprehension, particularly on the relationship between religious life and the apostolate. Fr. Antonius de Winter began with the Dutch report and advised that although the Dutch were blamed for much, others were to watch out, for what was reported from Holland would follow in other parts of the congregation. With what could be described as "gallows humor," he likened

---

38. Ibid., 605–13. The visit of Pope Paul VI to Uganda took place during the second session of the chapter and was followed on television by the capitulants.

39. Ibid., 497–99.

40. *GB* 52 (1970), supplement, 6. O'Carroll's account, written *post factum*, gathered some common themes from the minutes of the fifty assemblies. These he summarized as: the nature of our society; the modality of our apostolate; a new understanding of religious life and formation for this life; the importance of personal values; and structures which embody ideals rather than existing for their own sake.

the Dutch province to the first child in the family to get the flu. The others spoil the child in the hope that the flu would pass and they would not be affected. But De Winter warned that each province had enough microbes of their own that would result in what he reported from Holland. He painted a rosy picture of the past and an ominous one for the future. With only 452 Dutch Spiritan priests, 160 brothers and 36 scholastics, the province was in decline. In spite of this, the recently concluded provincial chapter pledged its commitment to mission and to only accept new members committed entirely to the missions. He also remarked that throughout all the discussions at the Dutch chapter, not one reference was made to the general chapter documents of the first session.[41]

The Irish provincial Fr. Vincent Dinan, CSSp, reported that the congregation was the largest missionary society in Ireland, with 776 members of which 170 were working in Ireland, particularly in schools from which most of the vocations had come (over 500 of the 776). He noted that of the twelve young confreres ordained in 1969, ten had come from Spiritan schools. Dinan regretted that the chapter had not accepted education as a means of evangelization. There was "general agreement in the province that the documents were relevant and worthy, though the confreres recognized that in some there was considerably room for improvement and far too much verbiage." He also appealed for the second session to place a "greater emphasis on our spiritual renewal and on our religious life with definite guidelines for formation."[42]

Fr. George Hargar, provincial of USA West, reported that the chapter documents had been distributed and studied at group meetings throughout the province. He noted that "the great majority had hoped for more definite, concise and more practical results. Too much theorizing with many wordy statements were vague and confusing so that it was very difficult for many to absorb or even attempt to understand the documents." He wanted the chapter to define the nature of the congregation as religious with three public vows.

Fr. Alphonse Soucy of Canada reported on the closing of the junior seminary and that the novitiate building was up for sale as "it is too large for the purpose, is too monastic in character and no longer suits the mentality of today's youth." He spoke of a new model for the novitiate experience that was shared with four other congregations. The major seminary had been transformed into a missionary center which not only trained young Spiritans for the missionary priesthood but also laymen who intended to work

---

41. *GB* 52 (1970) 45–51.
42. Ibid., 39–44.

in international development projects. Soucy saw value in a shared training approach as young Spiritans "will be forced to clarify, for themselves and for others, what is their proper role in missionary service."[43] With a decline in vocations, and drop in financial support for missionaries, this initiative would be repeated in the following years by other provinces. The traditional support for missionary activity in countries like Canada was increasingly channeled into support for international aid organizations seen as "a new and more acceptable way of relating to the world."[44]

The chapter recognized the challenge of maintaining unity in the congregation while allowing experimentation and increased pluriformity through the process of decentralization. While it was agreed to continue with the principle of subsidiarity, the question remained as to how the congregation could continue as a single entity. There were two approaches to this question. The first was to maintain a focused approach with a single specific end, a common life, and the vesting of real authority in the general council. The alternative was a much broader approach posited on service to the local church and the primacy of the local and the individual. A resolution to these apparently different approaches could be found through an "organization set-up from bottom to top" with central government responsible for implementing general policy.[45]

Debate on the organization of provinces and districts gave rise to two different approaches to authority. In the first, the superior governed with the assistance of a council. In the other, the council governed, with the superior acting as its spokesperson. Perhaps, some capitulants argued, each circumscription would decide for itself which model to adopt. Put to a vote the first option was accepted by 71 votes to 25 votes. What then of provincial chapters? What is their mandate? And, more importantly for many capitulants, what would any future relationship between province and district look like? There were many individual interventions on this issue and, as the chronicler noted, the solution eventually agreed as expressed in the final chapter documents *Chapter Directives and Decisions (CDD)* 202, was "a judicious compromise."[46] The compromise was that the provincial, with his council, would assign members to works in the province, also to the districts, and other works of the congregation in consultation with the superiors involved. It was the prerogative of the superior general and his council to make first appointments, but in consultation with all concerned.

43. *GB* 52 (1970) 177–85.
44. Ward, "Christianity, Colonialism and Missions," 87.
45. *GB* 52 (1970), supplement, 17.
46. Ibid., 31.

The question that eluded resolution at the first session was on the nature of the congregation. "How are the apostolate and religious life mutually related?" Fr. Lécuyer intervened to report that at a recent meeting between the Sacred Congregation of Religious and the Union of Superiors general it was established that religious life could not be subordinated to the apostolate. This intervention influenced the decisions reached on the nature of the congregation which were added to what had been agreed during the first session on its specific end. This combination formed the first chapter of CDD, "The Specific End and Nature of the Congregation."[47]

Agreement on the Spiritan habit was more difficult to reach with strong emotions raised. One capitulant asked about being buried in the habit. The moderator "replied that this might be difficult in the case of an air accident!" Humor relieved the tension and the decision given in CDD 286 was "the wisest compromise acceptable."[48] Involvement in schools was also a contentious issue with some advocating the inclusion of school work in the paper on the apostolate. But what of disengagement? And then, what of those whose lives had been spent as Spiritans in school work? A vote was taken with 43 against the inclusion and 35 for it. The chronicler, who himself spent a life-time in Blackrock College, noted that the chapter returned to the issue with the three moderators proposing a motion which was approved (CDD 291).[49] The role of the moderators in maintaining harmony among capitulants was an important one.

The second session of GC XIII concluded on 10 September 1969 with an address by Fr. Lécuyer. He endorsed the work of the capitulants saying that "we can be satisfied that our chapter has achieved something truly useful to the church and to our apostolic work." He recognized that the congregation had weathered a storm of division and a great time of turmoil and confusion. It had grown in the process of "giving birth" to a new understanding of the Spiritan apostolic life. In this it remained faithful to the founding vision of Libermann. He gave thanks to

---

47. CDD 1–17.

48. CDD 286 reads: "It pertains to the provincial and district chapters to determine what the Spiritan habit entails, taking into account the demands of poverty, the regulations of the local ecclesiastical authorities, and the usage prevailing among the clergy and religious of the region."

49. CDD 291 reads: "The general chapter recognizes that works of education in the provinces and in the districts can be an efficacious means of fulfilling the specific end of the congregation. It will be the duty of the provincial and district chapters to subject such works to periodic examination to see if they really correspond with the specific end."

> all who wholeheartedly placed at the service of the chapter their zeal and their knowledge, who tried to be makers of peace and mutual understanding, who refused to allow themselves to be narrowed by the famous dilemmas—youth or elders, conservatives or progressives, essentialists or existentialists, verticalism or horizontalism, particular or universal church. They are false dilemmas: the church is one and complete including all these in her embrace.[50]

In the concluding remarks to his chronicle of the second session which lasted eight weeks and three days, Fr. O'Carroll spoke from the heart.

> We achieved a remarkable degree of unanimity in thought, will and heart. The votes which I have narrated tell of the first. As to the will and heart I can say with utter honesty that there was a marvelous atmosphere of fraternity, friendliness, trust, mutual help. We spoke out our opinions freely and fully in the assembly and then either in the bar (relatively harmless, I may say, as to consumption) or in the dining room, sat down, or walked in the recreation, with a minimum, practically, no trace, of rancor, bitterness; without triumphalism or defeatism.[51]

Chapter Directives and Decisions (CDD)

The GC XIII documents were published on 8 December 1969. Frs. Bouchard and Moore, the secretaries to the chapter and of the post-capitular committee tasked to prepare the documents, noted the significance of chapter 1, "The Specific End and Nature of the Congregation," as it "forms a class apart." They declared, "It is the most fundamental [chapter] and serves as a basis for all the others."[52] The more inspirational documents came next. They deal with the Spiritan apostolic life, community, the evangelical counsels, and prayer.

Chapters on the organization of the congregation, temporal goods[53] and training followed. *CDD* concluded with guidelines for reflection on the

---

50. *GB* 51 (1969) 627.
51. *GB* 52 (1970), supplement, 62.
52. *CDD* 8.

53. The bursar general's report on the temporal state of the congregation was not published in *CDD* but appeared in the *General Bulletin*. In it he states that "the annual surplus is not sufficient to meet the growing needs of the works of the congregation" and proposed a financial structure for the financial stability of the congregation. *GB* 52 (1970) 19–27.

apostolate. They were intended to assist individual confreres and groups to "enter into the views of the universal church on missionary questions, to remind them of the missionary thinking of Father Libermann, to stimulate them to keep themselves informed and to be ready to propose to the local hierarchy new methods of approach corresponding to the signs of the times."[54]

These guidelines were in three sections. The first section, "Our Missionary Activity," spoke of (1) different stages of our missionary activity; (2) presenting the message; (3) forming the Christian community.

The second section, "Our Style of Missionary Life," highlighted the aspects of (1) the apostolic spirit; (2) being all things to all men; (3) being a community of destiny; (4) living the paschal mystery; (5) community life; (6) apostolic strength and patience; (7) obedience to the word of God, and to the Holy Spirit.

The third section addressed "The Place of Our Apostolate in the Church Today" and considered this first, in relation to the sending church and second, in relation to the receiving church (the bishop and episcopal conferences, the major superior, contracts, disengagement, the local clergy, other congregations, *fidei donum* priests and ecumenism).

Fr Lécuyer, in presenting *CDD*, pointed to three basic ideas around which all the documents revolved. The first was the fundamental Spiritan calling to evangelization and the founding of new churches. Second, each confrere should be able to fulfill this missionary vocation and, third, to live the evangelical counsels freed from elements alien to the Spiritan apostolic life. Finally, he pointed out that the application of *CDD* was *ad experimentum* and subject to review at GC XIV, the next ordinary chapter due in 1974.[55]

The inter-sessionary period was an interesting time. It was designated as an opportunity for capitulants to return to their communities and present the documents so far agreed, and in process of being agreed, by the chapter. The feedback given at the second session of the chapter indicated a resistance to what was presented. Different reasons were suggested. It became clear that change proposed from "the top," that is, the chapter, needed acceptance from those "at the bottom," the ordinary foot-soldiers, as it were, if change was to happen.

Congar's study on true and false reform in the church, demonstrated from church history that reforms introduced by church councils were often ineffective as they only mobilized bishops and theologians. This was also the case for religious congregations. It is one thing for capitulants to gather

---

54. *CDD* 378.
55. *CDD* 3–5, "Letter of Presentation by the Superior General."

in chapter and make decisions. It is another thing to communicate these decisions, and the reasoning behind them, to others. Without persuasive communication, the likelihood of any change being implemented and taking root is remote. One old Irish missionary in The Gambia, reflecting on Vatican II, remarked, "All those bishops in Rome writing documents about the church and about priests. But who rings the church bell in the morning? who opens the church door? *The l'abbé!*" (the priest). There is need for the clergy and the laity to be involved in decision-making about change. A gap can develop between those "who govern" and those "who are governed" that alienates and prompts resistance. A popular movement was needed to flow into and from GC XIII for its decisions to be accepted and lived. This common-sense rule is now usually applied in the preparation for a chapter, either provincial or general, and in the dissemination of the chapter document to the membership. Thinking back to the Fourth Lateran Council (1215), Congar mused about what its legacy might have been were it not for "a current of spiritual reform strong enough to make its decrees a vital part of the wider church."[56]

3. Understanding the Experience

As with Vatican II, there were two competing understandings of development at play in the Spiritan congregation during the 1960s. The one advocated by Lefebvre resisted *aggiornamento* and wanted gradual change in incremental steps that only made necessary and practical accommodations to changing situations. The extent and depth of renewal within the life of the church authored at Vatican II had not been realized by many capitulants who supported him. They wanted the continuation of the cautious approach to change taken at GC XII. The reformers wanted the congregation to engage as fully as possible with the spirit of the council and advocated radical change by an uncompromising identification with first evangelization as the specific end of the congregation. This approach was based on the logic of *ressourcement* or return to the source, claiming first evangelization as the founding intention of Libermann for his congregation.[57] It was expressed by

---

56. Congar, *True and False Reform*, 243.

57. It must be noted that no reference is made to the earlier tradition, beginning with the founding of the congregation in 1703. The Spiritan story did not begin with Libermann but with Poullart des Places. Recognition of the fuller story might well have allowed for a less divisive solution to the dualism of religious life and the apostolate.

a break with the recent past (with its emphasis on religious observance) and a return to the congregation's original missionary inspiration.[58]

The reformers were active before the first session began. They concluded that the 1962 chapter made a mistake in electing Mgr. Lefebvre as general and were determined to correct that mistake. The first vote of the chapter marked a turning point when his influence over the chapter was curtailed. His extreme response to absent himself alienated him, and perhaps, more importantly, also prevented those sympathetic to his position from robust engagement in the chapter deliberations.[59] Change usually involves a certain amount of ambiguity. The letting go of cherished understandings and practices is rarely a straightforward exercise. Congar suggested that once "ambivalent insight or affirmation is held within the church's communion, it benefits from the regulation of the whole and is complemented by different values within the whole."[60] Otherwise a one-sided approach develops and this tends to skew the understanding in favor of one position over another.

Was GC XIII sufficiently informed and influenced by the way bishops at Vatican II had conducted their business? They encountered many challenges that were addressed through prolonged debate and what was, for many bishops, "a steep learning curve." For them, it was the first time to participate in an ecumenical council. The experience was strange, particularly for bishops unaccustomed to the workings of the Roman Curia. The four sessions of the council over four years was the laboratory for change that would be injected into the Catholic Church throughout the world. Congar, anticipating Vatican II wrote that "the conditions for the Spirit's gifts (we might even say for the Spirit's work) are essentially communal. The Spirit operates within the mutual love of the faithful as a Spirit of love and fraternal communion. True faith does not exist without a fraternal communion."[61]

58. The "original missionary inspiration" of the congregation was expressed by *CDD* (1969) no. 1: "to preach the gospel of Christ and to implant his church among peoples and groups who have not yet heard or have only scarcely heard the gospel message."

59. Lefebvre returned on 28 October for the visit of Cardinal Agagania n, prefect of the Sacred Congregation of Propaganda, and attended the papal audience in the Clementine Hall on 11 November 1968.

60. Congar, *True and False Reform*, 208. Congar suggested four conditions for authentic reform without schism in the church. These are adapted to apply to an analysis of the 1968–69 chapter, a chapter of renewal understood as reform. Congar's conditions are: (1) the primacy of charity and of pastoral concerns; (2) remain in communion with the whole church; (3) having patience with delays; (4) genuine renewal through a return to the principle of tradition.

61. Congar, *True and False Reform*, 230–31. Can Vatican II's call for renewal in religious institutes be interpreted as a call to reform in Congar's sense? Cardinal Avery Dulles recognized the influence Congar's book had on the council. He pointed out that the council avoided using the term "reform" and preferred to speak of renewal. Once

The bonds of fraternal communion were severely tested at GC XIII and so it could not provide the laboratory for change the congregation needed.

GC XIII did not follow the pattern of previous chapters: an orderly progression of propositions, recommendations made and capitulants returning to their provinces and districts leaving the work of "tidying up" to a commission guided by the general and his council. It took its role seriously as the supreme legislating body called upon to implement Vatican II renewal in the congregation. The vacuum created by Lefebvre's unexpected withdrawal was filled by those who seized the opportunity to give new direction to the congregation's life and mission. Congar suggested that the reformer (he spoke of "the prophet") "is not concerned with the balance or the harmony of his message; he is more inclined to overstate it in an absolute way."[62] Perhaps the absence of a corrective and strongly argued alternative point of view to that of the reformers resulted in a one-sided document being passed by the chapter which was rejected or, perhaps, ignored by some confreres and groups throughout the congregation.[63]

The strong assertion by GC XIII that first evangelization was the congregation's raison d'être alienated many. Allied with that was a downgrading of traditional religious practices. Certainly, the form of religious life practiced in the congregation had become regimented in style and at odds with the understanding of Christian vocation and human dignity espoused at Vatican II. The decisions of GC XII, for example, were over-prescriptive in regulating the lifestyles of confreres of different cultures. But did GC XIII

---

in the Decree on Ecumenism (*Unitatis Redintegratio*, 6) it spoke explicitly of reform. "*Christ summons the church, as she goes her pilgrim way, to that continual reformation of which she is always in need insofar as she is an institution of men here on earth.*" It balanced that statement by saying that "*every renewal of the church essentially consists in an increase of fidelity to her own calling.*" Dulles went on to apply Congar's writing on true and false reform in the church to true and false reform in religious institutes. His understanding of reform in the church can be applied to the reform of religious institutes in terms of the essentials of the institute's charism being preserved; putting right that which had gone wrong and implementing a new way to express the charism's essentials. Renewal of religious institutes is a work of reform in the sense that there is organic continuity with the past in preserving its substance. See Cardinal Avery Dulles, "True and False Reform," *First Things*, August 2003, https://www.firstthings.com/article/2003/08/true-and-false-reform.

62. Congar, *True and False Reform*, 215.

63. This seems to have been the case particularly following the first session of 1968 and the interim documents it produced. The Dutch provincial reported to the second session of the chapter what one young confrere said to him in the presence of many others: "When we are at a loose end about amusing ourselves, we read one of the documents of the general chapter." *GB* 52 (1970) 51.

"throw out the baby with the bath-water?" Was sufficient time allowed for capitulants to make sense of the changes that were taking place?[64]

Lécuyer, at the end of the chapter, called for loyalty and professed surprise "by certain stands taken, by certain statements made, or rather by certain attitudes of mind, against which I would like you to be vigilant. Some people speak about theological, pastoral, and moral questions as if the thinking of the church as a whole, of the hierarchy as a whole, and of the pope, had no importance whatever."[65] As an eminent theologian, he was, perhaps, understandably annoyed at the "complacent ignorance" displayed by several confreres in matters of theology. But was sufficient attention given to persuade rather than cajole others into a new frame of mind and a new world view? GC XIII probably overestimated what could be achieved in such a short time. Further discussion among the membership would be needed to ensure the proper implementation of what GC XIII had decided.[66]

4. Finding a Way Forward with *CDD*

GC XIII defined the specific end of the congregation as "missionary activity among peoples and groups whose material and spiritual needs are greatest and who are the most neglected, a service for which the church has difficulty in finding apostolic workers" (*CDD* 4). Because of this the congregation required a disengagement from works not in line with this end (*CDD* 8) and would only accept members committed to this end (*CDD* 9).

The Dutch, at their provincial chapter, decided "to accept only those members who are ready to engage themselves entirely in missionary tasks." This "engagement" was defined as "renouncing marriage, renouncing all material interests, and wishing to live in fraternal groups (teams)."[67] The reformers at the general chapter had already suggested that a renewal of fidelity to the congregation's specific end of first evangelization and the establishment of local churches would stem the tide of departures and at-

---

64. Le Gall's report on the first session suggests that some capitulants came to the chapter much more prepared than others.

65. *GB* 51 (1969) 629.

66. The first session of GC XIII laid out a blueprint for consultation and decision making at every level within the congregation. We have seen that the principle of subsidiarity was accepted as a principle of the congregation's general organization and that the new general council issued directives devolving its authority on to provincial and principal superiors. This process of decentralization would be the subject of evaluation at future general chapters.

67. *GB* 52 (1970) 47. Note the use of secular language here to refer to the evangelical counsels.

tract new members. Fr. Lécuyer referred to this in his letter to bishops and superiors. He wrote, "Many capitulants are even of the opinion that the number of vocations to the congregation will be in proportion to its fidelity to this specific end."[68] Was Lécuyer impatient with the status quo and eager to move on with the implementation of decisions by a chapter that had not yet concluded? Was there also an oversimplification as to the problems being faced? A new form of governance was taking shape and it would take time for all to work well. New directions only develop over time and require a maturation process that comes with experience.

Congar, analyzing the conditions for true reform in the church, suggested that patience was a virtue. "What is needed is a spiritual and mental disposition that understands the meaning and necessity of delays. This is a kind of humility and spiritual flexibility that is conscious of imperfections and even of deadly compromises."[69] Perhaps the Generalate in Rome with its new team was haunted by the very recent memory of its previous occupant. The "handing over" of the office of superior general was not easy. Lécuyer was Lefebvre's procurator to the Holy See but was not trusted by him. Lefebvre commented on hearing of his election, "He's the best of a bad lot." We can take it that there were few "hand-over" opportunities by Mgr. Lefebvre to Fr. Lécuyer.[70] It has also been suggested that Lécuyer's general council "was never really a team amongst themselves and with the superior general, so their impact on the congregation as a whole was limited."[71]

Congar postulated that great tension accompanied reform. A temptation of the reformer was to oversimplify issues and push through reform. One side of the argument is overlooked and the virtues of one's own side alone considered. The proposition that first evangelization was the key to open all doors of possibility for the congregation was wide of the mark and risked unity within the congregation. For Congar a condition for true reform in the church was to remain in communion with the whole church. He wrote that "even the most powerful religious experiences and the most

---

68. Letter of 25 February 1969. Was it this letter that prompted feedback at the second session from the Irish provincial pointing out the importance of maintaining the Spiritan schools in Ireland in order to ensure vocations? The downward trend in vocations would not be so easily reversed. In 1970, membership had dropped by 148 from the previous year to a total of 4,775 members. Significantly the number of seminarians had dropped to 496 (a fall of 96 from the previous year).

69. Congar, *True and False Reform*, 266.

70. Tissier de Mallerais, *Marcel Lefebvre*, 374–75.

71. Timmermans, "New Spring," 58.

deeply felt truths risk becoming heresies if they are not regulated by the faith and the life of the entire *Catholica*."[72]

A tragic drama unfolded at GC XIII that threatened the unity of the congregation. On the one hand, there was Mgr. Lefebvre, who broke communion with the congregation and subsequently with the church. His actions seem out of step with Fr. Libermann who submitted his plan for a missionary congregation, the Immaculate Heart of Mary, to the Holy See in Rome. In this Libermann followed Ignatius of Loyola's example when founding his society. "*Sentire cum ecclesia*" (to have the sense of the church) is the grounding for all apostolic initiatives that are guided by the Spirit of God.[73] On the other hand, did those opposed to Lefebvre, "the reformers," overlook the need to maintain unity in the congregation at a time of profound change? A complaint sometimes heard from those trained before Vatican II is "this is not the congregation I joined," and, "I am not a Spiritan; I am a Holy Ghost Father and will die a Holy Ghost Father." Changes rarely bring everyone along with them. GC XIII relied on the loyalty of the membership while failing to adequately communicate its vision and foster unity in the congregation.[74]

Lécuyer's address at the end of GC XIII touched on the difficulty involved in maintaining the balance between constancy and change. "Perhaps in our effort to bring about the necessary updating of our institute, in our anxiety to discover the wisest and best adapted human methods to be employed in the contemporary world, we are sometimes tempted to forget that without Christ all these are nothing, and to substitute little by little our human wisdom for the wisdom of God."[75] He identified with Fr. Libermann's advice to the superior of the Missionary Sisters of Castres.

> Obviously, we must work with all our energy in the accomplishment of the tasks which God has entrusted to us, but we must be on our guard against making them our own work. Let us employ all the means he puts at our disposal for the perfect accomplishment of what may be for his glory but tranquilly, and unworried about success. It is for us to plant and water but for

---

72. Congar, *True and False Reform*, 233.

73. Ibid., 253.

74. The Jesuits held two general congregations with a space of some seven years between them to allow the new ideas and changes to filter through to all members. The first, which elected Fr. Arrupe as general was held in 1967 and the second was held from 2 December 1974 to 7 March,1975. It was at this second assembly that the unifying theme for all aspects of the Jesuit apostolate, "Doing the Works of Justice," was adopted.

75. *GB* 51 (1969) 631.

him to give growth and harvest the fruits. Since the fruits belong to him, since the field is his, and since even the workers are his property, He is the Master who decides how to employ us and for what end. He is the Master who decides whether we are to be productive or sterile, whether we are to work or remain idle. Let us remain before him ready to be, in his hands, the kind of instruments he wishes us to be.[76]

This quotation from Fr. Libermann captures his missionary strategy. The mission is God's mission and it is with trust in divine providence that missionary work proceeds and bears fruit. Many concepts, such as that of *missio Dei*, were developed since 1969 and give new insight to the writings of Libermann. In turn, the rediscovery of Claude Poullart des Places and the Spiritan story since 1703 provided a basis for appreciating mission as a multi-faceted reality that could be understood, among other things, as evangelization, inculturation, struggle for liberation, reconciliation, option for the poor and working for justice, peace and the integrity of creation.

In discerning the original spirit or charism of the congregation we need to look not only to des Places and Libermann, but to all that has contributed to the Spiritan story since then. We can, perhaps, apply Congar's writing on liturgical reforms to Spiritan reforms. "Returning to tradition means absolute respect for ecclesial expressions that are permanent and always viable, and a critical and intelligent respect for transitional forms, in a spirit of loyal respect and affection for all the forms."[77] A discernment is needed that distinguishes what is of the essence of Spiritan mission and what are accidental accretions acquired in different times and places. Future general chapters would engage with mission as a polyvalent concept and go beyond the restricting limits set in *CDD* which understood missionary activity in the geographical terms of sending church and receiving church (*CDD* 416–27). Yet GC XIII gave a direction to Spiritan life and mission that generated new understandings to Spiritan mission and life.

The Apostolate and Religious Life

The tension between the missionary and religious dimensions of the Spiritan vocation was a source of conflict in the post *CDD* years. Was it possible to be both? Stories from retired Irish missionaries tell of being sustained through the strict semi-monastic regime of their seminary days in Kimmage by the great expectation of extending their "missionary wings" when

76. Ibid.
77. Congar, *True and False Reform*, 295.

appointed to "the missions." However, it was not unusual for them to experience a community regime similar to that of Kimmage when they arrived at their first appointment. The "father-in-charge," the cloister-like regulation of the house and formality of life seemed to them an extension of the seminary. Some found ways around these strictures. It is little wonder then that younger confreres with such an experience of religious life welcomed the *CDD* assertion of the missionary nature and end of the congregation.

CDD, in its first articles (1–12) listed the different aspects of being a missionary society. Its specific end was to preach the gospel of Christ and to implant his church. All its activity and resources were ordered to that end. First evangelization, assisting young churches, and promoting missionary activity were its priorities. Spiritans would go only to the poorest and most neglected places where the church had difficulty in finding apostolic workers; they would withdraw from works not in keeping with that specific end and only accept new members committed to it. All Spiritans were entitled to appointments in accordance with this specific end while recognizing that those appointed temporarily to ancillary roles in support of it also fulfilled their missionary vocation.[78]

With Spiritan mission defined, *CDD* addressed the relationship between the "missionary-religious" dimensions of the Spiritan vocation (*CDD* 13). The way of the evangelical counsels was followed and members lived in community, "working together, pooling their abilities and the fruits of their labors." Fervor of life and apostolic zeal were the values of such mission communities. In its second chapter, *CDD* continued with eight articles describing Spiritan apostolic life. They began with Libermann's definition of the apostolic life which laid the foundation for the well worked out formula

---

78. *CDD*'s definition of the congregation's specific end and nature marked a significant departure from the pre-Vatican II Rules and Constitutions precisely on the issue of the primacy of the apostolate over religious life and the relationship between them. Constitutions 5, 6 and 7 defined the Nature and Aims of the Congregation:

"[5]—The congregation is a religious institute dedicated to the apostolate. It is classified as a religious congregation with simple vows, of pontifical status and non-exempt (Can. 488, 2°, 3°).

[6]—Its primary and general aim is to procure the glory of God and the sanctification of its members, by the practice of the vows of religion and the observance of its Rules and Constitutions (Can. 487).

[7]—Its specific and distinctive aim is to undertake humble and toilsome ministry for which the church less easily finds apostolic workers, especially the evangelization of infidels, and, in particular, of those of the black race. Apart from this, only such work as is expressly requested by the Holy See shall be accepted, and also, by way of exception, other work which is both useful to the church and in keeping with the interests of the congregation."

of the chapter that united this apparent dualism at the heart of the Spiritan vocation. In *CDD* 20 we read,

> Missionary activity and the religious life—which may exist separately in the church—are united for the Spiritan in the concrete unity of one and the same response to "God who calls him to give himself entirely to the work of the gospel" (*Ad Gentes* 24). It follows that, for us, the religious spirit belongs to the nature of the apostolic life which it animates, and this in turn belongs to the nature of the religious life.

CDD 21 declared that membership of a religious community strengthened the link between a committed life and the choice of missionary activity. Missionary activity and religious life were combined in the apostolic life with the religious spirit animating the apostolic life. "Spiritans dedicate their whole lives to the Father who seeks his glory in the happiness of men." This vocation came from Christ who united all the aspects of that vocation—missionary work, prayer, apostolic initiatives, obedience, poverty, joys, and trials—and all is ordered toward Christ (*CDD* 22).

Nothing human was alien to this vocation. "The culmination of human progress, as it has been revealed to us in Christ, coincides exactly with the final goal of missionary activity" (*CDD* 23). There was but one ideal for this vocation, to be "a humble and faithful servant of the church and of its mission" (*CDD* 24). The Spiritan apostolic life was thus summarized as "Spiritan and ecclesial, humanitarian and Christianizing, active and prayerful, missionary and religious" (*CDD* 25). *CDD* 26 to 35 applied this ideal to the day to day lives of Spiritans. The starting point was the apostolate which "is the basic reason for our common life" and, as such, needed to be determinative of how the common life is lived (*CDD* 26). To highlight this and avoid any dualism between the apostolate and religious life, vows would be celebrated in the context of the consecration to the apostolate (*CDD* 27).

The tension between prayer and action was to be addressed through a "practical union" that brought prayer into the apostolate and the apostolate into prayer (*CDD* 28). A periodic review of a community's apostolic work "would be a sign that we have achieved brotherly existence in community" (*CDD* 29). Active participation in development work for people should continue as it "has always been an integral part of our evangelizing mission" (*CDD* 30). A missionary spirituality was needed and "our rule of life should give expression to those spiritual qualities which flow from our missionary dedication to those in the greatest spiritual and material need" (*CDD* 31). Spiritans should not only be concerned with building up their own community but "should always strive to be ourselves builders of communities for the benefit of those around us" (*CDD* 32).

The primacy of the apostolate should be evident in spiritual formation "and not be a mere copy of monastic training" (*CDD* 33). The missionary spirituality espoused by *CDD* needed the nurturance that would come from studying the teaching of Libermann (*CDD* 34), and the forthcoming rule of life "should give the essential guidelines for our apostolic life, while leaving to the provinces and districts the responsibility for working out the application to communities" (*CDD* 35). In the years following *CDD*, there was a revision of the relationship between the missionary and religious dimensions of the Spiritan vocation.[79] The preferred order in 1969, "missionary-religious" (*CDD* 13), was definitively inverted to "religious-missionary" at GC XV in 1980.[80]

The Reorganization of the Congregation

A central issue at Vatican II was the identification of the locus of authority in the church. Authority was no longer the preserve of the few but the responsibility of all. This shift in understanding put in play a respect for the dignity of every individual and each local church; it demanded attentiveness to the working of the Holy Spirit and prompted a decentralization of authority. The local church was recognized as "fully church" and not an outstation of the Church of Rome. The process of decentralization was also at work in the congregation empowering the periphery and reinterpreting the center as servant to the periphery. Lefebvre had been "opposed to episcopal collegiality, which he had already labelled in October 1963 as 'collectivism,' and found it impossible to reconcile the new ecclesiology of Vatican II with an ecclesiology heavily marked by an ultramontanist and hierarchical

---

79. An example is the report from a meeting of superiors of Central Africa in Libreville from 8 to 10 January 1974 which noted that too great an emphasis was put on "first evangelization" *GB* 55 (1974), 43.

80. See *SL* 4, 85, 98, 111, 150, 154, 155, 170, 197, and 207. Interestingly GC XIV (1974) in *Guidelines for Animation* used "religious-missionary" twice. The first is in relation to confreres who did not live habitually in Spiritan communities because of their service to the local church. They were "united to the congregation as to a place of religious-missionary renewal, and as an agent of dialogue between churches" (*GA* 79b). The second in defining the role of the general council: "to strengthen our spiritual and our religious-missionary life according to the spirit of our founders and the living traditions of our congregation" (*GA* 121). Can this reordering by GC XIV be explained by its stated aim to seek general agreement on the direction of the congregation for the next six years?

mentality" which he espoused.[81] Applying the new ecclesiology of Vatican II, *CDD* articulated general principles for the organization of the congregation. These included the dignity of the individual and the realization of unity through subsidiarity and decentralization.

GC XIII defined the congregation as a group of members "drawn to it by a common vocation as the result of a special grace from God" (*CDD* 144) and that its unity "depends on the fidelity of all its members to the grace of the Holy Spirit" (*CDD* 145). Therefore, all the members were to be consulted and represented in all that concerned them. This applied particularly when appointing superiors and the holding of councils and chapters (*CDD* 151). Each member had a right to be consulted on how the congregation was to fulfill its mission in the world. This was the process engaged at Vatican II in discerning the promptings of God's Holy Spirit and the signs of the times. Up to this time the prevailing culture was that of "mother knows best" or, in the Spiritan context, "the superior as the voice of God."[82] For GC XIII, authority had two sources: first, from the membership, and second, from the hierarchy (*CDD* 146). In the case of the first, it is exercised in a spirit of service that unites and inspires the membership so that all live and work well together (*CDD* 148).

The organogram for the congregation that can be deduced from *CDD* is a "bottom-up" one with the exercise of authority understood to begin at the individual and local levels. It left to "individuals and intermediate bodies initiative and responsibility in the tasks proper to them," with higher authority tasked to "sustain and encourage the efforts of the intermediate bodies" (*CDD* 149). This approach represented a radical change in the exercise of authority previously vested entirely in the superior general. All provincial appointments (community superior, directors of formation, etc.) were made by him. *CDD* spoke of collaboration among the membership. Solidarity could be "realized all the more perfectly when it is the fruit of the collaboration of all" (*CDD* 150). The organization of the congregation was seen to be in service of its mission. The different sections of the congregation—provinces, vice-provinces, and districts—were living units enabling members to "participate according to their special vocation in the general missionary vocation of the church" (*CDD* 191).

Administration at these levels was modelled on the way the congregation operated in general chapter and at the level of superior general and

---

81. Faggioli, *Battle for Meaning*, 31.

82. There is a story of one such superior who had held office for longer than any of his confreres could remember. At a conference with his community, he remarked that, as superior, he was with Jesus, upon the cross. A voice was heard to come from the back of the room, "and he doesn't want to come down oh!"

council. Each one would have a superior and council elected by the membership in the same way that the general chapter elected the superior general and general councilors. Provincial chapters would meet every three years and operate within the general statutes of the congregation as "the highest authority for the affairs of the province" (*CDD* 194). "The provincial, with his council, administers the province in accordance with the directives given by the general council and the provincial chapter. He presides at meetings of both the chapter and the council" (*CDD* 199). His role was not only administrative. He was also to be "a leader who inspires the members . . . take a personal interest in all the members . . . responsible especially for the direction of those activities which can further the development of the province and of the congregation" (*CDD* 200). The purpose and functions of district chapters and principal superiors were similarly described (*CDD* 211–23).

Going Beyond the Province—District Model

Provinces were established to recruit and train missionaries for the mission territories confided to the congregation by the *jus commissionis*.[83] Each province had its own mission territories which relied on the "home" province for personnel, material support, accommodation, and renewal for missionaries on "home leave," and more long-term provision for ill and retired confreres unable to serve in their districts.[84] The province from which the members came and to which they would return was an important point of reference for a district. The districts of the Irish province, for example, were identified as "Irish Districts." Confreres identified with the district to which they were appointed. They made it their "home" as they familiarized themselves with the local culture and took up positions in the local church. Appointment to

---

83. *Jus Commissionis* is the system by which *Propaganda Fide* regulated relations between ecclesiastical and religious superiors in mission territories (*Quum huic AAS*, 1930, 111–15). This usually meant entrusting a mission territory (apostolic vicariate) to a missionary institute to provide mission personnel and assume responsibility for its evangelization and the establishment of a local church.

84. The Irish province made provision for this purpose by building the Mission House at Kimmage Manor which opened in September 1959. A history on Kimmage Manor points out that this was eleven years after discussions on the need for such a facility began. Missionaries home on a three months leave were required to spend one month in the house with two hours study each day from 10:00 a.m. to noon. Otherwise they followed the ordinary regulations of the community. See Ryan, *Kimmage Manor*, 97–102.

a district was understood to be for life and any further appointment outside the district was exceptional.[85]

The need for collaboration throughout the congregation, but particularly between neighboring provinces and districts was recognized and acted upon after GC XIII. The *General Bulletin* reported that regional meetings were held from January 1972 with the first meeting of Superiors of Southern Europe (Spain, Portugal, Switzerland, France, and Poland) coming together, with formation and animation personnel in attendance. The group agreed to meet on an annual basis. Other regional meetings were held at that time, usually with a representative of the general council present. The superiors of USA East and USA West, Ireland, England, Canada, Puerto Rico, and Ontario met in 1972 in Trinidad and began their preparations for GC XIV. The superiors of French-speaking Central Africa (Bangui, Doumé, Gabon, Congo, Yaoundé) came together with representatives from France and Holland. The superiors of East Africa (Bagamoyo, Kilimanjaro, Kenya, Malawi) met from 21 to 22 April,1972 in Tanzania. Fr. Joe De Boer gave a paper on "Africanization" and the meeting decided that all present would proceed with a vocations and formation program.

The development of relations between founding provinces and neighboring districts was particularly challenging as these had often functioned in the past as self-sufficient entities.[86] The complex network of relationships to promote cooperation between circumscriptions and then of circumscriptions with dioceses advanced quickly in accordance with *CDD* 224–47. The congregation had taken the first brave steps in reimagining its mission, life, and organizational structures in the spirit of Vatican II.

---

85. I recall two elderly missionaries walking along the avenue at St. Mary's School, Nairobi, during the annual retreat in 1978. One had just returned from Ireland and told the other that he had bought a new suit in Dublin. "How much was it?" he was asked. "Forty Irish pounds," was the reply. The other confrere, who had not been back to Ireland for many years and the Kenya shilling had become his measure of value, asked, "But what is that in Kenya shillings?" The Kenya district was second only to the "flag ship" district of the Irish province, the District of Eastern Nigeria.

86. *GB* 54 (1972) 78.

Chapter 4

Continuing the Journey of Renewal

1. Apostolic Religious Life in a Vatican II Church

VATICAN II'S DECISIONS AND subsequent regulations for the implementation of change throughout the Catholic world impacted more significantly on the lives of some Catholics than others.¹ Three categories especially affected were: religious, missionaries, and priests. New understandings of what it meant to be a religious, a missionary and a priest needed to be assimilated and understood. The council's proclamation in *Lumen gentium* located the religious vocation within the more fundamental call to holiness addressed to all the baptized.

The council's openness to the world expressed in its documents—the pastoral constitution, *Gaudium et spes*; the right to religious freedom declared in *Dignitatis humanae*; the positive relations desired with non-Christian religions (*Nostra aetate*); the desire for dialogue with other Christian churches expressed in the council's decree on Ecumenism, *Unitatis redintegratio*—required a radical review of missionary thinking and activity. What was the role for a missionary institute in the light of the council's decree on missionary activity, *Ad gentes*, which recognized that the local church was the primary agent for mission and that all Christians by their baptism were missionary?²

---

1. Andrew Greeley commented, "Anyone save an academic or a bishop would have anticipated that, when you change that which was unchangeable for 1,500 years, you are going to create a religious crisis. Attempts to put together a new system of religious symbols were half-hearted, unplanned and, most of all, insensitive to the actual religious needs." Quoted in Stark and Finke, *Churching of America*, 263.

2. The Third General Assembly of the World Council of Churches at New Delhi in 1961 presented the vision of one church proclaiming one gospel as the responsibility

What of religious life? Religious life did not form part of the structure of the hierarchical church but stood in dynamic tension to it through its prophetic witness to the realization of kingdom values. In defining "laity" Vatican II distinguished between "all the faithful" and "those in holy orders and those in the state of religious life specially approved by the church" (*LG* 31). How was the religious vocation to be understood and lived in the years following the council? This question was asked not in the legalistic sense as applied before the council but in the light of the council's understanding of church as mystery experienced through relationship with God and with one another. Was the religious vocation peripheral to the Vatican II understanding of church? How were religious to relate to all others in the building up of the body of Christ? Many religious also exercised priestly ministry. The Decree on the Ministry and Life of Priests, *Presbyterorum ordinis*, gave new understanding to priesthood. While maintaining the traditional understanding of priest as *sacerdos*, "offering gifts and sacrifices for sins," the decree, in an exercise of *ressourcement*, drew from a more ancient tradition and spoke of the priest as *presybter*, as "minister of Christ among the people" for the ministry of the word, of sacrament and of the parish. Priestly ministry was understood primarily in function of the people of God. Service of God's people made ministerial priesthood a relational term defined in terms of its service within the people of God.

Lumen gentium affirmed specific vocations within the church particularly when it concluded that "the state which is constituted by the profession of the evangelical counsels, though it is not the hierarchical structure of the church, nevertheless, undeniably belongs to its life and holiness" (*LG* 44). Consecrated life was seen to play a constitutive role in the life of the church. Religious institutes would continue their mission both renewed by the teaching of the council and the inspiration of their founders. They did so conscious of their historical nature and as such engaged with their history in critical self-examination and radical self-renewal. Blessed Pope Paul VI reminded religious of this role in his apostolic exhortation on the renewal of religious life, *Evangelica testificatio*.

---

of the *whole* church. "Mission and service belong to the whole church. God calls the church to go out into the world to witness and serve in word and deed to the one Lord Jesus Christ, who loved the world and gave himself for the world." *Approved Report on Unity* (1961) 15. The Faith and Order Lima declaration on *Baptism, Eucharist, and Ministry* in 1982 recognized the responsibility of all the baptized to bear witness to Christ and work for the establishment of God's kingdom in the world. "As they grow in the Christian life of faith, baptized believers demonstrate that humanity can be regenerated and liberated. They have a common responsibility, here and now, to bear witness together to the gospel of Christ, the liberator of all human beings." *Faith and Order Paper* 111 (1982) 10.

> How can the message of the gospel penetrate the world? What can be done at those levels in which a new type of culture is unfolding . . . ? Dear religious, according to the different ways in which the call of God makes demands upon your spiritual families, you must give your full attention to the needs of men, their problems, and their searching; you must give witness in their midst, through prayer and action, to the Good News of love, justice, and peace. . . . Such a mission, which is common to all the People of God, belongs to you in a special way.[3]

While Vatican II affirmed the place of religious life within the church it was left to individual religious institutes to discern their future within its mission. This exercise was more difficult for some than for others. Many apostolic religious institutes were founded at a time and in a place to attend to a need of that time and place. As Sr. Sandra Schneiders, IHM, expressed it, congregations typically began "in the charismatic experience of one or more founders who feel impelled to give themselves to God and God's work, almost always in response to some historically pressing need. Subsequent members respond to a personal call to join the founders in this divinely originated enterprise."[4]

Vatican II's call for each religious institute to live according to its founding charism was particularly challenging for those institutes founded to meet a historically pressing need that no longer existed. How were they to justify their existence as religious, particularly as the call to perfection which formerly distinguished religious life within the church was recognized as the prerogative of all the baptized? This was the case for some women religious institutes who "had come into being not because of any charism handed on by a founder, but rather because of a ministerial need, and at the invitation or mandate of a bishop or other founding cleric."[5] One such institute in the USA was founded in a parish with a school, but no teachers, "and where no religious were forthcoming from any of the local religious congregations. The comment of the parish priest at the time was, 'We cannot obtain nuns? Then let us make some.'"[6] Some religious institutes arose then, not so much from a founder's charismatic response to divine initiative, but more, on an *ad hoc* basis, to carry out a task for a local church.

---

3. *Evangelica testificatio* (1971) 52.
4. Schneiders, *Prophets*, 100.
5 Confoy, "Religious Life," 330.
6. Ibid.

From 1965 onward, several religious institutes, particularly female teaching communities in the United States, would declare their "*Nunc dimittis.*"[7]

2. A New Missionary Epoch

Missionary activity since the 1960s was no longer understood primarily as "growing the church" through increasing its membership but rather as Christian service to the world. The 1960s was "the decade of the secular" with the church alert to the problems of poverty and inequality in the world. The Latin American bishops at Medellin spoke of being "on the threshold of a new epoch." Technology and new collaboration between nations opened new possibilities for combating inequality and the eradication of poverty. A better world for all seemed attainable and the church provided the theological underpinnings for this new enthusiasm. Blessed Pope Paul VI in *Populorum progressio* coined the expression "peace is not the absence of war." Development was the new word for peace.

> When we fight poverty and oppose the unfair conditions of the present, we are not just promoting human well-being; we are also furthering man's spiritual and moral development, and hence we are benefiting the whole human race. For peace is not simply the absence of warfare, based on a precarious balance of power; it is fashioned by efforts directed day after day toward the establishment of the ordered universe willed by God, with a more perfect form of justice among men.[8]

Were the Christian churches ready to take sides and make the preferential option for the poor? The Peruvian philosopher and theologian Fr. Gustavo Gutiérrez, OP, in his groundbreaking work, *A Theology of Liberation*, made the case for taking the side of the poor. This book, and liberation

---

7. The documented case of the conflict between the Immaculate Heart of Mary Sisters and Cardinal McIntyre of Los Angeles came to a head when the cardinal refused to accept their chapter of renewal decisions (1968) giving more autonomy in choice of ministry, choice of dress and prayer with a new leadership style and formation program. The sisters appealed to the Vatican which upheld their right to hold a chapter of renewal and make the decisions they did. However, Cardinal McIntyre interpreted the implementation of the changes as an affront to him and the tension increased. He appealed to the Vatican which then upheld his decision. This resulted in a division in the community with 400 sisters seeking to be dispensed from their vows and reconstituted themselves as a lay community in the church. Only 50 sisters complied with the cardinal's wishes and remained within the Los Angeles Catholic Schools system. See Ebaugh, *Women in the Vanishing Cloister*.

8. *Populorum progressio* (1967) 76.

theology in general, pioneered a new course for the church, not just in Latin America, but everywhere. Vatican II had challenged scholars to renew their theological and biblical studies. Gutiérrez did that by examining the concept of God and the scriptures within the Latin American reality of extreme poverty and systemic injustice. That led to a renewed realization of Christ's presence among the poor and oppressed, especially in their struggle to end poverty and oppression.

The 1971 Synod of Bishops spoke of working for justice as a constitutive element of Christian discipleship and "no peace without justice" entered the lexicon of Catholic Social Teaching.

> The uncertainty of history and the painful convergences in the ascending path of the human community direct us to sacred history; there God has revealed himself to us, and made known to us, as it is brought progressively to realization, his plan of liberation and salvation which is once and for all fulfilled in the paschal mystery of Christ. Action on behalf of justice and participation in the transformation of the world fully appear to us as a constitutive dimension of the preaching of the gospel, or, in other words, of the church's mission for the redemption of the human race and its liberation from every oppressive situation.[9]

The synod boldly outlined the role of missionaries as being the advocates for justice and the voice of the oppressed, empowering them to find their voice and speak out against the grave injustice of a world order that kept the poor, poor, so that the rich could remain rich. Remaining neutral in the struggle for the rights of the poor was not an option. The synod, again put it clearly.

> The present situation of the world, seen in the light of faith, calls us back to the very essence of the Christian message, creating in us a deep awareness of its true meaning and of its urgent demands. The mission of preaching the gospel dictates at the present time that we should dedicate ourselves to the liberation of people even in their present existence in this world. For unless the Christian message of love and justice shows its effectiveness through action in the cause of justice in the world, it will only with difficulty gain credibility with the people of our times.[10]

The rediscovery of the gospel of the poor transformed the thinking and practice of mission and demanded a radical review of the church's alignment with the rich and powerful in the world.

---

9. Synod of Bishops, *Justice in the World*, 6.
10. Ibid., 35.

The "trickle down" economics of the 1960s did not have the desired effect of a more just distribution of wealth and a narrowing of the gap between rich and poor. If anything, the gap was widening, to the point in the 1980s when 20 percent of the world's population controlled 80 percent of the world's wealth and conversely, 80 percent of the world's population had access only to 20 percent of the world's wealth. These figures pointed to the reluctance of the wealthy nations of the northern hemisphere to share wealth and more importantly, the means to create wealth with the poorer nations of the global south. "The theory was that the Third World would be empowered without the West having to give up any of its power and privilege; however, even if the West had intended to relinquish power in favor of the Third World, it would have been impossible, given the contemporary asymmetrical relationship between the north and the south."[11] A disillusionment with "development" as the way to tackle poverty led to the recognition that there was a causal link between wealth and poverty. There was poverty because there was wealth.[12]

The 1974 Synod of Bishops addressed the theme of evangelization. The landmark apostolic exhortation of Blessed Pope Paul VI on the evangelization of peoples (*Evangelii nuntiandi*) in 1975 was the result. It spoke of the transformation of culture and society recognizing that the Lord commissioned the church to bring gospel values into contact with the way people live, think, and make judgments.

> For the church, it is a question not only of preaching the gospel in ever wider geographic areas or to ever greater numbers of people, but also of affecting and as it were upsetting, through the power of the gospel, mankind's criteria of judgment, determining values, points of interest, lines of thought, sources of inspiration and models of life, which are in contrast with the Word of God and the plan of salvation. (*EN* 19)

The missiologist Fr. Donal Dorr, reflecting on these words, noted that "just as Jesus took flesh in a particular place and time, so the good news has to become 'embodied' or incarnated in the different cultures within which people live."[13]

11. Bosch, *Transforming Mission*, 357.
12. The principle "preferential option for the poor" originated among Latin American theologians, and was first explicitly adopted by an ecclesiastical assembly at the General Conference of Latin American Roman Catholic bishops at Puebla, Mexico, in 1979. The phrase has since appeared in papal encyclicals, letters of bishops' conferences and synods, and in the writings of various authors. It is a key principle of Catholic Social Teaching.
13. Dorr, *Mission in Today's World*, 94.

The Synod and the Apostolic Exhortation on Evangelization "marked the beginning of the rebirth of the Catholic missionary movement. Coming through the moment of crisis and insecurity, *Evangelii nuntiandi*, developed many of the fundamental principles of *Ad gentes* in light of the reflections and experiences of the first post-council decade."[14]

Whereas *Ad gentes* identified the "who" of mission as "the church," *Evangelii nuntiandi* defined the "what" of mission. The mission of the church was to bring about the reign of God in the world. It involved a dynamic and complex interplay between proclamation, witness of life, incorporation into the church community, and the sending out of new evangelizers. Blessed Pope Paul VI recognized the imperative for the church to proclaim the gospel to those who had never heard the good news of Jesus Christ (*EN* 51) as well as "to make ever more mature" through a catechesis full of gospel vitality the faith of those who had already received the gospel (*EN* 54) and to those who did not practice their Christian faith (*EN* 56). The church needed to be present in society engaging with secularism and new forms of atheism (*EN* 55). The profound links between evangelization and human advancement were recognized in terms of development and liberation (*EN* 31).

Evangelii nuntiandi gave the Vatican II church the *"magna carta"* for evangelization. Written ten years after the close of the council, and in its spirit, it recognized that the starting point for evangelization was that the church is herself in need of evangelization (*EN* 15). It would bring the gospel into all strata of society (*EN* 18) through witness of lives well lived and filled with the joy of the Risen Lord (*EN* 21). The mission mandate, to make disciples of all nations, still stood; but was reinterpreted to apply to the conversion of peoples and nations, not only individuals. "Being church" is not about numbers but rather about being the "salt of the earth," the leaven in the mass of society. The church was in a diaspora situation, scattered throughout the world. Development work to be truly human and integral needed the complementarity of mission work. Mission work and its salvific function were intimately tied up with the quest for peace and unity among human beings.

A holistic anthropology was at work in *Evangelii nuntiandi* that connected salvation with development, well-being on earth with an eternal destiny and proclaimed an evangelization that was truly liberating of the human person.

> Peoples, as we know, engaged with all their energy in the effort and struggle to overcome everything which condemns them to remain on the margin of life: famine, chronic disease, illiteracy,

---

14. Bevans and Schroeder, *Constants in Context*, 253.

poverty, injustices in international relations and especially in commercial exchanges, situations of economic and cultural neo-colonialism sometimes as cruel as the old political colonialism. The church, as the bishops repeated, has the duty to proclaim the liberation of millions of human beings, many of whom are her own children—the duty of assisting the birth of this liberation, of giving witness to it, of ensuring that it is complete. This is not foreign to evangelization. (*EN* 30)

3. Animation for Spiritan Renewal and Collaboration

As a religious, missionary, and clerical institute the Spiritan congregation "sat up and took notice" of the teachings of Vatican II not only in a spirit of compliance with what was juridically required but to find through it a new way of being missionary religious priests and brothers. How was it to fulfill its ecclesial vocation in a post-Vatican II world? This was a question the congregation had faced many times in its long history. As Anthony Gittins, put it, "Since our foundation three hundred years ago, Spiritans of every generation have interpreted the 'missionary' scene, according to prevailing mission theologies, within the context of particular times and places, and out of personal and collective bias or inspiration."[15]

The 1968–69 Chapter of Renewal decided on significant changes to be made. It is one thing to decide, it is quite another to put that decision into practice. The long Spiritan history of survival and sacrifice grounded the *ad experimentum* period of change and strengthened the congregation's resolve to choose life, not death.[16] On the solid foundation of ages past, and on the decisions of GC XIII, the Congregation of the Holy Spirit seized the moment to proceed on the path of renewal mapped out by Vatican II. It did so through an internalization of the spirit of the council; a judicious self-examination and adaptation of lifestyle, new evangelical engagement, and commitment to justice and peace in the world.[17]

15. Gittins, "Root, Shoot and Fruit," 97.

16. See Koren, *To the Ends of the Earth*, a general history of the Spiritan congregation.

17. Libermann understood the missionary work in the French colonies and in Africa as a work of justice. Writing in 1847 to Fr. Pierre Percin, recently ordained at Saint Sulpice and parish priest of Port-au-Prince, Haiti, he had this to say about the injustices suffered by the people of Haiti and the black race in general at the hands of their white colonial masters: "The race (the blacks) has suffered so much from us proud Europeans that it would give me the greatest pleasure to do all I can to make reparation for the injustices committed by the whites" (ND IX 158). Translated by Gay, *Jew According to*

Following GC XIII Fr. Lécuyer wrote to the membership calling for a "Joint Examination of Conscience." He asked all to recognize that "we are individually and jointly responsible for safeguarding our Spiritan heritage." Each one carried out his work both within the congregation and in communion with the entire church. He regretted that some members were "unsympathetic" to the need for renewal and asked, "Are not some prejudiced against the decisions of the general chapter as though nothing good could come from it."[18] He complained that some members had not even seen a copy of the chapter documents and that it was responsibility of superiors to ensure that members study the documents for the desired transformation—from communities of observance (of rules) to communities of true brotherhood in the Lord—to take place.[19] In pre-Vatican II days, the letter of the law prevailed over the spirit behind it, with institutions and customs imposed to shape members's behavior (*habitus*).

The need for animation in the congregation was clear. Lécuyer had frequently commented in his visitation reports to different circumscriptions of confreres being "out of touch" with the changes introduced since Vatican II. This applied particularly to the mission districts where he reported that apostolic activity was the priority for the members but they "pray little or not at all . . . perhaps the apostolic activity is their prayer?"[20] But how was the change to a more thoughtful and considered approach to apostolic work to be achieved? In mission territories where most of the clergy were Spiritan, the general practice was that training and updating happened within the context of the diocese rather than the congregation.[21] In his reflections over the six years of his leadership of the congregation, Lécuyer, on the eve of GC XIV, wrote to the membership:

> Those who were present at the first session of the last chapter will recall the particular difficulties involved in taking on the succession at such a crucial time, the controversial atmosphere, the deep diversity of varying and sometimes opposed currents of thought, which simply reflected a corresponding diversity

---

the Gospel, 90.

18. *GB* 52 (1970) 328–35.

19. "It is the fault of superiors at all levels if this necessary study of *CDD* has been neglected and no time should be lost in remedying the situation where necessary." *GB* 54 (1972) 62.

20. *GB* 74 (1973) 266.

21. *GB* 54 (1972) 104. This practice originated with the *ius commissionis*. This was the arrangement by which mission territory was entrusted to a missionary congregation or society. This practice was replaced by the establishment of dioceses and the appointment of diocesan bishops.

> throughout the whole Congregation. . . . Everything has not been easy and I recall many visits I have begun in deep distress, and again others from which I have returned in grave anxiety.

Lécuyer went on to express his appreciation for the many welcomes he received on visitation, the admiration he had for "the generosity of so many Spiritans and the spirit that animates them" and the confidence he had despite the

> sources of deep preoccupation that exist for us, as for all congregations—numerous departures . . . the uncertainty and disarray of quite a few in face of changes; the attitude of calling everything in question; the discussions on the nature of the religious and missionary vocation; the violent controversies in the bosom of the church herself; and then the impatience of others with the slowness of an evolution that they consider urgent and indispensable and that they wish to be much more deep and radical; the decrease in vocations and the impression that the way we live the religious and missionary life no longer attracts the young, etc.[22]

Lécuyer's successor, Fr. Frans Timmermans, elected in 1974, focused on the challenges facing Spiritans as missionaries in Africa. Writing on the 1974 Synod of Bishops on evangelization, he saw reason for Spiritans to rejoice as "Christianity in Africa has experienced the greatest constant numerical growth of any continent or period in history." Referring to Blessed Pope Paul VI's call at Kampala in 1969 for an African Christianity, he added, "We expatriate missionaries know and accept with joy that from now on our role is to offer service and assistance as collaborators." The "from now on" suggests that Timmermans, as Lécuyer before him, saw the need for a change in attitude and practice among Spiritans in search of what he termed "a new equilibrium," enabling confreres "to play our full part as members of the presbyterium centered around the bishop, in genuine, fraternal dialogue with our colleagues of the country."[23]

At that same synod, Fr. Arrupe spoke on behalf of the Union of Superiors General. His words, for Timmermans, coincided with the concerns and challenges addressed at GC XIV.

> Religious today need to show much greater spiritual strength and human equilibrium than in other times. Evangelical radicalism, self-denial and self-sacrifice, availability, and definitive

---

22. *GB* 55 (1974) 34–38.
23. *GB* 55 (1974) 62–65.

commitment make religious qualified evangelizers. . . . They must further strengthen their relations with the local church, with a view to collaboration in diocesan pastoral work. The international character of religious institutes is also an ecclesial aspect of great importance for evangelization and for the pastoral progress of the local church.[24]

Spiritans could look back with pride at their history of involvement in and building up of the church in so many parts of Africa. But nostalgia was no substitute for new ways of thinking and acting which the present demanded. These new ways were embodied in germ by Vatican II which signaled a new beginning for the church, and, for missionaries, a new way of being on mission.

Massimo Faggioli, theologian, and commentator on Vatican II, reflected on a lecture given by Karl Rahner in 1965 during the last weeks of the council, in which he proposed a hermeneutic of the council as ushering in a new era or "macroperiod" in the life of the church. For Faggioli, Rahner interpreted the close of the council not so much as an end and conclusion of a process, but rather as a beginning.[25] Faggioli's reflection can be applied to the congregation as it prepared to agree a rule of life. GC XIII, the chapter of renewal, and its document *CDD*, marked not the end and conclusion of a process, but rather, a new way of being Spiritan and a new way of being on mission. The challenge, recognized by Lécuyer and Timmermans, was to embed the "new way" in the minds and hearts of the members and devise structures of organization and an understanding of mission consonant with the spirit of Vatican II as captured by *CDD*.

The tensions identified at GC XIII, particularly between religious life and the apostolate remained. The implementation of changes required renewal, but this was resisted by some who wished to "return purely and simply to our way of life before Vatican II." Others, under the pretext of implementing *CDD* and "out of so-called fidelity to Vatican II, [seek] the complete overthrow of all that goes by the name of structures—common

---

24. Ibid.

25. Faggioli, *Battle for Meaning*, 120–21. "The beginning of a turning point of renewal for Catholicism, an unprecedented event, similar only to the Council of Jerusalem in chapter 15 of the Acts of the Apostles. In this interpretation, the shift made possible by Vatican II takes over the role that both Rome and Athens played in the history of Christianity—both in the history of its theological language (the Greek *logos* and the Roman law) and the history of its institutional development between the Emperor Constantine and the nineteenth century (the Imperial Church) and the church as a *societas iuridice perfecta*, a 'perfect community.'"

life, poverty, obedience, celibacy, etc."[26] The French scholar Michel Dortel-Claudot, SJ, involved in assisting institutes with renewal in general and the revision of their constitutions, recognized many difficulties for mainly French-speaking institutes "with challenges to the authority of superiors, a fall-off in sacramental life and prayer life, encroachments on poverty and the common life, an increase in the number of members living alone, and so on."[27] He saw that following the "special chapter" (for Spiritans this was GC XIII) there was need for subsequent chapters (the Spiritan GC XIV and GC XV) to "deal with this situation, so that in many cases—and particularly with regard to community life, poverty, and obedience—they approved texts highlighting the requirements of religious life that had tended not to be stressed by the special chapters."[28]

4. GC XIV: Guidelines for Animation[29]

GC XIV (1974) held at Chevilly-Larue, recognized that change was causing conflict and tension in the congregation. It gave an analysis of the situation. "Profound changes are apt to cause insecurity and fear, emotions to which both old and young can be vulnerable. Such insecurity often finds its expression in an aggression which may be masked by a passionate or intransigent defense of a theological position, or by a repressed silence."[30] The different discourses underway in the congregation around change required evaluation to distinguish the wheat (sincere difference) from the chaff of emotional frustration and opposition. Communities needed to appreciate difference as a source of enrichment, rather than a cause of division.

---

26. *GB* 54 (1972) 94–96.

27. See Dortel-Claudot, "Revising the Constitutions," 101. His "*Que mettre dans les nouvelles Constitutions, règles de vie ou normes des congrégations religieuses?*" acted as a reference for the congregation's rewriting of its Rules and Constitutions.

28. Ibid.

29. The newly elected general council included an "Introductory Note" at the beginning of the GC XIV document explaining, among other things, why *Guidelines for Animation* was chosen as its title. "The chapter of 1974 set itself a limited objective: to produce some *guidelines for animation* which would answer to the difficulties and problems which face us in our present situation. . . . The word *animation* will raise the eyebrows of many English-speaking confreres. It has nothing to do with animated cartoons. It is a French word which is beginning to gain currency in English because we lack a single word to translate the concept. It has a lot to do with what in English we call 'leadership.' An *animateur* possesses among other qualities those which would be attributed to a good organizer."

30. *GA* 86.

Spiritual renewal and professional retraining would help members in their adjustment to change (*GA* 91).

GC XIV refocused attention on the membership and the building up of community when it prefaced its quotation of *CDD* 1 with the statement, "Our congregation is a fraternal community" (*GA* 3). Community came first, as it could only be from community well lived that the mission would be achieved. The chapter recognized the human qualities needed by Spiritans on mission that are nurtured through living in community (*GA* 4). It understood mission as involvement "in the human situation in which the betterment of human life is achieved" (*GA* 5). The first issue of the new *Information/Documentation* (*I/D*)[31] produced by the Generalate team in 1975 chose "Building the Christian Community" for its theme. This choice was in line with the priority for mission strategy expressed in *GA* 12.[32] One contribution included from the District of Gabon put it well. "The Second Vatican Council reemphasized the primitive concept of the church as the People of God, the body of Christ. Its highest law, its style of life and its bond of unity and interpersonal love is true fraternal charity, lived and exercised in Christ. Its ministries and services are the sustaining points, the channels of divine goodness, spread out everywhere among the People of God."[33]

Community-building was understood to be vitally important for the Spiritans who, like other congregations, were experiencing a hemorrhage of membership at that time. From 1964 to 1974 one hundred and sixty priests were laicized. This represented 4.4 percent of the total number of priests in the congregation. In the academic year of 1973–1974, thirty-eight scholastics, two with perpetual vows, left formation in Ireland. GC XIV acknowledged that such statistics represented difficult and complex decisions by individual members who decided to leave the congregation. "His confreres should be open and understanding, and there should be no

---

31. *Information/Documentation (I/D)* was set up by the general council as an instrument of animation for the congregation with the first issue published in November 1975. It was intended to facilitate discussion among confreres on matters affecting Spiritan mission drawing on the lived experiences of Spiritans. This was the method chosen to animate and build collaboration among members. It was succeeded in 2003 by *Anima Una*. The change of name indicated the goal of the new publication: to reinforce a sense of belonging among the membership to the same congregation and to develop a shared commitment to mission.

32. *GA* 12: "All our attention should be centered on the building of Christian communities which are rooted in the cultural milieu, and on the growth of a responsible and fully committed laity."

33. *I/D* (November 1975) 1.4

trace of condemnation in their attitudes. On the contrary, the departure of a confrere should be for us the occasion of an examination of conscience."[34]

The need to realize and be strengthened by a shared Spiritan identity grounded in the founding charism of the congregation was recognized. GC XIV asked that Libermann's writings be made available to the various language groups (*GA* 36); that specialists in Spiritan studies be brought together (*GA* 50); that knowledge of Spiritan spirituality be more widely communicated (*GA* 51); that formation programs provide for the study of Libermann and his writings and that they be discussed in communities, particularly on 2 February, the anniversary of his death (*GA* 53).

In November 1975, a congregation-wide survey was conducted by the Generalate entitled "What Does Libermann Mean to Us?" and the results were summarized in *I/D* 76 (1976) 1. The responses ranged from "nothing at all at the moment" to "I think of him occasionally" to "I look forward to reading him much more." The conclusion drawn was that "those who are searching for authentic religious missionary renewal are much more likely to turn to contemporary authors who know the problems, the needs, and the hopes of today's world" than to their founders.[35] It seemed as if Libermann was locked away in the nineteenth century and his teaching remained remote to Spiritans of the twentieth century. If so, what then distinguished Spiritans from other missionaries? What was it that united the congregation? This was the question that exercised the mind of Lécuyer in his final year as superior general. He wrote, "Are we as Spiritans sufficiently aware of our origins, of our continuity with a past from which we have received a particular inspiration and tradition of spirituality?"[36]

The Spiritan Studies Group

The general council sought to fulfill its mandate given in *GA* 50 by calling together a group of confreres expert in Spiritan Studies to a meeting in Rome from 28 December 1975 to 5 January 1976. These were: Frs. Joseph Lécuyer (former superior general), Joseph Bouchaud (the Generalate), Paul Sigrist (France), Myles Fay (Sierra Leone), Bernard Kelly (Ontario), Henry Koren (USA), Ramos Seixas (Barcelona) and Amadeu Martins (Portugal). The group agreed statutes and named themselves the "Spiritan Studies Group." Lécuyer was elected as chair. Martins, as secretary, would reside in Rome, and provide the cohesion necessary for the work. It would meet

34. *GA* (1974) 104.
35. *I/D* 76 (1976) 1.
36. *GB* 54 (1973) 286.

annually and gather together Spiritan texts from the different provinces and promote interest in Spiritan founders, history, and tradition. In this way, its goal would be achieved enabling "the members of the Congregation to become aware of its identity and its spirit by a better knowledge of its founders, of its history (i.e., the past) and its life (i.e., the present)."

The Spiritan Studies Group focused its attention at first on Francis Libermann, and second, on Claude Poullart des Places. The first issue of *Spiritan Papers* (October 1976) studied Fr. Libermann's writings on the building up of local churches in Africa. The group published three issues of *Spiritan Papers* each year for the next four years. It went on to publish twenty-two more issues from October 1976 to December 1988. The articles covered many aspects of Libermann's life such as his baptism and conversion experience; his year in Rome seeking approval for his missionary work; his commentary on St. John's Gospel; his nervous ailments and coping with suffering; his years as superior general at Rue Lhomond and his great respect for persons. Research on the writings and spiritual personality of Poullart des Places and his role as founder were also published. The group also proposed a publication giving the essential points of Spiritan history and the teaching of Spiritan founders to replace the old *Spiritual Directory*. The production of a Spiritan Calendar was also proposed to commemorate the principal anniversaries of the congregation.

I/D 9 (January 1977) was devoted to *"Libermann–missionary."* The focus was on him as founder of an important missionary movement in the nineteenth century. While well known as a spiritual director, this aspect, his missionary dedication, needed to be highlighted. It is particularly as a missionary strategist that he left a "patrimony" that deserves to be preserved. Interestingly, the first reference to Claude Poullart des Places in the Spiritan documentation of this time is found in *I/D* 13 reporting on the first International Meeting of Young Spiritans. This meeting was held in 1977 at the Spiritan novitiate, Aranda, Spain from 1 to 15 August. It was attended by 134 young Spiritans from thirty different countries.

They acknowledged "the inspiration we find in Claude Poullart des Places, in Francis Libermann, and in other great Spiritan personalities like Bishop Joseph Shanahan. Still, to live in the spirit of our tradition does not mean to reproduce yesterday's mission today, but rather to be fully involved in today's mission." The young valued community life with one group report at Aranda stating, "The community is the source of our strength and our support. In missionary situations, our community life can be looked upon as our first witness and our first proclamation of the gospel."

International Collaboration and New Foundations

GC XIV recognized a willingness and a need in the congregation for more unity, internationality, and sharing in finance and personnel. A new structure, the "Enlarged General Council," to meet every two years was proposed (*GA* 131–34). Its purpose "is to improve communication and co-operation between the different provinces, districts, and groups and to promote the unity of all with the generalate" (*GA* 131).[37] The first meeting was held at the Generalate in Rome on the day after the Ascension, 1976. The subject for consideration was solidarity. At first it was proposed that the meeting would split into two language groups, but all quickly agreed to work together as one. A great "sense of co-responsibility or collegiality of the major superiors in their work, the orientation and the commitments of the congregation" was reported in *I/D* 7 (June 1976). The meeting recognized that the congregation could only undertake new missions through collaboration between provinces and districts. It was on the eve of Pentecost that three mission projects, Angola, Paraguay, and Pakistan, were accepted as mission priorities for the congregation. Three projects on three continents—internationality had arrived!

Internationality would benefit the congregation which was "too Western," too much influenced by the colonial past with, for example, French confreres sent to French colonies, and Portuguese to Portuguese colonies. It will be remembered that Libermann favored founding an Irish province (then part of the United Kingdom) as Irish missionaries would be more readily accepted in British colonies than missionaries of other nationalities. For most Spiritans, the congregation meant "our province." One participant remarked, "Internationality could well be the test of whether or not we are, and will continue to be, a living congregation."[38] Initiatives by some provinces had already led to the expansion of the congregation in the southern hemisphere. A minor seminary was opened in Ihiala, Nigeria, in 1953. Trinidad was set up as a Vice-Province with its own seminary in 1961, and became the first southern hemisphere province in 1968.

The Generalate team reported on substantial development of Spiritan Foundations in the Congregation:

---

37. The enlarged council comprised the general council, provincial superiors and eight delegates from the districts, one each for South America, West Indies and Guyana, Portuguese-speaking Africa, English-speaking West Africa, English-speaking East Africa, French-speaking Africa, Madagascar/Reunion/Mauritius and one representing African Spiritans (*GA* 134).

38. *I/D* 7 (1976) 2.

- *The Brazilian foundation* (six districts) began in 1970 and had 19 students, 5 priests;
- *The East African Foundation* (Tanzania, Kenya, Uganda, Zambia, Malawi, with the integration of Kongolo-Zaire being considered) also began in 1970 and had 37 students, 9 priests;
- *The Central African Foundation* (Cameroon, Gabon, RCA and Congo) began in 1977 and had 8 students, 3 of whom would be ordained in 1981;
- *The Puerto Rican Foundation* began in 1978 and had 11 pre-novitiate students and 3 novices;
- *The West African Foundation* (Senegal, Gambia, Sierra Leone, Ghana, Makurdi, Kwara-Benue) began in 1980 and had 15 students;
- *The Indian Ocean Foundation* (Madagascar, Mauritius, Reunion) began in 1981 and had 6 prospective novices for the novitiate which was due to open in September 1982.[39]

Superiors in East Africa came together in the East African Foundation to facilitate a program for vocations and formation for their region. There were 11 students in the orientation program, 9 novices, 7 students in philosophy and 9 in theology. Nigeria, Angola, South Brazil, USA West, and Puerto Rico also reported varying degrees of progress in their efforts to promote vocations and develop a common formation program. This growth of foundations in the countries of the south contrasted with a drop-off in vocations and an older membership in the "countries of the north." However, the financial strength and expertise of the congregation was in the established provinces while the demands on resources for recruitment and formation were in the new foundations. Solidarity required a collaboration that included making the congregation's resources available to the new foundations.

GC XIV had already called on provinces to make adequate provision for a pension fund. A fund was also to be centrally administered to coordinate a reallocation of finances in the congregation to overcome the "very real inequalities in the standard of living of Spiritan missionaries. Glaring inequalities should be reduced, without attempting to reach an unattainable equality" (*GA* 172 a). Districts and groups in need were to be subsidized and the on-going formation of confreres was to be funded. It was envisaged that the training of lay leaders would take precedence over buildings

---

39. *I/D* 28 (1981) 1.

and development projects. A brief mention was made of providing for the formation of young Spiritans.

The second enlarged general council meeting held at Knechtsteden, Germany in 1978 analyzed the issue of co-responsibility in relation to international teams. "It was easy to visualize a few small teams. With the cooperation of the provinces, the general council could have its international teams just as the provinces have their districts." The thinking went along parallel rather than intersecting lines, with provinces responsible for districts while also supporting the general council's oversight of international teams. Recognizing a flaw in this approach the general council put an important question,

> If the concept of co-responsibility for the common missionary project of the congregation is to grow in meaning, we must think in future of the mission of the congregation as a whole, and see the needs of our particular Spiritan circumscription in this context; and we must not see the missionary priorities of the congregation as a sort of alms-box to which we contribute when other personnel needs have been fulfilled.[40]

The theme of solidarity was prominent in 1974 at GC XIV and again at subsequent enlarged general council meetings of 1976 and 1978 where discussion was on co-responsibility. The general council led that discussion privileged with an overall view of the congregation and its mission. In proposing an agenda for GC XV it raised challenging questions on co-responsibility as an expression of solidarity. Two of the questions put to the members for reflection in preparation for the chapter were directed toward attitudes and behavior in relation to new foundations and the increasing membership from former mission territories. These were:

> "How ready are those in the older circumscriptions to allow themselves to undergo change, when necessary, because of the inter-dependence required when living and working with Spiritans from other cultures?" And, "what is the response in your circumscription to appeals from the new Foundations for assistance: personnel, financial aid, welcoming and supportive acceptance of their members who come for part of their studies?"[41]

---

40. *I/D* 18 (1978).

41. *Our Spiritan Life*, a pre-capitular document from the general council, April 1979.

5. GC XV: "Mission Today"—Justice and Peace

Since the institution of the diaconate in the Acts of the Apostles (Acts 6:16) the church has provided for the care of those in need. Bevans and Schroeder explained the need that developed in the late twentieth century for the church to go beyond the alleviation of the effects of poverty and challenge their causes. "Not only was the church to engage in the corporal works of mercy through charitable service, but it was also to be involved in human development, the practice and establishment of justice, and the struggle for liberation."[42]

GC XV reflected this new understanding in its sixty articles on contemporary mission published with the title *Spiritan Life* (*SL*). There was a noticeable development in thinking from the experience of the six intervening years since GC XIV. The methodology also had evolved. An analysis of the context was given (*SL* 8–25) that reflected first on the changing world and a deepening of renewal in the church. In that context, "a new age of mission" was recognized characterized by the shift of its center of gravity, both in terms of numbers and vitality, to the southern hemisphere. GC XV also accepted that the changes had brought difficulties and tensions. This was especially true in the development of the young churches. Spiritans as missionaries were no longer the leaders but rather collaborators with the local church. It was difficult to figure out how to take up a different role in the churches of Africa so recently founded by Spiritans or other missionaries. The return of many confreres to Europe and North America had a negative impact. The scripture passage, "The harvest is great, but the laborers are few" (Luke 10:2), was applied to the challenging situation.

GC XV recognized "a great desire to strengthen unity" among the confreres as witnessed by the renewal of community life in many places; growth in solidarity within the congregation and in co-responsibility. Concrete signs of hope and new life were: the growth of foundations; confreres adapting to new situations; the founding of small Christian communities; growth in team ministry; educational works promoting justice and peace; more involvement with ministry to migrants and refugees; positive experiences of disengagement and the taking up of new works. "All these signs show us clearly the action of the Spirit, which gives us life in the midst of our trials and human weakness" (*SL* 46).

The Spirit, at work in GC XV, guided the capitulants to recognize a call to work for justice and peace in the world. Situations of injustice in the world were reviewed (*SL* 69–74) and principles for action enunciated.

---

42. Bevans and Schroeder, *Constants in Context*, 370.

Spiritans were called to serve the marginalized of the world who suffer as a result of an unjust economic system that keeps the poor, poor; and the rich, rich. The congregation committed itself to working for a justice that would bring peace in fidelity to the teaching of the church and Libermann's call to be the advocates of the weak.[43] The new justice and peace ministry required ongoing conversion. "Every Spiritan, whether he is working directly for the poor or not, must know the urgency of inculcating and maintaining in his whole way of life a great sensitivity to Justice and Peace" (*SL* 79). Each Spiritan community should be a living witness to the "kingdom of justice and peace" by the quality of life lived together in mutual understanding and forgiveness, sharing and hospitality. They were to be free from any form of discrimination so that the justice preached was the justice lived. The capitulants agreed that animation was needed to mobilize the whole congregation in the work of justice and peace. This was to be conducted by the leadership of provinces and districts and by the Generalate team (*SL* 82, 83).

A congregation-wide report on Spiritan witness to justice and peace recognized many examples of confreres "who hunger and thirst for justice" (Matt 5:6).[44] In war-torn Angola, brave witness was given by missionaries who remained with their people. One confrere wrote,

> On all sides there was guerrilla warfare, political tensions, hardships. . . . An attack could come any day. . . . I simply could not abandon the mission and these people, as they were in such distress. Day and night they were with me. I tried to find food and drink and medicines for them. Could I leave, when they depended on me? . . . I am convinced that sooner or later we shall have to speak out clearly and take a clear stand on behalf of the poor and oppressed. . . . What will the congregation do with its statement on justice and peace? . . . Will the congregation have the courage to risk its personnel? . . . The congregation should speak out clearly if it is to be truly missionary.[45]

The French province was involved in chaplaincy for African students in Paris. An account of that work was given in the province's bulletin *Province et Mission* in June 1977 and reproduced in *I/D* 27.

> We are in regular contact, here in the community and in their homes and meeting places, with about a thousand African

---

43. In this GC XV remained true to Libermann's provisional rule of 1849 that Spiritans must be "the advocates, the supporters and the defenders of the weak and the little ones against all who oppress them" (N.D. X.517).

44. *I/D* 27 (1981).

45. Ibid., 1.

students. They have been plunged into a world completely different from their own and often hostile to them in their daily life. They are up against all sorts of problems and difficulties, simply from the fact that they are "colored"—difficulties in finding accommodation and work, difficulties with registration forms and bureaucracy. . . . Many of them have to study by day and work by night, or vice versa. . . . This cannot but concern us. We try to respond by being present among them, welcoming them, showing solidarity with them, and taking concrete action. . . . It is important to help them stand up for their rights, and to denounce racism wherever we find it. . . . As for the church structures and communities in France, they find nothing there but indifference to them, segregation, and conscious or unconscious paternalism. . . . Has the congregation a clear program for the assistance of African students and workers in France?[46]

An event two years after this report gave an example of the Spiritan leadership of France acting for justice. The enlarged provincial council meeting decided to suspend its session (25 June 1979) for members to join a silent protest march through Paris against a government bill which would seriously undermine the rights of immigrant workers. The Senate voted against the bill.

An example from Brazil was reported in *I/D* 27. A Dutch Spiritan working in the small village of Itamarati, Amazonia, produced a local monthly newspaper, the *Journal of Itamarati*, aimed at pastoral care, the building up of a sense of community, and the conscientization of these isolated people, threatened by various kinds of disease and oppressed by the rubber industrialists.

> In the face of such injustice [the confiscation of lands] the paper does not hesitate to go into specifics, giving simple and clear questions and replies:—"If someone buys land, has he a right to expel the peasants who are living on it?" Reply: "Never."—"Has the Brazilian peasant a right to a plot of land of his own in this immense country?" Reply: "The constitution guarantees him such a right." The *Journal de Itamarati* leaves no doubt, therefore, about the church's position. It tries to make the people realize that they have rights and that they must defend them.[47]

In New York, USA, the Brooklyn community

---

46. Ibid., 2.
47. Ibid., 3.

> comprises three Spiritans and a Haitian secular priest. Since 1971, they have been working for the Haitian refugees in New York, who number about 40,000 at present. . . . There is obviously a political side to some of the activities. It could hardly be otherwise when trying to help people who are rejected both at home and in their new place of refuge. Conflict with civil authorities is inevitable, and even with priests who see things from a different angle and would prefer a "purer" ministry, with no ambiguities.

The major superiors of North America and the Caribbean at their January 1981 meeting in Puerto Rico wrote an open letter to the Prime Minister of the Bahamas. It noted that

> the Holy Ghost Congregation has ministered to the Haitian people since the mid-nineteenth century. . . . We have learned during these days that your government has set January 18, 1981, as the date after which all Haitians in the Bahamas are subject to immediate expulsion . . . in the name of God, of our common Christian traditions of compassion for those in need, and of respect for the dignity of all human beings, we now appeal to you to rescind or at least to postpone this order. Such a postponement would give international agencies time to arrange for other nations to help in receiving these unfortunate people.[48]

The Generalate team in reviewing these and other reports of particular actions for justice in the congregation also noted that "real commitment is a duty for each Spiritan, and not merely for a privileged elite. It would be too easy for us to soothe our consciences with the thought that some Spiritans are living in dangerous situations." This advocacy for justice was seen by many in the congregation as particular to the few among them specially called and especially heroic. But how did it fit in with mainstream Spiritan mission and the many committed to continuing with traditional works of charity? The general council was clear about its intention. These instances of commitment to justice were shared so that all members would be conscientized into the way of justice. "Otherwise we may become lethargic and stifle the anguish that gripped the heart of a Poullart des Places or a Libermann. Perhaps we have too often heard warnings about what we should not do rather than encouragement to do the things we should."[49] The tension between the ready acceptance of the ministry of charity and resistance to the

---

48. Ibid., 4.
49. Ibid.

doing of justice was captured in the saying of Dom Helder Camara of Recife, Brazil, well known and much loved by Spiritans working in Brazil. "When I give food to the poor, they call me a saint. When I ask why the poor have no food, they call me a communist."

The New Foundations and Formation

GC XV recognized the "growing awakening of southern hemisphere churches to the religious and missionary vocation" (*SL* 105) and a significant portion of its final document addressed "New Foundations" (*SL* 104–38). It quoted from the International Missionary Congress held in Manila in 1979, "We have reached a decisive turning-point in the history of Mission in the Third World. . . . A new era has begun: that of Mission by the Third World" (*SL* 104). While the initiative for a new foundation was the responsibility of the founding districts, "the supply of personnel and finance is a matter for the whole congregation" (*SL* 114). The work of building up the new foundations was one of mutual service between the congregation and the local church "a service that is a preparation for evangelization in the new era, an invitation to take part in it, and an expression of coresponsibility in mission" (*SL* 117).

GC XV gave significant attention to formation (*SL* 139–213). It provided an outline of what formation in the congregation should look like and who was responsible (the general and provincial councils) but it is difficult to figure out which contexts the capitulants had in mind when they were thinking about formation. Were they focusing on the older provinces or on the new foundations? The decisions seem abstract and theoretical. The general council was charged with "giving dynamism and unity" (*SL* 183) to formation throughout the congregation. This meant that the general council's authority in relation to formation in the congregation was restricted to drawing up general guidelines and fostering collaboration "in a spirit of efficient coresponsibility" (*SL* 183). The tough questions about resourcing and ensuring authentic Spiritan formation were not directly addressed.

Fr. Joseph De Boer, a founder of the East African Foundation, was called to Rome in 1979 to spearhead a strategy to provide for the development of the new foundations. *I/D* 28 (1981) reported that he made contacts with various funding agencies, which were generous in their support, and the annual *Cor Unum* allocations from the Generalate had also helped. The report also noted that a spirit of self-reliance was needed as "the foundations will be truly African only when they can dispense with outside help." Efforts were being made at being self-supporting and the example was given of a self-help project in Tanzania where 140 acres of arable land at Tengeru was being farmed.⁵⁰

The third enlarged general council meeting in 1982 was held at Carcavelos, Portugal. Stress was laid on decentralization and putting responsibility for the common project on the circumscriptions and regional conferences of major superiors. This was in response to a fear expressed by some that the congregation was taking on new commitments while unable to resource existing ones. The meeting identified tensions emanating from a resistance to internationality that made it difficult to set up international teams. These included the challenges to renewal of community life particularly where there were cultural differences. It was reported that long-standing habits and "*de facto*" situations also stood in the way. However, signs of hope were also celebrated. It was reported that the three new international communities in Angola, Paraguay, and Pakistan were progressing well. The meeting resolved to strengthen bonds of solidarity in the congregation, especially with confreres experiencing real need, "those who live and work among the poor."⁵¹

Revising the Rules and Constitutions

GC XV entrusted the process for revising the Rules and Constitutions to the general council (*SL* 236) which, in turn set up a committee of four confreres, Frs. Georges-Henri Thibault (France), chair, Anthony Geoghegan (Ireland), Joaquim Ramos Seixas (Spain) and Antoine Mercier (Canada) to undertake the initial work. Their first meeting was held in Rome from 6 to 11 April 1981. The committee devised a program in four stages:

A. Distribution of an outline to all confreres for the revision with a questionnaire; all replies to be worked upon and a report based on the replies prepared for the EGC in 1982.

B. Appointment of a committee for the writing of a first draft of the constitutions; the distribution of the first draft to all confreres between 1982 and 1984; the committee receives comments and revises the first draft (this work to be presented to the EGC in 1984).

---

50. The report continued: "However, our record with farm projects has not been encouraging, and some have questioned the suitability of farming as a means of raising money for the foundations. Other productive projects could be considered, but, whatever the means adopted, there should be serious attempts to reduce the need for funding from abroad."

51. The report on the enlarged general council meeting of 1982 was entitled "Take Courage" and given in *I/D* 32 (1982).

C. Between 1984 and 1986 a second draft would be composed taking account of remarks and suggestions made on the first draft; the second draft would be made available to capitulants in advance of GC XVI so that the opinions of confreres are gathered for consideration at the chapter; amendments and approval of the constitutions by GC XVI.

D. Approval by the Holy See.

The outline distributed at the first stage was in five parts: (1) The Congregation and Its Founders; (2) Spiritan Life; (3) Initial and Ongoing Formation; (4) Spiritan Authority and Service; (5) Temporal Goods.[52]

The process of consultation on the revision of the constitutions was accompanied by a program of animation by the general council which can be traced through *I/D*'s issued from June 1981 to April 1986. The five years of animation were likened to a pilgrim journey undertaken in hope and moving in four complementary directions: towards the periphery; greater universality; renewal of life; and "into the future with hope."[53]

It was at the periphery, in abandoned or difficult areas, that first evangelization and work for migrants, refugees, the marginalized, the abandoned, and oppressed minorities was taking place. "It is hoped that the movement towards the periphery, already visible in many of our commitments, will continue to grow in importance to meet the demands of our times, to rejuvenate the ideals of the congregation and to confirm it in its special vocation." The congregation's attention to new situations indicated a movement toward greater universality. The opening to Asia; attention to dialogue, especially with Islam; research on new forms of membership; openness to internationality in formation, and solidarity between circumscriptions were all evaluated as positive signs of life in the congregation. "A new spirit of universality is moving through the congregation and will get stronger still because of the young provinces and foundations." It was predicted then that a more universal membership and growing numbers of appointments to mission from the new circumscriptions would enable the congregation to incarnate the Spiritan charism in new cultures resulting in a diversification and internationalization of the Spiritan presence on all six continents.

---

52. Timmermans in his report to GC XVI (1986) could confirm that the rewriting of the constitutions had been "an operation involving the entire membership in three general consultations." He further confirmed that the exercise was conducted "obedient to the church's call to spell out for our day and age the Spiritan vocation coming from a long tradition in order that it may bear fruit for the church and the world today." Superior General's Report (1986) 1.

53. The general council offered an analysis in *I/D* 34 (December 1983), *I/D* 35 (February 1984), and *I/D* 36 (October 1986).

The move from being a Western, European-centered congregation to a truly "world congregation" required a renewal that could only come "from the spiritual depth that is in the hearts of the saints." The congregation had journeyed through a renewal of ideas where its charism was rediscovered, rethought and in the process of reformulation. That renewal provided the basis for a deepening spirituality and a rediscovery of the Holy Spirit inviting all to experience the very source of apostolic life as expressed by Libermann, "that life of love and holiness which the Son of God lived on earth." But would the invitation be taken up by all? The realistic evaluation of the general council was given. "The difficulty of adapting to this period of transition can be seen in confreres who no longer feel at ease in the congregation and who seek their spiritual nourishment elsewhere." Despite that observation, the congregation could look to the future with hope. The general council presented a complex report on outcomes of the renewal process. "We do not think that we are being deceived when we say that the signs of life seem to be stronger than the signs of death and that our progress is keeping step with developments in the world." This affirmation of hope was immediately followed by a *caveat*. "Our optimism does not, however, make us ignore the shadows that there are nor the conversions that still have to be made. We are still at an early stage in the renewal of institutes, and of our own in particular. That is why it is important to fix our gaze on the vitality that is being shown, so as to move with it and reinforce it."[54]

A frustration at the slow pace of change is evident from the documentation of the time. Timmermans's report to GC XVI expressed concern.

> The overall impression received from looking at the reports from the circumscriptions gives reason for concern.... The religious/spiritual dimension is greatly lacking in the description of our missionary presence. One can certainly draw the conclusion that there is an overall problem regarding the religious life, religious life and apostolate, and community life.... We seem to be rather remote from Libermann: he is hardly referred to ... remote also from the Spiritan way of life as presented in the new constitutions.

Timmermans identified three difficulties facing the spiritual renewal of the congregation. These were: first, the dispersion of personnel which is a fruit of the past; second, the work-oriented attitudes of confreres; and third, the pressure of pastoral tasks. He also spoke of a new stage in Spiritan history with the call to de-westernization as one of the biggest challenges facing the congregation. "If the congregation shows itself worthy of this new graft, it

---

54. *I/D* 34 (1983).

will be led into profound changes and thus live out an important aspect of what we have called in our own publications, 'a new foundation.'"⁵⁵

Prophetically the general council of 1980–86 wrote in the last *I/D* of its administration:

> In the distant future, with fewer vocations in the northern hemisphere, African Spiritans will be in the majority. This development will help us to open up more to universal mission, to enter the era of mission as cooperation and communion between churches, to be witnesses of the brotherhood of peoples. African dominance will ensure in a new way what was "the preferential option for Africa" of our origins.⁵⁶

6. The Spiritan Brother and Lay Spiritan

The Spiritan Brother

Libermann defined the Congregation of the Missionaries of the Holy Heart of Mary as a society of priests devoting themselves to the proclamation of the Christian gospel and the establishment of the kingdom of God among the poorest and most neglected in the church. The nature of the congregation's work required that "at least some of its members be endowed with priestly dignity" but that there will also be brothers who "can be very useful and they can cooperate for the attainment of the end of the congregation."⁵⁷ Libermann's first plans for missionary activity in Africa included collaboration between priests and brothers.

In his transcription of Libermann's conferences on the rule, Fr. Lannurien noted Libermann as saying, "We must, therefore, act in a saintly way towards them and treat them as good brothers who are willing to share our labors for the glory of God and the salvation of souls."⁵⁸ The spirit of fraternity and commonality of membership was expressed in a move from "a society of priests" to a "religious institute dedicated to the apostolate" (Rules and Constitutions, 1959). But a disparity of status between brothers

---

55. Ibid., 62.

56. *I/D* 41 (1986). Statistics of membership given for new provinces and foundations were: 133 priests and 12 brothers, 288 students in higher education in 1985 and a forecast of possibly 550 students in 1990. Most of these new Spiritans were African. The province of Nigeria alone had 80 priests, 4 brothers and 99 students doing higher studies in 1985.

57. *Provisional Rule of Fr. Libermann*, 37.

58. Ibid.

and priests was noticed for some time in the congregation. Submissions to GC XII (1962) expressed concern at a clerical mentality prevailing with the status of brothers perceived as less than that of priests. The editor of *Spiritus*, Athanase Bouchard, wrote an article entitled "*Sommes-Nous Frères?*" He noted that "we the priests who have almost a monopoly of the offices and responsibilities in the congregation, we are culpable for this situation and we need to have the basic courage to begin to recognize this." He admired the Jesuit superior general, Fr. Arrupe, who pointed out publicly the sin of racial segregation among American Jesuits. For Spiritans, the segregation was clerical in nature.[59]

These concerns had been addressed with GC XIII's reiteration of Constitution 189. "All the members of the congregation, who have made their consecration to the apostolate, whether definitive or temporary, participate in the same benefits and advantages spiritual as well as temporal" (*CDD* 280).[60] The status of brothers was changed with *CDD* clearly stating their "new position in the congregation." That position was based upon the congregation's traditional recognition that although priests and brothers had different roles in community and on mission, they equally committed their whole lives through religious vows to the service of the gospel. "Indeed, to be really efficacious, missionary activity has need of apostles who combine a living witness and active presence of Charity with the preaching of the gospel" (*CDD*, introduction to section entitled "The Brothers," 96). Any semblance of a two-tiered membership of the congregation was to end. "All the members of the congregation, fathers and brothers, who have completed their training, have the same rights and the same obligations. With due allowance for the exigencies proper to each office, and excepting cases for which the priesthood is required, brothers as well as fathers are eligible for all positions of responsibility" (*CDD* 273).

GC XIII further called on superiors "to take practical steps to bring about the full integration of brothers into community activities; sharing responsibilities, participating in councils, united in community prayer, sharing the common table, and for brothers who so wish, the abolition of distinguishing signs (name, dress)" (*CDD* 274). An important note is given at the beginning of *CDD*. It referred to *CDD* 273 which warranted a clarification from the Sacred Congregation of Religious (27 November 1969) pointing out that brothers could be appointed to administrative posts that

---

59. Athanase Bouchaud, CSSp, *La Fin D'Une Réforme*, 108.

60. Constitution 189 reads: "The congregation makes the newly professed member a partaker in the benefits and advantages, spiritual as well as temporal, which all its members enjoy."

had no direct relation to priestly ministry, but they "may not be appointed as superior or vice-superior, either at general, provincial or local level."

GC XIV recognized that a greater effort was needed on both the side of the priest and the brother for attitudes and ways of acting to change (*GA* 56, 57). At that time, the congregation had six hundred and three brothers and three thousand, four hundred priests. A community experiment was conducted in Chevilly, Paris, based on the *CDD* principle that the consecrated laymen were not "lesser clerics," but rather, men who had received a specific call to be missionaries. The result of the experiment was reported at the EGC of 1978. It showed that "the brothers realized that the difference between vocations was not between priest and non-priest but was to be understood in terms of ministries to be done and the charisms necessary for the growth of the community."[61] Discussion at the meeting concluded that what mattered most was that all Spiritans would see themselves as missionary-religious.

> There may be an unconscious assumption amongst us that the priesthood is more "important" than the religious life, that the fathers are mainly priests, and that the brothers are—religious. Until the members of the congregation accept, existentially as well as theoretically, that we are all brothers sharing the same religious commitment, there will always be a certain alienation in the congregation.[62]

GC XV heard from the superior general of a continuing decline in the number of brothers. "With the number going down by 20 a year, we shall have no brothers in 20 years' time." It proposed that "one of the primary objectives of animation over the next six years be the nature of membership, i.e., that we are, before all else, a religious-missionary congregation in which all members live as brothers" (*SL* 97).

Lay Spiritans

The raising up of a mature Christian laity (*AG* 21) was prioritized in *CDD*'s plan for building up the local Christian community in mission countries. "Hence from the very beginning, missionaries should collaborate closely with lay-people, whom they train for the apostolate and teach to form their judgments by the light of faith" (*CDD* 401). Catechists and youth were recognized as categories of people deserving of special attention in building up

---

61. *I/D* 18 (1978) 2.
62. Ibid.

the local church. It was part of the missionary task to "be on hand to help and train, out of their own experience, those who will devote themselves to missionary activity for a time" (*AG* 27). The possibility for associate membership was given in *CDD* 14 which authorized major superiors to accept "priests and laymen who wish to consecrate themselves to the work of the congregation by adopting our way of life."[63]

GC XIV in referring to *CDD* 14 encouraged the experiments that had begun to continue and asked about lay people who not only wished to collaborate in Spiritan mission, but also in its spirituality? The chapter welcomed "other links" with those interested in the Spiritan life of prayer and spirituality, who wished to share temporarily in the life of the community and help in the missionary apostolate (*GA* 63). While a green light was given for exploring forms of associate membership, the energy and commitment was directed toward awakening and fostering vocations to the priesthood and brotherhood. The Dutch and French strategy was to have open communities welcoming to youth. The English and Irish provinces set up teams to promote vocations and to preach school retreats. The U.S.A. West province called for parish directors of vocations to work with its full-time vocation director.[64]

The capitulants at GC XV recognized that "we are, before all else, a religious-missionary congregation in which all members live as brothers" (*SL* 97). Because of this they wanted to promote the vocation of "the Spiritan Lay Religious-Missionary" (*SL* 99). It acknowledged that "some circumscriptions have begun experiments with new forms of membership in the congregation" (*SL* 101) and called for an account of these experiments to be prepared for the next EGC meeting in 1982. It was not yet time to legislate for this as these initiatives were "mostly still at the stage of a loose form of association."

The 1982 EGC acknowledged difficulties with the development of lay forms of membership. These were "the clerical status of the congregation, financial problems, and mentalities that are not open enough to change."[65] Undaunted by these difficulties, the general council was committed to

---

63. Lay participation in Spiritan mission and life was a reality before 1968. Reference was made in 1962 at GC XII to the increasing role for lay coworkers in Irish Spiritan schools as the number of confreres available for that work decreased. These schools had among their staff those who already had an association with the congregation as former teacher volunteers in Africa or as former professed members. Statutes of GC XII (1962) *GB* 47, supplement, 53*.

64. *I/D* 8 (1976) 4.

65. *I/D* 32 (1982) 4.

finding the best way forward for new forms of membership. Their report on the 1982 EGC ended with an aptly chosen quotation from Fr. Libermann.

> We are just a bunch of poor folk brought together by the will of the Master, who alone is our hope. If we had powerful means at our disposal, we would achieve nothing worthwhile; but, as we have nothing and desire nothing, we can form great projects, for our hopes are founded not on ourselves but on him who is all-powerful.[66]

---

66. *N.D.* IV.303.

Chapter 5

Writing a Rule

1986 WAS AN IMPORTANT year for the Spiritan congregation as it completed the *ad experimentum* period and gave definition to its place in the church and world after Vatican II. It was almost twenty years since Archbishop Lefebvre convoked the extraordinary general chapter of 1968–69. That significant event followed by the general chapters of 1974 and 1980 and led by the prophetic figures of Lécuyer and Timmermans, advanced the renewal agenda through a decentralization of authority, the building up of collegiality, and a rediscovery of the congregation's mission and way of life.

The role of leadership in bringing the congregation through the troubled waters of change while maintaining the unity necessary for mission was vital. Lécuyer rose to "the challenge of helping the congregation to adapt its missionary vision to the directions outlined by the Second Vatican Council."[1] It was the task of his successor, Frans Timmermans, "to give energy and direction to the congregation."[2] Speaking many years later, Timmermans remembered the strategy that he and his council adopted in leading the congregation through an important time of change. "We had decided to do all our visits as a group, and, in the spirit of the Second Vatican Council, we were responsible for helping confreres to buy into the new vision of the mission of the church, based on the return to evangelization and the return to the charism of the founders. . . . We had to continue the work begun by Fr. Lécuyer, to write the spirituality of the congregation."[3]

---

1. From an interview with Fr. Frans Timmermans, CSSp, at the Generalate Rome in 2016 by Baba Gaston Temgoua, CSSp, and published in the quarterly bulletin of the Generalate, September 2016.
2. Ibid.
3. Ibid.

This chapter begins with setting the scene in the 1980s for the writing of the new rule of life regarding the reception of Vatican II in the church, by religious institutes in general and the Spiritans in particular. The stages involved in writing the rule of life (*SRL*), GC XVI (the general chapter that agreed the rule's final draft), and its approval by the Holy See, will each be considered in turn. The chapter ends with an appreciation of the new rule of life.

1. A Changed Ecclesial Context

The 1980s was a time of confusion in relation to the reception of Vatican II. In 1985, twenty-five years after the council, and the year before GC XVI, Pope St. John Paul II called an extraordinary assembly of the Synod of Bishops to "celebrate, reaffirm, and carry forward the work of the Second Vatican Council." The calling of the synod was viewed with suspicion in some quarters. The *Tablet* (a Catholic paper in Britain since 1840) expressed three reservations for the success of the synod in the context of the John Paul II papacy.

First, the synod system wasn't working. This was particularly the case for the Synod on the Family held in 1980. It was argued that the resulting papal document, *Familiaris Consortio*, bore little resemblance to the conclusions reached in the synod hall. Second, the papacy asserted its role of central authority in the church without recognizing that, as an institution, it was a stumbling-block to Christian unity. Third, the article also noted the pope's stated commitment to the council. "But the whole trend of his papacy testifies to his reservations. They arise because he feels that in opening its arms to the world, the church let the world in too much, thus blunting the cutting edge of its proclamation."[4]

Cardinal Silvio Oddi, the prefect of the Vatican's Congregation for the Clergy, was part of the chorus welcoming the synod. But his reasoning was ominous: there were postconciliar errors to be corrected. Suspicions were confirmed! In contrast, Cardinal Basil Hume, as president of the Council of European Bishops' Conferences, spoke positively of Vatican II, making the argument that it was not so much that the council had failed but that the council's changes in relation to collegiality were not fully implemented. "We have not yet accepted the changes of attitude and practice that are demanded of us, whether we be laity or ordained ministers. We still lack adequate

---

4. *Tablet*, 2 February 1985, as quoted in Hebblethwaite, *Synod Extraordinary*, 6–7.

structures and procedures for the exercise of collegiality in the church, and the proper consultation of every part of the church."[5]

The extraordinary assembly of the Synod of Bishops concluded that "the council is a legitimate and valid expression and interpretation of the deposit of faith as it is found in sacred Scripture and in the living tradition of the church." It also recognized that there were "deficiencies and difficulties in the acceptance of the council. In truth, there certainly have also been shadows in the post-council period, in part due to an incomplete understanding and application of the council."[6]

The Distinctive Spiritan Way of Living and Acting in the World

Renewal was not a sentimental journey into the past but rather a living out of the big vision of the founder in "the today" of the congregation. The challenge for Spiritans, like other religious apostolic institutes, was to respond generously and creatively to the council's call to mission and find new paths of cooperation in carrying on the mission of the church.[7] Spiritans had journeyed for almost twenty years through a rediscovery of their charism to a deeper understanding of their religious consecration lived in the active apostolate. During that time, much that had been accumulated over the years was set aside as a more radical living of the Spiritan vocation was embraced. "Challenged by the developments of the past twenty years, the congregation has started on a new journey, walking on a difficult road towards a still unknown country."[8] The decisions and directives taken by GC XIII and their development by GC XIV in 1974 and GC XV in 1980, gave shape to a new way of being Spiritan and of being on Spiritan mission. This was the context for GC XVI charged with the task of bringing the period of

---

5. Ibid., 34.
6. *Final Report of the 1985 Extraordinary Synod*, 1.3.
7. *Ad gentes* 40, challenged apostolic religious institutes. "Institutes of the active life, whether they pursue a strictly mission ideal or not, should ask themselves sincerely in the presence of God, whether they would not be able to extend their activity for the expansion of the kingdom of God among the nations; whether they could possibly leave certain ministries to others so that they themselves could expend their forces for the missions, whether they could possibly undertake activity in the missions, adapting their constitutions, if necessary, but according to the spirit of their founder; whether their members are involved as totally as possible in the mission effort; and whether their type of life is a witness to the gospel accommodated to the character and condition of the people."
8. *I/D* 34 (1983) 2.

experimentation to a conclusion by the writing of a new Spiritan rule to celebrate, reaffirm, and carry forward the work of renewal in the congregation.

The time had arrived for Spiritans to give definition to their vocation in the light of Vatican II. But the congregation was not one, but rather consisted of many "journeys" within the one "Spiritan Journey." Each confrere had experienced the journey differently. In 1982, the congregation's journal, *Spiritans Today*, gathered together a collection of interpretations of Spiritan life from several confreres on mission. They each transmitted an enthusiasm and energy for Spiritan mission, but in a different way. One spoke of "divesting oneself of Western categories to receive and appreciate the African way of living." Another was committed to his mission with little hope of tangible results. "Are not these situations the ones most in conformity with our specific end? To work without seeing the results, to die like the seed in the earth—is that not one of the characteristics of our charism?"[9] One confrere wrote of his prayer life:

> I understood that for me the desert of prayer was necessary because I was loving the Lord for myself and not for him. Then I discovered the tenderness of God for all men and found once more the joy and peace of my first gift. . . . I saw very strongly the tenderness of the Father revealed by Jesus Christ in Mary. I feel myself much more fragile, less sure of myself, but with total confidence in God.[10]

A testimony to "Spiritan availability" was given.

> The characteristic of the Spiritan for us has been his availability to serve wherever it was most difficult or where there were not enough workers. The Spiritan has always been the initiator, "*in manibus superiorum paratus ad omnia*," and sometimes we dared to say "*aptus ad nihil*"—prepared for nothing in particular and ready for everything. Here the Spiritans accepted manifold services and responsibilities that others did not want, in difficult

---

9. Quotations are taken from a selection of reflections from confreres on their experiences of renewal in *Spiritans Today* (1982). "Investigation of our Spiritan Way of Life," 7–27.

10. *Spiritans Today* 1 (1982) 10–11. *Spiritans Today* was produced by the Spiritan Research and Animation Center and ran to five issues from 1982–87 with the task of stimulating reflection and sharing among Spiritans on Spiritan mission. It was followed by *Spiritan Life* in 1989 which continues to be published. Each issue of *Spiritan Life* typically reports on a topic related to an aspect of Spiritan mission considered by an international meeting of the congregation.

and dangerous missions, refused by other missionary congregations. This is what impresses me most in my confreres.[11]

In 1984, the Spiritan Animation and Resource Centre in Rome issued a general invitation to young Spiritans in formation to share with the congregation their dreams and hopes for their future lives as Spiritans.[12] Some two hundred replies were received from Angola, Brazil, Cameroon, Canada, the Central African Foundation, the East African Foundation, England, France, the Indian Ocean Foundation, Ireland, the Netherlands, Nigeria, Portugal, Poland, Puerto Rico, Spain, Switzerland, Trinidad, the United States, and the West African Foundation. Common themes were noted. First, loyalty to the congregation was expressed, with some recognizing their role in the church as that of humble service; others saw themselves taking leadership in their countries and being a leaven in the mass for local churches.

One young confrere wrote, "Spiritan life is essentially a spiritual pilgrimage, the mystery of which invites us to penetrate ever more profoundly its wealth of meaning."[13] Another defined teamwork and co-responsibility as

> the ability to work together, to be co-responsible in building up communities which are a true sign of God's love for all men and women. This demands a great respect for the confrère and the ability to trust him. It also demands that our communities be open ones, that those with whom we work, brothers, sisters, lay men and women, be included in the warmth of our fellowship.[14]

The Spiritan vocation to the poor and being in solidarity with the poor was central to many responses.

> I feel we must be present to people who are victims of the world economy, side by side with them. I think of all that is going on in Latin America, priests who are close to the landless peasants exploited by land-owners. There is a place for us, or in the most economically disadvantaged African countries, which our western governments oppress in different ways.[15]

---

11. Ibid., 17.

12. In 1981 the Spiritan Centre for Research and Animation succeeded the Spiritan Studies Group; it was under the direction of Fr. Alphonse Gilbert, assisted by Fr. Myles Fay and joined by Fr. Anthony Geoghegan in 1985.

13. This and subsequent quotations are taken from *Spiritans Today* 3 (1984) 51–83.

14. Ibid., 55.

15. Ibid., 57.

The importance of community life was recognized by many as the source from which members "draw the power to accomplish Christ's mission." With great hope and expectation for the future one respondent said that the Spiritan vocation is "to live a life of fraternity in such a way that the Spiritan community becomes a place where the kingdom grows. Let it be the seed of the new world we all wish for. Let the world's power structures never enter it." But community life is "not merely living under one roof but having the Christian vision which we share among ourselves and which is the springboard of our apostolic actions."

The replies clustered around four fundamentals of Spiritan vocation: holiness, religious life, community life and the apostolic life. One respondent combined these by saying,

> The different fundamental aspects boil down to what I call a love-union formed by apostolic life, religious life and community life. I see the apostolic life holding a place, the first place, in my objectives. It stems from Jesus' parting message: "Go, teach all nations; make disciples. And I am with you all days until the end of time." It is a mission in joy that assures us of the permanent presence of him who sends us, Jesus Christ.[16]

Reflecting on the survey among the young, Timmermans, speaking as "an elder," recognized his dreams in the visions of the young. "Their overall outline of the Spiritan vocation is in the best traditions of Libermann: apostolic life with Jesus-Apostle as model, a life that draws its vitality from intimate union with Christ, an apostolic life lived in community, at the service of the poor."[17] Speaking from experience he went on to recognize what all Spiritans knew deep down within themselves.

> We well know how, in the run of daily ministry and commitments, some elements become more sharply focused than others. . . . But these oppositions between prayer and action, community life and response to the needs of those we serve, concern for unity and struggle for the disinherited—these are born of ourselves, twists in what is fundamentally one reality. This unity does not seem to pose a problem for our young people.[18]

Whether old or young, the dynamic between adaptation of the Spiritan way of life through contact with its founding charism and tradition was needed for renewal in the spirit of Vatican II. Spiritans share a common charism with an inner dynamism which energizes their mission and brings it to fulfillment. The currents of change at any one time are strong and need to be understood and

16. Ibid., 81.
17. *Spiritans Today* 3 (1984) 86.
18. Ibid.

negotiated. The many confreres caught up in the traumatic time of change since Vatican II and who came together to find a new way for Spiritan life and mission were prophetic figures whose good deeds live on after them (Rev 14:13). They have left those who follow them a rule that gives direction and energy to Spiritan life and mission today.

2. Writing and Approving a Text

The general council stipulated that the new rule of life should be inspirational; give a good reflection of renewal in the church, in mission, and in religious life; and be open to the signs of the times and to the future.[19] Much had changed in the congregation over the previous twenty years. The great challenge was to harvest the treasure of individual experiences and be true to them in a formula of words that would speak to all and in which all would recognize their own Spiritan reality. The hope was that a rule could be written through which the energy of God would be infused into Spiritan life and mission for the future. In his report at the beginning of GC XVI, Timmermans referred to the process of rewriting the congregation's Rules and Constitutions.

> The past six years—the time it has taken to rewrite our Rules and Constitutions—have been a rather unusual period in the congregation's long history. The rewriting has been an operation involving the entire membership in three general consultations. A large number of confreres from all circumscriptions and continents has been intensely caught up in a complex process of study, analysis of surveys, evaluation, and text-writing. This has been an intensive and costly activity, carried out in obedience to the church's call to spell out for our day and age the Spiritan vocation coming from a long tradition, in order that it may bear fruit for the church and the world today. Never has the whole body of the congregation been asked to concentrate for so long and in such a systematic way, on its own identity. Moreover, the exercise was not devoid of serious dangers, as it could possibly have turned the community in upon itself.[20]

That exercise is here considered in five stages: first, the synthesis of replies to the initial questionnaire; second, the production of a first draft; third,

---

19. Letter of general council to the members of the special commission for the constitutions, 11 June 1983.
20. Superior General's Report (1986) 1.

a constitution commission; fourth, a second draft for distribution to the membership; fifth, a third and final draft for consideration by GC XVI.

I/D 31 of February 1982 reported that a group at the Generalate was working on the feedback received from confreres to the open-ended questionnaire on the revision of the constitutions. The thirty-one questions looked for essay type answers and some 1,200 replies were received, or 32 percent of the congregation's total membership. The report quoted Pope St. John Paul II: "After several years of experiments with a view to updating religious life in accordance with the spirit of each institute, the time has come to evaluate these efforts objectively and humbly so as to bring out the positive elements, set aside any deviations there may have been, and prepare a stable Rule of life, approved by the Church."[21] This would, he went on to say, "provide members with a stimulus for a deeper knowledge of their commitments and a life of joyful fidelity."

A committee of four then synthesized all the replies (6–11 April 1982) and proposed an outline and a content for the revised constitutions to the enlarged general council meeting held in Carcavelos, Portugal, in May 1982. That meeting recognized several different ways of looking at the relationship between the Spiritan apostolate and religious consecration. "The tension at the heart of the description of the Spiritan as a 'religious-missionary' was thus clearly felt."[22] The desire for the process of decentralization to continue within the congregation and gain expression in the new constitutions was also recognized at the 1982 meeting.

Two confreres, Georges Henri Thibault of France and John Daly of Ireland, were commissioned to write a first draft of the new constitutions following the 1982 EGC meeting. Their draft would provide the basis for the work of a constitution commission. In the preface to their draft of May 1983 Thibault and Daly wrote, "We set out to produce a scissors-and-paste draft, a sort of concordance of the various constitutional documents which would serve as an *instrumentum laboris* for the work of the commission."[23] The first draft was in the form of two books: the basic text (referred to as the "Rules") and the "Constitutions" (norms subject to change over time).

The general council studied the text prepared by Thibault and Daly and in October 1983 named twenty-three confreres to form a constitution commission to meet in Carcavelos, Portugal, from 20 December 1983 to 6 January 1984 and "work on the constitutions." The commission's task was to

---

21. Address to 600 women superiors general during the fifth general assembly of the UISG, Sistine Chapel, 14 November 1979.

22. *I/D* 32, October 1982.

23. Farrelly, "Revising the Rules and Constitutions," 12.

prepare the ground for the second draft of the new Rules and Constitutions. The conflictual issues identified at the enlarged general council meeting of 1982 needed to be addressed and resolved before a new draft could be written that would command the respect and agreement of all confreres.

The Carcavelos Commission and a Second Draft

A careful selection of members for the commission ensured inclusion of diverse opinions, positions, and cultural backgrounds. The twenty-three members with a secretariat of three confreres and facilitator/moderator, Fr. Thomas M. Farrelly, CSSp, came from twelve countries on four continents (Brazil, Cameroon, Canada, France, Germany Holland, Ireland, Nigeria, Portugal, Tanzania, Trinidad and the USA). Each member was also competent in different disciplines such as Scripture, theology, sociology.[24] The commission set about achieving its task of preparing for a second draft of the new constitutions by:

1. adopting general orientations related to the major options;

2. structuring the form and content of the constitutions in accordance with the orientations adopted;

3. composing a text which would clearly express the agreed form and content with the editing of a final text left to a drafting committee.[25]

The commission recognized that the general orientations for the second draft should be the Spiritan vocation understood in a dynamic rather than theoretical way. That dynamism would have four dimensions:

---

24. The members of the Carcavelos Commission were: Frs. Ferdinand Azégue, Cameroon (foundations and African context); Paul Chuwa, Tanzania (foundations and African context); John Daly, Ireland (theology and co-redactor of the first text); Anthony Geoghegan, Ireland (theology/seminary and pastoral); Manuel Gonçalves, Portugal (theology/seminary and pastoral); William Headley, USA (sociology/planning); Pedro Iwashita, Switzerland (Brazilian context). Bernard Kelly, Canada (spirituality of Libermann); François Nicolas, France (Spiritan studies); James Okoye, Nigeria (sacred Scripture); Patrick Peters, Brazil (theology/seminary and pastoral); Felix Porsch, Germany (sacred Scripture, especially the Holy Spirit); Paul Sigrist, Switzerland (Spiritan studies/theology); Georges-Henri Thibault, France (canon law and co-redactor of the first text); Eugene Uzukwu, Nigeria (theology, and African culture); Michel Verteuil, Trinidad (theology/justice and peace); René You, Algeria (dialogue with Islam). Brother Christian Roberti, Zaire (the brothers, medical services in Africa); Fr. Thomas Farrelly acted as facilitator/moderator; Fr. Vincent O' Grady was secretary and Frs. Gerald Walsh and Armand Burghard were translators and secretarial assistants.

25. The Report of the Constitutions Commission which was presented to the superior general and general council on 6 January 1984.

(1) a biblical perspective, (2) the context of the charism of the founders, (3) the Spiritan historical identity and (4) the congregation's multicultural membership.[26]

There were two phases to the commission's work. First, it confronted the major issues that needed to be resolved before progressing to a second draft. "While consensus was aimed at in this phase, it was not an overriding concern. The Holy Spirit can speak through minority opinions! The main concern was that each person should be able freely to express his point of view and be listened to with respect."[27] It was agreed that dissenting opinions could be included as "alternative options" in the final text.

> Differing viewpoints were freely aired with fervor and conviction. Gradually a common ground was reached as attempts to define our charism in the juridical language of general and specific ends were abandoned and the language of vocation was adopted. Ideas and attitudes finally crystalized around the concept of our Spiritan vocation according to the charism of our founders, Claude Poullart des Places and Francis Libermann.[28]

Farrelly reported that the first chapter, although short, was the key that opened the door to an understanding and agreement on all that followed. The work of the commission was completed by an editing committee which met at Chevilly, Paris at the end of February 1984.[29] In this way, a second text of the Rules and Constitutions was written. It was distributed to all confreres for a further consultation between May to December 1984. The general council, in its introduction to this draft, recognized a few unresolved difficulties and pointed to some possible solutions. It stated that the issue of Spiritan charism should not be locked into a categorical definition but rather described in terms of its essential characteristics. It also noted that the difficulties associated with defining the Spiritan apostolate to the poor in different contexts could be addressed through the prism of justice and peace as proposed at GC XV. The general council further proposed that the apparent tension between religious life and the apostolate could be resolved by appreciating religious life from an apostolic and prophetic perspective.

How was Spiritan community to be understood? Given the different conceptions—Francophone, Anglophone, Lusophone, African, and South American—the way forward was to speak of Spiritan community

26. Ibid.
27. Farrelly, "Process of Revising the Rules and Constitutions," 14.
28. Ibid., 14–15.
29. The Editing Committee members were: Frs. Bernard Tenailleau, James Okoye, David Regan, and Manuel Gonçalves.

as open, fraternal, and apostolic. Another issue was that of governance. The Carcavelos meeting did not fully address this, but the general council accepted the editing committee's suggestion that the organization of the congregation should be considered in the context of service, solidarity, and co-responsibility.

The common orientations that emerged at Carcavelos, on inspiration and on openness to diversity among its membership and to the signs of the times, were evident in the text it produced. The Carcavelos meeting also gave the Rules and Constitutions a distinctive Spiritan orientation. The word of God permeated them; they were filled with the breath of the Spirit and were reflective of des Places, Libermann and the enduring Spiritan tradition. The council commended the draft as it fulfilled the expectations set out at the beginning of the process.

Consultation on the second draft was concluded by 15 December 1984. There were 1,406 replies from almost 40 percent of confreres to the consultation. These responses were analyzed by the "Analysis Commission" in January 1985.[30] The commission found overall agreement with the 1984 text although some amendments were proposed. The general comments were summarized as focusing mostly on the need for greater precision in defining the Spiritan vocation. A more appropriate weighting between the "juridical" and the "prophetic" was needed. The religious and the apostolic aspects of the Spiritan vocation were to be amplified and many forms of the Spiritan apostolate were to be included along with the option for the poor. A few responded that they could not recognize the reality of their own mission situation in the text. For some, it was too idealistic.

Following the work of analysis, a further editing was carried out. The editing committee responded to some of the suggestions/amendments by shortening and simplifying the text and provided greater precision concerning what was specifically Spiritan.[31] Points made by the committee about some parts of the text were included with the publication of the third and final draft of the Rules and Constitutions approved and distributed by the general council to all confreres. This publication also acted as the working document for GC XVI. In his letter accompanying the text and observations of the editing committee, Timmermans called for further study and discus-

---

30. The Analysis Commission members were: Frs. J. Hogema (Holland), A. Le Flo'ch (France), F. Lopes (Portugal), S. Moore (Ireland). T. Farrelly, the coordinator of the project, assisted the commission.

31. The members of the Editing Committee met in Rome during March–April 1985. They were Frs. M. Gonçalves (Portugal), J. Okoye (Nigeria), T. Geoghegan (Ireland), A. Le Flo'ch (France). Fr. R. You (Algeria) agreed to perfect the literary style of the final French draft.

sion. "It is especially important to clarify the essential points concerning our Spiritan vocation which will be the subject of debate at the chapter. The more explicit the thinking of the confreres on these important questions, the easier it will be for the capitulants to carry out their discernment together in fidelity to our heritage and to the call of the world and the church in our day."[32] Farrelly likened the writing of the Rules and Constitutions to an exodus experience for the congregation. But he added, "This is not to imply that there is some Promised Land called 'Renewal' in which we can find rest. The Second Vatican Council has taught us that the church is a pilgrim people, the process of revision and renewal continues under the guidance of the Holy Spirit."[33]

Finalizing the Rule of Life

Eighty-One Spiritans gathered in general chapter (GC XVI) at Chevilly-Larue on 1 July 1986 to approve the final text of the congregation's new Rules and Constitutions.[34] This intercultural, multilingual international gathering (111 confreres in all) was the congregation in microcosm from

---

32. Superior General's Letter, Pentecost 1985, which accompanied "The Draft of Our Rules and Constitutions" (1985 edition). Three guideline questions for discussion prepared by Fr. Farrelly were included in the Introduction to the 1985 draft Rules and Constitutions. These corresponded to the three levels of reflection and decision (the levels of vision, mission, and commitments) to be undertaken by the 1986 General Chapter. They were: (1) How would you express your vision of the congregation and the Spiritan vocation in the light of the charism of our founders? (2) How would you express the mission of the congregation today and for the future? (3) How would you describe the commitments to be made in view of accomplishing our mission?

33. Farrelly, *Spiritan Papers* 18 (1984) 18.

34. The capitulants were from the Generalate (9 de jure members) and from the provinces, 35 elected capitulants (7 from France, 6 from Ireland, 3 from Holland, 2 each from Angola, Germany, Nigeria, Portugal, and USA East; 1 each from Belgium, Canada, England, Poland, Spain, Switzerland, Trans-Canada, Trinidad, and USA West). Thirty-one capitulants were elected by the districts (Alto Juruá, Amazonia, Bagamoyo, Bangui, Brazil Central, Brazil South, Brazil SE, Brazil SW, Cape Verde, Congo, Doumé, French Guiana, Gabon, Gambia, Ghana, Guadeloupe, Kenya, Kilimanjaro, Kongolo, Kwara-Benue, Madagascar, Makurdi, Martinique, Mauritius, Puerto Rico, Reunion, Senegal, Sierra Leone, Southern Africa, and Yaoundé). There were 6 capitulants elected by Foundations and Groups (the Brazilian, Central African and East African Foundations; the groups represented were Pakistan, Paraguay, and Zambia). Thirty confreres joined the capitulants as the chapter staff. These were moderators (2), facilitator (1), liturgy (2), bursar (1), secretaries (3), translators (7), documentation (4), the manager of the secretariat (1), assistants (6), information and communication (3).

four continents united by one charism for one important task: to agree a final text for the new Rules and Constitutions.[35]

Timmermans noted in his report a tendency in many responses to the consultation on the new Rules and Constitutions "to evaluate the proposed text too exclusively in the light of local conditions, without sufficient attention for the greater variety of situations and commitments in which we are involved."[36] He presented themes of his administration, and asked that "the capitulants accept to transcend their own local viewpoints and approach the matter at the very level of the congregation as such. We must be equally conscious of our own—often implicit—points of departure, in order to arrive at a common conception of the constitutions, and at common criteria."[37] GC XVI set out to achieve that task through eight commissions with ten delegates in each commission. The chairs elected by each commission, along with the moderators (Frs. Maurice Piat[38] and Gaétan Renaud), the superior general or a member of his council, the facilitator (Fr. Thomas Farrelly) and Fr. Sammy Moore (the chapter manager) formed the Central Commission. Each commission was responsible for reworking a particular chapter of the constitutions, but had at the same time to review and comment on the work of the other commissions. Each chapter had to come before the general assembly three times for voting. All the chapters were passed with near unanimity. The finished work was entitled *The Spiritan Rule of Life*. An editorial committee was approved to produce the official version (in French) for submission to the Holy See for approval.[39]

The other task of GC XVI was then addressed with the election of Fr. Pierre Haas as superior general on the afternoon of 24 July by an absolute majority on the third ballot (50 votes out of 80). The election of the general councilors followed. They were Frs. Michael Doyle (Irish/Canadian), James Okoye (Nigeria), Manuel de Sousa Gonçalves (Portugal), Denis Wiehe (Mauritius), Francois Nicolas (France) and Peter Marzinkowski (Germany).

---

35. The full list of delegates and chapter staff is given in *Spiritan News* 61 (March–April 1986). Several changes were made in delegates and staff who attended the chapter. The changes are noted in *Spiritan News* 63. This issue of *Spiritan News* gave a report on the 1986 general chapter which forms the basis for what is presented here.

36. Superior General's Report (1986) 75–76.

37. Ibid.

38. Fr. Maurice Piat, CSSp, became bishop of Port-Louis Mauritius in 1993 and was named one of 17 cardinals on 9 October 2016 by Pope Francis during his regular Sunday address to St. Peter's Square. He was joined in that announcement by another Spiritan, Dieudonné Nzapalainga, CSSp, archbishop of Bangui in the Central African Republic. They are the first Spiritans to be named as cardinals.

39. The Editorial Committee members were: Frs. Manuel Gonçalves, Vincent O'Grady, Georges-Henri Thibault, and René You.

Frs. Doyle and Okoye were both elected on the second ballot. They were subsequently elected first and second assistant, respectively.[40]

Finally, guidelines for the next six years, 1986–1992, were to be drawn up. A questionnaire was circulated to delegates before the chapter by Fr. Farrelly who analyzed the responses. Regional commission meetings—Europe, North America, South America, West Africa, Central and Southern Africa and the Indian Ocean, Oceania, and Asia (which had only two capitulants)—were held to address the issues identified by the analysis. Each commission drew up priorities for their region. The resulting guidelines under five headings of New Provinces and Foundations, New Forms of Mission, Community, Solidarity, and Justice and Peace were discussed and approved by the general assembly on 1 August.

One of the outgoing general councilors, Fr. Norman Bevan, on his return to America as newly elected leader of the USA East province, distributed an "unofficial" translation of the new *Spiritan Rule of Life* to his confreres. He recognized that it was a great gift to the congregation and "invited the province to use this document as part of the ongoing process of renewal which we are called to as a congregation." He echoed the description given by his predecessor, Fr. Vernon Gallagher of GC XII in 1962, when he described GC XVI as "a deeply enriching experience to live in Spiritan community for five weeks with confreres from over fifty countries—to share a vision and a hope for the future of the congregation, to share a conviction that who we are and what we do as Spiritans is worth the commitment of our lives."[41]

Approval and Publication of the Rule of Life (*SRL*)

In his 1987 Pentecost Letter to the Congregation from Gentinnes, in Belgium, the new superior general Fr. Pierre Haas announced that the Congregation for Religious had approved the *Spiritan Rule of Life*. Haas pointed out the significance of the date which marked the opening of the Marian Year and the twenty-fifth anniversary of the Kongolo Martyrs.[42] He wrote, "This witness of our Spiritan brothers continues to challenge us: the total giving of our life is a fundamental parameter of our missionary vocation—whether

---

40. The *Spiritan News* report on the chapter also noted that Fr. Okoye was appointed by the Holy See to the ITC.

41. Circular Letter, 12 August 1986 (Archives, USA Province, Bethel Park).

42. 20 Spiritans (19 Belgian and 1 Dutch) were abducted from their mission in Kongolo (in present-day Democratic Republic of Congo) and murdered on 1 January 1962. A shrine at Gentinnes commemorates their martyrdom.

this life is given day by day or required of us suddenly, in the prime of life, while generously fulfilling our duties." Haas included two other recently deceased confreres in his remembrance. The first was twenty-nine-year-old Fr. Jean-Étienne Wozniak, who was "shot down in Angola on the road from his mission to an outstation to celebrate Mass two years earlier, on Pentecost Sunday."[43] The other, Fr. Nicolaas Ligthart, who only two weeks before, had "also paid with his life for his dedication" in Angola was also remembered. Among the documents found in his car was the expression, "A boat is much safer in port, but boats are not made to stay in port."[44]

The congregation weathered the storm of renewal and adaptation and the time of experimentation had drawn to a close. With the new *Spiritan Rule of Life*, it now had a sure guide for future mission as it journeyed with peoples it was called to serve in so many parts of the world. Fr. Haas introduced *SRL* confident of it being a gift from the Holy Spirit. "By the Holy Spirit's grace, it can become for each one who lives it in spirit and in truth, a road to apostolic holiness."[45] This, he pointed out was confirmed by the church through the beatification of two Spiritans, Jacques Laval and Daniel Brottier. "It represents the application of the charisms of the founders to the church of our times and the modern world—God's present day—an application made possible by the research that has been going on in our congregation since the 1968 general chapter."[46]

The newly elected general council produced *A Handbook for the Spiritan Rule of Life* in 1987. The acceptance of the new rule and putting it into effect was one of its most important priorities. "To accept this new rule of life in faith is surely an occasion of grace for each Spiritan. It is also an invitation to a renewal of life, personal, apostolic and community, and a

---

43. Jean-Étienne Wozniak was a French Spiritan who arrived in war-torn Angola in 1984. Before his departure for Angola his provincial expressed concern about his appointment to a place of war. Did he not fear for his life? Wozniak replied, "Si un Spiritan n'est pas prêt a donner sa vie, est-il encore Spiritain?" ("If a Spiritan is not ready to lay down his life, is he still a Spiritan?"). Accompanied by Irish Spiritan, John Kingston, they were approaching Kiwaba N'zogi mission, 100kms. North of Malanje on 26 May 1985 when they were caught in a Unita ambush. Fr. Wozniak died in the attack and Fr. Kingston was shot and captured but later released (See *Informations Spiritaines*, 186. April–June 2012. CSSp Maison généralice, Rome). Fr. Kingston went on to serve on the general council, 2004–2012.

44. Letter from the Superior General, Pentecost, 1987.

45. *SRL* (1987) introduction.

46. Ibid. Blessed Jacques Laval (1803–1864), the Apostle of Mauritius, was beatified by Pope St. John Paul II on 24 April 1989. His feast day is 9 September. See *Spiritan Papers* 9 (1979). Blessed Daniel Brottier (1876–1936), missionary in Senegal and restorer of *Apprentis d'Auteuil*, Paris, was beatified by Pope St. John Paul II on 25 November 1984. His feast day is 28 February. See *Spiritan Papers* 17 (1984).

rediscovery of the happiness of the Spiritan vocation."[47] General council members selected the chapters they were most familiar with and wrote on them. The individual writings were shared within the council and reworked to produce the handbook for which it took collective responsibility.

3. The *Spiritan Rule of Life* (*SRL*)

Our Spiritan Vocation

This is the shortest (only 7 articles) and most profound chapter of *SRL*. "Chapter 1 is the Rule, as it were, in germ. The other chapters unfold what chapter 1 contains in a very condensed manner."[48] It was introduced with the Scripture text "the Spirit of the Lord is on me . . ." (Luke 4:18–19), quoting Isaiah 61:1–2. This text has become synonymous with Spiritan mission in different contexts and at different times. It was intended to be "expressly evocative, open to many meanings, yet evoking depths beyond any of the readings."[49] Fr. Michael Cahill, CSSp, while recognizing the dangers associated with the inclusion of Scripture passages in *SRL* (for example, a text can be taken out of context or placed in an inappropriate juxtaposition with another text), saw in the use of Scripture an acknowledgment "that we are recipients of a gracious self-revelation of God. We read as members of the community of the faithful who have been given the Scriptures as a norm for living."[50]

Henry Koren located *SRL* in the line of succession of the congregation's charismatic foundation with des Places and Libermann. "Always open to the Spirit, both Poullart des Places and Libermann remained ready for everything that living the gospel of Jesus appeared to demand of them and their followers in the changing course of history. It is in faithfulness to that Spirit that we update ourselves in our era."[51] The handbook suggests that

47. *Handbook for the Spiritan Rule of Life*, 3.

48. Ibid., 15

49. Ibid., 9. The full list of Scripture references is given on pp. 138–39 of *SRL*. There are 40 texts from the Bible either quoted or referred to in *SRL*. As well as being used to introduce chapter 1, Luke 4:18–19 is also referred to in article 4 of that chapter when defining the purpose of the congregation as the evangelization of the "poor."

50. Cahill in a study of *The Use of Scripture in the Spiritan Rule of Life* also noted that "each chapter of the Rule is headed by one or two biblical quotations. Sometimes sections of chapters, for example the ones dealing with charity, poverty, and obedience in chapter 4, have their own introductory citations. . . . Scripture quotations (in French) are all from the New Jerusalem Bible, it being the best-known text in all languages." Document for private circulation. USA Spiritan Archives, Bethel Park, 13c-11-4.

51. *The Spiritan Rule of Life in Light of Our Founders*, by Henry Koren, CSSp, 2.

this was the first time the congregation affirmed not only that it had two founders but also, a "double charism" with Poullart des Places associated with an outreach to the poor (chimney sweeps and poor seminarians) and Libermann associated with the evangelization of Africa.[52]

The handbook helps the reader "to unpack" the deep Trinitarian understanding of the Spiritan vocation. "Spiritan life and apostolate comes from and moves back into the life of the Trinity. The two poles of this life and apostolate are missionary (sent) and religious (consecrated), deriving from Christ who was himself 'anointed' and 'sent'. It is in this sense that Spiritan life is a following of Christ."[53] The unity of the Spiritan life was finally achieved in the third paragraph of "Our Spiritan Vocation" with apostolic life seen as encompassing all its fundamental elements. There is a unity of task, obedience, and self-sacrifice in the life of the Spiritan as seen in the life of Christ. The apostolic life includes three essential dimensions: the proclamation of the Good News, the practice of the evangelical counsels and a life in fraternal and praying community (*SRL* 3). "The debate which had been going since the 1968 chapter on the relative importance for us of apostolate and religious life, apostolate and community is now ended—all are to be held in creative tension."[54]

Whereas chapter 2 of *SRL* listed works that, at the time of writing the rule, were part of Spiritan mission, here the "why" of Spiritan mission is given: "the evangelization of the poor." This explains why first evangelization is Spiritan because "it is a ministry to people in dire spiritual need who very few want to help or are equipped to help."[55] For the same reason education can be a work of the congregation when it is related to the evangelization of the poor. Fr. Vincent Donovan, CSSp, commented that there were "cultures and sub-cultures all around us in desperate need of evangelization."

Private circulation. USA Spiritan Archives, Bethel Park 13c-11-4.

52. Jean Savoie, CSSp, established that the general chapter held in 1919 and presided over by Mgr. Le Roy had already recognized Poullart des Places as founder of the congregation. This was due more to a legal requirement than an acknowledgment of his charism influencing the congregation. "In 1919, the general chapter recognized Poullart des Places as the founder of the Congregation of the Holy Spirit and Libermann as the second founder and spiritual father." This was encapsulated by Mgr. Le Roy in his famous saying: "Without one of them we would not have existed, without the other we would no longer be in existence." Savoie, "Cause for the Beatification," 5.

53. *Handbook*, 10.

54. Ibid., 13.

55. Ibid., 14. The handbook brought attention to the dropping of the term "poor and abandoned." Since the Carcavelos meeting it was recognized that the word "abandoned" gave a pejorative interpretation to the "poor" at a time when it is preferable to say "working *with* the poor" than "*for* the poor."

One of these cultures, the scientific-technological culture, merits special attention and mention, in light of our many educational works, and in light of the fact that this particular culture is spreading across the world even to our most remote foreign mission fields. The *Spiritan Rule of Life* calls for us to have special concern and care for those who have not yet heard the gospel message. If there ever was a culture that fits this description, it is the scientific-technological culture.[56]

Our Mission

The two scriptural texts introducing this chapter of *SRL* on Spiritan mission refer to the Risen Lord's sending out of the apostles (John 20:21–22) and their bearing witness to him in the power of the Spirit (Acts 1:8). Mission can only happen in the power of the Holy Spirit empowering a following of the One sent by the Father.

> The Rule tells us that the spirit of the Risen Lord gives life and direction to our apostolate. The evangelization of the world is related directly to the Resurrection. It was only after the Resurrection that the mandate to make disciples of all nations was given to the apostles. Things were different after the Resurrection. Some found that difficult to take. Mary Magdalene clung to the Lord on Resurrection morning. She was told not to do so. She had to let the Lord go to rise to the Father so that he could send out his Spirit on all humankind. And so must we. The vocation of evangelization calls on us to let go of the familiar and the comfortable in our relation to the Lord, to let the Lord rise and go to the Father to send out his Spirit on all humankind, no matter how frightening and unfamiliar that might seem to be.[57]

GC XVI recognized a danger in being too prescriptive when specifying Spiritan mission. Given the diversity of how the Spiritan apostolate is lived in different parts of the world a "catch all" definition remained elusive. This problem is addressed in *SRL* by recognizing the Vatican II principle of mission that "the responsibility for carrying on Christ's mission belongs in each place to the local church" (*SRL* 13) and by referring to what the church "is currently stressing in mission" (*SRL* 13.1): the universal mission expressed

---

56. Vincent Donovan, CSSp, author of the acclaimed *Christianity Rediscovered*, has written on *Evangelization and the Spiritan Rule of Life* (private circulation, USA Province Archives, Bethel Park, 13c-11-4).

57. Ibid.

locally; evangelization and the founding of new churches; empowerment of and dialogue with others; the inculturation of the gospel message in each local church. It would be for future general chapters to decide "important mission objectives" for their time with circumscriptions agreeing on "regional objectives" (*SRL* 26).

GC XVI solemnly declared the great commitments of Spiritan mission present in germ in the heart of des Places and coming to fruition in Libermann's writing. The Spiritan apostolate gives preference to being one with "those who have not yet heard the gospel message or who have scarcely heard it; those oppressed and most disadvantaged, as a group or as individuals; where the Church has difficulty in finding workers" (*SRL* 12). Spiritan mission is no longer understood geographically and first evangelization is expanded to embrace many newly emerging mission situations. Spiritan mission then was no longer seen as

> a going out from one's church of origin, for our mission exists in every place—and this is true too even for first evangelization. Our mission is a job that does not finish, must always be repeated, facing up all along to fresh problems. . . . When we look about us, we see first evangelization calling us to go everywhere: to the youth, with its special group culture; to the intellectual world, marked by modern thought and neo-paganism. The very rate of demographic increase surpasses our ability to evangelize. There are great masses of people untouched by the gospel—so very, very many situations that are a challenge to missionary initiative.[58]

Solidarity is a defining dimension of Spiritan mission. In the eighteen years since *CDD*, it was only through unity and solidarity expressive of the congregation's motto, *Cor Unum et Anima Una* (One Heart and One Soul) that Spiritans could meet the demands of the new mission era. Mission is about sharing life with the people to whom we are sent so that we can be "in solidarity with their joys and sorrows" (*SRL* 16.2). Spiritans are community builders wherever they find themselves. A simple lifestyle enables a "closeness to the poor" which "brings us to hear afresh the gospel that we are preaching" (*SRL* 24.1). Our communities provide the locus for "variety and complementarity" that enables mission (*SRL* 24.2) and welcome those who wish to share in that mission (*SRL* 24.3).

One of the challenges that faced GC XVI in giving definition to Spiritan mission was the fact that "mission theology evolved in function of a reality that is itself developing and mutating—(the life and times of humankind),

---

58. *Handbook for the Spiritan Rule of Life*, 25–26.

moreover theology develops both in how it is worded and what it deals with."[59] For example, the language of *missio Dei* is not used in *SRL*. In a commentary on this chapter, Gittins took issue with its title, "Our Mission," since he preferred to conceptualize Spiritan mission as a sharing in God's mission. He wanted to remind his confreres that God is the subject of mission. For Gittins, Jesus is the model missionary who did mission and models discipleship for all his followers in four ways: encounter with all kinds of people; being with and bringing people together in table fellowship; foot washing, the great symbol of loving reverential service; and boundary crossing which singled him out from the other rabbis of his time.[60] *SRL* worked from the understandings of mission current in the mid 1980s. It spoke in broad and inclusive terms consistent with future thinking on mission.

The understanding of a cosmic mission and the importance of the environment and the integrity of creation are topics for later mission discourse. For example, the Sacred Heart Missionary Fr. Diarmuid O' Murchu, recognizing the emerging paradigms for mission in the new millennium, could propose that "the Witness required in the name of mission is to the God who co-creates across the entire spectrum of creation, across time and history, forever inviting humans to collaborate in that global and cosmic process of birthing possibilities for new hope."[61] While such language is not found in *SRL*, it is not excluded from its broad and inclusive vision for Spiritan mission.

Community Life

The quality of Spiritan community life was considered in 1980 by GC XV. It resolved that the general council would "promote research on community life in the congregation and on its development in the church and in the world" (*SL* 96). The task was entrusted to the Research and Planning Service, established at the Generalate since 1983. In his report to GC XVI, Timmermans pointed out that a Community Life Commission had been set up by the general council in March 1984 with the task of developing a process for the renewal of community life in the congregation. He reported that a two-year plan in two phases had been implemented. The first was a

59. Ibid., 16.
60. https://www.youtube.com/watch?v=lOuCEU5Kccw. See the Spiritan Trans-Canada website YouTube series of reflections on *SRL* at https://www.youtube.com/user/SpiritansTransCanada. The title given in the 1985 draft text to chapter 2 was "The Spiritan Mission." For further development of these ideas see Gittins, *Way of Discipleship*.
61. O'Murchu, *Religious Life*, 133.

survey of 125 Spiritan communities throughout the world. The second was Farrelly's analysis of the survey's findings published in a report for GC XVI (the French version was available at the chapter).[62] The report contained practical principles for the renewal of community life and activities for implementing renewal in communities.[63]

GC XVI's deliberations on Spiritan community life were framed not only by the reality experienced but also by Vatican II's ecclesiology of communion. The general council's handbook to *SRL* commented on this.

> The church itself, and every church community, is more than the structures. It is shared experiencing of Christ's death and resurrection in a communion of solidarity, of prayer, of belief and of sharing. We find, if we look that these two ideas of "paschal mystery" and of "communion" as a single base for the kingdom have been woven into the texts of the rule that treat of our religious apostolic community way of living.[64]

There is an ecclesial dimension to the Spiritan community in that it is called to model Christian living in response to the inspiration of the first Christians, united in heart and soul (Acts 4:32). Like them, Spiritans were called to remain faithful to the teaching of the apostles, the brotherhood, the breaking of bread and to the prayers (Acts 2:42).

SRL envisaged each Spiritan community in dialogue with the world about it and with the congregation. It directed that communities were to meet regularly to discern God's will and organize fraternal life; to plan and evaluate their activities; and to deliberate in shared responsibility for the life of the community and its apostolic outreach (*SRL* 44). *SRL* understood authority in terms of a service of leadership and animation that maintained unity through consensus in decision making. All this is best achieved when there is mutual esteem and kindness, with each one working in a genuine spirit of co-responsibility (*SRL* 46–49). The transition from pre-Vatican II

---

62. Superior General's Report (1986) 81.

63. The manual, "Experiencing Community," was published in *Spiritans Today* 5 (1987). The issue is entitled *Spiritan Community*. Alphonse Gilbert in his introduction to the work says that "it contains three elements: sources, guidelines and instruments. The first part presents the results of research into sources which include our Spiritan tradition, contributions from the human sciences, and the theology of Vatican II. The guidelines follow from that; the third part contains a set of instruments, i.e., suggested methods for activities and experiences, to assist the process of putting the guidelines into effect. An effort is made to balance the pages of practice with those of theory. A survey in the congregation dating from 1984 throws light on the life of our communities." Ibid., 7.

64. *Handbook*, 29–30.

to post-Vatican II community living would take time. There were those who regretted the casting aside in the 1960s of what were for them, the three symbols of Spiritan life: the mortar board (education), the biretta (priesthood) and the pith helmet (missionary work) and suggested that these have not been replaced![65] *SRL* was the replacement, particularly with its template for apostolic community living. But for that to happen, practices that embodied expected patterns of behavior were needed in the congregation. Deep spiritual living was the condition necessary for dynamic encounter, dialogue, and discernment in community to empower mutual learning and support for creative and faithful mission.[66]

A familiar term throughout the congregation by which members refer to each other is *confrère*. It is not only a reminder of the congregation's beginnings in France, but, more importantly, of Poullart des Places bringing together under one roof a group of individuals who, through the working of the Holy Spirit, were formed into a community. "In our community, each and all are looked upon as confreres, received from the Lord" and each "one has gifts from which all draw benefit" (*SRL* 34). Libermann's last words are a constant challenge to Spiritans to live together in charity. *"Above all charity . . . charity above all . . . charity in Jesus Christ. Charity through Jesus Christ . . . charity in the name of Jesus Christ; fervor . . . charity . . . union in Jesus Christ. The spirt of sacrifice . . . "* (*SRL* 38). *Confrère* was surely a term of affection and endearment for Libermann for which he set practices to embody expected patterns of behavior. In his Provisional Rule of 1841, he devoted a chapter to "Rules of Conduct towards Others" which began with right conduct between confreres. "The conduct of our members among themselves must be that of children of the same family, that is, children of Jesus and Mary. We shall regard as done to our Lord himself all that we do to our confreres, and we shall do towards them what we would have done towards Jesus and his Blessed Mother."[67] Libermann's novice at Le Neuville, Louis Marie Barzer de Lannurien, faithfully transcribed the comments given by Libermann on this rule.

> We must look upon everything we do to our brethren as being done to God. This is not an exaggeration. It is our Lord himself who has said it. What you do to the least of his disciples he considers as done to himself. *A fortiori*, what is done to one of our

---

65. The mortar board, biretta, and pith helmet featured on the dust cover of an early edition of Koren's *Spiritans*, published in 1958.

66. Interview with Donald J. Nesti, CSSp, 4 November 2016. St. Thomas University, Houston, Texas, USA.

67. *Provisional Rule*, 217.

confreres, who is in a special manner consecrated to him, he considers as done to himself in a very special way.[68]

Libermann's thinking on how confreres were to relate to one another had developed when it came to his writing on the duties of members of the congregation toward each other in the *Règlements* (sect. 2, div. 1, ch. 3, art. I–XXI) of 1849. Daly, in his commentary, recognized this as "another fine chapter."

> He first gives the reasons for the unity of members of the congregation amongst themselves. We are one family because we have one faith. We have a certain way of loving each other in the name of Christ and in our work, we have the same objectives, apostolate, mission; we share the same means to attain these objectives—thus community and religious life form a way of living which is proper to us. We have the same models, Jesus, Mary, the apostles, and we share the same attraction for the Holy Spirit. Then Libermann gives two fundamental rules for living this unity: we should have unity of spirit and unity of heart: hence the motto of the congregation, *cor unum et anima una* (one heart and one soul).[69]

Here are two key emblems or symbols to express and sustain Spiritan community life. Each member is a confrere and all live together in community with one heart and one spirit.

Religious Life

The first set of rules written by Poullart des Places was for a community of poor students preparing to be priests, some of whom would become religious priests. The community and each member were consecrated to the Holy Spirit. They were not formally established as a religious community but all lived in community and they were poor. "The students (often enough the text of the Rules calls them the individuals) are not religious. They have small sums of money with which they can buy extra wine, pay for the laundering of personal linen, and have fixed any windows they may break. . . . The house furnishes the necessary food, clothing, and shoes for all."[70]

Libermann's congregation, the Missionaries of the Holy Heart of Mary, was primarily "a society of priests" which also had brothers as members

---

68. Ibid., 219.
69. Daly, *Spiritan Wellsprings*, 202.
70. Lécuyer, "On Re-reading Poullart des Places," 13.

who occupied themselves with the community's material needs.[71] They lived according to "the Spirit of religion which must be the soul of community life and the apostolate." The conditions at the time did not allow for the making of the three customary vows. However, individuals could have the consolation of making secret vows in the congregation but only "under the condition that the superior general of the congregation has the power to annul the vow when he judges it proper to do so."[72] It was not until 1855 that Spiritans made public religious vows.

SRL placed the chapter on religious life after the articulation of the Spiritan apostolic vocation lived in community. In keeping with the ecclesiology of Vatican II, it understood Spiritan religious life in the broader context of the People of God and the sacrament of baptism (SRL 50). "All the baptized in fact have this calling of disciple and the other one of witness of the kingdom of God."[73] Words were carefully chosen to value religious life for Spiritans as "gift," "free act," "joy," "discovery," "liberation," and "adoration." Religious consecration was not a burden to be carried but rather fully lived, the key that opened the door to true liberation in Christ that came from the discovery "that God's love can fulfil all our desire" (SRL 53). It is the Father who "gave us his Son, pledge of his love" (SRL 56) and who sends us out to preach a salvation that is a "gift from God" (SRL 11). Every facet of the calling that is ours, the way we share, the way we love, our practice of chastity in the single state (SRL 39, 60), the discernment that operates our obedience (SRL 76), the way our life of prayer resonates all through our apostolic activities (SRL 86), "all these are gifts from the Holy Spirit."[74]

The ideal presented in the poetry of SRL can be traced back to the concrete life experience of the first Spiritan community at Rue des Cordiers and later, from 1705 on, in the larger accommodation at Rue Neuve-Saint-Étienne in Paris. Poullart des Places provided the ideal for that community in his rules and regulations.

> They all live like poor men, eating at the same table and having the same food—of which a part is leftovers from the Jesuits. . . . But this poverty has to be accepted freely: everybody must always eat with thankfulness what is placed before him; they will be content with what is served to them and will not go looking

---

71. *Provisional Rule*, 71.

72. Ibid., 120–21. A note was added between article III which did not impose the taking of the three customary vows and article IV which allowed for the taking of secret vows. The note dated 21 March 1846, read: "Father Superior (Libermann), explaining that Rule, declared that henceforth making the vows would be obligatory."

73. *Handbook*, 39.

74. Ibid., 41.

for something better; they will never talk about what they like or don't like. They will neither praise nor criticize what they have had to eat. It is unworthy of a true Christian to think too much about all these things, to enjoy them or to complain about them, but for a religious or a cleric it is much more unmortified to fall into these faults. They will not ask the bursar to buy such or such a thing. . . . They will never complain that things are badly prepared, that such or such a seasoning is missing. . . . A man who is a little bit mortified, of the type we should have here, eats with indifference whatever he is given. He finds everything good when he recalls that his God quenched his thirst with gall and vinegar.[75]

The practice of religious life changes over time and "takes on different forms among different peoples or in various cultures" (*SRL* 55). And yet it is the one spirit of simplicity, hospitality, sharing, openness, and willingness to serve, that constitutes Spiritan living. It transcends all historical periods and cultures and is as truly lived and quickly recognized when experienced whether in Europe or Africa, the Americas, Asia, or Oceania.

Spiritan Prayer

The second draft (1984) of the constitutions that emerged from the Carcavelos meeting included a chapter on prayer. The general council, in presenting this draft for discussion asked the question: "should there be a special chapter on prayer, or not?" Feedback from confreres showed overall agreement with the inclusion. "The fact that a special chapter on prayer was written into the rule should be seen for what it is. It does not mean that prayer is a separate something, a reality off on its own, in our life. Neither does it imply that prayer is a set of exercises to be repeated in addition to or apart from our life in the apostolate."[76] It was pointed out that the first pronouncements on prayer in *SRL* were grounded in the person of Jesus "and the Holy Spirit who consecrates him" (*SRL* 83).

Fr. Bernard Kelly, CSSp, a capitulant at GC XVI, speaking about *SRL* many years later, asked, "Can it be that prayer is not principally about us? Prayer helps us to realize that our life is not our own. We are part of a grand

---

75. Lécuyer, "On Re-reading Poullart des Places," 14–15. Here Lécuyer compressed des Places's rules to provide an experience of the way community life was lived in that first Spiritan community. The rules, in order, are: 227, 58, 78, 105–6, 111–12, 66, 70, 72–78.

76. *Handbook*, 45.

design of God that is masterfully laid out in *SRL* 1."[77] Kelly goes on to say that "when we struggle to express our calling, our identity, we realize that it is not principally about us. Our Spiritan identity emerges from the life of the Trinity; from the love of God made human in Jesus; from our being caught up in the Spirit of mission. If we don't see our life as emerging from the life of the Trinity we are in danger of having an identity crisis; of not knowing who we are."[78]

GC XVI had two diverging approaches to the place of prayer in *SRL* and in the life of the Spiritan. One approach saw prayer as personal to each member and not to be regulated by the rule. The other wanted guidelines and practices for Spiritan prayer to be included in the rule. Both approaches were honored in the final text which spoke of Spiritan prayer in terms of "the Spirit of Christ who 'comes to help us in our weakness' (Rom 8:26), who leads us along missionary paths and who prays in the depth of our hearts. We are genuine apostles to the extent that, in our daily living, we entrust ourselves entirely to him" (*SRL* 85).

The confreres gathered in general chapter "valued times of quiet prayer but in a busy world they knew that prayer was frequently a casualty among claims for a place on the daily time-table."[79] That was why *SRL* laid down concrete obligations for each Spiritan to factor in times for prayer in the rhythm of life with annual retreats (*SRL* 96), the Eucharist which "commits us to a genuine solidarity with the poor" (*SRL* 93) and a "hotly debated" specification of a half an hour personal prayer each day (*SRL* 91). Some argued that this was already adequately covered in *SRL* 90 which called for "a substantial time for prayer, deeply united to Jesus."

Spiritan spirituality gives pride of place to Mary, the first disciple of Jesus. She "is our model of willing obedience and of faithfulness" (*SRL* 89). Here we draw close to the great mystery of the incarnation. Mary, as Mother, was venerated by des Places as he gathered his first members around the statue of *Notre Dame de Bonne Deliverance* in 1703. The statue is of mother with child. The shrine to our Lady, *Notre Dame des Victoires*, also depicts Mary as Mother. *Notre Dame des Victoires* is the shrine associated with Libermann's founding of the Holy Heart of Mary and his contact with Bishop Barron. It is a copy of this statue, placed in the niche over the high

---

77. Fr. Bernard Kelly, CSSp, well-known Libermann scholar, was a delegate to GC XVI as provincial of Trans-Canada. He was the "runner-up" to Fr. Haas in the election for superior general. His reflections on chapter 5 of *SRL* can be accessed at the Trans-Canada website, https://www.youtube.com/user/SpiritansTransCanada. Or on YouTube at https://www.youtube.com/watch?v=L0C9ZelNXeE.

78. Ibid.

79. Ibid.

altar, which catches the eye on entering the chapel of the Mother House in Paris. The same applies to the chapel of the first Spiritan work in Ireland at Blackrock College, Dublin.

Libermann, inspired by the Holy Spirit, decided to dedicate his new congregation to the Holy Heart of Mary. Its first lines, "All for the greater glory of our heavenly Father, in Jesus Christ, Our Lord, through his divine Spirit, and in union with the Holy Heart of Mary," are testimony to this.[80] SRL described Libermann's practical union as a "dynamic of prayer and activity that is at the heart of all Christian living, a 'practical union'—a habitual disposition of fidelity to the promptings of the Holy Spirit" (SRL 88)—that gives expression to a fundamental option committing the Spiritan to seek light and strength in the mystery of God. This fundamental option puts us at the disposal of the Holy Spirit in all things.

> It is apprenticeship in spiritual poverty, an ever more and more complete putting of our self into the hands of God. If we allow ourselves to be led and set free by the Spirit of God, as all who are truly poor do, then more and more frequently will the Lord come to stay with us. He will break into our life in moments of failure or depression, by entering into our joys and elations when we are with the poor who are "evangelizing" us. These are the moments when we shall experience this practical union, which is one of the joys of life as a missionary. It is a perfect state that we enter little by little, it is a destination in the direction of which we should steadfastly strive.[81]

Formation

SRL's chapter on formation defined the purpose of Spiritan formation as "the continual deepening of our 'apostolic life' (see SRL 3 above) under the influence of the Holy Spirit and in keeping with the spirit of our founders, our living tradition, and the present needs of the world" (SRL 100). The handbook pointed out that this chapter was not to be read in isolation but rather in the context of the entire rule as formation was centered upon the essential aspects of the Spiritan vocation: the following of Christ; intimate union with him as it was for his first disciples; living an apostolic lifestyle

---

80. Libermann had taken Le Vavasseur's suggestion of naming his society in honor of the Holy Cross. It was Tisserant who wanted the congregation named "The Holy Heart of Mary." Once Libermann sided with Tisserant, "the ink flowed." See Van Kaam, *Light to the Gentiles*, 94.

81. *Handbook*, 46.

that is "of Christ"; carrying on his mission in the church and being able to come together in "fraternal and religious life" (*SRL* 101).

Formation was recognized as an integrated process with various stages (*SRL* 102). The individual was valued, recognized as "a gift from God" that enriches the congregation (*SRL* 103). Formators accompany those in formation helping them "to respond freely under the influence of the Holy Spirit to the call addressed to them by Christ and to commit themselves to follow him in the Spiritan way of life" (*SRL* 104). The steps in this process of intellectual, religious, and missionary formation (to include missionary experience) were outlined (*SRL* 105–36): the discernment of vocation; the novitiate; first profession (made for three years which is renewable, but not to exceed nine years); perpetual profession, with candidates for the presbyterate making their perpetual profession before receiving the diaconate. Studies in initial formation were to be carried out with a view to mission and, for those called to ordained ministry, the requirements of church law were to be fulfilled (*SRL* 137–40). As the congregation was worldwide, "our formation prepares us both for living in a community and in a situation that is intercultural" (*SRL* 141).

GC XIII had recognized the importance of ongoing formation for all members (*CDD* 366–67). Developing this idea, GC XVI "emphasizes that ongoing formation is both a personal responsibility and a community one. What has to be acquired right from the beginning of formation is an attitude to personal development in every aspect of our calling."[82] This emphasis in *SRL* on the responsibility of the individual for his formation is a new departure in the congregation's legislation on formation and reflects the zeitgeist of the age with emphasis on the dignity of the individual human person as fashioned in the image and likeness of God. "In our day, there is a livelier awareness of the dignity of the human person. More and more people are claiming for man the possibility of acting in terms of his own choices and with full freedom and responsibility—not under pressure or constraint— while still being guided by knowledge of his duty."[83]

The task of attuning Spiritan language to that of Vatican II began with *CDD* in 1969 and was brought to a certain completion by *SRL* in 1986 with words such as "gift," "free act," "joy," "discovery," "liberation," and "adoration." While this vocabulary is different to Libermann's language of "detachment," "self-sacrifice," and "holy indifference," yet they both point to the same reality: union with God and service of neighbor. They are at one in acknowledging the human as the meeting point with the divine. The

---

82. Ibid., 57.
83. *Dignitatis humanae*, 1. Vatican II, Declaration on Religious Liberty.

time-honored wisdom of Tertullian remains valid, "*caro salutis est cardo*" (the flesh is the hinge of salvation).[84]

The Organization of the Congregation

SRL's extensive legislation on the organization of the congregation has been described as "the skeleton which holds the body together." The 121 articles in chapter 7 (from 148 to 269) provide the structure for "the accomplishment of our aims and objectives and even to providing a framework within which the prophetic voices may be heard."[85] The Carcavelos meeting had completed the preparation of a text entitled the *Norms for the Spiritan Community and Temporal Goods* for further development by the drafting committee and general council. In preparation for the third draft (1985) several questions had to be addressed. What were the titles and criteria of province, district, foundation, and apostolic group? What was the role of the enlarged general council? How was solidarity between circumscriptions to be coordinated? There were problems too, such as the canon law requirements of a "clerical institute." There were evolving problematic situations such as districts which were growing smaller and foundations growing bigger. How was the congregation to legislate for these developing situations?

The increasing complexity of the congregation as a decentralized worldwide, intercultural apostolic institute in the church was carefully addressed. Its status as "a clerical religious institute of pontifical right, comprising clerics and consecrated laymen" and its direct dependence on the Holy See's Congregation for Institutes of Consecrated Life and Societies of Apostolic Life was stated (*SRL* 148).

The congregation comprised individuals and communities assembled in circumscriptions "under the authority of the superior general and his council" (*SRL* 150). Different types of communities were described (*SRL* 151–54) and the service of authority defined for each one (*SRL* 155). The congregation was organized in circumscriptions which could be provinces or groups with their own superiors, councils, and bursars (*SRL* 156–74). Regulations for provincial and group chapters were given (*SRL* 175–83). Provision was made for circumscriptions sharing a geographical area or a common language to form "Unions of Circumscriptions" (*SRL* 184).

The general administration of the congregation was outlined by defining the roles and responsibilities of the superior general, general council, general bursar, secretary and procurator to the Holy See and services

---

84. Tertullian, *De resurrectione carnis* (Treatise on the Resurrection) 8, 2.
85. *Handbook*, 60.

provided by the Generalate were defined (*SRL* 185–210). Regulations concerning the general chapter including the election of the superior general and council followed (*SRL* 211–26 and appendix 1, *SRL* 235–244.3). Legislation was also written to cover the administration of material goods; the management of circumscriptions and of the general administration; and a process for the resolution of disputes and the making of contracts was outlined (*SRL* 227–234.4). Appendix 2 attended to the competencies of the various councils of the congregation (*SRL* 245–248.6). Appendix 3 dealt with absences or separations from the congregation (*SRL* 249–269). The general council's handbook concluded with a salutary admonition.

> Finally, it is to be hoped that the Rule of Life and this accompanying commentary may be of help to all of us in deepening our commitment to the Spiritan way of life and in becoming better servants of the kingdom. Both documents, as products of fallible human beings are flawed, but at this moment they are the best effort of the chapter and of the general council. Let us celebrate them together with one heart and one soul.[86]

4. New Beginnings

"If we stay on the road we are on," a Chinese proverb teaches, "we shall surely get where we are going!" Looking back over the years from GC XII (1962) to GC XVI (1986), it can be concluded that the journey was both difficult and life-giving for the congregation. The road of renewal and adaptation was long and hazardous, with many casualties along the way.[87] Numbers were decreasing but in the years between 1980 and 1986 Timmermans could report at GC XVI that a total of 183 first appointments were made.[88]

The capitulants of GC XVI departed from Chevilly-Larue on 2 August 1986 content at a job well done. They could look back and appreciate that the congregation had come a long way since 1962. The congregation had, at

---

86. *Handbook*, 65.

87. The superior general's report to GC XVI included statistics for membership of the congregation for the three years of general chapter, 1974, 1980, and 1986. There was a total membership of 4,222 in 1974; 3,806 in 1980, and 3,491 in 1986. The total decrease in membership from 1974 to 1986 was 731.

88. First appointments were made from the following provinces and foundations: Angola 3, Brazil 9, Central African Foundation 10, East African Foundation 25, England 4, France 15, Germany 6, Ireland 36, Holland 3, Nigeria 35, Poland 10, Portugal 2, Puerto Rico 1, Spain 3, Switzerland 5, Trinidad 1, Trans-Canada 1, USA East 6 and USA West 5.

last, a new rule providing "a road to apostolic holiness" for each individual member and the congregation as a whole. The congregation set out on this road in 1986 fortified by a new identity, a firm resolve for unity and solidarity, and a clear understanding of Spiritan mission.[89]

Spiritan Life

The Spiritan engagement with Vatican II between the election of Mgr. Lefebvre as superior general in 1962 and the 1968 extraordinary general chapter fell far short of what was required for the congregation's renewal. Some in the congregation even doubted its ability to survive in the context of radical change evident all about them and required by the spirit of Vatican II. There was need to articulate a new understanding of the religious apostolic life for Spiritans. The jourey of renewal from 1968 to 1986 set about that articulation, culminating in *SRL* which gave expression to the Spiritan following of Jesus Christ and the living of the gospel. Liturgical renewal and the restoration of the place of Scripture in liturgy was another fruit of renewal which gave shape to Spiritan spirituality. Spiritans came increasingly to recognize the personal need for study of Scripture as many had, in the old formation program, only acquired a passing knowledge of God's word.[90]

The old ways of praying with a manual of prayers was replaced by the Prayer of the Church and the rote lining up for a free side altar to "say Mass" was overtaken by community concelebrations of the Eucharist. Sr. Joan Chittister, OSB, a prophetic and controversial commentator on the renewal of religious life, described the prayer practices of women religious in the United States of the time before Vatican II as "more recitation than reflection, more quantity than quality, more a collection of formulas than a sharing of faith experiences or a response to the realities of the time."[91] Spiritans could identify their own experience of community and personal prayer before the Vatican II renewal with that description.

---

89. One Spiritan, Donald Nesti, spoke of *SRL* as "an inspired document." In a reflection on *SRL*, he said, "Having given many retreats to other congregations and having read their constitutions before the retreats, I can tell you that every time I come back to this document I am very happy that I am a Spiritan and share this vocation." The Benedictine, Fr. Henry O'Shea of Glenstal Abbey, conducting the Kimmage Manor Community retreat in June 2016 similarly praised *SRL* as an inspiring rule of life.

90. Significant to the transition from was American Spiritan, Lucien Deiss, CSSp, (1921–2007) a noted scripture scholar, liturgist, and composer of religious music. He brought the scriptures alive in compositions such as "All You Nations" and "Keep in Mind." Scripture studies became a priority in Spiritan formation.

91. Chittister, "Amazing Journey," 82.

The radical assertion of the Spiritan vocation as a call to first evangelization at GC XIII while appreciated as prophetic was also seen as divisive. The hoped-for increase in vocations with this radical reinterpretation did not materialize. A confusion of Spiritan identity undermined efforts at a renewal in life and mission. An elderly confrere is remembered saying at the time, "I took my vows under the black book [the old Rules and Constitutions]. Why do I have to change now?"[92] A human cost applied to the dramatic changes that were underway in the 1960s. Chittister pointed out at this time that although the candidates for traditional religious congregations were few, yet "young people go on giving their lives to great human endeavors year after year after year."[93] While religious spoke of a "vocations crisis," she countered that the real crisis was to discover the significance for religious life in the contemporary world. It was a crisis of spirituality.

> Religious life is at the brink of renewal and faced with two choices: personal comfort or prophetic presence, individual commitments or charismatic congregations. Neither choice is an easy one but one does not preclude the other. The problem for the future is no longer the structures of religious life. Structures have been bent to the breaking point. The problem for the future is the commitment of religious themselves.[94]

SRL provides the Spiritan congregation with the way to apostolic holiness. It is for each Spiritan and each Spiritan community in every age and place to recommit to the rule that gives life.

Spiritan Community

The election of Frans Timmermans in 1974 as superior general heralded twelve years of leadership to strengthen unity of purpose and of life in the congregation. *CDD* had decentralized the congregation's authority structure to provinces and districts. The general council's role was seen increasingly as one of animation, operating with moral rather than juridical authority. Timmermans embraced this role as a polyglot Dutchman of remarkable charm. With consummate patience, he, alongwith his general council members, traveled to all corners of the congregation meeting individual members in their place of mission. This had not been done before. The development of regional meetings between superiors opened new possibilities

---

92. Interview with Donald J. Nesti, CSSp, 4 November 2016.
93. Chittister, "Amazing Journey," 90.
94. Ibid.

for collaboration between circumscriptions. A deepening knowledge and interest in the Spiritan charism and of its founders was promoted with the founding of the Spiritan Studies Group that developed into the Spiritan Mission and Animation Centre. The need for communication was recognized with the general council understanding itself as the "Generalate team" and so modelling the unity it sought to promote throughout the congregation by its mode of operation. It also led congregation-wide discussion on topical missionary issues and informed the membership of new initiatives happening in its different parts.

When an organism is under threat it contracts, hardens its outward defenses, and turns in on itself for protection. The congregation's response to change, in some parts and at different times, took on this posture of self-protection. An organization's preoccupation with its own survival is the death knell of any organization. This is especially the case, for a religious institute consecrated to mission in the world. Initial, localized contractions occurred at that time in the congregation. Fr. Patrick J. Ryan, CSSp, carefully reported on the situation of the Irish province in the early 1970s. He provides an account of the internecine strife of the time which left scars and mortal wounds that were difficult to heal. The dissipation of energy on family quarrels detracted from constructive engagement with the world outside the congregation. This navel-gazing and destructive behavior was symptomatic of a malaise sapping life from individuals and communities. At that time, the drop-out rate of young professed members from the seminary at Kimmage alarmed many. The councilor for formation reported at the 1976 Irish Provincial Chapter that between 1965 and 1970, 39 percent of students between first profession and ordination had left the congregation.[95]

The Timmermans leadership was less inclined to embroil itself in local squabbles. Perhaps the hard work of putting out bush fires had already been attended to by Lécuyer and his council. Whatever the case, the Timmermans's initiative of the congregation taking on new missionary projects is well documented. He built on the solidarity that had grown both at the general chapters of 1974 and 1980 and the enlarged general council meetings of that period. Perhaps Timmermans recognized that the antidote to internal squabbling and what would give new life to the congregation was to both look beyond particular problems to survey the horizon of possibility for Spiritan mission and to forge the unity necessary to realize those possibilities.

---

95. See Ryan, *Kimmage Manor*, 127–34. The report pointed out that this was in keeping with the situation at the time in major missionary and diocesan seminaries throughout Ireland.

Spiritan Mission

Vatican II set in motion a positive appreciation of the working of the Holy Spirit in the world. The kingdom of God was no longer restricted to the boundaries of the visible church in the world. God's grace was at work everywhere. The way the church did business had changed and gave new energy and hope to religious and missionary institutes, such as the Spiritans. They followed the example of what the bishops had done at Vatican II, and broke out of what might be termed a "ghetto-like" mentality to address the world in a more open and confident way. The *Pastoral Constitution on the Church in the Modern World* was taken seriously. Quotations from it such as, "We must be aware of and understand the aspirations, the yearning and the often dramatic features of the world in which we live," and, "Our eagerness for dialogue, conducted with appropriate discretion and leading to truth by way of love alone, excludes nobody . . . ," gave impetus to positive engagement with the modern world.

The understanding of mission and the role of missionaries in the church developed in the 1970s and 1980s with a growing collaboration between institutes, e.g., the founding of SEDOS[96] and the Union of Superiors General. The reimagining of mission in terms of evangelization and working for justice and peace enabled a widening of the Spiritan missionary perspective from the narrow first evangelization position adopted by GC XIII. Irish Redemptorist and journalist, Fr. Tony Flannery, recalled the excitement for religious immediately following Vatican II.

> The impact of this on the imagination of religious is now hard to assess, but at the time it was immense. Suddenly, the world was our oyster. Closed doors, high walls, enclosures, were to be tolerated no longer. Why shut out this world with which we were called to enter into dialogue? How can we come to know it, to understand its yearnings and aspirations, if we are locked away from it? This was a dramatic change.[97]

For Spiritans, the Vatican II renewal process led to a new relationship of cohesion within the congregation and solidarity with new movements working for the integral development of peoples and justice and peace in the world. The congregation was also expanding in these years in Africa

---

96. SEDOS began during Vatican II with informal meetings of 7 missionary societies in Rome to exchange information and views on the mission of the church. A permanent secretariat was established in 1964 in the Divine Word Missionaries (SVD) College in Rome.

97. Flannery, *Death of Religious Life?* 30–31.

where former mission territories had become a source of vocations for the congregation.

The Initial Reception of *SRL*

T.S. Eliot's poem, *Little Gidding*, has the chastening lines: "We shall not cease from exploration, and the end of all our exploring will be to arrive at where we started and know the place for the first time."[98] Is there a sense that the congregation in 1986 had come full circle and returned to the charism of its founders and there recognized its true apostolic and evangelical identity in the light of Vatican II? Is the congregation a qualitatively different reality after its adaptation and renewal program than before?

A certain amount of cynicism was associated with the efforts made by leadership teams and chapters to bring about renewal in their congregations. A Spiritan quip about a capitulant returning from a chapter was sometimes heard. On being asked, "Tell us what happened?" the capitulant would respond, "It was an incommunicable experience!" Gerald Arbuckle SM, a cultural anthropologist, researched the value of general chapters during the *ad experimentum* period. "In the years immediately following Vatican II, religious congregations in a burst of euphoria and hope spent considerable time and energy preparing for, and then holding lengthy general and provincial chapters of renewal. Somehow, we thought, these chapters would give us the revitalized vision and reform we needed."[99]

Before Vatican II renewal the style of religious life lived by the Spiritans and the Marists was like other congregations. For Chittister, "to enter pre-Vatican II religious life was to take on a kind of time-capsule in which people too often lost touch with life, with issues of personal growth and with their own needs."[100] The glue of centralized authority, religious ritual, and rigorous discipline held the religious world together. The fall-out from the decentralization of authority, the relaxation of community regulation and personalization of the spiritual life was immense. The old symbols, authority structures and rituals that held everything together, had lost their meaning and were cast aside. The publication of *SRL* marked the end of the *ad experimentum* period with the acceptance of ways by which the life and

---

98. Quotation from *Four Quartets*, T. S. Eliot (New York: Harcourt, 1943).

99. Arbuckle, *Out of Chaos*, 151. Arbuckle offers a case study on his own congregation, the Fathers and Brothers of the Society of Mary (the Marists). A similar pattern to that of the Spiritan process of renewal can be detected.

100. Chittister, "Amazing Journey," 77.

mission of the congregation would be sustained. These can be summarized as:

- a deepening knowledge and love for the Spiritan charism,
- the building of bridges of communication within the congregation,
- the broad redefining of the Spiritan apostolate,
- the understanding of authority as service and
- a new emphasis on the dignity of each member and the spiritual renewal of each one.

Chapter 6 gives a Spiritan view of the world at *SRL* and beyond, told through the reports of the superior general to the general chapters from 1986 to 2004. A brief account is given for each of these general chapters and the enlarged general council meetings associated with them. Chapters 7–9 recount the congregation's progress along the trajectory set for it in *SRL* by a reading of the chapter documents (GC XVII–XIX) on the three distinctive and inter-connected themes constitutive of Spiritan life and mission: Spiritan mission, community, and religious life. Chapter 10 celebrates the rediscovery of the Spiritan charism and the renewal of Spiritan spirituality. It offers a hermeneutic of the Spiritan renewal process through the lens of Vatican II's interpretation and implementation and outlines the challenges that lie ahead.

Chapter 6

From *SRL* to GC XIX (1986–2004)

1. The Superiors General Reports (1992-2004)

THE "SPRINGBOARD" FOR FR. Pierre Schouver's report to the Dakar EGC in 1995 was a Libermann quotation which he would repeat in his report to GC XVIII of 1998 at Maynooth. It conveys the spirit by which the congregation should place itself in service of the gospel "as the world moves on."

> The trouble with the clergy in recent times, is that they have got stuck in the ideas of the past. The world moves on, and our enemies have adapted their armory to the spirit of the age while we are left way behind! Without abandoning the spirit of the gospel, we must get up to date, do good and combat evil in the world as it is today.[1]

Schouver's reports, as superior general, and that of his predecessor, Fr. Pierre Haas (1992), give a bird's eye view of the world as seen through the Spiritan lens as it strives to "do good and combat evil in the world as it is today." Haas, introducing his report in 1992, acknowledged the collaboration of his council in drawing it up.

> Each assistant, in function of his responsibilities within the council and of his familiarity with the congregation through visits or his correspondence, has contributed his part. In this we have kept faith with the method of working we have been using right through our six years. We have, as a team, gone over all

---

1. *N.D.* X (1848) 151.

the different contributions so as to arrive finally at this finished version.²

Haas also noted that, for the first time, the report was sent to capitulants several weeks before the chapter. His successor, Schouver, maintained this practice, sending his 1998 and 2004 reports two to three months before the chapter.

The time of general chapter is an occasion for the congregation to reflect seriously on its mission in the world. In the spirit of Vatican II, it must be "really and intimately in solidarity with the human race and with our history. From now on we can no longer think of mission without taking the time to look about at the world and without seeking to understand its deepest questioning."³ Situations need to be analyzed (*SRL* 14.1) and the life experience of those we are called to serve be respected and accepted in all its depth (*SRL* 16.2).

The Haas Report (1992)

Haas quoted an estimated projection of the world population in 2025 to be 8.2 billion people. His chief concern was the same one expressed by Timmermans in 1986: the uneven growth in world population with accelerated population growth in the less developed countries commensurate with a decreasing population in developed countries.⁴ How would this impact on the well-being of future generations, particularly the poor? The world divide between a "rich North" and a "poor South" was of significance to Spiritans who found themselves on both sides of this divide. Haas pointed out the 1991 membership statistics for the congregation which had 1,750 Spiritans living in the northern hemisphere and 1,570 Spiritans "living in the southern hemisphere, either working there or originally from it." He recognized in the membership of the general chapter a microcosm of this divided world and asked, "Do we not have a message to communicate that might get a hearing beyond our congregation? Do we not have a duty to help resolve the North-South divide by putting the reconciliation of humanity into living practice—between ourselves?"⁵

2. Superior General's Report (1992) 1.
3. Ibid.
4. The 1992 Superior General's Report contrasted the rate of population growth between sub-Saharan Africa which is projected to be 1.257 billion people to the twelve European community member states of 1992 with Switzerland, Austria and the Scandinavian countries projected to be 396 million people.
5. Ibid., 21.

The movement in world population was increasingly to the cities. Haas referred to the phenomenon of a "megalopolised world." He noted that demographic studies projected that by 2025, 78 percent of the population of industrialized countries would be urban dwellers, with 57 percent living in developing countries. He reflected on the phenomenon of the modern city.

> In the towns, people come together from everywhere. They live in an atmosphere of diversity, change and disorder. Complex social networks are created which favor the freedom of the individual, a freedom which can be very attractive. Some communities integrate very quickly, others retain their separate identity over a long period. . . . From the religious point of view, there is a multiplicity of cults from which people can choose the one that best answers their needs. . . . Many end up living not only without religion, but also without any moral standards or order. The ensuing frustration leads to conflicts and violence.[6]

The Catholic world population stood at 18 percent to 19 percent and the Muslim world population at 17 percent to 18 percent in 1992. "Other Christians are said to be 16 percent. Hinduism is in fourth place. It should be noted that 15 percent to 16 percent of the world's population say that they do not belong to any religious affiliation."[7] The report referred to some estimates showing that over the following ten years (from 1992 to 2002) Muslims would outnumber Catholics.

Haas quoted an estimate of migrants and refugees as fifty million and twenty million, respectively.[8] The problem was worsening. He maintained that 50 percent of all refugees and displaced persons were in Africa due to internal conflicts in Liberia, Chad, Sudan, and Somalia, with the possibility of further displacement in the event of the escalation in frontier disputes between Senegal and Mauritania. The report noted the discrimination suffered by refugees. "There are many reasons for this: their origin, not knowing the language of the country where they are living, unfamiliarity with their entitlements under the law, the discriminatory legislation of many states, the precarious sort of jobs they do, their religion, the way their culture and their identity are looked upon."[9]

---

6. Ibid., 4–5.

7. Ibid., 15.

8. These figures are quoted from a world congress on migration and refugees held in Rome by the Pontifical Council for the Pastoral Care of Migrants and Itinerants, from 30 September to 5 October 1991.

9. Superior General's Report (1992) 13.

Haas recognized a growing inequality between the "wealthy North" and "poor South" caused by world debt.

> During the last 30 years, the gap between the poor countries of the South and the rich countries of the North has widened dramatically. Today the 20 percent of world population that lives in the North is enjoying 80 percent of world GDP and the 80 percent living in the South, 20 percent. This imbalance is without any doubt going to get worse, except for a few countries in the North and South, to a point where it will create unsustainable tensions that will put world stability at risk.[10]

He proposed a historical perspective suggesting that it was the northern developed countries that were in debt to the developing countries of the southern hemisphere. His question was, perhaps, a rhetorical one, but important to ask, none the less. "If we took into account the real cost of the historic and present debt of the North to the South (added value for slavery, contribution to the war efforts in Europe, damages for colonialism, present underpayment for primary materials etc. . . .), would the South then really be the debtor . . . ?"[11]

GC XVII in 1992 was the first Spiritan general chapter to attend to environmental issues. It was incumbent on an international missionary congregation present on six continents to promote global collaboration. World problems required global solutions. Haas maintained that "the tragedy of a Bhopal or a Seveso or a Chernobyl demonstrates that there is no country that can look upon itself as sheltered from ecological catastrophe, even if it has no part directly in causing it."[12] Haas called on the chapter to take account of data showing a heating up of the atmosphere caused by human activity that endangered the ozone layer leading to the extinction of many species of plants and animals. This activity includes a proliferation of industrial waste, some of which is radioactive, proving dangerous for future generations. "At Paris in July 1989 a summit of the seven wealthiest countries—the G7—for the first time issued a declaration on the topic of the safeguarding of the atmosphere, underlining the urgency of getting this question sorted out before the future of mankind is compromised."[13]

Haas acknowledged a worldwide increase in religious movements, many of which could be classified as sects. They were feeding off the human desire for the transcendent evident among populations in industrialized

10. Ibid., 8.
11. Ibid., 11.
12. Ibid., 3.
13. Ibid., 4.

countries and those not yet industrialized. He quoted a statistic, that 57 percent of Americans prayed daily and 78 percent prayed once a week. Traditional religions, he reported, were also experiencing a rebirth. "The quest for a more complete meaning to human existence, for some transcendent quality, for a 'better-being' can create an opportunity for religion and for the Christian faith." But, he also asserted that "unfortunately this openness towards the transcendent, which could be a lever towards an authentic meeting with God, often stops at superstitious practices, in divination, in astrology or it takes refuge in the irrational."[14]

He reflected particularly on the plight of urban youth in developing countries. He recognized the importance of education in meeting their needs.

> In many countries of the southern hemisphere, young people drop out of school having failed their first examinations. At the same time the entire school system—imported from the North—no way prepares them for the social and economic needs of the country. The creation of alternate forms of schooling is becoming an urgent duty, as is the rescuing of those who have to live with failure in schooling.[15]

Haas went on to describe the terrible discrimination against the poorest children such as in São Paulo, Brazil where police officers employed by commercial companies murder street children to put an end to petty theft.

The Schouver Reports (1998, 2004)

Schouver, in his 1998 report to GC XVIII in Ireland, spoke out against attitudes in the developed world to the migration of people from less developed countries.

> The northern countries barricade themselves against certain categories of migrants, especially the poorest. They use strategies that are both simplistic and ineffective: the blocking of frontiers, and ever more annoying checks. Restrictive legislation and repressive measures against immigrants are on the increase. They are based on the supposed danger of an uncontrolled invasion which will threaten the rich and stable societies.[16]

---

14. Ibid., 17.
15. Ibid., 22.
16. Superior General's Report (1998) 13.

Economic strength generated cultural domination. Schouver maintained that the very continuity of minority cultures was in question. Young people were particularly affected. "They are going around in circles in Africa, unemployed, responsible for nothing, and therefore powerless. There is no place for them in the corridors of the world economic system, which alone moves money around and creates employment."[17]

In his 2004 report Schouver spoke of the human cost of migration to the cities.

> The towns attract people with the promise of light, beauty, riches and an enhanced social life. But many who in the past oriented their lives by their culture and religion now find themselves in huge cities with others who come from all over the place. Deprived of the ambience to which they were accustomed, they often feel a void within; they are in danger of going to places where they will find no real community or any meaning to their lives. The great cities also have areas of great poverty; new arrivals often end up in the outskirts, with families piled in together wherever they can find somewhere to live.[18]

Schouver was encouraged by the change in practice by some development NGO's that involved local people in decision-making to take account of the cultural context in which they operated. Six years later he acknowledged the emergence of civil society's reaction to the dominance of the global market, some of which is positive. "The G7 or G8 meetings are regularly confronted by enormous crowds of protestors, some of whom become violent. Such reactions point to the negative side of our globalized world; they are trying to indicate other ways of living together and of directing the world economy."[19]

The Schouver report (1998) was hopeful that the UN Conference on the Environment and Development held in Rio de Janeiro (the "Earth Summit") of 1992 and its declaration on the environment and development would deal with major ecological concerns: patterns of production and impact on the environment; alternative sources of energy and water as a finite resource. The report also counselled caution as "changes in policy regarding the management of natural resources and the protection of the environment are slow in coming, because such changes would be a move against free market forces."[20] This caution was justified and, in 2004, Schouver again re-

17. Ibid., 7.
18. Superior General's Report (2004) 5.
19. Ibid., 6.
20. Superior General's Report (1998) 12.

ported that nature continued to be threatened by the domination of market forces.

> The integrity of nature is under increasing threat. However, many groups, and even many countries, are aware of the degradation that the globalized world is causing. More and more movements are developing and policies are being integrated into the political program of some countries, e.g., Germany and many others, to counteract this destruction that the world economic system is producing.[21]

As the production of goods is globalized, human society is also globalized. This economic inspired globalization generates misery. "Globalization results in the domination of market forces at the level of the planet. It is the law of the strongest, not the right of individuals, which prevails. It conditions the lives of people without taking into account the totality of what it means to be human."[22] The apparently unstoppable demand for the production of consumer goods has a detrimental effect on the natural order of things. A bleak picture for the future was given as serious consequences for the environment were outlined.

> The consumption of meat calls for an increase in cattle production with the consequent deforestation of large areas to create more pasture. The trade in expensive timber brings in huge profits. The governments of developing countries, which are always looking for cash to pay off their debts, allow companies to destroy vast areas of forest to get hold of a few tree trunks. Illegal groups use the same methods of felling. Industrial growth is producing enormous amounts of waste, which not only defaces the countryside but also pollutes rivers and soil. Cars and lorries pollute the atmosphere. The nuclear power stations, which are sometimes constructed and maintained without sufficient supervision, can represent a threat to life in large areas.[23]

Schouver commented in 1998 on the place of religion in contemporary societies.

> Religion is no longer the basis [for society] but just one of many components. All our experiences develop in a context of human autonomy, a spirit of criticism, the liberty of the individual, and the mastery of nature. . . . Secularized society has allowed

---

21. Superior General's Report, (2004) 6.
22. Superior General's Report (1998) 10.
23. Ibid., 12.

people to free themselves from the yoke of tradition, with all the narrowness and oppression that it dragged along with it. It has raised their standard of living."[24]

In 2004, a different approach was taken. Schouver made secularization the top challenge facing the congregation's mission in the world. He noted that in France many parishes no longer had regular Sunday mass. The payment of the religious tax in Germany was greatly reduced. Cult was reported to be increasingly secularized and, in France, a militant secularism was attempting to remove all religious symbols from society. Atheism was well established in some former communist countries of Europe. In Africa, a type of secularization formed part of the response to the religious impositions of the past. In Latin America, the phenomenon of emotional and sometimes sectarian communities was also in evidence partly in reaction to an oppressive experience of church.[25]

Schouver recognized a general "disenchantment" of Western society resulting in a life experience increasingly divorced from the beauty of nature and from the affirming symbols and rituals of traditional society. "People feel as though they are imprisoned by a system; Parisians sum it all up in their saying '*métro, boulot, dodo*' (tube, work, sleep). . . . Out of their global experience they seek a meaning to life, a mutual support and solidarity that goes beyond purely economic considerations."[26] This search for meaning was an uphill one, as society was increasingly dominated by a media that kept people passive and manipulated public opinion. "We are in danger of being reduced to uninvolved spectators of the life of our world. The media can so easily encourage dependence, assimilation, and a climate of consumerism."[27]

Schouver however saw possibilities for gospel witness. There were "new signs of the times" grounded in a reawakening of the human spirit. This reawakening was expressed in the form of "people power" setting out to change the world. "There is an increased insistence on integrity and responsibility. . . . It is in this world on the move, with its good and its bad side,

---

24. Ibid., 1–2. In this Schouver was following the Haas Report (1992). Haas referred to Blessed Pope Paul VI's *Evangelii nuntiandi*, which spoke of secularization as an "effort in no way incompatible with faith or religion, to discover in creation, in each thing or each happening in the universe, the laws which regulate them with a certain autonomy."

25. Superior General's Report (2004) 2–3.

26. Superior General's Report (1998) 2.

27. Ibid., 16.

that we have been called to witness to the gospel, together and in collaboration with others, to the ends of the earth."[28]

2. General Chapters Following *SRL* (GC XVII–GC XIX)

Introduction

General chapters are moments when the entire congregation meets through representation to reflect, evaluate, and decide on the apostolic and religious vitality of the membership and its missionary activity. The post-Vatican II identity and mission of the congregation expressed in *SRL* is the point of reference for all decision-making in the congregation. As general chapters are charged with "protecting the patrimony of the institute" (Can. 631.1) so they look to *SRL*, the repository of the Spiritan patrimony, for direction and inspiration. "The general chapter is the supreme authority in the congregation" (*SRL* 211) with the responsibility "to check that the congregation has remained faithful to the mission that it has within the church" and to examine the financial state of the congregation (*SRL* 213). Enlarged general council meetings, although only consultative, are also significant in that they meet at least once between two ordinary general chapters to "check on the implementation of the decisions of the general chapter"; consider new means for achieving the congregation's objectives and strengthen collaboration between circumscriptions and with the general council (*SRL* 205.3).[29]

Successive general administrations have invested significant resources of time, personnel, and finance in the preparation for general chapters and in a follow-up animation of the membership presenting the orientations adopted by the chapter to the membership. *SRL* stipulates the convocation of a general chapter to be announced "at least one year before the opening day" (*SRL* 216.1) allowing sufficient time for the agenda to be drawn up in consultation with the circumscriptions (*SRL* 216.2/3). The general chapter, working within the constraints of canon law, is self-determining with the aim of promoting "the spiritual and apostolic vitality of the congregation and to ensure its unity in fidelity to its charism, for the better service of the church." For this to happen,

---

28. Superior General's Report (2004) 8.
29. A significant development in understanding of the role of the enlarged general council has taken place since it was first instituted at GC XIV. At that time its membership had a deliberative vote (*GA* 133) and met every two years (*GA* 137). The first enlarged general council meeting took place in 1976.

the members of the chapter enter into a process of discernment to learn how the Lord is calling the congregation today. It is a gathering where each member is attentive to the movement of the Spirit within, while listening also to what the Lord is saying through the other members as all seek to discern the direction to be taken in the coming years. The general chapter is an experience, a journey in faith that the members are called to undertake.[30]

General chapters were held every six years (*CDD* 157) since 1968.[31] The question of the length of the mandate of the superior general and the frequency of general chapters was considered at the Duquesne EGC in 2001. It was proposed to extend the time between chapters to eight or nine years. Accordingly, the superior general and council's mandate would be likewise extended, but not renewable. This proposal was put to GC XIX in 2004 and accepted.[32] It was agreed that with the increase in regional meetings and meetings of those engaged in similar specialized apostolates, general chapter and enlarged general council meetings could be less frequent and so reduce expense. It was also agreed that eight years would give time for the superior general and his council to gain a more complete knowledge of the complex reality of the congregation and contribute positively to that reality. A nonrenewable mandate ensured a turnover of personnel in leadership with fresh ideas.[33]

GC XVII (1992). Itaici, Brazil

The general chapter following the promulgation of *SRL* was the first to be held outside Europe. Apart from GC XIII in Rome, all others took place in Paris, France. GC XVI, while grateful to the French province for hosting general chapters in the past, decided that different venues should be arranged to better reflect the congregation's internationality. GC XVII was

30. McHenry, *General Chapters*, 55–56.

31. This was the practice up to 2004, with chapters held in 1974, 1980, 1986, 1992, 1998 and 2004. *CDD* stipulated that every ordinary chapter is elective with the superior general elected for six years. He could be reelected "as often as the chapter decides" (*CDD* 173) provided he secured two-thirds majority of the votes. This practice was adopted by *SRL* in 1986.

32. *SRL* was hence amended by a vote of 51 for the amendment with 19 against and 1 abstention. *Spiritan News* 153 (2004) 7.

33. Torre d'Aguilha (2004) 8.1. The length of provincial and district superiors' mandates was not similarly extended or the frequency of circumscription chapters altered.

held in Itaici, Brazil, to coincide with the five hundredth anniversary of the evangelization of Latin America.[34] *Spiritan News*,[35] reporting on the chapter interpreted the significance of its location some 70 kms from São Paulo in the "Vila Kostka" Center for Spirituality (a former Jesuit novitiate) as "removing ourselves from the center to the periphery was, ultimately, an invitation to each Spiritan to uproot, to up-anchor himself in a new approach to mission, to the respectful encounter with peoples and cultures and to acceptance of Spiritans of other origins."[36]

Twelve experiences of contemporary Spiritan mission were shared at Itaici: (1) dialogue in Pont-Praslin, Mauritius; (2) inculturation among the Huastec Indians, Mexico; (3) solidarity with the poor and oppressed, Haiti; (4) engagement with the Baka pygmies, Lomié, Cameroon; (5) a parish on mission, St. Laurent Du Maroni, Guyana; (6) in service of religious and ethnic minorities, Pakistan; (7) caring for disadvantaged youth, Auteuil, France; (8) birthing a new province, East Africa; (9) education by respectful intervention, Servol, Trinidad; (10) ecumenical option to evangelize with the Orthodox, Gamu Gofa, Ethiopia; (11) new life of service among youth and the homeless in an old province, England; (12) option for the poor and marginalized, São Paulo, Brazil.

Following the inductive method adopted by the Haas leadership during the previous six years, GC XVII engaged in an exercise of listening to the reality of Spiritan mission as experienced and lived in twelve different contexts. The symbolism of twelve "significant experiences" and "acts" situated the Itaici gathering within the apostolic church tradition. The introduction to the Itaici document refers to the assembly of believers gathered to listen to Paul and Barnabas (Acts 15:12). "As at Jerusalem, we tried to look at the full picture; the disappointments, the misunderstanding, even within our own family. And again, as at Jerusalem, we decided to use our lived

---

34. There were 115 participants: 77 capitulants and 38 functionaries. The capitulants, 9 were ex-officio (superior general, 6 assistants, the general bursar and general secretary), 31 delegates elected by the provinces; 26 elected by the districts and 11 elected by the foundations and groups. The 38 functionaries included 3 moderators, Frs. Jenkinson, Piat and de Verteuil (it will be remembered that Fr. Piat and Fr. De Verteuil also moderated the 1986 chapter) and 3 facilitators Frs. Headley, Regan and Schouver. Schouver also preached the opening retreat.

35. The *CSSp Newsletter*, addressed to all confreres in the congregation, and offered in French and English was prepared during GC XIII. The first issue is dated 31 March 1969 This tentative first step at mass communication in the congregation under Lécuyer became a central means for animation adopted by Timmermans and his council and those that would follow them. The newsletter (a stenciled production) was upgraded to printed form and entitled *Spiritan News* in March 1994.

36. *Spiritan News*, 93 (1992), supplement.

experience, with all its joys and sorrows, as the starting point in the search for the paths down which the Spirit might be calling us."[37]

In answer to the question, "What did we hear at Itaici?" the first part of the chapter document summarized the fruit of that hearing. The capitulants heard:

- much about listening and respect
- what inculturation meant from those who live it
- about dialogue in many different forms
- about justice and peace as a constitutive part of evangelization
- about community in the context of Spiritan mission
- of renewal in mission in the older parts of the congregation
- a call for an extension of Spiritan missionary activity in the Asiatic world
- about the role of education in the experiences shared.

All hearing requires a response. The Itaici capitulants discerned where the Spirit was leading the congregation. Part two of the chapter document summarized those responses. They provide the "anatomy of Spiritan mission today":

- "where we are weak, there we are strong"
- we are being led along the path of a greater openness to others
- consists far more in listening than in talking
- presumes a willingness to let the gospel take on different forms in different places
- the modern missionary can expect to be questioned
- we are being led along the paths of liberation
- the Spirit is leading us on the road to death and resurrection
- the Spirit is guiding us along the path of faith
- is about the renewal of the church
- the Spirit invites us to take the road of communion and solidarity.[38]

Vatican II spoke of the whole church as missionary and the local church as primarily responsible for mission. In that context Itaici deliberated on

37. Itaici (1992) 3–12.
38. Ibid., 13–25.

two realities in the organization of Spiritan mission that had already been discussed at the Arusha EGC and were in a state of becoming since GC XIII: new foundations/provinces, and, regionalization.

GC XVIII (1998). Maynooth, Ireland

Reflecting on the general chapter which was held at Maynooth from 12 July to 8 August 1998, the reelected superior general, Fr. Pierre Schouver, had this to say:

> The most impressive thing about the chapter was undoubtedly the unanimity of the delegates and invited guests who came from so many different corners of the world, from such different age groups, cultures, and skills. It was not so much what we achieved ourselves as what happened to us in an almost miraculous way. It was not difficult to believe that the Spirit of the Lord was at work amongst us. He was clearly leading each of us to the source from whence comes everything that is close to love. We had a concrete spiritual experience of our congregation: our mission, our life together, our collaboration with many different partners, and our sources of inspiration. We tried to discern and formulate this experience of the congregation so as to give an idea of the meaning and challenges it has for us.[39]

Schouver was reelected virtually unanimously and rapidly. Elections for the general council also went quickly, with five councilors elected on the first ballot. The councilors elected were: Frs. John Fogarty from Ireland, elected also as first assistant; Michael Onwuemelie from Nigeria, elected also as second assistant; Jean-Michel Jolibois, from France; Rogath Kimaryo, from Tanzania; Gabriel Mbilingi, from Angola and António Farias, from Portugal.[40]

Maynooth had four main themes: Spiritan mission, sources of inspiration, living together in community and collaborative ministry.[41] The chapter

---

39. *Spiritan News* 123 (1998).

40. Ibid. There were 72 capitulants (9 were ex-officio; there were 63 elected members representing forty-eight circumscriptions; and 3 lay associates who were invited). There were 32 functionaries consisting of 3 moderators (Frs. B. McLaughlin, P. Jubinville and A Torres Neiva); 16 translators (oral and written) using the three official languages of the congregation, (French, English and Portuguese); 8 secretaries (with Fr. P. Roe, over-all secretary to the chapter); there were 5 others: the general manager to the chapter, Fr. D. Kenny, assisted by a bursar, and confreres responsible for liturgy, the chapter retreat, and for information.

41. Preparations for Maynooth included a questionnaire from the general council

first identified the distinctive characteristics of Spiritan mission and then specified areas for its engagement. The training, the resources, and coordination needed to progress Spiritan mission were then deliberated upon.

GC XIX (2004). Torre d'Aguilha, Portugal

Torre d'Aguilha, near Lisbon, was a Spiritan seminary up to 1975, with accommodation for more than a hundred seminarians and was refurbished to function as a conference center. It became home to sixty-two capitulants and thirty-three functionaries from 20 June to 17 July 2004 for GC XIX, which elected Fr. Jean-Paul Hoch, present at the chapter as one of the three moderators (the others being Frs. Manuel Gonçalves and Eugene Uzukwu), as the new superior general on 8 August. The election of the general council followed. With Frs. John Kwofie, Ghana, and Eduardo Miranda, Portugal, elected first assistant and second assistant, respectively. Others elected were James McCloskey, USA/East; Christian Berton, France; Michael Onwuemelie, Nigeria, who had served on the previous administration; and John Kingston, Ireland.

The importance of the "team" approach to leadership in the congregation was highlighted in Fr. Hoch's first message as superior general. "Who am I, a moderator coming from the far-off island of Taiwan, to capture this 'spirit' [of the chapter]; how can I live by it myself and then help my brothers and sisters to live by it? It was only after the election of the general assistants and, from amongst them, the first and second assistants that peace was restored to my heart."[42] The outgoing general, Schouver, introducing his report, had set the theme: "Authentically living the Spiritan charism today." The outgoing administration had developed a pre-chapter document with this title giving three main headings for chapter deliberations: (1) rediscovering Spiritan apostolic life in the contemporary world; (2) the increasingly international membership of the congregation; (3) maintaining unity in diversity. Feedback to the document suggested a consensus "that it is time to

---

to the 69 circumscriptions. The joint replies from 49 of them, together with some individual replies were analyzed by an *ad hoc* committee. This process resulted in the prioritization for the chapter's agenda of "four strands of Spiritan life."

42. *Spiritan News* 153 (2004) 2. The report gave a biographical note on the new superior general. Jean-Paul Hoch was born in 1945. He made his profession in 1963 and completed a licence in philosophy in Rome in 1967. His formation included two years in Congo Brazzaville (1967–1969) and one year at Saverne. He was ordained in 1978 and served in the Central African Republic from 1978 to 1988. He was French provincial assistant from 1988 to 1991 and elected provincial in 1991. He was a member of the international team in Taiwan since 1998.

look more closely at some of the issues that affect significantly how we live the vision of Maynooth. Many have called for a bridging of the gap between our vision and our lived reality."[43]

The emphasis at GC XIX was on the evangelizers themselves. What are "the 'pebbles in our shoes' that frustrate and hold us back from following more faithfully the charisms of our founders?"[44] The response was recorded in eight parts: (1) spiritual renewal of the congregation; (2) life in international communities; (3) justice, peace, and the integrity of creation; (4) joys and challenges of new circumscriptions; (5) joys and challenges of older circumscriptions; (6) formation; (7) finance; (8) Spiritan rule of life. The inductive method, initiated at Itaici and employed at Maynooth, was the means used by Torre d'Aguilha in addressing these issues.

Fr. Hoch's introduction to the chapter documents noted the diversity of the capitulants, with thirty-seven being native Europeans and North American, twenty-two being native African, Latin American and Caribbean. He also welcomed the possibility for the involvement of all Spiritans in the chapter deliberations through the internet. This initiative of the outgoing administration, he said, "certainly needs to be developed in our congregation so that there will be a larger and better participation by all in making decisions that affect everybody."[45]

3. Enlarged General Council Meetings following *SRL*

EGC 4 (1989). Arusha, Tanzania

The first enlarged general council meeting following the promulgation of *SRL* was held in Africa, at Arusha, Tanzania. The meeting was an occasion to celebrate the transition from the East African Foundation, established in 1973, to the more stable reality of the East African Province (EAP) on 2

---

43. Torre d'Aguilha (2004) 17.

44. Ibid. This question was asked in light of the celebration of the Spiritan Year held from February 2002 (commemorating the one hundred and fiftieth anniversary of Libermann's death) and Pentecost 2003 (commemorating the three hundredth anniversary of the founding of the congregation by Poullart des Places).

45. Ibid., 11. This sentiment reiterated Schouver's invitation to all confreres to become involved in an "interactive chapter." He wrote: "a general chapter is an event that involves and challenges every single member, young and old, of our Spiritan family. While only a restricted number of elected delegates can take part in the proceedings, it is essential that the chapter discussions reflect the joys, the concerns, and the hopes of the entire congregation. The final orientations and decisions of the chapter should speak to each individual member in the reality of his Spiritan life and mission." *Spiritan News* 151 (2004) 4.

February 1989. Before the EGC meeting, Fr. Haas opened and blessed the new novitiate of the EAP dedicated to Claude Poullart des Places at Magamba, in the Usambara Mountains, 300 kms southeast of Arusha. During the EGC meeting, Fr. Renatus Assenga, CSSp, was ordained to the presbyterate by Bishop Dennis Durning, CSSp. He was the forty-fifth member of the new province to be ordained. The EGC event was a strong visual reminder that the demographic center of the congregation was shifting from Europe to Africa.

The *Spiritan News* of May–July 1989 recorded the reflection of one participant. "It is only now that I realize the profound change that is taking place in the congregation." The article continued, "When one considers that, of the 648 young men at present in formation, two-thirds are from Africa and three-quarters from the 'southern' hemisphere, it is not hard to imagine that in 20 years' time the congregation will be southern, and largely African, rather than northern."

EGC 5 (1995). Dakar, Senegal

As the Arusha EGC in 1989 prepared the way for GC XVII at Itaici in 1992, so also the Dakar EGC of 1995 set the course for the Maynooth preparations (GC XVIII). Dakar was chosen as the EGC location to remember and celebrate the one hundred and fiftieth anniversary of the arrival of Libermann's missionaries on the West Coast of Africa. The gathering assembled on 7 May 1995 with the general council joined by twenty-seven delegates and a staff of sixteen. The meeting agreed new missionary initiatives: to work with refugees in Guinea; an international group for Mozambique and a possible new project in Asia.

The meeting also approved a guide for Spiritan formation and reviewed the congregation's organization, providing guidelines for the evolution of its structures as groups (mostly international) were replacing the traditional districts, and regional collaboration between circumscriptions was on the increase. At global level, the northern provinces looked for a new dynamism through closer collaboration with the new circumscriptions of the south and welcoming confreres on mission from there.

One of the tasks of the Dakar EGC was to identify the spirit energizing Spiritans at that time. A reply to the pre-EGC Questionnaire suggested that the true spirit of the congregation was "to be at the service of the poor, to be open to where the Spirit is leading us, to read our tradition into the actuality of today's mission, to renew our community life and to live in mutual support of each other."[46] An EGC participant attested to a "feeling of solidarity" empowering participants to collaborate together in a shared Spiritan mission.

> It was the Holy Spirit who brought us together despite all our diversities. In our congregation, differences do not disappear; it is hardly surprising if everything does not end in one clear and distinct orientation. But one is nevertheless left with a feeling of solidarity, which unites in the same mission both the old and sick missionary and the one who still enjoys the vigor of youth in the front line of missionary engagement.[47]

EGC 6 (2001). Pittsburgh, USA

As with its predecessors, GC XVIII (2004) was prepared by a general consultation of the membership, the circumscriptions, and an enlarged general council meeting which was held in Pittsburgh, USA, in 2001. Duquesne University was the venue and the US East province the host for the sixth EGC held from 24 June to 7 July 2001. A community of fifty-four formed the EGC consisting of the 8 members of the general council (the superior general, six councilors and the bursar general), 26 representatives from Europe; North America 6 and the Caribbean 3; French West Indies 1; South America 2; Northwest Africa 1; Central Africa 2; West Africa 4; Angola 1; East Africa 2; Southern Africa 1; Indian Ocean 1; Asia 1; and Oceania 1. Seven young students in formation were invited to participate, as formation and first appointments were topics under discussion.[48]

Regional coordinators of the History and Anniversaries Commission were also invited to join Fr. Christian de Mare, CSSp, (the Generalate coordinator) and report on their meeting held in Rome from 18 to 25 January 2001. These were Frs. Jose Altevir da Silva (Latin America), Bernard Ducol (Europe) and Casimir Nyaki (East Africa). One representative of the lay associates, Marie Reine Guilmette (Canada) was invited and two representatives from Vietnam, along with twelve functionaries made up the number involved in EGC 6.

46. *I/D* 52 (1995) 9.
47. Ibid., 9–10.
48. The seven students were: Benedict Iheagwara (Nigeria—W. African Region) who made a presentation to the EGC on behalf of the group; Hugo Castillo Salinas (Mexico—N. American/Caribbean); David Mwaura Thuku (EAP—East African Region); Yvon Edward (France—Europe Region); Leonardo da Silva Costa (South America Region); Alain Boubag (Central Africa Region) and Zacarias Camulele (Angola Region).

The choice of location was symbolic. Duquesne, a university of the congregation associated with formation since its foundation in 1878, provided the setting for a meeting to address "formation in relation to our mission today; interdependence in our congregation today (along with the collaboration and solidarity that this demands); the inspiration that we receive today from our founder and our history."[49] The general council gave a report in *I/D* 58 (December 2001) on the meeting. The following aspects of formation were discussed: relationships (based on mutual confidence, trust, transparency, freedom, and responsibility); the length of the formation program; formation for Spiritan spirituality; and, the ministry of formation.

---

49. *Spiritan News* 138 (2001) 1.

Chapter 7

Spiritan Mission

1. The Ecclesial Context for Spiritan Mission since *SRL*
Redemptoris missio

IN 1990, CELEBRATING THE twenty-fifth anniversary of *Ad gentes*, Pope St. John Paul II acknowledged the role of mission institutes in the church's missionary work. His encyclical, *Redemptoris missio*, pointed to the demographic change that had taken place in traditional mission institutes which benefited from a flourishing of vocations and new life in the former mission territories to which they first brought the good news and established the church. *Redemptoris missio*, with a strong focus on mission *ad gentes*, had the promotion of missionary vocations as one of its main objectives.[1]

> The special vocation of missionaries "for life" retains all its validity: it is the model of the church's missionary commitment, which always stands in need of radical and total self-giving, of new and bold endeavours. Therefore, the men and women missionaries who have devoted their whole lives to bearing witness to the risen Lord among the nations must not allow themselves to be daunted by doubts, misunderstanding, rejection or persecution. They should revive the grace of their specific charism and courageously press on, preferring—in a spirit of faith, obedience, and communion with their pastors—to seek the lowliest and most demanding places. (*RM* 66)

Historically, missionary institutes came into being in churches located in traditionally Christian countries, and utilized by *Propaganda Fide* for the

---

1. Zago, "Commentary," 71.

spread of the faith and the founding of new churches. In the new missionary era these institutes were receiving more and more candidates from the young churches they founded. This validated the continuing relevance of these institutes. They remain necessary, not only for missionary activity *ad gentes*, in keeping with their tradition, but also for stirring up missionary fervor both in the churches of traditionally Christian countries and in the younger churches.

Redemptoris missio also addressed the relationship of the church with other religions and the proclamation of the gospel. Missionary activity proclaimed the mystery of Christ (*RM* 44) in a dialogical way by respecting the freedom of the human person (*RM* 7, 35, 39, 46), cultures (*RM* 24, 34, 37, 53), and religions (*RM* 5, 9–11, 28, 46, 55, 91). "Preaching constitutes the church's first and fundamental way of serving the coming of the kingdom in individuals and in human society (*RM* 20, 31, 34, 40, 44–47, 55, 58, and 83)."[2] The Pontifical Council for Inter-Religious Dialogue and the Congregation for the Evangelization of Peoples published *Dialogue and Proclamation* shortly after *Redemptoris missio*. As the encyclical commemorated Vatican II's *Ad gentes*, this document celebrated twenty-five years since Vatican II's *Nostra aetate*. While the encyclical had the promotion of missionary evangelization as its purpose, *Dialogue and Proclamation* set out to show that interreligious dialogue and the proclamation of the gospel were distinct, yet related elements of the evangelizing mission of the church. The church fosters interreligious dialogue through proclamation as it "aims at guiding people to explicit knowledge of what God has done for all men and women in Jesus Christ, and at inviting them to become disciples of Jesus through becoming members of the church."[3] In this it reiterated Vatican II's teaching (*UR* 3, *AG* 7) that dialogue "should be conducted and implemented with the conviction that the church is the ordinary means of salvation and that she alone possesses the fullness of the means of salvation" (*RM* 55). The *magisterium* position was that dialogue and proclamation were complementary and no necessary conflict existed between proclaiming Christ and engaging in interreligious dialogue (*RM* 55).

The encyclical sought to uphold the Catholic Church's positive appreciation for other religions and cultures as expressed at the Pilgrimage of Peace in Assisi when the pope met with leaders of different churches and religions and spoke of being with them on "a fraternal journey in which

---

2. Ibid., 87

3. *Dialogue and Proclamation: Reflections and Orientations on Interreligious Dialogue and the Proclamation of the Gospel of Jesus Christ* (1991) 81. See Dupuis, "Theological Commentary," 120.

we accompany one another toward the transcendental goal."[4] It also upheld that the church is the sacrament of salvation for all humanity (*RM* 20). Gittins interpreted this as an identification of the church with the kingdom and as problematic for genuine dialogue. "We Christians should, of course, remember the treasure we hold and not treat our faith disrespectfully. But we may also need to be reminded of the creative tension that will obtain between openness to dialogue and respect for our own heritage."[5]

Spiritans approached this creative tension guided by the spirit of Vatican II which in *Gaudium et spes* acknowledged the working of God's grace in "all men of good will in whose hearts grace works in an unseen way" (*GS* 22). In the great variety of situations of mission in which they have found themselves since the 1960s and the new challenges facing them both in relation to their mission and their life as members of an international congregation, Spiritans, in service of the kingdom of heaven, demonstrated the ability of the householder in the gospel who could "bring out of his treasure what is new and what is old" (Matt 13:52).

The New Evangelization

Pope St. John Paul II first used the phrase "new evangelization" shortly after his election when he traveled to Poland in 1979. His focus seemed firmly fixed on the "older" churches where membership and practice was in decline and there was a drop in religious vocations.[6] The Spiritan family recognized that the "evangelizing impulse" of Vatican II demanded a new missionary impetus. As Congar pointed out, the teachings of previous reforming church councils were promoted and sustained by the dominant apostolic movements of their time—the Fourth Lateran Council (1215) by the Franciscans and the Dominicans; the Council of Trent (1546–1563) by the Jesuits. Similarly, Vatican II needed its advocates. Missionary congregations in the post-Vatican II period, identified by the pope as a time of "new evangelization," were called upon by the church to fulfill the missionary mandate given by the Risen Lord, "Make disciples of all nations!" (Matt 28:19).

---

4. Quoted in Zago, "Commentary," 79. The Assisi Meeting of the leaders of the world's religions was hosted by Pope St. John Paul II in 1986.

5. Gittins, "Missionary's Misgivings," 221.

6. The Center for Applied Research in the Apostolate (CARA) estimated a 41 percent weekly Mass attendance of Catholics in the USA in 1980. The estimate for 1965 was 55 percent (Gallup estimates). A 1993 study of religious orders in the USA reported a drop of nearly 43 percent in the membership of brothers and sisters' congregations and 18 percent in clerical religious congregations. See Nygren, *Future of Religious Orders*, 142.

2. Organization for Spiritan Mission

Young Provinces and Foundations

A working paper entitled "Young Provinces and Foundations," with a focus on the transition from foundations to provinces, was presented at the Arusha EGC in 1989 by two general councilors, Frs. Okoye and Wiehe. This was a pressing matter for consideration as in Angola three districts had formed the province of Angola; one of Brazil's six districts (Brazil South) would become a province on 2 February 1990; Nigeria had a province and two districts and the area covered by the East African province had three districts. There were new foundations in Puerto Rico, Central Africa, West Africa, Southern Africa, and the Indian Ocean. "The relations between districts and new provinces were discussed at length, as well as the criteria for becoming a province, the formation needs of the young provinces and foundation, and the making of first appointments."[7]

New foundations and provinces gave expression to the missionary character of their local churches. It was important to resource these. But what about going on mission outside one's own culture and country? A balance was needed between sending members to mission *ad extra* while keeping others "at home" to build up a home base.

> All Spiritans are for mission—difficult and urgent pastoral situations, the poor and oppressed, especially transcultural mission. Some foundations have thus sent most of their members to other countries and cultures. On the other hand, vocations often grow because there are indigenous members to identify with, the work itself of vocations and formation requires some indigenous input as well as the setting up of a self-reliant network for the care of missionaries and mission projects, the sick and aged. ... For these necessary works, foundations retain some of their members or recall some after only a short period on mission. The Arusha EGC considered that tension would diminish if the principle were established that in normal circumstances first appointments would last for at least three years. Agreement of the general council and of the two superiors concerned would

---

7. *Spiritan News* 77 (1989) 5. The transition from "foundation" to "province" was quite a rapid affair. This contrasts with the sixty-two years it took for the Irish Spiritan communities (which began in 1859) to be formally declared a province on 21 January 1921. Perhaps the establishment of the Irish province in 1921 was prompted by the anticipated declaration of an Irish Free State toward the end of that year (6 December 1921).

be required to recall or transfer one on first appointment before the three years expired.[8]

The superior general's report to GC XVII at Itaici in 1992 proposed a set of criteria for the establishment of a province within the congregation. It should have between fifteen and thirty members with perpetual vows; enough "native-born" formators; personnel for the necessary administration; two-thirds of the "native-born" members are in favor; has a mission program outside of its own area; can meet at least 50 percent of its current expenses; has the agreement of the neighboring circumscriptions; and its statutes are clearly expressed. Recognizing that some flexibility could be applied in the interpretation of these criteria, the chapter accepted them. It also called on new provinces to have the long-term goal of financial independence with the congregation's *Cor Unum* fund helping them to achieve this according to its means.[9]

Haas in his GC XVII report asked that the congregation with its multicultural and ethnic membership witness to the possibility of people from different cultures and ethnicities living and working together as brothers in the One Lord. As Blessed Pope Paul VI challenged in *Evangelii nuntiandi*, the evangelizer must first be evangelized. The chapter agreed. "In a world where ethnic strife and discord are all too prevalent, we feel it important as missionaries to give a Christian witness of unity and interracial harmony. For this reason, we strongly encourage maximum collaboration between districts and foundations and even fusion, as in the East African Province, Angola, and Brazil."[10]

---

8. *I/D* 45 (1989) 2.

9. Financial solidarity within the congregation was required to support the new provinces. The General Bursar's Report at the Arusha EGC (1989) acknowledged the gift of the German province for the establishment of a Formation Fund from the sale of one of its formation houses. The interest from the capital invested was used for the construction of the Spiritan International School of Theology in Nigeria (SIST) and the novitiate and house of philosophy at Ejisu, Ghana. In 1989, the *Cor Unum* fund distributed a total of $943.176. Over 60 percent of this went to the foundations and new provinces which fell far short of what was needed. It was reported that no foundation has a capital fund and only a few had any form of insurance for confreres. A good response was made to the general council's call for the older provinces to make 5 percent of their reserves available to meet the costs of establishing the foundations and new provinces.

10. Itaici (1992) 89.

Collaboration in Spiritan Mission

GC XVII quickly recognized that the missionary agenda was greatly influenced by the world in which the missionary lived and was called to serve. Spiritans live and work in "many worlds" to which they seek to respond. The quality of the response is much better when working collaboratively within a region. Regionalization developed from the need to pool resources and to share ideas on issues of common concern. Typically, regional collaboration developed to establish the congregation and provide formation. The result was a foundation for which some circumscriptions had responsibility. This process developed organically as needs arose and benefited from animation to stimulate solidarity, encourage creativity and foster cooperation rather than the establishment of any new set of structures.[11]

The success of the congregation's projects required solidarity among its constituent parts: general council, provinces, districts, foundations, and groups. With decentralized in place since 1969, this could only be achieved through collaboration and mutual support. "More and more we feel the need for channels of communication and exchange. We could be mutually enriched through this diversity, strengthened in our apostolic commitment and in our Spiritan life at the service of this commitment to provide mutual help in combined apostolic projects."[12] Itaici acknowledged the importance of collaboration at congregation level and echoed the rule of life. "Our mission is always that of the congregation, recognized as such through a process of discernment and accepted in obedience in accord with the rule of life" (*SRL* 22). Regions then were expected to interconnect, to cross their own boundaries "and join in solidarity at the level of the congregation worldwide, under the responsibility of the general council. International meetings, promoted by the general council, are to be further encouraged."[13]

Solidarity for mission developed both within the congregation and with other missionary institutes in the 1990s. The European Centre for Co-operation and Development (CSECD) was founded in Belgium in 1997 to assist with the development of the foundations and new provinces. Portuguese Spiritan Fr. Firmino Cachada was the first director. He also directed another organization for Spiritan solidarity, the Program of European

---

11. The congregation's Planning Service conducted a survey amongst 16 religious congregations and their structures for regionalization. A report was given to the Arusha EGC outlining different models. One contrasting model had general councilors as regional superiors residing in the region but traveling regularly to Rome for general council meetings.

12. Superior General's Report (1992) 115.

13. Itaici (1992) 95.

Spiritan Solidarity (CESS) which was established as "a way of coordinating financial aid which each European province can engage in, over and above its participation in the *Cor Unum* fund for the benefit of circumscriptions from the South which make an express request for this."[14] CSECD is also known as "Kibanda."[15] Kibanda has as its goal the assistance of Spiritans in need of funding for development projects in their missions. The office is strategically based in Brussels to access European Union funding. The expertise acquired by the office is availed of by many confreres enabling them to successfully apply to appropriate funding organizations with the required documentation. Irish Spiritan Fr. Brendan Smyth was appointed director of CESS and Kibanda/CSECD in 2005.

Solidarity with other mission institutes, particularly for the promotion of justice, is a feature of Spiritan mission since *SRL*. Fr. John Skinnader, CSSp, Generalate Justice and Peace Coordinator, reported to GC XVIII that there was "more and more collaboration in all areas related to social justice." Because of this he called for a "strengthening of the networking that has already begun among congregations and lay groups."[16] Spiritans joined with forty-seven other missionary societies and congregations in 1988 and established the Africa/Europe Faith and Justice Network (AEFJN), "to promote economic justice between the European Union and Sub-Saharan Africa so that the poor of Africa may look forward to a better future."[17] AEFJN directs its efforts toward bringing about a more equitable and just relationship between the peoples of Africa and Europe. Fr. Schouver in his 2004 report affirmed the participation of confreres in the Swiss and French provinces in working for JPIC within the larger faith-based international network provided by AEFJN in their respective countries.[18]

The Spiritans collaborate with eleven other missionary congregations in Vivat International, an organization founded by the Sisters Servants of the Holy Spirit (SSpS) and the Society of the Divine Word (SVD) in November 2000. The Spiritans became permanent members in January 2009. Vivat International is a non-governmental organization (NGO) with consultative status at the United Nations. It is committed to serving the global community by bringing the spiritual and ethical values of the member congregations to the United Nations and other international organizations.

---

14. Superior General's Report (2004) 66.

15. A Swahili word which means "little workshop" or "shelter without walls" and used as a place of meeting in Tanzanian villages.

16. Maynooth (1998) section 1.5.

17. See AEFJN website, http://aefjn.org/en/home/.

18. Superior General's Report (2004) 78, 81.

3. Dialogue and Inculturation in Spiritan Mission

Dialogue

GC XVII (Itaici, 1992), the chapter of listening and of dialogue, considered "three kinds of dialogue": interfaith dialogue, dialogue with other Christian churches, and dialogue within the Catholic Church. The considerations were in response to the significant experiences that began the chapter event and gave direction to its deliberations.

> Mission is dialogue, a word that is so full of meaning and implications for action and attitudes. It breaks down barriers of ignorance, indifference, self-satisfaction, and egoism. Our confreres, who are led along this path by the Holy Spirit, can no longer live as if Hinduism, Islam, African religions, and other forms of Christianity do not exist or are irrelevant to their personal vocation. And being swept along by the dynamism of this dialogue, they will also want to apply it within our own church.[19]

Dialogue within the Catholic Church was required by Spiritans committed to a *nouvelle image* (new image) for the parish of St. Laurent in French Guyana where they served. They diagnosed their parish as being "a little too introverted, cut off from the great generality of baptized persons and too little open to other groups (immigrants, Amerindians and Afro-Americans) who live near the town."[20]

Dialogue with other Christian traditions and churches was prompted by contemporary Spiritan experience of close collaboration with Orthodox clergy and laity in Ethiopia. Rather than "going it alone" to evangelize the Hamar nomads, they opted to form a joint first evangelization program with the Orthodox bishop, Abuna Zakarias. In this the Spiritan group of five Irish and one French, were keeping faith with Vatican II's esteem for the Orthodox churches as "sister churches" whose "entire heritage . . . belongs to the full catholic and apostolic character of the church" (*UR* 17). The joint project resulted in the establishment of three Orthodox parishes. In his sharing at Itaici, Fr. Brian O'Toole said that the Congregation for the Evangelization of Peoples (*Propaganda Fide*) was opposed to this ecumenical experiment. They wanted the Spiritans in Ethiopia to work independently of the Orthodox Church and to set up new Roman Catholic communities. He commented that "this is a missionary approach that returns to the 'only the flock of St. Peter is the Church' ecclesiology, and does not admit that the

---

19. Itaici (1992) 17.
20. Ibid., 46.

Orthodox Church is the traditional expression of the Church of Christ in Ethiopia."[21] The chapter voted a declaration of support for the ecumenical approach of the Spiritan group in Gamu-Gofa, Ethiopia.

Spiritans in Mauritius continued Laval's legacy of engaging with all its citizens through inter-religious dialogue. The population of 580,000 on this small island nation in the Indian Ocean was multireligious, with 32 percent Christian, 50.6 percent Hindu, and 16.3 percent Muslim, which suggested the need for dialogue between neighbors. Finding the way to achieve this was not easy. The initiative to set up a center for dialogue between the religions, the Pont-Praslin Reception Centre, encountered many difficulties. "Very few Christians were ready for such an experiment and our Hindu and Muslim friends were very hesitant." Undeterred, in 1987, the group decided to offer introductory sessions to all-comers on the various religions and cultures of the island. From this initiative, Fr. Raymond Zimmerman, CSSp, reported that a strong team of some thirty members was in place to run the center. In addition, some of these wished "to consecrate themselves more definitively to the service of the mission and felt the need for a closer union between themselves, the better to perform their mission."[22] He noted that this group was seeking a closer association with the Spiritans and was in the process of writing its own rule of life.

The Spiritan presence in Pakistan since 1977 was a beginning for the congregation in Asia. Recognized by Pope St. John Paul II as a missionary priority, "*ad gentes*," for the Catholic Church (*RM* 37), Asia required greater attention from the congregation. Fr. Haas, in his report, asked: "Is the Spirit not moving us to 'enlarge the place of our tent' (Isa 54:2) and to commit ourselves resolutely down the road towards opening a new mission in Asia?"[23] Itaici answered in the affirmative.

> Asia contains the majority of the world's poor and its non-Christians and it is the home of all the great world religions. As yet the message of the gospel has scarcely found a home there. These facts cannot simply be overlooked by an international missionary congregation. Hence the plea that the congregation should consider another initiative in Asia. The ultimate aim of this initiative would be to contribute to making the Asian church more missionary and self-evangelizing.[24]

---

21. Ibid., 62.
22. Ibid., 30.
23. Superior General's Report (1992) 113–14.
24. Itaici (1992) 12.

Inculturation

Poullart des Places not only helped poor seminarians with alms, but entered their world, became one with them and shared in their life. He renounced a comfortable life with good career opportunities, preferring to live with the poor. Spiritans strive to continue this countercultural witness by lifestyles in solidarity with the poor in society. "Our closeness to the poor brings us to hear afresh the gospel that we are preaching. It becomes an unceasing summons to conversion and an invitation to adopt a simple style of life" (*SRL* 24.1).

GC XVII acknowledged and celebrated instances of Spiritans seeking to incarnate the gospel within different contexts. The first beatified member of the congregation, Fr. Jacques Laval, was proposed as a model of inculturation. He was one with the Mauritian people through his service and love of them. "He made a point of always sitting with his door wide open to the street so that people could come and go as they wished and feel perfectly at home and welcomed."[25] American Spiritan Fr. Vincent Donovan championed the principle of inculturation in more recent times. His letters, addressed to "relatives and friends" who supported his missionary work in Tanzania from 1957 to 1973, describe his journey into the life and culture of the peoples he had come to evangelize and which inspired his acclaimed book *Christianity Rediscovered*.[26] Donovan came to understand that "a missionary's primary job is to bring the Christian message."[27] He maintained that if the missionary was successful in this, then the church could be established. In a letter dated April 1969 he described his engagement with four villages of the Sonjo people (a traditional people living in the Maasai region of northwest Tanzania), each with a unique identity, and hence, requiring a particular evangelical approach. "Each community seems to have a different character, a different personality, a different face—differences which you would normally associate only with individuals."[28]

---

25. Ibid., 4. Inculturation was considered at a conference on first evangelization held at Chevilly-Larue in November 1991. One of the meeting's conclusions was that a long period of living with the cultural group in question was a prerequisite to understanding and appreciating the culture. The engagement of missionaries, thus inculturated, can help those they are with to discover the gospel and to identify for themselves "those elements of their religion and of their traditions which can find fulfilment in Christianity and those which are negative, which stand in need of salvation, of being liberated by the good news" (Superior General's Report 1992, 122).

26. Bowen, ed., *Missionary Letters of Vincent Donovan*.

27. Ibid., 180.

28. Ibid., 141.

One educationalist recognized a Spiritan pedagogy at work in Donovan's approach to the Sonjo. "Fr. Donovan did not adopt a 'telling' mode with the people to whom he ministered. . . . This refusal to 'tell' implies a willingness to learn from the other."[29] For Donovan, the missionary is a "fellow traveler" with those to whom he/she is sent. In a shared searching, God is found. When asked if he had "found the High God? If he had known him?" Donovan heard himself answering, "No! We have not found that High God, not even those of us who have been sent to tell you about him. We have not known him. But we believe he exists, and we have a certainty about that belief. I have come to ask you to join me. Let us search for him together. One day we may find him."[30] For Laval and for Donovan, Spiritan mission was about being one with people. There is a model here for all Spiritans who strive to incarnate the gospel message where they are. The Christian anthropology underpinning the discussions at GC XVII reflected the thinking of *Gaudium et spes* as developed by the ITC.

> The human person is a community being who blossoms in giving and receiving. It is thus in solidarity with others and across living social relationships that the person progresses. Also, those realities of nation, people, society, with their cultural patrimony, constitute for the development of persons a "definite, historical milieu which enfolds the man of every nation and age and from which he draws the values which permit him to promote civilization" (*GS* 53).[31]

Missionaries take seriously the different cultures they are called to experience. The words of Yahweh addressed to Moses from the burning bush are often applied to the missionary entering a new place. "Put off your shoes from your feet, for the place on which you are standing is holy ground" (Exod 3:5). It is God who makes holy. Who are we to say otherwise (Acts 10:15)? "Creation is the reflection of the glory of God: man is its living icon, and it is in Christ that the resemblance with God is seen. Culture is the scene in which man and the world are called to find themselves anew in the glory of God."[32]

The inculturation of the gospel message depended on the context. In Africa, given the continent's colonial past, cultural identity and belonging prompted the development of small Christian communities and inculturation of liturgy. Another context, that of Latin America, involved another

---

29. Harden, "Spiritans for Today," 81.
30. Bowen, *Missionary Letters*, 143.
31. ITC, "Faith and Inculturation," 6.
32. Ibid., 30.

discourse, that of liberation from oppression and social ills. "Every local church inhabits a cultural, political, and socio-economic context. That church's link to this context is an essential element of the local church. Being rooted in a human community wherein the Christians are living has faith value, for this is the setting within which the Christian has to bear witness to his faith, of which he is salt and light."[33]

The much-quoted advice of Libermann to the European missionary was reiterated in contemporary language at GC XVII when it spoke of mission consisting far more in listening than in speaking.[34] The danger of "cultural arrogance" was recognized. It "can nestle insidiously in the cracks between our theories and our actions, without our being aware of it. It can lie behind our unwillingness to admit that we are all culturally conditioned."[35] Culture was not defined but rather appreciated by reference to the many examples of inculturation given in the twelve presentations. Itaici recognized the importance of anthropological studies for missionaries. The missionary seeks only to plant a seed that will be nurtured by the earth that receives it, and so bring forth the fruit that lasts (John 15:16).[36]

> Inculturation that is directed by the expatriate will always have its limits. It will be, of its essence, an intervention from outside. This shows, in a certain way, the "otherness" of the word of God, which "cuts like a double-edged sword" the culture of both the announcer and the hearer. We must be ready always to recognize and rejoice in the constant newness that the Spirit brings forth where ever he is at work. The missionary brings the seed of the gospel; he must discreetly withdraw into the background so that those who have welcomed the word can live and celebrate it in their own way.[37]

---

33. Superior General's Report (1992) 25.

34. In a letter of 1845 to Fr. Bessieux in Guinea, Libermann wrote: "Strip yourselves of Europe, its customs and spirit. Make yourselves black with the blacks in order to train them as they should be trained, not European-style but preserving their own particular ways; be to them as servants to their masters in order to perfect and sanctify them and make them people of God." See Van de Putte, *Spiritual Letters*, 165.

35. Itaici (1992) 15.

36. Eugene Hillman, CSSp, understood inculturation in terms of a "radical incarnation" as "the full acceptance of the people where they are, in their own time and place, in everything except sin. Such is the incarnational economy through which God embraces humankind from within." Hillman, *African Christianity*, 84.

37. Itaici (1992) 17.

4. Spiritan Mission: Justice, Peace, and the Integrity of Creation (JPIC)

Spiritans respond creatively to the needs of evangelization of their time (*SRL* 2). In this they remain faithful to Fr. Libermann's flexible and dynamic approach by responding to changing needs in the world. What Libermann advised the priests of the association of St. John in Paris can be applied to his confreres. "Today new needs are felt everywhere. Every priest, without abandoning his assigned position, must study those needs, probe society's wounds, and grasp every opportunity offered by his position to provide remedies or alleviations for those wounds and needs."[38] The congregation of des Places and Libermann continues to identify "society's wounds" and strives "to provide remedies." It is that process of identification and action inspired by the Spirit that drives Spiritan mission and validates its place in God's mission. Without the appetite for and willing commitment to mission for engagement with the needs of evangelization of their time and place, Spiritans die.

> If we die, Spiritans may cease to exist, but mission continues, because God will raise other witnesses. Without change, we cannot keep up with God's mission. This has always been the church's problem. How do we keep up with God when doors shut and institutions decay and die? How do we discern God's mission in a changing world? Either the Spirit of God speaks and we hear and respond, or we muzzle the Spirit.[39]

SRL identified the evangelization of the poor as the Spiritan purpose (*SRL* 4) consisting in the "integral liberation" of people, action for justice and peace, and participation in development (*SRL* 14). Evangelization is the key concept for Spiritan mission as it reflects the church's thinking on mission found in the apostolic exhortation of Blessed Pope Paul VI *Evangelii nuntiandi* of 1975 and the "new evangelization" initiated by his successor, Pope St. John Paul II. It has a wide connotation covering a range of activities which are expressive of Spiritan mission: dialogue, inculturation, liberation, communion, education, JPIC, and formation for mission. Evangelical availability is at the heart of the Spiritan vocation and has been defined as

---

38. *N.D.* XI.536. Translated in Van Kaam, *Light to the Gentiles*, 263. Van Kaam surveyed the addresses and interventions made by Libermann at the association's regular weekly meetings from 3 January 1849 to 30 April 1850 as collected by his secretary Fr. Lannurien. He noted that Libermann "always seemed to offer surprisingly fresh approaches to the problems with which these Parisian priests were wrestling in that difficult post-revolutionary era." Ibid., 254.

39. Gittins, "Mission Today," 97.

"remaining attentive to the Holy Spirit at work in the concrete expressions of life."[40]

GC XVII

The superior general's report to GC XVII at Itaici showed a wide range of varying responses within the congregation to the mission of justice and peace.

> In North America and Europe, it will be a matter of protesting against North-South injustices, of struggling for the protection of the environment.... In Africa, the emphasis will be on ... integral development which is culturally adapted, on protest at worsening "trade terms," on respect for the common good. For Latin America, the concern will be with problems of land, the liberation of the poor from conditions bordering on slavery. ... All these different aspects constitute a wealth which demonstrates justice and peace in context and provides reference points for the various continents and countries in their respective approaches.[41]

In developing countries, Spiritans were doing what they could in their own situations. A range of activities, such as helping to diversify one-crop economies, teaching self-help skills, effecting a transfer of appropriate technology, etc., could be enumerated. In developed countries, many Spiritans were engaged in direct service to the poor. These examples of Spiritan mission for justice and peace were in accord with the Spiritan rule of life (*SRL* 14) which called for "integral liberation" to include both action for justice and peace and participation in development. *SRL* acknowledged that the awakening of an understanding of justice was a principal Spiritan activity (*SRL* 18). If "the cry of the poor" was to be heard, then "ongoing conversion" (*SL* 79) was required. This challenged Spiritans to review their attitudes, choices, availability, and lifestyle. The congregation explicitly associated Spiritan mission with responding to the injustices, oppressions and exploitations experienced by the people Spiritans were called to work for and live with (*SL* 83).

GC XVII put it that Spiritan mission is about nothing less than the transformation of the world in Christ. "So our mission cannot be reduced to the transmission of a doctrine, of a law, a ritual, of structures. It is above all a commitment, in the name of Jesus Christ, to the total liberation of all people

---

40. Koren, *Essays*, 15.
41. Superior General's Report (1992) 120.

from all those things that enslave them. The gospel is not just a message; it is a project of love aimed at transforming the world, to struggle for justice and peace."[42]

GC XVIII

GC XVIII at Maynooth in 1998 understood Spiritan mission as evangelization of the poor. But it asked, "How does this evangelization take place?" The methodology employed to address this question was, like GC XVII, grounded in the congregation's experience at the time. Twenty-three presentations gave expression to the wide range of experiences representative of Spiritan mission. Reflection on these experiences resulted in a consensus around the style of mission rather than its substance already articulated in *SRL* and at GC XVII. Deliberation on these experiences in the light of God's word and the congregation's charism (*SRL* 1) suggested seven qualities to define Spiritan mission.

1. Spiritan mission was about *being present* with people. "We go to people not primarily to accomplish a task, but rather to be with them, live with them, walk beside them, listen to them and share our faith with them. At the heart of our relationship is trust, respect and love."[43]

2. The Spiritan was *in solidarity with* different people and neglected groups. "We are called to a practical solidarity with the people amongst whom we live, especially those who are most poor, vulnerable and excluded from society" (Maynooth 2.2).

3. *Spirituality* was at the heart of being present and being in solidarity with others. "Our present understanding of mission means that we must look again at our personal and community life regarding the kind of relationship we have with God, our lifestyle and the way we look at the world around us" (Maynooth 2.3).

4. Mission was no longer understood geographically but rather as the *crossing of frontiers and openness to new horizons*. Spiritans continue to reach out to the abandoned, excluded, and oppressed in society. This can be best achieved through international communities (Maynooth 2.5–2.6).

5. *Collaboration* was an essential dimension of contemporary mission. "Such is the complexity of mission today that we cannot effectively

---

42. Itaici (1992) 20.
43. Maynooth (1998) 99.

accomplish it in isolation. Working with others strengthens us in our commitment and benefits those with whom we collaborate in the pursuit of common objectives" (Maynooth 2.7).[44]

6. *Dialogue and proclamation* were necessarily complementary for authentic mission amid other religions and where religious indifference and unbelief challenge missionary assumptions (Maynooth 2.8, 2.9).

7. The Spiritan role in *local churches* was to bear witness to their call to universal mission, to justice and fraternity amongst peoples. This can be done by consciousness-raising; working for Spiritan vocations and encouraging other forms of missionary involvement (Maynooth 2.10).

GC XVIII also prioritized specific contexts in which Spiritan mission was lived.

1. *First Evangelization* in the service of the kingdom remained central to Spiritan mission. "It is an evangelization which begins beyond the frontiers of the church. When the gospel has been planted in a particular place, it can continue to be carried beyond frontiers by targeting individuals and groups who have not so far been touched or very little."[45]

2. *Education*, both formal and informal, was integral to Spiritan mission. Two reasons were given. First, it brings freedom to the poor and promotes their dignity as children of God and, second, the contact education gives with the world of young people "provides an opportunity for passing on the good news, above all through the witness of the life of the educator."[46]

3. Concern for *Justice and Peace* issues had greatly increased in the congregation and "each circumscription will draw up a program for

---

44. Ibid., 121.

45. Superior General's Report (1998) 98. The report elaborated an understanding of first evangelization to encompass mission as a witness to the kingdom where the cultural context does not allow for the establishment of the church. Can secularized societies where some people have forgotten or have never really heard the Christian message and a youth culture little influenced by the gospel be understood as areas of first evangelization?

46. Maynooth (1998) 102. One of the capitulants elected to the general council, Fr. Rogath Kimaryo, CSSp, reflecting after GC XVIII wrote about committing to a "quality education" especially for mission in Africa. "It is this type of training that will liberate and free African men and women from ignorance and equip them with the tools for managing their environment. In a world of globalization, Africa cannot exist in isolation. While protecting its identity and values, it has to enter a competitive world which is largely defined by economic interests." Kimaryo, *Project of the Blacks*, 70.

justice and peace" (Maynooth 2.17). Collaboration with others to influence local, national, and international political decision-making; an expression of practical concern for refugees and migrants; the role of women in the church; reconciliation and conflict resolution and training of personnel to act for justice and peace were all initiatives to be undertaken "over the next six years" (Maynooth 2.18–24).

The principles enunciated at general chapters on dialogue and respect for others was modelled in many difficult missionary situations. One such situation was the Spiritan mission to the post-communist society of East Germany. Following the fall of the Berlin wall and the reunification of Germany there was much church rebuilding to do. The Spiritans were involved in the city of Rostock in the archdiocese of Hamburg. One of these, Irish Spiritan John B. Doyle, CSSp, (1937–2014), reflected on his presence there.

> Someone has said that if you want to talk to people today about God you need a previous exchange on the level of humanity. Not, I would suggest, an exchange of ideas, but an exchange in a relationship—what I might call a "whether or not" relationship. A friendly, open, personal way of relating to people that says in effect, "I accept you whether or not I admire your lifestyle. I'm interested in you whether or not you believe in God. I've time for you whether or not you go to church. I listen to you, whether or not I believe what you say.[47]

GC XIX

The 2004 general chapter at Torre d'Aguilha recognized that Spiritans choose poverty to be in solidarity with the poor who struggle to break out of the cruel, soul-destroying cycle of structural poverty that weighs them down. "This option for the poor makes us different in a society that excludes large sectors of the population who suffer poverty" (TA 35). Here GC XIX gave a contemporary interpretation to the rule of life. Practical efforts of solidarity were expressed in working for justice and peace. "To empower poor people, we need to avoid creating situations of paternalism and dependency. Money from outside can help, but it can also do much harm. . . . As an international congregation, we are called to play a role in establishing a more just relationship between developed and developing countries" (TA 36).

John Kilcrann, CSSp, JPIC coordinator at the Generalate, reflected on GC XIX and its contribution to the construction of a truly Spiritan

---

47. McLaughlin, "Spiritans for Today," 77.

spirituality of justice, peace, and the integrity of creation. He saw that it developed Maynooth's thinking on mission spirituality in terms of pilgrimage, adventure, contemplation, and discovery of the Spirit at work. In the language of GC XVIII, mission was "a crossing of cultural boundaries and a reaching out to groups of people who are abandoned, excluded and oppressed" (Maynooth 99–100).

Following this line of thinking he outlined a progressive realization of the Spiritan option for the poor with four distinctive moments of (1) pilgrimage into the world of the other, the poor; (2) being present in a mutually enriching relationship, (3) being of service one to another, and (4) solidarity.

> Conscious that Christ's Spirit is already present and active in the cultures to which we are sent, mission becomes a pilgrimage of mutual enrichment, where together we identify and seek liberation from the chains that impede the full realization of God's kingdom. . . . This understanding of mission today requires of missionaries a deeper, more contemplative spirituality. (TA, 18)

Mission is primarily God's work, it is the *missio Dei*. It is for the missionary to participate in the paschal mystery of the kingdom. This demands a capacity to contemplate and so discern the action of God and learn how to cooperate with that divine action. Spiritans strive to build up communities of witness wherever they are, as mission exists not for its own sake, but for the sake of God's reign.

GC XIX recognized that the missionary's own spirituality is deepened through encounter and relationship with those to whom they are sent (TA, 34). A strong bond and relationship grows between missionaries and the people they serve.

> Through our presence with migrants and refugees, we come close to the oppressed and disadvantaged . . . our outreach makes them feel at home, our advice and training eases the pain of their transition. Our presence . . . is a small voice calling for genuine human equality. We speak with and on behalf of the victims of gender and racial inequality, overlooked in a prevailing atmosphere of individualism, materialism, and rampant consumerism. (TA, 57–59)

Spiritans were called upon to live a faith that does justice. Solidarity is "a lived consequence of our choice to journey to and take up our residence in the world of the poor."[48] The poor are best served by working in collabora-

---

48. Kilcrann, "Constructing a Spiritan Spirituality," 76.

tion with them and other groups similarly committed to defending the poor and protecting their rights. Kimaryo gave personal testimony to the Spiritan vocation following the example of des Places and Libermann. "We give ourselves generously to go and to meet the poor in their own environment and experience with them the daily struggles of their lives. We give ourselves wholeheartedly for their cause. We assist them to liberate themselves and build their own viable and secure future."[49]

The chapter retreat pointed realistically to the challenges facing Spiritans as they set out on mission to be in solidarity with the poor and marginalized in society. How was the congregation to translate its spiritual patrimony into valid apostolic projects?

> Today we are faced with extreme situations of need and urgency, but the sources that fed our spirituality, and which were powerful in the past, are now neutralized, which creates a spiritual conformity at odds with our world in transformation. We live a protected spirituality in contrast to the difficulties that the majority of the people on the margins face. We live on the defensive, if not protecting our patrimony, at least protecting our integrity. We lack the living of a solid spirituality of the margins, of justice and peace, of frontiers, of conflict and risk. We lack prophets. (TA, 111–12)[50]

One of the Torre d'Aguilha capitulants, Antonio Gruyters of Holland, gave a moving account of a Spiritan prophet he lived with in Brasilia, Brazil, from 1970 to 1982, Ângelo van Kempen.

> Ângelo took the option for the poor very seriously even though he did not trust very much the fancy ideas of some liberation theologians. He recognized in the poor his masters and teachers. One could see in him the gift of interior liberty and joy. He insisted on giving a good welcome to all who knocked on his door (and they were many), without making distinction between people. . . . Ângelo showed that our baptism takes place when we patiently lose ourselves in the lives of the poor. They helped us to see the deficiencies of our formation; they taught us a spirituality of which we had thought that we were the experts. Many of the poor live love. They know that they have little or no control over what may crash in on their lives. There is much sin amongst the poor, but without doubt what is much more impressive for those who know how to contemplate it is the

---

49. Kimaryo, *Project of the Blacks*, 35.
50. The GC XIX retreat was given by Fr. Adelio Torres Neiva, CSSp. See TA, 109–20.

great holiness of the People of God. . . . In 1991 he returned to Holland where he was killed by a drug addict who got into the Spiritan house where Ângelo lived. This happened in February of 1996.[51]

Kilcrann's reflections pointed to the emergence of a "solid spirituality of the margins, of justice and peace, of frontiers, of conflict and risk" as lived by Spiritan Ângelo Kempen. He recognized this emergence as a process with the potential to give meaning, energy, and direction to the Spiritan option for the poor. "This is a rich process which helps us understand our charism more profoundly and re-read it in the light of today's call to mission. The vibrancy of the resulting spirituality has become more obvious in recent years."[52]

GC XIX associated the importance of working for the integrity of creation with the Spiritan Justice and Peace mission. Before 2004, the importance of the integrity of creation was not a focus for the congregation. This area of concern received comprehensive coverage in issue 19 of *Spiritan Life* (2012) entitled *Spiritan Mission and the Integrity of Creation*. Other aspects of Justice, Peace, and Integrity of Creation (JPIC) were identified by GC XIX: "Special attention is drawn to tasks, such as peace building, conflict resolution, reconciliation, dialogue, lobbying and advocacy in favor of the poor and marginalized, work for liberation of the oppressed and for the integrity of creation" (TA, 48). Mission in this area was described as an "Areopagus" (Acts 17:16–34) or what could broadly be described as a new, different, and groundbreaking call to mission.

Fr. Rogath Kimaryo, CSSp, outgoing general councilor at GC XIX, listed new initiatives in service and empowerment of the poor throughout the congregation. These included the orphans at Auteuil, France; a center for asylum seekers in Dublin, Ireland; the Centre Energie at Antananarive, Madagascar; a refugee center in Durban, South Africa; and the flying medical doctor service in Okokola, Tanzania. In all these works the Spiritan strategy is to empower others while avoiding the trappings of paternalism and dependency.[53]

---

51. Gruyters, "Contemplation and Action," 111–14.

52. Kilcrann, "Constructing a Spiritan Spirituality," 78.

53. See Kimaryo, *Project of the Blacks*, 36. Rogatus Kimaryo, CSSp, was ordained bishop of the Diocese of Same, Tanzania, on 13 June 2010.

5. Education as Spiritan Mission

Beginning with Poullart des Places, Spiritans have been involved in providing education for those most in need. The rule of life speaks of education in three ways: the preparation of the laity; as an apostolate in its own right; and as a response to the needs of youth (*SRL* 18, 18.1). Spiritan involvement in the education apostolate in the early 1990s was varied. Initiatives such as SERVOL in Trinidad, *Capacitaçao da Juventude* in Brazil, and *Casa dos Rapazes*, Angola, operated in the nonformal sector and engaged directly with those most in need in society. At the high school level: Spiritans in Europe, North America, the Caribbean, and Africa were engaged as owners, administrators, teachers, and chaplains of many schools. At tertiary level, some Spiritans ministered as chaplains, lecturers and administrators in universities, institutes of technology and teacher training colleges. Duquesne University was the only Spiritan University at the time. A third-level program in development studies was offered to Irish and overseas students at Kimmage Manor, Dublin. It was seen that involvement in education helped to build good social relationships and gave a status to the local church in countries like the Gambia and Sierra Leone where Catholics were a small minority. In "first" world countries, Spiritan schools provided many vocations for the congregation.

GC XVII

The engagement of Spiritans in formal and nonformal education was prominent in some of the twelve significant experiences presented at Itaici. The chapter recognized their role as truly Spiritan. "Education is a Spiritan charism that is as old as the congregation itself. There are Spiritan schools in several provinces, and in one, a university. Education is still an important vehicle of evangelization in many of the missions where Spiritans work."[54] The year before GC XVII, a worldwide symposium (the first) on Spiritan education was held at Duquesne University of the Holy Spirit, from 24 to 28 June 1991. Ninety-eight delegates engaged in the Spiritan educational apostolate, both formal and nonformal, representing twenty different countries, gathered for the symposium. They recognized that they were meeting at a crucial turning point in the history of the Spiritan education apostolate which faced many challenges. Delegates recommitted themselves to providing education and access to all, especially to the poorest in their societies.

---

54. Itaici (1992) 12.

One of the challenges was remaining faithful to the Spiritan charism of care for the poor. This applied particularly where Spiritan schools served middle and upper middle class students. The Irish delegation to Duquesne acknowledged the challenge. Spiritan schools in Ireland were endeavoring to develop "a faith that does justice" program. Its purpose was to engage participants in "a critical analysis of society and of the consumerist/secularist values it portrays; students and staff should be involved at a practical level in the promotion of a just society. . . . Missionary awareness too will be continued in line with the healthy traditions of the colleges."[55] Such initiatives required lay participation as the number of Spiritans working in education was on the decline and the continuation of Spiritan schools was increasingly in the hands of lay people.

A way forward could only be secured through the involvement of lay collaborators in the articulation of goals, the formulation of vision statements, and reflecting with the congregation on the nature and direction of the Spiritan mission in education. Examples of progress in lay participation were reported. These included the appointment of Duquesne's first lay president, and lay principals leading some Spiritan schools in Ireland, Trinidad, and Canada. The continuation of Spiritan mission in increasingly lay staffed and managed institutes would be facilitated by mechanisms assuring a Spiritan involvement, such as representation on the governing board of Auteuil in France and elected Catholic school boards in Canada. The congregation established a board of trustees for Templeogue College, Ireland, and for Holy Spirit School, Mauritius.

The Duquesne meeting ended with a statement of intent, expressing confidence

> that, with the guidance of the Holy Spirit, the charisms bequeathed to us by Poullart des Places and Francis Libermann will enable us, religious and laity, to adapt our educational mission to the challenges of a changing world, which seeks global peace and communication across cultural diversity, where poor and marginalized seek a share in global prosperity and a say in decisions which affect their future, and where education becomes a continuing and life-long project.[56]

---

55. *I/D* 49 (1992) 3.
56. Ibid., 4.

GC XVIII

GC XVIII at Maynooth affirmed the importance of formal and informal education for Spiritan mission. "It is an integral part of our mission of evangelization." The chapter explained the basis for this assertion. "On the one hand, this social ministry to the poor brings them freedom and promotes the dignity that is theirs as children of God; on the other, the contact it gives with the world of young people provides an opportunity for passing on the good news, above all through the witness of the life of the educator."[57] One statement made by Maynooth (1998) to describe Spiritan mission as "presence" and being with people was taken up some years later and reflected upon as a base for a Spiritan pedagogy by some collaborators in Spiritan education.[58]

6. Formation for Mission

SRL provided a general orientation for formation as "the continued deepening of our 'apostolic life' under the influence of the Holy Spirit and in keeping with the spirit of our founders, our living tradition, and the present needs of the world. It is both a personal task and a shared responsibility" (*SRL* 100). This post Vatican II approach to formation is in contrast with what preceded it. One of the contrasts is the acceptance of a diversity of formation experiences within the congregation due to its international character. "Up to 1968, almost all houses of formation throughout the world followed the same formation scheme.... With the coming of the theology of the local church and the emphasis placed on inculturation . . . for all practical purposes, each province and foundation established its own program and trained its own formators."[59]

GC XVII

The general council wrote a paper on *Spiritan Formation Today* in 1989 outlining "the Spiritan religious and missionary ideal" for those in formation.

---

57. Maynooth (1998) 102.

58. Maynooth (1998) 99 reads: "We go to people not primarily to accomplish a task, but rather to be with them, live with them, walk beside them, listen to them and share our faith with them. At the heart of our relationship is trust, respect, and love" For a follow up on this development, see Duaime, "Heartbeat," 107, and Hansen et al., "Spiritan Pedagogy."

59. Superior General's Report (1992), 128–29.

In the year 2000, the Spiritan will continue to commit his life to sharing the sufferings and hopes of the poor. He will have learnt to be particularly close to the abandoned persons and groups that our world is producing in increasing numbers: immigrants and refugees, the young, the casualties of urbanization . . . those who have not yet heard, or have hardly heard, or who no longer hear, the good news. He will work with them and will be able to analyze the moral and social causes of their suffering. He will have been trained in educational techniques, in the social sciences, in defending the integrity of creation. He will commit himself, with courage and discernment, to changing unjust structures.[60]

Three years later, in his report to GC XVII at Itaici, Fr. Haas wrote: "The 600 young Spiritans in formation throughout the congregation are certainly a source of joy, of confidence in the future of Spiritan mission, or indeed of mission in general. But they also constitute a great responsibility: the quality of formation today will determine the kind of missionary family we shall be tomorrow."[61]

Spiritan discourse since 1986 on the style of formation, its objectives and content, was inclusive and well considered. It involved formators, students in formation, congregational leadership, and the general membership.[62] A consensus emerged in the form of the *Guide for Spiritan Formation* (1996) that linked preparation for mission with the nature of mission itself. The pre-1968 model of formation has already been described. The Dublin meeting of novice masters in 1989 spoke of three styles of novitiate operating in the congregation: (1) an "instruction model" with emphasis on courses and exercises and limited personal free time; (2) an "induction model" with fewer courses and greater emphasis on the novices' own experience; (3) an "insertion model" with emphasis on interaction with the environment and

---

60. *I/D* 44 (1989) 1.

61. Superior General's Report (1992), 128. The responsibility was taken seriously with many formation meetings held including a Spiritan formation congress in Saverne (July 1982), a novice masters meeting in Dublin (July 1989), formators at SIST, Enugu (July 1991) and at Chevilly (July 2002); a pan-African meeting of superiors and formators at Yaoundé (September 2002). Formation was central to the agenda of the Dakar and Duquesne EGC meetings in 1995 and 2001, respectively, and at GC XIX in 2004.

62. Regional meetings of formators were regularly held. A commission of six formators was set up by the general council (first meeting, April 1992) to (1) collate the various reactions to these meetings, analyze them and make recommendations; (2) establish guidelines for a common formation program; (3) examine formation in the congregation and explore possibilities for greater effectiveness and solidarity.

guided reflection on the apostolic experience. Was there a congregational preference for one model over another?

A growing diversity with each circumscription devising its own formation program was a feature of the *ad experimentum* period. While respecting the need for such diversity, a common outline for formation was also needed to ensure the maintenance of congregational unity through an authentic interpretation of the Spiritan apostolic life (*SRL* 3).

> The central concept that gives unity to our life is that of our apostolic life, the values of religious and community life. Three characteristics of mission—solidarity with the poor and oppressed, mission in union with the people of God, and the incarnation of Christ in different cultures—have an impact on our formation program.[63]

GC XIX

Torre d'Aguilha recognized the good fortune of the congregation to have "young people who wish to share in our mission" and the challenge of a changing world calling for new types of mission and witness. It asked for all training programs to "adopt more of an apprentice style approach, giving students opportunities to have personal experience of missionary life today."[64] The students, in return, needed to be open to guidance by their formators who accompany them on their journey. This form of training is a way of learning through experience, empowering participants to witness what they preach.

The formator's role was of central importance in this formation model. The guide for formation (1997) distinguished between the role of teacher/professor and that of formator in formation communities. While both had a formative role, the latter was primarily responsible for accompanying the candidates and young members in the way of vocation discernment. But skilled formators were in short supply. The general council reported in 1999 that "a good number of confreres are currently training to be formators so within a few years the situation will be somewhat improved. During this summer, the Pan-African Region organized a short course for formators at

---

63. Report on EGC Dakar, 1995. *Spiritan News* 108 (1995) 3. The discussion on formation at the Dakar EGC led to the publication in 1997 of a *Spiritan Guide for Formation*. The guide was written in three parts dealing with (1) general orientations for initial and ongoing formation; (2) initial formation to the Spiritan religious apostolic life lived in the light of *SRL*; (3) ongoing formation.

64. Torre d'Aguilha (2004) 63–64.

SIST in Nigeria."⁶⁵ The general council also pledged financial assistance for the training of formators and to reestablish a secretariat for formation at the Generalate.

Torre d'Aguilha identified "holiness of life and a spirit of sacrifice in the service of mission" as the primary objective of formation which is complemented by mature human relationships and a capacity to live mission collaboratively in international community.⁶⁶ It adopted a developmental model of formation ordered in stages of first cycle, novitiate, "stage" (pastoral and practical mission experience) and second cycle. The first cycle emphasized the human development of the candidate. It introduced him to living in community and growing in faith. The novitiate continued the work of first cycle with a deepening of knowledge and appreciation for Spiritan spirituality and history. "Stage" was an essential element in the Spiritan formation process and consisted of mission experience in a transcultural situation among the poor. The second cycle focus was academic with the study of theology and particularly missiology, anthropology, inter-religious dialogue, social analysis, and other areas immediately relevant to contemporary mission challenges.

However, "while academic excellence is an essential part of our formation, the intellectual content will not be over-stressed to the detriment of the human, spiritual, and pastoral dimensions. The integral development of the whole person will characterize our formation process."⁶⁷ It needed to be, as advocated by Libermann, "an affair of the heart." As he wrote to Monsieur l'Abbé Mangot at the Seminary of Amiens on 5 March 1837: "We must study all the subjects in our curriculum, but we must put our trust in God alone. We shouldn't allow our hearts to become tied up in the sciences. God wants us to study. He wants us to study with every ounce of energy and attention. But we've got to study in view of God and solely for love of him."⁶⁸

A recurring theme in discussion on formation was the valuing of those in formation as "a gift from God" (*SRL* 103) and how best to accompany them in their formation journey. The limited resources available for formation and the increasing numbers in formation in the new circumscriptions were recognized as a major challenge for the congregation. This was discussed at Maynooth (1998), at a formators meeting (2002) and at Torre d'Aguilha (2004).

---

65. *I/D* 56 (1999) 7.
66. Torre d'Aguilha (2004) 64–65.
67. Ibid., 67.
68. *N.D.* I.279. Translated in van Kaam, *Light to the Gentiles*, 57.

Maynooth recognized a disparity between the wealthier provinces and the new circumscriptions "on the frontline of mission" and chose not to impose a system of levies to reduce this disparity, but rather opted to "rely instead on the spirit of our tradition of *cor unum et anima una* to spark our solidarity into action."[69] This approach was also adopted for the funding of formation in the new circumscriptions. The general council was "invited" to use its moral authority "to achieve a better distribution of personnel, particularly for new projects and for formation."[70]

The 2002 meeting frankly acknowledged a "disparity existing in regard to material resources and the urgent need for more effective collaboration among circumscriptions. However, financial and material constraints only served to fuel the desire to search for a way forward and to deepen the sense of our Spiritan identity."[71] It was a scandal to some that the wealthier circumscriptions of the North with few vocations had greater resources, while the poorer ones in the South had many vocations with fewer resources. The northern provinces contributed generously to the *Cor Unum* fund. Yet, this generosity was insufficient. Fr. Schouver pointed to this in his report to GC XIX. "Most formation houses in the South exist on the minimum, with poor facilities, while the picture is completely different in the houses in the northern hemisphere. What is the rationale for maintaining, in some instances, very costly structures with a handful of vocations? Is there a better way of organizing our resources of personnel (formators) and finances?"[72]

GC XIX asked for a feasibility study on the centralization of second cycle formation and for a careful study of financing and resourcing of second cycle formation and the role the general council could play in ameliorating the disparities that were identified at the chapter. The meeting also recognized the need for "a common approach to formation" and that the value of future Spiritan missionary commitment depended to a large extent on the nature and quality of the formation the congregation offers to its candidates.

---

69. Maynooth, (1998) 137.
70. Ibid., 140.
71. *Spiritan News*, 144 (2002) 2.
72. Superior General's Report (2004) 107.

Chapter 8

Spiritan Community

1. The Importance of Community Life

FR. LIBERMANN'S PROVISIONAL RULE for the Holy Heart of Mary (1840) made it "an important and fundamental rule in the congregation that its members should live in a community, be subject to a common rule, and that they should never work separately and alone outside their community."[1] The *Reglèments* he wrote for the Congregation of the Holy Spirit connected the two wings of the congregation's mission (the apostolate) and life (religious life) through a community life that was apostolic and religious.

SRL recognized the importance of community life for its members and its mission. "Community life is then an essential element in the Spiritan way of life. It is a privileged means of practising the evangelical counsels in the service of the good news" (*SRL* 28). Good community life was recognized as a precious and, perhaps, rare gift. General council reports and general chapter documents described model communities. They also gave instances where community life was problematic. Is there such a thing as a model Spiritan community? Or is it a case that "true community is always a goal for which we strive."[2] How was this goal to be achieved? These questions were a focus of attention for the congregation's leadership as it finalized the new rule of life.

GC XVI was presented with an overview of community life in the congregation and approved a program for community renewal.[3] However, the

---

1. *Provisional Rule*, 187.
2. *I/D* 42 (1987) 4.
3. GC XVI recognized community renewal as one of the five important concerns that the chapter asked the incoming general administration to consider. The other

transfer of insight and commitment from the center to the periphery, that is, to the grass-roots, would prove difficult. While the theory was clear and well understood, the practice was less easy. And yet the renewal of community life was vital to the congregation's mission as good community life provided the base and support for the individual missionary vocation to find expression and play its part in the church's mission and the building up of the kingdom of God.

Before taking up his appointment to the new mission of Mozambique in 1996, Portuguese Spiritan Fr. Pedro Fernandes remembered a conversation he had with an elder confrere who told him, "The heaviest thing is not the difficulties, the challenges, and trials that you will encounter; the most decisive thing will be the manner in which you live together through these difficulties. If community is guaranteed, whatever difficulties you meet can be confronted without too much penalty! More than the 'what to do,' will matter the 'whom to be with.'"[4] The elder confrere recognized that good community life enables good missionary work. Yet it was also recognized that despite the importance for Spiritans to live in community for missionary effectiveness the reality was otherwise. It was often reported that many Spiritans lived alone.

A study of the 1993 "État du Personnel" suggested that almost one third of confreres did not live under the same roof with other Spiritans. The concept of "regional communities" was discussed and affirmed as the needs of the apostolate very often required that confreres lived alone, or in small groups (CDD 254–56). Fr. Vincent O'Toole, CSSp, of the English province and working at the Generalate, was concerned that young Spiritans could not reconcile the reality of Spiritan living with what *SRL* said about it. "We are still a long way from that return to our founders's inspiration that was so much insisted upon by Vatican II."[5]

SRL and Living in Community

SRL made a causal link between community living and the apostolate. "We seek to work together in the service of the gospel" (*SRL* 29). The community did not exist for itself but to accomplish a mission. As the church was not to

---

concerns were the foundations and new provinces; new forms of mission; solidarity; justice and peace. The priority given to community renewal was in response to the document "Experiencing Community," presented to the chapter. See *I/D* 42 (1987) 3–4.

4. Fernandes, "Constructing Religious Community," 25.
5. O'Toole, "Libermann's Impossible Dream," 11.

be equated with the kingdom of God neither was community to be understood as an end but a witness to that kingdom.

> The church is not its own end, but, as sacrament of the Incarnate Word, is "for us men and for our salvation." Similarly, for us Spiritans, our community life is not just for its own sake. It is for the support and perfection of our apostolic life. It follows that the Spiritan community does not see itself as a static institution, a kind of sanctuary standing apart from history, turned in on itself and away from the world.[6]

The community's apostolate determined the community's lifestyle and the lives of its members. It was not so much that the community was formed for a mission, but that individuals gathered together and formed community in response to a common mission. The way in which Spiritans understand community and live it is different to the way other religious understand and live community life according to their traditions.[7]

The kernel of Libermann's understanding of Spiritan community was quoted at the beginning of chapter 3 of *SRL*. Spiritans live in community "to bring the apostolic life—for which Spiritan life is intended—to its perfection, to assure the continuance and the development of the works in which it engages and to foster the holiness of its members, the congregation has adopted life in community as its founding principle. Its members shall all live in community at all times."[8] The apostolate and the holiness of members were recognized as the twin goals for community living.

Before Vatican II, the religious life aspect of the Spiritan vocation had come to be so emphasized that the apostolate was understood to be the work of the community and secondary to it. Justification for this interpretation was found in Libermann who emphasized the importance of community

---

6. *Spiritans Today* 5 (1987) 102. This quotation is part of the conclusion to the research on Spiritan community presented at GC XVI which approved *SRL* in 1986.

7. The determining influence of the apostolate on the lifestyle of the community can be taken as something distinctively, though not exclusively, Spiritan. The Marianists, for example, recognized that their "*Rule of Life* calls us to live a common life of prayer, shared faith and transforming relationships. It is a life that helps us witness to the gospel here and now." See https://www.marianist.com/community-life. Another example is the Congregation of the Holy Cross. Its constitutions understand community as a support for individuals who come together for mission. "Our calling is to serve the Lord Jesus in mission not as independent individuals but in a brotherhood. Our community life refreshes the faith that makes our work a ministry and not just an employment; it fortifies us by the example and encouragement of our confreres; and it protects us from being overwhelmed or discouraged by our work." *Constitutions of the Congregation of the Holy Cross*, 33.

8. Rule of 1849. N.D. X.454, as quoted in *SRL* 27.

for his first missionaries sent to the West Coast of Africa. His concern at that time was for their survival. Libermann thought that the support of a cohesive, united, and well-ordered community was vital for their health and well-being. There were many dangers associated with living for the first time outside one's own culture. While urging a "casting off" of all that was familiar to them for the sake of the apostolate, a strong base was needed to secure the future of the mission. Hence, he cautioned against deviating from community regulation for the sake of apostolic expediency.[9]

The distinctions made between the three dimensions of the Spiritan vocation were central to the challenge of renewal for the congregation. Which was more important? Some emphasized one over the other. The task of renewal was to integrate them and recognize the synergy that could come from that integration. The integrating principle—the apostolic life—was achieved by SRL adopting the quotation from the Rule of 1849 which defined the Spiritan vocation as "that life of love and of holiness lived on earth by the Son of God to save and sanctify the people. By it he continually sacrificed himself, thereby glorifying the Father and saving the world" (SRL 1).

Internationality and Living in Community

The movement away from national blocks to a more international way of mission was a strategy initiated during the Timmermans era (1974–1986). GC XIX spoke of the congregation as one big "rainbow" family with a membership on all continents (25 countries in Africa, 12 in Europe, 9 in the Americas and the Caribbean, 2 in Oceania and 2 in Asia). This development gave rise to a great diversity, yet a unity is maintained through the Spiritan characteristic of "evangelical availability" or as Torre d'Aguilha put it, "not for ourselves but for the mission to which we have been called"[10] whereby each one forgets himself for the sake of the kingdom of God. "We are given the strength of unity in a world which is perturbed by individualism, egoism and terrorism. This is the profound meaning of our religious family and our spiritual history—to make us, by those means, witnesses to the love of God."[11]

The demographic shift with fewer vocations coming from the traditional provinces and more from the new foundations and young provinces occasioned greater internationality in the congregation. The foundations, destined to become provinces, needed the support of experienced

---

9. *Provisional Rule*, pt. 2, ch. 5, art. 1–11.
10. Torre d'Aguilha (2004) 94.
11. Ibid., 95.

missionaries for their establishment, particularly for administration and formation. First appointments, made by the Generalate, were increasingly needed to build up the new foundations as well as sending young confreres *ad extra*, that is, on mission beyond their own region. New mission projects in Paraguay, Angola, and Pakistan, were undertaken and included experienced missionaries as well as those on first appointment. These international teams with specific projects and working where the congregation had not been before, became the new model for mission. They were international, intercultural, and intergenerational and looked to the Generalate for direction and support.

The individual Spiritan was coming more and more to identify with the congregation as an international community of which his own national community was a part. International teams promoted a sense of belonging to the congregation that transcended the particularities of nation, culture, and race. All first appointments were made by the Generalate and an increasing number of projects were undertaken in the name of the congregation. Older provinces which in the past operated with a large measure of independence came to value inter-dependence in the congregation, particularly as they relied on appointments from the foundations and young provinces to maintain their traditional works and take on new mission initiatives. In turn, the young foundations and provinces welcomed the congregation's solidarity as they built up their own "home base" and formation program.

The congregation's motto, *Cor Unum et Anima Una* (one heart and one soul) which was, prior to Vatican II, ensured through a uniformity of lifestyle and a centralized authority, was, in the years since Vatican II, promoted through a growing collaboration between provinces coordinated by the Generalate in Rome ensuring a sharing of resources for the global building up of the congregation and extension of its mission. The language of "family" was increasingly used to describe this worldwide Spiritan community. "Variety and complementarity are commonly characteristic of our communities. The sick, the healthy, the young, the old, the priest, the Brother—together we are but one family, intent on one mission" (*SRL* 24.2).

Community Living: Authentic Community for Apostolic Witness

GC XVIII at Maynooth (1998) recognized that while general chapters had interpreted the principle of community differently as time and circumstance required, being a community-minded and committed person remained an identifying mark of what it was to be a Spiritan. Community living is an essential source of inspiration for Spiritan mission. Each one is strengthened through a community that prays together, enables its members share their faith journeys together, and where the members offer friendship and support to one another (Maynooth 3.8). The individual Spiritan vocation is nurtured through sharing in the common vocation of the community that is increasingly an international, intercultural, and intergenerational experience.

Maynooth recognized the challenges associated with community life. "The fact that confreres live together under one roof is no guarantee that they are living an authentic community life; a quality of presence, of communication and sharing, is called for" (Maynooth 115). The challenge of living together and the positive outcomes from meeting those challenges was highlighted by the Congo-Brazzaville experience. Capitulant René Tabard, recounting the experience of "different nations, ethnic groups and cultures living in community," pointed out that "to live in community is something which involves both mind and heart. It presupposed in each confrere a conviction: I need the others to better fulfil my mission, a mission which is beyond my individual strength."[12] Community is developed by all being around the same table; praying together; doing community planning for the apostolate; sharing of resources; having transparency of management. This, Tabard said, was a demanding menu, but he added, "Whoever wants to eat the food of his own village should remain in his own diocese!"[13]

Confreres needed to be prepared for living together in international community for mission. The community needed to agree structures to facilitate true sharing for a good quality of life to be enjoyed by all the members. Such living together was valued as it bore witness to the human possibility of reconciling differences and living in harmony by overcoming conflict, racism, and the cult of the individual. "In this way, our community life is an integral part of our mission and a powerful witness to the message of the gospel."[14]

GC XIX at Torre d'Aguilha (2004) considered Spiritan community life as "a lived reality." Like a natural family through which its members develop their human capacity to live well with others, so also for the members of the congregation. They acquire through community living the social skills needed for respectful and positive interaction, and the spiritual aptitude for patience and the tolerance of difference. Leadership "has an essential role to play," but as was said at Maynooth, living under the same roof did not

12. Maynooth (1998) 63.
13. Ibid., 65.
14. Ibid., 117.

constitute a community, but rather community building "has to be worked at and the contribution of each member to this process is considered vital to healthy community life and personal growth."[15] GC XIX made a strong connection between authentic community living and apostolic witness. "What we preach should reflect a reality that we already live. Only in this way is the gospel message credible. Community and mission go hand in hand."[16]

2. Diversity of Membership

The congregation, as a clerical religious institute, faced particular challenges in its renewal. Commentators on renewal of religious life claimed that "clerical congregations committed to ministry forget more easily the prophetic and charismatic dimensions of religious life."[17] Fr. Desmond O'Donnell, OMI, writing in preparation for the 1994 Synod of Bishops on consecrated life in the church, noted a growing awareness among the leaders of clerical religious institutes that renewal was "intimately dependent on their understanding of how the ministry of priest religious will be exercised in the church of the future."[18] He called on the synod to distinguish between the different kinds of religious families, from the contemplative to the active lay and active clerical, and address issues like prayer and community as specific to each. Monks, lay religious, and clerical religious do not pray or live in community in the same way. The type of religious life influences how the religious vows are practised.

The final message of the 1994 Synod of Bishops responded to this concern by enumerating multiple forms of consecrated life in the church. "Each form of consecrated life has its proper style of life and specific apostolic commitments, from the desert to the city, from the cloistered retreat to contemplation on apostolic frontiers, from fleeing the world to embracing its cultures, from an attentive silence to creative social communication, from monastic stability to mobile mission."

The Spiritan congregation continued with its proper style of life and specific apostolic commitments and redefined itself in 1986 as a religious missionary institute (*SRL* 2). Since then it has fashioned a new model for

15. Torre d'Aguilha (2004) 20.

16. Ibid., 33.

17. Benito Blanco, SJ, president of the Conference of Latin American Religious, at a meeting of the Union of Superiors General (28–29 May 1992). See O'Donnell, "Clerical Religious," 6.

18. Ibid.

Spiritan life and mission. But *SRL* also defined the congregation as "a clerical religious institute" (*SRL* 148). In this it remained true to Poullart des Places whose mission was to train priests to serve the poor and to Fr. Libermann who defined the congregation he was founding as "a Society of Priests who, in the name of Our Lord Jesus Christ and as sent by him, devote themselves wholly to announce his holy gospel, and to establish his reign among the souls that are poorest and most neglected in the church of God" (*Provisional Rule*, pt. 1, art. 1).[19]

Many candidates are attracted to the congregation because they want to be priests like the Spiritan priests they came to know in their parishes or their schools. Most Spiritans live three distinct vocations in the church: that of priest, religious, and missionary. It can be difficult to distinguish between the religious and secular priest particularly in the context of pastoral ministry. Living the Spiritan vocation within such a context was recognized as a growing reality in the congregation.[20] While pastoral ministry can be Spiritan, fulfilling the role of the secular priest as part of hierarchical church structure without losing sight of one's religious and missionary identity is not without its difficulties.

The *SRL* index does not list "cleric," "ordination" or "priest." The entry on "orders" refers mostly to formation with the requirement that perpetual profession is made before receiving the diaconate (*SRL* 134); a common period of formation is provided for all (*SRL* 135); those called to an ordained ministry are to comply with the requirements of the general law of the church (*SRL* 138). Does this coverage of the clerical dimension of the congregation adequately address the missionary and religious identity of the Spiritan priest? We have seen the inexorable fall in the number of brothers in the congregation since the 1960s that suggests the clerical dimension of the Spiritan identity had eclipsed the religious and missionary aspects.

Spiritan priests are ordained for the "missionary priesthood" (for the mission entrusted to the congregation) which means a freedom from

---

19. It is to be noted that Libermann's commentary recognized the need for brothers following the establishment of the society. Libermann's *Règlements* of 1849 defined the purpose of the Holy Ghost Congregation in terms of the apostolic life—"the salvation of the most needy, and the most abandoned people," and does not make mention of priests. This, perhaps, is because the congregation was already established as a clerical institute. See Daly, *Spiritan Wellsprngs*, 68, 164–65.

20. Summarizing a collection of reflections on Spiritans in parish ministry, "The Missionary in the Parish," *Spiritan Life* 7 (1997) 61, the editorial team wrote: "Many of us, perhaps the majority, live out mission in a parish: one that is newly-born, growing up, or already well-developed. Bearing in mind the renewal of the church and her mission, the question is not, or is no longer, whether we can live our Spiritan vocation in a parish setting, but rather how we can do it."

restriction to one local church and a readiness to go where the church's need for priests is greatest, particularly to those who have not heard, or scarcely heard the message of the gospel (*SRL* 4). As it is for brothers and lay associates, so also for Spiritan priests, the apostolic life is the integrating principle of the different dimensions to the Spiritan vocation.[21] It is also the key principle unifying formation for Spiritan life and mission. Schouver, introducing the *Guide for Spiritan Formation* (1997) said that it outlined "the main stages of the journey through which everyone must travel at some point or another. It tries to ensure that all Spiritan pilgrims are tuned in to the same frequency, listen to the same words and the same music."[22] "All Spiritan pilgrims" referred to here encompasses not only differences of culture and context, but also the difference of cleric, brother, and lay membership.

The Spiritan Brother

The congregation had journeyed a long way from its pre-Vatican II days toward the integration in community of priests and brothers in the 1980s. The pre-Vatican II Rules and Constitutions were divided into two parts. Part 1 covered the general organization of the congregation which distinguished between cleric and lay members. Part 2 was entitled "Rules Common to All Members." Part 1 spoke of "various classes of members," namely, clerics and lay religious, known as "brothers" who came after the clerics in precedence (8.47). Brothers, once professed, could not become priests (21.190). "The mission of the Brothers is to assist the Fathers" (24.221). In houses where brothers are sufficiently numerous, they were to perform their exercises apart (24.223).

Vatican II renewal called into question the vocation of the brother in clerical institutes. A new approach to the vocation was needed. Spiritans responded to this challenge through the development of a common life and mission for both brothers and priests within the congregation. GC XIII had legislated for a "full integration of brothers into community activities" (*CDD* 274), acknowledging full rights for brothers and their full participation in a shared community of life and of work.

The decline in the number of Spiritan brothers since 1969 was of concern. GC XIV and GC XV approached this issue differently. The line taken in 1974 (GC XIV) was that of "diversity in unity," seeing difference as enrichment and contributing, each in its own way, to the one common project. Although the equality of priests and brothers was acknowledged, there

---

21. Ibid., 39.
22. *Guide for Spiritan Formation*, 3.

was still some way to go to bring about a change of attitude and behavior to unite all in one fraternal community. The 1980 emphasis (GC XV) was on the religious-missionary identity of Spiritans with all members of the congregation responding to that one vocation and, as such, being brothers living in community. Commitment to this vocation did not necessarily include the desire to be a priest. Research on this vocation was required, and experimentation on new forms of membership was to continue.

SRL defined the Spiritan vocation in terms of religious and missionary life. While recognizing a distinction of roles between priest and brother members, all "are to bear witness to a kingdom of justice and peace." And this is to be achieved "by living together in community" (SRL 24). It made no mention of ordained ministers as such. The Spiritan vocation is lived in community where "each one and all are looked upon as confreres, received from the Lord. Each individual according to his gifts—young, old, in health, in sickness—each one has gifts from which all draw benefit" (SRL 34). Since 1986 the Spiritan brother "sees himself and wishes to be seen as a full partner in the work of evangelization, as indeed the Rule of Life would have it."[23] The Spiritan brother is mentioned in SRL in a collective sense with the priest members jointly engaged in bearing witness and living together in community (SRL 24). The perspective of complementarity is applied in appreciating the different forms of participation in the one Spiritan family (SRL 24.2).

A three-day congress of Spiritan brothers, hosted by the French province, was held at Chevilly-Larue, France, from 3 to 5 July 1989, bringing together a total of 75 brothers, of whom 51 were from the French Province itself, 11 from French Districts, 6 from Holland, 3 from Belgium, 3 from Portugal and 1 from Ireland. The congress was originally planned for the French province only, but the other European provinces were invited to send representatives. The congress heard that at one time in the nineteenth century, there were more Spiritan brothers than priests. In 1989, they formed only 11 percent of the congregation. Of the 377 brothers, 138 were from the French province, with 72 from Holland, 45 from Portugal, 35 from Germany and 30 from Ireland. None of the other circumscriptions had more than 7. One of the things stressed at the congress was the special vocation of the Spiritan brother and his mission as a consecrated layman, and that the validity of this vocation should be presented by the congregation to generous young men.[24]

The sharing of several experiences of community life at GC XVII, Itaici 1992, proved a significant moment in bringing the SRL ideal to life.

23. Superior General's Report (1992) 135.
24. *Spiritan News* 78 (1989) 3–4.

In the Pakistan group, there were ten Spiritans, four were brothers and six were priests, with a brother as superior. "The community life is such that all share in the pastoral activity, with each person's particular charism being respected."[25] Brothers were superiors in formation communities in Brazil and Paraguay. "With very few exceptions, there seems to be no separation between brothers and priests in the congregation. In some places, the titles 'Father' or 'Brother' are no longer used"[26] Itaici envisaged the establishment of apostolic teams comprising three kinds of vocation: priests, brothers, and lay associates. In doing so it recognized that in the past the status of brothers was lower than the the status of priests. Distinctions in leadership between brothers and priests should be avoided in the congregation. It will be remembered that *CDD*'s effort to include brothers at all levels of leadership in the congregation was curtailed by canon law which did not allow the appointment of a brother as superior or assistant superior at local, provincial, or general level in clerical institutes.

A Nigerian Spiritan brother, Joseph C. Mba, CSSp, was invited to attend GC XIX, Torre d'Aguilha 2004, to speak on the continued validity of the role of the Spiritan brother. His presentation began with the recognition that

> the vocation to the brotherhood in the congregation is dwindling. Looking at the overall statistics, one cannot but agree that in a short time, membership to the brotherhood will be a thing of the past. One cannot deny that in Africa, and particularly in Nigeria, there is a "vocation boom," especially to the priesthood.[27]

Brother Joseph pointed out the missionary needs that could be met by brothers. These included catechetics, education and hospital visitation, work with prisoners, refugees, technical and mechanical work.

Torre d'Aguilha suggested a causal link between a growing clericalism in the congregation and the drop in the number of Spiritan brothers. It hoped that the brother's vocation would not disappear and called for the elimination of "any hint of discrimination amongst us." Its near-extinction was a consequence of a failure to adequately value the vocation and the need to give it fresh impetus was acknowledged. "Having played such an

---

25. Itaici (1992) 76.

26. Ibid.

27. Torre d'Aguilha (2004) 68. The vocation boom led to a restructuring of the Nigerian Province. On 2 October 2010 four circumscriptions replaced the one province of Nigeria. They were the Province of Nigeria South-East; the Province of Nigeria North-East; the Foundation of Nigeria North-West and the Foundation of Nigeria South-West.

important role in the history of the congregation, the vocation of brother, 'this branch of the same tree,' must not be allowed to perish."[28] The capitulants voted that the vocation of the Spiritan brother should be explained and recommended to young people interested in becoming Spiritans; that the need for brothers with professional skills be publicized; and that suitably qualified brothers would be appointed to formation teams. Exclusive terms that gave a false image of the congregation, such as "Holy Ghost Fathers" or "seminaries" were to be avoided.[29]

Spiritan Lay Associates

The Spiritan charism of mission to the poor was not the exclusive preserve of the professed members of the congregation. The involvement of lay Spiritans in the process of collaboration and sharing in Spiritan mission and life accelerated since the 1970s mostly in the Northern provinces.[30] In the 1980s the different groups of associates in North America had regular contact with each other deepening their commitment to works of Justice and Peace. The first International Meeting of Lay Spiritans and Associates was held in 1991. This was the initiative of the USA/East Province, which hosted the gathering at Bethel Park, Pittsburgh, from 17 to 21 June 1991. The preparatory committee included Fr. Norman Bevan USA/East provincial, John and Anne-Marie Hansen (USA/East), Raymond and Denise LaBelle (Canada), Anne MacGregor-O'Neill, Dermot and Deirdre McLoughlin (Trans-Canada). Thirty lay and seventeen professed Spiritans assembled from seventeen Spiritan circumscriptions. Fr. Michael Doyle represented the general council at the meeting. Nineteen children were also in attendance and as one participant remarked, "It was interesting to be engaged in group discussions while five- and six-year-olds wandered in and out to inform their parents of the terrible things that their older brothers and sisters had done."[31]

The meeting explored ways to advance lay participation in Spiritan life and mission. It delineated two main types of lay association, that of the "Lay Spiritan" and "Spiritan Associate." The lay Spiritan made a long-term

28. *Spiritan Life*, 15 (2006) 116–19.

29. Torre d'Aguilha (2004) 69.

30. Lay participation in Spiritan mission and life was a reality before 1968. Reference was made in 1962 at GC XII to the increasing role for lay coworkers in Irish Spiritan schools as the number of confreres available for that work decreased These schools had among their staff those who already had an association with the congregation as former teacher volunteers in Africa or as former professed members (Statutes of GC XII [1962] *GB* 47, supplement, 53*).

31. *Spiritan News* 88 (1991) 1.

commitment to share the Spiritan ideals and spirituality in community life or through regular contacts and prayer in common.[32] It was Fr. Doyle who, as provincial, invited Dr. Dermot and Deirdre McLoughlin, on Pentecost Sunday 1974, to form the nucleus of a community of lay Spiritans in Trans-Canada. The meeting also recognized many forms of involvement and support for Spiritan mission in the different provinces.

An evaluation of the meeting confirmed the value of bringing like-minded people together to share their experiences and pool their resources. It was agreed that an important value of the meeting was enabling lay Spiritans and associates from different countries to get to know each other. One participant reported, "For the first time we were able to see the international nature of the associate movement. We no longer feel as we once did that we must be crazy for wanting to be associated with a religious community. Pulling associates from isolation around the globe was important affirmation for us."[33]

The following year an invitation was extended to Dermot and Deirdre McLoughlin to take part in GC XVII. Their participation brought awareness to the issue of lay involvement in Spiritan life and mission. "The witness of the two lay people present at the chapter made a deep impression on the assembly" (Itaici 38.1.1). Twelve years later a North American regional meeting of lay associates was held in April 2004 at the Spiritan center in Montreal. The participants gave expression to their mission as lay associates. "We see ourselves as a community gathered together under the strength of the Spirit; we give special attention to the poor, the vulnerable, and the excluded in our society, and we work beside them in their efforts to free themselves from the deprivation in which they live."[34]

---

32. Spiritan Associates typically made a short-term commitment of two to three years to mission service with the Spiritans. Examples of such involvement were the VICS (Volunteer International Christian Services) program in Canada, which was running since 1971; the "Missionar auf Zeit" (MaZ) of the German province, which started in 1982; and the Spanish province which had prepared and sent some twenty-five volunteers on Spiritan mission. Other provinces planned for short-term voluntary commitments on an *ad hoc* basis.

33. Ibid., 2.

34. The theme of lay involvement in the Spiritan education mission received a lot of attention in Europe in the 1990s. Representatives of Spiritan schools in Europe met in Knechtsteden, Germany (from 11 to 14 April 1996). The meeting recognized that "it is clear that the laity in our colleges have brought their own experience, thoughtfulness and realism. It is the laity who will have the responsibility to ensure the survival and development of our Spiritan charism in Spiritan schools. Structures must be put in place which will facilitate this." The meeting represented 40 schools with 12,000 students and 2,000 staff. *Spiritan News* 114 (1996).

Meetings of lay associates from across Europe have taken place in different locations since 1997. The 2004 meeting, held at Le Bouveret, Switzerland, from 29 April to 2 May, prepared a report and elected a delegate to attend GC XIX. In one of the "other documents" of that chapter there is an extended reflection on "Lay Spiritans." It recognized that as in previous general chapters—Itaici and Maynooth—the chapter membership included lay associates. "The sharing of our spirituality with lay people, as well as new forms of communion and co-responsibility in mission, are already part of the congregation's heritage" (TA 99). It spoke of Spiritan laity as "a branch of the Spiritan tree" acknowledging that "a real ecclesiology of communion and participation is created by an attitude of shared responsibility in the task of building up the kingdom of God" (TA 101).[35] Here Torre d'Aguilha was concluding the work of Itaici which called for a formation program for lay associates without the imposition of structures (Itaici, 92); and Maynooth which called on communities to be welcoming and collaborative with lay brothers and sisters.[36] Fr. Schouver's report amplified the theme of lay collaboration in Spiritan mission.

> The emergence of the laity in the church is without doubt one of the most fruitful intuitions to emerge from Vatican II. It is the hope that the laity will be a line of force in the third millennium. One of the domains which is actually developing in the church is the closer relationship between religious and lay people. The laity, men and women, celibate or married, desire to be nourished by the richness of the charism of the consecrated life in its three dimensions: spiritual experience, specific mission, and community life.[37]

Schouver was following the lead given by *Vita consecrata* which spoke of the "sharing of gifts" and the "sharing of charism" by religious with the laity and of new possibilities, rich in hope, opening up in the relationship between consecrated persons and the laity (*VC* 54). Schouver concluded, "A

---

35 Maynooth also called on lay Spiritan groups to form their own structures according to their particular contexts (Maynooth 119).

36. See *Anima Una* 62, 41–50. A questionnaire was sent to all circumscriptions in November 2007 inviting information with a view to setting-up a data base on lay Spiritans. There were sixteen replies with the information that there were many forms of association and a great variety of formation programs and levels of relationship with the communities concerned. Analysis of the responses indicated significant lay collaboration with a diversity of understandings. It was reported that 105 Spiritan Associates had written contracts with their circumscriptions that were also registered with the general council.

37. Superior General's Report (2004) 117.

mutual enrichment emerges from this relationship, and we believe that new aspects of the Spiritan charism can emerge from this sharing; the congregation will come to know a new spiritual and missionary upsurge, thanks to the contribution of the laity."[38]

---

38. Ibid.

Chapter 9

Spiritan Religious Life

1. Different Religious Identities in the Catholic Church

MANY LAY PEOPLE IN the church are fascinated by the diversity of religious identities and the distinction between "regular clergy" and "secular clergy." Monica Verploegen Vandergrift[1] interrogated this diversity by tracing the development of different forms of religious life each with its attendant distinctive spirituality. She delineated broad categories featuring orders/congregations from the monastic (Augustinian, Benedictine and Cistercian), to the mendicant (Franciscan, Dominican and Carmelite), to the ministerial and active apostolic (the Jesuit, Redemptorist, Salesian and Marist), to the missionary (Spiritan, Maryknoll, and Society of African Missions).

Vandergrift identified *monasticism* with community and contemplation. "It is traditionally seen as a conservative lifestyle that requires us to go away to a place dedicated to foundational practices of solitude, silence, and scripture. . . . Monasticism emerged in the fourth century as a reaction against the institutionalization and alignment of Christianity with the Constantinian Empire."[2] The *mendicant* orders were initially popular lay movements. They attracted people who wanted to dedicate themselves wholeheartedly to improving the conditions in the world and spreading the Christian message. "Mendicants abandoned the surety and protection of

---

1. Monica Verploegen Vandergrift is codirector of TATENDA International (*tatenda* is the Shona for "thanks"), based in Boston, USA. TATENDA International is a trust offering a "rejuvenation in the Spirit" experience to formation communities in the developing world. "

2. Verploegen, *Legacy of the Founders*, 3.

monastic enclaves and formed communities that took on the gospel challenge to rebuild the church, one that was aligned with the poor, the outcast, and the sick."³ The *ministerial and active apostolic* spirituality, associated with Ignatius of Loyola and Alphonsus de Liguori among others, "was a combination of an internal call to dedicate one's life to God, manifested through external expressions of that conversion."⁴ The conversion was expressed by addressing the needs of the poor of their time through catechetics and a variety of social work.

Verploegen's review concluded with the *missionary* congregations "that exclusively were formed to travel to foreign countries to serve peoples beyond their home countries.... Historically, missionary spirituality grew out of the spiritual impulse to go out with the gospel vision and better the world. It is as ancient as the gospel."⁵ In her description of the Spiritans, Verploegen identified a providential connection between the two founders.

> Both Des Places and Libermann attended to the directives of the Holy Spirit within the historical milieux in which they lived. Their great conviction that the Holy Spirit spoke through the persons, places, and events of life was a common bonding between them, despite the century and a half that separated their lives. Availability to the Spirit's invitation became a key feature of the zealous men who gathered around each of these men. The radical willingness to listen faithfully and respond wholeheartedly to the Holy Spirit within the concrete circumstances of life characterized their charism and their spiritual approach. Part of the legacy of Des Places and Libermann, therefore, included evangelical availability, evangelical poverty, and active self-disposal to the Holy Spirit.⁶

Verploegen was attracted to the Spiritan model of religious life. Quoting from Koren she interpreted the vows of poverty and obedience in terms of evangelical availability. Celibate love was understood by her as "active self-disposal" enabling the Holy Spirit to be at work. The Spiritan vocation was centered on "the Holy Spirit with a call to evangelical availability and evangelical poverty. Like many missionary communities, they see

---

3. Ibid., 34.

4. Ibid., 63. Verploegen continued her description of the ministerial and active apostolic spirituality: "Active ministerial spirituality was evident in Christianity in its earliest days. The example of instruction and active attentiveness to the needs of the people was best seen in the human figure of Jesus Christ himself. He was not only interested in feeding people's spiritual lives, but also in nourishing them in other ways." Ibid., 63.

5. Ibid., 99.

6. Ibid., 106–7.

themselves going where others will not go. As their name indicates, there is an emphasis on the Holy Spirit in these encounters. There is a value placed on experience, flexibility, and personal dignity in this tradition."[7]

Claude Poullart des Places moved from Collège Louis-le-Grand to form community with poor students; Francis Libermann moved from the Eudist novitiate to form a society with Tisserant and Le Vavasseur to evangelize "les pauvres noirs" (the poor blacks). Both transitioned from formal religious and clerical environments to a new apostolate in response to God's call. The apostolate was the purpose; religious life became the means to fulfill the purpose. Des Places wrote a set of rules for his community to preserve and promote Christian living; Libermann wrote a provisional rule making "the spirit of religion" the soul of community life and the apostolate (*Provisional Rule*, pt. 2, art. 1). Libermann's commentary on this article, provided by Lannurien, reads: "the spirit of religion is the source-principle which must give life and activity to it, the reason being that our end and goal is wholly supernatural and it is all for the glory of God."[8]

2. Spiritan Religious Life since *SRL*

An elderly Irish confrere recalled taking final vows in the congregation many years ago. He was a seminarian "prefecting" in one of the Spiritan colleges in Ireland at the time. It was at night and he was supervising a dormitory full of young students. His superior called for him saying that his temporary vows expired at midnight and that he could make final profession if he wished. He did wish to do so and made his way to the college chapel with the superior who invited him into the sanctuary and opened the door of the tabernacle on the main altar. He was given a form with the words of perpetual profession and asked to speak them to the Lord present in the Blessed Sacrament. The forms were signed, the tabernacle closed, and the newest finally professed member of the congregation returned to the supervision of a rowdy dormitory.

This brief recollection is given to highlight a pre-Vatican II attitude to religious life in the Irish province. The goal of a Kimmage formation was ordination to the priesthood and appointment to the missions. External observance of the seminary regime with a monastic regularity, severity and silence, was the price paid to "get to the missions." Religious life was experienced from the time of the novitiate as an exercise in external observance of rules for the formation of the Spiritan *habitus*. The recollection

7. Ibid., 132.
8. *Provisional Rule*, 119.

exemplifies the taking of vows as a legal requirement with obligations of external observance. In this, it partially followed Libermann's *Règlements* of 1849 which addressed religious life on two levels. The first revolved around external observance. The second was at the level of virtue with a vowed life chosen to symbolize a total self-giving and consecration of self to God.[9] Part 2, "Rules Common to All Professed Members" of the pre-Vatican II Rules and Constitutions similarly distinguished between the vow and the virtue for each of the vows.[10]

From the 1970s a new way of understanding religious life and in living a vowed life emerged in the spirit of Vatican II. O'Donnell pointed out the significance of new social mores affecting the understanding and living of the three vows.[11] The observance of the vow of poverty, he maintained, was especially complicated for clerical religious who had to manage parishes, administer church funds, keep a personal bank account, and use a credit card, as modern living demanded. He asked, how could clerical religious with such a lifestyle live their vow of poverty in the traditional way? It can be added that this question applied equally to the religious brother. O'Donnell maintained that the vow of obedience needed rethinking given the dialogical culture that had developed in religious life. Living the vow of celibacy (a term more commonly used than chastity) also needed to be reimagined as contemporary psychology increasingly pointed to the need for healthy personal relationships to strengthen and support the celibate option.

While religious consecration had a juridical aspect in the *Spiritan Rule of Life*, it was understood theologically as a personal commitment made in continuity with the baptismal call to holiness and the carrying on of Christ's mission (*SRL* 50). It is a gift of the Holy Spirit (*SRL* 51) experienced through encounter with Jesus and a desire to witness to the kingdom of God (*SRL* 52). The fruit of this experience and self-giving response is joy and liberation of self for service of others (*SRL* 53). This vocation is lived in reliance on God's faithfulness (*SRL* 54). *SRL*'s emphasis on the divine initiative in calling and sustaining a joyous and liberating response can be contrasted with the pre-Vatican II Rules and Constitutions's utilitarian understanding of the vows which were taken to achieve the "aims" of the congregation. "To ensure the sanctification of its members, and to prepare them more

---

9. See Daly, *Spiritan Wellsprings*, 208. The taking of public vows in the congregation began in 1855.

10. Rules and Constitutions. The Vow of Poverty (from 239 to 246), the Virtue of Poverty (from 247 to 254); the Vow of Chastity (from 255 to 256), the Virtue of Chastity (from 257 to 264); the Vow of Obedience (from 265 to 268), the Virtue of Obedience (from 269 to 274).

11. O'Donnell, "Clerical Religious," 9–10.

effectively for the apostolic life by developing in them dispositions of self-denial, generosity, and union with God, the congregation requires them to take and to practice the three vows of religion."[12]

In Chastity for the Kingdom

SRL also differs from the Rules and Constitutions presentation of the three vows which began with poverty, then chastity, and then obedience. SRL begins with "In Chastity for the Kingdom." SRL 56 set the foundation for a Spiritan living of the vow of chastity: God chose an intimate relationship with humankind through the mystery of the incarnation. This divine act inspires a voluntary response of love for God and neighbor (SRL 56). The single state is chosen by Spiritans and lived chastely in fraternal community and in communion with all (SRL 57, 58). The high ideal set is difficult to realize and all who take this path do so trusting in God's mercy and love and the support of a fraternal community (SRL 59). "Our celibacy is a sign that the kingdom has already come" (SRL 60).

SRL's emphasis on the relational nature of celibacy reflects not only contemporary psychology's understanding of the human person but also the mind of Libermann. The Règlements highlighted the relational nature of the vow and presented the behavior expected of one consecrated to God.

> Their bearing will be modest, their manner serious, their tone of voice moderate, and they will be peaceful and reserved in their actions and words. ... In everything they will be serious, peaceful, and of good conduct. They must avoid, however, a manner which is austere, hard, rude, or unfeeling in tone. Their gravity, if spiritual in origin, must have charity as its inspiration.[13]

O'Donnell referred to the church scandals among its celibate clergy and religious and the urgent need to understand that the living of the charism of celibacy is predicated on healthy psychosexual living. Spiritan leadership since SRL promoted among the membership the values of total self-giving, honesty, and integrity in relationships. As in SRL, the topic was approached in an inspirational and compassionate way.

---

12. Rules and Constitutions 8.

13 Daly, *Spiritan Wellsprings*, 152. The *Règlements* of Francis Libermann, pt. 2, sec. 3, ch. 4, art. 7, no. 518. Daly commented that Libermann is not fearful of sexuality or excessively prudent: "Libermann felt himself free with the people he met and he expressed for them a real affection, which showed no signs of a fearful frigidity and stiffness. He was at ease in personal relationships because he had made himself free." Ibid., 213.

> Our religious consecration is a journey of discovery: despite moments of weakness and doubt, we gradually come to know that God's love can indeed fulfil all our desires, we learn to let go of our inborn longings for possessions and power and we experience a new freedom to serve God and our brothers and sisters. It is also fundamentally a journey of conversion, if we are to try to live fully for the Lord and for the people he has called us to serve.[14]

Libermann's practical wisdom of the nineteenth century can be directly applied to contemporary child safeguarding issues. In the *Règlements* he made specific reference to how missionaries were to relate with children.

> The missionaries will avoid those attentions and too natural feelings of affections which come so spontaneously because of their innocence and the other qualities of childhood. They should also avoid too affectionate shows of tenderness, such as embraces, kisses, etc. Nor should they seek satisfaction in friendship with children any more than any other relationship. . . . They must, however, show children much kindness and affection after the example and in the spirit of our Lord Jesus Christ.[15]

In Poverty for the Kingdom

The Spiritan, in imitation of Jesus, takes on "the condition of the poor" to be one with those he is called to share the gospel (*SRL* 61). This free self-donation is realized in community where everything is held in common (Acts 4:32) for the sake of the apostolate (*SRL* 63). The Spiritan rule, while attending to the practicalities associated with vowed poverty (*SRL* 64–69), maintains the visionary approach to the vows by setting it in the context of God's self-emptying in Jesus and the response in love expressed through complete self-giving in service of the poor.[16] The vow of poverty is taken

---

14. *I/D* (2002) 59. Letter of the superior general, Pierre Schouver, CSSp, on behalf of the general council.

15. Pt. 2, sec. 3, ch. 4, art. 13; in Daly, *Spiritan Wellsprings*, no. 524.

16. This contrasts with the opening statement on the vow of poverty in the Rules and Constitutions which was legalistic and negative. "By the vow of poverty, the members of the congregation bind themselves not to dispose of any temporal goods without the permission of their lawful Superior" (Constitution 239). *SRL* returned to Libermann's connection of the vow with the apostolate. He wrote, "The members of the congregation will consider poverty as one of the most important and fundamental virtues of the apostolic and religious life. . . . Poverty affects the sanctification of its members and makes them fit for service of the people whom divine providence has confided to them."

and lived in solidarity with those subject to "an unchosen poverty" and professed as a sign of God's kingdom where there is no more injustice and no more poverty. Libermann's challenge to those who come after him to be with the poor "as servants with their masters" continues to be the Spiritan ideal.[17] Spiritans choose to live away from the security of family and culture and so witness to the riches that come to those entrusting themselves to divine providence (*SRL* 70).

SRL, like the Rules and Constitutions before it, proposed a simple and modest lifestyle for Spiritans. Each reflected the language of its time and both were grounded in the established rule of a balance between "abundance and destitution" (Rules and Constitutions 248). The Spiritan intentional choice of a simple and modest lifestyle to be in solidarity with the poor was given explicit expression (*SRL* 71). All aspects of Spiritan life both personally, in community, and globally as a congregation, were "at the service of our apostolic life" (*SRL* 72). Becoming poor with the poor is a liberating experience empowering a full self-giving for the service of the good news (*SRL* 74).

An inevitable tension exists between what Spiritans profess to be and what is actually the case in their individual, communal, and congregational living. Membership of an international congregation provides opportunities for communication and travel; means to access funding for projects, and network with other agencies in development work. The level of education achieved by members as required by church law and the nature of the apostolate confer social status. Spiritans have access to a security and standard of living beyond the reach of many they are called to serve.

"Living the vow of poverty today" was recognized as a constant challenge. A substantial reflection on this challenge was made in 2008 by the general council addressing it under four headings:

1. the vow of poverty as a means to overcome poverty;
2. taking the vow of poverty to be like Christ;
3. taking the vow of poverty to live together as a congregation;
4. forming oneself in the vow of poverty.

These four headings were addressed at the three levels of the individual, the local community, and the circumscription (*Anima Una* 61 [2008]).

The key approach to the challenge of living the vow of poverty is choosing to live simply in a community that orders all that it has toward its purpose: the evangelization of the poor. This intentionality, itself a gift of the

---

Règlements, pt. 2, sec. 3, ch. 3, art. 1.
17. *N.D.* IX.330.

Spirit, enables life-giving choices that allow Spiritans to be fashioned into the likeness of Christ who emptied himself taking the condition of a slave (Phil 2:7). "Identifying with the poor Christ begins with the slow recognition of one's own limits and continues with a dying to oneself, until one is no longer controlled by desire for worldly goods. Having achieved this self-emptying, the Spiritan candidate is ready to undertake his mission."[18]

In Obedience for the Kingdom

Jesus Christ is the model of total availability (*SRL* 75) that can only be imitated through the power of the Holy Spirit (*SRL* 76). The concept of discerning God's will through dialogue is the innovation of the new Rule of Life that distinguishes its directives on obedience from its predecessor, the Rules and Constitutions, which predicated obedience on the just interpretation of the rule by the superior. Their contractual language was replaced by the inspirational language of *SRL*. There is a shift from "conform" and being "placed over" to discernment and dialogue (*SRL* 77).[19] The individual member is part of a community and is free to submit his plans and make suggestions to the community and it's superior. However, the mission belongs to the community and he is prepared to set aside his own preferences for what is agreed through community discernment. *SRL* introduced new dimensions to deciding God's will: what is asked by the local people; the signs of the times interpreted in the light of the gospel; and community discernment.

Libermann in the *Règlements* only referred to the rules of the congregation and its superiors. "Perfect obedience consists in renouncing one's own judgement and will to submit oneself with love to the will of God as manifested by the rules of the congregation and its superiors." Libermann also advocated a blind obedience, directing that "superiors will be obeyed

---

18. *Anima Una* 61 (2008) 26. I recall a general assembly of Spiritans in Kenya arguing on how to live the vow of poverty. Some regretted living in concrete houses when the majority of their parishioners's dwellings were made of mud or of wood. A visiting Tanzanian confrere, Fr. Josephat Msongare, CSSp, settled the argument by saying that Africans did not mind the size of house their priests lived in or what it was made of. What mattered was that its doors and windows should be open in the spirit of *karibu* (welcome).

19. Constitution 30 of the Rules and Constitutions on the vow of obedience begins: "By the vow of obedience, the members of the congregation contract the obligation to obey the formal commands of their lawful superiors in all that bears directly or indirectly on the observance of the Rules and Constitutions." The virtue is similarly understood as binding professed members "to conform to what is laid down in the Rules and Constitutions, and to the orders and directions of superiors and functionaries placed over them" (Constitution 31).

even when they order things which might be against the rule or against its spirit."[20] But this reference to Libermann's advocacy of blind obedience needs to be balanced by his respect for the individual and his practice of discernment. In a letter dated 8 June 1845 to Fr. Briot, a young member of the Holy Heart of Mary waiting at Bordeaux to go with others to the mission at Dakar, Libermann counselled a process of community discernment to better decide on the direction their mission should take.

> When you are about to begin something important, consider and discuss the matter together in the presence of God. Begin by removing all prejudice for or against the venture. . . . Weigh well what you think you ought to do in a spirit of faith but at the same time reason things out. . . . When you discuss what should be done, your heart must not rule over your head. . . . Always be guided by your faith, basing your conduct solely on the principles of the gospel. But while your mind is tuned into the things of God, it should also reason things out and act after mature reflection and deliberation. . . . Leave nothing to chance, but once you have taken every precaution, place your trust in God alone.[21]

Since *SRL*, the Spiritan understanding of the vow of obedience is of an obligation freely undertaken with confidence in the faithfulness of God and for the sake of the apostolate (*SRL* 78). Spiritans commit themselves to the Rule of Life and subsequent decisions made by the congregation "in pursuit of its apostolic goals" (*SRL* 80) in service of the kingdom of God. As part of the body of Christ that is the church, the congregation's members remain loyal to the teaching of the church and its authority (*SRL* 81).[22]

Obedience is not a burden but liberation for those who freely and responsibly embrace as their very own what is required of them as members of the congregation. The fruit of intentional obedience is an inner freedom which liberates the individual from a desire for power over others enabling him to grow into the full likeness of Christ (2 Cor 3:18). The general council produced a document on obedience to be studied throughout the congregation in 2011. In it they meditated on Jesus as showing forth the way to a life-giving obedience (*Anima Una* 63 [2011]).

> Jesus shows the path of obedience—a free acceptance of God's plan, making his own life an act of service of the Father and of

---

20. *Règlements*, pt. 2, sec. 3, ch. 5, art. 1 and 5.

21. *Spiritan Anthology*, 267.

22. *SRL* also makes provision for the explicit giving of an order "under the vow" that requires compliance (*SRL* 79).

the Father's plan for the world. For Jesus, as for all of us, this path is marked with setbacks. Did he not "learn obedience through what he suffered" (Heb 5:8) by saying and doing only what the Father gave him to say and do? He encountered a lack of understanding from the members of his own family who concluded that he was "out of his mind" (Mk 3:21). He had to face conflict from the religious practitioners of his own land and had to endure being treated as a blasphemer. The scene in the Garden of Gethsemane highlights the dilemma—"Not what I wish but what you wish" (Matt 26:39). To persevere in listening to the Father at that particular moment becomes a real interior struggle, an "agony." By becoming "obedient to death, the death of the cross" (Phil 2:8), Jesus does not engage in blind obedience but rather his obedience is the liberating act of a free person.[23]

Missionaries who know what it is to sacrifice their own will and well-being for the sake of the gospel can identify with this meditation and draw strength from the one who not only calls them to mission, but who goes ahead of them to Galilee (Mark 14:28).

---

23. *Anima Una* 63 (2011) 6–7. The theme of obedience was understood under four headings: (i) Obedience: Learning to Listen; (ii) Obedience: School of Liberty; (iii) Obedience: The Path of Communion; (iv) Obedience at the Service of Mission. The reflections were addressed to the three levels of the congregation, the individual, the local community, and the circumscription which, together make up the congregation.

Chapter 10

The Rediscovery of the Spiritan Charism

1. In the Power of the Holy Spirit

FR. SCHOUVER RECALLED ATTENDING an evening meal with Pope St. John Paul II and other religious superiors at the Vatican during the first Synod of Bishops for Africa in 1994. He reported that the pope sent good wishes to every Spiritan, with the words, "Well, in your case at least, things have got to be fine—you have the Holy Spirit!"[1] The Holy Father was not speaking infallibly with this remark! Spiritans, usually good at self-criticism, and knowing themselves quite well, might accept the Holy Father's words *cum grano salis* ("with a pinch of salt"). The journey of renewal and adaptation within the church and the congregation's finding its place in the world was a difficult one that upset the old certitudes and strong institutions that sustained Spiritan self-esteem in the past.

In 1979, Bernard Kelly, CSSp, spoke of the traumas experienced by some Spiritans since Vatican II. "It is no secret that over the past fifteen years some members of the Congregation have been having second thoughts about what it means to be a Spiritan. During this time, things have not been turning out as they had expected. Some may even feel themselves strangers in the congregation where they had expected to always feel at home."[2] Another confrere, Fr. Heliodoro Machado, CSSp, writing in 1980, suggested that the confusion experienced by some in the congregation stemmed from forgetting the experience and teaching of Libermann, the missionary.

---

1. *Spiritan News* 102 (1994) 2.
2. Kelly, "Who Would Have Thought," 40.

Do we Spiritans walk along the same path as Libermann did? Are we not in the process of cutting ourselves off from our origins? Should not the uniting force of Libermann's personality always be the source of our inspiration and our joy? Undoubtedly, each age has its own specific problems; those of our own times are different from those which Libermann knew, but I think that we can continue to ask ourselves: Are the demands of the gospel not the same today as yesterday? Do they not continue to call the Christian to make the cause of the poor his own?[3]

Machado went on to describe the "new era of mission" primarily as the emergence of local churches from former mission territories. The changed times required new approaches, different to those taken in Libermann's time, yet requiring the same fundamental missionary orientation that he proposed. The Spiritan heritage was a strong support for the mission endeavor of the new era. "Adaptation to the new stage of evangelization in the local churches according to the Spiritan charism will be the guarantee of a promising future for the mission of Jesus for all those who wish to follow in the footsteps of Libermann and Poullart des Places."[4]

Even after the years of experimentation and the writing of the new rule, with contentious issues addressed, the challenge to maintain unity in an increasingly diverse congregation was keenly felt. GC XVIII, at Maynooth in 1998, asked, "Where do our communities which are so diverse and are in such a constant process of change, find a stable point for their unity?" The congregation, a community of communities, in the first order of its reality as a missionary religious institute, trusts in the providence of the God of life and of mission. "Only the Holy Spirit, living and praying in us, can bring about this astonishing miracle of keeping in unity a group of men, prone to weakness and to sin, which, left to itself would be more likely to fall apart."[5] Maynooth spoke in terms of a mission spirituality echoing the sentiments expressed by Libermann in his encouragement to the missionaries of his day. "The Spirit goes ahead of us on the path of mission, and signs of his presence accompany our work. Mission is therefore a pilgrimage, an adventure, contemplation, and discovery of the work of the Spirit. It is, above all, a witness through the quality of our lives. We are called to conversion and transformation by a process of *kenosis*."[6] The trials and difficulties involved

3. Machado, "Dream Realised," 5.

4. Ibid., 18.

5. Maynooth (1998) 72. The quotation is taken from the report of Fr. Jean Paul Hoch, CSSp, French provincial, who would be elected superior general at Torre d'Aguilha in 2004.

6. Ibid., 99.

in remaining faithful to a life of conversion and transformation were met through the congregation's rediscovery of its charism.

A Spiritan Spirituality Is Given Expression

GC XIX, at Torre d'Aguilha in 2004, attended to the question of "handing on the Spiritan charism." The superior general, Fr. Schouver, CSSp, set the theme for the chapter with his report entitled *Authentically Living the Spiritan Charism Today*. The general council presented a pre-chapter document with this title giving three main headings for chapter deliberations: (1) rediscovering Spiritan apostolic life in the contemporary world; (2) the increasingly international membership of the congregation; (3) maintaining unity in diversity. Reactions to the document suggested a consensus "that it is time to look more closely at some of the issues that affect significantly how we live the vision of Maynooth. Many have called for a bridging of the gap between our vision and our lived reality."[7] The emphasis was placed on the evangelizers themselves. What are "the 'pebbles in our shoes' that frustrate and hold us back from following more faithfully the charisms of our founders?"[8]

The program of animation since GC XIV, in 1974, resulted in the recognition of a Spiritan spirituality and charism originating in the founders and articulated in *SRL* as a "double reality" by which the Spiritan is consecrated to deep communion with God and service of others, especially the poor. Spiritan life and mission are grounded in the Holy Spirit who, Libermann tells us, is the source of happiness and a wellspring of love. Spiritans are open to and respectful of the people to whom they are sent to share life. "Conscious that Christ's Spirit is already present and active in the cultures to which we are sent, mission becomes a pilgrimage of mutual enrichment, where together we identify and seek liberation from the chains that impede the full realization of God's kingdom."[9]

I/D 60 (2007), entitled *Living Spiritan Spirituality*, provides a summary of thinking in the congregation of a distinctive Spiritan spirituality grounded in the apostolic life. It recognized that up until Vatican II Spiritans did not talk about the congregation's "charism." The rediscovery of the example and teaching of Poullart des Places and Francis Libermann set the foundation for a Spiritan spirituality as one of contemplation and action. In them was found the double desire of total submission to God's will

---

7. Torre d'Aguilha (2004) 17.
8. Ibid.
9. Ibid., 18.

expressed by effective missionary work. Libermann's "practical union" with God in the apostolate was the means of sanctification for Spiritans. Spiritan life was understood as a life of prayer and of apostolic service. Spiritans live in community exercising openness, availability, and docility to God's Spirit at work in them. A Spiritan is one who is sent by the community on mission. The Spiritan goes willingly as one on pilgrimage, setting out in search of a greater value and so responding to a deep inner need for dialogue, service, and solidarity with others, especially with the poor and those who suffer.

The congregation had come to recognize a distinctive Spiritan spirituality in 2007. This can be contrasted with the publication in 1985 of *Towards a Missionary Spirituality for Today (I/D 40)* which marked the tentative beginnings of a "missionary" spirituality, rather than a distinctively Spiritan one.[10] The writing of a new rule of life made it possible for the congregation to acknowledge a distinctive Spiritan spirituality.[11] "Looking at the writings of our founders and our response to mission situations over the generations, we became aware that despite our enrichment from many other sources we do indeed have a spirituality that can be called 'spiritan.'"[12]

New terms were incorporated into the Spiritan lexicon—"Pilgrimage," "Justice, Peace and the Integrity of Creation," "Solidarity"—that can be read as a reconfiguration of traditional terms such as "Exodus," "Foundation,"

---

10. The Generalate team in 1985 proposed that a renewed spirituality among the members was a necessary condition for a new apostolic dynamism in the congregation. Seven features of such a renewed spirituality were explored. They were: (1) an experience of God as the Absolute; (2) An openness to the "signs of the times"; (3) great docility to the Holy Spirit; (4) recognition that Spiritan mission is to the poorest; (5) that mission, the work of God, is inseparable from the paschal mystery; (6) that community life is essential for maintaining the religious spirit; (7) that only apostolic holiness can sustain missionary work. The apostolic dynamism required a capacity for (1) exodus—that is a movement from the familiar structures of mission to the development of new ones; (2) foundation—new missionary beginnings among those who "have not yet heard the gospel message or who have scarcely heard it"; (3) apostolic availability—a readiness to leave the work to others and go to meet new needs in new places; (4) welcome—all that the Spirit is doing in the young churches and cooperating with that Spirit; (5) contemplation—being able to see God at work in different cultures, in history and in the signs of the times; (6) insecurity—being unable to see what the future will bring and being able to embrace all the uncertainties of that future; (7) community—an involvement with others that bears witness as it is a life-giving experience; (8) universality—openness to the wondrous diversity of cultures, philosophies, religions and ways of life that engenders communion with all; (9) frontier situations—engaging with what is new, unknown and unsettling, yet recognizing the presence of God in all that is.

11. Michel's biography of Poullart des Places in 1962 and many studies on Libermann became more widely available within the congregation. See "Inventaire Critique des Études Historiques sur Libermann," in Coulon, *Libermann*, 133–60.

12. *Living Spiritan Spirituality*, 5.

"Insecurity." The key classical concepts of Spiritan spirituality articulated in des Places and Libermann of apostolate, community, and religious life remained as the fundamental source for the generation of terms to express Spiritan mission and life. The dynamic between the founding principles of the congregation and the exigencies of contemporary mission shows a characteristic openness to the Spirit of God at work in the every-day events of life. Des Places and Libermann would not have used terms as "lobbying," "networking," and "advocacy," but they knew what it meant to be on the side of "the weak and the little ones," to work for them in collaboration with others and to be their advocates. Words change but the underlying reality to which words give expression remains the constant source of inspiration for mission. Not only is Spiritan spirituality a lived reality; it is a living spirituality, which, like all that lives, adapts to the demands of mission in changing times. These permutations, born of the Spirit, give rise to new expressions of the treasure bestowed by God to the church through the Spiritan founders.

The changes in life and mission undertaken in that journey impacted greatly on Spiritans. The first painful steps of change taken in 1968 set a course that was not always easy to keep as new ways for religious and missionary living required a language appropriate to those new realities. Fluency in that language of mind and heart was only achieved through the rediscovery of the Spiritan charism and attentiveness to the Spirit's guidance into a new era of mission. Can the period between 1968 and the writing of *SRL* in 1986 be interpreted as a "third founding moment" for the congregation?

2. Interpreting the Spiritan Journey of Renewal in 2018

While enthusiasm for debate on the Spiritan interpretation of Vatican II and its journey of renewal has long abated, the fiftieth anniversary of GC XIII provides an opportunity to revisit that debate and appreciate again the significance of the *ad experimentum* period in shaping the Congregation of the Holy Spirit as it exists today. An analysis by a noted theologian and commentator on Vatican II, Massimo Faggioli, on the meaning of Vatican II from its opening in 1962 to its fiftieth anniversary in 2012 according to significant moments offers a hermeneutic to propose parallel moments for the Spiritan congregation's journey of renewal.[13]

---

13. See Faggioli, *Vatican II*, 3–19.

- The first moment was that of the council itself (1962-65). The parallel moment for the congregation was the holding of the Extraordinary General Chapter of Renewal (1968-69).

- The second moment was a time for commentaries and the early implementation of the council (1965-80). The parallel moment for the congregation was the period of experimentation marked by two general chapters, GC XIV 1974 and GC XV in 1980.

- The third moment, from 1980 to 1990, was marked by a reassertion of the church's central authority over the process of implementation which Faggioli associated with the early years of Pope St. John Paul II's papacy.[14] The parallel moment for the congregation was the conclusion of the period of experimentation marked by GC XVI in 1986, finalizing the text of the new rule of life *SRL* and its approval in 1987. There was a gradual reassertion of authority by the general administration at the congregation's center.

- The fourth moment was characterized by scholarly interest and debate on the significance and meaning of the council, with the publication of many histories on the council (1990-2000).[15] The parallel moment for the congregation was the period of implementation of *SRL* marked by two general chapters, GC XVII in 1992, and GC XVIII in 1998 and studies on the congregation's heritage.

- The fifth moment (leading up to and following on from the fiftieth anniversary of the council) was dominated by the revisionism of Joseph Ratzinger both as cardinal prefect of the Congregation of the Doctrine of the Faith and as Pope Benedict XVI. The interpretation of the council as a paradigmatic event representing discontinuity with the past was rejected. Instead, he maintained that the council is properly

---

14. With the ending of the period of special experimentation mandated by *Ecclesiae sanctae II*, many religious institutes dedicated to works of the apostolate were engaged in a review of their experience. With the approval of their revised constitutions and the coming into effect of the newly formulated Code of Canon Law, they were moving into a new phase of their history. At that point of new beginning, they heard the repeated pastoral call of Pope St. John Paul II to evaluate objectively and humbly the years of experimentation to recognize their positive elements and their deviations (Address to the International Union of Women Superiors General, 1979; and to Major Superiors of Men and Women Religious in France, 1980). This was the context for tension within religious congregations between the two approaches, one referred to as "traditional" and the other as "progressive."

15. Faggioli recognized Giuseppe Alberigo's five-volume work, *History of Vatican II*, as "a major scholarly and historiographical exploration of the debate on Vatican II." Faggioli, *Vatican II*, 15.

interpreted in the context of the whole history of the church and in continuity with its past.[16] The parallel moment for the congregation was the celebration of the Spiritan Jubilee Year 2002–2003, marking the three hundreth anniversary of the founding of the congregation by Claude Poullart des Places in 1703 and the one hundred and fiftieth Anniversary of the death of Francis Libermann in 1852. The general chapter of this period, GC XIX, was held in 2004 with the theme, "*Faithful to the gift entrusted to us*" by which the continuity of the congregation's 300 years' history was acknowledged.

The sequence of events with a parallel sequence for the congregation since GC XIII as outlined above can be variously interpreted. GC XIX understood the fifty years of renewal in the congregation as a time of rediscovering its charism as a living reality evident in "the way we live, the way we pray and participate in the mission of the church and the whole congregation."[17] The congregation changed much since 1968 but remained the one unique congregation in continuity with the charism of its founders through creative fidelity to its mission in the church.

What interpretation applies in 2018 to the Spiritan journey of renewal since 1968? Can the many developments outlined in these pages be understood in terms of a rediscovery of an identity and mission for an apostolic community gifted and sustained by the Spirit of God and given to God's church for the evangelization of the poor? Does this period of renewal constitute a third founding moment (from that of des Places in 1703 and of Libermann in 1848) for the congregation when its identity as a worldwide community was realized and its mission widened to encompass the *oikoumene*, the whole wide world? The narrative proposed here speaks a story of metamorphosis: from law to Spirit; from missions to mission; from institutions to community; from an aggregation of provinces to an international congregation. It tells a story of change in creative fidelity to the congregation's founding charism.

---

16. The church is fundamentally a mystery, "*whose nature is such that it always admits new and deeper exploring*" (Blessed Pope Paul VI, *Opening Address for the Second Session of the Second Vatican Council*, 29 September 1963: *AAS* 55, 848). While Vatican II changed much in the church's thinking and practice, yet, the church remains one, holy, catholic, and apostolic. Its identity, constituted in the mystery of God's self-communication as Father, Son, and Spirit, is itself ever open to new and deeper understanding. One such exploration is the understanding of the church as communion and the relationship between the local churches and the church universal. See the "Ratzinger-Kasper Debate" in the Jesuit magazine *America*. April-November 2001.

17. Torre d'Aguilha (2004) 37.

3. The Journey Continues

The Spiritan story which began in 1703 continues to be lived and told. The charisms of Claude Poullart des Places and Francis Libermann were the seed that germinated into a wonderful plant (borrowing the analogy for religious life given in *Vita consecrata*) or the analogy followed here, the unfolding story of unique charisms for mission in the church. The continuing narrative of God's Spirit at work in individuals coming together in religious community for mission to the poor has extended far beyond the seedbed of France and grown into a truly international family. The diversification of membership and works since Vatican II is expressive of the congregation's creative fidelity to its original inspiration in changing circumstances and new ideas. Like the Hasidic tale, Spiritans still know their story, and how to tell it. However, the concern, often expressed during that time, about the handing on of the congregation's charism across generational and cultural differences remains a challenge.

The Challenge of Identity

Fr. Schouver, in his report to GC XIX, asked the question, "How well do we live together in this great and complex organization which is the congregation?"[18] The general chapter recognized a great diversity in its membership, variety in its commitments and different forms of organization.

> Amongst Spiritans, you can find those who are super-active and others who are rather people of listening, of contact and dialogue, of contemplation. Some have been marked by the trials of life; perhaps they have made them more human, more serene, and open to others. Others carry the wounds of contradiction and incomprehension. Sometimes we can feel weighed down by the burden of our differences, of the complexity of the congregation spread across the continents and fashioned by so many cultures, religions, and visions of the world.[19]

What is it that unites Spiritans from different parts of the world; with different temperaments and life experiences; different expectations and hopes for their lives? A shared identity that comes from common participation within the one Spiritan story is a powerful "spiritual adhesive" that

---

18. Ibid., 93.
19. Ibid., 93–94.

connects the many into a coherent unity which channels individual talent and enthusiasm through solidarity in the one Spiritan mission to the poor.

The Spiritan identity has its foundation in a story, common to all, which unfolds from its origins in des Places and Libermann: the experience of the love of God and being captivated by that love for mission. It is through the "telling the stories of the founders and other Spiritans who lived out this spirituality in their work"[20] that the Spiritan charism is passed on from one generation to the other.

The many and varied efforts made to develop the Spiritan identity in a post-Vatican II Church culminated with the inspirational *SRL*. Its approval marked not only the conclusion of a process, but a new beginning for the congregation. Like the church, the congregation is always in need of renewal. Those intimately engaged in the process of writing *SRL* were keenly aware of this. Leadership in the congregation continues to be guided by it as it animates the membership toward an ever deeper love for God, for one another, and the poor through the congregation's many and varied missionary engagements in the world.

GC XIX (2004), held after the celebration of the Spiritan Year (2002–2003), recognized that Spiritan identity is sustained through the handing on of the Spiritan charism. This is achieved at congregational level through "the study of its foundations and history applied to our way of life and spirituality,"[21] and at local community level, through "a style of living together and working for the kingdom."[22] All Spiritans are guardians of the Spiritan identity found in *SRL* and confirm its truth as they give expression to what it says in their lives and mission.

The Challenge of Belonging

The human being needs to belong. In the 1970s, psychologist Abraham Maslow recognized that the rapid changes in American societies gave rise to a great human hunger. Any good society, if it is to survive and be healthy, must satisfy the need for belonging. This was necessary "to overcome the widespread feelings of alienation, aloneness, strangeness, and loneliness, which have been worsened by our mobility, by the break-down of traditional groupings, the scattering of families, the generation gap, the steady urbanization, and disappearance of village face-to-faceness, and the resulting

---

20. Ibid., 39.
21. Ibid., 37.
22. Ibid.

shallowness of American friendship."[23] Religious families before Vatican II met the need for belonging by ensuring certitude in and validation of vocational choice (the call to perfection); an unambiguous lifestyle (religious habit and strict observance of regulations) in unquestioned obedience to religious authority (the superior as "the voice of God"). The renewal of religious life in the light of Vatican II's positive anthropology put emphasis on the interior dispositions and personal vocational choice of each individual member. GC XIX recognized that this growth was primarily achieved in and through community living.

> Community living helps us to grow. In community we are obliged to listen to other ideas and perspectives; we cannot impose our own vision of things. God allows us to be pruned by others so that we can give greater fruit and become strength for the group. In community we learn to serve and our personal gifts are recognized and welcomed as a service to all . . . The ideal is important; it encourages us to strive for greater perfection in real life situations where tensions and conflicts are part of the human condition and can have redemptive and maturing value. Nevertheless, community building does not take place spontaneously but has to be worked at.[24]

Individual Spiritans have many loyalties in their lives, such as their family, age group, professional bodies, social groups, and local church. Loyalty to the congregation and its mission can be denied its rightful place, at the center of their lives. A sense of belonging to the congregation can decrease in intensity the further removed we are from our formation days. The congregation can be reduced to a sorting house for appointments, a point of reference for a position in a local church. In this, we can be reminded of the loose Spiritan identity associated with the congregation in the eighteenth and early nineteenth centuries. The priests trained at the Holy Ghost Seminary in Paris were referred to as "Holy Ghost Fathers," although they were secular priests working in the French colonies.

The hybrid nature of the congregation as clerical and religious can result in a clerical mentality oriented more toward the lifestyle of local clergy than that of the Spiritan community.[25] This was one of the challenges to unity recognized in the days of Vatican II renewal. It is particularly the task for congregation leadership to maintain the sense of belonging among the

---

23. Maslow, *Motivation*, 43.
24. Torre d'Aguilha (2004) 33–34.
25. The Spiritan religious habit was set aside by *SRL* and replaced by "the dress of the clergy, in keeping with canon 284" (*SRL* 73).

membership, building up an esprit de corps that does not end with formation but continues all through life.

GC XIX presented a motivation for Spiritan belonging that is true, not only when first written in 2004, but will continue to challenge future generations of Spiritans. It highlighted a key characteristic of the Spiritan family as "a forgetting of self" and a giving of all, "even our lives" to partake in the death and resurrection of Christ (*SRL* 10).

> It was precisely to live such a vocation and to be faithful to such a commitment that we entered this religious family. The congregation lives by the charism of our founders: they certainly set the bar very high but they have continued to inspire us for the last 300 years. Their spirit is passed on to us through our life together. Thanks to the spirituality they left us and the communion between ourselves in our work and prayer, we live a life which is quite extraordinary but which, without this help and support, would be completely beyond us.[26]

The Challenge to Mission

The creative fidelity to the Spiritan vocation demonstrated in the post-Vatican II era offers inspiration and instruction for future generations of Spiritans. The founding charisms of des Places and Libermann for evangelization of the poor found new expression as Spiritans journeyed from *CDD*'s focus on first evangelization to *SRL*'s portrayal of the apostolic life as a multi-faceted and diverse reality. The many examples of this apostolic life since *SRL* confirmed the Spiritan vocation as a gift from God to the church in service of the *missio Dei*. The evangelization of the poor is the distinctive Spiritan task within the *missio Dei* (*SRL* 4). It is through respectful entry into the world of the poor and walking in solidarity with the poor that the story remains authentically Spiritan.

GC XIX recognized the ongoing tension involved in the congregation remaining true to its founding purpose. It wanted the prophetic voices to be heard; the charismatic dimension of consecrated life reawakened; and the minority groupings—in some places it is the youth, in others, those in primary evangelization and those on the margins—to be listened to and learned from.[27] The Spiritan is "set apart (Acts 13:2) to follow Jesus and to announce the good news of the kingdom" (*SRL* 1). The authentic Spiritan

---

26. Torre d'Aguilha (2004) 94.
27. Ibid., 117–20.

community needs "to experience the gospel, the experience of a faith shared; the celebration of this faith, the sharing of goods and services and the fidelity to an accepted communal project."[28] As an international congregation, the Spiritans are strategically placed to "make a difference" in a divided world by bringing "the haves" and the "have-nots" together in mutual respect at the one table of humanity served by the God who, in Jesus wrapped a towel around his waist and washed the feet of his disciples (John 13:1–17). The example has been given and Spiritans through the ages have chosen to take up the towel and do as the Master has done.

GC XIX sought to encourage the "new life" coming to the congregation through the young provinces. It drew a parallel between the injection of life given to the old Poullart des Places Congregation by the youthful Libermann Society of the Holy Heart of Mary, and the old provinces receiving new life from the young foundations of the South.

> Today we live in similar times: the older provinces have their glorious past, their structures, their values, their legal status, their financial supports, but the new provinces have the new personnel, the new understanding of mission, they have the strong wind coming from the south. They are a grace and a gift offered to the congregation which we must not devalue, but need to believe in, because that is where the future lies.[29]

The Spiritan story of self-emptying in service of others and thereby finding one's true self, told by des Places and Libermann, continues to challenge and draw people to explore the Spiritan vocation either as priests or brothers, as lay associates, or collaborators in mission. The future, like the recent past narrated here, will require fidelity to the church, confidence in the Spiritan charism, loyalty to the congregation and commitment to its mission. Present and future Spiritans are part of a great story reaching back over three hundred years that continues to be lived in them. Their commitment to one other and joy in a shared vocation will sustain them in mission and will, with Poullart des Places, Francis Libermann, and all their forebears, make this a story worth telling and a road worth traveling.

---

28. Ibid.,119.
29. Ibid.,119–20.

Bibliography

Achebe, Chinua. *Anthills of the Savannah*. New York: Anchor, 1987.
Alberigo, Giuseppe. *History of Vatican II*. Maryknoll: Orbis, 2006.
———, ed. *The Reception of Vatican II*. Washington, DC: Catholic University of America Press, 1987.
Arbuckle, Gerald A., SM. *Catholic Identity or Identities? Refounding Ministries in Chaotic Times*. Collegeville: Liturgical, 2013.
———. *Out of Chaos: Refounding Religious Congregations*. New York: Paulist, 1988.
Bane, Martin J. *Catholic Pioneers in West Africa*. Dublin: Clonmore & Reynolds, 1956.
Béguerie, Philippe. *Vers Écône: Mgr. Lefebvre et les Pères du Saint-Esprit*. Paris: Desclée de Brouwer, 2010.
Bevans, Stephen B., SVD. "Revisiting Mission at Vatican II: Theology and Practice for Today's Missionary Church." *TS* 74 (2013) 270–84.
Bevans, Stephen B., and Roger P. Schroeder. *Constants in Context*. Maryknoll: Orbis, 2004.
Beyer, Jean, SJ. "Life Consecrated by the Evangelical Counsels." In *Vatican II: Assessment and Perspectives; Twenty-Five Years After (1962–1987)*, edited by René Latourelle, 3:64–89. New York: Paulist, 1988.
Bosch, David J. *Transforming Mission*. Maryknoll: Orbis, 1991.
Bouchard, Athanase. *La Fin, L'Urgence et Les Moyens D'Une Réforme*. Paris: Cahiers de Spiritualité Missionaire, 1968.
Bowen, John P. *The Missionary Letters of Vincent Donovan, 1957–1973*. Eugene, OR: Pickwick, 2011.
Bromley, Geoffrey W. *Theological Dictionary of the New Testament*. Abridged ed. Grand Rapids: Eerdmans, 1985.
Brown, Raymond E. *The New Jerome Biblical Commentary*. Englewood Cliffs, NJ: Prentice-Hall, 1990.
Canadian Canon Law Society. *The Code of Canon Law*. Grand Rapids: Eerdmans, 1983.
Catholic Church. *Catechism of the Catholic Church*. London: Catholic Truth Society, 2016.
Chittister, Joan. "An Amazing Journey: A Road of Twists and Turns." In *Religious Life: The Challenge of Tomorrow*, edited by Cassian J. Yuhaus, 75–92. New York: Paulist, 1994.
Cleary, Hugh, CSC. "The Consecrated Life: Witness to Destiny." In *Apostolic Religious Life in America Today: A Response to the Crisis*, edited by Richard Gribble, CSC, 144–54. Washington, DC: Catholic University of America Press, 2011.

Confoy, Maryanne, RSC. "Religious Life in the Vatican II Era: State of Perfection or Living Charism?" *TS* 74 (2013) 305–30.

Congar, Yves, OP. *True and False Reform in the Church*. Translated by Paul Philibert, OP. Collegeville: Liturgical, 2011.

Congregation for Institutes of Consecrated Life and Societies of Apostolic Life. *The Service of Authority and Obedience*. 1998. http://www.vatican.va/roman_curia/congregations/ccscrlife/documents/rc_con_ccscrlife_doc_20080511_autorita-obbedienza_en.html.

Congregation for Religious and Secular Institutes. "Essential Elements in the Church's Teaching on Religious Life as Applied to Institutes Dedicated to Works of the Apostolate." 1983. http://www.vatican.va/roman_curia/congregations/ccscrlife/documents/rc_con_ccscrlife_doc_31051983_magisterium-on-religious-life_en.html.

Congregation for Religious and Secular Institutes, Congregation for Bishops. *Mutuae relationes*. Directives for the mutual relations between bishops and religious in the church. Washington, DC: United States Catholic Bishops Conference, 2004.

Congregation of the Holy Spirit. *A Handbook for the Spiritan Rule of Life*. Rome: Generalate, 1987.

———. *General Chapter 1968–1969: Directives and Decisions*. Rome: Generalate, 1970.

———. *General Chapter 1974: Guidelines for Animation*. Rome: Generalate, 1974.

———. *General Chapter 1980: Spiritan Life*. Rome: Generalate, 1980.

———. *General Chapter 1992: "Where Is the Spirit Leading Us?"* Rome: Generalate, 1992.

———. *General Chapter 1998: "Launch Out into the Deep."* Rome: Generalate, 1998.

———. *General Chapter 2004: "Faithful to the Gift Entrusted to Us."* Rome: Generalate, 2004.

———. *Guide for Spiritan Formation*. Rome: Generalate, 1997.

———. *Rules and Constitutions of the Congregation of the Holy Spirit*. Dublin: Holy Ghost Fathers, 1959.

———. *Spiritan Anniversary Diary*. Rome: Generalate, 2003.

———. *A Spiritan Anthology: Writings of Claude-François Poullart des Places and François Marie-Paul Libermann*. Chosen and presented by Christian De Mare, CSSp. Rome: Generalate, 2011.

———. *Spiritan Rule of Life 2013*. Rome: Generalate, 2013.

———. *2000 Years of Evangelization, 300 Years of Spiritan Mission*. Strasbourg: Éditions du Signe, 2000.

Corecco, Eugenio. "Aspects of the Reception of Vatican II in the Code of Canon Law." In *The Reception of Vatican II*, edited by Giuseppe Alberigo, 248–75. Washington, DC: Catholic University of America Press, 1987.

Coulon, Paul, ed. *Histoire & Missions Chrétiennes* 10 (2009).

Coulon, Paul, and Paul Brasseur. *Libermann 1802–1852*. Paris: Les Éditions du Cerf, 1988.

Daly, John, CSSp. *Spiritan Wellsprings: The Original Rules, with Commentaries of the Holy Ghost Congregation*. Dublin: Paraclete, 1986.

De Jong, Albert. *The Challenge of Vatican II in East Africa*. Nairobi: Paulines, 2004.

Deretz, J., and A. Nocent, OSB, eds. *Dictionary of the Council*. London: Chapman, 1968.

Dorr, Donal. *Mission in Today's World*. Dublin: Columba, 2000.

Dortel-Claudot, Michel. "The Task of Revising the Constitutions of the Institutes of Consecrated Life, as Called for by Vatican II." In *Vatican II: Assessment and Perspectives*, edited by René Latourelle, 3:90–130. New York: Paulist, 1989.

Duaime, Jeff, CSSp. "The Heartbeat of Spiritan Education in the US." In *The Heartbeat and Ethos of Spiritan Education*, 101–14. Duquesne: Center for Spiritan Studies, 2013.

Duffy, Stephen J. *The Dynamics of Grace: Perspectives in Theological Anthropology*. Collegeville: Liturgical, 1993.

Dupuis, Jacques, SJ. "A Theological Commentary: Dialogue and Proclamation." In *Redemption and Dialogue*, edited by William R. Burrows, 119–60. Eugene, OR: Wipf & Stock, 1993.

Ebaugh, Helen Rose Fuchs. *Women in the Vanishing Cloister: Organizational Decline in Catholic Religious Orders in the United States*. New Brunswick: Rutgers University, 1993.

Eke, Casimer I., CSSp. *Evangelical Availability: A Contemporary Spiritan Theology and Spirituality of Mission in the Light of Spiritan Living Tradition*. Ann Arbor, MI: ProQuest, 2008.

———. "Re-inventing the Spiritan Charism for Contemporary Mission." *Spiritan Horizons* 1 (2006) 40–47.

Eke, Casimer I., et al. In *The Footsteps of Our Founder: A History of the Spiritan Province of Nigeria 1953–2006*. Onitsha: Spiritan Province, 2006.

Faggioli, Massimo. *Vatican II: The Battle for Meaning*. New York: Paulist, 2012.

Farragher, Seán P., CSSp. *Irish Spiritans Remembered*. Dublin: Paraclete, 1998.

———. *Led by the Spirit: The Life and Work of Claude Poullart des Places*. Dublin: Paraclete, 1992.

Farrelly, Thomas, CSSp. "The Process of Revising the Rules and Constitutions." *Spiritan Papers* 18 (1984) 7–18.

Fernandes, Pedro, CSSp. "Constructing Religious Community: A Spiritan Rereading." *Spiritan Horizons* 8 (2013) 25–38.

Fitzmyer, Joseph A. *First Corinthians: A New Translation with Introduction and Commentary*. New Haven: Yale University Press, 2008.

Flannery, Austin, OP, ed. *Towards the 1994 Synod of Bishops*. Dublin: Dominican, 1993.

———. *Vatican Council II: The Conciliar and Postconciliar Documents*. Rev. ed. Collegeville: Liturgical, 1996.

Flannery, Tony, CSsR. *The Death of Religious Life?* Dublin: Columba, 1997.

Fransen, Peter. *The New Life of Grace*. New York: Herder & Herder, 1972.

Gay, Jean. *Libermann: Jew according to the Gospel (1802–1852)*. Paris: Beauchesne, 1977.

———. *The Spirit of Venerable Libermann*. New York: Society of Saint Paul, 1954.

Geoghegan, Anthony, CSSp. "The Mission of the Irish Province in a Time of Change, 1968–1998." In *Go Teach All Nations*, edited by Enda Watters, CSSp, 159–225. Dublin: Paraclete, 2000.

Gilbert, Alphonse, CSSp. *A Gentle Way to God: The Spiritual Teaching of Francis Libermann, CSSp*. Translated by Myles Fay, CSSp. Dublin: Paraclete, 1990.

———. *You Have Laid Your Hand on Me*. Rome: Spiritan Animation and Research Centre, 1983.

Gilbert, Alphonse, CSSp, and Myles L. Fay, CSSp. "Spiritan Vocation." *Spiritans Today* 2 (1983) 15–18.

Gittins, Anthony J., CSSp. "Mission Today Call and Response." In *Spiritan Anniversary Lectures 1703-2003*, compiled by the Anniversaries Commission, 87–99. Dublin: Paraclete, 2004.

———. "A Missionary's Misgivings: Reflections on Two Recent Documents." In *Redemption and Dialogue*, edited by William R. Burrows, 216–22. Eugene, OR: Wipf & Stock, 1993.

———. "Root, Shoot and Fruit: From *Missio Dei* to Mission Today." *Spiritan Horizons* 1 (2006) 32–39.

———. *The Way of Discipleship*. Collegeville: Liturgical, 2016.

Gobeil, Maurice. "A Life-Experience under the Breath of the Spirit." *Spiritans Today* 4 (1985) 29–48.

Gribble, Richard, CSC, ed. *Apostolic Religious Life in America Today: A Response to the Crisis*. Washington, DC: Catholic University of America Press, 2011.

Gruyters, Antonio, CSSp. "Contemplation and Action." *Spiritan Life* 15 (2006) 111–15.

Gutiérrez, Gustavo. *A Theology of Liberation*. New York: Orbis, 1986.

Haight, Roger, SJ. *The Experience and Language of Grace*. New York: Paulist, 1979.

Hansen, Stephen, et al. "Spiritan Pedagogy in Practice." *Spiritan Horizons* 10 (2015) 99–113.

Harden, Janie Fritz. "Spiritans for Today: Vincent Donovan." *Spiritan Horizons* 10 (2015) 75–86.

Hebblethwaite, Peter. *Synod Extraordinary*. New York: Random, 1986.

Hillman, Eugene, CSSp. *Toward an African Christianity*. New York: Paulist, 1993.

Homan, Helen Walker. *Star of Jacob: The Story of the Venerable Francis Libermann*. Kent: Paraclete, 1953.

Howell, Patrick, SJ. "The 'New' Jesuits: The Response to the Society of Jesus to Vatican II, 1962–2012: Some Alacrity, Some Resistance." In *Conversations on Jesuit Higher Education* 42 (2012) 7–11.

International Theological Commission. "Study on Faith and Inculturation." 1988. http://www.vatican.va/roman_curia/congregations/cfaith/cti_documents/rc_cti_index-doc-pubbl_en.html.

Jenkinson, William, CSSp. "Mission Outreach of the Irish Province during 1900–1960." In *Go Teach All Nations*, edited by Enda Watters, CSSp, 111–58. Dublin: Paraclete, 2000.

Jurado, Manuel Ruiz, SJ. "Consecrated Life and the Charisms of the Founders." In *Vatican II: Assessment and Perspectives; Twenty-Five Years After (1962–1987)*, edited by René Latourelle, 1:6–28. New York: Paulist, 1988.

Kelly, Bernard, CSSp. "Who Would Have Thought That Things Would Turn Out Like This?" *Spiritan Papers* 10 (1979) 37–44.

Kilcrann, John, CSSp. "Constructing a Spiritan Spirituality of Justice, Peace and the Integrity of Creation." *Spiritan Horizons* 2 (2007) 71–78.

Kimaryo, Rogath F., CSSp. *Venerable Fr. Francis Libermann's "Project of the Blacks."* Arusha, Tanzania: Holy Ghost Fathers Provincialate, 2005.

King, Jason, and Shannon Shrein, eds. *God Has Begun a Great Work in Us*. New York: Orbis, 2015.

Koren, Henry J., CSSp. *Essays on the Spiritan Charism and on Spiritan History*. Bethel Park, PA: Spiritus, 1990.

———. *The Spiritans: A History of the Congregation of the Holy Ghost*. Pittsburgh: Duquesne University Press, 1958.

———. *The Spiritual Writings of Father Claude Francis Poullart des Places*. Pittsburgh: Duquesne University Press, 1959.

———. *To the Ends of the Earth*. Pittsburgh: Duquesne University Press, 1983.

Koupal, William. "Charism: A Relational Concept." *Worship* 42 (1968) 539–45.

Küng, Hans. "The Charismatic Structure of the Church." *Catholic World* 201 (1965) 302–6.

Küng, Hans, et al. *Council Speeches of Vatican II*. New York: Paulist, 1964.

Kwok, Wai-Luen. "Narrative Therapy, Theology, and Relational Openness: Reconstructing the Connection between Postmodern Therapy and Traditional Theology." *Journal of Psychology & Theology* 44 (2016) 201–12.

Lécuyer, Joseph, CSSp. "On Re-reading Poullart des Places (Continued)." *Spiritan Papers* 5 (1978) 3–20.

Lee, Bernard J., SM. *The Beating of Great Wings*. Mystic, CT: Twenty-Third, 2004.

Libermann, Francis. *Provisional Rule of Father Libermann*. Translated by Walter van de Putte, CSSp. Pittsburgh: Center for Spiritan Studies, 2015.

Lienhard, Joseph T., SJ. "Signs of the Times: Signs, Symbols, and Meaning in Religious Life." In *Religious Life in America Today*, edited by Richard Gribble, CSC, 91–100. Washington, DC: Catholic University of America Press, 2011.

Lindbeck, George. "A Protestant Point of View." Address to international conference on the Theological Issues of Vatican II, University of Notre Dame, March 20–26, 1966.

Machado, Heliodoro, CSSp. "A Dream Realized by the Power of the Spirit." *Spiritan Papers* 12 (1980) 3–22.

Malinowski, Francis X., CSSp. "The Holy Spirit in Francis Libermann." Unpublished manuscript, 1996.

———. "The Holy Spirit in the Writings of the Venerable Francis Libermann." *Spiritan Horizons* 10 (2015) 7–18.

Martins, Amadeu, CSSp. "When the Spirit Inspires a Work." *Spiritan Papers* 7 (1978) 3–25.

Maslow, Abraham. *Motivation and Personality*. 2nd ed. New York: Harper & Row, 1970.

McHenry, Dairne, RSCJ, ed. *General Chapters: A Guide for Facilitators, Planners and Participants*. Newry, Northern Ireland: CreateSpace, 2014.

McLaughlin, Brian, CSSp. "Spiritans for Today: The Journey of a Non-Hero's Hero? John Doyle, CSSp." *Spiritan Horizons* 11 (2016) 68–79.

McLeod, Hugh. *The Religious Crisis of the 1960s*. Oxford: Oxford University Press, 2007.

Michel, Joseph, CSSp. *Claude-François Poullart des Places*. Translated by Vincent O'Toole, CSSp. Pittsburgh: Center for Spiritan Studies, 2013.

Nardoni, Enrique. "Charism in Paul." *CBQ* 55 (1993) 68–80.

O'Carroll, Michael, CSSp. *A Priest in Changing Times*. Dublin: Columba, 1998.

O'Collins, Gerald, SJ. "Does Vatican II Represent Continuity or Discontinuity?" *TS* 73 (2012) 768–94.

———. *Living Vatican II*. New York: Paulist, 2006.

O'Donnell, Desmond, OMI. "Clerical Religious: Taking Stock for the Synod." In *Towards the 1994 Synod of Bishops*, edited by Austin Flannery, OP, 4–16. Dublin: Dominican, 1993.

Okoye, James Chukwuma, CSSp, ed. *Meeting the Holy Spirit in the Writings of Father Francis Libermann, CSSp*. Collected and translated by Francis Xavier Malinowski, CSSp. Pittsburgh: Center for Spiritan Studies, 2015.

O'Malley, John W. "Priesthood, Ministry and Religious Life: Some Historical and Historiographical Considerations." *Theological Studies* 49 (1988) 223–57.

———. *What Happened at Vatican II.* Cambridge: Harvard University Press, 2008.

O'Murchu, Diarmuid. *Consecrated Religious Life: The Changing Paradigm.* Maryknoll: Orbis, 2005.

O'Toole, Vincent, CSSp. "Libermann's Impossible Dream." *Spiritan Life* 8 (1999) 3–12.

Padberg, John W. *Together as a Companionship.* Saint Louis: Institute of Jesuit Sources, 1994.

Pannier, Guy. *L'Église de Pointe-Noire.* Mémoire d'Églises. Paris: Karthala, 1999.

Perrin, Luc. "Mgr. Lefebvre, D'Une Élection á Une Demission (1962–1968)." *Histoire & Missions Chrétiennes* 10 (2009) 139–72.

Pollard, John. *The Papacy in the Age of Totalitarianism 1914–1958.* Oxford: Oxford University Press, 2014.

Pope John XXIII. *Ad Petri cathedram.* Encyclical on truth, unity and peace, in a spirit of charity. 1959. http://w2.vatican.va/content/john-xxiii/en/encyclicals/documents/hf_j-xxiii_enc_29061959_ad-petri.html.

Pope John Paul II. *Redemptionis donum.* Apostolic exhortation to men and women religious on their consecration in the light of the mystery of the redemption. Boston: St. Paul Editions, 1984.

———. *Redemptoris missio.* Encyclical on the church's missionary mandate. London: Catholic Truth Society, 1990.

———. *Vita consecrata.* Post-synodal apostolic exhortation on the consecrated life and its mission in the church and in the world. Washington, DC: United States Catholic Bishops Conference, 1996.

Pope Paul VI. *Ecclesiam suam.* Encyclical on the church. 1964. http://w2.vatican.va/content/paul-vi/en/encyclicals/documents/hf_p-vi_enc_06081964_ecclesiam.html.

———. *Ecclesiae sanctae.* Apostolic exhortation implementing Vatican II decrees. 1966. http://w2.vatican.va/content/paul-vi/en/motu_proprio/documents/hf_p-vi_motu-proprio_19660806_ecclesiae-sanctae.html.

———. *Evangelii nuntiandi.* Apostolic exhortation on evangelization in the modern world. 1975. http://w2.vatican.va/content/paul-vi/en/apost_exhortations/documents/hf_p-vi_exh_19751208_evangelii-nuntiandi.html.

Prévotat, Jacques. "La Condemnation de l'action française et les Spiritains: Le cas du Séminaire français." *Histoire & Missions Chrétiennes* 10 (2009) 69–93.

Rahner, Karl. "Towards a Fundamental Theological Interpretation of Vatican II." In *TS* 40 (1979) 716–22.

Ratzinger, Joseph. *The Ratzinger Report.* With Vittoria Mesori. San Francisco: Ignatius, 1985.

Rodriguez, Alphonsus, SJ. *Practice of Perfection and Christian Virtues.* London: Manresa, 1929.

Ryan, Patrick J. *Kimmage Manor: 100 Years of Service to Mission.* Dublin: Columba, 2011.

Sacks, T. Howland, SJ. "A Church That Can and Cannot Change: The Dynamics of Tradition." *TS* 76 (2015) 302–10.

Savoie, Jean, CSSp. "The Spiritual Personality of Claude Poullart des Places." *Spiritan Papers* 10 (1979) 3–26.

Schillebeeckx, Edward. *The Real Achievement of Vatican II*. New York: Herder & Herder, 1967.
Schneiders, Sandra M. *Prophets in Their Own Country*. New York: Orbis, 2011.
Schreiter, Robert J. *Constructing Local Theologies*. Maryknoll: Orbis, 2008.
Stark, Rodney, and Roger Finke. *The Churching of America, 1776–2005: Winners and Losers in Our Religious Economy*. New Brunswick, NJ: Rutgers University Press, 2005.
Synod of Catholic Bishops. *The Church, in the Word of God, Celebrates the Mysteries of Christ for the Salvation of the World*. Final report of the 1985 Extraordinary Synod. https://www.ewtn.com/library/CURIA/SYNFINAL.HTM.
———. *Justice in the World*. 1971. https://www.cctwincities.org/wp-content/uploads/2015/10/Justicia-in-Mundo.pdf.
Timmermans, Frans, CSSp. "A New Spring for the Congregation." *Spiritan Horizons* 3 (2008) 57–68.
Tissier de Mallerais, Bernard. *Marcel Lefebvre*. Kansas City: Angelus, 2002.
Toffler, Alvin. *Future Shock*. New York: Random House, 1970.
Van Kaam, Adrian, CSSp. *A Light to the Gentiles: The Life Story of the Venerable Francis Libermann*. Denville, NJ: Dimension, 1959.
Verploegen, Nicki. *Legacy of the Founders: From Monks to Missionaries*. Cambridge: Lutterworth, 2012.
Ward, Kevin. "Christianity, Colonialism and Missions." In *The Cambridge History of Christianity*, vol. 9, *World Christianities 1914–c. 2000*, edited by Hugh McLeod, 71–88. Cambridge: Cambridge University Press, 2006.
Ward, Maisie. *France Pagan? The Mission of Abbé Godin*. New York: Sheed & Ward, 1949.
Wiesel, Elie. *The Gates of the Forest*. Translated by Frances Frenaye. Reprint. New York: Schocken, 1995.
Wittberg, Patricia, SC. *The Rise and Fall of Catholic Religious Orders: A Social Movement Perspective*. New York: State University of New York Press, 1994.
Wulf, Friedrich. "Declaration on the Adaptation and Renewal of Religious Life." In Herbert Vorgrimler, *Commentary on Vatican II*, 2:346–58. London: Burns & Oates, 1968.
Yuhaus, Cassian J., ed. *Religious Life: The Challenge of Tomorrow*. New York: Paulist, 1994.
Zago, Marcello, OMI. "Commentary on *Redemptoris missio*." In *Redemption and Dialogue*, edited by William R. Burrows, 56–92. Eugene, OR: Wipf & Stock, 1993.

www.ingramcontent.com/pod-product-compliance
Lightning Source LLC
Chambersburg PA
CBHW071243230426
43668CB00011B/1563

I0316726

Plain Truth for Plain People

"For several years, Dr. Brad Estep was my pastor. I heard his sermons week after week, and found myself challenged every time. This book comes from the heart of a pastor, the mind of a scholar, and the wisdom of a teacher. It should be on every pastor's reading list."

—Jesse Middendorf, General Superintendent Emeritus, Church of the Nazarene, Executive Director of the Center for Pastoral Leadership at Nazarene Theological Seminary

"Here is a veritable feast of preaching for the Christian year from a master preacher in the spirit of John Wesley. Brad Estep offers us a book of sermons that is deep in the Scriptures. I highly recommend this book for anyone seeking to bring the Christian calendar to the life of their congregation."

—Steven Hoskins, Professor of Church History and New Testament Greek at Trevecca Nazarene University

"While there is no magic formula to convert the novice into a mature preacher, Brad Estep's collection of sermons shows the way toward thoughtful, biblical, and engaged preaching that is faithful to the Christian calendar, corporate worship, and the Wesleyan-Holiness tradition."

—Bryon McLaughlin, Former Executive Editor, *Grace and Peace Magazine*

"One of the common exhortations of Martin Luther King Sr.—'Daddy King'—to preachers filling his pulpit at Ebenezer Baptist Church was a fervent: 'Make it plain! Make it plain!' In *Plain Truth for Plain People*, Estep offers sermons preaching to plain people, some of whom had PhDs and MDs. Over his career, he has taken preaching seriously. He has taken pastoring equally seriously. He has known congregants coming desperate for a bit of good news. As you scan, read, or re-read these sermons, you will find your mind saying, "Now, *how* did he say that?" These are not sermons extracted from filing cabinets or laptops and repackaged as a book. These well-crafted, well-preached sermons deserve a second or third hearing . . . or reading!"

—Harold Ivan Smith, Bereavement Specialist, International Speaker, and Author of *Eleanor: A Spiritual Biography*

"Dr. Brad Estep is one of the top ten Wesleyan preachers of our day. He packs more content into one sermon than most of us can in a six-message series. This is a must read for every pastor dedicated to proclaiming the realities of the Spirit-filled life."

—Larry D. Dennis, District Superintendent of Florida District Church of the Nazarene

"Lean into the pastoral, prophetic, and wise words of the preacher whose sermons unfold in these pages. As you read, open your minds to creative, theologically deep, and edifying sermons. As you are edified, you will also discover a collection of sermons that will enhance and shape your own preaching in a way that edifies your flock in your local church context."

—Tara Beth Leach, Pastor of First Church of the Nazarene, Pasadena, California and Author of *Emboldened*

"In *Plain Truth for Plain People*, Estep carefully moves from historical context to present day application. This is a great resource for the local pastor who desires to help their congregation live out the implications of God's Word."

—Rick Harvey, Pastor of First Church of the Nazarene, Bethany, Oklahoma

"For eight years, I sat under the ministry of Brad Estep. He consistently held my attention, gave me insight into a biblical passage, and spiritually challenged me. These fifty sermons, which guide us through the Christian year, do the same. One could hardly ask more from a preacher. This book is a valuable tool for any pastor's library."

—Darius Salter, Retired Professor of Preaching and Pastoral Theology at Western Evangelical Seminary and Nazarene Theological Seminary

"Dr. Brad Estep was my pastor for over nine years. Not one time did he fail to miss the mark in the sermons he preached—inspiring, encouraging, challenging me on a weekly basis. I highly recommend this book because I know the thoughts Brad expresses will spark the imagination of preachers in the Wesleyan tradition as they prepare their own sermons for the Christian year."

—David Wilson, General Secretary of the Church of the Nazarene

"The first sermon I heard Brad Estep preach provided a Christian perspective on suffering. Years later, it still stands out among the thousands of sermons I've heard. Estep takes seriously the preaching life. Sermons in this collection bristle with biblical and theological insight and illuminate how sound exegesis, an understanding of culture, and the words chosen by a preacher all work together to facilitate the proclamation of good news. This stirring collection models how to preach through the Christian year and how to express the great themes of Christian theology to our contemporaries."

—Stan Ingersol, Historian and Archivist for the Church of the Nazarene

"In a world that is rediscovering the art of preaching, it's refreshing to find a resource such as this by Brad Estep. The challenge of preaching through the church year is tackled well as Estep provides us with a variety of ways in which to contextualize the message. This is a valuable resource for those who are committed to preaching through the church year, from the entire Bible, and from passages that may make us uncomfortable."

—Carla Sunberg, General Superintendent of the Church of the Nazarene

"As a parishioner fed by Pastor Estep's preaching for nine years, I am thrilled that these sermons will reach a broader audience. His vivid storytelling and faithful exposition of the text of Scripture make this collection a substantive resource for any preacher wanting to be both deep and accessible."

—Doug Hardy, Professor of Spiritual Formation at Nazarene Theological Seminary

"God has uniquely gifted Dr. Estep in the proclamation of the Word. He is truly a craftsman in preparing succinct and powerful messages that make the Word applicable to our daily living. His knowledge of the stories of antiquity, his understanding of the history of our people, and his familiarity with the culture of the day provide him the ability to weave examples and illustrations into the sermon that help make the message clear and direct. Now we are blessed to have some of these gems in writing to read and study."

—Charles Davis, Retired Judge from the Florida Second District Court of Appeal

"As two of the 'plain people' privileged to hear Pastor Brad year after year preaching plain truth sermons to our congregation, we are pleased that they are now available for others to share and be inspired. These messages were tried, true, and tested in our daily lives as Pastor Estep preached through the Christian year. The biblical presentations of truth were enhanced with insight and inspiration drawn from history, literature, science, and real-world experiences. We believe others can benefit greatly from Pastor Brad's intense study of Scripture, his creative approach to preaching, and the faithful clarification of plain truth."

—Jerry and Verla Lambert, parishioners from First Church of the Nazarene, Kansas City, Missouri

Plain Truth for Plain People

Sermons for the Christian Year from the Wesleyan Tradition

Brad Estep

FOREWORD BY
Dan Boone

PREFACE BY
T. Scott Daniels

WIPF *&* STOCK · Eugene, Oregon

PLAIN TRUTH FOR PLAIN PEOPLE
Sermons for the Christian Year from the Wesleyan Tradition

Copyright © 2019 Brad Estep. All rights reserved. Except for brief quotations in critical publications or reviews, no part of this book may be reproduced in any manner without prior written permission from the publisher. Write: Permissions, Wipf and Stock Publishers, 199 W. 8th Ave., Suite 3, Eugene, OR 97401.

Wipf & Stock
An Imprint of Wipf and Stock Publishers
199 W. 8th Ave., Suite 3
Eugene, OR 97401

www.wipfandstock.com

PAPERBACK ISBN: 978-1-5326-6093-1
HARDCOVER ISBN: 978-1-5326-6094-8
EBOOK ISBN: 978-1-5326-6095-5

Manufactured in the U.S.A.

To the parishioners of Trinity Church of the Nazarene (Richmond, Virginia), Victory Church of the Nazarene (St. Petersburg, Florida), First Church of the Nazarene (Winter Haven, Florida), First Church of the Nazarene (Kansas City, Missouri), and Sun City Church of the Nazarene (Sun City, Arizona) who encouraged me to give my best time and energy to the vital work of preparing to preach and preaching. To all of them, I am forever indebted.

Contents

Foreword by Dan Boone | xi

Preface by T. Scott Daniels | xiii

Acknowledgments | xv

Introduction | xvii

Section 1

Sermons for Advent and Christmas Eve

1. The Kidnapping of Advent | 3
2. Highways, Exile, and Advent | 8
3. How Will God Come to *You*? | 13
4. Advent as Preparation | 18
5. Is *This* the Christ You're Expecting? | 23
6. What About Joseph? | 28
7. Christmas Eve: Angels and Christ's Coming | 33
8. Christmas Eve: *The* Savior . . . to You | 35

Section 2

Sermons for Christmas, Epiphany, and
the Non-festival Time Before Lent

9. Everything New | 41

10. Epiphany, the New Year, and a Holy Life | 47

11. Why is the Water Boiling? | 52

12. Being Found, Following, and Finding | 58

13. Relentlessly Pursues, Recklessly Merciful | 63

14. Firsts, Miracles, and the Kingdom | 68

15. Beside Jesus? Or, the Target? | 73

Section 3

Sermons for Lent and Good Friday

16. Command, Invitation, and Prayer | 81

17. Important, but Forgotten | 86

18. A Sanitized and Sanitizing Jesus | 91

19. Ascending from Dreams to Joy to Hope | 96

20. That was *Mine*! | 101

21. Hope and Change: Jesus Style | 106

22. Songs, Swarms, and Love | 111

23. Good Friday Meditation 2016 | 116

24. Good Friday Meditation 2015 | 118

25. Good Friday Meditation 2014 | 120

Section 4

Sermons for Easter Sunday, the
Easter Season, and Pentecost

26. Darkness, Confusion, and Seven Words | 125

27. Bunnies, Words, and Degrees | 129

28. Thomas, Translation, and Trust | 134

29. Fact, Interpretation, and Result | 139

30. Adjectives: Good, Other, and One | 144

31. Witnesses of These Things | 149

CONTENTS   ix

32. There's Something About Newness | 155

33. Pentecost is About Power | 160

34. Rushing In and Pushing Out | 165

35. Greeting Cards, the Center Section, and Centrifugal Force | 170

Section 5

Sermons for Post-Pentecost Non-Festival
Time Before Advent

36. The Year Uzziah Died | 177

37. Nic at Night | 182

38. Little Words, Huge Deal | 187

39. Soda, Seeds, and the Kingdom | 192

40. Amazement, Aesop, and a Faith that Follows | 197

41. Like Tumbleweed Dipped in Saltwater | 202

42. The Wise Life | 207

43. Turning Points | 212

44. Hygiene, Hypocrisy, and the Heart | 217

45. Cochlear Implants, Bo Jackson, and Signs | 222

46. The Jesus Way in a World of Selfies | 227

47. Jericho, a Cloak, and a Question | 232

48. Navigating the 613 | 237

49. *Not* Out of Obligation | 242

50. Big Stones and Birth Pains | 247

Bibliography | 253

Foreword

Preaching seems so anemic at times. By anemic, I mean non-biblical ranting, entertainment drivel, borrowed sermons without context, popular opinion ditto-head, and so many other forms of sermons that show up in the pulpit of the people of God every week. This anemia dwarfs the body of Christ because it robs the people of God of the defining narratives that tells us who we are in the world.

There is very little that we face in the world today that has not already been faced by the historic people of God. Our technology may be better and our attention span shorter, but God's people have already been everywhere that the kingdoms of a dark world are at work. We are not the first to face racism, poverty, bad politicians, depression, disease, or selfish desires. Our problems are in the Bible, dressed in ancient clothes. But God has given us preachers to take us there and open to us the same grace that saved our much older friends.

I must admit that I am often disappointed by the low priority and shoddy work ethic that goes into sermons. For me, the sermonic moment is the single opportunity each week to use the gifts bestowed on me by God for the sake of the church at a time when the whole church could benefit. Counsel was offered to a few people each week, visitation to a handful, administrative wisdom to a board or team, but in the preaching moment, all the church is gathered as one to be formed by the miracle of anointed preaching. This challenge is worth doing well and it is hard work to be a lifelong preacher who keeps showing up well-prepared to serve.

This is why I am glad to commend the work of my friend, Brad Estep. He is not the flashy pulpiteer or the flaming evangelist. He is the pastor who has lived for decades between the world of Scripture and the world of his parishioners. He knows the beauty and grace of that moment when the Spirit has something to say to the gathered church. He is a trained theologian who

practices the discipline of study, yet he delivers truth that is contemporary and contextualized to the given community.

The sermons that follow flow from the Wesleyan understanding of God and the Scriptures. Because we believe that past history, present experience, and solid reasoning guide our understanding of the Bible, these sermons express equal regard to the past, present, and future. They are actually written for real people in real time. We get to overhear what the Spirit said to a particular church. I have found this to be a helpful practice—listening to other men and women practice the sermonic craft in their particular place. I have learned much from a few model preaching friends and from attending their sermons over the years. I commend Brad Estep to you as such a friend.

These sermons are marked by structure that is proven over time to communicate. The delayed anticipation of some sermons is intended, the room at the end for questioning is purposeful, the tension around an issue that we wish were black and white is planned. More is going on in these sermons than meets the eye. I always like to ask of a sermon that moved me: "What was going on here? How did this preacher draw me into the web of examination?" These sermons provoked those questions.

Given the oddness of the competing calendars that we live by, I think it is wise for us to allow the story of God to guide us through a given year. Our national calendar is based on the honoring of empire leaders in Ancient Rome while the Christian calendar is based on a Christian story. Followers of Jesus need to be at home in the Christian story, even when the world's calendar tells them it is a different time. In short, I'd like to say that this is what good preaching looks like today. I hope it exposes you to the formative story of God.

Dan Boone, President of Trevecca
Nazarene University, Nashville, TN

Preface

"I have no life-rhythm," he said. That seemed like a very strange answer to the very simple question, "How are you doing?" My former student went on to explain that since graduating from the university a few months earlier, his internal timing and tempo just felt off. "For twenty-two years," he expounded, "I have danced to the beat of the academic year. And now the music is just different. I haven't figured out the pattern yet."

My young friend was describing a phenomenon that I've seen happen in many former students when they leave school and go find a job. Beginning in kindergarten, their life is shaped by the rhythms of the academic year. Life begins in late August with visits to the local office-supply store for new folders and pencils. There are short breaks that come in December and March, and it all ends with a long and glorious gap of rest beginning in mid-May. Each day starts early but it ends by three o'clock. The pattern of academia gets engrained deep in the bones.

However, when post-college work-life begins, for most people a whole new pattern of living comes with it. Work still starts early but it ends much later. There may still be a break on the weekend for most, but vacation is now two weeks long and can come anytime in the year. For most workers, August can feel just like February and May feels just like November. When your body has been shaped by twenty-two years of tests and tardy-bells, it takes some time to adjust to the life of the market.

My point is simply this: we are creatures of habit (including the habit of marking time). This truth is at least part of the reason why—in the wisdom of the Christian tradition—living in the rhythms of the liturgical year has been an important aspect of worship. There is something deeply formative in the patterns of Christian time. The practices of anticipation and waiting during Advent lead into the celebrations of the in-breaking light during Epiphany. However, those who now walk in the light also must experience the shadows of sin and death present during the observation of Lent. But

xiii

as deep as darkness can grow—reaching an apex on Maundy Thursday and Good Friday—Easter and Eastertide remind God's people that darkness doesn't get the last word, light does. Sin doesn't get the last word, grace does. Evil doesn't get the last word, goodness does. And most importantly, death does not get the last word, resurrection life has the final say. Celebrating this new creation life of the resurrection gets capped off with a birthday party for the people called church, who are now a foretaste of the new creation at Pentecost, and with the adoration of the God who is eternally revealed in the mysterious Trinitarian community of the Father, Son, and Holy Spirit. The church then leans into life in the extraordinarily ordinary time in-between the times, until we start all over again.

This keeping of time is meant to shape the gathering called the body of Christ into a people who live and move with the rhythms of a new creation. There is much in the following sermons from Brad Estep to love. Brad's preaching is thoughtful, insightful, helpful, and often deeply profound. Brad is a skilled exegete of the Scripture. But what I love most about the sermons offered to us here is that they are formative and transformative. Which is exactly what makes them "Wesleyan." Sermons preached in a "Wesleyan way" are not just sermons preached from a particular theological perspective that emphasizes the gifts of free will, grace, and holiness (although they certainly do that). Sermons that are Wesleyan are more concerned with experiencing the transformation of God's grace than just receiving the information presented to us in the Bible. That is why I also think it is beautiful that Brad offers these sermons to the church in the flow of the liturgical year. There is something about keeping time immersed in the language of the Scripture that ought to form our holy imaginations at the deepest and most life-shaping parts of our being. That is the gift that I believe Brad offers the reader in the pages to follow. He offers us not just helpful insights for laypeople or good sermons starters for preachers. He is offering opportunities for people of faith to learn to dance to the rhythms of grace.

May you be blessed as you read, and may you be shaped into a reflection of the Christ who is exalted in every word.

T. Scott Daniels, Pastor of College Church
of the Nazarene, Nampa, Idaho

Acknowledgments

To my wife, Dawn, who has partnered with me in ministry for more than twenty-five years. Thank you.

To my children, Chris and Kat, who have listened to their dad's sermons, provided feedback, and helped me better understand the constantly changing cultural realities.

To my parents who have encouraged my preaching ministry in so many ways. My father modeled good preaching in my growing up years and gave me opportunities to preach even before I had any idea what I was doing. My mother's curious and keen mind helped me think deeply and her devotion to prayer provided a clear example.

To my brother, Kent, who has journeyed with me on the path of pastoring.

To Roger Hahn who encouraged me, as a young college student, to go deeper and study homiletics and the sacraments at the graduate school level.

To Jesse Middendorf who chose Fred Craddock's *Preaching* for my undergraduate homiletics class and sent me out all over Northwest Oklahoma to hone my craft on unsuspecting parishioners.

To Bryon McLaughlin who encouraged me to put a collection of sermons together and helped convince me that it could be a tool for learning, both for myself and for others.

To Stan Ingersol and Mark Graham who, with Bryon, formed "the amigos." Thank you for your presence and encouragement through the ups and downs of ministry. I cherish our friendship.

To all my associate pastors over the years who have helped to lead and oversee parish ministry so that I could give some of my best time to the task of preaching.

Introduction

Preaching is similar to the parables of Jesus. It seems plain to understand, but there's always a mysterious aspect to it. You think that you have it in your grasp and yet it slips through your fingers. I've wrestled with this part of preaching for more than twenty-five years even though I've been preaching for about thirty-five years. My father was a pastor and when I acknowledged a call to preach, he let me. Actually, he did *more* than let me. He put me on the church calendar. He encouraged me. He helped me. He ran advertisements in the local newspaper that I would be home from college and would be preaching in the upcoming services. I really had no idea what I was doing or even *trying* to do at that time, but I was learning about willingness, communication, courage, and so much more that is involved in preaching.

When I was in college, the overseer of all of my denomination's churches throughout Northwest Oklahoma was a family friend and a contemporary of my parents. He and his wife had attended the same college at the same time as my parents. His wife was a bridesmaid in their wedding. Having preached beginning at sixteen years of age and wanting to preach more, I asked this leader and family friend if he would help me find opportunities to preach. He was willing and encouraging. When a small church in the area needed someone to fill in because their pastor was sick or away on vacation, he sent me off onto the backroads of northwestern Oklahoma to preach to people that I didn't know. In the process, I learned about congregational personalities and peculiarities. I learned about the value of pastoral connection and preaching. I learned about different expectations and how location, history, education, and relationship impact the content and form of preaching.

During this same time, the church overseer and family friend was asked to teach the introductory course on preaching. Little did I know at the time, but a "new homiletic" had been born and was growing into

adolescence. One of the monumental homileticians of that burgeoning movement had just published some of his thought and study after fifteen years of reflection. It was simply titled *Preaching*.[1] Within a year of its publication, I was introduced to the thought, writing, and preaching of Fred Craddock. This book and this course was when the study of homiletics began to form the trajectory of my life. An entirely new world of analysis and reflection was being opened to me and I was excited about it. My New Testament professor, who was a very accomplished preacher himself, sensed my excitement for the field and began to encourage me in this direction. He also planted seeds about study of the sacraments and the liturgical context for preaching. He hinted that, after seminary, I should go on to do doctoral study in this area.

I completed a bachelor's degree by the time that I was twenty years of age and stayed an additional year to complete a master's degree in religion. I was engaged to be married and my wife was finishing her degree. So, by the time that I was twenty-one, I was married and was headed to seminary to pursue a master of divinity degree. While at seminary, my love of preaching continued to grow. I had more opportunities to preach and I was becoming more familiar with the literature that was coming out of the "new homiletic" movement. While I was in seminary, Fred Craddock came to town to do a lecture series at a local church. I went and met this diminutive man who was a giant in the field. In the process, I learned some more about voice inflection, substantive content, and the power of anticipation. Looking back, my one great regret was that I didn't cross-register at a neighboring seminary and take a homiletics course or two from another giant in the field—Eugene Lowry.

Throughout my seminary years, I wrestled with the idea of whether I should go into the pastorate or continue to further my education. At the time, there were very few universities or seminaries that were offering PhD level studies in preaching or a closely related field. The options were fairly limited. There were a few places where you could try to design your own program, but I didn't want to tackle that. Having decided to pursue more education, I discovered that Union Theological Seminary in Virginia was planning to introduce a PhD program in practical theology with emphases in christian education, pastoral counseling, or preaching and worship. This, I thought, was exactly what I wanted. In addition to the hurdle of being chosen for admission, the entering class would enter in the fall of 1992. I was to graduate from seminary in the spring of 1991. What would I do during that intervening year? I decided that I would apply to Union's ThM program

1. Craddock, *Preaching*.

INTRODUCTION   xix

in church history for the academic year from fall of '91 through the spring
of '92. If I was accepted, that would give me a year to get acclimated to the
school, become acquainted with some of the professors, and get settled into
my new surroundings. Also, I thought that it would help me get admitted
into the PhD program if I had a year to show that I could cut it. During that
year in which I worked on a ThM in church history, I had the opportunity
to take an elective course in preaching from Elizabeth Achtemeier. What a
treat. She was an Old Testament scholar and had written extensively about
homiletics.[2] Additionally, she was such a powerful preacher. Her focus in
that particular course revolved around language, word selection, and imagery. I have utilized much of what she taught me about preaching on a weekly
basis throughout my pastoral ministry.

But by the time that I was twenty-five, I had finished college, earned an
MA, an MDiv, and a ThM in church history, and I had been admitted into
the PhD program in practical theology at Union. I was thrilled and excited
about the future and my love for preaching was continuing to grow. However, having moved to a new place, my opportunities to preach had become
less frequent. I was reading, studying, learning languages, and writing for
my education, but I was longing to preach more and more. While in the first
year of my PhD coursework, a small church across town lost their pastor. I
was invited to fill in for a week or two in the fall of 1992. After one of the
Sunday morning services, a layperson asked me if I would have any interest
in being their pastor. I was thrilled by the possibility. They had already asked
a retired minister to fill in during January and they weren't even sure, at that
point, if the church would remain open. He told me, however, that he would
be in contact with the overseer of the district churches and would get back to
me. The retired minister ended up filling in until Easter Sunday of 1993 and
I began serving as pastor of that small congregation on the following Sunday. Essentially, in the early days, my primary tasks were to plan the worship
service and to preach. I was learning about liturgy, the Christian calendar,
lectionaries, the weekly demands of preparing to preach, and preaching substantive, meaningful, and interesting sermons.

Since starting pastoring in April of 1993, I have preached on a weekly
basis for the last twenty-five years. Except for one twelve-week sabbatical,
I have preached almost every week and have rarely missed two weeks in a
row because of vacation or illness. In some pastoral settings, I have preached
as often as four times a week. During most of my pastoral career, I have
preached a least two unique sermons per week. In one particular year, my
records indicate that I preached in 115 different services—that's too much.

2. Achtemeier, *Preaching as Theology*.

I have pastored smaller church and larger ones. My journey has led me to small towns and heavily populated cities. The churches that I have served over the years have been in at least three distinctly unique areas of the country. My experience, I think, has been varied and broad.

Regardless of the different congregations, my basic convictions about preaching have remained the same: the place to start is to have something to say. John Wesley called this "plain truth." Having something clear and grounded to say on a weekly basis requires lots of listening, study, prayer, reading, thought, and preparation. What is to be said should be scriptural, sound, and significant. Preaching begins and must be grounded in a scriptural text. This is the starting place. This is the source from which you have something to say. But since preaching isn't simply quoting Scripture, the preacher must select her or his words with a concern for sound theology. Preaching is not the place to be theologically novel. Additionally, the preacher must say something significant. This is not the time or the place for trivialities and trifles. Humor and creativity can have an important role, but it must be utilized in service to something significant if the preaching is going to be worthwhile. These foundational issues revolve around the content of preaching, but what is said must also be said in an interesting way. Interest must not only be captured, it must also be sustained in some way. There must be an element of suspense or anticipation. Ultimately, preaching must solicit response. It must call us to engage in some new way of thinking and living.

Over these decades of study, practice, reflecting, and occasional teaching, I have learned a few things about preaching. Much of that is reflected in the sermon manuscripts with accompanying analysis that make up this book. I have always tried to have something scriptural, sound, and significant to say when I've stood to proclaim the Word. And, I've always tried to say it in a way that was interesting by utilizing suspense, sustaining interest, and soliciting response. My aim has been to preach "plain truth" to people in a particular context who were eager to hear something that was meaningful and that directed their attention to the presence and ongoing work of God in their lives. In other words, I was trying to preach "plain truth" to "plain people." Whether that was accomplished in the accompanying sermons is left for you to determine.

I would like to point out a few things about what you will read in the proceeding pages. First, these sermons are not meant to be read silently. They are meant to be heard. As I prepared them, I was preaching them and hearing them in my own ear.[3] If something sounded odd or not quite right

---

3. I practiced this intuitively, but much of this concept was captured so articulately in Robin Meyers' *With Ears to Hear*. He wrote, "The process of self-persuasion begins in the ear and is completed by the compulsion to speak. The speaking brings a new hearing and

INTRODUCTION

in terms of content, word choice, timing, or emphasis, I would change it on the spot in my own hearing until I heard it the way that I wanted my listeners to hear it. That process is difficult to capture in writing, but these sermons are the end product of it. For me, sermon preparation is a constant re-hearing, clarifying, and articulating for the purpose of more moving, impacting, interesting, and persuading speech. Throughout the manuscripts, you will find words that are italicized. This is a way of trying to make clear where the emphasis should lie in the sentence in order to be heard with the proper meaning. Creating my sermon manuscripts with these visual clues helps me communicate more effectively. Again, these sentences are meant to be heard, so reading them out loud may be the best way to hear them for yourself. Move the emphasis around in the sentence and listen for yourself to how it changes the meaning.

Second, these sermons were written for a specific congregation in a specific place on specific Sundays. These were not sermons that were written for some unknown or generalized group of listeners to be preached on any Sunday.[4] I have made no attempt to make them such for publishing purposes. Part of the reason for that is because specific references and particular events have more power and stick better in a person's mind than generic references or stories. Good stories are always specific. These sermons are meant to exemplify pastoral preaching in a specific context to a specific people, week after relentless week. These are not "sugar stick" sermons that were preached multiple times and honed to perfection. They were the product, for good or ill, of that particular week's preparation, reflection, and diligence. Now, let me say that this specific context and congregation (like every context and congregation) is unique. Some of what makes it unique is the variations in the constituents of the congregation. For example, half of the local seminary's faculty was a part of the church. That's unusual, but sitting alongside them were people with little or no formal education beyond high school. Sitting next to these biblical scholars and theologians were junior high and high school students. The range in biblical and theological acuity was quite striking. Additionally, the broad span of the socio-economic spectrum was also present. With people living on fixed incomes, the unemployed, and the under-employed, there were folks present who lived in million-dollar homes in one of the most affluent neighborhoods in all of the Midwest. Although the church was across

---

effects subsequent speech. It is almost impossible to determine where one ends and the other begins, but this much is certain: the acoustics of delivery are dependent upon the acoustics of conception. A sermon not spawned by the ear may be stillborn on the tongue. Listen, then speak, then listen to yourself speaking." Meyers, *With Ears,* 43-44.

4. "Those sermons marked 'Good for Any Occasion' are really good for none." Meyers, *With Ears,* 69.

xxii INTRODUCTION

the street from a very affluent community, as a whole, the congregation was not particularly affluent. Most of the people drove in from other parts of the metropolitan area because they could not afford to live in the residential areas immediately surrounding the church. This "drive-in" aspect of the church was a great obstacle to developing close-knit community within the congregation. People who came a long distance and drove past scores of churches along the way found it difficult to connect and make lasting friendships with people who were doing the same thing from the opposite side of the city. Another point of uniqueness for this particular congregation was its historic influence and heritage. The church where these sermons were preached was over one hundred years old and had seen its pastors be elected to positions of leadership and authority within the congregation's denominational structures. Time after time this had happened. In the first fifty years of its history, and because of its proximity to the denominational headquarters and seminary, this congregation functioned, essentially, as the church for all the denomination's leaders. During the second fifty years, this reality had faded dramatically, even though it remained in the church's collective memory. These issues and a host of others formed the milieu in which these sermons were crafted.

Third, the vast majority of these sermons were preached from a text that was recommended by the Revised Common Lectionary for that particular Sunday. With four passages assigned to each Sunday, my practice was to select one for proclamation knowing that these same passages would appear in the cycle again in three years. The index of sermons in the front of the book identifies the date the sermon was preached and where that Sunday appeared within the Christian calendar for that year. If there is no indication related to the Christian calendar then the text was not recommended by the lectionary and it was simply a text from which I chose to preach that week.

Finally, all of these sermons were written for the purpose of inviting response from the congregation. Most of them were written with the celebration of communion as the intended response. This may or may not be typical of many congregations, but it became more typical within this setting over the last several years. In some places, I have offered an "alternative ending" to provide examples of how a sermon could be directed toward a different response depending on the circumstances and practices of any particular congregation. I have not done this in every instance, but simply to model how it could be done.

These sermons are offered for the purpose of analysis, criticism, exploration, and learning. They have been written and reflect my own speech patterns and rhythms. They reflect my own theological heritage and educational influences. I share them with humility, but also with the hope that

INTRODUCTION

they may be of use to other pastors, students, and laity who are interested in the craft of preaching. As Walter J. Burghardt wrote in the prelude of his text on preaching, I too wish to say,

> "Like Jeremiah, 'I do not know how to speak' (Jer. 1:6). I can only trust that, as with Jeremiah, the Lord has at certain gracious moments put His words in my mouth. Please God, the effort in this volume to recapture the charism that is preaching will stimulate other preachers to wrestle with words and the Word, to enflesh the word the Word spoke, to fling it out to our world with conviction and courage, with imagination and passion."[5]

I have given much of my life to preparing to preach and to preaching. It has been simultaneously a great joy and a heavy burden. The results are sometimes hard to measure and difficult to grasp. It has been like the parables of Jesus—a tiny seed here and a handful scattered over there. I wouldn't trade it for anything.

Brad Estep, PhD
Advent 2018

---

5. Burghardt, *Preaching,* 2.

Section 1

Sermons for Advent and Christmas Eve

SERMON I[1]

The Kidnapping of Advent[2]

Matthew 24:36–44

A dvent is prone to getting kidnapped. It gets taken hostage by busy-ness and frenetic activity. It's the first Sunday of Advent in 2016 and I've learned through trial and error that the season will "run me over" if I don't intentionally and consciously *refuse* to allow that to happen. Advent, of course, is about much more than gift-buying, tree-decorating, eggnog drinking, and fighting for the empty space in the Target parking lot. It's much *more* than that. Advent is about purposeful, intentional, and spiritual preparation for the *coming* of Jesus. You see, that's what "advent" means. It means *coming* and it's not just about his *coming* at Bethlehem, but it's *also* about his coming *now* to us in ways that we may not expect. It's also about his coming *again*—his *second* coming—for which we must be prepared. Jesus spoke about that very issue and I want to direct your attention to his words as relayed to us in chapter 24 of Matthew.

Matthew 24:36–44

Part of what Jesus is talking about here is the need and necessity of making preparation—of being prepared. The example that Jesus uses is the story

1. Preached at First Church of the Nazarene in Kansas City, Missouri on November 27, 2016 (Advent 1; Year A).

2. Part of what made this sermon interesting was the strangeness of the text. We simply are not accustomed to these kinds of images and ideas. Oftentimes, I am away from my congregation on the first Sunday of Advent because it is almost always the Sunday right after Thanksgiving in the U.S. This passage or a similar one is always assigned by the Revised Common Lectionary for this Sunday of the year. Like Advent itself, these kinds of texts can get "kidnapped" for uses other than their intended pur-pose. My attempt was to hear the passage in an Advent context and to allow it to speak its counter-cultural message without resorting to scare-tactics or manipulation.

3

of Noah and the building of the ark. God had told Noah that flooding and destruction was going to happen but that he had a plan to save Noah and his family. *That* plan wasn't going to just fall "whole-cloth" from the sky. *That* plan was going to involve painstaking, time-consuming, and labor-intensive preparation. It was going to involve Noah building a boat that is one-and-a-half football fields long and had storage space equal to 370 railroad boxcars. Have you seen the replica of the ark that has been built in Kentucky somewhere? It's a tourist attraction and it is massive.

Building something like that requires *preparation*—daily, diligent, and determined preparation. As I read this passage again this week, there was a verse that struck me. It's verse 39. It says that "they knew *nothing* about what would happen until the flood came." That's interesting to me. It's undoubtedly true that people who were distant from the site of the ark's construction had no clue about what was going to happen. That's clear. But my mind is drawn to those people who *knew* Noah and lived *near* Noah and who *associated* with Noah's family. What about them? They *had* to know that *something* was about to happen. I mean, here's this thing going up that is forty-five feet high and 450 feet long. *Something's* happening. Or at the least, Noah *believes* that something's going to happen. But people simply went about their business. Jesus says, "Eating, drinking, marrying, and giving in marriage" was "business as usual."

The city of Pompeii was completely and utterly decimated in 79 AD. Mount Vesuvius erupted. The volcanic ash and the superheated gasses destroyed *everything* with its intensity. Scientific scholars have confirmed what Roman writers recorded in the first century regarding Vesuvius: people *could have* prepared. The mountain had been rumbling for weeks. There was a minor eruption and a plume of smoke that was clearly visible several *days* before the explosion. Preparation was *possible*. It's just that people went about their daily routines—busy, working, parenting. It was "business as usual"—*unprepared*.

Preparation for the coming of Jesus for *us* won't involve building a boat or escaping a volcano. It will involve *daily, diligent*, and *determined* obedience to the Lord. It will mean faithfulness to the Word. It will involve service and compassion in his name. *This* is what preparation for Christ's coming looks like *before* and *after*. When the trees are gone, the sales are over, the lights are taken down, and the radio stops playing Bing Crosby and Mariah Carey, preparation for the coming of Jesus continues. Preparation for his coming is a daily, year-round, ever-present reality.

Jesus, in these verses, not only draws attention to our need to *prepare* for his coming, but he emphasizes the *suddenness* or the *quickness*—the *surprise*—with which he can come. Jesus uses an example that is taken from

THE KIDNAPPING OF ADVENT 5

first century culture. Men are working the field. Women are working at the mill. They're talking, conversing, and working together, and then one's taken and one's left. It happens *suddenly*. *All* of us know the pain, surprise, and confusion when tragedies and circumstances come upon us quickly. We can hardly catch our breath and life as we know it is radically changed in an instant. Thanksgiving wasn't the same. Christmases won't be the same and everything's different because it happened so suddenly. There's an empty chair. There's the heavy weight of grief. There's the life-changing new reality that was inconceivable just months or even weeks ago.[3]

Do you know about "el camino de la muerte"? It's called the "road of death" and it's in Bolivia. From the city of La Paz, which is at an elevation of twelve thousand feet, the road descends about forty miles to the edge of the Amazon River basin which is at sea level. On average, twenty-six vehicles a year fall off the road, and between two-hundred and three-hundred people lose their lives. Cliffs. Dropoffs. No guardrails. Rain. Fog. Inferior roadways. Mudslides. All kinds of complications make the road so dangerous.[4]

But listen. The "most dangerous road" in the world—*spiritually*—is the "road of un-readiness" or living in a "business-as-usual" kind of way, when what God wants for us is for us to live in a real, life-changing, sins-forgiving, daily-following relationship with Jesus. That's what this final image that Jesus uses in these verses is meant to convey. Jesus says essentially: "If you know when the burglar is coming, then you won't be caught off guard. You'll be watching and waiting. You'll be *expecting* his arrival." Again: It's about *not* being *spiritually* asleep. It's about *not* being distracted *spiritually*. We live in a world that is devoted to distraction. T.S. Eliot, the poet, once used a phrase describing people when he said that we can be "distracted *from* distraction *by* distraction" and T.S. Eliot died in 1965. Can you *imagine* what he would say about the distractions *today*?[5]

It's been a little more than twelve years ago, now. We were living in central Florida. It was late summer of 2004 when three hurricanes lined up between the coast of Africa and the peninsula of Florida. Their names will forever be imprinted in my mind: "Charley," "Frances," and "Jean." The area in which we lived was devastated by those hurricanes. Thousands upon thousands of people were without electrical power. Some people had

---

3. There were people within the congregation who had gathered for Thanksgiving or were preparing to gather for Christmas for the first time without their spouse, parent, child, or friend who had died within the previous year. Terribly painful times.

4. Gori, "Thrills."

5. The impact of technologies on people's lives and attention spans is difficult to overestimate. Neil Postman's *Amusing Ourselves to Death* has proven to be more and more prophetic with every passing year.

generators and they began to put them to use. Of course, they knew or were instructed not to use them in a closed-in space, because running generators need ventilation. During the aftermath of one of those storms, a guy in our town had his generator stolen as it was running outside of his house. He was in the house and he didn't even discover it until he went out to put some gasoline in it. If you've ever heard the racket that a running generator makes, you might wonder: "Well, how could that happen? Why didn't he hear it being shut off?" Here's why. The thieves took his riding lawn mower and started it beside the generator. Then, they left *it* running while they made off with the "prized" generator. It was all about *distraction*. And that's the kind of world that we live in today—a world of distraction. It's a culture of noise. Our world is bent on distracting us from the things that are most important. To borrow a phrase from Quaker, Thomas Kelley: We live in a world that takes "time *far more seriously* than eternity."[6]

The messages that compete for your attention and for mine revolve around *things* and *stuff* and bigger things and bigger stuff and more experiences. They have everything to do with *this* world, *this* life, immediate gratification, and temporary things. Like a counter-cultural beacon of light in a world of darkness, Jesus wants to warn us that while we're being distracted by all those non-essential, non-eternal pursuits and priorities, his coming is at hand, our lives are so fragile, and we must be ready. Verse 42 says: "Watch, because you do not know on what day your Lord is coming." The Scripture says that only God knows the time. No one else knows. The television preacher doesn't know. The prophetic expert doesn't know. The guy on the street corner who can quote the book of Revelation doesn't know. Only God knows. But this we *do* know: the coming of Jesus in glory or our going to meet him is closer *today* than it has ever been.

Early this year, they moved the "Doomsday Clock" ahead by two minutes. A magazine called the *Bulletin of Atomic Scientists* created the "doomsday clock" in 1947. It's a symbol—a way to measure how close the world is to the "midnight" of some nuclear or environmental apocalypse. As of January of 2015, the clock is at 11:57 pm. Back in 1953 after the United States tested a hydrogen bomb, the clock was at 11:58. When the Soviet Union fell in 1991, the clock was moved back to 11:43.[7] Over the years, the clock has been moved forward and backward depending upon world events, environmental issues, and political unrest. As we live in Advent and anticipate the coming of Jesus—not just in Bethlehem as a baby—but into our lives and someday in glory, the timing of Jesus' coming doesn't get more distant or further out

6. Ortberg, *The Life*, 82, emphasis added.

7. Ray, "Doomsday Clock."

THE KIDNAPPING OF ADVENT

there in the future. It simply gets *closer and closer.* Part of Advent preparation is about coming to grips with that reality and living from day-to-day with that reality clearly in view. What would *that* kind of preparation look like in *your* life during this season which leads us to Christmas?

Would it mean setting some things aside and giving your attention more fully to the things of God? Would it mean making restitution for something? Would it mean trying to mend that relationship that has broken down? Would it mean a fresh devotion to reading and meditating on God's Word? Would it mean reaching out to a friend, neighbor, or co-worker and sharing the love of Jesus in some tangible way with them? Is it possible that Jesus might come to you and speak to you or prompt you to some action even as you prepare for his coming? Would you invite the Spirit of God to come to you with forgiving grace, with encouragement, with strength for the struggles, or with comfort for the pain? As we gather at the Table of the Lord today, would you invite the Lord to come to you and to *give* to you—through the bread and the cup—what your soul truly needs?

Amen.

SERMON 2[1]

Highways, Exile, and Advent[2]

Isaiah 40:1–11

Have you tried to drive on 435 out at the I-35 interchange lately? K-7? It looks like a giant-sized pile of spaghetti made out of steel girders and concrete. Fly-over bridges. Cranes and bulldozers. Piles of rock and traffic cones everywhere. Here we are on the second Sunday of Advent and the Scripture will speak today of "making straight in the wilderness a highway for our God." This "highway building" is difficult stuff. This is not something that happens easily or naturally.

1. Preached at First Church of the Nazarene in Kansas City, Missouri on December 6, 2015 (Advent 2; Year C).

2. This sermon was patterned or structured along the lines of Eugene Lowry's "loop" which he describes in his classic, *The Homiletical Plot: The Sermon as Narrative Art Form*. The first part of the sermon was to "upset the equilibrium." Lowry calls this the "oops" section. The "oops" in this particular sermon ran from the beginning through the description of the Babylonian exile. Then the sermon moved into the "ugh" section where the problem was analyzed or diagnosed even further. This was the section on the Exile's similarities to the state of the Western church in the early twenty-first century. The "aha" (or "disclosing the clue to resolution") was the confession that God is still at work even in exile—God was at work then and is at work now. "Aha" is followed by "whee!" where Lowry says that the "gospel is experienced." This section is the "good news" and in this sermon it took the form of identifying the qualities (found in the text) of this God who does not abandon us in our time of exile. After "whee!" comes "yeah!" where "plot-wise," according to Lowry, "it is the stage of effecting closure." In this sermon, this was the section where the congregation was called to respond to the "good news." In this setting and on this occasion, the congregation was invited to gather around the Lord's Table and to taste the faithfulness, power, and compassion of God in the bread and cup of Christ.

8

Isaiah 40:1–11

It's virtually impossible to read this passage from Isaiah 40 without *hearing* one thing and *seeing* something else.[3] The thing you *hear* is the voice of a tenor beautifully vocalizing these verses as a part of Handel's "Messiah." What *most* of us *see* is some mental image that we have constructed of John the Baptist. We *do* that because this passage shows up in the gospel stories and *that* is not insignificant. In fact, this is one of the few things that shows up in *each* of the four Gospels.

The story of the birth of Jesus is in Matthew and Luke, but not in Mark and John. *That's* a pretty important story. Or, Jesus' famous "sermon on the mount"? The longest and most complete version is in Matthew. Luke has *some* of it. Mark has very little and it's scattered here and there throughout his gospel. John has *none at all*. If you think the raising of Lazarus from the dead is extremely important then you would agree with the Gospel of John, but *not* with Matthew, Mark, or Luke. Other than the resurrection of Jesus, there's only *one* miracle story that shows up in all four of the Gospels and that's the "feeding of the five thousand."[4] Very little, ultimately, shows up in *all* four of the Gospels in our Bibles, but portions of this passage from Isaiah does. Because of that, when we hear it, we jump out of the original context for it and we push it right into a context like the New Testament. Even though it's two thousand years ago, the New Testament's context is much more familiar to us than the *original* context. I wonder if it would be possible to intentionally try to avoid doing that today. *If* we did, would there be something that we could hear that would help us, teach us, or *shape* us?

In 722 BC, the "northern kingdom"—often referred to as Israel—was overrun and destroyed by a neighboring "super power" of the time. The "ten lost tribes of Israel" were wiped off the map. The people were either killed, became slaves, or were transplanted to another place never to return. They were wiped out. For years and years, they had been disobedient to God and had chased after idols. They had embraced the wicked practices of their neighboring nations and, in 722 BC, it all came to an end for Israel. At the same time, the little "southern kingdom"—the kingdom of Judah—was spared. It became clear, however, that they *too* were following the wayward path of their brothers and sisters in Israel. There were periods of time when there were attempts at faithfulness. There were calls for repentance, but the general pattern was the same. They rejected the one, true, and living God

---

3. "Oops" section begins.

4. Matt 14:13–21; Mark 6:32–44; Luke 9:10–17; John 6:1–13.

10   SECTION 1: SERMONS FOR ADVENT AND CHRISTMAS EVE

who had redeemed them and provided for them and they replaced that with chasing after the gods of their pagan neighbors.

In 586 BC, about 140 years *after* Israel was destroyed, another "super power" invaded Judah, ransacked the city of Jerusalem, destroyed the temple, and took the people who were "worth taking" into captivity as slaves and servants. This is called the "Babylonian captivity" or "the exile." The people of Judah were removed from the places, the people, the things, the patterns, the routines, the smells, and the land that they loved. They were forcibly re-located to a place and to ways of living that were foreign to them. Uncomfortable. Filled with change. Nothing made sense. Everything was different and it was terribly upsetting to them. If there is a time and if there are circumstances in the Scripture that run "parallel" to the time in which we live today—to the circumstances that the church faces in America—the parallel is biblical "exile."

The church used to be the "center" of every community's life and activity.[5] *Changed. Gone.* Churches used to be respected, revered, and given a special place in society. *Changed.* The Church and her ministers were honored, consulted, and invited to lead in the shaping and decision-making of the culture. *Gone.* Our "special day"—Sunday—was cherished and protected. Commerce was discouraged. *Long gone.* The Church could set up "nativity scenes" wherever she wanted and pray Christian prayers in the name of Jesus at public events, whenever and wherever she wanted. The Church could put up crosses in national parks and in government offices as often and whenever she wanted. But you know and I know that those days are *gone.* The patterns, routines, and ways that have been so valued and cherished by the church are no longer supported and encouraged by our society or by the civic organizations that form its fabric. We haven't been forcibly relocated *geographically* like the people of Judah in the sixth century BC, but the Church *is* in exile. Make no mistake about it.

Isaiah 40 is a message to a people in exile and the message is that God is still at work.[6] God *came* to us, *comes* to us, and will *continue* to come to us. God didn't abandon his people to their Babylonian captors as much as it may have felt that way at the time. He had not abandoned them. As their world was being turned upside-down, it certainly *seemed* that way. There are some things that Isaiah reminded them about God while they were in exile, and these same things can be an encouragement to us in these days.[7] Verse 8 says: "The grass withers and the flowers fall, but the word of our

5. "Ugh" section begins.
6. "Aha" section begins.
7. "Whee!" section begins.

God stands forever." God is faithful even when it seems that everything else is fading away or changing.[8] When virtually everything around us is getting older, no longer working, being replaced by something shiny and new, only to be replaced next year by the next "something" that is shinier and newer—when that kind of pattern prevails all around us in exile, *God remains true and firm and stable.* He is *faithful* and "his word *stands forever*" (Isa 40:8, emphasis added).

Here in Kansas City, we're still basking in the fact that the Royals won the World Series this year. This Tuesday night, we're having our church board Christmas party and we're having a "Royals theme." Let me remind you: the Royals hadn't won the World Series since *1985*. Thirty years ago, I was at the seventh game of the World Series that year. I was in the upper deck down the left field line. It seems like such a long time between World Series Championships. But thirty years is really *nothing*. It's the "blink of an eye." In God's sight, a *thousand* years is like a *day*.[9] "The grass withers and the flowers fall, but the word of our God stands *forever*." He's *faithful.* That's good news for people in exile.

He's also *powerful*. Look at the end of verse 9: "Say to the towns of Judah, 'Here is your God!' See, the sovereign Lord comes with *power* and his arm rules for him." When *we* think of "power," our mind skips to things like souped-up hot rods, muscle-bound weight lifters, or even to "shock and awe" displays of military weaponry. But, there is a *different kind* of power. There is a power that moves and works and transforms "behind the scenes," under the surface, and from within. There's a "power" that enables a boy to fell a giant[10] like a lumberjack fells a Douglas fir. There's a power that makes city walls fall down at the sound of shouts and trumpet blasts.[11] There's a power that pushes followers of Jesus into the streets of Jerusalem to proclaim the "good news" of the risen Christ.[12] Power doesn't always look the same or display itself in the same way. It's a *different* expression of power that "enfleshes" divinity in a peasant's womb, births him into the world, and puts him into the arms of a teenager.[13] This kind of power doesn't get the "press" like shows of force and choreographed parades of might. There's a power

8. Hirsch, *Forgotten Ways,* 16: "The truth is that the twenty-first century is turning out to be a highly complex phenomenon where terrorism, paradigmatic technological innovation, an unsustainable environment, rampant consumerism, discontinuous change, and perilous ideologies confront us at every point."

9. Ps 90:4.

10. 1 Sam 17.

11. Josh 6.

12. Acts 2.

13. Luke 2.

12   SECTION 1: SERMONS FOR ADVENT AND CHRISTMAS EVE

that submits and surrenders and hangs on a tree so that the same kind of power can be set loose in those who receive it—in those who welcome it. Power—God-given power—will look like this in exile much more than it will look like displays, parades, and "shock and awe." It's "good news" to us that our God is forever faithful and uniquely powerful.

And, then, clearly, God is *compassionate* in verse 11: "He tends his flock like a shepherd: He gathers the lambs in his arms and carries them close to his heart." What a picture of compassion. Sometimes when things aren't going the way that we want them to go, we are tempted to think that God must not care or that God must not be concerned about us. Ever had that thought? You may be going through one of the most difficult times in your life. Your health, or that of a loved one, may be failing. Your job may be hanging in the balance. Your kids or grandkids may be charting a course that is destructive and dangerous. I don't know. But that doesn't negate or nullify the *compassion* that God has for you and me. He loves us like a shepherd loves his sheep. Do you see the verbs in that verse? Tends. Gathers. Carries. Those are *actions.* Not just *feelings.*[14]

In Advent, we anticipate and celebrate the *action-taking* love of God that *came*—that *comes* to us even now—and that has promised to *come* again.[15] But, we must also remember and re-affirm that God's *coming* in Jesus would lead to other action-taking expressions of his compassion— namely suffering, dying, and rising. At the "spaghetti-like" crossroads of Advent, Sunday worship, your pain, my struggles, societal shifts, and the church's exile, there is a table. It's a place where we touch and taste the *faithfulness,* the *power,* and the *compassion* of God in the bread and the cup of Christ. "Comfort, comfort *my people,*" the Scripture says. Hear the "good news." We *are* God's people regardless of where we stand in the culture or in the eyes of the world. God's "word stands forever" and his subtle, subverting power is at work in *us. We* are the objects of his loving provision in Christ. So, come. Eat and drink at the Table of our faithful, powerful, and compassionate God.

---

14. *Alternative ending if not calling the congregation to the Lord's Table:* In Advent, we anticipate and celebrate the *action-taking* love of God that *came*—that *comes* to us even now—and that has promised to *come* again. But, we must also remember and re-affirm that God's *coming* in Jesus would lead to *other* action-taking expressions of his compassion—namely suffering, dying, and rising. At the "spaghetti-like" crossroads of Advent, Sunday worship, your pain, my struggles, societal shifts, and the church's exile, God invites you to experience, for yourself, his faithfulness, his power at work in your life, and his love as revealed in Christ. We have a place of prayer here where you can bring your needs and burdens to the Lord. Here you can be reminded of his faithfulness, touched by his power, and assured of his love.

15. "Yeah!" section begins.

SERMON 3[1]

How Will God Come to *You?*[2]

Ezra 1:1–4; 3:1–4, 10–13

Babylon was a bully. Around 586 BC, Babylon ransacked Jerusalem, destroyed Judah's prized-possession—Solomon's Temple—and took the able-bodied people into captivity. They killed most of the rest and left the old and crippled to fend for themselves in a burned-over landscape of scarcity and death. But like most bullies, at *some* point they meet their match. Somebody finally stands up to them and discovers that they may not be as powerful as they *think* they are. It was King Cyrus and the Persians who stood up to Babylon, the bully. There was a "new sheriff" in town and his name was Cyrus. We pick up the story around 538 BC or about fifty years *after* the destruction of Jerusalem and the temple.

Ezra 1:1–4; 3:1–4, 10–13

Part of the excitement and thrill of the Advent season is anticipation. Some of you are counting the days until you head for home—wherever that is. Some of you are waiting for the big premiere of the Star Wars

---

1. Preached at First Church of the Nazarene in Kansas City, Missouri on December 13, 2015.

2. Part of the effectiveness of this sermon revolved around the images, stories, and language that was utilized. Everyone has had some experience with a neighborhood bully. Everyone has had the experience of disappointment after having inflated expectations. Everyone has seen someone treated differently or unfairly because of their status or accomplishments. These familiar images were used to open up the text and bring the issue of expectations to the foreground. The sermon culminated in the powerful question: "How do you expect Jesus to come to you?" Essentially, the challenge presented here was to align our expectations with the ways of God that we see in his revelation in Christ—humble, surprising, atypical. This sermon in some ways relied on its countercultural message and call to maintain interest and engagement.

13

movie.[3] Some of you are looking forward to having family members arrive from all over the country, gather around *your* table for dinner, and share together around *your* Christmas tree. With confidence, I can say that there are children and teenagers anxiously awaiting that particular gift or that special "something" that they've been hoping to receive. They will hurry to the tree on Christmas Eve or early on Christmas morning and they'll come *expecting*—hoping and anticipating.

As I read this relatively unfamiliar story from the Old Testament in preparation for preaching on this third Sunday of Advent, the verse that jumped out to me was verse 13 in chapter 3: "No one could distinguish the sound of the shouts of joy from the sound of weeping." When the "exiles" began making their way *out* of their captivity at the generosity of King Cyrus and headed *back* to their homeland—*back* to Judah after fifty years—there was a conflict on the horizon. *This* conflict was different from the one when Babylon invaded and took them captive. *This* conflict was different from when the Persians overpowered the Babylonians and became the new "bully" on the block. *This* new conflict was a conflict not between ancient "super-powers" fighting over control of kingdoms, but it was a conflict between *expectations* and *reality*. And that's a conflict that is not confined to a particular time, place, or people. *That's* something that we *all* have to deal with. Ever had that happen to you—when expectations were so high and the reality just didn't measure up?

I was talking to someone this week who was telling me about a particular experience in their life. For months they had planned and anticipated going on a cruise as a family. It was their first cruise—ever. Mom, Dad, and the three kids—all together for a cruise. It was going to be amazing. The ship was enormous. The food was going to be fabulous. The itinerary included all of the great sites and stops in the Caribbean. *This* was going to be the trip of a lifetime. Expectations were high. Sadly, on the *first* stop at the *first* excursion in San Juan, Puerto Rico, Mom slipped on a slick sidewalk and broke her ankle. There was no time to go to the hospital because the boat *will* leave without you. They made it onto the ship and the ship's doctor confirmed that it was broken, but nothing could be done about it until the next stop in St. Thomas, Virgin Islands. For the rest of the trip Mom was in a wheelchair and on pain-meds. There was no frolicking in the waves. There was no playing with the children on the beaches under the Caribbean sun. Somewhere in that split-second between slipping on the sidewalk and hitting the pavement, those high and lofty expectations met a new and not-so-lofty reality.

---

3. "Star Wars: The Force Awakens" premiered on December 18, 2015. It earned more than $2 billion at the box office.

HOW WILL GOD COME TO YOU?   15

It's happened to you and it's happened to me, hasn't it? It happened when some of the Judean exiles made their way back to Jerusalem after fifty years of Babylonian captivity. When the foundation of the temple was laid again after having been destroyed, the people who remembered the former glory *wept*. Their hopes and expectations were being dashed on this new and not-so-lofty reality. *This* temple—sometimes referred to as "Zerubbabel's Temple"—went half-completed for at least *twenty* years and many of the people who returned to Jerusalem from exile *never* saw it completed.

The season of Advent, in many ways, revolves around anticipation and expectation. Right? If you have an Advent calendar, with every day you open a new little cardboard window or put a new figure into the nativity scene, you are cultivating expectation. We count down the days. We turn the pages until we arrive at Christmas Eve and Christmas Day. Much of this "marking" of time points to hope and expectation. But *part* of the problem is that the story has become *too* familiar to us. It has become *too* common. We sing: "Joy to the world the Lord has come" and that *is* "good news," but we *cannot* and we *must not* skip over the hard reality that the way God comes to the world is downright *shocking*. It's disappointing in an "ankle-breaking" and Zerubbabel's-Temple kind of way. We're getting ahead of the season a bit, but the very fact that the angels make an appearance and they sing their song to a bunch of *shepherds* on a hillside is mind-blowing. *These* guys are the *first* to hear about the world-changing news? Shepherds were the lowest of the low. I used to try to make some comparison into our culture and sometimes I would say that the shepherds were like the garbage collectors of their time. It was a misguided attempt to capture the perceived "bottom" of the societal structure. I think that analogy breaks down. I'm leaning toward comparing the shepherds of the first-century to the politicians of our day, but that might be a slight to the shepherds.[4] Maybe I should use telemarketers or something similar. I don't know.

What I *do* know is that our familiarity with the story serves to "shield" us from the abrasiveness—the shock-value—the hard and lowly reality of it. Nobody expected God to come in a stable surrounded by flying fur and animal feces. Nobody expected God to come through the womb of a peasant girl. Nobody. This is not how *we* would write the story, but this is how *God* writes the story. This is how God enfleshes himself in the world. Who would have ever dreamed that God would be there in backwater Bethlehem, and in the helpless, vulnerable, messy, fussy cries, and coos of an infant? We *all* would have expected something *more*—something *better*.

This phenomenon of a lofty expectation and a simultaneously disappointing reality wasn't limited to the *birth* of Jesus, but became evident even

---

4. Having preached weekly in this congregation for seven years at this point, they understood my "tongue-in-cheek" humor.

in his earthly ministry. His critics and the religious "insiders" labeled him as a "drunk" and as a "friend of sinners and prostitutes."[5] Some thought him a rag-tag teacher from a non-descript town with a bad reputation.[6] With noses turned up and eyes in scornful gaze, they would say: "Who does he think he is?" But even his own disciples had expectations that were not and *would* not be fulfilled by Jesus. Peter got the *title* right—Jesus *was* the "Christ,"[7] but he had loaded that label with hopes and expectations that in the end would be nailed to a tree. Peter wanted and expected something much more grandiose, something mightier. He expected something overwhelming and overpowering. Peter wanted Rome thrown down, Jesus crowned, and all things clear and readily apparent. God had chosen a different way—an upside-down way. It's a mustard-seed, tiny, yeast-in-the-dough, lay-down-your-life kind of way. Some see it. Some perceive it. Others miss it entirely. For many, it's like tripping over a stone. It sounds and seems foolish to so many—a God who is enfleshed in a baby and grows up to die on a cross as a criminal? When you hear the thud of the cross being dropped into a hole on the brow of a mountain that looks like a skull, it is the sound of expectations hitting a new harsh reality. Peter, the leader of the disciples, felt it like a kick in the gut. He had initially promised faithfulness to the death,[8] but when push came to shove, he cursed and denied, the cock crowed, and he ran away weeping.[9] The disciples weren't prepared for Jesus' death even though Jesus had walked and talked with them about it on multiple occasions. Even though the religious leaders and Roman authorities thought that they had eliminated a threat and squashed a revolt—"No one could distinguish the sound of the shouts of joy from the sound of weeping" (Ezra 3:13).

When God, through an unlikely channel like King Cyrus of the Persians, delivered his people and allowed them to go back, resettle in Jerusalem, and rebuild the temple, the lofty expectations met a new and harsh reality. When God, through an unlikely channel like a virgin peasant girl, entered the world in human flesh, grandiose expectations were confronted in the nighttime squeals of a restless baby. When God revealed himself most clearly and profoundly in the death of Jesus, the Christ, on a Roman cross, expectations of "messianic" glory and power were spilled onto the ground, like water and blood from an open wound. So, I ask you: How is it that you want God to come to *you* this year? Maybe the question should not be:

5. Luke 7:34.
6. John 1:45–47.
7. Mark 8:29.
8. Mark 14:31.
9. Mark 14:66–72.

HOW WILL GOD COME TO YOU?

"How do you *want* him to come?," but rather, "How, in light of the Scripture, should you *expect* him to come to you?"

Many of you have read some of the books of Max Lucado. Before he was travelling around preaching and writing books on a full-time basis, he pastored a church in San Antonio, Texas. Every now and then, one of the most famous people in San Antonio would show up at church, unannounced. Not only was he famous, but he was also seven-feet tall. It was David Robinson, the center of the San Antonio Spurs, and one of the greatest basketball players of all time. In between the two worship services, Lucado says that boys and dads flocked around the star athlete and asked him to autograph whatever they could find—worship folders and offering envelopes. Eventually, the crowd would disperse and Robinson would make his way out of the sanctuary and the second worship service would begin. On the *same* day, right at the beginning of the second service, a homeless man with his backpack and assorted belongings came down the center aisle and found the best seat in the house. He sat right in the front row. Heads turned and eyes followed him all the way to the front. Nobody swarmed him or flocked to him or asked him to sign their bulletin. After an awkward minute or two, one of the leaders of the church got up from his seat, walked over, sat down beside him, and patted him on the shoulder. Lucado says that it was in *that* moment that a question came into his mind: "Who touched Jesus today?"[10]

How do you expect Jesus to come to *you*, in Advent, this year? It seems to me that, in all likelihood, it won't be in some grand display that is undeniable and overwhelming. It won't be where there are *only* shouts of joy and all is obvious. Probably not. My guess is that God will come to you like God most often comes—in the unexpected places and unexpected ways. He comes in the cries of the hurting and in the faces of the "least of these." He comes in the humility of children. He comes, not in grandiosity and pomp, but in grace and brokenness. You see, *this* is how he comes to us in the bread and cup here at the Table of the Lord. On the road to Emmaus on the day of Christ's resurrection, Jesus walked with a couple of disciples but they didn't recognize him. It was only when they shared a meal together that their eyes were opened and they *recognized* him "in the breaking of the bread."[11] May it be so among us today. May *our* eyes be opened. May *our* minds perceive that God *is* coming to us here, during Advent, in humble faces and in broken places with his grace and presence.

Amen.

10. Lucado, *Touch of Christ,* adapted.

11. Luke 24:13–35.

SERMON 4[1]

Advent as Preparation[2]

Matthew 3:1–12

I've been teaching an introductory class in preaching over at Nazarene Theological Seminary during this fall semester. An issue that always comes up in discussion revolves around how much *time* it takes to prepare to preach on a weekly basis. Students want to have some guess at the number of hours. It reminds me of a story that I read about the great Reformer, Martin Luther. It was a busy time in his life and he read those verses from Luke: "Do not worry about. . .what you will say, for the Holy Spirit will teach you at that time what you should say."[3] For Luther, that was permission to work on his commentary on the book of Psalms rather than on his sermon for that week at the Wittenberg Cathedral. On Sunday morning, he climbed up into the pulpit and looked down on all those upturned faces and he said that the Spirit *did* speak to him in that moment. The Spirit really did speak. The Spirit whispered in his ear: "Martin, you didn't prepare."[4] Advent is about *properly preparing* for Christmas. Interestingly, Church won't allow us to go to Bethlehem without *first* going out into the desert and listening to this guy named John. I invite you to turn to Matthew 3.

1. Preached at First Church of the Nazarene in Kansas City, Missouri on December 14, 2016 (Advent 2; Year A).

2. In this sermon, part of what I tried to do was to recapture the biblical meaning and message of repentance. In some circles or traditions, the concept has become so narrow or minimized. Oftentimes, it's limited to a "once-in-a-lifetime" that is way back in the past somewhere. This is just not in line with the biblical witness or the realities of experience. The church calendar and lectionary will not allow us to bypass "repentance." Every year, we are called to face John the Baptist and his message. This was my attempt to recapture the positive message of repentance in a time and place where it has, for the most part, been portrayed in negative terms and images. Part of the challenge was to reconceptualize repentance as "good news" for everyone.

3. Luke 12:11–12.

4. McKenzie, "Advice on How."

18

Matthew 3:1–12

Have you ever dreamed of living off the grid? You know what I mean: grow your own food, have a water source, heat your house the old-fashioned way. Some people are energized by that kind of stuff—by living off the grid. Well, John the Baptist was *that* kind of person in the *first* century. He was part of a group of people called the Essenes. They lived off the first-century grid—out in the desert. They ate bugs, harvested wild honey, and dressed themselves in animal skins. John was off the grid and out there preaching a message of repentance. He was also baptizing people in the local water source—the Jordan River.

John was a prophet, a preacher. He was interesting and fascinating and filled with the Spirit of God. By virtue of that combination of things, people from all over wanted to hear him, see him, and watch him in action. Now, prophets don't typically mince words. They don't have the "people-pleasing" gene, if there *is* such a thing. They've been liberated, somehow, from the concern that they might hurt somebody's feeling. For whatever reason, prophets probably don't have empathy as one of their higher qualities or strengths.[5] From later in the Gospel of Matthew, we learn that John's ways and his preaching got him in trouble with the king. John confronted Herod with his sin and eventually Herod tired of it and had John thrown into prison. While John was doing his time, Herod's birthday rolled around and there was a big birthday bash. During the birthday party, Herod's niece provided the entertainment. She was a dancer and Herod liked it. In fact, he liked it so much that he told her he would grant any wish she had. And while everybody was standing around eating birthday cake and Vienna sausages, she asked her Uncle Herod to have John the Baptist beheaded. Herod complied.[6]

But before any of *that* happened, John was out preaching in the desert and Matthew 3:2 essentially records his entire message: "Repent, for the kingdom of heaven is near." In the English translation that I read today, it's eight words. In the Greek, it's only seven. Of course, it's that *first* word that's difficult: "repent." You might say: "Repent? That's the message of those crazy preachers in Times Square with the weird signs and the megaphones." Or, "Repent? Why does the church—every single year—make us read this story about John from one of the gospels?" Or maybe, "Repent? I did that a long time ago—way back there when I was a young person—in that little country church where I was raised." Repentance has

---

5. A popular analytic tool that identified a person's "strengths" was quite popular and fairly common, at the time, in this congregation.

6. Matt 14:1–12.

become a "throw-away" word in our culture. It's "out of date." It's old. It's not a part of anybody's vocabulary anymore. Even though it's a biblical word, it has lost much of its meaning even in the church. It's been so "narrowed" or "compartmentalized"—restricted to "one time" and "way back there"—that now it can be set aside. I have "good news" for you today. Repentance is a wonderful word. It's a *good* thing. It's not a "throw-away" word. It's for *us*—today—even on the way to Bethlehem.[7]

People from all over the region came out to the river bank to hear John preach and he preached about repentance. Repentance is multifaceted. It's not monochrome or bland. It's got several aspects to it and *one* of those is the aspect of *removal*. In repentance, the wrongdoing or our self-chosen waywardness from God's design is removed in the sense that we separate ourselves *from* it. There's an old rabbinic saying that goes like this: "If a man has an unclean thing in his hands, he may wash them in all the seas of the world, and he will never be clean. But if he throws the unclean thing away, just a little water will suffice."[8] Do you understand that? As long as whatever "it" is is in your life, then feeling sorry, feeling bad about it, or trying to punish yourself for it will not address it. *None* of that will set you free from it because it's still there to be held, turned back to, or experienced again. Too often, repentance has been narrowed down to mean simply regret or remorse. It's much *more* than that. Repentance means, that with the grace and help of God, I'll remove myself from or separate myself from the situations, temptations, and occasions that lead me down the path of waywardness from God. Repentance involves *removal*. As one theologian put it: Repentance is a "sign of our readiness to allow God to continue His work within us."[9]

Repentance involves removal, but it also means *re-direction*. It means to turn away from sin and waywardness and to turn *toward* God. It is a change of direction and purpose. It is indicative of a re-orientation of our priorities and values. It's a "course-correction." Repentance means re-direction and that's something for *all* of us regardless of how long we have been followers of Jesus. When you and I are driving our car down the road, we're headed in a certain direction, but all along the way, we are making "course-corrections," right? Even if the road is perfectly straight, you can't take your hands off the wheel for very long at all because there's a need to make almost constant adjustments—redirecting the vehicle and keeping it between the lines. *This* is repentance. It's not *bad*. It's good. It

---

7. This was a way of referring to the journey and weeks of Advent.

8. Barclay, *Matthew*, 54.

9. Williams, *John Wesley's Theology*, 66.

ADVENT AS PREPARATION

keeps us out of the ditches and away from the guard rails. It helps us miss the bridge supports and the other speeding cars on the road. Repentance is *re-direction* that protects and preserves us. That's "good news" for folks like you and me. Repentance is for us. It's about removal and re-direction which leads to the best news of all which is *renewal.* The goal of repentance is renewal. You may or may not care for Eugene Peterson's paraphrase of the Bible but, like it or not, it's always interesting.[10]

> When John realized that a lot of Pharisees and Sadducees were showing up for a baptismal experience because it was becoming the popular thing to do, he exploded: "Brood of snakes! What do you think you're doing slithering down here to the river? Do you think a little water on your snakeskins is going to make any difference? It's your *life* that must change, *not* your skin! And don't think you can pull rank by claiming Abraham as father. Being a descendent of Abraham is neither here nor there. Descendants of Abraham are a dime a dozen. What *counts* is your life. Is it green and blossoming? Because if it's deadwood, it goes on the fire.[11]

The Pharisees and Sadducees—the most religious and God-fearing people of that time—thought that tracing their family tree back to Abraham would be enough. But John—also a descendent of Abraham—was preaching repentance that led to *spiritual renewal* or *life-change.*

Have you ever given thought to some of things that we may claim from time to time? We say: "We're good, law-abiding citizens. We haven't hurt anybody or cheated on our taxes. We even come to church. We pray. We give some of our time and money to the work of God in the world." Maybe if the "bold Baptist" from the Jordan were to stand among us today, he would say: "God can raise up good people, Sunday school teachers, church-attenders, and even preachers from *anything!* What do you and I claim? Are *our* lives being constantly molded to the ways and patterns of Jesus? Are we being *changed* and *renewed* by the grace of God to become more and more like Jesus?"

Repentance involves *removal.* It means *re-direction.* It includes *renewal.* Sometimes we get so caught up in associating repentance with punishment and the past that we fail to realize that repentance is about *renewal* and the *future.* Repentance truly is about our agreeing with God that the *past* will *not* have power over the present and the future. Repentance is

---

10. Within this congregation were several biblical scholars who looked askance at paraphrases.

11. Peterson, *Message,* 1748; Matt 3:7–10.

the "road to renewal." It's about *preparation*. It's about "preparing the way of the Lord" in our own lives. It's about readying the highway of our own hearts here in Advent so that Christ can come in renewing and refreshing ways into our own lives. Every year, John the Baptist stands on the road between us and Bethlehem and says: "Repent. For the kingdom of heaven is near." I want to paraphrase the Grinch from Dr. Suess fame. Here goes: "Advent came to Who-ville without ribbons or tags without boxes or bags. Maybe Advent doesn't come from a store. Maybe Advent means a little bit more."[12] It *does* mean more—a *lot* more. Advent is a journey of preparation that means *repentance*—i.e., removal, re-direction, and renewal. John the Baptist says that part of repentance is "producing good fruit." Peterson calls it a life that is "green and blossoming." It's a life that is "renewed" and alive with the presence of God. That's why we point you to Jesus. That's why we center our lives around the life, death, and resurrection of Jesus. We do it because he is the source of our living. We "bear fruit" like a branch that is connected to a vine—like a branch that is connected to the vine, Jesus the Christ.[13] It is not coincidental that the Church points to this meal—a piece of bread and some fruit of the vine—and the Church says: "God is at work in you." How will you invite God to work in you *today*? Could God free you from the guilt and shame that you have dwelled in for so long? Maybe you need comfort, strength, or endurance from God like you have never needed it before. Maybe you come to eat the bread and drink the cup as an expression of thanksgiving for the sustaining, forgiving, freeing, and empowering grace of God that is at work in you. David Lose says: Repentance is "about a re-orientation, a change of perspective and direction, a commitment to turn and live differently."[14] Maybe "the turn" for you could happen here at the Table—today.

12. Seuss, *How the Grinch,* 29. "Advent" has been substituted for "Christmas" in the quotation.

13. John 15:1–5.

14. Lose, "Hoping for More."

SERMON 5[1]

Is *This* the Christ You're Expecting?[2]

Mark 1:1–8

It's kind of hard to believe, but this is my seventh Advent season as pastor here at First Church. On the second Sunday of Advent—every year without fail—John the Baptist shows up. It might be Luke's Gospel or Matthew's, but this year it's Mark's. It's like what we used to say when we were playing hide and seek: John says, "Ready or not—here I come," and here he is—again. Matthew and Luke start their gospels with birth stories. Not Mark. He launches in and John the Baptizer is fully grown, bearded, and preaching repentance. Jesus is thirty years old and standing on the edge of the stage waiting to make his appearance. It's as if Mark doesn't have time for babies and birth narratives. The clock is ticking. Time's a-wastin'. He leaps headlong into the story. Let's look together at Mark 1.

Mark 1:1–8

There's something attractive about John the Baptist. He's one of those characters who marches to his own drum. He wears what he wants to wear. He eats what he wants to eat. No doctor is going to tell him to lower his cholesterol or reduce his sodium intake. John lives his life on his own terms. He's out in the desert with bugs between his teeth and honey dripping from his beard. He's got fire and brimstone on his lips. He has a mission and a

---

1. Preached at First Church of the Nazarene in Kansas City, Missouri on December 7, 2014 (Advent 2; Year B).

2. Here is another sermon on John the Baptist. I wanted to include it as a way of showing that similar passages can be preached in different ways. There were similarities, but also differences between this sermon and the other that revolves around John's ministry and preaching. In the end, I think the effectiveness of the sermon rested in two things: the redefinition of "power" as the humble strength that we see in Jesus and the image of Jesus as the "Christ of the dirty fingernails."

23

message and nobody's going to stop him from proclaiming it. There's something attractive about that. Mark's Gospel confirms it with a bit of hyperbole in verse 5: "The *whole* Judean countryside and *all* the people of Jerusalem went out to him" (emphasis added). You may have a mental image of what that looks like in your mind. I know that *I* do. What John does, how John lived, and what John looked like is all of interest to me, but I'm *most* interested in what John had to say—John's message. Mark says in verse 7: "This was his message: 'After me will come one more powerful than I, the thongs of whose sandals I am not worthy to stoop down and untie. I baptize you with water, but he will baptize you with the Holy Spirit.'"

I've been pastoring for over twenty-two years and preaching for more than thirty years. *Most* of the time, John's message is condensed down to "repent and be baptized." Mark's Gospel doesn't specifically use the word "repent," but *that,* along with "baptism," seem to be the focus of preaching when it comes to the story of John. Afterall, he *is* "John, the Baptizer" or "John, the Baptist." Some of you grew up in churches that were named after him. But it's the *first* part of John's message that intrigues me today. When John says, "there is coming someone who is more *powerful* than I am," what does he *mean* by that?

The word translated "powerful" is the word *iskuroteros* in Greek. It gets translated in a variety of ways. In some of the older English translations it shows up as "mightier"—"one *mightier* than I." Sometimes it gets translated as "stronger" or "greater." Have you ever wondered why John chose *this* adjective to describe the one who would come after him? Why not, "After me will come one more *holy* than I," or "more *loving* than I," or "more *godly* than I," or something else? Why "more *powerful* than I"? And if Jesus is more *powerful* than John, what does that really *mean?* Is it some kind of reference to the miracle-working power of Jesus that John apparently didn't possess or practice? Is *that* what this is about? If it was really about *that* kind of power, would John or Mark have chosen *this* word in Greek when there were *other* words like *dunatoi,* from which we get English words like "dynamite," words that mean and connote *power?*

When I was a kid, our home was the place where my mother's side of the family gathered for Thanksgiving and Christmas. My mom was the youngest of five children and her closest sibling was ten years older than her. One of her older sisters was married to a man named Don, which made him my uncle. When my brother and I were teenagers, we thought Don was a wimp. We had never seen him throw a ball, kick a ball, or hit a ball. He was kind of a small man with a very slim frame. When we would watch football on television, he would express his concerns when two guys ran their heads

IS THIS THE CHRIST YOU'RE EXPECTING?

into each other.[3] Back *then*—in our teenage minds—it was synonymous with "wimpy-ness." I'm not saying it was *right*. I'm just saying that's what we thought. I didn't know *then*, what I know *now*. My "wimpy" uncle had been shot out of a plane over France during World War II and when he parachuted to the ground, some French farmers hid him in a barn. Then, they hid him in another house and then in another place until someone betrayed them and my uncle became a "prisoner of war" along with several other Allied soldiers. The Germans put them for a while at the Buchenwald concentration camp where they were deprived and neglected. They were fed loaves of bread that were one-third sawdust along with their soup that was full of bugs. Wimp? I don't think so.

There are different kinds of "power" and "strength," aren't there? There's "power" like the biblical Samson who was the original "strong man." He killed wild animals and defeated armies with the simplest of weapons.[4] He pushed over building-supporting pillars with his bare hands.[5] There's *that* kind of power; but when John says that Jesus will be more "powerful" than him, *that's* not what he's talking about. Or, when Gideon or David led armies into battle and defeated other nations, there's *that* kind of "power." But, is *that* what John the Baptist is talking about?

As I've pondered this Scripture, I've come to the conclusion that John says more than he really understands when he speaks of the "coming One's power." There is a kind of power that runs through the biblical witness that has nothing to do with military might or with physical feats of strength. It has nothing to do with elevation of status or authority, but it has *everything* to do with humility and sacrifice. There's a power that the world does not know or recognize that is found in humble service and obedience. There is a "greatness," as Jesus says, that is found as a "slave,"[6] in the "least,"[7] and as the "last."[8] There is a God-like and godly weakness that is stronger than human strength in all its bravado and bluster. There is a power that Jesus modeled that is hinted at by John in his confession of unworthiness when John said: "I am unworthy to untie his sandals."

What's the big deal with untying sandals? This is a problem for *us* because it requires an awareness of first-century life in Palestine. You and I put

---

3. This was, of course, long before the current on-going conversation about the long-term impact of multiple concussions.

4. Judg 14:5–6 and 15:1–17.

5. Judg 16:25–30.

6. Matt 20:26–28.

7. Matt 25:31–46.

8. Matt 20:16.

on our socks and shoes in the comfort of our carpet-covered homes with vacuum-cleaned rugs. We step onto sidewalks or concrete-floored garages and into our carpeted automobiles. We do our very best to avoid dirt and mud and the idea that we might walk through the sewage of our city is beyond our comprehension. It's just *not* a factor in our daily lives. But, in the first-century, there were no sidewalks, carpeted-homes, or socks. People lived and walked every day in sandals through the dirt, mud, and sewage of the town. Animals, that we never encounter except at the petting zoo or on the school-trip to the farm, lived in the town, were tied to the house or sometimes *in* the house, and did in the streets and houses what animals do. Avoiding that *entirely* was impossible. It was accepted as a part of life. It was simply the way the world worked.

As one biblical scholar says: "Untying the master's sandals was the one demeaning task never required of a Hebrew servant. To be unworthy of such a task would be to lower oneself *below* the status of a slave."[9] Why was it the *one* demeaning task never required of a Hebrew slave? Why? Because untying sandals that are caked with dirt and feces is about as gross, difficult, and "unclean" as anything might be. Yet, *this* is the very thing that *Jesus* did for his disciples when they gathered in Jerusalem on the night before he was crucified. The arrangements for the meal had been made. The various food items had been prepared.[10] The room was ready, but there was no slave, no servant. No one was prepared or willing to untie the dirty sandals and wash the filthy feet of Jesus and his followers. But John the Baptist said: "After me will come one more *powerful* than I," and on the night that Jesus was betrayed by one of his companions, he took a towel and a basin and the "more powerful One" got down on the floor and did the one demeaning task that was never required of a Hebrew slave.[11]

Is *this* the Christ that you are awaiting in Advent? Is *this* the Jesus that you're anticipating? Is he the one on the floor with feces under his fingernails, with a towel wrapped around his waist, and washing the feet of his disciples? Is *that* the one you're looking for? You *do* understand that *this* Jesus doesn't sell much at Walmart? He doesn't help the bottom line at Target or even at Bed, Bath, and Beyond.[12] John helps us to remember that the Jesus we await is the child born to some peasants in a cave-like stable filled with barnyard animals and stench. His crib was a manger, but

9. Guelich, *Mark,* 24, emphasis added.

10. Matt 26:17–19.

11. John 13:1–17.

12. The shopping explosion that happens in the U.S. between Thanksgiving and Christmas Eve was in full swing. I chose some local retailers with which everyone was familiar.

IS THIS THE CHRIST YOU'RE EXPECTING?

even *that* has lost its edge. His parents repurposed a feeding trough for the animals and wrapped their shivering newborn in strips of cloth—the clothing of a poor infant. The Jesus of Advent is the Christ of the stable, the dirty sandals, and the cross.

When Jesus laid down his life—when he "humbled himself and became obedient unto death, even death on a cross,"[13] as the apostle Paul says it in Philippians—the grown, adult Jesus was simply continuing the pattern and story of the newborn, infant Jesus when God became flesh and "pitched his tent"[14] among us. Those of us who have experienced more than our fair-share must ever be reminded that when God "pitched his tent," he pitched his tent among the poor. When Jesus rested his head as a baby, he did it in a borrowed barn. When he rested his head as a traveling preacher, he did it in the open air at the hospitality of others. Jesus said about *himself*: "Foxes have holes and birds have nests, but the Son of Man has nowhere to lay his head."[15] When they laid his bruised and lifeless body in the tomb, it was in someone else's.

In a time and culture that is so focused on consuming, acquiring, and collecting, the Christ of Advent comes to us as the "more powerful One," yet he comes in the power of humility, brokenness, and service. I don't guess it should surprise us that the word "humility" comes from a Latin word—"*humus*"—which means "soil" or "dirt." What would Advent look like for you and me if we focused on the One who came to serve, to sacrifice, and to humble himself? One of the great Old Testament prophets summarized life following God in this way: "What does the Lord require of you?" and then he answers his own question—"To act justly, to love mercy and to walk humbly with your God."[16] You and I cannot do that on our own. We cannot live that way or respond that way without the invading grace and power of God. Not a grace or power that came to us "once upon a time," but a grace and power that comes to us and helps us on a day-to-day basis. As we gather at the Lord's Table today, may you receive grace and strength to expect the Christ of the dirty fingernails this Advent. In the bread and the cup, may you receive help to live *this* week acting justly, loving mercy, and walking humbly with God.

Amen.

---

13. Phil 2:8

14. John 1:14. Sometimes translated as "tabernacled" or "dwelt" or "made his dwelling."

15. Luke 9:58.

16. Mic 6:8.

SERMON 6[1]

What About Joseph?[2]

Matthew 1:18–25

Why does *Mary* get all the attention and all the press? An angel visited her and she said, "I'm willing,"[3] and now universities are named after her. There's a church near Disney World in Orlando and this is the name of it: "The Basilica of Mary, *Queen of the Universe.*" Joseph gets a hospital down the street and a little town in Missouri.[4] What's going on here? Mary is the "Queen of the Universe" and Joseph is the "carpenter from Nazareth." Where's the justice in *that*? The Gospel of Luke is focused on the story of Mary, whereas the Gospel of Matthew gives much more attention to Joseph. Today, on this fourth Sunday of Advent, we look together at the story from Matthew 1.

---

1. Preached at First Church of the Nazarene in Kansas City, Missouri on February, 18 2016 (Advent 4; Year A).

2. Some of the references in the opening "tongue-in-cheek" section were local and therefore particular to the place in which this message was preached. That was intentional because, as one homiletics theorist suggests, specifics stick in memory better than generalities. Almost every community would have some connection or reference to Mary or Joseph. In this particular year, Christmas Day fell on a Sunday. As a result, I felt comfortable preaching from the story of Joseph on the fourth Sunday of Advent, and saving aspects of the story that revolve around Mary for Christmas Eve and/or Christmas Day. Sometimes I think alliteration can be forced, but in this case, I thought "match, messenger, and meaning" came quite naturally out of the story.

3. Paraphrase of Luke 1:38.

4. This is a reference to St. Joseph Medical Center in Kansas City, Missouri and the city of St. Joseph, Missouri.

28

WHAT ABOUT JOSEPH?

Matthew 1:18–25

This story brings to light, in some ways, the difficulties of translation from one language to another along with some first century Jewish cultural practices that are very different from our own. I don't know about you, but "betrothal" or being "pledged to be married" is not typically a part of my weekly vocabulary. In all likelihood, Joseph and Mary were *matched* together by their families. Once that "match" takes place, there are certain things that happen and certain things that are *not* supposed to happen. Joseph and Mary have entered into a "legal agreement" in which they are "matched" together, and if one of them were to die, the *other* would be considered a "widow" or a "widower." Yet, during this same period, they are not living together and sharing sexual intimacy. Intimacy, under normal circumstances, would not happen until *after* their wedding ceremony which would conclude this prior time of "betrothal," or this legal arrangement in which they have pledged themselves to each other. The use of the English word—"engagement"—is simply inadequate and doesn't convey what was really going on in the cultural context of first century Palestine.

During this time of being "matched"—but before their "wedding ceremony"—Mary becomes pregnant. Verse 18 says that she "is found to be with child." Now, they didn't have pregnancy tests that you could buy at Walgreens, but neither were the people of the first century completely ignorant. They had a clear understanding of how children were conceived. They didn't have access to 3-D sonograms, but women of the first century were closely in tune with their own bodies. Additionally, we learn from Luke's Gospel that Mary was visited by an angel who filled her in on what was going on. It was miraculous and mysterious, yet she trusted the angel's word. She believed what Joseph was yet to be told. You and I, however, can imagine what Joseph must have thought. Presumably, Joseph is told by Mary what has happened. She's pregnant. An angel told her that this is from God and that this child will be called the "Son of the Most High." Wow. What Joseph knows for sure is that *he* isn't the father. As a result of that one fact, the "match"—the legal agreement—can be voided. The translators of Matthew 1 use the word "divorce" even though they hadn't had a "wedding ceremony" yet. The point is that Joseph has options. He can embarrass Mary. He can shame her, because who's going to believe a story involving angels, God, and conception without sexual union?

But Joseph doesn't want to do that. He doesn't want to shame Mary, but rather, he wants to "divorce her quietly," Matthew says. The "match" will be broken. Joseph will go his way and Mary will go hers. But then, there's a *messenger* who comes to Joseph. I use *that* word on purpose because that's

what the word "angel" means in Greek. "Angels" were "messengers." They delivered news. They came with news from God and this happened quite frequently to Joseph. *This* passage in Matthew 1 is the first of *four* different occasions in the first and second chapters of Matthew when Joseph is the recipient of a "message" from God via an "angel."

Like most angelic messages, the first instruction is "fear not" or "don't be afraid." I looked up the admonition, "do not be afraid," and I found seventy different times in the Scripture where this is said. Sometimes it's said by God, an angel, in a vision, or by Jesus. Other times it's said by Moses to the people, by Joshua, or by somebody else. Typically, when Moses, Joshua, or some person other than Jesus says, "do not be afraid," it is usually followed by a reference to Pharaoh's army or the inhabitants of some land that is yet to be conquered. Someone might say: "Do not be afraid of the Jebusites or the Canaanites," or something similar.

But forty-five of the seventy references are instances where God comes to someone in a vision, sends an angel, or Jesus is speaking. In *most* of those passages, the person who is receiving the message must be assured that *they* need not be afraid in that moment. Apparently, these were naturally frightening experiences: seeing an angel, having a vision, or being talked to by God. So, when Joseph has this "angelic visit," the first thing that he is told is "do not fear" or "do not be afraid." It's as if *that* is the angel's way of saying: "hello." It happens to Mary in Luke. It happens to Abraham in Genesis. It happens to Joseph in Matthew.

Once *that* is out of the way, the "news" for Joseph is mind-boggling. The angel arrives to say that what Mary has been telling him is *true*. She *is* pregnant. She hasn't been "fooling around." This miracle is the *Lord's* doing. Now, if *that's* not enough to wake Joseph from his dream, the next part of the message will surely snap him out of it. Get this. The child to whom Mary will give birth will be named "Yeshua" or Jesus, the angel says, because he will save his people from their sins. Matthew doesn't include these details, but I think Joseph woke up like he'd been hit by a bolt of lightning. His pupils were dilated. His forehead was covered with sweat like only happened when he was chopping wood. His nerves were on full alert. The message had been received and Matthew tells us that "when Joseph woke up, he did what the angel of the Lord had commanded him" (Matt 1:24). It was like Joseph had received his marching orders and he obeyed. The *match* of him and Mary, which had almost been broken, was now preserved and secured because of the message that Joseph received via an angel sent from God.

It's a great story. It's a miraculous and mysterious story. But the *meaning* of the story is what makes it important for you and me and for the world. I want to summarize that *meaning* in three simple phrases that

WHAT ABOUT JOSEPH?   31

I hope you can ponder during this week before Christmas. Are you ready? Here's the first phrase: "*To* us."

In the birth of Jesus, God is sending his Son *to* us. It's the miracle of incarnation. The most memorized verse in all the Bible says it *this* way: "God so loved the world that he *gave* his one and only Son, that whoever believes in him shall not perish but have eternal life."[5] God *gave* his Son *to* the world—*to* us. If you or I had been doing the giving, we probably wouldn't have done it *this* way. Would we have sent Jesus into the world through the womb of a young, peasant in Palestine? Would we have put him into the care of a carpenter from Nazareth? Would we have had him be born in a Bethlehem barn? It boggles the mind and is mysterious beyond our comprehension, but we confess that God, in his wisdom and at just the right moment,[6] "en-fleshed" the eternal word in a baby and he was given *to* us. The New Testament says that Jesus is the "radiance of God's glory and the exact representation of his being."[7] In other words, if you want to know what God is like, then the answer is Jesus.

After the service last week, someone mentioned to me a great, current theologian and writer by the name of N.T. Wright. I think he goes by "Tom" among his friends. He was asked an interesting question not too long ago. He was asked what he would tell his children on his deathbed. His answer was: "Look at Jesus," and like most theologians, he couldn't stop *there*. He elaborated on why. He said: "If you want to know who God is, look at Jesus. If you want to know what it means to be human, look at Jesus. If you want to know what love is, look at Jesus. And go on looking until you're not just a spectator, but part of the drama that has *him* as the central character."[8] God has come *to* us in Jesus and this is part of the meaning of Advent.

Another aspect of the meaning of this message that Joseph received in his angelic vision is summarized by the phrase—*for* us. This baby that Mary would birth will be named "Jesus" because he will save his people from their sins. The purpose of his coming is salvation, healing, wholeness, and peace *for* us. Salvation is not something that you and I can acquire for ourselves or achieve by ourselves. Salvation is provided *for* us by God through the life, suffering, death, and resurrection of Jesus. Jesus died the death that we deserved. We are guilty and he provides pardon. We have sinned and he provides forgiveness. We are "dead in our trespasses,"[9] and

5. Paraphrase of John 3:16.

6. Allusion to Rom 5:6.

7. Heb 1:3a.

8. Watling, *Marriage of Heaven*, 129.

9. Paraphrase of Eph 2:1.

32 SECTION 1: SERMONS FOR ADVENT AND CHRISTMAS EVE

he gives life. We are restless and he brings peace. We are lost and he leads us home. Part of the meaning of Jesus and his coming is what he did and what he will do is *for* us. He *came*—for us. He *died*—for us. He was raised from the dead—*for* us. And he will come again *for* us. He came *to* us in the incarnation. He came *for* us to provide salvation. He is also *with* us. As Matthew cites the prophet Isaiah: Jesus is the fulfillment of the name "Emmanuel" which means "God *with* us!"[10]

Lauren was five years old and her favorite Christmas decoration was a tiny nativity set that her parents kept in a little metal box similar to one of those little containers for mints. One day before Christmas, in a panic, she rushed in and blurted out: "Daddy! Jesus is missing! We've looked everywhere and can't find him." The search was on. They looked under the couch and in the toy box. They looked behind the book case. No Jesus. Then Dad zeroed in on the backpack. Down among the hairbrushes, the plastic wallet, the random stuffed animals, and the empty gum wrappers, *there* was the little figurine of Jesus.[11] Jesus wasn't really "missing." He was just in the ordinary places among the daily stuff. He wasn't on the mantel piece—pretty and displayed. No. Jesus was in the middle of life and living—down in the bottom of a crowded and dirty backpack.

Where will you see Jesus in this last week before Christmas day? He *is* with us. By the power of the Spirit, Jesus is with us in the mundane and routine. He's with us in the highs and lows. In the middle of your pain, in the middle of your confusion, or in the midst of your anxiety—down in the bottom of the backpack—Jesus is there *with* you. He slipped into the world under a cover of darkness on the backside of a sleepy little village. He was found among the straw, surrounded by the stench of animals, and in the arms of his tired and wondering mother. He was among the ordinary and common things.

This is *part* of the reason why Jesus instituted what we call communion or the Lord's Supper with bread and wine—common things, cross-cultural things. Some would call them staples. These things that are for everyone everywhere and always have been. In a way, they convey that Jesus is *with* us in the ordinary things and in the daily stuff—no matter where we are or what we're facing. I announce "good news" to you today. Jesus has come *to* us and *for* us and he's *with* us here, now, and always.

Amen.

10. Matt 1:23.

11. Asimakoupoulos, "Jesus is Missing," adapted.

SERMON 7[1]

Christmas Eve: Angels and Christ's Coming[2]

Hebrews 2:16

I've been preaching from some strange passages of Scripture during these weeks of Advent leading up to Christmas, and since you've already heard the story from Luke sung and read tonight during this service, I thought I would continue that pattern. But, *before* we read a verse from Hebrews, I want to draw your attention to something that you already know about the Christmas story. There's this "thread" running throughout that points to the important presence of angels. Have you noticed that? An angel appears to Mary and tells her what's going to happen. She's been chosen. She's going to give birth to the messiah. She doesn't understand it all, but she is willing, and so Mary becomes this amazing example of trust in God. Joseph, however, has to be convinced and, sure enough, an angel appears to him as well. Joseph is told to take Mary as his wife and not to divorce her privately because of her pregnancy, which Joseph apparently had every right to do. Later in the story, the magi—sometimes called "wisemen"— are warned in a dream to take another route home.[3] In all likelihood, they were instructed by an angel. Even later in the story when Joseph and Mary and the baby Jesus flee to Egypt, the "warning" comes to Joseph from an angel.[4] And, of

---

1. Sermon preached at First Church of the Nazarene in Kansas City, Missouri on December 24, 2015.

2. This Christmas Eve meditation was set in the context of a "Carols by Candlelight" type of service where scriptural texts were read and familiar carols were sung in response to them. The effectiveness of this homily was the interplay of the prominence of angels in the story set against the verse from Hebrews. The "rub" of the persistent presence of angels against the scriptural witness that Jesus' salvific purpose was not for angels, but for human beings like us is what made the sermon interesting and turned the congregation's attention to foundational meaning of Christmas.

3. Matt 2:12.

4. Matt 2:13.

33

course, while the shepherds are in the fields outside of Bethlehem, angels come to share the news about the birth of Jesus and give them clues about how they will *know* that they've found the right baby.[5] Remember the clues? He will be "wrapped in strips of linen and lying in a manger." Angels have made their way into the hymnody of the church particularly at this time of year. "Angels We Have Heard of High" and "Hark! The Herald Angels Sing" are two of the most often sung carols that we have. There is this "thread" of angels and angelic messages that runs throughout the story.

But *tonight*, I want to emphasize that the story is *not really* about angels. You know that. The story is about God coming to us in the baby born in Bethlehem who is the Son of God. He is "Emmanuel"—which means "God *with* us." This child is the Christ, the promised Savior from heaven. He grows up and matures. Eventually, he launches out into a public ministry for several years surrounded by a select group of disciples. Ultimately, he is arrested, tried, and crucified on a Roman cross outside Jerusalem. The "even-better-news" is that he was raised from the dead—never to die again—and he is at the right hand of God even now making intercession for us.

I haven't forgotten about the strange text for tonight. It's over in the book of Hebrews. Hebrews affirms that Jesus "shares our humanity"[6]—that Jesus was "flesh and blood" living in the world like *we* are living in the world—almost immediately we come to our text: "For surely it is not angels he helps, but Abraham's descendants."[7]

Did you catch that? Angels bring messages. Angels form choirs in the heavens. Angels give warnings and appear in dreams, but God has not come in Jesus to help *angels*. No. God has come to help people like you and me. Tom Troeger says it *this* way: "Yes, the angels are indeed lovely, but their heavenly splendor must not distract me from the core of the gospel: Christ has come not for the sake of angels but for us human creatures, fragile and broken as we are."[8] Hear the "good news" again on Christmas Eve: God has come in Christ for *you* and for *me*. Not for angels, but for *us*—to save and redeem *us*.

Amen.

5. Luke 2:8–12.
6. Heb 2:14, paraphrased.
7. Heb 2:16.
8. Troeger, *Sermon Sparks*, 10.

SERMON 8[1]

Christmas Eve: *The* Savior . . . to You[2]

Luke 2:11a

Tonight's text comes from a familiar passage at this time of year: Luke 2.

Luke 2:11a

Next year will mark the three-hundredth anniversary of his death. He died in 1715. There won't be any celebrations or commemorations. He is essentially unknown. When he died, he was confined in an institution for debtors. He hadn't paid his bills for a long, long time. He had earned a fair amount of money, but apparently, he had spent it or wasted it. He died penniless and institutionalized. *But*, fifteen years before his death, he wrote one of the hymns that we have sung tonight. His name was Naham Tate and his song is probably the most biblically literal Christmas hymn that we have. It is essentially a paraphrase of the verses from Luke that we have been reading tonight. Ironically, the lyrics that Naham Tate wrote were set to the music of George Frederick Handel. Of course, Handel wrote the famous "Messiah," which includes the climactic "Hallelujah Chorus." He was a musical genius, but similar to Tate in that he was a monetary mis-manager. Handel went bankrupt much like Tate had done. The two never met and Tate never heard his lyrics sung to the music of Handel. He died before it happened.

---

1. Sermon preached at First Church of the Nazarene in Kansas City, Missouri on December 24, 2014.

2. This brief homily from a Christmas Eve service was meaningful because of its emphasis upon Jesus as "Savior" in a world of competing "saviors" and answers. The concluding thought that "these others things just won't do" is a sentiment that many felt and of which others needed to be reminded. Part of the sermon's power was that it was focused on the simple and foundation message that God became incarnate in Jesus in order to save us, and that this is the essence of Christmas.

His famous song is "While Shepherds Watched Their Flocks by Night." It's the lyric from verse 3 which is drawn from verse 11 in Luke 2. Here it is from the song: "To you in David's town this day is born of David's line, the Savior who is Christ the Lord."[3]

I don't want to make *too* much of this because the witness of the Scripture in its entirety is very clear. But, the lyricist *did* change the words of the Lukan text a bit. Luke makes reference to "*a* Savior" who is Christ, the Lord. Actually, in the Greek text, there is not even an "*a.*" It's just—"Savior"—*soter* in Greek. The lyricist, however, says: "To you is born *the* Savior." Again, there are plenty of places in the New Testament where Jesus is identified or identifies *himself* as *the* Savior or *the* Messiah—not just *one* among many. When Jesus says, "I am *the* Way, *the* Truth, and *the* Life," it's very clear. I simply point this out tonight because when we sing this famous Christmas song, we are making an incredible faith-claim. We are confessing that *Jesus*—born in Bethlehem centuries ago, walking the dusty streets of Palestine in the first century, dying on a Roman cross as a criminal, raised from the dead by the power of God—*he,* we sing, is *the* Savior of the world. *Not* a democratic government. *Not* a better educational system. *Not* more NGOs giving away international aid. *Not* bigger armies or better intelligence operations. *Not. . . not. . . not.* Make your own list. *The* Savior is *Jesus* whose birth we celebrate tonight.

Hear it from a British journalist who writes for the *London Times.* Ironically, he is an avowed atheist. His name is Matthew Parris. In the quotation that I'm going to read to you, he refers specifically to Africa because he was looking into the impact of the humanitarian aid that has flooded into the continent over the last few decades. Although he refers specifically to Africa, his comment, I believe, is applicable to the world and to us. Here's what he said:

> Now a confirmed atheist, I've become convinced of the enormous contribution that Christian evangelism makes in Africa; sharply distinct from the work of secular NGOs, government projects and international aid efforts. These alone will not do. Education and training alone will not do. In Africa, Christianity changes people's hearts. It brings a spiritual transformation. The rebirth is real. The change is good.[4]

The message of the church at Christmas is that "these other things just won't do." The gifts under the tree, the time together, the beautiful snowfall, the trip to Colorado, the cookies and cider—*all* are wonderful things, but *alone,* they just won't do.

3. Osbeck, *Amazing Grace,* 379.
4. Greer and Horst, *Mission Drift,* 36.

Hear again the Christmas news. To Africa, to Asia, to the entire world, and to *you* is born *the* Savior who is Christ, the Lord.

Amen.

Section 2

Sermons for Christmas, Epiphany, and the Non-Festival Time Before Lent

SERMON 9[1]

Everything New[2]

Revelation 21:1–6a

C an you believe it? 2012. The Mayan calendar says that this is going to be the *last* year[3] and some are stockpiling supplies like it's Y-2K all over again.[4] I thought that I'd better preach—at least *once*—from the book of Revelation. Today's the day. "Revelation" comes from a Greek word, *apokalupsis*—apocalypse. It means an uncovering or a disclosure, a revelation. This vision happened to a man named John on an island off the coast of what is today called Turkey. In the first century, the island was called Patmos. Now, it's called Patino—all thirteen square miles of it. It was like the first-century Alcatraz. Rocky. Spartan. Hard labor with little reward and lots of suffering. Exiles barely survived on the island of Patmos. The entire book of Revelation is a "tale of two cities."[5] One's the "harlot" and one's the "bride."

1. Preached at First Church of the Nazarene in Kansas City, Missouri on January 1, 2012 (1st Sunday after Christmas; Year B).

2. In this example, I intentionally used Paul Scott Wilson's "Four Pages of a Sermon" method of structuring the sermon. I have, however, included an introduction which Wilson does not explicitly advocate, because I thought it was necessary to introduce the strange writings of Revelation. The "first page" names the theological problem or issue that gives rise to the text, and this section is noted in the manuscript. According to Wilson's schemata, the "second page" articulates analogous trouble in the contemporary world. This section was tied closely to world news that was happening at the time, and particularly the regime change that was happening in North Korea. The "third page" identifies the good news at the center of the text. Then, the "fourth page" helps the congregation experience and respond to God's grace in today's world. The beginning of the "four pages" are indicated by the presence of a footnote.

3. Stories about the Mayan calendar were all over the news. Some were serious. Some were not.

4. This was a reference to the end of 1999, when some believed that computer systems all over the world would crash because they were not prepared to transition to the year 2000.

5. Of course, *A Tale of Two Cities* was Charles' Dickens' famous novel set in the

41

42   SECTION 2: CHRISTMAS, EPIPHANY, AND THE TIME BEFORE LENT

With all the images of beasts, horns, dragons, and bowls—there's just a host of metaphors that run together and are overwhelming. It's *meant* to be so, but the *outcome*—the *end*—is never in question.

Part of that comes through in chapter 21.

Revelation 21:1–6a

John is banished to Patmos for a reason.[6] He says in the first chapter of Revelation that he's there because of the "word of God and the testimony of Jesus."[7] [1:9]. You see, John was walking in the way of Christ. He was following Jesus and his following of Jesus resulted in the same things that happened to Jesus—persecution and suffering. It was the time of Domitian, and even though Domitian was the supreme ruler of the Roman Empire, he was not very secure. He was easily threatened. His father, Vespasian, had been the emperor which meant that, for the most part, he was absent from Domitian's life. After all, it's tough to be the emperor and military leader—ruler of an empire that spans thousands of miles—and, at the *same* time, be a caring, present father-figure to your children. It just didn't happen.

In addition to that, Domitian's mother had died while he was just a child and this only further exacerbated his isolation and insecurities. Simultaneously, he was living in his older brother's "shadow." Titus, his brother, ultimately succeeded his father as emperor. Titus was the guy who laid siege to Jerusalem and ultimately destroyed the city along with the temple in 70 AD. But after being emperor for only a couple of years, Titus died of a fever. So, at the age of thirty, the young, insecure, isolated Domitian became the ruler of the expansive Roman Empire.

When Domitian was a teenager, Emperor Nero wanted to renovate and rebuild a portion of Rome. There were, however, *people* living there and working there. Nero didn't care. His sinister solution was to burn that part of the city to the ground so that he could rebuild it to *his* own liking. Homes burning. Shops burning. People dying. Nero's answer was to blame the fire on the "Christians"—those followers of a long-gone preacher who claimed to be some kind of a savior. "Blame it on *them!* Then as punishment, have them killed for it. Feed them to the dogs. Crucify them along the streets of Rome." All of this for a tragedy that they didn't cause. You see, for Roman emperors, Christians were an easy target.

---

midst of the French Revolution.

6. This marks the beginning of Wilson's "page one" which articulates the theological problem or issue that gives rise to the text.

7. Rev 1:9.

EVERYTHING NEW

43

John was banished to Patmos during Domitian's reign and was enduring his own measure of suffering. His friends and fellow-followers of Jesus who were scattered in cities throughout Asia Minor were facing threats and persecutions and dangers of all kinds. They had known, personally, Christians who were pulled from their homes and made to pay with their lives for someone else's crimes. They knew what it was like to gather up the remains of a loved one who had been burned, stoned, or crucified. They were living in a world that was in moral free-fall. Their world was filled with violence, death, and decay at every turn and it certainly *seemed* that the brunt of the evil was being borne by the peace-loving, cheek-turning, grace-filled people who named Jesus as "Lord." It certainly seemed, felt, and looked as if the world was spinning out of control—that it was without direction or guidance.

I wish I had paid attention to his name but I didn't.[8] He was one of those "talking heads" who was being interviewed on one of the news channels as I was clicking past on my way from one football game to another one. For some reason, I stopped and listened for a moment or two. He was an expert of some kind. He had several titles and several connections to a "think tank" in some prominent place. He was being asked about Iraq-Iran relations in the aftermath of several bombings on the streets of Baghdad. Of course, *that* conversation took place in an environment where nerves are on edge on the Korean peninsula and beyond because Kim Jong Il, North Korea's dictator, has died[9] and now the "reins of power" have been transferred to a twenty-something-year-old kid with access to nuclear launch codes and the potential to destroy half the world.

Vladimir Putin in Russia—another nuke-laden power—is fixing elections[10] while European economies are imploding and dragging the rest of the world with them. Multiplied millions around the world and even in the United States are wondering what they'll eat tonight for dinner. Nazarene pastors in India are being beheaded for their faith. Martyrs in sub-Saharan Africa are fertilizing a growing church with their own blood while churches in America are declining in impact, being closed or sold, and our culture fights about whether kids should be suspended from school for "Tebowing" in the hallways.[11] It's a broken-world that we live in, isn't it?

8. This marks the beginning of Wilson's "second page" which outlines analogous trouble in the contemporary world.

9. Kim Jong Il died on December 17, 2011 as reported by North Korean state television.

10. This, of course, is *not* a reference to the 2016 presidential election in the U.S. (because the sermon was preached in 2012), but a reference to an election in Russia, at the time, which gave Putin an overwhelming majority.

11. Tim Tebow, a college football star and outspoken Christian, would kneel and

44   SECTION 2: CHRISTMAS, EPIPHANY, AND THE TIME BEFORE LENT

Anyway, this "talking head" was on television to say that, in all likelihood, as a result of the conflict between Iran and Iraq and the departure of
the U.S. and others who were trying to "keep a lid" on a very volatile situation, the minority Christian population in Iraq, Afghanistan, and other
places in the Middle East will disappear completely in the next few years,
through annihilation or by being driven entirely "underground." There's
an old saying: "If it ain't broke, don't fix it." But, pardon my grammar:
What if it *is* "broke"? Maybe Newt can fix it?[12] Or, Mitt?[13] Or a second
helping of "hope and change"[14] from the president? When you really think
about it and take time to reflect, how *old* and *tired* does all that sound to
you? Pain and brokenness. Suffering, disengagement, and fear—this is a
painted picture of our world.

But John on Patmos caught a glimpse of God's glory.[15] Between the
back-breaking labor and the barely hanging on, John heard the voice of
God say what he and his Jesus-following friends so desperately needed to
hear. God said: *"I am making everything new."* When you look closely at the
book of Revelation, you notice that God had spoken in the eighth verse of
chapter *one* when he said: "I am the Alpha and Omega." But now, it's been
twenty chapters since he last spoke. There have been twenty chapters of
John's vision of fires and horses and of horns and harlots. Not until chapter
twenty-one does the Lord God speak again. This is what he says: *"I am
making everything new."*

When Rome has his "thumb" on you, she wants to hear you say: "Caesar is Lord." Rome wants to see you live as if "Caesar is Lord" and wants to
make you think down deep in the recesses of who you are that "Caesar *is*
Lord." But it's *good news* when God speaks again and says: *"I am making
everything new."* When you've gathered up the charred bones of your mother
or father and you've watched as your friends have done the same thing for
their brother or sister, and it's all because they claim that *"Jesus is Lord,"* it's
world-shaking, empire-crumbling news when God says: *"I am making everything new."* When your kids are hungry and you haven't been able to buy

pray after a touchdown. Children and teenagers were imitating this action at their
schools all across the country.

12. Newt Gingrich, an American politician, who was running for president at the
time.

13. Mitt Romney, an American politician, who was running for president at the
time. These two were chosen because of the uniqueness of their first names and they
needed no explanation.

14. This was the theme of President Barack Obama's presidential campaign.

15. This marks the beginning of Wilson's "page three" which identifies the good
news at the center of the text.

EVERYTHING NEW 45

food at the city market, not because you don't have any money, but because the sellers won't sell to someone who's a "Christian," an enemy of the empire. When your life is ebbing away and your children are suffering, you better believe that it's *good news* when God announces: *"I am making everything new."* In a world of decay and degeneration, death is used by the empire to serve as entertainment in the colosseum and as a threat and deterrent on the streets of Roman cities. In *that* kind of world, God's word is *"I am making everything new."* When crying, mourning, pain, and suffering are as consistently experienced as the rising and setting sun, God speaks into that world and says: *"I am making everything new."*

And, don't you want to ask, "Where?[16] When? *Where* are You making things new? And, *how?*" Jeremy Begbie tells the story about a young, American man who attended a worship service in one of the extremely poor townships of South Africa. Before the service started, he was told "that a house around the corner had just been burned to the ground because the man who lived there was a suspected thief. A week before *that,* a tornado had cut through the township, ripping apart fifty homes"[17] and killing five people. Then he was told that "the very night before, a gang hounded down a fourteen-year-old, a member of the church's Sunday school, and stabbed him to death."[18] He said that at the beginning of the worship service, the pastor began to pray: "Lord, you are the Creator and the Sovereign, but *why* did the wind come like a snake and tear our roofs off? *Why* did a mob cut short the life of one of our own children, when he had everything to live for? Lord, we are in the midst of death."[19]

As he prayed, the congregation groaned and wailed and sighed. But once he finished praying, very slowly they began to sing. At first it was quietly and softly, but then it grew louder. And they sang—song after song of praise and thanks—to a God who, in Christ, plunged into the very worst the world had to offer and became obedient unto death, even death on a cross.[20] As Begbie tells it: "The singing gave the congregation a foretaste of the end."[21] He goes on to reflect: "Christian hope isn't about looking around at the state of things now and trying to imagine where it's all going. It's not about trying to calculate the future from the present. It's about breathing

16. This marks the beginning of Wilson's "page four" which helps the congregation experience and respond to God's grace in the text and sermon.

17. Willard, *A Place for Truth,* 232.

18. Willard, *A Place for Truth,* 232.

19. Willard, *A Place for Truth,* 232, emphasis added.

20. Phil 2:8.

21. Willard, *A Place for Truth,* 232.

46   SECTION 2: CHRISTMAS, EPIPHANY, AND THE TIME BEFORE LENT

now the fresh air of the ending, tasting the spices and sipping the wine of the feast to come."[22]

On this New Year's Day, with some gathered here who are living in the midst of grief and despair, with others having suffered recent loss, with many struggling with pain or fear or discouragement, can *we* hear God say, *"I am making all things new"*? Can we *hear* it? Can we *taste* it? Around the Table, we gather today to eat the bread and to sip the wine—all as a foretaste of the feast that is yet to come.

Amen.

---

22. Willard, *A Place for Truth*, 232.

SERMON 10[1]

Epiphany, the New Year, and a Holy Life[2]

Matthew 2:1–12

We emphasize Epiphany today. Epiphany is actually on January 6. It happens every year on the twelfth day after Christmas. But we thought we'd celebrate it today since it would be rather difficult to get all of you together on Tuesday morning. In some cultures, January 6 is when folks exchange gifts. That makes more *logical* sense because the "gift-giving" is related to the story of the Magi. Of course, we've got this whole "Santa thing" going and who, in *our* culture, wants to wait twelve long days to get the new video game, the high-definition television, or whatever was under your tree this year? I didn't grow up marking Epiphany. I didn't even know what the "12 Days of Christmas" meant. I heard the song, but I didn't really *get* it. Frankly, I didn't care much about "geese a laying" and "pipers piping."[3] Christmas lasted from about 5:00 p.m. on Christmas Eve when we arrived at my grandparents' home until about 7:03 a.m. on Christmas morning when all the presents had been opened. Every year, the passage most closely connected to Epiphany is the story of the Magi or wisemen. It's found in Matthew 2.

---

1. Preached at First Church of the Nazarene in Kansas City, Missouri on January 4, 2015 (Sunday closest to Epiphany; Year B).

2. Part of the strength of this sermon was its honesty. From acknowledging the unfamiliarity of Epiphany to naming the problem of infrequent and irregular participation in corporate worship, this sermon tried to name the "elephants in the room" in a straightforward but gracious way. In addition, the sermon was helpful in trying to give "handles" to the meaning of a holy life. In seeing these through the actions of the Magi, this sermon helped to show that "holiness preaching" is not restricted to certain texts or certain times of the year, but is a persistent and pervasive theme throughout the Scriptures and the Christian calendar.

3. This is a reference to some of the lyrics from the song.

47

48   SECTION 2: CHRISTMAS, EPIPHANY, AND THE TIME BEFORE LENT

Matthew 2:1–12

I've preached from this passage in Matthew on the Sunday before January 6 for the last three or four years here at First Church. As I looked back on those sermons, I've had the opportunity to say much about Herod and his paranoia. I've spoken about the journey of the Magi and all that it entailed. *This* year, I want to set the story of Matthew 2 in conversation with a verse from 2 Timothy. Listen: "It has now been revealed through the appearing of our Savior, Christ Jesus, who has destroyed death and has brought life and immortality to light through the gospel."[4] The word for "appearing" here is the Greek word for "epiphany." To paraphrase: "God has made all of this plain or revealed it to us by the *epiphany* of Christ Jesus."

Of course, the question must be asked: "What does all of this mean?" When 2 Timothy 1:10 says that "it" has been made plain or revealed, what is "it"? The place to look is the previous verse. In *that* verse, 2 Timothy tells us that God has "saved us and called us to a holy life—not because of anything we have done but because of his own purpose and grace."[5] *This*—the grace of God in Christ—has been revealed in the "appearing" or the coming of Jesus in the flesh into the world. If God's gracious work through Jesus is to *save* us and *call* us to a holy life, then what does a "holy life" look like? What does a "consecrated" or "separated" life look like? What does a fully devoted or God-filled life look like?

I want to offer the response that we see in the Magi around the Christ-child as a template for living and as a way of marking a life of devotion to God. When the star appeared and led them to where Jesus was, the Scripture says that they were "overjoyed." It's kind of a weird word, isn't it? The King James translation says: "They rejoiced with exceeding great joy!" Another translation says that they "were filled with delight."[6] Part of the reason that translating this word from the Greek is difficult is because the form of the word is passive. In other words, it's something that happens *to* them rather than something that they actually *do* themselves. I imagine it in some ways like an ocean wave. You can be carried along and ride it or you can try to resist it or fight against it. When the TNIV uses "overjoyed," I think it's an attempt to capture that this "joy" is not something that the Magi *generated* from within themselves, but it was a *gift*. It was a *wave*. It was something that happened *to* them and wasn't *from* them.

4. 2 Tim 1:10.

5. 2 Tim 1:9.

6. Jerusalem Bible.

EPIPHANY, THE NEW YEAR, AND A HOLY LIFE

Living a life of joy is not something that you and I can *make* happen. It's a bit like sleeping. You can't *make* yourself go to sleep. Anybody with insomnia knows that. But you can do certain things that make sleeping more likely. You can stop eating after a certain time at night. You can stay away from caffeine-filled drinks after a certain time. You can make the room darker, the bed softer, or the air cooler. There are things that you *can* do that will make sleeping more likely to happen. It's kind of like joy. It's a gift from God. It's a "wave" that comes our way, and it lifts us when we are *open* to it and *receptive* of it. There is a joy—a deep, peaceful sense of gratitude—that does not come and go like happiness or excitement. Does anybody remember the little acronym for "joy" that some of us were taught as kids? It was a priority list for life and living that was based on the letters "j," "o," and "y"? The answer is: "Jesus, others, and you." If you think about life in *this* order: number one, Jesus; number two, others; and number three, yourself, then you will have a shot at a life of joy. When 2 Timothy says that "it" has been made plain to us and the "it" is a "holy life," *part* of what that life looks like is *joy*.

Another quality or characteristic that we see in the Magi in Matthew 2 is this: A life of worship. When they came to the house where Mary and Jesus were, verse 11 says: "They bowed down and worshipped him." What if this year, for *you*, was a year of regular, persistent, and intentional daily worship of God in Christ? What if your personal practices of worship were viewed as an extension *of* and preparation *for* the community of faith's worship on the Lord's Day? What if your worship was *not* perceived as *one* hour on *one* day that is *optional*, if inconvenient? Rather, what if your worship of God becomes the prism through which *all* of life is viewed? What would happen? I don't think the songs we sing, don't sing, or how often we sing them would be nearly as important. I don't think our schedules of when we can gather, whether we can gather, or how often we can gather would be such factors. Just so you know: I'm working from a definition of "regular" participation in corporate worship which, I'm told, is defined now as 1.9 Sundays per month over the course of a year. I can't do that math in my head, but for those of you who may be trying to do the calculation—it's about twenty-three Sundays per year. Please understand what I'm saying. There are things that happen: there are work schedules, there are illnesses, and there are family events that sometimes prevent *all* of us from being a part of the community that is gathered for worship on Sunday. I recognize that. But, twenty-nine absences a year and *this* is still considered "regular" attendance? Listen. I want you to be here as a part of our corporate worship as often as you can for a reason: *so* that you are

50   SECTION 2: CHRISTMAS, EPIPHANY, AND THE TIME BEFORE LENT

reminded as frequently as possible that worship is for *every* day and *every* moment because God is *worthy* of it.

What could be overlooked in the story of the Magi is what is connected to their worship. The Scripture says that they "bowed down." This is an expression of humility. It finds a variety of cultural expressions and has for centuries. Sometimes it means kneeling. Other places it means bowing one's head or not making eye contact. Regardless of the cultural expression, it's humility. On January 14, I will invite you—the congregation of First Church—to enter into a period of forty days of prayer and fasting in preparation for our special services of revival and renewal that will begin March 1. The lost and neglected practice of fasting is a conscious, intentional, purposeful way of humbling ourselves before the Lord. It's a way of *focusing* our attention. Fasting can take a variety of forms and I've prepared a calendar with suggestions on how each of us may participate in this forty-day process. You'll see as you're given a calendar today that the time between January 14 and March 1 is actually forty-six days. There are six Sundays, and on *those* days, there is no planned fasting element.[7] When Jesus taught his disciples about fasting, he never referred to it as an option. He didn't say, "*If* you fast." No. Jesus said, "*When* you fast."[8] Hopefully, these forty days of prayer and fasting will be a time when we discover or re-discover the value and practice of fasting so that it may become an on-going part of our life of humility and worship of God. We don't fast to score points with God. We fast to focus our attention. We fast to humble ourselves. We fast to enhance our worship of the God who gave his only Son for our redemption. An integral part of a "consecrated life"—a "holy life"—will undoubtedly be *worship* of our Creator who has revealed himself in Jesus, the Christ.

Another thing that I want you to see is the thing for which the Magi are most famous: gift-giving. They brought gifts across the desert, over the river, and through the woods—not to grandma's house—but to the home of Joseph, Mary, and Jesus. Although I don't want to speak specifically to gift-giving, I do want to speak to an aspect of a holy life—a life fully given to God—and that is a life of *generosity.* If our lives are going to be God-filled and godly, then we will certainly practice what God, himself, did and does. These astrologers from Iraq *did* what *God* did. They *gave.* The story of God's creation and interaction *with* his creation is a story of *generosity.* God creates, blesses, fills, and gives. God is gracious and kind. He is abundant and self-sacrificing. *Because* he loved his world so much, he *gave* his one and

7. The calendar included a scriptural passage, prayer concern, and fasting suggestion for each day. Fasting suggestions included things like meals, coffee, social media, or entertainment.

8. Matt 6:16.

EPIPHANY, THE NEW YEAR, AND A HOLY LIFE   51

only Son that we might have true life—*real* life.[9] Generosity isn't confined to gift-giving and tangible resources. That's almost laughable. Some of the most generous, giving, sacrificial people you and I have ever known were people who had the least amount of financial means in the world. No, generosity is an attitude and a *way* of living. It's not a check cut or cash in an envelope. Don't get me wrong: A life of generosity will greatly impact your checkbook and your cash flow. No doubt about it. But it's not *limited* to that. Generosity is about your spirit, your time, your attention, your priorities, your talents, your efforts, and your attitude. Generosity is about *who* you are and to *whom* you will give your life and devotion. What if *this* year you intentionally and consciously looked for opportunities to be generous in spirit, in care, in resources—in *all* ways? What would *that* kind of year look like?[10] At the cross-section of Epiphany, the new year, Matthew 2, and 2 Timothy 1, I've highlighted three issues: joy, worship, and generosity. Those aren't the *only* aspects of a holy, consecrated, God-filled life, but they cover a lot. The good news is that that kind of life is possible, but it's possible *only* through the power and presence of God at work within us. *You* can't do it. *I* can't do it. But *God* can do it as he lives the life of Jesus through us. When we come to the Table of the Lord, we come to give thanks for the greatest action of generosity in the history of the universe—when God gave his Son for us. The table and these gifts of bread and cup are the tangible expressions of God's generosity to us in Christ. We come to the table with joy. We come as an expression of our worship. And we come to offer *ourselves,* humbly and generously, to the Lord and his work in the world.

Amen.

---

9. John 3:16 paraphrased.

10. *Alternative ending if not calling the congregation to the Lord's table:* At the cross-section of Epiphany, the new year, Matthew 2 and 2 Timothy 1, I've highlighted three issues: joy, worship, and generosity. Listen. *Those* aren't the only aspects of a holy, consecrated, God-filled life, but they cover a lot. The good news is that that kind of life is possible, but it's possible *only* through the power and presence of God at work within us. *You* can't do it. *I* can't do it. But *God* can do it as he lives the life of Jesus through us. Has the Spirit called you to fully give your heart and life to God today? We have a place of prayer where you can consecrate yourself to the ways of God.

SERMON II[1]

Why is the Water Boiling?[2]

Genesis 1:1–5

Last week, I preached to you from the book of Revelation, the *last* book of the Bible, and today, I want to jump back all the way to the *first* book of the Bible—the book of beginnings—the book of Genesis.

Genesis 1:1–5

It's 2012 which means it's an election year. Lots of polls, statistics, and surveys will be dispersed. Debates and competing claims are in store for us in this coming year. One of the things that is always interesting to me is when a political candidate is asked a question that they don't want to answer. It's fascinating to see how they navigate that situation. Often what happens is they simply begin giving an answer to a different question that they really *wanted* to be asked. They talk about what *they* want to talk about regardless of what the original question was. The reality is that a question, even a *simple* question, can have different answers that are *both* true. John Polkinghorne, a world-class scholar, asks the question: "Why is the water in the tea

---

1. Preached at First Church of the Nazarene in Kansas City, Missouri on January 8, 2012 (First Sunday after Epiphany; Year B).

2. This sermon from the first chapter of Genesis was an opportunity to emphasize the theological and foundational purpose of the "creation narrative." In a culture and context of great disagreement and argumentation about "origins," this sermon was energized by the primary message of the text which is captured in the first words of the Bible—"in the beginning, God created." The acknowledgement that we are tempted to ask the Bible to answer questions that it was not intended to answer was a powerful starting point and one that some may have never considered. The twist at the end of the sermon was to simply call attention to the fact that the Creator is worthy of our worship and that there are competitors of every stripe and color that are vying for that in our lives.

52

WHY IS THE WATER BOILING?   53

pot boiling?" He says that *one* answer is because of the burning gas under the pot that is heating the water. The molecules of H2O are being compelled to move faster and faster and further apart and will eventually take the form of steam when it reaches 212 degrees according to the Fahrenheit method of measurement. Now, that's *one* answer to the question. But *another* answer to the question—"Why is the water boiling?"—is just as true, and the answer is: "Because I'm going to make a cup of tea with it."[3]

A similar kind of thing happens whenever we turn to the book of Genesis. As human beings living in an intricate and sometimes confusing world, we have questions that Genesis isn't interested in answering. We have questions that seem so important, vital, and critical to *us*, but are not important, vital, and critical to Genesis. We are fascinated, intrigued, perturbed, or possibly confused by the when, the how, the design, the intricacy, and the timeline of creation. Yet, Genesis seems to be focused squarely on the "that" and the "who" of creation. When Genesis 1 starts out, "In the beginning, God created," the emphasis is that what you see, even what you *cannot* see, what you experience, and all that *is*, stretching from heaven to earth, has been created by God. For the Bible, God—the Source and Creator—is an *assumption*. For *us*, God—as "maker of heaven and earth"—is an *affirmation* of our faith. We *believe* it. We confess it. We believe it to be logical. We believe that it makes sense. We believe that this affirmation does not run contrary to the discoveries and illumination of science, but rather, we believe that this affirmation is *enhanced* by scientific discovery. The amazing intricacies of creation and the on-going discoveries of the size, shape, and expansion of the universe all serve to *re-affirm* the place of an infinitely imaginative and creative God *in* and *behind* it all. Francis Collins, one of the world's leading scientists, is a leader in genetic study. He was head of the "human genome project" which mapped the structure of DNA. In a recent book, he wrote: "In my view, there is no conflict in being a rigorous scientist and a person who believes in a God who takes a personal interest in each one of us."[4]

I know embarrassingly little about the Heisenberg uncertainty principle, the six flavors of quarks that makeup neutrons and protons, or gene sequencing inside the double-helix of a DNA strand, but I *do* know that you don't have to ignore those things, avoid those things, or try to explain away those things because you believe in a creator who has revealed himself most clearly in Jesus Christ. As a Jesus-follower, you are *not* asked to disengage your brain, unplug your gray matter, or relegate science and discovery to some other compartment of life, as if you could stick your head in the sand

3. Giberson and Collins, *Language of Science*, 107.
4. Collins, *Language of God*, 6.

54   SECTION 2: CHRISTMAS, EPIPHANY, AND THE TIME BEFORE LENT

and hope it all goes away. No way. *God is the creator.* Scientific discovery is helping us understand in ever-so-finite ways the amazingly intricate universe and world in which we live today. In my preparation for this message, I was struck by the number of different ways that writers tried to calculate the probability of the world's intricacies to having just *happened*—purely by chance—over a long period of time without *any* direction or design. One of the fascinating ways that someone tried to prove or disprove the idea that "time + chance = life" was based on an actual experiment done by the British National Council of Arts. Here's the question: "How long would it take for an infinite number of monkeys pounding on an infinite number of typewriters to compose a sonnet by Shakespeare?"

Without an infinite number of monkeys and without an infinite number of typewriters, somebody took *six* monkeys and let them hammer away on a computer keyboard for a month and over that period of time, the monkeys produced fifty pages of text. The results were amusing. In *all* the typing, there was not *one* single word—not even an "a" or an "I" with a space on both sides—in all fifty pages of text. Not *one* single word.[5] It's really just another way of trying to say and affirm what the psalmist offered in praise thousands of years ago: "When I consider your heavens, the work of your fingers, the moon and the stars, which you have set in place, what are mere mortals that you are mindful of them?"[6]

We pray prayers like: "Oh God, when we put DNA under a high-powered microscope, when we point a high-powered telescope into the vastness of the universe, when we watch the aero-dynamic acrobatics of a hummingbird, when we more closely examine the intricacies of the human brain, and when we begin to better understand the constants of the universe that *must* exist to make life even possible—when we catch just a tiny glimpse of *all* that—we confess that you are Creator and Lord. Even though we see 'through a glass darkly,'[7] as Paul wrote, *even still* we turn to praise and thanksgiving: '*You* are the Creator. *You* are the Maker of heaven and earth.'"

The Scripture also teaches us that God's creation is *good*. In the surrounding verses of our text, there is an emphasis that shows up over and over throughout Genesis 1. God creates and then announces or affirms that it is good. It happens in verse 4, verse 10, verses 12, 18, 21, 25 and then, in verse 31, his creation is "*very* good." God's creation is good. Scholars teach us that "good" has the additional implication of "beauty." God's creation is "beautiful" and "intricate," but the word that is translated as

---

5. "Former Atheist."

6. Ps 8:3–4a.

7. 1 Cor 13:12.

WHY IS THE WATER BOILING?

"good" is a *purpose* word at its core. As H. Ray Dunning wrote: "the Creator pronounced His handiwork good because it perfectly fulfilled the purpose that He had in mind."[8]

So, *what's* the purpose? Listen to a few verses from Psalm 148 and see if you pick up on a theme:

> O praise the Lord. Praise the Lord out of heaven; praise him in the heights. Praise him, all his angels; praise him, all his host. Praise him, sun and moon; praise him, all you shining stars; praise him, heaven of heavens, and you waters above the heaven. Let them all praise the name of the Lord, for he spoke the word and they were created; he established them for ever and ever by an ordinance which shall never pass away."[9]

The creation's purpose is *praise* of its Creator. The world, the heavens, the universe, the trees, the fields, the black holes of outer space, the electrons spinning in orbit around their nuclei, waves of light streaking across the universe at 186,000 miles per second, you and I—*all*—are created for praise. We've been given life for the purpose of worshipping our Creator.

Augustine, the great theologian of the fourth century, helped us see that "our hearts are restless until they find rest" in God.[10] We've been created with an emptiness in our lives that can only be filled by the presence of our creator. We've been formed and fashioned for worship of God. *That's* why, in our world as understood through the lens of Scripture, the number one problem and sin that shows up time after time and in place after place is idolatry or worshipping anything and everything *other* than God. Idolatry: we don't use that word much anymore in the church or anywhere else, but it is *lived* and *practiced* in the church and everywhere. You don't have to look very far or very long to observe idolatry. It's all around in every shape, form, and fashion that can be imagined. I have often quoted an idea that came from John Calvin, the Protestant Reformer of the 1600s, when he said: "The human heart is a factory of idols."[11]

That reality has its roots in the affirmation that we have been created by God and for God's purpose of worshipping him. The question is not "*Will we worship?*," but rather, "*Whom* or *what* will we worship?" Will we worship ourselves, our own desires, and our own wants? Will we bow at the shrine of pleasure, leisure, or the "Almighty dollar"? Will we sacrifice our lives on the

---

8. Dunning, *Grace*, 239.

9. Ps 148:1–6.

10. Augustine, *Confessions*, 1:1, paraphrase.

11. Calvin, *Institutes*, 1:11.

altar of "success," experiences, or the "pursuit of happiness"[12] in all its varied manifestations and misguided endeavors? *What* or *whom* will we worship? That's the real question.

A few weeks ago, Tim Keller came to Kansas City to speak to a bunch of pastors and community leaders. Keller is an author and pastor serving a church in New York City. He wrote a book a couple of years ago called *Counterfeit Gods*. In it, he tells the story of a young woman named Mary who had attended his church. She was an accomplished musician, but she was troubled by psychiatric issues. They were complex issues which required the involvement and expertise of a therapist. Mary gave Pastor Tim permission to speak to her therapist and it's how the therapist described some of Mary's issues that caught my attention. The therapist said: "Mary virtually *worships* her parents' approval of her and they always wanted her to be a world-class artist."[13] She "worships her parents' approval." We're *made* to worship and we will *search* for something, *find* something, or even *manufacture* something to worship. Ricky Gervais, an actor, comedian, and avowed atheist says that he just needs a reason to live and "imagination, free will, love, humor, fun, music, sports, beer, and pizza are all good enough reasons for living."[14] Really? Our ancestors in the faith have tried to help us. They have tried to point us in the right direction. They want to help us answer the question: "What *is* the chief or the primary 'end' or purpose for human beings like us?" The answer has been: "To glorify God and enjoy him forever."[15]

A loving,[16] creating God has made and shaped us for himself. We've been created for relationship with him and there are all kinds of competitors for our worship that are vying for ultimate importance in our lives. Would you like to talk to someone about those kinds of issues in your own life? There's a card in the corner of your worship folder. It's a way of making a commitment and saying, "I want Pastor Estep to call me, email me, or set a time to visit with me about this very issue—about *whom* or *what* I will wor-

12. This phrase come from the U.S. Declaration of Independence and is listed along side life and liberty as an "inalienable right."

13. Keller, *Counterfeit Gods,* 148–9.

14. Gervais, "A Holiday Message."

15. Westminster Shorter Catechism (Question 1).

16. *Alternative ending for concluding the service with the celebration of communion:* A loving, creating God has made and shaped us for himself. We've been created for relationship with him and there are all kinds of competitors for our worship that are vying for ultimate importance in our lives. When we gather around the Lord's Table, we come with thanksgiving for what God has done for us through the life, death, and resurrection of Jesus, but we also come to confess again that "Jesus is Lord," that God in Christ is the one to whom we are giving our worship—our lives. So, come.

ship." There's a place for your name, an email address, and a phone number. Maybe you would like to simply take that card, fill it out, and hand it to me after the service. You could mail it. Or, you could bring it up and place it on the altar now as we conclude this service with singing.

Amen.

SERMON 12[1]

Being Found, Following, and Finding[2]

John 1:43–51

The story that we'll read this morning from the Gospel of John is the story from which our church gets its name. Not the "First Church" part, but the "Nazarene" part. Almost 120 years ago, a Methodist minister by the name of Phineas Bresee started a church and the church needed a name. The church was ministering in Los Angeles, California, among the marginalized and poor of the urbanized core of the city. One of Bresee's friends, a medical doctor named J.P. Widney, suggested the name "Nazarene" because Jesus was raised in the town of Nazareth. The town, according to this story from John 1, was not a place of high regard or much respect. What better name for a church that's going to minister to the disrespected and poor than a church named after Jesus, the "Nazarene"? The story is in John 1.

John 1:43–51

In the Scriptures, there are many places and the names of these places have meaning. Sometimes these things are lost in translation or simply passed over by folks like us who don't read and write in Hebrew and Greek. Bethsaida is one of these places. Like Beth-lehem, Beth-el, and Beth-phage,

---

1. Preached at First Church of the Nazarene in Kansas City, Missouri on January 18, 2015(Second Sunday after Epiphany; Year B).

2. In this sermon, I tried to reaffirm some of the basic doctrines and practices that have always been a part of Wesleyanism and, specifically, the Church of the Nazarene. Prevenient grace, discipleship, and evangelism have been some of the crucial aspects of the church. Even though the story toward the end of the sermon was specific to Kansas City First Church, every church, if you look closely enough, has a similar story somewhere in its history. Part of the reason for using a story from one's own church and history was to call the church to be more authentically what it has always been—a graced community that follows Jesus and invites others to do the same.

these places all begin with a Hebrew word that means "house." Beth-lehem, for example, can be translated as "house of bread." Beth-el is "house of God." Beth-saida means "house of fish," and this town on the edge of the Sea of Galilee was the home of several of the first disciples of Jesus. Some were among "the twelve" and others may not have been, but it was this fishing village—this "house of fish"—that Andrew, Peter, and Philip all called home. It was *there,* in the "house of fish," that John 1:43 says: "Finding Philip, [Jesus] said to him, 'Follow me.'"

It would be easy to skim over the first part of the verse and jump right to the second, but that would be to miss a major theological issue and idea. To go directly to the "follow me" part is premature. The "finding Philip" part goes to a core, theological characteristic of God. It speaks of God's prevenient, pursuing, or reaching grace. God in Christ doesn't wait on us to get it together. God doesn't wait on us to "clean ourselves up." No. *God* does the finding. He does the *pursuing*—the *reaching.* We sometimes make the same mistake that Philip did in this very story. Even after John tells us that *Jesus* found Philip, when Philip goes to Nathanael, did you see what he said? He says to Nathanael: "*We* have found the one Moses wrote about."[3]

No, you didn't, Philip. *You* didn't find Jesus. *He* found *you.* Even this language is metaphoric and eventually breaks down because it somehow implies that God doesn't know where we are and that he has to *find* us. The language is a bit problematic, but the underlying truth is that God, in his grace, extends himself to us *first, ahead of,* and *before* we ever respond to him. That's part of what we have to understand and it makes all the difference in the world. *We* don't pursue God as if God doesn't care, isn't concerned, or only responds to us when we take the first step. It's just not true. One of my favorite verses in all of the Scripture puts the nail in that false and faulty understanding. Romans 5:8 says: "God *demonstrates* his love for us in this: While we were still *sinners,* Christ died for us."

Don't make the same mistake that Philip made when he told Nathanael that "we have found" the Messiah. No. The Savior has found *you.* Over and over, Jesus told stories throughout his ministry that reaffirmed this idea. There was a story about a shepherd leaving the "99" to go in search for the "one lost sheep."[4] There was a story where a woman sweeps the house, turns everything upside-down and searches for the lost coin that was so precious to her.[5] This is Jesus drawing a picture of what *God* is like. Over and over again, the Scriptures tell us how Jesus lives before us

3. John 1:45, emphasis added.
4. Luke 15:3–7.
5. Luke 15:8–10.

in ways that portray the seeking, searching, ahead-of-time-loving, grace and mercy of God. That grace is at work in your life already, whether you recognize it or not. So, wake up to the grace of God at work and available to you. God is at work in your life. God's grace is reaching, pursuing, guiding, confronting, and challenging you even now. Tune in to the prevenient grace of God that is *already* at work.

Part of "tuning in" is doing what Philip did when Jesus called him and that is: *following*. Phillip followed after Jesus. He went with him even though he didn't know the outcome or the end. It was an act of faith. It was faith put into action. It was day-to-day and routine. It wasn't glamorous, always exciting, or void of difficulties. Phillip was becoming a "disciple" which was primarily characterized by living *with* Jesus and listening *to* Jesus. Joseph Nye teaches at the Kennedy School of Government at Harvard University. He says that one of the characteristic features of our post-modern culture is, what he calls, the "paradox of plenty." Nye says: "A plenitude of information leads to a poverty of attention. . . Those who can distinguish valuable signals from white noise gain power."[6] I'm not so much interested in Nye's take on how to "gain power," but I'm interested in the interaction of the abundant information that constantly streams into our lives and the scarcity of attention that we are able to give to it. In response to these ideas, Leonard Sweet writes: "Paying attention is the highest form of opening to life and to God. Unarguably the greatest gift you can give another is your attention. . . The greatest gift we can give God is our passionate attention, which is another name for prayer."[7] I think it's another name for following or discipleship.

This is one of the four main things[8] that we as a church have identified for defining who we are and to what we want to give ourselves and our energies. Along with worship, community, and compassion, we are focused on discipleship. We are committed to following Jesus and giving him and his ways our "passionate attention"—to use Sweet's language. Relationships are difficult to maintain and they certainly have difficulty thriving when there is a lack of attention given to them. The same thing is true of our relationship with Jesus. If we ignore it, forget it, or don't consider it to be important, our relationship won't grow and thrive. It appears from multiple stories in the New Testament that the disciples of Jesus didn't always understand everything correctly and didn't always grasp what he was trying to do, but generally, it does seem that they gave him their "passionate attention." They

6. Sweet, *Nudge*, 54.

7. Sweet, *Nudge*, 54.

8. These core values of worship, community, compassion, and discipleship had been articulated by the church board and were referenced in a multitude of ways throughout the life of the church.

BEING FOUND, FOLLOWING, AND FINDING   61

left things behind to *follow* him—to be *with* him and to listen *to* him. They were *found* by the reaching, pursuing grace of God and they *followed* Jesus as he called them to give attention to him and his ways.

Then what happened in John 1? Philip, who was following, goes and finds Nathanael. John 1:45 says: "Philip *found* Nathanael and told him, 'We have found the one Moses wrote about in the Law.'" As I mentioned earlier, I think Philip got it wrong when he describes what happened as them finding Jesus, but what is clear is that part of Philip's following of Jesus meant finding others to join them on the journey. It would be one thing if this was the only story where this happened, but if you were to look at the preceding story, you would see much of the same thing. In John 1:40, it says: "Andrew, Simon Peter's brother, was one of the two who heard what John [meaning John the Baptist] had said and who had followed Jesus." So, Andrew had followed Jesus. John 1:41 says: "The first thing Andrew did was to find his brother Simon and tell him, 'We have found the Messiah.'" Part of following is finding others to lead to Jesus. *This* is the mission of the disciples of Jesus in the world.

It happened not far from this very location in an apartment complex called Nob Hill over off of 71 Highway. There was a couple living there who had come to Kansas City to go to Nazarene Theological Seminary. They had been found and were followers of Jesus. One of their neighbors was a single mom with two little twin girls—both with beautiful, but oddly spelled, Irish names. The girls were about three years old and the seminary couple reached out to this single mom with the love of Jesus. They knew that a part of following was finding others who were in desperate need of God's love and care. The grace of God was going ahead of them and before long, Sandy had received Christ into her heart and life. The people who led her to the Lord—like Philip had led Nathanael—were a part of this church family. Sandy knew that she needed to surround herself with people who would love her, support her, disciple her, and share the gospel with her children, so she started bringing those kids here. Individuals came alongside them. Some mentored them. Others prayed for them. Others helped those girls navigate the teenage years. All watched them grow in their relationship with Jesus. Then, one of those twin girls married a big, tall young man who had moved to Kansas City to attend Nazarene Theological Seminary. He graduated and they went off to the other side of the country to pastor a church. Later, they left the US and crossed the border into Canada to pastor a different church. Just recently, they've crossed the Pacific Ocean to serve as missionaries in the Philippines where they continue to follow Jesus and are helping to find others who need to be brought to him. God in Christ found them at Nob Hill apartments through the love of a couple

who has served as missionaries in Kenya for the last twenty plus years. *Now*, one of those twin girls who they helped find and bring to Jesus will be serving across the globe among hurting and broken children in the metropolis of Manila. What a story of God's reaching grace, transformation, and the path of discipleship.[9]

It's the pattern that I want you to see because it's the pattern in which *all* of us are meant to participate: being found by Christ, following him on the path of discipleship, and finding others to bring to Jesus. The bad news is that you and I can't do that on our own, but the good news is that God's Spirit living within us can make it happen. We gather around the Lord's Table to give thanks that God, in his mercy, has *found* us. God pursued us, reached out to us, and rescued us through the death and resurrection of his Son, Jesus. We gather around the table to receive grace and strength and help to follow Jesus, to live as his disciples in the world, and to be about the mission of finding others and bringing them to him.

Amen.

---

9 *Alternative ending if not leading to the eucharist:* What a story of God's reaching grace, transformation, and the path of discipleship. Where are *you* on the journey? Are you resisting the "pursuing grace" of God even now? Maybe today is the day that you abandon yourself to his love and mercy. Has the Lord brought you to this place and this moment for this very reason? Would you like to pray about that or have someone pray with you?

SERMON 13[1]

Relentlessly Pursues, Recklessly Merciful[2]

Jonah 3:1–10

April of this year will mark the 100th anniversary of the *Titanic's* maiden, famous, and *only* voyage. Last week off the coast of Italy, the *Costa Concordia*, with more than 4,200 passengers and crew hit a rock, slid forward, spun around, and capsized in the shallow waters near Giglio, Italy. Ships can be a dangerous place to be. It was one hundred years ago. It was last week. And it was in *biblical* times. Whenever we turn in the Scriptures to the book of Jonah, we're reminded that this prophet—this preacher— tried to escape the plan of God by boarding a ship and heading across the Mediterranean. I invite you to turn to Jonah 3.

Jonah 3:1–10

Many of us have grown up with the story of Jonah.[3] If you were raised in the church, somewhere along the way, you were told this amazing and

1. Preached at First Church of the Nazarene in Kansas City, Missouri on January 22, 2012 (Third Sunday after Epiphany; Year B).

2. In this sermon, I chose to use a "pattern" for preaching based on the work of Paul Ricoeur, a hermeneutical theorist. It's a three-fold pattern: first naivete, critical reflection, and second naivete. In "first naivete," the text is dealt with in a pre-critical way. The world of the text is experienced on its own terms. Its pictures, values, behaviors, and ideas are not questioned, but are treated straightforwardly and simplistically. In the "critical reflection" portion, the text is examined and questioned. Are there issues that are difficult, hard to understand, inexplicable, counter-cultural, or otherwise contrary to one's held beliefs in the contemporary setting? In the final section which is termed "second naivete," the preacher and community return to the text with the potential "distractions" set aside. Attempt is made to identify ways that the text "names the world" or "shakes us up" or asks us to confront difficult truth. For purposes of clarity, I have noted in the manuscript the beginning of each section which utilizes Ricoeur's rubric.

3. "First naivete"—encountering the text in a pre-critical manner.

63

64 SECTION 2: CHRISTMAS, EPIPHANY, AND THE TIME BEFORE LENT

mind-bending story. Alongside the stories of Noah with his ark and David with his sling, you heard of Jonah and the "big fish." While others were being told stories from the Brothers Grimm, Aesop, or even Disney, some of us learned very early the story of the rebellious prophet who tried to escape the call of God upon his life. That's the way the story was told. The issue was God's call on Jonah. God's direction for Jonah was to go and preach and Jonah chose to run from that call. That's *part* of the story but I don't think that this is really the *essence* or the heart of the Jonah story. So many times, when we read or listen to someone preach from the story of Jonah, the emphasis gets placed squarely on the "big fish." We are prone to find that part of the story fascinating. Like you, I like big fish stories. Every now and then when I can't find a basketball game as I'm surfing the channels, I'll stop at *River Monsters*.[4] It's a show about a guy who travels around trying to catch huge, dangerous, and potentially man-eating fish in the rivers and waterways of the world. It's an interesting, intriguing program and almost *totally* about big fish. But, that's really not the point with the story of Jonah. Don't get me wrong. The "big fish" plays an important role in the story and it has been used as a way of talking about the miraculous power of God—that God could and would send a fish to swallow his rebellious prophet. That's an important *part* of the story, but it's not the essence or at the *core* of the story.

I looked back into my history as a pastor and preacher and tried to see if I had ever preached about Jonah *before,* and I discovered that I *had.* As I was looking at what I had said in regard to this story, one of the things struck me in particular—and I *believe* it—but neither is *it* at the core of the story. It's the idea that prayer can be offered from anywhere at any time and God *hears* it. Chapter one in Jonah gets a lot of attention. Chapter three doesn't get as much, but some. Chapter *two* gets very little at all because chapter two is essentially the prayer of Jonah while trapped in the fish's gullet. Jonah's *prayer* and praying while *inside* a fish is a pretty odd place to pray which helps to teach us that prayer can happen anytime and anywhere. That's *true,* but it's just not the real "heart" of the story. It's not why *Jonah* is a part of our Scriptures. It's a good lesson, but it's not the core. Do you understand what I'm saying? The story of Jonah is a wonderful, intricate, ironic, even comedic story and there are many lessons that can be drawn from it and all kinds of interesting angles that come out of it, but *beyond* those things—or maybe *underneath* those things—is the real reason or the real *essence* of the story.

I guess that conclusion or that way of understanding is grounded in the basic idea that, when we read the Scripture, what we're really looking to

---

4. *River Monsters* is a British and American wildlife documentary-type program produced for the Animal Planet channel.

RELENTLESSLY PURSUES, RECKLESSLY MERCIFUL 65

see or hear or understand is this:[5] What does this say about *God?* The book is named after Jonah, but really if Jonah were to be awarded a Golden Globe or an Oscar, he would have to be considered in the category of "supporting actor." That would be true of the "big fish," the other sailors on the boat, the plant that shoots up in chapter four, the people of Ninevah, the worm that eats the precious plant, and Jonah, himself. Those are all "supporting" roles because the main character—the protagonist of the story—is *God.* What does this story tell us, show us, or reveal to us about God?

That question is a question that must be brought to every portion of the Scripture. The story of Moses is an incredible story. It's like a huge, panoramic tale. From the threat of infanticide to being rescued by the Pharaoh's daughter and from the heights of power to tragedy and isolation, the Moses story has monumental swings of the pendulum. There are lessons of faith, of blessing, of the consequences of anger, of willingness to serve, and a host of other things, but the issue is: What does this story tell us about God? Some of you may remember that in the late 1990s, Dream-Works came out with the story of Moses in animation and it was called, *The Prince of Egypt.* I went on the internet and pulled up the movie trailers and listened again to the main song of the film. It was a song called: "When You Believe." The main lines went like this: "There can be miracles / When you believe" and "Who knows what miracles / You can achieve / When you believe."[6] There's not a single mention of God. Miracles are wonderful and believing is important, but that's *not* what the story of Moses is about. Moses, like Jonah, is a "supporting character" alongside the main actor—the main "mover" of the story—*God.* And it's a story in which God is director, producer *and* protagonist.

When we read the third chapter of *Jonah,* there's a clue in verse 1 that tells us something about God.[7] Verse 1 says that the "word of the Lord came to Jonah a *second* time." There's a clue. You see, the "word of the Lord" had come to Jonah before and that's when Jonah said: "I don't want any part of that. I don't want to be involved in that." God had told Jonah that he wanted him to go to Ninevah and "preach against it."[8] You see, Ninevah was the capital city of the Assyrian Empire at that time and for Jonah and other Jews like him, just the *thought* of Ninevah and the Assyrians made their blood boil. The Assyrians were the most violent, pagan, evil, hideous, awful, horrific,

5. "Critical reflection"—the text is examined and questioned.

6. Mariah Carey and Whitney Houston, "When You Believe."

7. "Second naivete"—returning to the text for "difficult truth" with "distractions" set aside.

8. Jonah 1:2.

66   SECTION 2: CHRISTMAS, EPIPHANY, AND THE TIME BEFORE LENT

mean, and shameful people that Jonah could ever imagine. They were the scum of the earth. They were the Nazis, the Vietcong, al-Qaeda, and suicidal-terrorists all rolled into one. Jonah *hated* them. Now God was telling him to go and preach to them for a second time.

A lot had happened between the first time and the second time. After the first time that God told him to go to Ninevah, Jonah went down to the closest port city—a place called Joppa—and he got on a boat that was headed in the *opposite* direction from Ninevah. Ninevah was a journey of 550 miles in a north-easterly direction over land, but Jonah got on a boat and headed in a westerly direction. He was headed to a place that some scholars believe was on the southern edge of Spain some 2,500 miles across the dangerous waters of the Mediterranean. You know what happened next. The storm comes. The ship is about to go down. The crew does everything that they know to do to save the vessel and then Jonah says: "I'm the problem. If you'll just throw me in, this will all work out."[9] They did and it *did* because God, as 1:17 says, "provided a huge fish to swallow Jonah." Between the first time and the second time, Jonah spent part of three days and three nights inside the fish, wrapped with seaweed, until finally, God commanded and the fish vomited Jonah on the beach. After three days, the fish spewed out a half-digested, fishy-smelling, salty-tasting, now-ready-to-be-obedient prophet. Jonah has been relentlessly pursued by God. God wouldn't let him just walk away. He wouldn't let him run and hide, bury his head in the sand, and live without the confrontation of his own prejudices and bitterness. Like a poet said so many centuries later, it's like God is the "hound of heaven"[10] and he's on Jonah's trail, relentlessly pursuing.

But what is true of God toward Jonah is *also* true of God toward these people of Ninevah. By the time Jonah picks the seaweed out of his hair and the sand out his clothes, God has brought the issue of Ninevah to him *again*. Pardon the simile, but it's like God has OCD[11]—this compulsive, relentless pursuit of his wayward children—even toward Nazis and terrorists and people like the people of Ninevah. So, Jonah obeys. He goes and he preaches. It's not much of a sermon really. It's only five words in Hebrew: "Forty days more, Ninevah destroyed."[12] That's it. It wasn't very eloquent. It wasn't much of a sermon, *but* the people repent and the king repents and they *all* put on sackcloth which was a signal of repentance. They even make the *animals* wear sackcloth. Repentance and revival breaks out in Ninevah

---

9. Jonah 1:12, paraphrase.

10. Allusion to Francis Thompson's poem, *The Hound of Heaven*.

11. Obsessive compulsive disorder.

12. Jonah 3:4, paraphrase.

RELENTLESSLY PURSUES, RECKLESSLY MERCIFUL 67

like Jonah could never have imagined. They give up their violent ways. They stop their evil practices and they "call urgently"[13] on the Lord. Their repentance is so genuine, so authentic, and so *powerful* that something incredible happens: *God repents*. Now the translation that I read doesn't capture that, but let me read Jonah 3:10 from the Revised Standard Version which follows the original language much more closely. Here it is: "When God saw what they did, how they turned from their evil ways, God *repented* of the evil which he had said he would do to them; and he did not do it."[14] The Assyrians changed their mind and the direction of their ways and so God changed his mind about what he had intended to do to them. What we see is a God who is recklessly merciful. God is extravagantly gracious and Jonah doesn't like it. It makes him angry. Jonah essentially says: "That's why I headed for Tarshish in the first place because I *knew* that you, God, would do something like this because you are gracious, merciful, slow to anger, and abounding in love."[15] In fact, a preacher like Jonah might say: "You're the kind of God who would send your only Son in human flesh to die on a Roman cross and be raised from the dead so that people like me could be forgiven and transformed and filled with all the fullness of God's Spirit."[16] As the great hymn-writer put it, "There's a wideness in God's mercy like the wideness of the sea."[17] We gather at the Lord's Table to celebrate, give thanks for, and bask in the presence of our God who relentlessly pursues and is recklessly merciful. Amen.

13. Jonah 3:8.

14. Jonah 3:10, emphasis added.

15. Jonah 4:2, paraphrase.

16. *Alternative ending for the sermon if not leading to the celebration of communion:* As the great hymn-writer put it: "There's a wideness in God's mercy like the wideness of the sea." Maybe you've been running from the Lord like Jonah. Maybe you would perceive yourself to be evil and obstinate like the people of Ninevah. The good news is that God loves you and pursues you. In his mercy, he has revealed his love to you in Jesus. Have you come to the place where you would like to surrender your life to the love of God?

17. Faber, *There's a Wideness*.

SERMON 14[1]

Firsts, Miracles, and the Kingdom[2]

Mark 1:21–28

They gave it to me for Christmas because they know that I like reading presidential history. The title was simply "41."[3] Some of you knew immediately that George Herbert Walker Bush was the forty-first president of the United States. His son, by almost the same name, was "43." There aren't many US presidents that are known in this way, right? My guess is that *most* of you could not quickly name the twenty-third president[4] of the U.S. or the thirtieth.[5] *Some* of you would know Abraham Lincoln was the sixteenth president. But I would dare say that *all* of you would know the name of the first president of the United States—George Washington. Firsts are important. The first person or persons to fly a plane: the Wright brothers. The first person to run a sub-four-minute mile: Roger Bannister. The first person to set foot on the moon: Neil Armstrong. Firsts are important. The passage for today is from the first chapter of Mark's Gospel and is the story of Jesus' first miracle.

---

1. Preached at First Church of the Nazarene in Kansas City, Missouri on February 2, 2015 (Fourth Sunday after Epiphany; Year B).

2. In this sermon, the challenge was to deal with a story from the Gospel of Mark which has very little initial resonance with post-modern and secularized people. In the current North American church context, this story could quite easily be dismissed and ignored. By reclaiming miracle stories as more than just about displays of power, they can help shape our understanding of God's will and mission as it has been revealed in Christ. Although possession language is not common to our vocabulary, the reality is easily recognized when it is couched in terms of jealousy, pride, prejudice and the like. By inviting people to consider where they see it in others, my hope was that the door was opened for them to see it in themselves.

3. Bush, *41*.

4. Benjamin Harrison.

5. Calvin Coolidge.

68

FIRSTS, MIRACLES, AND THE KINGDOM   69

Mark 1:21–28

Mark's Gospel doesn't have time for baby stories, Magi from the East, and 12-year-old boys who camp out in the temple. Mark doesn't tell us about that stuff. Mark's Gospel doesn't tip-toe into the room. Mark barges in. He knocks the door down. Things happen "immediately" or quickly in Mark.[6] Before Jesus has dried off from his baptism, he has preached a brief sermon, called four disciples, and burst into the synagogue at Capernaum as the unannounced, but guest rabbi for the day. The teaching of Jesus was "amazing"—and *not* because it was something crazy—but because of the authority of it.[7] There was something about it. There was something compelling or captivating and it revolved around his authority. I don't guess that this should surprise us in light of the fact that he had just called four fishermen to follow him and they left *everything* to do it. They walked away from their boats, their workers, and even their father. Apparently, there was a quality of authority in Jesus' speaking, calling, and teaching. The disciples had witnessed it and experienced it for themselves. The people in the synagogue of Capernaum *heard* it and recognized it. But, they weren't the only ones.

Mark 1 tells us that even "evil spirits" or "unclean spirits" knew it. The word that sometimes is translated as "evil" and sometimes as "unclean" is the word *akatharton*. The "a" at the beginning of the word means "not" and *katharton* is the word from which we get "catharsis" or "cleansing." So, a "not-cathartic" or "not-cleansed" spirit recognized the authority of Jesus. Right in the middle of his teaching, this un-named man who was "possessed by an evil spirit" interrupted Jesus: "Have you come to destroy us? I know who you are—the Holy One of God."[8] Jesus hadn't said anything about destruction or annihilation. At least, Mark doesn't tell us anything about it. But this man somehow knew the authority or knew the power of the one who was in their midst. "Silence," Jesus said.[9]

I must have looked up ten or more different translations for what Jesus said. They ranged from "hold your tongue" to "hush up" to "be muzzled." I couldn't find a single translation that said "shut up," which seems to be the intention of the word. "Silence," "hush up," or "quiet" is what Jesus said to the "wind and the waves" in another story and they obeyed.[10] This is what Jesus said to the man in the synagogue and then he delivers him or frees him

---

6. "Immediately" occurs twelve times in the NIV translation of the Gospel of Mark.

7. Mark 1:21–28.

8. Mark 1:24.

9. Mark 1:25.

10. Mark 4:39.

70 SECTION 2: CHRISTMAS, EPIPHANY, AND THE TIME BEFORE LENT

from the "unclean spirit" which possessed him. It's the *first* miracle story in the Gospel of Mark. Why?

I've got to tell you that as a preacher in this time which is such a secularized, scientific, and post-Christian culture, I do not "chomp at the bit" to preach from stories like this. These aren't my favorites stories. Give me a blind man healed and a crowd fed with fish any day. I've got something to say about that. But a man with an "unclean spirit" who interrupts Jesus in the synagogue? What do you do with it? What do you say about it? Sometimes we misunderstand the miracles stories of Jesus as just a display of his power or authority. "See," we say, "this *proves* that Jesus was divine and sent from God." We narrow the focus of the miracle to become simply a manifestation of power, kind of like the "magicians" in Pharaoh's court when Moses and Aaron came to town demanding that he let God's people go. Do you know or remember that story? It's in Exodus 7. Part of the story goes like this:

> The Lord said to Moses and Aaron, 'When Pharaoh says to you, 'Perform a miracle,' then say to Aaron, 'Take your staff and throw it down before Pharaoh,' and it will become a snake." So Moses and Aaron went to Pharaoh and did just as the Lord commanded. Aaron threw his staff down in front of Pharaoh and his officials, and it became a snake. Pharaoh then summoned wise men and sorcerers, and the Egyptian magicians also did the same things by their secret arts. Each one threw down his staff and it became a snake.[11]

The purpose of the miracle was to display or reveal power—miraculous power. In Mark 1 and throughout the New Testament, the miracles of Jesus are *more* than that. They're more than just evidence of divine power and authority. They are meant to reveal something about God's ways and God's will. That is certainly true here in Mark 1. What happens in this story from Mark is meant to provide insight into Jesus' first sermon. Earlier in the story, Jesus preached a short sermon: "The time has come. The kingdom of God is near. Repent and believe the good news."[12] Like preachers have done for centuries, sermons need good illustrations. Here it is: the "driving out" of this "unclean spirit" is Jesus *illustrating* that the kingdom of God is near. Jesus was saying that God's kingdom is breaking in to *this* time and *this* place and a man set free is evidence or an illustration of that.

For two thousand years, the kingdom of God has been breaking in. The life, death, and resurrection of Jesus announced it. Since then, it shows up. It invades. It captures. As the book of Revelation teaches us, there's still

11. Exod 7:8–12.

12. Mark 1:15.

FIRSTS, MIRACLES, AND THE KINGDOM
71

some fighting and battling to be done, but the ultimate *outcome* is no longer
in question. God's Kingdom is *here* and *near*. It's "already" and "not yet"
completed.[13] It's why we continue to pray: "Thy kingdom come and thy will
be done on earth as it is in heaven."[14] But, there are already signs and signals
of the inbreaking kingdom. It seems clear to me that part of what Mark
wants us to understand is that when the Kingdom breaks in, people are
liberated from what possesses them. We shouldn't be surprised by this. The
Gospel of Luke makes it very clear that this is how Jesus understood his
own ministry. It was in *another* synagogue—the one in his hometown of
Nazareth—where he read from the scroll of Isaiah: "The Spirit of the Lord
is on me, because he has anointed me to preach good news to the poor. He
has sent me to proclaim freedom for the prisoners and recovery of sight for
the blind, to release the oppressed, to proclaim the year of the Lord's favor."[15]
He rolled it up, handed it back, and said: "Today is the day of fulfillment."
Jesus was announcing his ministry which would be committed and devoted
to these things. When he said that he had come to "proclaim freedom for
the prisoners," this wasn't just about incarceration and jail time. This was
much larger and much broader than that. Jesus was "setting people free"
from what bound them. He was bringing liberation from what "possessed"
them. That is not a first-century problem, is it?

Have you ever done something or responded to someone and then
said: "I don't know what got into me. I don't know why I would *do* something like that." That's a saying with ancient roots that revolves around the
idea of something "possessing" us or taking control of us. We don't name
that as an "unclean" or "evil spirit" these days, but we all know that we
can be dominated by and captured by ways of thinking and living that are
harmful and unhealthy—even anti-Christian. You have a co-worker who is
"possessed" by jealousy and anger. She was abandoned by her husband and
left to fend for herself. Now, the anger boils just below the surface and it
bubbles up on a regular basis to be vented toward anybody and everybody
who's in the pathway. You have a son, a grandson, or a son-in-law who is
"possessed" by workaholism and greed. The driving force of his life is the
next dollar or the next deal. He lives embracing the Rockefeller answer to
the question "When is enough enough?" with the answer: "Just one dollar

13. One of the early proponents of inaugurated eschatology was biblical scholar
George Eldon Ladd. It has taken on many shapes and forms since his time and the
language of "already and not yet" has found its way into the lexicon of much of
evangelicalism.

14. Matt 6:10.

15. Luke 4:18–19.

more."[16] Or, what about the friend or colleague who is "possessed" by prejudice or racism? It comes out in the jokes around the coffee pot at work or in the emails forwarded from who knows where. The list of potential "possessors" could include despair, food, approval, or consumerism. You could make your own list. The message of Jesus is that, in the kingdom, he has come to set people free from what "possesses" them so that they can be filled fully with the presence of God.

Some of you know what I mean when I say Alka Seltzer. For others, that's a foreign language. Others of you know about products like Emergen-C or other similar things that help to boost your immune system. You take the tablets and drop them into some water and they fizz and fizz until they're dissolved. What would happen if you dropped the Alka Seltzer or the Emergen-C into the water without taking it out of the sealed package? Nothing would happen. It would be restricted from working because it's sealed up in the package. It's prevented by the package. Jesus has come and announced the kingdom of God in the world, died on a Roman cross in your place, and was raised from the dead by the power of the Father to *set you free* from the things that bind you, that possess you, and that restrict the work of the Holy Spirit in your life like a sealed packet.

In just a moment,[17] we're going to sing a song and while we're doing that, I'm going to invite you to find a place of prayer here at the altar. What "binds" you? What "imprisons" you today? Jesus has come to set you free by his grace and power. Amen.

---

16. Anecdotal story. No confirmed source.

17. *Alternative ending if concluding the service with the Lord's Supper:* Is today the day that you are set free? It could happen right here and right now as you come to the Table of the Lord. You could step out today in faith and seek the freedom from sin and shame that only God, through Christ, can provide. Maybe that's how you come to the Lord's Supper today. Others who have been following Jesus for a while may come seeking to be liberated from a controlling anger, a dominating sense of discouragement, or a possessing-prejudice. The good news is that you can be free because Jesus gives orders and possessors obey his command. So, come. Eat the bread and drink the cup and be free. Be filled with the presence of God.

SERMON 15[1]

Beside Jesus? Or the Target?[2]

Luke 4:14–21

In about ten days, it will be the 110th anniversary of the birth of Dietrich Bonhoeffer. He was born on February 4, 1906. He was hanged by the Nazis before he turned 40 years of age at the Flossenburg concentration camp during World War II. Many of you have read Bonhoeffer's writings, including his classics, "The Cost of Discipleship" or "Life Together." A friend of mine sent me a Bonhoeffer quote this week. Here it is: "The Church is the Church only when it exists for *others*" (emphasis added). It reminded me of another quote which comes from William Booth, the founder of the Salvation Army many years ago. He was scheduled to speak at an international convention, but because of sickness or travel problems he was unable to attend. He sent his speech for the conference via telegram and it was one word in large letters: "OTHERS."[3] I invite your attention this morning to the fourth chapter of Luke's Gospel.

---

1. Preached at First Church of the Nazarene in Kansas City, Missouri on January 24, 2016 (Third Sunday after Epiphany; Year C).

2. This sermon was preached toward the end of January 2016. Therefore, the historic references to Bonhoeffer made sense. In this sermon, I began with a brief introduction that highlighted the outward focus of ministry and service. In some ways, this was the "expected" message when a passage like Luke 4 is read to a gathered group of Jesus-followers on a Sunday morning for worship. The twist or surprise was in turning the message toward that same group and inviting them to see themselves as poor, oppressed, blind, and needy. In a congregation where some were fairly affluent and quite established, this move was the intriguing power of the message.

3. Anecdotal story. No confirmed source.

73

74 SECTION 2: CHRISTMAS, EPIPHANY, AND THE TIME BEFORE LENT

Luke 4:14–21

By the time we get to Luke 4, a lot has happened in the life of Jesus. He's been born to Mary and presented at the temple in Jerusalem where an old man and an old woman *both* make prophetic and amazing declarations about who this child is and what this child will be. Then Luke gives us the one story from Jesus' pre-teen years where he ends up teaching the teachers in the temple courts. The child prodigy is "schooling" the teachers for everyone to see and hear. Then Jesus is baptized by John the Baptizer and is led into the desert to be tempted for forty days and nights. I didn't even include the genealogies and other details that Luke covers, but *much* has happened by the time we get to Luke 4 where the public ministry and teaching of Jesus has begun in earnest.

I want you to notice how Jesus comes to Nazareth. He comes to Galilee, which is a region, and eventually to Nazareth, which is a village, "in the power of the Spirit," as verse 1 says. He had been led by the Spirit into the desert of temptation and, while being tempted, the Spirit had sustained him and enabled him to resist the temptation. Now, out of the desert he comes. He returns to Galilee, the place where he had been raised and where he had grown, as Luke 2 says, "in wisdom and stature, and in favor with God and others." Galilee and Nazareth, in particular, are the places where Jesus was known best. It was *there* where they knew his family. In all likelihood, this is where Joseph, his earthly father, was entombed. This is where his brothers and sisters were raised. Galilee and Nazareth were home for Jesus. He returns from being baptized in the Jordan, and from being tempted in the desert, in the power of the Spirit. The ministry of Jesus in his teaching, preaching, healing, and helping will be a Spirit-led and Spirit-empowered ministry. He comes to Nazareth in the power of the Spirit.

He also comes on a wave of praise. News about Jesus had spread "through the whole countryside" as Luke says. This was a "word-of-mouth" process. There were no advertising firms or marketing strategies. This was person to person to town-crier to traveling merchant to village "grapevine." Word was out about Jesus. He was teaching in the synagogues throughout Galilee and the end of verse 15 says: "And *everyone* praised him." That's a dangerous place to be when *everyone* is praising. Maybe Jesus headed for Nazareth to preach in his hometown synagogue for this very reason. Maybe Jesus wanted to "pop the bubble" of pervasive and persistent praise because when he preached in Nazareth, he chose a prophetic text. It was from Isaiah, the prophet. We would call it chapter 61, but that kind of notation comes much later. In addition to that, what Luke records here in chapter 4 is not *exactly* the text from Isaiah 61. There's no reference

BESIDE JESUS? OR THE TARGET?   75

to the "recovery of sight for the blind" in Isaiah. But with those details or differences acknowledged, Jesus reads from Isaiah this prophetic, hope-filled promise from God, and then he sits down.

Now, for *us*, when someone wants to make a speech or gain the attention of an audience, we stand up and go to a podium or to the front of the crowd. The posture for speech-making in our time and place is to stand and speak with boldness. When we read that Jesus sat down, we're tempted to believe that he finished. It's over. Case closed. But in the first century and in Jewish culture, the posture for speaking with authority and boldness was while being seated. For context, imagine a king on his throne making pronouncements. He's seated. Or, recall all the references to Jesus being "seated at the right hand of God, the Father." Sitting and speaking is the posture for authority. Notice how verse 20 says that after Jesus sat down, "the eyes of everyone in the synagogue were fastened on him." He had their attention. They were waiting for his authoritative pronouncement. They were giving their full focus to his teaching and to his words. Then Jesus says, essentially: "All these amazing promises from God, to preach to the poor, to proclaim freedom to prisoners, to give sight to the blind, to set the oppressed free, and to announce jubilee—all these things are and will be fulfilled in *me*."[4]

Wow. What a claim. Jesus is declaring that *this* is what his life and ministry are to be about. This is what he has come into the world to do. His hometown "fan club" calls for an immediate meeting. It concludes with them driving Jesus out of town and trying to throw him down a cliff.[5] You thought the wheels could quickly come off a twenty-first century *political* campaign. Well, Jesus' lost his luster in an instant and it was in his *hometown*, of all places.

I think that it's appropriate and accurate to point out that Luke includes this story in his gospel not *just* for the prophetic ministry of Jesus, but also to give direction for the Church and for the priorities of the Church. In other words, if the Church is going to follow Jesus, then the Church needs to be interested in the ministries that Jesus claims for himself. I think that is accurate and helpful for the Church, but I also think that when we read the story in this way, we automatically place ourselves *beside* Jesus in doing the work of the kingdom and joining him in his ministry. I think that's OK and can be helpful. *Where* you see yourself in the stories of the Scripture is a huge deal. But if you're always with Jesus, always on the winning team, and always on the God-side, then you probably need to re-think a story or two. If you're always the Good Samaritan who stops to help the man in need and you never see

4. Luke 4:18–21 summarized and paraphrased.
5. Luke 4:29.

yourself as the "religious person" who walks by on the *other* side of the road,[6] then you might have a skewed view or opinion of yourself. If you're *never* the "prodigal" who runs away[7] and *never* the sheep who wanders off[8] and *never* the coin that gets lost,[9] then you might want to re-evaluate what's really happening in your life. So, for today and in *this* story: what if we imagine moving ourselves from being *beside* Jesus and continuing the work that he has come to do in the world to rather being the *target* or the *focus* of his prophetic and hope-filled word from Christ? What if *we* are the poor ones who need to hear the good news that Jesus preaches?

"Poor? *We're* not poor! We live in the wealthiest and most powerful country in the world. We live in some of the wealthiest communities and counties in the country.[10] I could hit a pitching wedge from this platform into one of the most exclusive neighborhoods in Leawood, Kansas that is *filled* with multi-million dollar homes."[11] But, what if our own poverty was masked by an affluence that hinders us from hearing the gospel of Jesus as *good* news? What if our poverty was bound up in our own self-sufficiency to the place that we don't even sense a *need* for God or the *need* to be rescued or redeemed? We must come to the place where we humbly acknowledge our desperate need for God's life and touch. An awareness of our own poverty will be a crucial indication that renewal is coming or has come among us.

Instead of being *beside* Jesus and helping him do the ministry that he's come to do, is it possible for people like you and me to see ourselves as "prisoners" who need to be "freed"? Jesus said: "He has sent me to proclaim freedom for the prisoners." What is it that "imprisons" people like you and me? Are there expectations that constrict your life from being what God wants your life to be? Are you a captive to a way of life, to the views of others, or to the perceptions of your family or neighbors and somehow those opinions or perspectives chain you to a certain way of living? Prisons don't just come in the form of cinder blocks, bars, and locked doors. Like idols, prisons come in a variety of shapes and sizes that are as varied as our imagination and experience. Most often, they are of our own making. *We* construct the prisons that imprison us. They take the form of addictions and habits. They are patterns of thinking and responding which perpetuate themselves like

6. Luke 10:25–37.

7. Luke 15:11–32.

8. Luke 15:3–7.

9. Luke 15:8–10.

10. According to the 2010 U.S. census, Johnson County, Kansas (which is adjacent to Kansas City, Missouri) was the wealthiest county in the state and the thirty-first wealthiest county in the U.S.

11. Hallbrook Country Club was across the street from the church.

BESIDE JESUS? OR THE TARGET?

a wheel rolling downhill. When we truly hear the prophetic words of Jesus directed to *us*, we will recognize the chains that bind us and the prisons that constrict us. *Then*, we will seek the liberating presence and power of Jesus to be unleashed in our own lives.

What about blindness? Is that purely or strictly a physical need that Jesus addresses? Clearly, Jesus healed several people in the New Testament who were physically blind. Bartimaeus comes to mind,[12] along with others. But if today, *we're* the target of Jesus' prophetic and hope-filled word, we must ask ourselves, "How are we blind? What is it that we do not see?" Are we blind to our own pain-causing ways and words? Do we lash out without being aware of the consequences and then explain it away as simply our personality or our devotion to truth? Are we blind to our own prejudices or latent racism? Are we blind to the basic needs of others here and around the world? Leo Tolstoy, the great Russian writer, begins "Anna Karenina" with the sentence, "Happy families are all alike; every unhappy family is unhappy in its own way."[13] The thing that strikes me is that so often we are blind in our own way. We all would acknowledge, I hope, that we have blind spots. But when we are made *aware* of those blind spots by the Spirit of Christ or through the counsel of other followers of Jesus, how do we respond? Do we continue to live in our blindness and hold on to our blindness like it's something that we treasure? Or, do we let go of it with God's help and ask him to shine his light into those dark places in our lives? When we hear the prophetic word of Jesus, blind spots are exposed and dark places are illumined so that God can do his cleansing, healing, and restoring work in us.

Then there's this word about "oppression." Those "oppressed" will be "released," Jesus says. I hesitate to even suggest that folks like you and me would live under "oppression." It's not the same kind of "oppression" that many people of color live under, or what people working in sweatshops in China experience, or the tragedy of women caught up in the horrific world of sexual trafficking. Oppression, to paraphrase Tolstoy, happens "in its own way"—in a variety of ways. There is an "oppression" that accompanies the grind of work that isn't fulfilling or the pressure of bills that only seem to accumulate. What about an "oppression" that comes with the disappointment that closes in when dreams for ourselves, our children, or our grandchildren are squandered or intentionally cast aside? Jesus says, "The Spirit of the Lord is on me. . . to release the oppressed" (Luke 4:18). Renewal, revival, and release from oppression are related—not just linguistically—but also because they are *gifts* of God in Christ.

12. Mark 10:46–52.

13. Tolstoy, *Anna Karenina*, 1.

78   SECTION 2: CHRISTMAS, EPIPHANY, AND THE TIME BEFORE LENT

How shall we respond to God's word for us today? Let us gather at the table of the Lord around which followers of Jesus have gathered for centuries and across all the time zones on this particular Lord's Day. Let us eat and drink and recognize our own poverty apart from the presence of Christ. As we share, may be pray a prayer that says: "Lord, feed us with the food that frees us. Give to us the food that is your life and power and ways. As we partake, reveal to us our blindness—the ways in which we are not living fully in your light and life—and help us to surrender that blindness to your healing touch. If we are living under a sense of oppression in whatever form it has taken in *our* lives, may the power of your Spirit release us so that we might be instruments of the kingdom for the sake and cause of Jesus." Yes, the mission of Jesus is for others, but we, too, are the objects—the targets—of his life and love.

Amen.

Section 3

Sermons for Lent
and Good Friday

SERMON 16[1]

Command, Invitation, and Prayer[2]

Isaiah 55:1–9

M uch of my work is with words. I spend a lot of time reading them, writing them, thinking carefully about them, and speaking them. I get to offer them in prayers and in sermons. I speak them at funerals and over the telephone to comfort and to encourage. I use words to challenge and to console. Words—here and there and everywhere in between. Much of my working is caught up in words. It's a mixed bag. It's bane *and* blessing. Words are fleeting and yet sometimes they last. Today, we read in God's Word some ancient words from Isaiah 55 and I want to focus, frankly, on one *particular* word. Let's look and listen together to Isaiah 55:1–9.

Isaiah 55:1–9

Water has been, is, and always *will* be a matter of conflict and importance in our world. Just in the last few weeks, we've learned of this horrible problem in Flint, Michigan and other places where the water that has been provided to people's homes has been contaminated with lead for *years*.[3] The growth and development of children has been stunted because of poisoned water. It's infuriating, saddening, and unconscionable all at the same time. In situ-

1. Preached at First Church of the Nazarene in Kansas City, Missouri on February 28, 2016 (Lent 3; Year C).

2. This sermon was dangerous in the sense that it tried to confront a pervasive theological viewpoint about the basic character of God. The view is so commonplace that even raising questions about it is controversial and could prove to be problematic in a congregational setting. In essence, however, it is too simplistic and it is off-putting for those outside the church. At the crossroads of a contemporary water poisoning crisis, the prophecy of Isaiah, and that overly simplistic view of God, I tried to preach a meaningful and inviting word.

3. CBS/AP, "Water Crisis."

81

ations like that, we catch a tiny little glimpse of the importance or value of clean water. But, for the most part, it's not something that is at the forefront of our minds. Of course, we live with water at our fingertips. We carry it around in plastic bottles. Or, we watch it swirl down the drain as we brush our teeth almost without concern. We turn the knob or press the button on the fountain and we never expect it *not* to flow and to flow freely.

I did a little research this week. It wasn't difficult to find a few statistics related to average yearly rainfall in various places. Like here in Kansas City, which is certainly not one of the wettest places in the nation or on the planet, but even here, we get almost forty inches of rain per year. Jerusalem, Israel gets sixteen inches per year which makes it quite dry in comparison.

Death Valley, California gets 2.4 inches of rain per year which makes it very arid and dry.

Get this. Lima, Peru receives less than a third of *one* inch of rain *per year*. Can you imagine the value that is placed on water in Lima, Peru?

Of course, in biblical times, water had to be drawn from a well or carried from a river or stream in clay pots or jars. Water wasn't at the tap, piped in, or picked up at Walmart. Of course, when water is harder to get and harder to preserve, thirst is a much more familiar experience than with folks like us. When you and I are thirsty, typically within minutes we are able to quench our thirst. We rarely are thirsty for very long at all. Centuries and centuries ago in a much more arid and dry place, God said to his people in the prophecy of Isaiah: "Come. You who are thirsty. Come to the waters."

Sometimes the word "come" is a command. As a parent, I've used it that way: "Come, here," usually followed quickly by "right now." There is no time or place for conversation, argumentation, or negotiation. It is clear, pointed, and unequivocally a *command*. Some perceive that God functions in this way all the time with everything. This way of talking about God and how God acts is a way of emphasizing his power, his might, or his control over all that is. For some, it is the theological "filter" or the theological category that is predominant. It *must* be maintained and preserved at all costs. If not, God somehow becomes *less* than God. Some say, "God is in control and, therefore, God *must* command everything in the universe right down to the most miniscule of details. Otherwise, God is not God." There's an emphasis upon the sovereignty of God, the power of God, and that God is "in control" of anything and everything.

Practically, this way of thinking and these theological assertions show themselves when tragedies happen or illness strikes. All of a sudden, God gets credited with doing things that are horrible, painful, and difficult. All of a sudden, God is the one who "commands" a typhoon to develop and direct its

COMMAND, INVITATION, AND PRAYER   83

path right toward the tiny island of Fiji[4] to wreak havoc, death, and destruction when there are thousands of square miles of empty ocean where it could have spun and spun and done no damage at all. Or, God says "come" and commands cancer to strike this one, that one, or the ones we love. We struggle to understand how God—if he "controls everything"—could *do* such a thing.[5] We cry out, "Why? And why *me*? And why *them*?"

When "come" is a command—without room for pushing back or without room for questioning—God gets blamed for things that we wouldn't blame on the worst of our enemies. God becomes the cause of birth defects and Zika viruses.[6] He's the cause of lead poisoning in water,[7] brain aneurysms, and car crashes. All the while, folks try to tell us that "God is *testing* our faith" or "God is trying to *refine* our character" or some other rationale that might have a glimmer of truth. This way of thinking where God is "in control" of everything down to the smallest of issues is the prevailing, pre-eminent theological water in which our culture swims. It's everywhere around us. It's common and accepted. It's what gets spouted on the radio and in the best-selling books from prominent pastors in high-profile churches. It's the "theological fog" that pervades our culture. Or, as an old professor of mine used to say: "It's like water for a fish. The fish doesn't know anything else." When God, because he has to control everything down to the last detail, becomes the cause of tragedy, disaster, and defects, something is wrong. This is why I think that this way of thinking is biblically simplistic and theologically misguided.

When God says "come," it's not a command, but rather an invitation. When God says "come," it's not like when you or I are demanding that our child obey our command. It's more like an invitation given to someone who has been gifted with the freedom to accept it or to reject it. Theologically, it is a way of thinking that prioritizes the *love* of God, rather than the power or sovereignty of God. It's a way that lets go of control in order to trust. It lets go of simple answers in order to embrace a complexity that is often beyond our understanding or comprehension. When "come" is an invitation to those who are thirsty, and when "come" is an invitation to those who have no money—no resources, no solution, no ready-made-answers—then, the

---

4. Category 5 Cyclone Winston struck Fiji on February 20, 2016. Winston was the most intense tropical cyclone in the Southern Hemisphere ever recorded.

5. These are the foundational questions of theodicy.

6. Early in 2015, there was a Zika virus outbreak in Brazil that caused severe birth defects and other neurological problems. Some were fearful that it would impact the Summer Olympic Games which were held in Brazil in the summer of 2016.

7 Reference to the lead poisoning of water pipes in Flint, Michigan.

84   SECTION 3: SERMONS FOR LENT AND GOOD FRIDAY

invitation of God is an invitation to a relationship of giving and trust—of receiving and of his presence.

When Jesus walked along the shores of the Sea of Galilee at the beginning of his ministry, he called some men to become his disciples. Remember that? Was it command or invitation? Could they have said, "No, thank you"? Or, is that inconceivable? Sometimes when you read the stories of Jesus, it's like the disciples functioned as robots. There's such little detail offered by the gospel writers. Jesus comes down to the shore of Galilee and he sees Peter and Andrew fishing and he says to them, "Come, follow me and I will make you fishers of men. At once they left their nets and followed him."[8]

Now, you can read that in different ways, right? You can imagine that this was the very first time that Jesus even met Peter and Andrew. You can imagine that Jesus was so compelling and such a commanding presence that when he said, "Come, follow me," they dropped their nets like they were in a trance. They climbed out of their boats and chased after Jesus like there was no other option. That's one way to read the story. But, it's possible that Peter and Andrew had heard Jesus preaching. Mark 1:14 says that, after John the Baptist was imprisoned, Jesus went into Galilee proclaiming the "good news of God." Maybe Peter and Andrew had been there to hear Jesus preach. Maybe they had watched him among the crowds and had observed his spirit and demeanor. Maybe they had even talked to him about his mission, life, and plans. When he came along the shore and called them to be his disciples, they accepted his invitation and willingly made him their rabbi or teacher.

Isaiah 55 is set in the context of the exile where the inhabitants of Judah had been taken by force to a distant land. They had settled there. They had planted crops, built homes, and made a life for themselves. Now God was inviting them to come "home"—to come to himself. "Why spend your labor on what does not satisfy?," as verse 2 says.

This is one of those places where I see the ground from which the thoughts and ideas of Augustine are born. He lived at the end of the fourth and the beginning of the fifth centuries. Church historians and scholars were recently asked: "Other than the Bible, what are the 25 most influential writings since the time of Jesus?"[9] Get this: four of the twenty-five writings, including the *first* and the *fourth* spots, were penned by Augustine.[10] His most famous or most familiar quote is addressed to God and goes something like this: "You

---

8. Mark 1:18.

9. *Christian History* editors, "Did You Know?," 1.

10. Augustine, *Confessions, City of God.*

COMMAND, INVITATION, AND PRAYER

have *made* us for yourself, and our heart is restless until it rests in you."[11] When God invites the exiles to "come to the waters"—to "come, buy and eat"—what God is really saying is that they are invited to "come home"—to "come and rest"—to live in a life-transforming relationship with him for which we were created and shaped. Verse 3 may say it best: "Give ear and come to me; hear me, that your soul may live." A loving, gracious God who has gifted us with freedom *invites* the exiles and you and me to *come* to him—to rest in him and to abide in his presence. Is that what you need?

It's not a commanding "come," but it's the gentle invitation to come to God and receive exactly what you need. It may be for your spiritual thirst to be satisfied. It may be for your hunger for a deeper relationship with God to be met. Maybe what you need is comfort, encouragement, healing, freedom from the past, or courage for the present moment. God's invitation is for you to come. What about us? What is *our* response?

I think our response is captured in a word from the New Testament which is based in two Aramaic words. Many times, it isn't even translated. It's left in a Greek form of an Aramaic expression. When you hear it, many of you will be familiar with it. It's the word "maranatha."[12] It's a prayer that gets translated in most places as "Come, Lord." It's a prayer. Hope and help in our time of thirst and need is when God's invitation to "come" is met by our prayerful response that says, "Come, Lord."[13] Almost every Lord's Day, we are invited to come to the Table and to receive grace and strength, help and hope, courage and comfort. It's as if the cross of Jesus is the arms-wide-open invitation of God to come to him so that our souls may live and that we may find our rest in the one who created us. In essence today, our response in coming to receive the bread and the cup is captured in our prayer—"maranatha"—"Come, Lord"—"Come to me, I pray. Come to heal. Come, to forgive. Come, to free and transform, O God!" In a dry and desert place, water is priceless and God doesn't command, he invites. God says to you and to me, "Come, all you who are thirsty, come to the waters." Come.

---

11. Augustine, *Confessions*, 1:1, paraphrase.

12. 1 Cor 16:22.

13. *Alternative ending if the response to the sermon is not intended to be at the Table:* God's invitation is to "come." He has already reached out to us with grace through the provision of Jesus' life, death, and resurrection from the dead. His death brings us life, but we have to receive it for ourselves. Maybe that's what "coming" will mean for you today.

SERMON 17[1]

Important, but Forgotten[2]

Joshua 5:9–12

Important, but forgotten: is it possible for those to go *together*? Appomattox Courthouse in rural Virginia is a forgotten place and yet it is one of the most important places in the history of the United States. It's where the Civil War was ended when Robert E. Lee and Ulysses Grant shook hands in the parlor of the McLean House on April 9th of 1865. I've been there in the parlor of that place and yet, for the most part, it's been forgotten.

The Great Smoky Mountain National Park was visited in 2014 by more than ten *million* people. Almost five million went to the Grand Canyon. Over four million rode the ferry out to see the Statue of Liberty. Those were the 3rd, 10th, and 17th most visited national parks or historic sites in 2014. Do you know where Appomattox Courthouse ranked in number of visitors? 151st.[3]

It's important, but it's been forgotten. One of the most *important* places in all of the Old Testament is also one of the most *forgotten* places. It's a place called Gilgal and we'll read about it today in Joshua 5.

1. Preached at First Church of the Nazarene in Kansas City, Missouri on March 6, 2016 (Lent 4; Year C).

2. This sermon, based on a fairly unfamiliar passage, was an opportunity to speak to one of the huge issues in the scriptural witness—that of *remembering*. Of course, God provided the people of Israel with a physical "marking" to help them remember. Circumcision is not the easiest thing to talk about on a Sunday morning and my attempt to do so may or may not have been effective. You can decide. The turn, however, to baptism as the church's form of circumcision was important and helped to recover a portion of the meaning of baptism from simply being a way to testify to something that happened in the past. I wanted to emphasize that baptism must become something for each day in the present moment and for the future, as well. Similarly, the eucharist is not meant to be a random, very occasional remembrance. This sermon tried to point to the sacraments as the Church's tried and true ways to be marked and to remember.

3. Statistics gathered from pleacher.com/np/visits/allnpsv.pdf.

IMPORTANT, BUT FORGOTTEN   87

Joshua 5:9–12

The story needs some set up so let me pick a place to start and I'll try to summarize very quickly. God's people were slaves in Egypt and then God raised up Moses to lead them out. It was a miraculous deliverance. They celebrated the very first Passover. God had told them to mark the door frames of their homes with the blood of a lamb. That night, when the angel of death came through to strike down the firstborn of every home in Egypt, the places marked with blood would be passed-over. *That* event was what led the King of Egypt to say to Moses and God's people: "Get out. Go." And so, they did.

On their way toward the promised land, they got trapped between the sea and Pharaoh's approaching army. The Pharaoh had changed his mind about letting his entire workforce leave the country. But, just in the nick of time, God parts the sea, the Israelites go through on dry ground, and the Egyptian army is drowned as God reverses the miracle. Then, God leads his people right up to the edge of the land that he has promised to give to them. That's why it's sometimes referred to as the "promised land" or the "holy land." Moses sends a group of spies—twelve of them—into the land. They are charged with checking things out and bringing back a report. When they come back, they all have great things to say about the land and its fertility and abundance, but ten of the twelve are frightened by the walled cities and the strong people who are already living in the land. In a sad case where the majority swayed the day, the people refused to go into the land that God had promised to give to them. For those of us who cherish democracy and the democratic model, here's a biblical example of where the idea of "majority rules" went terribly wrong.

As a result of this faithless decision, God's people wandered in the wilderness for forty years, and all the adults of that generation—other than Caleb and Joshua, the two spies who offered the minority report—everyone of that generation died and were not allowed by God to enter the promised land. During those forty years, God continued to provide for his people. He fed them. He gave them water to drink. He sent manna from heaven six days a week, and he sustained his people physically and in every other way. But, during those forty years in the desert, God's people forgot *who* they were and *whose* they were.

"Why do you say that, Pastor?" Well, you have to read the first eight verses of this chapter which I chose *not* to do this morning because some of you parents would have to go home this afternoon and explain it to

88   SECTION 3: SERMONS FOR LENT AND GOOD FRIDAY

your children.[4] Here's a possible suggestion. Call up *Toy Story* on Netflix or remind your kids of that scene where Woody is being "refurbished" by a doll-doctor. His arm gets stitched back on. His hair and facial features are cleaned up. Then, the bottom of his boot is re-painted and, as that's done, you see Andy's "mark"—his name—being painted over. Woody was Andy's possession and Andy had made that clear by putting his name or a mark on the bottom of Woody's boot.

Similarly, God had chosen a certain way to mark or identify his people and it was a mark that was painful, but distinctive. It was done to every male in that patriarchal society and culture. But during those forty years in the desert, God's people weren't faithful to continue this very distinctive practice that God had given to them. They quit doing it. They had forgotten *who* they were and, in so doing, they had forgotten *whose* they were. It wasn't until Joshua, the successor to Moses, led the people through the Jordan River on dry ground by a miracle of God that the people ended up in this forgotten place called Gilgal. Before the river began running again, God told Joshua to send twelve men into the river bed and for each of them to pick up a large stone and carry it on their shoulder out of the river. Then, they were to pile those twelve stones together at Gilgal. Why? For this reason: when someone asks about this pile of stones, you can then tell them about how God stopped the Jordan and led us through. "These stones are to be a memorial to the people of Israel forever."[5] Later in chapter 4, Joshua expanded on the reason when he said: "'What do these stones mean?' tell them, 'Israel crossed the Jordan on dry ground. For the Lord your God dried up the Jordan before you until you had crossed over. The Lord your God did to the Jordan just what he had done to the Red Sea when he dried it up before us until we had crossed over. He did this so that *all* peoples of the earth might know that the hand of the Lord is powerful and so that you might always fear the Lord your God.'"[6]

If that was all that happened at Gilgal, it would be important. But that's not all. The first part of chapter 5 tells the story of Joshua leading the people in reclaiming and beginning to practice again the "marking" of God's people that had been abandoned for the last forty years. Gilgal, the place where God's people had forgotten *who* they were and *whose* they were, became the place where they remembered again. Gilgal is one of the most important places in all of the Bible. It was where the people of God entered into a new era. An old way and an old era came to an end at Gilgal. The manna

4. The topic is circumcision.

5. Josh 4:7.

6. Josh 4:21–24.

IMPORTANT, BUT FORGOTTEN

stopped. The manna that had been provided day after day for forty years ended. When the people passed through the Jordan on dry ground, they were being told again that the God who delivered his people from Egyptian bondage and led them through the Sea, this same God was delivering them *again*. In combination with the story of circumcision in the first verses of this chapter, God's people were being "marked" again. They were being chosen and claimed again.

You and I must understand that our baptism—our passing through the waters—is our "marking" or "claiming" by God. We become God's people in baptism. It's *more* than just you giving a testimony about your faith in Christ. It's *more* than just a "profession" of a past decision that you have made. As the apostle Paul says, in baptism, we are buried with Christ. An old way or old life dies and a new way and a new life is resurrected. If you haven't been baptized, I want to encourage you to take this step and pass through the waters to be "marked" and "claimed" as a child of God with billions of other Christians around the world and throughout the centuries. We will baptize folks on Easter Sunday morning. What better day to be buried and resurrected out of the water than Easter? If you want to take this step, please call me or email me. The information is there in your worship folder and we can talk together about it. If you've already been baptized, but between then and now your life in Christ has been renewed or restored, you may want to openly and publicly "reclaim" your baptism.[7] I would love to talk with you as well about how we might help you to do that. This is also something that we have planned for Easter Sunday morning.

Not only do we have this once-in-a-lifetime experience and "marker" upon us, but we also have other ways that regularly and constantly bring before us who we are and whose we are in Christ. The season of Lent—this time where we are moving toward Holy Week and Easter—is an intentional time to ponder and to examine who we are and whose we are. We're a lot like the people of God wandering in the desert, aren't we? We're prone to forget. It's easy to *not* remember. It's our tendency to let things slide, to get distracted, and to not give the proper attention to what is most important. We do that, don't we?

The Church, as much as it is maligned and often dismissed, is the only institution in our culture and world that is determined and purposed to remind you of who you are and whose you are. We don't have a secret handshake or an encrypted password. We have two main things to accomplish this great task. We have baptism where we are "marked" and where God's

---

7. I was trying to preserve the Church's historic teaching and practice that rejects re-baptism.

grace for our salvation in all of its fullness is celebrated. We pass through the waters where old things die and new things are born. The Church has baptism to help you know who you are and whose you are. The Church has two primary practices and the first is baptism. The second thing that the Church has is the Lord's Supper. Sometimes we call it communion, the eucharist, or the "great thanksgiving." Here at the table, along with millions upon millions of other Christians around the globe, it is proclaimed that Christ came, lived among us in the flesh, and died on a cross outside Jerusalem in *our* place. He was crucified for our sins and he was raised from the dead as the "signal" or "first-fruits" of our own resurrection. Sometimes when I'm scrolling through Facebook photos or memes, I'll see a picture of some historic event—of 9/11 or Pearl Harbor or some other important moment—and down at the bottom of the picture, there will be a phrase: "We will never forget" or "We will always remember." The Church has been doing that very thing for two thousand years here at the Table. There's a Greek word for it: it's *an-amnesis*—literally translated—"not or no amnesia." In Luke 22, when Jesus is sharing his last meal with his disciples, Jesus says, "Do this in remembrance of me"—the word is *an-amnesis*. In effect, "Do this . . . with no amnesia. Remember *who* you are and *whose* you are."

The people of Joshua's time were led to Gilgal—an important, but forgotten place—where they re-discovered and renewed who they were. There's an old song that some of you know. It's almost one hundred years old now and the chorus goes like this: "Lest I forget Gethsemane, / Lest I forget Thine agony; / "—then comes the best part—"Lest I forget Thy love for me, / lead me to Calvary."[8] So, come to the Table. Remember. Be assured of God's love. Receive his grace today in this *important* and *not* forgotten place.

Amen.

8. Hussey, "Lead Me to Calvary."

SERMON 18[1]

A Sanitized and Sanitizing Jesus[2]

John 2:13–22

I met a friend for lunch this past week in Overland Park, just off of Metcalf. Like most restaurants, I was greeted, led to a table, presented a menu, and then I was given a big, plastic bottle of germ-killing sanitizer "for my convenience," as the hostess said. After all, I was going to be sticking my fingers into the same basket of corn chips as my friend. When I visit someone in the hospital these days, there are dispensers of sanitizing foam at every turn, at every elevator, and at every door handle. Even at the gym where I try to exercise from time to time, the showers have sanitizers hanging on the walls. Gone are the days of leaving a bar of soap to be used by whomever for however long it lasts. We live in a world concerned with sanitizing, don't we? Sanitized. Cleaned. Cleansed. Today's story from John 2 is often referred to as the "cleansing of the temple"—the "sanitization" of the temple. Let's hear it again.

---

1. Preached at First Church of the Nazarene in Kansas City, Missouri on March 11, 2012 (Lent 3; Year B).

2. In this sermon, I utilized four paintings. The first three can be from any famous artists. I chose paintings that I thought people might recognize. The fourth painting was the one that was so important for the sermon. It helped to convey an image of the "sanitized" Jesus which is so different from what was portrayed in John 2. Typically, I rarely use visual images in sermons. The primary reason is because I want my hearers to be constructing or calling up their own mental images. I want them to be engaged in the process and in the sermonic moment. I don't want to do the work for them. But in this case, I thought it was helpful, maintained engagement as they tried to identify the artist, and then surprised them with this incredibly familiar painting from a virtually unknown artist. The Sallman painting helped convey the idea of the first section of the sermon where Jesus is "nice, kind, and neatly groomed."

91

John 2:13–22

Don't you find it interesting that this story for most of us is *not* the story that first comes to mind when we begin to think of Jesus and his ministry. We think of Jesus feeding the five thousand, delivering the Sermon on the Mount, praying in the garden of Gethsemane, or performing some miracle of healing. I think that *part* of the issue is that we don't really know what to do with a whip-wielding, table-turning, angry-eyed Jesus. It's like when Dr. David Banner gets angry and turns into the Incredible Hulk. Do you remember what he says just before the transformation? He says: "Don't make me angry. You wouldn't like me when I'm angry." For whatever reason, we just don't like the angry Jesus of John 2. Have you ever thought about that? When most of us think about Jesus, we have an entirely different picture or mental image of Jesus in mind.

Just for a moment, let's take a little twentieth century art quiz. No worries. This won't cost anything and will be a little different from what you're used to. I'm going to have the video folks project a painting onto the screen and then I'll ask you to identify the artist. You don't have to know the name of the painting just the artist who painted it.

Painting #1—Norman Rockwell

Painting #2—Pablo Picasso

Painting #3—Andy Warhol

Those are three, familiar artists from the twentieth century, but *none* of them were identified by the *New York Times* in 1994 as the "best-known artist of the century." Can anyone identify the "best-known artist of the century" as named by the *New York Times*?

His name is Warner Sallman[3] and his most famous painting is the one called "The Head of Christ" and it was painted in 1941. In some form—cards or trinkets or illustrations—it has sold more than 500 *million* copies. It's *this* picture—*this* mental image of Jesus—that predominates in most of us. He's clean. He's stoic. He's respectable. He looks like he's had his eyebrows waxed. His eyes are blue and his hair's been highlighted. He's kind of a "sanitized" Jesus. He doesn't get angry. He doesn't offend. He doesn't turn over tables or scatter greedy merchants in the temple courtyards. He's the "acceptable" Jesus. He's the Jesus who doesn't upset things, challenge the status quo, or demand too much. The Sallman or "sanitized" Jesus is the Jesus that we add to our lives and it doesn't make much difference or require much change. Life pretty much moves along like it always

3. Grimes, "*The Man.*"

has, but we can always pull this Jesus out of our pocket like a lucky rabbit's foot. But the Jesus of John 2 is just *not* that kind of Jesus.

This story—the story of the "cleansing of the temple"—is told in *all* of the Gospels. Every Gospel—Matthew, Mark, Luke, and John—tells this story. There aren't a lot of stories where that is true. I mean, two of the Gospels don't even have stories about Jesus' birth. They don't all have Jesus' most famous sermon. Besides the resurrection, only one of the miracle stories is in every one of the Gospels. This must be a very important story, right? But what makes it particularly unusual is that Matthew, Mark, and Luke tell it near the end of their Gospels and toward the end of Jesus' life and ministry, while John's Gospel puts this story right at the beginning of Jesus' ministry. John tells it like it's the second thing that Jesus does once his ministry has gone public. He changes the water into wine at a wedding feast[4] and then, like a horse bolting out of the gates at the Kentucky Derby, Jesus bursts into the temple courts in Jerusalem and starts "taking names." It's like John wants us to know right from the beginning that Jesus is not some placid, stoic, milquetoast-Messiah. The "Deliverer from God" has arrived on the scene and life is going to change. Old wineskins won't do the job anymore. Systemic evil will no longer go unchallenged. Predatory practices that take advantage of the weak, poor, and marginalized must be destroyed and dismantled. You see, Jesus walked in on the most lucrative and fixed scheme of the first century. This was a scheme of which Bernie Madoff[5] would have been proud. The religious leaders of Judaism had a corner on the market and it was a monopoly. The temple was the place to make sacrifices and just *any* animal was not acceptable. You couldn't bring one from the family farm because it wouldn't be approved by the ones in the temple who made the rules. The only option was to purchase an animal from the ones who approved the animals. Of course, when there's a monopoly, there's always a "mark-up." So, people were at the mercy of the dealers when it came to animals for sacrifice. Additionally, temple-taxes had to be paid in a certain currency, and the only place to change unacceptable currency into acceptable currency was in the temple courtyards by those who controlled the currency. Like at the bank or in the customs area of the airport, exchanging currency comes with a fee, a price. In the first century in Jerusalem, it came with a heavy price. So what you see in John 2 is a God-ordained prophet—a God-sent Savior—stepping boldly into a system of evil that is

4. John 2:1–11.

5. Madoff, an investment advisor and financier, was the mastermind of a multi-billion dollar Ponzi scheme. He was arrested for securities fraud in 2008. He pled guilty in 2009 and was sentenced to 150 years in prison.

94   SECTION 3: SERMONS FOR LENT AND GOOD FRIDAY

taking advantage of the poor, abusing the oppressed, and adding insult to
the injuries of the broken. He steps in to turn the tables.

In the Gospel of Luke, the *first* thing that Jesus does after he has come
out of the wilderness of temptation is that he goes to his hometown of
Nazareth. He goes to the synagogue and he reads from the scroll of Isaiah
where it says: "The Spirit of the Lord is on me, because he has anointed me
to proclaim good news to the poor. He has sent me to proclaim freedom
for the prisoners and recovery of sight for the blind, to set the oppressed
free, to proclaim the year of the Lord's favor."[6] That's the first thing that
Jesus does in his ministry in Luke. Well, in John, right at the beginning,
Jesus is not in Nazareth and he's not in a synagogue. Rather, he's in Jerusalem in the temple courts. Instead of a scroll from Isaiah, John's Jesus has
a whip in his hand, but the message is the same. And the message is not
about "sanitizing" the temple courts. The message is about announcing the
heart and pulse of God. It's about reclaiming what God is truly about. In
the words of the prophet Micah, it's about "acting justly, loving mercy, and
walking humbly with God."[7]

When Jesus bursts into Jerusalem's temple courts, the animals begin to scatter, coins are in mid-flight, and the legs of tables are pointing
toward the sky—and you can almost hear the voice of the prophet Amos
saying: "I hate, I despise your religious feasts; I cannot stand your assemblies. Even though you bring me burnt offerings and grain offerings, I will
not accept them. Though you bring choice fellowship offerings, I will have
no regard for them."[8] As priests and religious teachers are scurrying to
safety and wondering about who this is who comes to the temple courts
with fire in his eyes, can you hear more of the words of Amos? "*Away* with
the noise of your songs! I will not listen to the music of your harps. But *let
justice roll on* like a river, *righteousness* like a never-failing stream."[9] Here
in these opening scenes of John, Jesus is announcing that he had not come
to "sanitize" or to "clean up." In fact, later in the New Testament, Jesus
preaches and teaches against the kind of "cleaning up" that the Pharisees
and religious leaders of the time were engaged in. As Jesus said, they were
"white-washed tombs."[10] They had been "sanitized" outwardly, but inside,
they were a pile of filth and bones. In a sense, when Jesus comes into the
temple, surveys the scene, and then begins to unleash the righteousness

6. Luke 4:18–19.

7. Mic 6:8.

8. Amos 5:21–22, emphasis added.

9. Amos 5:23–24, adapted.

10. Matt 23:27.

A SANITIZED AND SANITIZING JESUS   95

of God, what we see is a glimpse into the purpose of Jesus' coming and
ultimately into his death. Jesus has come to call God's people back to the
heart of God's mission—back to the reason that God has called a people to
himself—to be a blessing and to be a light to the nations.

When God chose Abraham and Sarah and told them that they would
have a child in their old age,[11] the reason for God to have a family in the
earth and the reason for them to be blessed was so that they could, in turn,
be a blessing. The writer of Hebrews captures the idea that Jesus has come for
more than just to "sanitize" our lives. This is how Hebrews says it: "Jesus suffered outside the city gate *to make the people holy* through his own blood."[12]
Holy people. Christlike people. People who love God with their whole heart
and love others with a reaching, touching, serving love.

If the temple-cleansing Jesus were to storm into your life today, what
"tables" would be overturned in you? What would happen? If you were
driven out from your routines and ways, where would that push you? Into
what places of need would you be pushed? Would you think for a moment about that co-worker who is broken and hurting? Would you call to
mind that classmate who is lonely and needy or that family member who
is devastated and distraught? What would ministry look like through you
to them? You see, Jesus has come to truly set you apart and make you holy
for his purposes in the world. He's come to free you from the power of sin
and use you to extend his love in a broken world. Is he turning some stuff
over in you today?

Amen.

11. Gen 18:10–12.

12. Heb 13:12, emphasis added.

SERMON 19[1]

Ascending from Dreams to Joy to Hope[2]

Psalm 126

Living in exile is kind of like having your teeth cleaned. It's unpleasant. It's painful. You can't wait to get out of there and when you do get out of the chair and back to your car in the parking lot, the sun is always brighter and the sky is always bluer. It's almost like a dream. When the hygienist had me leaned back, mouth wide open, with a sharp-pointy-thing scraping the most tender of areas, my mind was on other things. Between the lightning strikes of pain that were shooting throughout my body, I was dreaming of my soon-to-be freedom.

Have you ever been in a place where you dreamed of a better day and a better time? This, I think, is a common human experience and it's one that shows up in Psalm 126. Let's listen to these ancient words.

Psalm 126

This psalm, along with all the psalms numbered from 120 through 134 in our Bibles, are subtitled or identified as "songs of ascent." Many scholars believe that these songs were sung as pilgrims made their way up the hills and pathways toward the city of Jerusalem for certain festivals throughout the year. Literally, people were *ascending* or walking uphill as they were singing these songs. These psalms were for people on the move—for people walking

1. Preached at First Church of the Nazarene in Kansas City, Missouri on March 13, 2016 (Lent 5; Year C).

2. This sermon was an attempt to try something different. It was a chance to allow the setting of the text as a song of ascension to influence the structure of the sermon. The idea of "ascending"—not just physically and literally, but in a progression of ideas captured in the text—was the intent. Along the way, I had the opportunity to rebuff the prosperity gospel and to expose people to the amazing story and thought of Jurgen Moltmann.

96

ASCENDING FROM DREAMS TO JOY TO HOPE

forward and leaving footprints on the roads to the holy city. William Faulkner, an American writer from the twentieth century, described footprints as "this is where I was when I moved again."[3] We won't be climbing the hill toward Jerusalem this morning, but we are on a journey toward Holy Week and Easter. We are moving through the season of Lent and our footprints are being left as we make our way toward the cross and the tomb.

I see in this passage a pattern of "ascent" in the ideas that I want to share this morning. Beginning with the lowest or the starting point, I want to simply acknowledge with Psalm 126 that we, too, are people who dream. You have dreams and I have dreams, right? The dreams that you have today might not be the dreams that you had in the past, but we all are people who dream. About a week ago, Dawn and I went to a twentieth anniversary banquet for the school that our kids have attended here in Kansas City. It was kind of an auction and dinner to celebrate the anniversary, and one of the auction items was a collage of photographs. Each student in the second or third grade class was pictured. Each of them was holding a small chalkboard on which they had written what they wanted to be when they got older. You won't be surprised that two of the boys in the class wrote "baseball player." I once shared that dream. If you had asked me about my dreams when I was a kid, it would have involved playing second base for the Cincinnati Reds on a team like the "Big Red Machine" from the mid-1970s. My dreams from 1976 are not my dreams for 2016. *I've* changed. My *dreams* have changed. My guess is that the same is true for you. But, we are people who dream dreams.

God's people were living in exile. They had been forcibly removed from their homeland. They were defeated and in despair,[4] yet they dreamed of going home. And eventually, that dream came true or was realized through some very odd and unexpected ways. They had been overrun and removed by the "superpower" of the day which was Babylon at that time. Sometimes this period in their history is referred to as the "Babylonian exile" or "Babylonian captivity" because Babylon did it. But, what the people could have never imagined was the way that God would deliver them *out* of this exile or captivity. God used the next "superpower" of the ancient Near East—the Persians—led by a man named Cyrus. This Persian pagan became the instrument to allow God's people to return to

3. Faulkner, *Town*, 29.

4. Klein, *Israel in Exile*, 3: "Exilic Israel nevertheless was a defeated nation that had lost its independence, its land, its monarchy, and its temple. There had been abundant pain and death, and it is hard to imagine that the economy was not completely topsy-turvy. Exile meant a host of physical and socio-economic problems. But the *theological* challenges and problems strike us as much more severe."

98   SECTION 3: SERMONS FOR LENT AND GOOD FRIDAY

their homes in and around Jerusalem. The people sang: "When the Lord brought back the captives to Zion, we were like people who dreamed" (Ps 126:1). They were "home," but the home that they returned to was *not* the home that they had left. The land had been devastated. The villages had been ransacked. The temple had been demolished and re-building it was going to be a long, difficult, and contentious project. They were people who dreamed and that's certainly true of us. We have dreams for our family and for our grandchildren. We have dreams for our church and for our businesses. We're dreamers. That's a part of who we are.

But, Psalm 126 "ascends" a little higher when it says that they were also people of joy. I think the critical verse is verse 3: "The Lord has done great things for us and we are filled with joy." Their joy was grounded in the faithful goodness of God. They recognized it and remembered it. They recalled it. The reason for their joy was God's loving care for them and the source of their joy was God alone. Notice how it says that they were "*filled* with joy." In other words, it wasn't something that they generated on their own. It wasn't a self-sufficient or self-generated joy. No. It was a *gift* from God. The story of humanity is the search for joy *apart* from God. In the church, we call that sin and it is a road that leads nowhere. When the exiles came back to the land, it was very different from when they left and yet they still experienced joy. Why is that?

I was reading this week about something that psychiatrists have identified as "the Paris effect." Back in September of last year, there was an article in the *Wall Street Journal* about this. It revolved around a Japanese psychiatrist who was living in Paris back in the 1980s. While there, he witnessed something that people from Japan were experiencing when they came to the French capital. The article said that people "expected a place full of romance, beauty, and wealth. Instead, they found pavements peppered with cigarette butts and aggravated commuters in packed metro trains," and "for some, the shock was too much to bear, prompting them to seek medical help."[5] When visitors to Paris discovered that daily life was not like a movie or a perfume commercial, disappointment and sadness set in. That could have happened to the returning exiles had they not recognized, remembered, and recalled the faithful goodness of God who gives joy even in spite of difficult circumstances in life.

Joy is not the same as happiness, right? Joy runs slow and deep. It sustains. Whereas happiness can come or go with speed and the slightest change. Joy is more like a long, deep river that "keeps rollin' along"[6] and

5. Berton, "State of Paris."
6. "Ol' Man River."

ASCENDING FROM DREAMS TO JOY TO HOPE 99

happiness is more like Brush Creek[7] that fills up and empties out almost as quickly. The returning exiles were people who dreamed like us. They were people of joy because of God's faithfulness and because they knew that their joy had been given to them by God. It's *one* thing to be a person who dreams—that's great. But it's something else to be a person of joy and to experience a joy that is long-term and that remains in spite of ups and downs and difficult circumstances. There's a difference between those things. It's almost like the ideas are "ascending" in priority or in importance. We're not walking up the hill to Jerusalem singing this song, but we're thinking about what the psalm says in an "ascension-of-ideas" kind of way.

As we focus on verses 4–6, let me summarize it this way: the people who returned to the land from exile were people with hope—from people who dream to people of joy to people with hope. When the captives returned to Judah and saw their villages, they were devastated. When they returned and saw the state of the temple, they were heartbroken. When they looked onto fields and vineyards that were now overgrown and useless, they ached with pain. When the people came home to Judah, they wept. As verse 5 says, they "sowed in tears." Or, as verse 6 says, "they went out weeping." Every pain, disappointment, or obstacle wasn't resolved or made right by their return from exile. Not even close. In fact, if they had wanted *less* pain, *less* disappointment, and *less* struggle, they probably would have stayed in exile. After all, they had settled there, planted crops there, and built homes there. But instead, they returned to a desolate land with burned out villages, a temple in shambles, and fields that were uncultivated and unproductive. They began watering the soil with their own tears.

This is not triumphalism. This is not some prosperity gospel where God makes everything easy. This is not some mind game that says that problems are really illusions and disappointments are just misguided expectations or misunderstandings. The people returning from exile in Babylon are *not* "Pollyannas."[8] They knew and *saw* the long road and struggle that was ahead for them, but simultaneously, they were people with hope. It wasn't wishful thinking or a positive mental attitude. It was *confidence* in the God who had done great things for them in the past, was filling them with joy in the present, and would accompany them into the future with *hope*. Look at verse 5 again: "Those who sow in tears *will* reap with songs of joy." Verse 6: "The one who goes out weeping, carrying seed to sow, *will* return with songs of joy, carrying sheaves with him."

7. A local creek prone to flash flooding.

8. Porter, *Pollyanna*. The title of this classic work of children's literature has come to mean an excessively optimistic or unreasonably cheerful person.

He was one of the most influential theologians of the last half of the twentieth century. He burst onto the scene in the mid-1960s with his book, "The Theology of Hope." Jurgen Moltmann had come a long way. He was raised in a completely irreligious environment in Germany. He was going to be a scientist, but in 1944 he was drafted for military service and was sent to the frontlines during World War II. He took the writings of the philosopher Friedrich Neitzsche with him to read during his spare moments. He tells this story about himself. He says that in 1945, as the war was winding down and the outcome seemed obvious, he surrendered in the dark to the very first British soldier that he met. For the next two or three years, he was a POW and was transferred from camp-to-camp in Belgium and eventually to Scotland. While he was in a Belgian camp, he met some followers of Jesus and while he was there, an American chaplain gave him a New Testament with the book of Psalms included in it. He began to read. He began to converse with Christians. He began to reconsider his life and re-think his approach. In the process, Jurgen Moltmann, a German POW with no religious training in his history, childhood, or growing up years, became a follower of Jesus. His testimony was this: "I didn't find Christ; he found me." Within only twenty years from that point, Moltmann wrote his monumental book called *Theology of Hope.* He wrote: "Totally without hope one cannot live. To live without hope is to cease to live. Hell is hopelessness," he said. "It is no accident that above the entrance to Dante's hell is the inscription: 'Leave behind all hope, you who enter here.'"[9]

The good news is that, like the returning exiles, we are people who dream and people of joy and people with hop*e* because God—as 1 Peter says—has "given us *new* birth into a *living* hope through the resurrection of Jesus Christ from the dead."[10] Biblical hope is a confidence and assurance in the faithful goodness and mercy of God. The psalmist declared: "The Lord has done great things for us."[11] When we gather around the Table we are rehearsing and re-visiting the great things he's done. Ultimately and specifically, we are "rehearsing" the giving of his Son, Jesus, *in* the flesh *to* our world *on* the cross *for* our redemption. Our hope is in him. It is a *living* hope. It is a present and resurrected hope. We've ascended up the mountain to the holy place of God as his people. Here at the Table, we are people who dream, people of joy, and people with hope in the mercy and grace of God.

Amen.

9. Moltmann, *Theology of Hope,* 32.

10. 1 Pet 1:3, emphasis added.

11. Ps 126:3.

SERMON 20[1]

That was *Mine!*[2]

Jeremiah 31:31–34

Do you know the ABCs of Israel's history? It's a great way to remember a portion of the story. While Saul, David, and Solomon were the kings, there was *one* kingdom. But, after Solomon, the kingdom was divided into a "northern kingdom"—often called Israel—and into a "southern kingdom"—often called Judah. The "A" is for Assyria. Assyria was an ancient "superpower" that came in and utterly destroyed the "northern kingdom" in 722 BC. They wiped it out. The "ten lost tribes of Israel" were obliterated by Assyria. The "B" is for Babylon. Babylon is another world "superpower" that will eventually come and take the people of the "southern kingdom" into captivity. "C" is for King Cyrus of the Persians who would later release the exiles from their captivity to return to Jerusalem.

Jeremiah prophesied between the "A" and the "B." It was during one of the most difficult times in the history of God's people. Israel, the northern kingdom, had been devastated and destroyed. Judah, the southern kingdom, had tried everything to avoid destruction. They had negotiated treaties with other kingdoms and betrayed their protectors. They had rebelled against powerful nations that surrounded them. They had forsaken God and turned

1. Preached at First Church of the Nazarene in Kansas City, Missouri on March 22, 2015 (Lent 5; Year B).

2. This sermon was an opportunity to address a huge biblical and theological idea—that of sin. Multiple images and metaphors were utilized, but the heart of the message rested in the emphasis upon our own participation in sin without anyone else to blame. Additionally, the realization that what we take hold of eventually takes hold of us was crucial. The image of addiction, which is so prevalent in our world, helped convey the meaning along with the recognition that, apart from God's provision in Christ, we are powerless to free ourselves from it. I imagined that for those who were familiar with the Bible, the ABCs at the front of the sermon would prove interesting. Additionally, in a city that was excited about its baseball franchise, I anticipated that the contract language would resonate.

101

to idols. They had sought security and protection from neighboring nations led by pagan leaders. They were headed in the same direction as their northern counterpart, Israel. It was a time of spiritual darkness, desperation, and imminent desolation. Very soon, the power and might of Babylon would be unleashed and the great temple of Solomon would be destroyed. The people of Judah would be killed or be taken captive. Their homes would be dismantled. Families would be divided. Villages destroyed. But Jeremiah, the prophet, had a message from God.

Jeremiah 31:31–34

In the darkest of times, Jeremiah had a message of hope from the Lord. It wasn't a message that Jeremiah had devised. It wasn't a message that Jeremiah would even see fulfilled. And it wasn't a message that meant the immediate resolution of the people's problems or struggles. It wasn't a quick-fix. Jeremiah didn't have a magic wand. His message was a message of hope and God's faithfulness throughout a future that would inevitably involve pain and suffering. This is a message for people like us. This is a message for people who are seeking to follow Jesus in a post-Christian culture that doesn't care one bit about Jesus or his ways. One of the things that you and I must be reminded of in this kind of an environment is that God is faithful to his promises. God had established a covenant with these people. He had chosen them—not because of their strength, not because of their number, and not because of their position in the world. No, God had chosen them *because* of their weakness, their smallness, and their obscurity so that his power and might could be put on display in and through them. When the church lets go of its strength, number, and position, God just might capture it and use it for his purposes again.

God made a covenant with these small, insignificant people. Now, a covenant is not like a contract between two equal parties. It's not like what you see today when a superstar athlete signs a new contract and then another superstar signs a *bigger* one.[3] The first guy decides: "Hey, I don't like this anymore. I'm going to hold-out or not show up for training camp while I demand that my contract be re-negotiated." That's *not* what's happening here. This is not contractual. God's covenant with the people of Israel is not a situation where they can provide something that God needs. They're not a power-hitting third baseman that God's team just can't win without. That's

---

3. Baseball spring training was underway. After losing the World Series in 2014, the Kansas City Royals fans were hoping for another great year. The Royals would beat the New York Mets in the 2015 World Series.

not the situation at all. God doesn't need them. God isn't desperate to sign them to his team. God has *chosen* them because he *loves* them. Out of sheer grace and mercy, he wants to use them as a vessel to share the news of God's compassion with the world.

A large portion of the Scripture is the story of the incredible lengths to which God will go to preserve that covenant and to sustain his chosen people. There's an allusion to that in the 32nd verse and the image is that of a loving, caring parent who is protecting and looking out for a child. It says that God "took them by the hand to lead them out of Egypt." You remember when you had small children. You'd come out of the grocery store or the department store and before you'd enter the parking lot, you'd say, "Take my hand." If I had my hands full of grocery bags, I'd say, "Grab Daddy's pocket until we get to the car." Why would we *do* that? Because the parking lot can be dangerous place and because children need guidance. It can be a child's tendency to run away, to wander off into danger, and to not see all the things that *we*, as parents, see. Right? This is what God has done for his children in the covenant. His plan is to guide them, direct them, protect them from dangers, and to keep them on the path. Over and over again, the Bible tells us about God's power and the incredible miracles that he performed in order to be faithful to the covenant. When these verses say that God "took them by the hand to lead them out of Egypt," that's a sentence that summarizes chapters and chapters in the book of Exodus. This is a reference to the monumental process which included ten plagues, miraculous signs, the death of the first-born, the parting of the Sea, and the destruction of Pharaoh's army—*all* in order for God to deliver his chosen people from hundreds of years of slavery and service to the pharaohs of Egypt. God led them out of Egypt. God was caring for, preserving, and sustaining his covenant people. But in stark contrast to God's faithfulness stands the *un*faithfulness of his people. Jeremiah 31:32 says that the people "broke my covenant." Verse 34 speaks to the people's "wickedness" and "sinfulness." God's people rebelled against him. They turned to idols. They turned to the gods of their powerful neighbors and they tried to secure their own place and future without reference to the God who had chosen them, sustained them, and delivered them. They looked to other sources for their hope, strength, security, purpose, and future. They hedged their bets. They wanted God and other securities. God said "either/or" and they wanted "both/and." That is as relevant a problem today as it was two-and-a-half millennia ago. God chose *them* and they turned away to go their own way. That's their story and it's *your* story. It's *my* story. It's the story of sin. Isaiah said it this way: "We all, like sheep, have

104   SECTION 3: SERMONS FOR LENT AND GOOD FRIDAY

gone astray, *each* of us has turned to his own way."[4] Waywardness, rebellion, and sin is not somebody else's fault. No. You chose it. I chose it.

I love the story about the little girl who had a younger brother and she just loved to tease him. She liked to pick on him. Most times, it would start out as playful and fun, but then it would end up in an all-out brawl. She was bigger and so she would usually win. She'd pull his hair and kick his shins. Finally, he would run to their mother and complain about what his sister had done to him. Mom would get them together and then she would say to the little girl, "Mary, *why* have you let Satan put it into your heart to pull your brother's hair and kick his shins? Why?" The little girl thought about it for a minute and then she answered, "Pulling his hair was Satan's idea, but kicking his shins—that was mine."[5]

We *chose* sin. It wasn't somebody else's idea. We did it and we worked at it. We practiced it and as a result, we got good at it. In fact, we became a slave to it. What we thought we had chosen to do and what we thought we could choose to walk away from had now captured us and we were bound to it. What we chose and practiced now had us in its grip. That's the story of your life and my life. We abandoned the covenant. We chose lawlessness and rebellion. We demanded our inheritance and we squandered it. What seemed so attractive at the time, and what we reached for and grasped, now had us in *its* grasp. It's like an addiction. It starts out as something random or something infrequent and then it *captures* us. It takes control of us. We invited it in and now it sets up shop, rearranges the furniture, and won't leave. As Paul says in Romans: "I do not understand what I do. For what I *want* to do I do not do, but what I *hate* I do . . . For I have the desire to do what is good, but I cannot carry it out. For what I do is not the good I want to do; no, the evil I do not *want* to do—this I keep on doing."[6] Like an addiction, it's so easy to take up, but so very hard—yes, humanly *impossible*—to set down. *That's* the power of sin. The power of sin had to be broken.

We are closing in on Holy Week which begins one week from today. When you examine the Gospels, you find that they are determined to tell us the story of how God in Christ broke the power of sin. Huge portions of the Gospels are devoted to the few days leading up to Jesus' death and resurrection. Entire decades of Jesus' life are passed over in the Gospels, but the story of how he broke the power of sin and death is front and center. God, in the fullness of time—at just the right moment[7]—revealed himself

---

4. Isa 53:6, emphasis added.

5. Honor Books, *God's Little*, 83.

6. Rom 7:15, 18b-19, emphasis added.

7. Allusion to Rom 5:6.

through Christ's death on the cross and his resurrection from the dead. As a result, the powers of sin, hell, and death have been defeated in Christ. As 1 Corinthians 15 says, "The sting of death is sin, and the power of sin is the law. But thanks be to God! He gives us the victory through our Lord Jesus Christ."[8] A *new* covenant was established. It is a covenant that is written not on tablets of stone or on parchments and paper, but on the hearts and minds of his people. It is written not with chisel or ink, but with the blood of Jesus. It's the *new* covenant. That's our hope today, and it's the only hope for the world. We trust *not* in our own ingenuity, *not* in our own goodness, *not* in peace negotiations, and *not* in the next election. That's not where our hope is found. "Our hope is built on nothing less than Jesus' blood and righteousness." Let me paraphrase: "You dare not trust the sweetest frame— translation: 'anything other than God's plan revealed in Christ' but wholly lean on Jesus' name!"[9] We recall the words of Jesus as recorded in Luke 22: "'This cup is the *new covenant* in my blood, which is poured out for you.'"[10] This is the *new* covenant that is written on our hearts with the cross as the pen and the blood of Jesus as the ink. It is written, not just for our blessing and benefit, but for the *world* to see and know that the one, true God *loves* them. He has revealed that love in the life, death, and resurrection of Jesus in order to break the power of sin in their lives.

Praise be to God. Amen.

8. 1 Cor 15:56–57.
9. Mote, "Solid Rock."
10. Luke 22:20, emphasis added.

SERMON 21[1]

Hope and Change: Jesus Style[2]

Luke 19:28–40

If you hadn't noticed, Holy Week and Easter come early this year. Is there anyone willing to admit that they haven't taken all their Christmas decorations down yet? It is possible for Easter to come even earlier than March 27, which is next Sunday. The *earliest* that Easter can happen in the Gregorian calendar[3] is March 22. It happened in 1761 and 1818 and it will happen again in 2285. We won't be here to celebrate that one. The *latest* that Easter can happen is April 25 and that happened in 1886 and 1943 and will happen in 2038. Some were here for 1943 and some will celebrate in 2038. Today, this Sunday, which begins this special week in the life of the church, is often called Palm Sunday and it has been called that for a long, long time. But, more recently, the church has added *another* title for this day. It's called Passion Sunday because Holy Week is the story of Jesus' entry into Jerusalem *and* his subsequent suffering. "Passion" is a Latin word which means "suffering." I want to read the story from Luke that is the "palm" part of the story and save some of the "passion" part for later in the sermon and for our Good Friday service.

---

1. Preached at First Church of the Nazarene in Kansas City, M on March 20, 2016 (Palm Sunday; Year C).

2. "Hope and Change" had been the theme for President Obama's political campaign in 2008 when he was elected to his first term as president. In early 2016, as a new election cycle was heating up, I used the context to frame a message from Jesus in Luke 19. It was a counter-cultural message. It was a holiness message in that it was a call to becoming more like Jesus as revealed in his death on the cross. The juxtaposition of our world's view of "hope and change" with Jesus' life and view was what made this sermon meaningful.

3. Don't make me explain that.

106

HOPE AND CHANGE: JESUS STYLE

Luke 19:28–40

If you hadn't noticed that Holy Week and Easter come early this year, you have *certainly* noticed that we are in the middle of an intense, often raucous, political campaign. Don't worry. I'm not endorsing anybody today. I don't intend to start a fight. That's the *last* thing that we need. I simply want to share an observation that accompanies every political campaign. It's stated in different ways. The language that is used is altered or adapted to the time or culture. But, for the most part, over and over again—every four years and regardless of the candidates—it's the same message. It was most succinctly and recently captured back in 2008 by the Obama campaign slogan, "hope and change." You may have voted for him or not—that's not the point this morning—but the core message was "hope and change." Essentially, it's the message of every political candidate and it's the message of every revolutionary or radical leader.

When Jesus entered Jerusalem in Luke 19, the expectations of the people who waved the branches, put their clothes on the ground in front of a donkey, and shouted "Hosanna" were hope and change. They were voicing their dreams, their hopes, and their expectations that Jesus was bringing change. These people were hoping for a better day. The Romans were oppressive. The tax-collectors were ruthless. The odds were stacked against them. It was virtually impossible to get ahead. Their children were staring at the same outcome or even worse than they were. The people lined up along the pathway leading to Jerusalem and they watched this man who had healed some of them, fed many of them, and taught most of them. He had confounded them with his wisdom and understanding. Now they shouted this word, "Hosanna." It was a cry that was born in the belly of hope. We sing it on days like this. The kids come through waving the branches to help us remember and celebrate what day it is. But the word "Hosanna" itself is a cry. It's a prayer from people in need of rescue and deliverance. If you were living in their time, if you spoke their language, and if you fell out of the boat on the Sea of Galilee, the word that you would scream is "Hosanna."

A great illustration of this is in Psalm 116 where the psalmist says: "The cords of death entangled me, the anguish of the grave came upon me; I was overcome by trouble and sorrow. Then I called on the name of the Lord: 'O Lord, hosanna!'—or 'save me!'[4] Simultaneously with this cry for help, the people along the streets waving the branches and shouting "hosanna" were also, in some way, indicating that they believed that Jesus was the answer to their prayers. They were shouting, praising, and acknowledg-

4. Psalm 116:3–4.

108   SECTION 3: SERMONS FOR LENT AND GOOD FRIDAY

ing that Jesus was their hope. He embodied their hope of a better day—a
new day. They harbored a hope that they would not have to continue to
live the way that they had been living. In order for that hope to be realized,
there had to be change.

But the story of Holy Week is the story of a people who cried for hope
and wanted change, however, it was not the kind of change that Jesus came to
bring. That's essentially what we mark, re-live, and remember during this special week of the year. Over this next week, we'll be reminded of changes that
God in Christ brought *about* or shined the light *upon*, but the people rejected.
Wednesday night, we'll gather for a Seder meal, and we'll think about, recall,
and recite the many ways that God has been faithful to his people and to us
throughout the centuries. In many ways, it's a rehearsal of something that we
often struggle against and that needs to change. It might be summarized as
a change from the illusion of self-sufficiency to the acknowledgment of utter
dependence upon God. Can you think of a change that is more radical than
that? The Seder meal and service, which draws from the story of the Passover, is a story that *defines* dependence upon God.[5] God's chosen, but captive,
people were instructed to put blood on the doorposts of their homes. The
"angel of death" would "pass over" them if they followed God's instructions.
They were utterly and completely dependent upon God and God's mercy.
They were slaves in Egypt. They couldn't free themselves or liberate themselves. They had no hope outside of the graciousness, presence, and power
of God who would do things for them that they could not do for themselves.
Part of the change that the story of Holy Week proclaims is that we are *not*
self-sufficient. We *cannot* "pull ourselves up by our bootstraps." We are not capable of "making our own way" and being "self-made" people. In our culture,
and in the current political environment, can you imagine someone making
that part of their stump speech or political platform? Can you imagine? But
this is at the heart of the story of Holy Week.

On Thursday night, we'll gather here in the sanctuary for a time of corporate worship revolving around the story of Jesus and his disciples in the
upper room of Jerusalem on the night that Jesus was betrayed. We'll share
communion together at the conclusion of the service. But the part of the
story that I want to highlight this morning, because it speaks to a changed
way of thinking and living, is the part of the story that happened *during* the
meal that they shared together. Remember? Typically, there was a servant
who, as the disciples gathered and entered the home, would have washed
their feet in preparation for the meal. As you know, the streets of the first
century were filthy. The streets served a variety of purposes including being

5. Exod 12.

the sewer system. While they were eating, Jesus pointed out what everybody already knew. Nobody's feet had been washed that night. So Jesus took a basin of water and a towel and proceeded to do for the disciples what none of them were willing to do for each other. You see, washing dirty feet was the lowest of the low. It was the job that no one wanted. The change that Jesus modeled and proclaimed was that life is best lived with an approach of humility rather than hubris. What a change. When we hear about "hope and change" in our world, is *this* the kind of change that they're talking about? I don't hear about or see modeled lives of humility, but I hear about and see lots of hubris. Of course, Jesus modeled this at other times than just in the upper room. Even the way that Jesus *entered* Jerusalem was an indication that Jesus was not going to bring what the people wanted or expected. Jesus came riding a humble, peaceful animal as opposed to entering like a militaristic revolutionary on the back of a stallion. The change that Jesus embodied was the call to humility and the rejection of hubris. This is a change that cuts across the grain of our culture and of our own nature. Only God, in the power of his Spirit, can actualize this change in your life and mine, and it's part of the story of Holy Week.

Then, of course, on Friday evening—Good Friday—we will gather for our traditional "service of shadows." As you might expect, the biggest change and the most counter-cultural, hard-to-grasp, mysterious change that Jesus brought about is that "all things are made new"[6] through his self-surrendering sacrifice at the cross. It was sacrifice rather than conquest. As you know from the story of Holy Week, when it became obvious to the people that this way—the way of suffering and death—was what Jesus would choose, the shouts of the people changed from "hosanna" to "crucify him."[7] The shouts moved from a prayer for salvation to a shout of death and violence. Politicians, change agents, and radical revolutionaries are always proclaiming the message of "hope and change." It may show up in slightly different terminology or expressions, but the message is always the same.

Holy Week is *also* about hope and change, but it's a hope grounded in the faithfulness and goodness of God. It's about counter-intuitive and counter-cultural change that Jesus modeled in humility and proclaimed in death. It's a change that looks like utter dependence rather than grasping for self-sufficiency. It's a change that views all of life from the perspective of humility rather than from hubris or pride. It's a change that wins by surrendering and sacrifice rather than by killing and violence. The story of Holy Week is that death and sin are defeated by the dying and rising of Christ. We've entered

6. Allusion to 2 Cor 5:17.

7. Mark 15:14.

into this special week which is like no other week in the entire year. It marks the message of "hope and change"—Jesus style.

I'm challenged by the writing of David Buttrick on this issue. He wrote:

> To step from Palm Sunday immediately to Easter Day retains the note of triumph we crave. The truth is that we are embarrassed by the crucified Christ. For if Jesus on the cross is the revealing of God, then the church may be called to a very different social role, namely, to suffer and die for the world . . . What if we were to stand before the cross of Christ and confess that there, there on Calvary, we see the full revelation of God's essential character? What then?[8]

I think the answer to the question, "what then?," is a prayer. It's a prayer that asks to be changed and to become more and more like Jesus. It's a prayer to be filled with his love, his humility, and his self-sacrificing ways. For the church, the place to pray that prayer is around the Table of the Lord. So, we come in humility to receive the bread and the cup and to be filled and empowered by the love of God. We come to confess our utter and complete dependence upon God. We come to reject any illusions that we might have of self-sufficiency or independence. We come to be shaped by the cross and the love that is revealed there as Jesus lays down his life for his friends and for the world. Yes. Jesus comes to Jerusalem to proclaim "hope and change," but it's not *of* this world. It's Jesus-style "hope and change" that is revealed in the cross.

Amen.

---

8. Buttrick, *Mystery and Passion*, 127.

SERMON 22[1]

Songs, Swarms, and Love[2]

Psalm 118:1–29

Did anybody else read the *Guinness Book of World Records* when they were a kid? I loved that stuff. There were photographs of the man with the longest beard and the woman with the longest fingernails. It was fascinating and crazy stuff. You may not know that the Guinness people have identified the three most popular songs in the English language and *none* of them are by Elvis. Number three is "For He's a Jolly Good Fellow," which is probably fading in popularity. Number two is "Auld Lang Syne," which is kind of funny since the title is not even English. You won't be surprised that number one is "Happy Birthday to You"—the song that is sung most often in the English language.[3]

This is Holy Week and we'll sing a lot of songs during these days and in our special services. But, we also should pay attention to the songs that were sung during the original Holy Week. Of course, the songbook for God's people over many centuries has been the book of Psalms. I invite you to turn to Psalm 118.

---

1. Preached at First Church of the Nazarene in Kansas City, Missouri on March 29, 2015 (Palm Sunday; Year B).

2. What made this sermon interesting, I think, was trying to move Psalm 118 from interpreting Palm Sunday to also helping interpret other events in Holy Week. As I made these discoveries in my own preparation, I was excited to share them with my people and emphasize that God's work in Christ was an expression of his love for us and for all.

3. The "Happy Birthday" song.

111

SECTION 3: SERMONS FOR LENT AND GOOD FRIDAY

Psalm 118:1–29

The lectionary assigns this passage to *this* day and it's virtually impossible to read it without hearing verse 26 as the "song" that the people sang as Jesus entered the gates of Jerusalem on that first Palm Sunday. There are only a few stories, teachings, or sayings that appear in all four of the Gospels. There are many that appear in *three* of the four, but not that many in all four. However, this "song" that the people sang as Jesus rode into the city on a donkey appears in *each* of the four Gospels. Psalm 118:26—"Blessed is he who comes in the name of the Lord"—is quoted or adapted in some way. Now in Luke, the word "he" is changed to "king"—"Blessed is the *king* who comes in the name of the Lord"—but, even there, clearly this is a quotation from Psalm 118. The people sang other things as Jesus rode into the city. They sang "Hosanna," which is a word that means "save us." My guess is that their song was sung to a blatantly patriotic tune with a snare drum and a brass section—maybe a first century John Philip Souza-type song. The people waving the branches and singing the songs were expecting a "revolutionary"—the leader of a coup that would topple Roman authority, at least in their little part of the empire.

We're not *that* far removed from similar kinds of hope and expectations these days. The internet buzzes with stories, cartoons, and dreams of the next leader who will take us back to some glorious heritage that has been lost. The story gets perpetuated when presidential candidates announce their plans in a packed auditorium on the largest of Christian campuses.[4] Of course, presidents and presidential candidates must conclude their speeches with the seemingly obligatory mantra: "and may God bless these United States of America."

The people of Jerusalem around 29 AD were seeking a solution and singing a song that was in direct contradiction to the plan and design of God in Christ. Of course, that would only become clear later in the week and later in the story. Much hinges on how you understand that word "blessed"—"Blessed is he who comes in the name of the Lord." If "blessed" means revolution, conquest, and power, then the song is misguided. But if "blessed" means suffering, poured out, and expended, *that's* a different story. But Psalm 118 doesn't just show up when Jesus rides into the city. Psalm 118 shows up when Jesus has gathered in the upper room for the Last Supper with his disciples. The scene is familiar to many of us. We see the famous Da Vinci painting with Jesus at the center of the table and six disciples on each side. Some are engaged in conversation while others are leaning

---

4. Donald Trump announced his candidacy at Liberty University in Lynchburg, Virginia.

SONGS, SWARMS, AND LOVE 113

into or away from Jesus. If that's the picture of the Last Supper in your mind, then *throw it out*. It's a beautiful painting. It's world-famous and all, but it's just not an accurate portrayal. It reflects less of the first century and more of the fifteenth century when it was painted. The first century setting was a meal. It was long and drawn-out with multiple courses at a leisurely pace. It was supposed to be *preceded* by everyone's feet being washed, but the disciples weren't willing to do that ugly, demeaning job. So somewhere during the meal, Jesus did it for them and used it as a teaching moment about humility, servanthood, and the kingdom of God. There were prayers, lessons, and what sounded like coded messages. There was anxiousness, fear, and talk of betrayal. Then there was the final cup of wine with bread and Jesus' famous words of institution where he says: "Take and eat; this is my body." Also, "This is the blood of the covenant, which is poured out for many for the forgiveness of sins."[5]

Many of us are familiar with all of those parts of the story, but there were songs and singing, as well. Scholars believe that in all likelihood the 113th and 114th Psalms were sung *before* the meal began. They were songs about how the Lord exalts the lowly and then about how God delivered his people from Egyptian captivity—the story of the Exodus. There was singing before the meal, but then there was singing at the conclusion of the meal as well. Most scholars believe that Psalms 115 through 118 were sung by Jesus and his disciples just before they left the upper room and went out to the Mount of Olives and to the garden of Gethsemane. Remember? Part of Psalm 118—"blessed is he who comes in the name of the Lord"—was sung as Jesus entered Jerusalem on the first Palm Sunday and *now*, on the night that Jesus was betrayed and at the conclusion of the Last Supper, Psalm 118, in its entirety, was sung by Jesus and his closest followers. Do you think as the events of Jesus' betrayal, arrest, trial, torture, and crucifixion happened over the next few hours that the lyrics from Psalm 118 came to the minds of Jesus' disciples? When Jesus prayed in the garden and he wept with such intensity as he faced his imminent death, did the words of Psalm 118 linger in his thoughts, "In my anguish I cried to the Lord, and he answered by setting me free. The Lord is with me; I will not be afraid. What can human beings do to me?"[6] When he cried out in the garden and prayed—"Lord, not *my* will, but *yours* be done"[7]—was that when the Father "set him free"? When the garden of Gethsemane was transformed from a place of prayer to a place of conflict as Judas betrayed his friend

5. Matt 26:26 and 28.
6. Ps 118:5–6.
7. Luke 22:42.

114   SECTION 3: SERMONS FOR LENT AND GOOD FRIDAY

into the hands of Roman soldiers, did more words from this psalm come to mind?—"They swarmed around me like bees."[8] Anybody ever been swarmed by bees? It's an awful and painful thing.

After dragging Jesus from place to place and trying to get him convicted on some "crime" that he had not committed, eventually he was sentenced to be beaten. This rebel or revolutionary was going to be taught a lesson by the power of the Roman Empire. Only as the soldiers abused him and whipped him with a cat of nine tails did Jesus lean on lyrics which they had sung just a few hours ago: "The Lord is my strength and my song; he has become my salvation."[9] Of course, eventually the bruised and beaten Jesus was brought before the people. Pilate *wanted* to release him, but the crowds called for his crucifixion. They wanted this preacher and healer executed, not primarily for what he had done but, more so, for what he had *not* done. He had *not* led the Messianic-revolution against Rome and succeeded. He had missed his chance and now he would be ground up by the empire that they wanted him to overthrow. With the shouts of "crucify, crucify" ringing in his ears, did Jesus re-sing the song?—"The stone the builders rejected has become the capstone; the Lord has done this, and it is marvelous in our eyes."[10] If he did, it would not have been the first time. The Gospel of Matthew tells us a story where Jesus offers one of those pesky parables.[11] He teaches about God's kingdom and points accusations at the religious leaders of his time. In this particular parable, he tells a story about a landowner who leased out his land but at harvest time would send a representative to collect his fees. Over and over again, the tenants would beat or kill the landowner's representatives. Finally, he decided to send his own son and the tenants—as Jesus said in the parable, "took him and threw him out of the vineyard and killed him." Earlier in the chapter, Matthew tells us that Jesus is doing this teaching in the temple courts and is surrounded by the chief priests and elders. Jesus asks them: "What will the landowner do to those tenants who treated his representatives and his son the way that they did?" The chief priests and elders answer with indignation: "He'll bring those wretches to a wretched end." And *then*, after a moment of silence and Jesus allowing their answer to settle in, he quotes from the 118th Psalm—"The stone the builders rejected has become the capstone." Psalm 118 was sung in the streets of Jerusalem as Jesus entered the city. Psalm 118 was sung in the upper room of the Last Supper just before Jesus' betrayal

8. Ps 118:12.
9. Ps 118:14.
10. Ps 118:22.
11. Matt 21:33–46.

SONGS, SWARMS, AND LOVE

in the garden. Psalm 118 can interpret the events of Jesus' arrest, trial, and suffering even as they were happening.

What about utilizing Psalm 118 now to look back on the life, death, and resurrection Jesus? Yes, in the primary affirmation that gets repeated over and over in this psalm there is the primary message of the cross. In the words that *begin* the psalm and in the words that *conclude* the psalm, there is this reason. Listen again to the opening verses: "Give thanks to the Lord, for he is good; his *love* endures forever. Let Israel say: 'His *love* endures forever.' Let the house of Aaron say: 'His *love* endures forever'" (emphasis added). Today, let those who reverence the Lord—like the folks gathered in the sanctuary of Kansas City First Church on Palm Sunday 2015—let them say, "His *love* endures forever." Then there is the final verse of this psalm. Does it sound familiar?—"Give thanks to the Lord, for he is good; his *love* endures forever."[12] Is there any doubt what this psalm is truly about? It's about the faithful, sacrificial, life-giving, enduring love of God. That is what this week—and the story that is captured in it—is about. The story of Jesus that culminates in his death on the cross and his resurrection from the dead is a story about God's enduring, faithful, life-giving love for you, me, and for the world. If you don't hear anything else that I say this morning, hear this: God loves you and has revealed the depth of his love in the death of Jesus at the cross. You might ask: "How so?"

The Bible and the church answer: because his death was for *your* sins. His death was in *your* place. His death was what you and I deserved but "the punishment that brought us peace was upon *him*"[13] as the prophet Isaiah says it. Instead of receiving what we deserve, we receive God's grace—his unearned favor and care. That's why we call this *good* news, and it's why the day of Jesus' death is called *Good* Friday. There's no other reason but the love of God for folks like you and me. When we gather around the table to celebrate the eucharist, we're doing exactly what Psalm 118 says because *eucharisteo* is a Greek word for "giving thanks." Listen to Psalm 118:29 one more time: "Give thanks to the Lord, for he is good; his *love* endures forever" (emphasis added).

Amen.

---

12. Ps 118:29, emphasis added.

13. Isa 53:5, emphasis added.

SERMON 23[1]

Good Friday Meditation 2016[2]

Isaiah 53:12

One of the benefits of using the same Scripture texts, the same songs, and the same readings year after year for this special service is that I'm given the opportunity to think about and offer some reflections on very specific portions or phrases in the Scripture. This evening, my attention is drawn to the reading which comes from Isaiah 53:12—particularly, the phrase where it says that "he poured out himself to death." Different translations say—"he poured out his *soul* unto death" or "he poured out his *life* unto death." Not to get too literalistic or even graphic but, what usually "pours out" of people that leads to their death is their blood. Clearly, the suffering and death of Jesus was an ugly, painful, brutal, and bloody event. The church has always sung songs about the "blood of Jesus." Songwriters for centuries have known and written about it because the Scripture speaks of it. It's a vital part of the story. Whether they were hemophobic or not, they wrote about the "power of the blood," or the saving qualities of the blood. Charles Wesley wrote: "And can it be that I should gain an interest in the Savior's *blood*?"[3] The famous hymn, "The Solid Rock," begins with these lyr-

---

1. Preached at First Church of the Nazarene in Kansas City, Missouri on March 25, 2016 (Good Friday).

2. The annual Good Friday service in this congregation was a form of the Tenebrae service, sometimes referred to as a "service of shadows." It was a service of Scripture readings, congregational responses, songs, and the extinguishing of several candles throughout the course of the service. Toward the end of the service, the sanctuary was almost completely dark with only the Christ candle burning. To conclude the service, the Christ candle was blown out and removed from the sanctuary in silence. It was a way of symbolizing the death and burial of Jesus. This meditation from Isaiah 53 happened about two-thirds of the way through the service.

3. Wesley, "And Can It Be?," emphasis added.

116

ics: "My hope is built on nothing less than Jesus' *blood* and righteousness."[4] In our Nazarene hymnal, there's a song with four verses and a chorus that asks a question. In one form or another, the question is asked no less than fourteen times in that one song: "Are you washed in the *blood* of the Lamb?"[5] The story of Holy Week, and particularly Good Friday, is a story about the "pouring out of Jesus' blood," of his life.

In April of 2015, there was an article in *Christianity Today* magazine about the *physical* qualities of blood and the *spiritual* work that is associated with the blood of Jesus. Let me quote from that article:

> Blood nourishes. Blood eliminates toxins. Blood protects us from pathogens. White blood cells sacrifice themselves. Blood heals our wounds. Blood identifies us. Blood unites us. Meanwhile, Christ's blood justifies, redeems, reconciles, sanctifies, cleans, frees, ransoms, bring peace, and unites us. There is not an aspect of the work of Christ that the New Testament does not connect to his blood.[6]

Soon, in the garden, Jesus will sweat drops of blood.[7] After he is arrested, very quickly the soldiers will beat him, flog him, and press a crown of thorns onto his head. All of this will involve significant loss of blood. As Jesus carries the cross through the streets of Jerusalem, his blood will be poured out along the way. Once he is pinned to the Roman tool of execution, in the end, his side will be pierced and out will flow a mixture of water and blood. The Scripture, the story, the church, and the hymnody will not allow you and me to get to Easter Sunday celebration without being confronted by the fact that Jesus "poured out his life—his blood—unto death." The good news even on this special Friday is found in the lyrics of William Cowper: "Dear dying Lamb, Thy precious blood / Shall never lose its pow'r, / Till all the ransomed Church of God / Be saved, to sin no more."[8]

He poured out his life unto death for you and for me and for the world. Amen.

---

4. Mote, "Solid Rock," emphasis added.

5. Hoffman, "Are You Washed?," emphasis added.

6. Olsen, "There's Still Power," 24.

7. This is a reference to one of the Scripture readings that would be read in the service shortly after the sermon was concluded.

8. Cowper, "There is a Fountain."

SERMON 24[1]

Good Friday Meditation 2015[2]

John 10:11

In the responsive reading that immediately preceded the hymn that we've just sung, there were frequent references to sheep. Most all of the references come from the writings of the prophet, Isaiah: "All we like sheep have gone astray . . ."[3] "Like a lamb that is led to slaughter . . ."[4] "Like a sheep that before its shearers is silent . . ."[5] Over and over again, and in many other places throughout the Scriptures, there are references to sheep and shepherds. For *most* of us—myself included—these images and practices are as foreign as raising emus or herding cats. It's just not familiar to us. I feel a bit like the pastor who discovered that not far from his church was a huge, modern, sheep farming operation. He had read about it in the newspaper and so he called to see if he could visit. Maybe he could have a conversation with someone about what it's like to be a present-day shepherd. He, of course, thought that this would help him in his understanding of the Scripture, his preparation

---

1. Preached at First Church of the Nazarene in Kansas City, Missouri on March 22, 2015 (Good Friday).

2. The annual Good Friday service in this congregation was a form of the Tenebrae service, sometimes referred to as a "service of shadows." It was a service of Scripture readings, congregational responses, songs, and the extinguishing of several candles throughout the course of the service. Toward the end of the service, the sanctuary was almost completely dark with only the Christ candle burning. To conclude the service, the Christ candle was blown out and removed from the sanctuary in silence. It was a way of symbolizing the death and burial of Jesus. One of the quotes from Troeger's story has been slightly adapted to fit my own speech patterns.

3. Isa 53:6.

4. Isa 53:7a

5. Isa 53:7b.

118

of sermons, and in providing pastoral care to his people. Tom Troeger, an author and preacher, tells this story.[6]

The sheep-herder welcomed the pastor to the ranch and took him out in the vast grasslands to show him the grazing sheep and to explain to him the challenges and difficulties of raising them. One of the most common frustrations was finding lost sheep—sheep that had wandered off from the flock. When that happened, the farmer would grab his cell phone and call his workers. Each one would take their pick-up truck to a certain area of the ranch. Each worker would drive around their portion of the ranch until one of them found the sheep, put it in their truck, and returned it to the group. He then told the pastor something surprising. He said, "If that same sheep wanders off a *second* time, we activate the same search, but once the animal is found, it's not returned to the flock. Rather, it's taken straight to the slaughter house. We simply can't expend the time-resources and the fuel-resources to keep searching for a sheep that is obviously prone to wandering off. It's just not *efficient* for us to do that." Troeger wrote: "Sheep beware: wander twice and the shepherd slaughters you because it is the efficient thing to do!"[7]

The story that you are about to hear[8]—maybe for the umpteenth time—is not a story about efficiency. This is a story about extravagance. It's about the extravagant grace and sacrifice of a loving and merciful God. Jesus himself said: "The *good* shepherd lays down his life for the sheep."[9] No one takes his life from him, but Jesus lays it down of his own accord and within his Father's plan for each and every sheep that has gone astray many more times than twice. The drama of Christ's betrayal, arrest, and death is a painful, brutal, blood-stained story and it's *not* about efficiency. It's about the extravagant grace of God for *you*, for *me*, and for every human being who has ever lived or *will* ever live. Listen closely to the story because this story is for a sheep like you.

Amen.

6. Troeger, *Sermon Sparks*, 60.

7. Troeger, *Sermon Sparks*, 60.

8. This was a reference to the Scripture readings in the remainder of the service which will tell the story of Jesus' suffering, crucifixion, and death.

9. John 10:11, emphasis added.

SERMON 25[1]

Good Friday Meditation 2014[2]

Isaiah 53:5

"By his wounds, we are healed"[3]—this phrase that was a part of our reading—is from the prophet Isaiah. The verses that precede and follow are some of the most familiar verses in the Old Testament. That's true partly because they are referenced and sometimes even quoted in the New Testament to point to the death of Jesus. All of that to say: the writers of the New Testament saw the preaching of Isaiah *fulfilled* in the crucifixion of Jesus. There is little, if any, doubt about that. But, what does it mean for us to affirm "by his wounds, we are healed"? When you step back and gain a little distance from it, it's a bit of an odd thought. Typically, wounds are in need of healing. Or, we go to the wound care clinic because they are not healing properly. But the idea that "wounds" are the avenue or the means of healing is almost backwards. It's at least counterintuitive. It's strange, even mysterious.

"By *his* wounds"—by the wounds of Jesus on a Roman tool of execution almost two thousand years ago which is marked annually on this day which somehow the church has deemed as "good"—by *his* wounds, we are

1. Preached at First Church of the Nazarene in Kansas City, Missouri on April 18, 2014 (Good Friday).

2. The annual Good Friday service in this congregation was a form of the Tenebrae service, sometimes referred to as a "service of shadows." It was a service of Scripture readings, congregational responses, songs, and the extinguishing of several candles throughout the course of the service. Toward the end of the service, the sanctuary was almost completely dark with only the Christ candle burning. To conclude the service, the Christ candle was blown out and removed from the sanctuary in silence. It was a way of symbolizing the death and burial of Jesus. Toward the end of the meditation, I made reference to a senseless shooting at a Jewish community center in the Kansas City area and the recent invasion of the Crimean peninsula in Ukraine by the Russian army. At that time, they needed no further elaboration.

3. Isa 53:5.

120

GOOD FRIDAY MEDITATION 2014

healed. When Isaiah says "his wounds," is that some kind of shorthand or code for Christ's death on the cross *in* our place, *for* our sins, and to reveal God's love for us?

Yes—if that's what is meant by "his wounds," then, yes, that *is* and will *always* be the means and provision for our healing. But, what does healing entail? What does that mean? Is it simply to be forgiven of sins? Can it be minimized to some crass image of a boarding pass or an admission ticket to heaven? What does it mean to be healed by the wounds—by the sacrificial death—of Jesus?

In a time of hate-crimes here,[4] and Russian aggression over there,[5] we must recognize what Stanley Hauerwas says: "Jesus is no less political than Caesar, but he rules not at the head of an army but from a cross."[6] Healing doesn't mean living without aches and pains. Healing isn't an exemption from suffering. Healing, by the gracious work of God, is identification with the crucified Christ. It is empowerment to respond to hate with love. It is enablement to confront darkness with light. Healing is God-given and grace-filled submission to the Jesus-way—the way of humility, suffering, and sacrifice. It is the way of the cross. And so, on this "night of shadows," let us move through the increasing darkness, but let us know assuredly, see clearly, and affirm with courage that "by his wounds, we are healed."

Amen.

4. A man with white supremacist views entered a Jewish Community center and a separate Jewish retirement center in Overland Park, Kansas and shot and killed three people on April 13, 2014.

5. Undercover Russian forces invaded the Crimean peninsula on February 27, 2014.

6. Hauerwas, *Without Apology,* 59.

Section 4

Sermons for Easter Sunday, the Easter Season, and Pentecost

SERMON 26[1]

Darkness, Confusion, and Seven Words[2]

Luke 24:1–12

$517 million in the *first* weekend. That was the world-wide ticket sales for *Star Wars: The Force Awakens*. It was the largest opening weekend for a movie—ever. Some of you waited in line for hours to see it and others don't know what I'm talking about. Someone from the *New York Times* asked a film studies professor why it was such a big hit. Why was it so successful? You may have your own answer. But here is hers. She said: "The studios finally seem to be remembering, after years of over-reliance on visual effects, that moviegoers like a *story*. It can be a story we are *familiar* with. It can be a *serialized* story. But give us . . . please! . . . we're begging you . . . a *story* of some kind!"[3] Friends, I want to read to you, this morning, the most profound, life-transforming, world-changing story ever told.

Luke 24:1–12

There are three things that I want you to notice about this story and the first is this: the story begins in the dark. Luke says that "very early in the morning" the women make their way to the tomb. They had a job to do that wasn't quite finished yet. And, we *all* know that if you want something done and done right, then you should ask a busy woman to do it. Am I right?

---

1. Preached at First Church of the Nazarene in Kansas City, Missouri on March 27, 2016 (Easter Sunday; Year C).

2. The value of this sermon was the overlaying of the Easter story with our own story and the conclusion which tried to capture the passion and excitement of Easter Sunday celebration. I ended the sermon with the particular phrase, "alive forever, amen," because the congregation's choir followed the sermon and concluded the service with a song that repeats that phrase on several occasions.

3. Barnes, "Star Wars," emphasis added.

125

126   SECTION 4: EASTER SUNDAY, THE EASTER SEASON, AND PENTECOST

Remember, now that Jesus had been executed on Friday afternoon and darkness descended on the scene. His body had to be prepared for burial and the Sabbath was getting ready to begin. The job had to be done before sunset. So they did the best that they could, as quickly as they could, with all the care that they could muster in the midst of their grief. They put him in a borrowed tomb because he had no possessions of his own. Then, they waited and waited and then they waited some more. The sun set and rose. It set and rose again, but the atmosphere, regardless of whether it was mid-day or mid-night, was *darkness*. The story begins in darkness.

The truth is that your story, my story, and the story of everyone begins in darkness. I'm not talking about physically. I'm not referring to that in-utero-darkness as we are growing and preparing to be born. What I'm talking about is the darkness of sin that *each* of us participates in and chooses for ourselves. Sin is an equal-opportunity controller. No one is exempt. No one can opt out. All of us and each of us has willingly plunged into the darkness of sin. You and I don't need to be reminded this week, in the aftermath of the Brussels bombing,[4] that the darkness pervades the entire world. We *cannot* excuse ourselves simply because we know that all the violence, pain, suffering, famine, and sickness in the world is *not* because of radical Islamic terrorism. We have enough in our own city and all around us that we can't blame it on somebody else. No. The story and *our* story begin in darkness.

Then the story moves from darkness to confusion. Not just here in Luke, but when you read the other Gospel accounts, it's very difficult to get a clear and precise picture of *exactly* what happened and when. The women arrive at the tomb and find something that they didn't expect. The stone is rolled away and the tomb is empty except for the fact that there are two "men in clothes that gleamed like lightning"[5] there, or a "young man dressed in a white robe,"[6] or maybe there was just one angel.[7] It depends on which gospel you're reading. Of course, Mary is crying at the time. Maybe she's not seeing clearly through her tears. Obviously, she mistakes Jesus for the gardener. Anyway, they hurry back to tell the disciples about what they've seen but their "words seemed to them like nonsense," Luke says in Luke 24:11. The word that gets translated as "nonsense" is the Greek word, *leros,* from which we get words like "delirious" or "delirium." The disciples didn't just jump to believing what the women were telling them. As one preacher put it, "If you

4. On March 22, 2016, three bombs were detonated by radical Islamist suicide bombers. Thirty-five people were killed and over three hundred were injured.

5. Luke 24:4.

6. Mark 16:5.

7. Matt 28:5.

DARKNESS, CONFUSION, AND SEVEN WORDS

don't find resurrection at least a little hard to believe, you probably aren't taking it very seriously."[8] The thing that strikes me about the story is that there was this confusion, initial disbelief, and differences in details. There doesn't seem to be any attempt to hype up the story, to embellish the story, or to make the story more convincing or overwhelming. Frederick Buechner says, "If the Gospel writers had wanted to tell it in a way to convince the world that Jesus indeed rose from the dead, they would presumably have done it with all the skill and fanfare that they could muster. [But] Here there is no . . . fanfare. They seem to be telling it simply the way it was."[9]

Your story and my story involves confusion, uncertainty, and sometimes running this way and that after things or experiences that we think will satisfy the craving for God and for meaning with which we've been created. My guess is that we've tried to embellish our stories. We've tried to make them appear better, bigger, more successful, or more whatever than they really are. Yet God is not fooled or mocked. God sees us simply and clearly. He sees us the way that we really *are*—without embellishment, exaggeration, photoshop, or a padded resume. God sees through to the heart and to the reality in your life and mine. He knows where we are and what we need. He knows the pain we experience, along with the frustrations and struggles that impact our lives. God knows that our story begins in darkness—begins in sin—and moves into confusion and into the search to fill the void in our lives. God *knows* that. That is why God sent Jesus in the flesh into our world. That's why God revealed himself clearly and powerfully in the life, death, and resurrection of Jesus, the Christ and Savior. It was because "he so *loved* the world that he *gave* his only Son."[10] A loving God gave his Son lovingly and sacrificially to save the world and to free each of us from sin and the selfishness that seeks to destroy us. As the old song says, "Jesus paid it all, / All to him I owe; / Sin had left a crimson stain, / Jesus washed it white as snow."[11]

John Ortberg tells a story about when he and his family were in southern California for the graduation of one of their children. As a part of all the commencement activities, they were invited to a smaller gathering of alumni, donors, and special guests—about fifty people. At that gathering, the president of the university brought out three of the graduating students and told their stories. Each of them was headed to India for two years to serve and work among the poorest of the poor. The president and those gathered wanted to commission them and pray for them. But then, the

8. Lose, "If It's Not."

9. Buechner, "Easter."

10. John 3:16, emphasis added.

11. Hall, "Jesus Paid it All."

president also revealed that someone wanted to bless these students in a completely unexpected and undeserved way. The president said, "There is somebody you do not know—an anonymous donor—who is so moved by what you're doing that he has given a gift to this university in your name and on your behalf." He invited the first student to the platform and said, "You are forgiven your student debt of $105,000." She started to cry. He invited the next student: "You are forgiven your debt of $70,000." More crying. The last student came: "You too are forgiven your debt of $130,000." By this time, *everyone* was crying. As Ortberg says it: "They were ambushed by grace . . . blown away that somebody would pay *their* debt!"[12]

That's part of what Jesus did for us through his death on the cross. It's the story of grace. Into the story of darkness and confusion comes grace—God's mercy and power at work. It is the greatest announcement in all of history. In Luke 24, in the English translation that I read this morning, it's only seven words: "He is not here. He has risen." Depending on the translation and the language into which it is translated, the Bible has between 750,000 and 800,000 words. Some of them are more familiar than others. Frankly, some of them are more important than others. Some of them have been memorized by some of you and others you might not even recognize. But, if you had to pick out only seven—this is where you should start. They give meaning to everything else that is spoken, written, and that happens: "He is not here"—meaning "confined to the tomb," "dead in the grave," or meaning "lifeless and powerless and without hope." No. "He is not here. He has risen." He has risen to forgive your sins, to indwell your life, to change your ways of thinking and living, and to empower your service for his kingdom. "He is not here. He has risen." He has risen to pay your debt, to ambush you with grace, to free you from the clutches and chains of sin, and to make you holy and pleasing to God. He has risen. He has risen to redeem all of creation. He has risen to bind up the brokenhearted, to set the captives free, and to fashion for his service a mighty multitude of his children. "He is not here. He has *risen*," meaning he has conquered hell, death, and the grave. He is the victor over all the enemies that would harm us and defeat us. He reigns as Lord of Lords and King of kings and he will come again to gather his bride to himself.

He has risen and he's alive and alive forevermore.

Amen and amen.

12. Ortberg, "Anonymous Donor."

SERMON 27[1]

Bunnies, Words, and Degrees[2]

John 20:1–18

"He is risen. **He is risen indeed.**"[3]

Easter is the highest and holiest day on the Christian calendar, but it is often misunderstood. Poke your head into the neighborhood Walmart and the biggest displays are full of multi-colored jelly beans and chocolate bunnies. Listen, I'm not a jelly bean snob. I'll eat the old waxy ones *and* the Jelly Belly frou-frou ones. I'll even eat the white ones. So, don't get me wrong. I love jelly beans, and who *doesn't* love chocolate in any shape or size? Of course, there's just something satisfying about when that chocolate ear breaks off and melts in your mouth. It's a great thing. You know what I'm talking about. But it's not really what Easter is about.

You've seen the shows or videos where they ask kids questions and wait for something funny to happen. On this particular episode, recorded a long time ago, they were asking children about their favorite Bible stories. This one little boy had *all* the details. He had clearly been to Sunday school and he wanted everybody to know that his favorite Bible story was the story of Jesus' resurrection. He leaned into the microphone and told how Jesus had been hung on a cross, how he had died, and how he had been buried in a cave. He told everybody how Jesus was in there for *days,* and he used

1. Preached at First Church of the Nazarene in Kansas City, Missouri on March 5, 2015 (Easter Sunday; Year B).

2. For faithful church people, stories like this often become too familiar. The power of this sermon, I think, was slowing down and paying attention to a few specific words within the text. Also, the illustration from Malcolm Gladwell's book was particularly effective because of the twist which took this familiar concept and turned it on its head to describe our relationship with God.

3. This was a traditional call and congregational response that was used in every service throughout the Easter season. The bold font indicates the congregation's part. This was also used at the conclusion of the sermon as a bookending technique.

multi-syllable words like "crucifixion" and "resurrection." I mean, this kid had it down except for *one* significant detail. He said that on the third day, Jesus rose up from the dead and came out of the tomb and then he saw his shadow and went back inside.[4] Somehow the story of Easter had gotten crossed up with Groundhog Day. Bunnies and groundhogs are *not* what Easter's about. So, let's hear the story from John's Gospel.

John 20:1–18

I was on 119th Street this past week and saw that, in addition to getting a very expensive sandwich at Dean & DeLuca, you can have your picture taken with a rabbit in a basket. It reminded me of a church sign that I saw many years ago in Richmond, Virginia. A church had made a banner and they had stretched it from one tree to another tree. On the banner was a photograph of a cute, fluffy bunny rabbit with a simple, but thought-provoking question: "Has Easter become a little fuzzy?" Part of my role as a preacher is to try to bring the true story into focus and eliminate the "fuzziness." That's what I want to do this morning by zeroing in on several important words in this passage from John.

The first word that I want to call attention to is translated as "taken" in verse 2. When Mary Magdalene goes out to the garden tomb on that first Easter morning, she is going there to complete the burial process. If you'll remember, late on Friday—just before sunset—Jesus had been hurriedly taken down from the cross and placed in the tomb. There was little time to get it done before the Sabbath began and so the whole process was done quickly. In Mary's mind, Jesus deserved better than that. So early on that first day of the week, she made her way to the grave. She was headed to a tomb that had been hurriedly borrowed from a man named Joseph of Arimathea.

Jesus, her Savior and friend, had been crucified less than seventy-two hours before. She had lived with the grief, pain, and sorrow of that experience for what seemed like an eternity. Jesus was the one who had changed her life. He had liberated her from her sin and her self-destruction. He was the one who had set her free to live in a *new* way with a *new* purpose and a *new* peace. When she got to that unfamiliar place, she noticed one thing immediately. She saw that the stone, which had blocked the entrance to the cave-like tomb, had been moved. The hole or entryway into the tomb was now open. The stone was pushed aside. The entrance to the tomb was open and Mary's conclusion was: "Somebody has taken the body of Jesus." Now, we shouldn't be too critical of Mary. Her conclusion or snap judgment

---

4. Anecdotal story with no confirmed source.

makes sense. I mean, everybody's knows that dead bodies don't stand up, don't push aside heavy stones, and don't walk away. Everybody *knows* that. Mary runs to tell the disciples what she has seen and concluded: Jesus has been *"taken."*

We know from the story that Mary goes *back* to the tomb after she had told the disciples what she had discovered, because verse 11 tells us that she was standing outside the tomb crying. It seems clear that Mary has yet to really *look* inside or *go* inside the tomb, but rather she's drawn her conclusions from the stone being pushed aside. Finally, in verse 11 she looks *into* the cave and sees two angels. *They* know that Jesus' body hasn't been stolen or taken. They know that Jesus is alive. They know that God has changed the world in Christ. They ask Mary, "Why are you crying?" But, Mary doesn't know what they know. She has her story and she's sticking to it. She says, "They've taken my Lord away and I don't know where they've put him." All she wanted to do that morning was come out to the tomb and give Jesus a proper burial. Now, there are disciples running around. The stone's been moved. There are grave-robbers on the loose. Strangers are inside the garden tomb. "What's going on around here?" She turns around, sees the caretaker of the garden, and thinks, "Maybe he knows something." But before she can ask him a question, he says, "Why are you crying?" Mary's had enough. "Listen. If you've moved Jesus' body somewhere, just tell me where it is and I will get him."

I want you to focus for just a moment on that last phrase from Mary: "I will get him," or "I will take care of it." Mary thought it was time for *her* to take control of the situation. People are running around confused. Everybody is seemingly more concerned about her crying than who's stolen Jesus' body. Gardeners are wandering around at the crack of dawn. She thinks, "Somebody needs to take control of this situation and figure out what's going on." Mary concludes that it's going to have to be her. In the process, Mary mistakes the risen Christ for the gardener. What she was looking for was right in front of her. He was right there with her, but it took something ordinary to help her see him. The word that Jesus spoke was "Mary," her name. Jesus called her by name and her eyes were opened in a new way. Instead of seeing an unknown gardener, she saw Jesus. It was personal. It was fresh. It was life-changing. Mary had missed seeing the risen Lord because she was preoccupied with the problem or with *fixing* the problem.

The truth is that we could miss it for the same reasons. Listen: you could miss new life, true joy, real meaning, and purpose for living because of a misleading distraction, a destructive habit, a self-centered absorption, an unresolved bitterness, a childhood memory, a long-past mistake, or something else. But it doesn't *have* to be that way. That's part of the

132   SECTION 4: EASTER SUNDAY, THE EASTER SEASON, AND PENTECOST

good news of Easter. Part of the good news is that Jesus knows *our* name. He knows us. As one author put it years ago, God is like the "hound of heaven."[5] He's pursuing us, coming after us, and tracking us down. He does that not to harm us or hurt us, but to save us from sin and from our own self-destructive patterns of living.

The last word that I want you to see is the word that is in Mary's second report to the disciples. Remember? The first time, she went to tell them that Jesus had been *taken*. That turned out not to be true and so she goes back to report a second time. It's the word "seen." She says, "I have *seen* the Lord." I would translate that for us in the twenty-first century—when Jesus is no longer walking around garden tombs in the flesh—as "encounter." You and I may not be able, like Mary, to see Jesus in the flesh, but we *can* encounter him by the Spirit. We can know him and experience his presence and help. We can live in a life-giving, sin-forgiving relationship with him. I was reading a bit from Malcolm Gladwell's famous best-seller from a few years ago.[6] He tells a story about a psychologist in the 1960s by the name of Stanley Milgram. You may have never heard of him, but you have heard of his experiment and the results. Milgram wanted to find an answer to what is called the "small-world problem." Essentially, it revolves around the issue of how human beings are connected in relationships—oftentimes in "web-like" relationships. Milgram had an idea. He was going to test this issue of human "connectedness" with a packet of information which he sent to 160 people in Omaha, Nebraska. Inside the packet was the name of a stockbroker who worked in Boston and lived in Sharon, Massachusetts. Each person within the group of 160 in Omaha were instructed to write their name on the packet, and *then* send it to someone who might get it relationally closer to this stranger in Boston. For example: Send it to a cousin in Rhode Island or send it to a stockbroker-friend in Chicago who might know some *other* stockbroker who might know this guy in Boston. Whatever. Try to get it closer—somehow. The idea was that everybody is connected in some way to everybody else. How many names were on the packet—by the time it arrived to that particular stockbroker in Boston—would be the number of "degrees of separation." Milgram's experiment is where we get the concept of "six degrees of separation." The idea is that there is no more than six people between you and anybody else in the world.

The "good news" of what God has done through Jesus Christ—through his life, death, and resurrection from the dead—is that there need not be a *single* "degree of separation" between you and Jesus. You can know him and

5. Thompson, "Hound of Heaven."
6. Gladwell, *Tipping Point*, 34–35.

live for him. You can live as a child of the Creator of all that is. If you want to know more about that, I'll be glad to talk with you after the conclusion of this service down here at the front. If you want to email me, my address is on the worship folder. If you want to talk with me on the telephone, the church's number is on the folder. If you want to learn more about what it means to *know* Jesus—not just know *about* Jesus—this church will help you and guide you on that path of discovery. But, know this: God loves you. His Son, Jesus, received the treatment that you and I deserved because of our sin and rebellion against God. Because of what Jesus did, you and I can be forgiven and our lives can be changed and transformed by his power. That's the message of Easter. Not bunnies, or jelly beans, or chocolate—as wonderful as all those things are. The truth is that he is risen. **He is risen indeed.**

Amen.

SERMON 28[1]

Thomas, Translation, and Trust[2]

John 20:19–31

When I say "Quasimodo," *most* of you will think of *The Hunchback of Notre Dame*—probably the Walt Disney version. Of course, that movie is based on the book by Victor Hugo which was first published in 1831. What I didn't know is that "quasi modo" are the first two words of 1 Peter 2:2 in Latin. That verse, traditionally, has been read on the Sunday after Easter morning. It was on that day in Hugo's story that this unnamed baby was dropped off on the steps of Notre Dame cathedral. That was why the priest named the baby "Quasimodo." In some traditions, since the words from 1 Peter are read on this Sunday every single year, this Sunday is called "Quasimodo Sunday." Most of the time, this Sunday revolves around the story of the disciple named Thomas. In other traditions, this Sunday is called "St. Thomas Sunday." In the time of Jesus, a week had passed since Easter morning and Thomas is living in the dark. Let's look at his story. I invite you to turn to John 20.

John 20:19–31

Where was Thomas on Easter Sunday evening? Have you ever thought about that? Jesus had been raised from the dead. The women who had gone to the tomb found it empty. Jesus, as John tells us, was thought to be the gardener

1. Preached at First Church of the Nazarene in Kansas City, Missouri on March 7, 2013 (Easter 2; Year C).

2. The introduction in this sermon utilized a technique which was articulated in the "new homiletic" movement in which preachers were encouraged to bring their research into the sermon in such a way that you present the process rather than just the results of the research and reflection. The Quasimodo story was a way of teaching something about the Christian calendar as well as provide an interesting way into the Gospel text assigned by connecting it with another name for the Sunday.

134

THOMAS, TRANSLATION, AND TRUST

by Mary Magdalene, but when Jesus calls her by name, she recognizes him. She and the other women go back and report the scene to the disciples. John runs to the tomb. Peter is chasing after. He gets there and goes right in. He finds the grave clothes, but not the body. Jesus is gone.

I don't know how you spent last Sunday afternoon. Maybe you spent it with family. Maybe you took a nap. Maybe you watched basketball. Can you imagine how the disciples and followers of Jesus spent the first Easter Sunday afternoon? What did they do? By evening time, we know what they were doing. They were huddled together in someone's home with the doors locked, fearing Jewish retaliation. Then Jesus appears to them and says, "Peace." But not everybody was there. Thomas wasn't there. Where was he? What was he doing? Why was everyone else there, but Thomas wasn't? Maybe Thomas was making a pizza run when Jesus showed up. Was he out getting donuts for everybody? Did he just have bad timing, other commitments, or a meeting somewhere on the other side of town? Because of the forms of some of the verbs that are used in this story, some scholars believe that Thomas was not present because Thomas had given up, had abandoned the group, or had walked away from this Jesus-movement. He hadn't betrayed Jesus like Judas had done. Maybe he had just kind of drifted away and concluded, "This is just not for me!"

From my perspective, that's a bigger problem and a bigger issue for twenty-first century followers than Judas-like betrayal. Don't you think? It just happens. You don't go into this Christian journey of trailing after Jesus thinking, "This is going to be hard. I'm going to get tired. I'm going to get worn down. Stuff is going to happen that is frustrating, heart-breaking, and confusing. Folks are going to fail me and disappoint me. At some point, I'm just going to fade away, lose interest, and disconnect." Nobody, that I'm aware of, goes into it thinking in that way, but somehow that's what happens in lots of people's lives. Maybe that's where Thomas was. Somewhere between Friday's crucifixion and Sunday's resurrection, Thomas got lost along the way. He didn't go to the tomb. He didn't hear the report of the women. He wasn't there when Jesus came to the other disciples and the doors were locked. Thomas was hearing it second-hand from these guys with whom he had lived for the last several years. They were excited. They had seen Jesus. They wanted him to share their joy, but he had walked away. He was through.

Can you hear that in Thomas' voice? When the disciples—thrilled and excited—say, "Thomas, we've *seen* the Lord," can you hear how Thomas feels in his reaction?: "Listen. Unless I put *this* finger into the nail-holes and *this* hand into his side, I will *not* believe." Thomas had not heard the resurrected Christ say, "Peace." He had not been there when Jesus breathed on them and said, "Receive the Holy Spirit." Thomas was off somewhere

136   SECTION 4: EASTER SUNDAY, THE EASTER SEASON, AND PENTECOST

else. He was busy or distracted or tending to his own wounds and disappointments. That's part, it seems to me, of what's going on here. But, there's another part that revolves around the complexities of translation from one language to another and I know just enough Greek to be dangerous. The wonderful thing about living when we do is the availability of resources to help us understand what's going on. But, obviously, translating the New Testament from Greek into English is not an easy or simple thing. All you have to do is get several English translations and lay them down side by side and see how different words are used in various places. One classic example in moving from Greek to English revolves around the word "love." In English, we've got one word. We love pizza. We love to go on vacation. We love our children and we love the Lord. We've got one word whereas Greek has at least three.

In this passage, the translation issue revolves around the word "believe" in all its various forms. It shows up everywhere in these verses. Thomas says, "I will not *believe*," in verse 25. Jesus says, "Stop doubting and *believe*," in verse 27. In verse 29, Jesus says, "Blessed are those who have not seen and yet have *believed*." The Gospel writer concludes in verse 31, "These [signs] are written that you may *believe*," and "that by *believing* you may have life in his name." The problem is that all these instances are verbs in various tenses and forms. But when this same word shows up as a noun, the English translation for it is "faith."

Do you see the problem? "Believing" is the verb and "faith" is the noun. They don't seem to be connected in English, but in Greek, they are the *same word*. The problem that this one translation issue has caused is enormous. In some ways, this is why, for centuries in the church, faith has been misunderstood as believing the "right" things, and by that we have meant, thinking about doctrine in orthodox or "proper" ways. That's *not* what the Bible means in almost every place by believing or by faith. We've made "believing" into a mental exercise when biblical "believing" is about *trusting*. It's about entrusting ourselves—our lives—to the Lord. There's a distinct difference between thinking the "right" thoughts and entrusting your life to Jesus.

Last October for my birthday, the staff took me to lunch for fried chicken at RC's in Martin City. While we were there, they gave me a gift. It was kind of a joke—a gag gift. They wanted to see how I would respond when they presented me with a certificate for a free hot-air balloon ride for two. Now, for *some* people, a hot-air balloon ride would be a wonderful gift and they would enjoy it immensely, but for me it would be a useless gift because I will *never* get into a hot-air balloon. Of course, I understand—I *believe*—that wicker baskets can be very strong. I have wicker patio furniture and when

THOMAS, TRANSLATION, AND TRUST

I sit on it, I have no fear that it will collapse or not be able to sustain my weight. So, I know that a balloon's wicker basket is strong. I also understand or *believe* that hot air rises. It's a well-known fact of physics. That's why the upstairs is always warmer than the basement. That's why the milk and butter case in the grocery store is down on the ground. Cool air sinks and hot air rises. I know all about that. I *believe* those things are true, but I am not entrusting my life into a hot-air balloon.

Listen. There's a difference, spiritually, between knowing the doctrines, understanding the truths of the Scripture, being familiar with all the Bible stories, knowing who Jesus is, and entrusting your life to him. What Thomas really was saying was this: "Until I see him and touch him, then I will not trust him." Then Jesus said, "Reach out and touch my side. Stop not trusting and trust." You see the word that is translated as "doubting" in verse 27 is simply the word for "trusting" or "believing," but with a negative prefix. It's not a different word entirely. It's simply the same word placed in a negative form. "Stop *not*-trusting—or *not*-having faith—and trust." Then Thomas comes out with one of the greatest affirmations of trust in all of the Bible when he says, "My Lord and my God." This ranks right up there with Peter's declaration to Jesus: "You are the Christ."[3] For a Jew in the first century to say about a man with nail-pierced hands and feet, standing right in front of him, "My God," is almost beyond what we can even fathom. Then Jesus says, "Thomas, you've seen me and trusted me and that's good. But, those who have *not* seen and yet have trusted me anyway, those folks are blessed."[4] When Jesus says that, those words are for people like you and me. We don't have the opportunity to put our finger in the wounds of Jesus. We're twenty *centuries* removed from touching his side, hearing him teach, or seeing him heal the sick. If there ever was a time when these words were important, insightful, and revolutionary, then it's *our* time. We live in a time that has led, as somebody has said, to a "tyranny of the eye."[5]

From the moment that Gutenberg began printing words on pages that were accessible to the masses, we have been enslaved to the eye. "What you can see is true. What you can read is factual and accurate. If it can't be seen, then it can't be known"—this is the kind of world that we live in today. Yet we simultaneously have proverbs like "There's more than meets the eye." We have become captivated by what we see and yet we know that there's something more. Our eyes can't always be trusted. The magician on the street corner

3. Mark 8:29.
4. My paraphrase.
5. Sweet, *Nudge*, 207.

138   SECTION 4: EASTER SUNDAY, THE EASTER SEASON, AND PENTECOST

can fool us with his sleight of hand. The stick in the water looks crooked, but when we pull it out, it's perfectly straight. We see but we don't see. John 20:29 is the misplaced beatitude from Jesus: "Blessed are those who have *not* seen and yet have *trusted* or *believed*" (emphasis added). It is true that we have not been afforded the opportunity to walk and talk with Jesus in the streets of Jerusalem and along the shores of Galilee. But, Jesus himself has provided, even for us, a way to see and to touch and even to taste the life and presence of our Lord. He invites us to his Table to receive bread and wine—emblems of his broken body and shed blood. When we come to his Table, we come to receive grace and help, but also to entrust again our lives, our plans, and our futures to him and to his care. At the Table, we break free from the "tyranny of the eye" and trust in a God that we have not seen but who has revealed himself in the death and resurrection of Jesus, the Christ.

Amen.

SERMON 29[1]

Fact, Interpretation, and Result[2]

Revelation 5:1–14

The book of Revelation is a bit like a birthday party at Chuck E. Cheese's. Have you been to one of these places? At Chuck E. Cheese's, they serve bad pizza, sugary drinks, and pizza crust desserts. Toddlers and elementary-age kids can't get enough of it. The lights are flashing. Animatronic robots are performing on stage. There's a person walking around in a bear costume hugging kids who will allow it and trying to comfort kids who are hiding behind their mothers. Disney tunes or something similar is blaring from the sound system. Ball pits and plastic slides are filled with laughing and screaming children. Chuck E. Cheese's is sensory overload *on steroids*. Do you have the picture? Sounds and smells, visuals and objects are going this way and that. Things are happening over here and now something else over there. It's kind of like the book of Revelation—sensory overload in biblical proportions.

Revelation 5:1–14

The scene is overwhelming and overpowering. There's a throne and, clearly, the One on the throne is revered. Creatures are bowing down. Revelation previously states that "from the throne came flashes of lightning, rumblings

1. Preached at First Church of the Nazarene in Kansas City, Missouri on April 10, 2016 (Easter 3; Year C).

2. Part of the effectiveness of this sermon revolved around some of the basic elements of the gospel. I wanted to point to "Christ-crucified" as the only hope of the world. In a world filled with distractions, that is our foundational confession. Often, it's not the "new" thing that speaks most powerfully in sermonic speech, but it is the truth that we know and have *always* known. I wanted to remind my people of this grounding truth.

139

140   SECTION 4: EASTER SUNDAY, THE EASTER SEASON, AND PENTECOST

and peals of thunder."[3] Fires are blazing. Strange, animal-like creatures—
hybrids of birds and other mammals—are chanting praises constantly and
loudly, "Holy, holy, holy is the Lord God Almighty, who was, and is, and is
to come."[4] Over and over again. As they do that, others are bowing down
around the throne and all the attention is focused on the throne where the
Lord God Almighty is seated. In his right hand is a scroll that is sealed.

You know how they used to seal things. In some form or another, they
would melt wax onto whatever they wanted to seal. Then, the king or the
person in charge would press his ring or some signature symbol into the hot
wax that would leave a distinct impression. Then it becomes easy to tell if
the seal or wax had been broken. While the hybrid animals are chanting, the
elders are bowing down, and the lightning is flashing, an angel steps forward
and asks in a loud voice—kind of like James Earl Jones—"Who is worthy to
break the seals and to open the scroll?" John says that he wept because no one
was worthy or came forward. Then, one of the elders who was bowing down
around the throne came to him and said, "The lion of Judah has triumphed
and he is able to open the scroll." "Of course," John thought. "The lion is able.
The fiercest and greatest in the animal kingdom is able. The one at the top
of the food chain can do it—the lion. That makes sense." Can you imagine
how silly it would be if the elder had pulled John aside and said, "Don't cry.
The raccoon has overcome." Or, "The squirrel or the camel has triumphed
and will open the scroll." But then, something happens for which John is
completely unprepared. Right after the elder says to John that the lion of
Judah is able to break the seal and open the scroll—*right* after that—John
sees a lamb, verse 6 says, "looking as if it had been slain." Can you imagine
the shock and the confusion? When you're *expecting* a lion and you *see* a
lamb? Then, the lamb steps forward and takes the scroll out of the hand of
the one seated on the throne. The instant that the lamb has the scroll in his
hand, the four "living creatures" (those hybrid-animals with wings) and the
twenty-four elders—*all* of them—fall on the ground and hide their faces in
an act of worship and humility.

Who knew that the elders were also musicians? They each break out a
harp and begin to play. They all begin to sing a new song that was written,
on the spot, for this occasion: "You are worthy to take the scroll and to open
its seals," they sing. The lion—the great symbol of power and might and the
one *expected* to take the scroll and open it—the lion of Judah *is* the lamb
who now is worthy to do what no one else could or can do. It's *not* the lion
and the lamb. No, the lion *is* the lamb. The revelation of God in Christ is

3. Rev 4:5.
4. Rev 4:8.

FACT, INTERPRETATION, AND RESULT   141

clearest, most lucid, and most obvious in the suffering and death of Jesus at the cross. In fact, the song that the elders sing around the throne of God articulates the reason that the lamb is worthy to open the scroll. Look at the first part of verse 9: "You are worthy to take the scroll and to open its seals, *because you were slain*" (emphasis added).

In most stories, under the usual rules of literature and story-telling, when the main character is betrayed, arrested, tortured, and murdered, that story is a tragedy—it's wrong. It's *not* hopeful or helpful. But with Jesus, things are different. The "lamb" is a title that is used *twenty-eight* times in Revelation for Jesus. His sacrificial death at the cross for the sin of the world is what makes him "*worthy* to open the scroll." Who would have ever dreamed or imagined that this is how it would happen? Who would have ever thought that "being slain" or being crucified would be what makes the lamb "worthy" to take the scroll and open the seals? As the apostle Paul said, "Jews demand miraculous signs and Greeks look for wisdom, but we preach Christ *crucified*: a stumbling block to Jews and foolishness to Gentiles."[5] One of the great temptations of the Church—any church and every church—is to somehow de-emphasize or minimize the scandal, the foolishness, and the shock of the cross. There was a time, during the years that I've been pastoring, where one of the hottest topics or questions was this: Should we mark our church building or our sanctuary with a cross? Maybe the question is still being asked in some places. I don't know. I don't pay much attention to that kind of stuff anymore. I think the very question itself is a deep—maybe even subconscious—recognition that a lamb who was slain is, in some way, hard to grasp, difficult to swallow, and even repugnant to our normal and natural ways of thinking. Almost eighty years ago now, a theologian described a form of Christianity in this way: "A God without wrath, brought people without sin, into a Kingdom without judgment, through the ministry of a Christ without a Cross."[6] The reality is that there is no Christianity without the cross.

Even with so many sounds, smells, and images going on, Revelation 5 is clear that the reason that the lamb is worthy to take and open the scroll is because he was slain. That Jesus was crucified on a hill outside Jerusalem around 30 AD is a historical *fact* that very few deny. The evidence that Jesus was executed at the hands of the Roman Empire is indisputable. But, Revelation 5 goes on to say something else about the lamb which is *not* a historical fact but is an *interpretation* of that fact. In verse 5, the lamb is worthy because he was slain, "and with his blood he purchased men and women for

---

5. 1 Cor 1:23, emphasis added.

6 Niebuhr, *Kingdom*, 193.

142   SECTION 4: EASTER SUNDAY, THE EASTER SEASON, AND PENTECOST

God from every tribe and language and people and nation." The meaning of Christ's crucifixion is that people have been "purchased for God." To use a theological and biblical term, they have been redeemed.

When the apostle Paul is reminding the church at Corinth about a life that is pleasing to God, and a life that reflects the presence of God's Spirit living within them, he writes, "Do you not know that your body is a temple of the Holy Spirit, who is in you, whom you received from God?" Then he says, "*You* are not your own; you were *bought at a price*."[7] When he was writing to the church at Ephesus, Paul said it this way: "In [Christ] we have *redemption* through his blood, the forgiveness of sins, in accordance with the riches of God's grace that he lavished on us with all wisdom and understanding."[8] The death of Jesus at the cross is a historical fact. That we are redeemed or "purchased" through his death is a faith-claim or a faith-affirmation about that historical fact.

But then, the elder's song in Revelation 5 sings even more. They sing that the lamb who was slain has purchased men and women from the whole world. Then, they sing that the lamb has made those people "to be a kingdom and priests to serve our God and they will reign on the earth." This is not the historical fact, nor is it the *interpretation* of that fact, but it is the faith-claim about the *result* of that fact. When we embrace the slain lamb, when we see and acknowledge that this is God's way and will for the world, and when we set aside or reject all other ways of being redeemed—through our own goodness because we are moral and do good things; we are kind and generous; we've "inherited" the Christian gene and we're better than our neighbors; or we've done certain things *for* God and the church—when we set aside *all* other reasons for being redeemed or ransomed, and when we embrace, as Paul said it, that "we are saved *by grace* through faith—and this is not of ourselves, it is the *gift* of God—not of works, so that no one can boast."[9] When that is true in us, then we are "made to be a kingdom and priests to serve our God" (Rev 5:10). The confession of the kingdom is this: "The lion *is* the lamb and the lamb is Lord." Our mission as citizens of the lamb's kingdom is to serve, suffer, and give ourselves away for God's purposes in the world.

It is quickly approaching commencement season. The graduation announcements are being addressed and sent out. Plans are being made. High schools and universities are busily getting the campus cleaned up and beautified for all the guests and alumni to return to their alma mater.

7. 1 Cor 6:19–20, emphasis added.

8. Eph 1:7–8, emphasis added.

9. Eph 2:8–9, emphasis added.

FACT, INTERPRETATION, AND RESULT

Hopefully, several will bring a hefty donation with them. I did a little search this week and found out that there will be some famous speakers at various commencements around the country. Michael Bloomberg will speak at the University of Michigan. The famous historian of baseball and the Civil War, Ken Burns will speak at Stanford. If movie-making is your thing, then Harvard is the place, because they'll hear from Steven Spielberg this year. A columnist from *The New York Times* says, "Commencement speakers are always telling young people to follow their passions. Be true to yourself. This is a vision of life that begins with self and ends with self. But people on the road to [character growth] do not find their vocations by asking, what do I want from life? They ask, what is life asking of me?"[10]

The real question, I think, is not, "What is *life* asking of me?," but rather, "What is *God* asking of me and calling me toward?" The answer from Revelation 5 is this: to participate in his kingdom, to worship him, and to serve others and the world around you. That is the calling for each of us and for *all* of us—wherever we work, study, or live these days. Many times when we hear the word "priest," we think "minister" or "clergy-person." But one of the great biblical principles of the Protestant Reformation was the "priesthood of all believers." What Martin Luther was emphasizing was that *each* of us and *all* of us are called to service in God's kingdom. No one is left out or excluded from service. Revelation 5 is set in the context of worship. Songs are being sung. Praises are being voiced. Prayers, like "golden bowls full of incense," are being brought before the Lord. The Lamb of God, slain for the world, is being worshipped because he is *worthy*.

When we gather around the Table of the Lord in this context of worship, we are aware in the broken bread and the cup of Christ that the lamb was broken and his blood was spilled at the cross for us and in our place.He died the death that we deserved so that we might live the life that only he can give. So, come with your prayers and praises. Come with your songs and sorrows. Come, knowing that you have been purchased for God and bought with a price. Come, realizing that you are a citizen of God's kingdom and your mission is to *serve*—to give yourself away in love to those around you and to the world. Come.

Amen.

---

10. Brooks, "Moral," SR1.

SERMON 30[1]

Adjectives: Good, Other, and One[2]

John 10:11–18

I have a calendar in my office that is kind of unique. It's different from a monthly calendar where you have a month on the bottom of it and then a photograph of a car, bird, or whatever else you are interested in. No, this calendar is set up according to the seasons of the Christian year. For example, an entire page is given to Holy Week alone. Then once Easter arrives, you flip the page and it has the seven weeks of the Easter season before arriving at Pentecost. I was slow in turning the page of that calendar until this week. I turned it and here was the artwork at the top of the calendar for the Easter season.[3] A sheep—staring at me. Why a sheep during Easter? One reason is the passage that we will read today. It comes from the tenth chapter of John.

John 10:11–18

Most of the time when this passage is studied, there is a focus on the fact that this is one of the "I am" statements of Jesus. Throughout the Gospel of John, at various times and places, Jesus says: "I am the gate."[4] Or, "I am the

---

1. Preached at First Church of the Nazarene in Kansas City, Missouri on April 19, 2015 (Easter 4; Year).

2. The value of this sermon rested, in my opinion, in how it paid attention to parts of the text that often are neglected. Two different tri-partite structures were intertwined. The what, for whom, and why questions were intersected with the adjectives (good, other, and one) in the text. This, I think, maintained interest. The conclusion drawn from Wesley was particularly relevant in an increasingly fragmented and divisive culture.

3. A photograph was projected of a sheep's face looking straight ahead.

4. John 10:7.

144

ADJECTIVES: GOOD, OTHER, AND ONE   145

way, the truth, and the life."[5] Or, "I am the resurrection,"[6] and others. These "I am" statements are incredibly significant in the Gospel of John because this phrase is so loaded with meaning and implications. It has its origin in the name that God revealed in the story of Moses and the burning bush. Remember? Moses asked, "What is your name?" God said, "I am who I am," or "I am that I am," or "I will be what I will be."[7] It's a complicated translation that is difficult to capture. Regardless, these "I am" statements by Jesus in John are very, very important and *most* of the time, this is what receives the bulk of attention.

I've preached from these passages and done that very thing. It's not what I want to focus your attention upon today. I want to zero in on three adjectives in the story and ask the question: What do these mean? Or, why are they significant? For example, when Jesus says, "I am the *good* shepherd," why is that important? Jesus doesn't simply say, "I am the shepherd," but rather, "I am the *good* shepherd." Of course, the story makes clear that Jesus is drawing a distinction between himself and the "hired hand," or the "hireling," as some translations put it. The key difference revolves around what the "good shepherd" *does*. It's not what the "shepherd" *says* or how the "shepherd" *thinks*, but it's what the "good shepherd" *does*. Jesus says—and the gospel repeats over and over throughout the passage—that the thing that the "good shepherd" *does* is that he "lays down his life for the sheep." That phrase, or some form of that phrase, appears five times in the span of these eight verses. As you know, and as I've mentioned on numerous occasions before, repetition in the Scripture is a clue to what is important because it is a way to emphasize certain things. They didn't have boldface type or letters in all caps. They didn't underline words or highlight them with a red pen. The way to emphasize was to repeat words or phrases.

Jesus says in verse 11: "The *good* shepherd *lays down his life* for the sheep" (emphasis added). Immediately, Jesus connects these two things together. Then in verse 15, in case you missed it, Jesus says, "I lay down my life for the sheep." Skip verse 16 for a moment. Just to repeat it again in verse 17: "The reason the Father loves me is that I lay down my life." Then to cap it off in verse 18, Jesus says—*twice*—"I lay it down"—referring to his life. What the "good shepherd" *does* is the "laying down of his life." That's what makes him the "good" shepherd and not just a "hired" shepherd, an apathetic shepherd, or a "run-away-when-the-wolves-come" shepherd. Jesus is the "sacrificial" shepherd. As the apostle Paul says it in Philippians 2, Jesus is the one "who

5. John 14:6.
6. John 11:25.
7. Exod 3:14.

146   SECTION 4: EASTER SUNDAY, THE EASTER SEASON, AND PENTECOST

became obedient unto death—even death on a cross."[8] He's the "my-life-for-your-life" shepherd. He's the "my-death-so-you-can-be-saved" shepherd. He's the "our-sins-on-him" shepherd. He's the *"good"*—loving, atoning, suffering-and-dying, take-our-place, and by-his-wounds-we-are-healed shepherd. That's what makes him the "good" shepherd—then, now, and forever. The "good" shepherd laid down his life for the sheep. That's what he did.

The next adjective that I want to draw your attention to is the word "other." It shows up in verse 16 where Jesus says, "I have *other* sheep that are not of this sheep pen. I must bring them also" (emphasis added). What's going on here? What is Jesus saying? Clearly, the Gospel of John begins with the affirmation, straightforwardly declared, that Jesus came into the world in human flesh with the primary mission to redeem and reclaim the chosen people of God, the people of Israel. We can never forget that Jesus came as the Messiah—the long-awaited redeemer from, to, and for God's chosen people. In the very first chapter of John, the Bible says: "He was in the world, and though the world was made through him, the world did not recognize him. He came to that which was his own, but his own did not receive him."[9] Jesus came *as* a Jew *to* the Jews and *for* the Jews, but the Jews, as John says, "did not receive him." Of course, Jesus understood his mission to the Jews in the same way that God had understood his mission for his people from the beginning. They were to be a "light to the Gentiles"[10] and the conduit through which the world would be blessed.[11] They were to be an instrument of ministry and mission to the world—to *all* people everywhere. God's mission was never meant—before Jesus or after Jesus—to be a restricted, exclusive, or narrow mission. Never. The people of God were "blessed" in order to be a "blessing" to others. So, when Jesus says in John 10 that "I have *other* sheep," he is reiterating the fact that God's plan is not limited to the Jewish people, but is for *all* people. We—non-Jewish people—are the "other sheep" from John 10. But now that we have been "grafted" in, as Paul would say,[12] and have *become* God's people—the Church and the followers of Jesus—our tendency sometimes is to "huddle up" and limit the mission to people like us. We do the same thing that the early Jewish church had the tendency to do which is to focus on us and limit God's big mission to the world.

8. Phil 2:8.

9. John 1:11.

10. Isa 49:6.

11. Allusion to Gen 12:2–3.

12. Rom 11:17–24.

ADJECTIVES: GOOD, OTHER, AND ONE   147

Maybe we should print what Jesus said and post it around: "I have other sheep." Some of you will remember when the Church of the Nazarene had a magazine by that very name, "Other Sheep." It was, of course, all about missionary work around the world. But the truth of the matter is that there are "other sheep" across the street, sharing a back fence, or working in your office. You don't have to go across the globe to find "other sheep." God is and has been bringing them to our doorstep for decades now, and his good news is for them. Who are the "other sheep" in your life, in your school, in your workplace, and in your neighborhood? Jesus laid down his life for them, too. Yes, we are the sheep for whom Christ died, but that is also true of all those around us. The good shepherd laid down his life for them.

What he did: the good shepherd laid down his life. That's what makes him the *good* shepherd and not just a "hired hand." For *whom* he did it: the "sheep," yes, but also the *"other"* sheep—those outsiders—which *we* ourselves used to be. The last question answered by last adjective is this: Why? *Why* did the "good shepherd" do what he did and for whom he did it? *Why?* Verse 16: "They too will listen to my voice, and there shall be *one* flock and *one* shepherd" (emphasis added). Does every sheep look alike? Of course not. Does every sheep sound alike? Of course not. Does every sheep think alike? I have no idea what goes on in an actual sheep's brain, as small as it may be, but if we're talking about followers of Jesus as the "sheep" then, of course not. We must let go of the notion that *I*, as a follower of Jesus, *you*, as a follower of Jesus, and followers of Jesus in Nairobi or Nashville or Nampa, Idaho—that we all must think alike, speak alike, and act alike. That's nonsense.But it doesn't preclude us from being "one flock." What is the key that binds us together? What is the key that makes us "one" in the Lord? The answer is a life defined and guided by love—love for God, love for each other in spite of our differences, and love for all the people of the world.

John Wesley, a Church of England preacher and evangelist in the 1700s, faced different issues than you and I face. It was a different time and a different place. He essentially lived on the back of a horse for decades. He travelled tens of thousands of miles that way. He lived by candlelight and actually read books that had pages. He wrote letters in longhand. It was a different time. Allow me to cite, at length, a portion of one of his sermons. It was written in 1750. Wesley wrote:

> I do not mean, 'Be of my opinion.' You need not: I do not expect
> or desire it. Neither do I mean, 'I will be of your opinion.' I can-
> not. . . I do not mean, 'Embrace my modes of worship' or 'I will
> embrace yours'. . . We must both act as each is fully persuaded
> in his own mind. Hold you fast that which you believe is most

acceptable to God, and I will do the same. I believe the episcopal form of church government to be scriptural and apostolical. If you think the presbyterian or independent is better, think so still, and act accordingly. I believe infants ought to be baptized; and that this may be done either by dipping or sprinkling. If you are otherwise persuaded, be so still, and follow your persuasion. . . I have no desire to dispute with you one moment upon any of the preceding heads. Let all these smaller points stand aside. Let them never come into sight. 'If thine heart is as my heart,' if thou *lovest* God and all mankind, I ask no more: 'Give me thine hand.'[13]

One flock united in love for God, each other, and for the world. Not uniform. Not identical. Not monolithic. Not a pallet of sameness. But *one* flock with *one* shepherd united in love. That's why the "good" shepherd did what he did for whom he did it. Good, other, and one. It's no coincidence that we are reminded when we share communion, as our ritual says, that "we are one at one Table with the Lord."[14] It is the love of God which sent his only Son into our world, the love of God which is revealed in his suffering and death of Jesus at the cross, and *his* love at work in *our* lives that unites us together as a people here and around the globe as followers of Jesus. May it be so, Lord Christ.

Amen.

13. Wesley, "Catholic Spirit," 2:89–90, emphasis added.

14. *Manual of the Church*, 260.

SERMON 31[1]

Witnesses of These Things[2]

Luke 24:36–48

It's the third Sunday of Easter. We're celebrating, sharing, and thinking together about the meaning of Christ's resurrection. We're considering what it means in your life and mine. Today we're confronted by a story from Luke 24. Let's look together at these verses.

Luke 24:36–48

We live in a world that is full of words, don't we? Words are everywhere. They're on screens. They're on signs. They're on paper. They're in books. They're in Kindles, NOOKs, iPads and tablets of all kinds. Words, of course, can change meaning over time. Here are three quick examples: 1) "artificial" at one time meant full of artistic or technical skill—something being "artificial" was a sign of quality. That's not true today; 2) "awful" at one time meant full of awe—something was wonderful, delightful, and good when it was "awful." That's no longer how the word is used; 3) "manufacture" comes from the Latin word with the meaning, to be made by hand. It has virtually the opposite meaning today.

This story from Luke 24 is an amazing story. There is so much to think about and deal with, but today I want to focus our attention on the last sentence of the text, and even more specifically on a certain word that also

---

1. Preached at First Church of the Nazarene in Kansas City, Missouri on April 22, 2012 (Easter 3; Year B).

2. Part of the power of this sermon was the invitation for the congregation to engage their senses and try to imagine the sights, sounds, and smells that were a part of the story. Also, reference was made to recent disasters around the world including an earthquake, tsunami, nuclear meltdown, and tornado. These references needed no explanation at the time. The sheer repetition of the word "witness" made the focus clear.

149

150   SECTION 4: EASTER SUNDAY, THE EASTER SEASON, AND PENTECOST

has changed meaning over time. In verse 48, Jesus says to his disciples: "You are witnesses of these things." What it really says is that you are "martyrs" of these things. Martyrs? When we hear that word, it means death by stoning, burning at the stake, or in the coliseum with the lions turned loose. Martyr, in Luke 24, means "witness." Only *later* did the word come to mean "someone who suffers death *because* of their witness." In these final words from Jesus in Luke—after having appeared to them, reaffirmed his presence with them, reassured them by inviting them to touch his hands, and sharing a meal of broiled fish with them[3]—after all of that, Jesus says, "You are witnesses of these things."

Have you thought about what the disciples witnessed? What had they seen and heard along the way with Jesus? They had felt the sand between their toes after some of them had pulled their fishing boats up on the shore and left everything.[4] They had *witnessed* Jesus say, "Blessed are you who are poor, for yours is the kingdom of God."[5] They had felt the grain between their hands as they rubbed them together, and they tasted the kernels on their tongues as they made their way through the field.[6] They had *witnessed* Jesus confound the Pharisees with a story from the Scriptures about David doing what was considered "unlawful" or "out of bounds."[7] It was in the town of Nain, where they heard the funeral dirges and the wailing of the mourners. They smelled death in the air, but then they *witnessed* Jesus stop the procession and speak to the corpse—miraculously, the young man was alive again.[8] Take a few moments this afternoon and wander through the Gospel of Luke and think about the sights, sounds, smells, tastes, feelings, observations, and experiences that the disciples of Jesus had. They were *witnesses*.

Of course, it wasn't all messages and miracles. Some of them were in the garden when they heard the sound of soldier's voices. They saw the dim light of torches in the night and the gleaming flashes of swords removed from their scabbards. They *witnessed* when Jesus was betrayed with a kiss into the hands of Roman injustice.[9] Some saw and heard from a distance the crack of a whip, the strike of a rod, and the grunts or moans of pain as

---

3. Luke 24:36–43.

4. Luke 5:1–11.

5. Luke 6:20.

6. Luke 6:1–2.

7. Luke 6:3–11.

8. Luke 7:11–17.

9. Luke 22:47–48.

WITNESSES OF THESE THINGS

portions of Jesus' beard were ripped from his face. They saw and heard.[10] They *witnessed* the suffering of their leader and Lord.

Etched into their minds and memories were the silhouettes of three crosses on a hill that looked like a human skull from a distance. They struggled to see through the darkness. They heard the cries. They felt the shaking of the earth.[11] They felt, heard, and saw the agonizing death of Jesus. They *witnessed* it. The despair of Saturday overwhelmed them. The grief and the confusion weighed heavy upon them. The hopelessness was palpable, but now it was dispelled by the risen Christ in their midst. He was talking and eating and touching. Jesus said, "You are *witnesses* of these things."

Somewhere in the first half of what we call the first century AD, the resurrected Jesus appeared to his disciples and emphasized to them the importance of their witness—of them sharing with others what they had seen and heard. Now, all these centuries later, and *here* in the first half of the twenty-first century AD, we can confidently assert that they *were* witness of those things. It's clear and obvious. It's apparent and powerful. For approaching two thousand years, the witness of those disciples has spread, grown, impacted, and changed the world as we know it. The world in which we live would not look anything like it does had it not been for the *witness* of those disciples who were in that room when Jesus appeared to them. Like a huge room of dominoes lined up one after another, they *witnessed* and moved the chain. One after one, each domino impacted the next one. Over and over again throughout these last twenty centuries, the progression of impact and influence has happened.

Without the Christian conviction and tenacity of William Wilberforce, millions of people may still be enslaved. Wilberforce and Wesley had great impact. You've heard of them. But, what about John Woolman? He was a Quaker from Philadelphia who had abolished slavery among Quakers a full *one hundred years* before Lincoln's Emancipation Proclamation of 1863. When you think of hospitals in our world, we have to acknowledge that the vast majority of them have been founded and operated by churches and Christians. Baptist hospitals, Lutheran hospitals, Seventh Day Adventist hospitals, and hospitals named after saints like Luke and Joseph are scattered throughout our metropolis alone.[12] What would the world look like without churches and believers who have started and funded hospitals here and around the world? This is an indication that

10. Luke 23:49.

11. Matt 27:51.

12. This was a reference to two prominent hospitals within the Kansas City metropolitan area. St. Joseph's Hospital is less than two miles from the church.

152   SECTION 4: EASTER SUNDAY, THE EASTER SEASON, AND PENTECOST

they were *witnesses* to those things. Or, consider the help agencies and the humanitarian organizations that are so prevalent in our world. Call to mind groups like World Vision, Doctors Without Borders, Mercy Corps, Feed the Children, Heart to Heart International, CARE, Nazarene Compassionate Ministry, and a host of others that are grounded in Christian faith and action. They're led by followers of Jesus who now stand at the far end of a long chain of witnesses. These agencies and organizations (and so many others) stand as a testimony that those disciples in that room with Jesus truly were *witnesses* to those things.

What happens when the cameras are turned off, the lights are packed up, the reporters from the newspapers and the TV stations check out of the hotels and climb aboard the planes that are leaving the scenes of disaster in Haiti, Indonesia, Japan, and Joplin?[13] Who's left? Who's still there working, helping, serving, feeding, and building? Who's there? The answer is *followers* of Jesus. The ones still there are *disciples* of Jesus—folks who have been impacted by the *witness* of those early disciples whose *witness* impacted another generation of disciples whose *witness* impacted another generation, and on and on it has gone.

More than one hundred years ago, a little cluster of Jesus' followers were gathered together. They were led by a preacher named A.S. Cochran,[14] and they were *witnesses* to what God had done in Christ and had done throughout the history of the Church. They knew what God had done in their own lives and they passed the message on with power. People's lives were transformed. They experienced for themselves the pardoning and forgiving grace of God. They grew up in Christ and surrendered themselves completely to his will and ways. They evangelized their neighborhood. They reached out in ministry to the marginalized—primarily young women who were giving birth to children without the support of fathers or family.[15] That group of Jesus-followers was the First Church of the Nazarene in Kansas City. Over the years and decades, this church—*our* church—has had pastors and preachers who have confronted the injustices in this city at great personal peril and cost. This church—*our* church—has given members and

13. A 4.8 magnitude earthquake struck Port-au-Prince, Haiti on March 8, 2012. An 8.6 magnitude earthquake happened off the coast of Indonesia on April 11, 2012 and triggered a tsunami warning which brought back memories of the horrible tsunami in 2004. The Fukushima nuclear disaster in Japan had initially occurred in March 2011. An EF5 rated multi-vortex tornado hit and destroyed significant portions of Joplin, Missouri on May 22, 2011.

14. Founding pastor of First Church of the Nazarene in Kansas City, Missouri which was started in 1911.

15. For several decades in its early history, the congregation funded and ran a home for unwed mothers.

WITNESSES OF THESE THINGS 153

families away so that other churches could be started in other parts of the city. As I discovered just a few months ago, this church—*our* church—has supported and given money for missional purposes around the world in amounts that exceed every church in the entire denomination except for five other churches.

Kansas City First Church—101 years into its life—stands as a testimony all these centuries later to those disciples to whom Jesus said, "You are witnesses of these things." The story of the centuries, and even the story of *our* century of existence, is a confirmation that they *were* witnesses of those things. Now, we must continue, with renewed strength and enthusiasm, to be witnesses of those things. We must continue the work. We must reach out, reach across, and reach down. We must preach and teach. We must help, serve, invite, and minister. It's *our* task to come alongside, befriend, and call folks into the future that Christ has for them. Everyone in this room knows what it is even though it was started in 1968, which was long before some in this place were even born. When I say "911," everyone knows that number is the emergency number. It's what you call when someone is having chest pains. It's the number you call when you are in, or witness, an automobile accident. 911 is the number when someone needs help, rescue, or assistance. We know that, but in April of last year, *Time* magazine wrote an article called "How to Fix 911."[16]

When the 911 system was established in 1968, the world was connected by landline telephones. Many of you used to have a landline phone. Who, in the last few years, has had their home telephone disconnected and now you function completely with a cell phone? It's possible that landline telephones may, one day, completely disappear. *Now*, when someone calls 911, typically they're on a cell phone. Usually they are in some kind of stressful situation. They're panicked. They're upset. The car has been rear-ended or flipped over and the adrenaline is racing through their body like they've never experienced before. Or, they're in pain. They feel like the proverbial elephant is standing on their chest and they're having trouble breathing, much less thinking or communicating with a 911 dispatcher. Sometimes, in the middle of the crisis, they don't even know where they are or they can't remember their location or address. What if they're in a high-rise office building or apartment complex and they can't remember which *floor* they're on? All kinds of complications may arise. The article in *Time* said:

"Such gaps leave us with a patchy emergency infrastructure that has become progressively less able to find people in need." Then, the article came to its concluding statement about the new reality. With the infrastructure

16. Kenneally, "How to Fix 911."

changing and technology changing and old ways of doing things no longer applicable, here's what the article concluded. It said: "Emergencies are best served by [smart] *people*."[17]

We live in a world with people hurting, lost, in danger, hopeless, helpless, and everything in between. In this new "church reality," the key is not going to be technologies, programs, productions, styles, or systems, but *people*. The key will be people who are committed, compassionate, compelling *witnesses* of what God in Christ has done at the cross, throughout the centuries, and *in our own lives*. We must be witnesses of these things. To be that kind of witness—just like the disciples in the first century—we need the presence and power of God within, poured on, and filling our lives. For that very reason, we gather around the Lord's Table to receive grace and strength and help in our time of need.

Amen.

---

17. Kenneally, "How to Fix 911," emphasis added, quote adapted by deleting "smart" in the last phrase.

SERMON 32[1]

There's Something About Newness[2]

Revelation 21:1–6

There's something about "newness." Some of you have experienced it. Others may not have experienced it. It's likely that the older you are means that you may have experienced it more often. Some may go their whole lives and never experience—what some call—the new car smell. Some think that it may be dangerous to your health. Essentially, it's a combination, I'm told, of glues, plastics, and materials in the car that have been recently applied. One study showed that the concentrations that make up the smell will decrease by about 90 percent over a three-week period. Not to be *too* cynical, but about the time that you have to make the first payment on that new ride is about the time that the new car smell goes away.

The Bible, and particularly the book of Revelation, has some things to say about newness. Let's look together at Revelation 21:1–6.

Revelation 21:1–6

By the time the story gets to chapter 21, much has already happened. There have been battles and bowls of wrath. There have been plagues and praising multitudes in the heavens. There have been wars and worship gatherings around the throne. By the time we get here to chapter 21, evil has been defeated and the final judgment has taken place. All that is left is to paint a picture of the new reality—the creation of God.

The first thing, I think, that we should understand is that John's vision or what John sees is also something that John has heard before. John is not

1. Preached at First Church of the Nazarene in Kansas City, Missouri on April 24, 2016 (Easter 5; Year C).

2. The key to this sermon was the connection of Revelation 21 with Isaiah 65 and the understanding that these centuries-old promises are also for us.

155

156   SECTION 4: EASTER SUNDAY, THE EASTER SEASON, AND PENTECOST

making things up out of whole cloth, out of thin air, or from his own imagination. No, there is a groundwork that has already been laid. We could say it this way. God is revealing to John, in many ways, the same kinds of things that God spoke to and through the prophet Isaiah.

Listen to Isaiah 65:17–25 and see if you hear the same kind of message as the passage that we've read from Revelation. Listen to it:

> Behold, I will create new heavens and a new earth. The former things will not be remembered, nor will they come to mind. But be glad and rejoice forever in what I will create, for I will create Jerusalem to be a delight and its people a joy. I will rejoice over Jerusalem and take delight in my people; the sound of weeping and of crying will be heard in it no more. Never again will there be in it an infant who lives but a few days, or an old man who does not live out his years; he who dies at a hundred will be thought a mere youth; he who fails to reach a hundred will be considered accursed. They will build houses and dwell in them; they will plant vineyards and eat their fruit. No longer will they build houses and others live in them, or plant and others eat. For as the days of a tree, so will be the days of my people; my chosen ones will long enjoy the works of their hands. They will not toil in vain or bear children doomed to misfortune; for they will be a people blessed by the Lord, they and their descendants with them. Before they call I will answer; while they are still speaking I will hear. The wolf and the lamb will feed together, and the lion will eat straw like the ox, but dust will be the serpent's food. They will neither harm nor destroy on all my holy mountain, says the Lord.

Doesn't that sound a bit like John's vision? You know, John has been referred to as the "disciple whom Jesus loved."[3] In fact, it seems to be John's favorite way of referring to himself. Now, we might look at that as boastful or braggadocious, as if John was saying that Jesus only "liked" his other disciples. It seems to us that John is elevating himself and minimizing the others. This is *not* what's happening. John is simply indicating what can be studied in the Gospel accounts—that Jesus and John had a very close relationship. John was a part of the "inner circle" of disciples which included Peter and James. He always seemed to be in close proximity to Jesus, as he was at the Last Supper. But as I thought and prayed about this passage this week, one of the thoughts that came to mind was that maybe another part of

---

3. I did not choose to share with the congregation that one scholar (Ben Witherington III) has argued that the "disciple whom Jesus loved" was Lazarus.

THERE'S SOMETHING ABOUT NEWNESS 157

the close connection between John and Jesus revolved around their mutual love and study of the prophecies of Isaiah.

In Luke 4, Jesus announced his purpose and his mission. It was a quotation from Isaiah. Remember that?—"the Lord has anointed me to preach good news to the poor . . . freedom for the captives . . . sight for the blind . . . release for the oppressed . . . and to proclaim the year of the Lord's favor."[4] That's from Isaiah. It seems that John, *too*, was a student of Isaiah because what God reveals to him in Revelation 21 is eerily similar to what he has heard read from Isaiah 65 in the synagogue over the years. In all likelihood, he and Jesus have discussed Isaiah as they have walked the pathways of Galilee and Judea. Revelation 21 in many ways is a reiteration or a re-emphasis of Isaiah 65, with a bit of a twist. When reference is made in Isaiah 65 to "my people" or "my chosen ones," the reference is to the people of Israel—this family that God had chosen in Abraham and multiplied over the centuries. They are the people that God has fed, sustained, delivered, exiled, rescued, and sustained some more. They were the people of Isaiah 65. But in John's vision, things have changed a bit. The outcomes are very similar: no more tears, no more suffering, and things made new, but the people for whom this promise is true are now the followers of Jesus—the Church.

The key, I think, is verse 2: "I saw the Holy City, the new Jerusalem, coming down out of heaven from God, prepared *as a bride* beautifully dressed for her husband." John mixes his images here. They seem to be coming at him or being revealed with such force and intensity that sorting them out or making rational sense of them is too much. For example, how can a *city* be "dressed as a bride"? What would that even look like? The image of a bride is the key. Jesus, in his own teaching in Matthew 22, made this same comparison, and when he did this, it was the final straw that convinced the Pharisees to try to trap Jesus in his words so that they could get rid of him. In a parable, Jesus compared the "kingdom" to a wedding feast given for a king's son. The ones who were initially invited—God's chosen people—refused to come. *Instead,* all kinds of people—the gentiles or all non-Jews—were invited and they *did* come.[5] In a similar way, the apostle Paul commandeered this imagery and idea in Ephesians 5 when he gave some instructions about relationships in the church and family. I don't want to go into everything that Paul says there, but I want you to see that this connection between "Christ/the husband" and the "Church/the bride or wife" is clear. Paul writes in Ephesians 5:25, "Husbands, love your wives, just as Christ loved the church and gave himself up for her."

4. Isa 61:1–2.
5. Matt 22:1–15.

158   SECTION 4: EASTER SUNDAY, THE EASTER SEASON, AND PENTECOST

Not just in the writings of John, but in Matthew and Paul's letters, the twist is that God's people and the promises of Isaiah 65 are now re-visioned in Revelation 21, and they are for the followers of Jesus—the Church. They are for *us*. The Church is the bride of Christ. The Church is the people of God. The glorious good news of Revelation 21 is that God has wonderful blessings in store for *his* people: "No more death or mourning or crying or pain, for the old order of things has passed away," John says.[6] To people who were being persecuted and watching their loved ones being martyred for the faith, this was good news. To people who were grieving the deaths of their fellow followers of Jesus, the promise of no more crying or mourning or pain was a vision almost beyond their comprehension. This was a vision and a promise where impossibilities become possible and where things incomprehensible become reality—like in Isaiah 65 where the "wolf and the lamb feed together" and the "lion eats straw like the ox."[7] It simply reminds me again that this is God's doing. This is something that God has to do. This is his work and task.

In a time and a place where so many things that used to be impossible have now become possible, and even familiar, we must hear these promises again. In the kind of world where, with the touch of a finger, we can send signals across the world, bounce them off satellites, and receive them back again in the palm of our hand—in *that* kind of a world, it would be very easy for me to think that I can do it. It's tempting to think that we can fix it or make it happen. It would be easy to believe that, with a little hard work, some long hours, and a bit of elbow grease, as they used to say, somehow, I can solve it or save it. Listen to what God says in Revelation 21: "*I* am making everything new" (emphasis added).

You have some things in your life that you are trying to solve, don't you? Frankly it's been that way for a while. I'm not suggesting that you give up or give in. There are Scriptures that say that we are "co-workers"[8] with Christ and "partners"[9] with him in the work and the gospel. But there's a stark difference between being a "co-worker" and being the "solution-finder," "problem-solver," or "answer" that is within myself or within my own control. This very issue was something that had to be faced by the man that we initially meet in the book of Acts as a man named Saul. Of course, he meets the risen Christ and everything changes. Eventually we come to know him as the apostle Paul who had a part in writing much

6. Rev 21:4.

7. Isa 65:25.

8. 1 Cor 3:9.

9. Phil 1:4.

THERE'S SOMETHING ABOUT NEWNESS

of the New Testament. From one perspective, Paul had reasons to boast. He was very devout from a very young age. He was diligent and devoted, maybe like few others have been. He said of himself that he was "blameless" when it comes to the law of God. He had an incredible history and heritage. But when he wrote to the churches in Galatia, he said, "May I never boast except in the cross of our Lord Jesus Christ, through which the world has been crucified to me, and I to the world . . . What *counts*," Paul wrote, "is the *new* creation."[10]

What is "old" in you that God wants to "make new"?[11] What is it? Can you hear God say to you today, "I am making everything new." Can you hear him say that to you? If so, then give praise to him. If not, then I'm inviting you to taste it, swallow it, and take it in. Here at the Table of the Lord, we have the opportunity to see, touch, and taste the work of God in Christ which was done for us, without our help, and long before we were even aware. "While we were still *sinners,* Christ died for us."[12] So, come and receive. God, even now, is at work in us, making everything new.

Amen.

10. Gal 6:15, emphasis added.

11. An invitation to pray at an altar or a kneeling rail as the way to respond to the message could be readily substituted at this point.

12. Rom 5:8, emphasis added.

SERMON 33[1]

Pentecost is About Power[2]

Acts 2:1–41

Is there anyone under fifty years of age who recognizes the name Garrison Keillor?[3] Anybody? Keillor is a writer and humorist. He's a storyteller and his long-running radio show—*A Prairie Home Companion*—has been on the air for more than forty years. *Newsweek* magazine, a few years ago, asked him to list, in his opinion, the five most important books in all of history. Number one on the list was the book of Acts. He didn't say the Bible, probably because it's a book *of books*, but he said, "The book of Acts."[4] Others, of course, would have a different list and a different number one. The funniest list that I saw this week came from NYUlocal.com (New York University). They compiled a list of the most important and influential books of all time. Number one on *their* list was *Madame Bovary* by Gustave Flaubert. So, depending on who you ask, you'll get a different list. The National Book Foundation put *Absalom, Absalom!* by William Faulkner at the top of their list. Why Keillor put Acts at the top rather than Romans or the Gospel of John, I don't know. But today on the day of Pentecost—this special day in the life of the church—I invite you to turn to Acts 2.

1. Preached at First Church of the Nazarene in Kansas City, Missouri on May 15, 2016 (Pentecost; Year C).

2. The discussion of different types of power was particularly interesting, in my opinion, because of the images that it evoked in the minds of the listeners. Additionally, the closing image of a river as a "dis-tributary," in all likelihood was an unfamiliar word or idea, but it captured so well the idea of God as the source of our strength for service and ministry.

3. This sermon was written eighteen months or so before Keillor was accused of sexually inappropriate conduct in November of 2017. If I was going to preach this sermon in some revised form today, I would change the bulk of the first paragraph of the introduction.

4. Newsweek Staff, "A Life in Books."

160

PENTECOST IS ABOUT POWER

Acts 2:1–41

The story of Pentecost is a story of power. Here in the Northern Hemisphere and particularly here in the Midwest, Pentecost almost always comes around each year during tornado season. *Because* of that, we know, in ways that others places don't, about the power of a violent wind. When Acts 2 says, "suddenly a sound like the blowing of a violent wind came from heaven and filled the whole house," we know that part of what this story is about is power. You and I are well aware that power comes in all kinds of varieties, forms, and expressions. I'm about the furthest thing from an auto-mechanic that you could find. But even I know that when gasoline is mixed with spark plugs and pistons and the internal workings of a combustion engine, the result is power. Or when the sky turns that crazy shade of green and the news interrupts the television program to say that the radar show lots and lots of red "storm-cells," beware or take cover because there's about to be the unleashing of power. When those "storm chasers" capture the footage of that funnel cloud spinning up debris until it turns brown and gray, you and I both know that we're observing power. Or, when a weightlifter reaches down and pulls on a bar that bends under the load on both ends, we're seeing power. When you're on that plane as it's barreling down the runway, when it lifts off and pushes you back into the seat, you're experiencing power. When candidates meet with political leaders and there are negotiations, press releases, and carefully worded statements, we're witnessing angles and plays for power. There are almost limitless forms, shapes, variations, and expressions of something we would name as "power."

When the Roman Empire, in cahoots with a nervous and self-preserving religious establishment, marched a traveling preacher outside the walls of Jerusalem to the local place of execution, it was an intentional and blatant display of power.[5] When they pinned the preacher down with spikes through hands and feet and then raised him up above the ground for potential "rebels" to see, the Romans were parading their power. In the glow of Rome's power, the disciples of Jesus had slinked into the shadows. Some had slipped away quietly, secretly. One in particular had gone away with the echo of his own boisterous denials ringing in his own ears.[6] But, eventually, *all* of them were aware that their leader and friend had been wrapped up in grave clothes, sealed with death, and buried in a borrowed tomb. They became acutely aware of their own powerlessness.

---

5. Luke 23:32–33.
6. Reference to Simon Peter.

162   SECTION 4: EASTER SUNDAY, THE EASTER SEASON, AND PENTECOST

Between then and Pentecost, however, the most important event in all of history took place: God raised Jesus from the dead.[7] Jesus was resurrected, never to die again, and he spent forty days walking with, talking with, and teaching his disciples. Obviously, something dramatic had changed, yet the disciples were still powerless. They were filled with joy and thankful that Jesus was alive. They were grateful for the additional time that they were allowed to spend with him. They were still trying to comprehend what God had done and was doing in Jesus, but they were essentially the same. Then, Jesus left them, returned to the Father and ascended into heaven.[8] For the last ten days, the disciples and other followers of Jesus—about 120 of them—have been in Jerusalem praying and waiting for the promise that Jesus gave them. He had told them to "stay in the city until you have been clothed with power from on high"[9] and that in a few days "you will be baptized with the Holy Spirit."[10]

Pentecost *is* about power, but a different power from the Roman oppression, threats, and saber-rattling. Pentecost is about the God-given, Father-sent power that comes through the filling of the Holy Spirit. Listen to what happens: They—meaning the disciples of Jesus gathered in Jerusalem—"saw what seemed to be tongues of fire that separated and came to rest on each of them. *All* of them were *filled with the Holy Spirit* and began to speak in other languages as the Spirit *enabled* them."[11] What I want you to see and notice is that this *power*—this "enabling" to do what they couldn't do before—is God-given. It is God-provided. The expression in Acts 2 was the ability to speak in all kinds of different languages so that the people who were gathered in Jerusalem from all around the known world could hear and understand the gospel message of Jesus. At other times throughout the book of Acts, and other places in the New Testament, there are examples of when it is the power of the Holy Spirit that makes things possible that were otherwise impossible. Sometimes it's miraculous healings, being delivered from prison, or people being converted who were hostile and resistant. In one of the writings of the apostle Paul (whose own conversion displayed the *power* of the Spirit) he wrote, "May the God of hope fill you with all joy and peace as you trust in him, so that you may overflow with hope by the *power of the Holy Spirit.*"[12] Having hope in the midst of situations of hopeless-

---

7. Luke 24:1–12.

8. Luke 24:50–53.

9. Luke 24:49

10. Acts 1:5.

11. Acts 2:3ff, emphasis added.

12. Rom 15:13 emphasis added.

PENTECOST IS ABOUT POWER

ness is the power of the Spirit. Having joy and peace in circumstances that would naturally call for discouragement and anxiousness is the power of the Spirit. Pentecost is about power, and specifically, it's about a God-*given* power through the indwelling or filling presence of the Spirit that is not self-generated. As one of my favorite preachers wrote, "Only in the power of the Spirit can you believe the unbelievable, hope for the grace beyond your grasp, [trust] the glory beyond the grave, [and] love with God's own love poured into your hearts."[13]

This brings me to the third idea this morning: the God-given power of Pentecost, then and now, pushes us out to serve. In Jerusalem, around 30 AD, it pushed the disciples into the streets to proclaim the good news of Jesus to those who had never heard. Much of Acts 2, as you heard, is a sermon by the most vocal, but often one of the most "wayward," of Jesus' disciples. Peter, who spent much of his time with Jesus removing one foot from his mouth in order to insert the other, becomes the *primary* and *key* spokesperson for the gospel. *That,* in and of itself, is a miracle of the Spirit.

It's like God blows a violent wind onto and into the disciples and it propels them out into the streets of Jerusalem for ministry, which takes the form of proclamation. But that's just the beginning. The rest of the book of Acts is the story of how God continues to blow and breathe his presence and power so that the disciples do what Jesus said would happen. Remember? Jesus said, "You will receive *power* when the Holy Spirit comes on you; and you will be my witnesses in Jerusalem, and in all Judea and Samaria, and to the ends of the earth."[14] Imagine an ever-widening circle of influence, ministry, and service. You can read the book of Acts and watch that happen. Immediately on the day of Pentecost, it's Jerusalem. In the next few chapters, the disciples are preaching, healing, serving, and being arrested and jailed in Jerusalem. Then, in chapter 7, Stephen—the first martyr for faith in Christ—is stoned to death.[15] Listen to what happens immediately: "On *that* day a great persecution broke out against the church at Jerusalem, and *all* except the apostles were scattered." Listen to *where* they were scattered: "*throughout Judea and Samaria.*"[16] By the end of Acts, the apostle Paul, who began as a persecutor of the church, has been transformed by the *power* of the Spirit to become the church's greatest missionary. By the end of Acts, Paul is headed to Rome with the intention of going on to Spain with the gospel. To them at that time,

13. Burghardt, *Lovely,* 62, adapted. The words "trust" and "and" were added for clarity and to better match my own speech patterns.

14. Acts 1:8, emphasis added.

15. Acts 7:54–60.

16. Acts 8:1, emphasis added.

164   SECTION 4: EASTER SUNDAY, THE EASTER SEASON, AND PENTECOST

Spain was the end of the earth—it was as far as they knew or could imagine. The power of the Spirit and of Pentecost is for ministry and service; it's for compassion to our neighbor and to the world. The power of Pentecost pushes us *out* and *to* and *for* others. But the power is not ours. It comes from the source of strength—from the presence of God.

For the first eighteen years of my life, I lived in a river town. Charleston, West Virginia sits on the banks of the Kanawha River. It's deep and navigable. Barges of coal are pushed downstream on the river as the river makes its way toward Point Pleasant, West Virginia. There, it empties into and adds to the strength of the Ohio River. The Ohio meanders its way in a westerly direction and forms the border between West Virginia and Ohio. Then it goes over the top side of Kentucky and eventually makes its way to Cairo, Illinois where it spills into the mighty Mississippi. Coming from the east, the Ohio River is the largest tributary for the Mississippi. Coming from the west, the largest tributary is the Missouri River. Over a course of hundreds of miles, the Mississippi rolls south toward New Orleans. It's the setting for Mark Twain's classic novels and many great, old songs. It is the signature river for our country.

The Mississippi drains over *one million* square miles of the nation—about 37 percent of the continental U.S. One source said that seven thousand rivers and streams eventually feed *into* the Mississippi. It's huge, long, powerful, and mighty. But, did you know that there are not only "tributaries" for the Mississippi but also "*dis*-tributaries"? The Atchafalaya River is a distributary—the opposite of a tributary. Its source is the Mississippi and the water that it carries is the Mississippi's. It has no life, no future, no power, and no source without the Mississippi. As a *dis*tributary, the Atchafalaya is pushed out with power to "distribute" the bounty and blessing of its source.

The church—Jesus' followers in the world—are *dis*tributaries who share the love of God as the power of the Spirit pushes them outward to others. Pentecost is about a different kind of power than what the Roman Empire or *any* empire understands. Pentecost is a God-given, God-sourced power through the presence of his Spirit. That power—the power of the Spirit—pushed the disciples out into the streets, and it pushes us out for ministry and compassion, for justice and service. On Pentecost, here at the table, we gather to be enabled and filled by our Lord's presence, the source of love and strength. We are filled so that we might be distributed to the world to do his will and for his purposes of compassion, proclamation, and love.

Amen.

SERMON 34[1]

Rushing In and Pushing Out[2]

Acts 2:1–13

Today is Pentecost Sunday. This special day on the Christian calendar doesn't get as much attention as Easter or Christmas, but it's one of the biggies. Every year on Pentecost, we read from the second chapter of Acts. I invite you to turn there in your Bible. This story happens on the first Pentecost after the resurrection of Jesus from the dead.

Acts 2:1–13

"Pentecost": the word means fiftieth, and the origin of Pentecost stretches back into the days and times of the Old Testament. Think back and try to remember some of those stories from the Old Testament that you may have learned as a child. You remember when the people of Israel were being held as slaves in Egypt. They were making bricks for Pharaoh. They had been there for hundreds of years and then God raised up Moses to lead them out of their bondage. God was going to send various plagues on Pharaoh and the Egyptians in order to encourage the Pharaoh to let the people go free. There were locusts or seventeen-year-cicadas,[3] flies, frogs, darkness, and all kinds of terrible things. In the end, the firstborn child in every family was killed *unless* you had spread blood from a lamb on the doorframe of your

1. Preached at First Church of the Nazarene in Kansas City, Missouri on May 24, 2015 (Pentecost; Year B).

2. The strength of this sermon was the portrayal of the contrast between "before" and "after" Pentecost in the life of Peter and the other disciples. This was an invitation for the listeners to relate more closely to one state of the disciples or the other. Near the conclusion, the confession of the overweight man is particularly poignant.

3. Missouri and Kansas were preparing at the time for the emergence of millions of cicadas.

165

166   SECTION 4: EASTER SUNDAY, THE EASTER SEASON, AND PENTECOST

home. These were God's instructions. God had commanded this action, and if you had done it, then the angel of death would pass over your home and your firstborn would be spared. That's the origin of what Jews all over the world still celebrate today as the feast of Passover. It was on *that* night that the people of Israel were freed from their slavery and Moses began to lead them across the desert and *through* the sea[4] on their way to the land that God had promised to them.[5]

So far, so good. Many people are somewhat familiar with that part of the story. Eventually, Moses led the people to the foot of Mount Sinai—God's holy mountain—and it was there that Moses received the law and instructions from God about all kinds of things. One of the stipulations of the law was that God was to receive an offering of grain, a bull, or a lamb as a way for the people to recognize and honor that everything they had and shared were gifts from God. This was meant to be offered at the culmination of the harvest festival and that was supposed to happen fifty days—note that—*fifty days* after the Passover. Pentecost became a great time of celebration. It was a feast. It was a festival. It was a time to gather together, to worship the Lord, to give him thanks, and to celebrate his miraculous, on-going provision for them. So, every year from all over the world, Jews came to Jerusalem to celebrate the conclusion of the harvest. They came to remind themselves of how the Lord had provided for them and cared for them throughout their history as a people. We have read the story of what happened on the first Pentecost celebration after the crucifixion, resurrection, and ascension of Jesus. Remember: Jesus was raised from the dead, he spent forty days with his disciples before he ascended to the Father, and then he instructed his disciples to go to Jerusalem to pray and wait. They did that for ten solid days. If you were to sit down with your calendar, you would discover that we celebrate Pentecost on the fiftieth day after Easter. If Easter is day one, then today is day fifty. Seven weeks ago *today* was Easter.

How could the disciples, on *this* day, preach the good news to all these people who were packed into Jerusalem from all the corners of the known world? How, on *this* day, were they so bold, when only days ago, they were fighting among themselves as to who would be the greatest,[6] and when only days ago they were denying that they ever *knew* Jesus[7]? How, on *this* day, could they proclaim the good news of Jesus Christ when just a few weeks ago they were hiding in fear behind locked doors and anxious for their lives?

---

4. The arguments over Red Sea or Reed Sea do not matter in the end.

5. Exod 7–12.

6. Mark 9:34.

7. Matt 26:70–72.

What happened to them? What transpired in them? What had taken place in their lives that resulted in this incredible transformation?

On the day of Pentecost, God poured out his Spirit on them and launched the Church of Jesus Christ in a dramatic and powerful way. On *that* day, the fearful, contentious, Jesus-denying, and Jesus-deserting disciples became the bold, unified, fearless preachers of the risen Lord. On Pentecost, the disciples were moved from spiritual paralysis to supernatural proclamation of the cause and kingdom of God. Miraculously, they moved from paralysis to proclamation. If we were to read further in Acts 2 today, we would hear how, through the preaching of Peter and the others, three-thousand became followers of Jesus the Christ and were added to the Church. *Three-thousand* became followers of Jesus in a single day in response to Peter's message. From being bound by fear, uncertainty, and caution, the disciples moved to bold, aggressive proclamation of and for Christ. How does that happen?

There is no reasonable or human explanation. The followers of Jesus hadn't called for a meeting, talked about it, strategized about it and decided, "We're just going to have to go out there and *make it happen.*" Kind of like when the basketball players huddle up on the sideline and they all put their hands together and somebody says. "One, two, three," and they all shout, "champions," or whatever. That's *not* what happened in the upper room on that first Pentecost after the resurrection of Jesus. The Bible says that the Spirit of God, like a mighty, rushing wind, came upon them. They couldn't control it, command it, or time it just right. They were not activators in the story, but receivers. If you've followed the news these past few weeks, you've seen pictures and heard stories about the power of wind. Tornadoes have touched down in all kinds of places throughout the Midwest. These are not unfamiliar events to folks like us. We live in "tornado alley." Hopefully, everybody here has a plan for where they'll go or hide when the sirens go off or the weather forecaster says that there's one on the ground in the area. We've even had experts come and tell us where the best places to shelter would be here in the church building. Tornadoes are sheer power. Cars get picked up and turned upside-down. Houses that were well-constructed and strong get blown away like they were made of sticks. Foundations are wiped clean as everything is taken away by the wind. Tornadoes are sheer *power.*

That's what the coming of the Spirit upon those disciples did for them. God empowered them as the Spirit came upon them like a mighty wind. The Spirit empowered them to do things that they could not have imagined doing in their own strength. The Spirit empowered them to do things that they simply could not do before Pentecost. Peter couldn't stand up to a teenage girl in the courtyard when she pointed her finger at

168   SECTION 4: EASTER SUNDAY, THE EASTER SEASON, AND PENTECOST

him and said, "You were with Jesus." He couldn't even admit that he was a friend of Jesus. Instead, he fumed, cursed, and denied that he even knew Jesus *before* Pentecost. Peter did not know and had not experienced the kind of power and fearlessness for ministry that he experienced through the poured-out, filled-up presence of the Holy Spirit in his life. *After* Pentecost, with his life empowered for ministry, Peter was willing and able to stand up in front of Jews from all over the world and in front of the most powerful religious leaders of his culture to proclaim the gospel of grace and life through Jesus, the Christ. *Before* Pentecost, he was powerless. *After* Pentecost, he had power. Had something changed on the outside for Peter? Was Peter a rugged fisherman *before* Pentecost and something different *after* Pentecost? Had his appearance changed? Had his mannerisms changed? Had the basics of his personality changed? No, of course not. On the outside, Peter was still rugged, sunburned, and tough. He still had the same personality traits and mannerisms, but *now*, Peter's life, gifts, and passions were empowered by the Spirit of God. The power was *within*. It was the Holy Spirit living and dwelling within Peter.

I remember a news story from several years ago that some of you may have followed. It was the story of a man who had a severe weight problem. I don't remember all the details or all the factors that were involved but, at one point, this man weighed in excess of one *thousand* pounds. He needed to be hospitalized. You've seen stories like this that involve some kind of intervention. His family and friends stepped in, sought out help, and eventually he was taken to a special hospital. At one point, this man had lost eight hundred pounds. He got his weight under control, but then he gained it all back. What is revealing about the story is the comment that he made about himself as he was being taken to the hospital for the second time. He said, "When I lost those eight hundred pounds, I only changed the *outside*. The *inside was still the same*."

Like Peter could have done, we can make changes to the outside. We can hide or alter the outside. But if we are to become overcomers *through* Christ,[8] become bold witnesses *for* Christ, live as empowered servants *of* Christ, then we will have to be changed from the inside. We will have to be empowered by the presence of the living God *within* us. We cannot make ourselves into more powerful witnesses or into more courageous disciples. That's not within our control. However, when we completely surrender *all* that we are to God, and prayerfully and persistently invite God's Spirit to rush in and fill our lives like a mighty wind, then that's when we'll be bold witnesses. That's when fear

8. 1 John 5:4.

RUSHING IN AND PUSHING OUT

will be overcome. That's when we'll be pushed out among the people and into the world for ministry and impact.

After Pentecost, the disciples wanted one thing: they wanted Christ to be proclaimed. They wanted Christ to be lifted up. They wanted Christ to be made known. Everything became secondary to Christ. The Holy Spirit rushed in and pushed everything else out. Their desire for greatness—at the right and left of Jesus—was pushed out. Their fear of disapproval by their contemporaries was pushed out. Their fear of the future was pushed out. Their overriding obsession with themselves was pushed out when the Holy Spirit came in with power. They were filled with God's Spirit and pushed out into their community with and for the good news of God's love revealed in the life, death, and resurrection of Jesus.[9] We gather around the Lord's Table on this Pentecost Sunday to be filled with God's presence and grace. We gather here, inviting the Spirit to rush in like a tornadic wind and push us out from these walls, so we can become the bearers and sharers of Christ's love and mercy to our world.

Amen.

9. If not responding to the message with the Lord's Supper, a song or hymn that revolves around the themes of Pentecost could be sung and the people commissioned to go and minister in the name and strength of Jesus.

SERMON 35[1]

Greeting Cards, the Center Section, and Centrifugal Force[2]

Acts 2:1–21

It's a "holy-day" weekend, as you know.[3] Over a period of just a few weeks, there are all these special days—special Sundays. Mother's Day was two weeks ago. Father's Day is three weeks from today and the greeting card companies would like to say "thank you."[4] Of course, when "you care to send the very best," you send a certain kind of card to Mom or Dad or whoever. Millions upon millions of cards have been crisscrossing the country. You can find cards for this and that and almost everything—every occasion, every celebration, and every holiday. But, what about *today?*

You didn't hear about it in the news, on television, or via Twitter, but *today* is right up there with Christmas and Easter for the Church. I'm told that about 57 million Easter cards are exchanged. I'm told that the card-count for Christmas is about 1.5 *billion*. The Pentecost card-count, I think, stands at zero. Yet, it is one of the three most important days in the whole Christian year. At its core, Pentecost is about power. It's about movement and force.

---

1. Preached at First Church of the Nazarene in Kansas City, Missouri on May 27, 2012 (Pentecost; Year B).

2. Part of the effectiveness of this sermon was the portrayal of the smallness of the group in Acts 2 and yet how God uses them to change the world. Additionally, the contrast of centripetal and centrifugal forces helped to illustrate the change in Jesus' disciples quite powerfully.

3. Memorial Day was the next day. The word "holiday," of course, is rooted in "holy day." I was utilizing a bit of sarcastic humor here, but I am confident that some did not perceive it.

4. Kansas City is the headquarters of Hallmark Cards.

170

GREETING CARDS, THE CENTER SECTION, AND CENTRIFUGAL FORCE   171

Acts 2:1–21

In John 16, Jesus tells his disciples that he is departing, but that the advocate—the Spirit—will be sent. Acts 2—the story of Pentecost—is the fulfillment of the prophet Joel's preaching and of Jesus' preaching. Acts 2 is a story of movement, force, and power. After the resurrection of Jesus, he spent forty days with his disciples. They talked together, travelled together, and ate together. They shared life for forty days and then Jesus said, "Go to Jerusalem and wait. Wait for the promise. Wait for the Spirit to be poured out."[5] So they did. They gathered together. They prayed and waited and waited some more. When the story of Acts 2 opens, they are, as verse 1 says, "all together in one place." Have you ever thought about that? From the beginning of time in the creative plan and action of God (over a span of years that is hard to even imagine), God had been creating, working, and moving. At *that* moment on the day of Pentecost about 30 AD, God had been shaping, leading, and using a particular people for *thousands* of years. He had chosen them, multiplied them, revealed himself to them, and delivered them from all kinds of dangers and perils. God had preserved them from extinction. God had given to them gifts of revelation, land, and purpose. Then, at just the right moment in the grand history of the universe and in the history of God's chosen people, God revealed himself in human flesh in Jesus of Nazareth. For *centuries*, the promised Messiah had been longed for and hoped for. *Now*, he has come into the world and into their lives.

Few saw it or recognized it.[6] But, for about three years, he lived, taught, preached, and healed. He gathered disciples with whom he shared his life. Throngs of people followed him from place to place. Thousands heard him teach and preach. In fact, in one place in the New Testament, Jesus fed more than five thousand people at one time from a boy's lunch.[7] The life and ministry of Jesus reached thousands of people, spanned at least three years, and covered hundreds of miles, most of them by walking. After touching *thousands* of people, spending *years* of time, and covering *hundreds* of miles, do you find it utterly amazing that on the day of Pentecost "all" were together in "*one* place"? In Acts 1:15, Luke—in kind of a parenthetical comment—tells us that there were about 120 believers. Really? Throughout the grand, majestic, long story of creation and salvific history, we come to this moment in God's great plan and we are left with a group of *120* people? We're left with a group that would fit comfortably

---

5. Paraphrase of Acts 1:5.

6. John 1:10.

7. Matt 14:13–21 and parallels.

172   SECTION 4: EASTER SUNDAY, THE EASTER SEASON, AND PENTECOST

in *one* section of this church sanctuary? Can you imagine that? Have you ever thought about that? The incredible plan of God at that moment in history fits in the center section at Kansas City First Church.[8]

Of course, the good news is that there's a wind that's blowing and fire that's falling and, as the Scripture says, they "were all filled with the Holy Spirit" (Acts 2:4). God took control of their lives like he never had before. The capacity of their lives was filled up with the Spirit—with the power and presence of the Creator and Redeemer. They became *more* than they had ever been before. There is this incredible and undeniable difference between what these people had been like *before* Pentecost and what they were like *after* Pentecost. It's like the difference between centripetal and centrifugal. Even though those words sound very much alike, the force and outcome are very different. Before Pentecost, the disciples could be described as centripetal. They were pushed or pointed inward. They were concerned about themselves. To use the Latin, they were *incurvatus in se*—"curved in upon themselves." They were navel gazers, self-preserving, and self-serving. They succumbed to centripetal force—a force that pushed them inward. But, then the wind and fire of the Spirit of God moved upon them. Something happened. Something *changed*. They went from being centripetal people to centrifugal people. Almost everyone in this room knows what it's like to be impacted by centrifugal force. If not, we can arrange for that to happen after service down on the children's playground. Right between the slide and the jungle gym is a merry-go-round. Any volunteers?

When I was a kid, we lived next to an elementary school. We had access to the playground almost year round. Back then, before bike helmets, elbow pads, and million dollar litigation, the object of the game was to get kids on the merry-go-round and then to get the thing spinning around so fast that the force would throw them off into the yard. If you were the last one thrown off, then you got to be the one to spin the merry-go-round the next time. We were experiencing centrifugal force—force that was pushing us out, away, and beyond.

Pentecost is a story of the centrifugal force of the Spirit. The Spirit came rushing in like a wildfire. When the Spirit was poured out, the disciples were pushed out. They were pushed out into the streets of Jerusalem. They were pushed out among all the peoples of the world gathered there. Eventually, they were pushed out beyond Jerusalem to Judea and Samaria and to the ends of the earth. Acts is the story of Spirit-generated, centrifugal force that compels the disciples *beyond* themselves, out from their little circle to the Jews first and then to the gentiles of the entire world. That story

---

8. Each local context would afford some way of capturing the size of 120 people.

GREETING CARDS, THE CENTER SECTION, AND CENTRIFUGAL FORCE   173

is the story of the church. It is the story of history since the birth of the Church on the day of Pentecost. It's the story of the good news of Jesus that is being proclaimed on every corner of the globe, translated into virtually every language and dialect on the planet, and lived by people of every race, color, and ethnicity in the world.

What will *this* local expression of church look like, act like, and commit itself to? How will *this* church reflect the world-wide, Spirit-driven, outward-directed Church that God planted on the day of Pentecost? We can be contributors to the Church's movement forward, to the life of Jesus in the world, and to the kingdom that has come and is coming. Or, we can worry about us, be curved in, and drag our feet as the designated brakes on the merry-go-round. Bishop Claude Payne wrote:

> Christianity grew at a phenomenal rate in the first century because the early Christians made effective and dramatic use of their social networks to [reach] new adherents to Christianity. They evangelized family members, friends, acquaintances, and friends of friends. They were open, accepting, and ultimately, externally focused. Their enthusiasm for the Good News and the transformations it had [brought about] in their lives carried them *out* into the world.[9]

When we gather around the Lord's Table, we are sharing something that is being experienced by Jesus followers around the world. When we gather at his Table, we are being nourished, strengthened, and fed by God's grace so that we might be scattered by the centrifugal force of the Spirit into the world as the hands and feet of love, care, and mercy.

Amen.

---

9. Payne, *Reclaiming,* 132, adapted.

Section 5

Sermons for Post-Pentecost
Non-Festival Time Before Advent

SERMON 36[1]

The Year Uzziah Died[2]

Isaiah 6:1–13

The Sunday after Pentecost is always Trinity Sunday. and one of the passages that is suggested for this day in the Christian lectionary is a portion of Isaiah 6. Part of the reason is the familiar cry of the seraphim—"holy, holy, holy"—three times, therefore "trinity." Are you convinced? Neither am I, but I want us to look together at this fairly familiar passage. The lectionary suggests that we only read through verse 8, but there's no way that we can stop there. We'll read the entire chapter.

Isaiah 6:1–13

It was the year the Twin Towers of New York City came crashing down in a twisted pile of steel and concrete that pulverized everything in its path. Do you remember that year? Do you remember how you felt on that Tuesday morning? We were glued to the television. We watched as people fled the billowing remains of the World Trade Center. Some can remember it like it was yesterday. Even now, we see the images in our mind. We can recount where we were, who said what, and the first person who we thought to call.

1. Preached at First Church of the Nazarene in Kansas City, Missouri on May 31, 2015 (Trinity Sunday; Year B).

2. The effectiveness of this sermon, I think, was in the descriptions of various "years" when things happened. Some were national events and some personal. Homiletically, the key was the intention that people would remember or recreate their own series of events in their mind. Also, the temptation that "bigger is better in all things" was rebuffed by the neglected verses of Isaiah 6, and also by the ways and story of Jesus. This was particularly meaningful in our culture, and specifically in a church culture, that often defines "success" by a larger, ever-increasing number of attendees and more dollars contributed. In a church that had understood itself in these ways, this was a challenging and difficult word. Within the entire collection of sermons, this is one of my favorites.

177

If we scratch deep enough, we can feel the emotion of the moment, hear the sounds of confusion, and taste the dryness in our mouth when our stress level shot through the ceiling.

It was the year the doctor used the "C" word in our family. She said it with such ease and familiarity. It rolled off her tongue so fluidly and so nonchalantly. "Cancer." The ease with which she said it was the polar opposite with which it crashed into our lives. It was like a train going 100 mph around a curve designed for 50 mph,[3] and coming off the tracks with such violence and force that our world was turned upside-down. "Cancer," she said. If you pause long enough, you smell the hospital room, cringe at the incessant beeping of the machines, and hear again the multi-syllable medical terms that used to be reserved for experts, but are now indelibly imprinted on your brain and in your vocabulary.

It was the year that "big D" didn't refer to Dallas, but to the divorce. Between the lawyers, the kids, and the convoluted stories of what he did and what she said, the weeks plodded along like an elephant in a pre-circus parade. Head down. Eyes closed as if in a trance-like state that seemed to never end. You got a lesson in deception and depravity like you never imagined was possible. Now, all these years later, you're *still* reaping the consequences of seeds that were sown in that year so long ago.

What year was it for you? Was it the year that your best friend died unexpectedly? Was it the year that the boss said—out of the blue—"We're making some changes. This is your last day"? Was it the year that your dreams to do a certain thing or achieve a certain goal dissolved? What year *was* it? What year did it crash in? What year did the darkness invade? What year were you knocked to your knees, needing and pleading to see something—*anything*—from God?

"It was the year King Uzziah died," Isaiah said. "I saw the Lord seated on a throne, high and lifted up." It was 740 BC and Uzziah had been the king of Judah for *fifty-two years.* Up to that point in the history of Judah and Israel, it was the longest reign of any king in either kingdom. There were some who reigned a year or two before they were killed off by their rivals. There was one king in Israel who lasted all of seven days. But, King Uzziah, referred to as Azariah in the book of 2 Kings, reigned for more than half a century in Jerusalem. During the last years of his reign, the king was a leper. He was struck with leprosy because he had insisted on burning incense in the temple when it wasn't his task to do.

---

3. This is an allusion to an Amtrak train accident in Philadelphia on May 12, 2015. The train was going 106 mph around a sharp curve. Seven people were killed and over two hundred injured.

THE YEAR UZZIAH DIED 179

We should not miss the stark contrast of Isaiah's vision. The weak, old, feeble, leprous, long-standing king of a tiny nation is dead, but the majestic, holy, powerful, awe-inspiring, exalted Lord Almighty—whose glory fills the whole earth—is shaking the temple of God in Jerusalem with his presence. Don't miss it. Isaiah is living in a time of horrible and tragic things. Death, disappointment, stress, and weakness are on display. Then, Isaiah's vision is redirected and refocused. It's interesting to me that in verse 5 Isaiah says, "My eyes have seen the King, the Lord Almighty." King Uzziah is dead, but the King—the Lord Almighty—is alive and is reigning over his world. He's surrounded by flying monsters too weird to fully describe. Smoke billows from his presence. The picture is one of awe, power, and holiness, and that picture must be set in contrast to the fragile, weak, leprous, death-certain condition of the frail, momentary monarch. Isaiah's vision is of the "wholly Other."[4] There's no buddy-buddy here. This is not the "man upstairs" or some other poor, transcendence-denying euphemism for the Almighty Lord of the universe. In the light of the glaring holiness of God, with flying creatures screeching their thrice-repeated praise, Isaiah became immediately aware of his impurity and *lack* of holiness. This recognition turns quickly to confession. He cried out, "I am ruined. I am unclean. I live among a people who is unclean."

Impurity can't stand up to the glare of social media and Facebook. What do you think would happen to it in light of the holiness of the one true and living God? Nothing will be covered up or hidden. As the old Scottish proverb says, "Confession is good for the soul." Isaiah confessed his uncleanness and God responded with cleansing. It came in the form of a hot coal pressed to his lips accompanied by the assurance, "Your guilt is taken away and your sin atoned for." It's good for the soul, but oftentimes painful. In our time and culture, it's very difficult for us to put "good" together with "painful" in any kind of meaningful way. For our culture, if it's good, then it's pleasurable. If it's painful, then it's bad. But when it comes to cleansing or being purified, like a surgeon's scalpel causes pain, God's response to confession also brings healing and restoration.

It's at this point where the story takes an unusual turn. Isaiah's vision of God's presence and holiness leads to his confession and cleansing. Then, we hear of Isaiah's willingness to be sent by the Lord on a mission. You know, this is great preaching material for motivating and challenging folks to get to work, serve, and help the church move forward with whatever ministries and programs that the preacher wants to push. My guess is that this is why, most often, we stop reading the passage at verse 8, but if we continue reading *beyond* verse 8, what we discover is that God

4. Otto, *Idea of Holy.*

has appointed, commissioned, and sent Isaiah on a pre-determined mission of failure. "Here's your message, Isaiah: The people will listen but not understand. They'll see but not really get it. They'll be calloused and dull and you'll never make much progress."[5]

Isaiah asks, "How long, O Lord?"

I remember when I was in grade school a long time ago. Occasionally the teacher would say, "Who wants to do me a favor?" Some of us would raise our hand like Horshack from *Welcome Back Kotter*—"ooh, ooh."[6] We were willing to do whatever would be requested. The teacher usually picked two of us—"you and you"—and occasionally, I was a part of the chosen two. *Then*—only after we had already agreed to serve—would she give us our assignment. She'd say, "I want you to gather up all the dirty erasers"— that were full of chalk dust from weeks of cleaning the chalk board—"and I want you to take them down to the basement and clean them." The job meant descending into the dark, musty basement of our old school building, clapping erasers together hundreds of times, and breathing chalk dust with no ventilation. What did I sign up for? Why? Sounds a bit like Isaiah. Frankly, it sounds a bit like the disciples of Jesus. "Come, follow me," he said. No explanation. No description of the job. No warning about having no place to lay your head. There was no promise of success and no indication that the leaders of the culture will be adamantly opposed to the mission. Jesus gave no clue that the people will be fickle. They will chant "hosanna" one day and "crucify" the next.

What is this way characterized by a willingness to serve, yet being called to step into the unknown—even onto a path that doesn't necessarily lead to "success"(whatever *that* means), but to disappointment and rejection? What is this way that focuses on a tiny seed that may one day produce something good? At the very end of Isaiah 6, God tells the prophet that even though "cities will lie ruined" and "the fields will be ravaged and ruined," like a tree when it's cut down, there's always a stump. There's always a little something left. There's something in the ground that may produce something good somewhere down the road.

It's interesting to me that Isaiah had this amazing vision of the greatness of the Lord. He saw the holiness and the magnificent power of God. Yet, at the end, God is calling him to focus on the seed and the stump—on the little bit that might turn into something someday. We should probably understand this better in light of God's revelation in the life of Jesus, the

5. My own paraphrase.

6. A very popular sitcom in the 1970s. Gabe Kotter was the teacher in an urban high school. His classroom was filled with a variety of interesting characters. Horshack wanted to please.

Christ. We should be clearer on this, it seems, when God enfleshed himself in a peasant's baby that was born in a backwater barn. We should pay close attention to the temptation that Jesus faced right after his baptism when the adversary challenged him to do something big and spectacular—"Throw yourself down off the pinnacle of the Temple. Everybody will see it. It will be like an awe-inspiring vision and everyone will instantaneously *recognize* who you are."[7] No, Jesus puts his head down and gathers to himself a few fishermen, a tax collector, and some other rag-tag men from the countryside of Galilee. He walks with them through a few months and years. He heals a blind man here and a leper there. He feeds a crowd or two, but when they want to make him the "Bread King,"[8] he slips off into the shadows. Toward the end, when the pressure has been turned up and the opposition is white hot, he's abandoned by the crowds and most of his inner circle. His mother sticks with him to the end like you would expect a mother to do.

In light of the cross of Jesus and in light of this being the way that God ultimately reveals his character and essence to us, maybe our desires should not be to have visions of grand, glorious, and powerful displays with smoke and flying monsters, but of smallness, humility, and sacrificial pictures of love. Maybe it's that year for you. It's the year that King Uzziah died. It's the year that it crashed in. Sometimes I wish that the Church could just "wow" you or overwhelm you with visions of power and assurance. I wish that the Church could make promises that everything will work out and turn up roses. But, that would be disingenuous. What the Church *does* offer to you is something small—a piece of bread and a few drops from a cup—but, *in it*, the *presence* of God and the promise to accompany you, by the Spirit, through every day and year regardless of what it holds. It was the year King Uzziah died and it is the year that I held the bread and cup in my hands. It's the year that I tasted the grace and presence of God.

Amen.

7. My paraphrase and interpretation of Matt 4:5–7.
8. John 6:1–15, specifically verse 15.

SERMON 37[1]

Nic at Night[2]

John 3:1–17

On this Trinity Sunday—the Sunday after Pentecost—we are directed to the third chapter of John. Within this story is the most memorized and most quoted single verse in all of the Bible. Most of the time, however, this verse is lifted out of its context—which is the story of Nicodemus. Let's look at that story together this morning.

John 3:1–17

As we look more closely at the story of Nicodemus, one of the things that we can infer is that Nicodemus had apparently been observing and tracking the ministry of Jesus. He had been paying attention to this travelling preacher from Nazareth. We might say that Nicodemus had been a *spectator*. He had been an *observer*. He apparently had been close enough to Jesus' ministry that he knew where Jesus would be staying on this particular night because he came to him and found him. He had been close enough to be aware of some of what Jesus was teaching and preaching. He had observed enough to know that many perceived Jesus to be a rabbi.

In verse 2, Nicodemus, a leader himself, says: "Rabbi, we know you are a teacher." How did they *know* he was a teacher and a "teacher who has come from God"? Part of the answer is that they were watching and tracking. They had been close enough to observe him. They knew at least *some* of what he

---

1. Preached at First Church of the Nazarene in Kansas City, Missouri on June 3, 2012 (Trinity Sunday; Year B).

2. The tripartite structure of spectator, seeker, and follower was, in my view, a particularly relevant and meaningful rubric to emphasize in this passage about Nicodemus. The illustrations involving Camus and Bonhoeffer were especially meaningful and captivating, it seemed to me.

182

was teaching. They knew that he was versed in the Law and the Prophets. They realized that he was familiar with their Scriptures. They were witnesses to the fact that he had gathered disciples and that crowds were following him and listening to him teach. They knew all that. In addition, they were aware that miracles were being worked through him. They either had witnessed miracles for themselves or they had received reports from people whom they trusted about Jesus' healing of the sick, opening of blinded eyes, and the cleansing of lepers. Nicodemus had been a spectator who was standing back and observing what Jesus had done and taught.

We live immersed in a spectating culture. Conversations around the coffee pot at work are devoted to what everybody watched last night on television. Bowling leagues, softball leagues, and tennis courts have dried up, stand empty, or go unused so that we can sit at home and watch others play games. Being a spectator of culture, sports, or television has become, for some, a full-time endeavor that dominates their lives.

You realize that there are lots of spectators in the twenty-first century when it comes to Jesus and the things of God? There are people all around who know *a little bit* of what Jesus taught. They have seen a few things that Jesus has done and may have a few questions about who Jesus is, but they never move beyond being spectators or observers. We live in a time and culture when being a spectator has been taken to new heights. But when it comes to Jesus, the kingdom, and the things of God, being a spectator isn't good enough. Being a spectator falls short of the goal. Being a spectator isn't sufficient. It's not God's plan for us. God wants us to move beyond being a spectator. Even Nicodemus moves beyond that.

When Nicodemus comes to Jesus to talk about certain issues with him, Nicodemus moves from being a spectator to what I would call a seeker. There's a definite difference between these things. Had Nicodemus simply been aware of Jesus, knew some of what he taught, been told about his miracles, then you and I would probably never have known anything about Nicodemus. There were lots of people who were aware of Jesus' teaching and even witnessed some of his miracles who never moved beyond simply observing. Nicodemus moved beyond that and became a seeker. He came seeking more. He came seeking answers and insight.

He came to Jesus "at night," the Bible says. There and then, Jesus began to teach him about the radical transformation that the kingdom of God would require and Nicodemus just couldn't get it. Jesus began to talk to him about being "born again," and Nicodemus couldn't make sense of it. He was trying to grasp what Jesus was saying in purely physical, logical, and tangible categories. Yet, Jesus was teaching him the "mysteries" of the kingdom. Even though Nicodemus wasn't fully understanding, he was seeking, and

184   SECTION 5: POST-PENTECOST NON-FESTIVAL TIME BEFORE ADVENT

seeking is crucial to the process. After all, Jesus said in his Sermon on the Mount, "Ask and it will be given to you; *seek* and you will find; knock and the door will be opened to you."[3] Seeking is *so* very important.

Howard Mumma was a Methodist minister from Ohio who served as a guest preacher at the American Church in Paris during several summers in the middle of the twentieth century. While there, he formed a friendship with a famous Frenchmen who had come to the church, mainly to hear the beautiful music played on the magnificent pipe organ. While he was there for the beautiful music, God began to speak to him through the preaching of Howard Mumma. Forty years later, when Mumma was ninety-two years old, he recounted what he had been told by Albert Camus. Camus said, "The reason I have been coming to church is because I am *seeking*. I'm almost on a pilgrimage—seeking something to fill the void that I am experiencing—and no one else knows . . . Deep down you are right—I am searching for something that the world is not giving me."[4] Albert Camus, of course, was a famous existentialist philosopher and atheist who had won a Nobel prize for literature in the late 1950s. "Deep down," he said, "I'm searching for *something that the world is not giving me*."[5]

We live in a world that is searching to fill the void that is within—a God-shaped, God-created void. People are searching in work, leisure, activity, possessions, drugs, and distractions. Folks are searching here, there, and everywhere. Being married to a Texan, I have to refer to President Lyndon Johnson from time-to-time just to keep the peace. LBJ is quoted as saying, "The answer for all our national problems—the answer for all the problems of the world—comes down to a *single word. That* word is 'education.'"[6] No, education won't "fill the void." Possessions won't fill the void. Pleasure won't fill the void. God has made us in such a way that only a living, vibrant, sins-forgiving, life-transforming, Spirit-filled relationship with him can fill the void. Only *his* presence can truly satisfy our heart's desire. There is no other answer for the void that is a part of each of our lives. Jesus said, "I am the Way, the Truth, and the Life. No one comes to Father but through me."[7]

We don't really know much about what happened to Nicodemus after this encounter with Jesus. I wish we had more details about his life and where he went from that nocturnal meeting with Jesus. He does help Joseph

---

3. Matt 7:7, emphasis added.

4. Mumma, "Conversations," 644.

5. Mumma, "Conversations," 644, emphasis added.

6. Whitaker and Lumpa, *Great Quotes*, 6, emphasis added.

7. John 14:6.

NIC AT NIGHT 185

of Arimathea prepare Jesus' body for burial.[8] What I *do* know is that being a spectator is not enough and that being a seeker is not enough. God wants us to be a follower—a disciple of Jesus Christ. We must be born again by his Spirit. We must be "born from above." We must "believe" in him, as verse 16 says, and give ourselves completely to him. We must trust him with our lives. That's what it means to be a follower—a disciple of Jesus. We give ourselves daily to the Lord. We ask him to use us for his purposes. We commit ourselves and our resources to him and for his kingdom in the world. Life begins to revolve around what *he* wants for us and what *he* desires for us. As someone said, "Christ is not looking for admirers but for disciples—those who will conform their lives to His."[9]

That's why we place such an emphasis upon discipleship and being a disciple of Jesus. That's why our mission as a congregation is to make Christlike disciples. That's why the Church of the Nazarene articulates its mission statement as to make Christlike disciples in the nations. Listen. The race will be completed by disciples. The "fight"[10] will be won by disciples. The obstacles and barriers will be overcome by disciples. Searching is good and necessary. Seeking is even better. But, discipleship is what Jesus calls us to and makes provision for through his life, death, and resurrection.

Dietrich Bonhoeffer was a Lutheran pastor in Germany. He was incredibly bright and talented. He pursued his education and excelled. He was a brilliant man with a brilliant mind. Then, onto the scene marched Adolf Hitler and Nazism to power in Germany. Bonhoeffer, as a young man, helped to begin what was called the Confessing Church. It was adamantly anti-Hitler and anti-Nazi. When World War II began, Karl Barth, Dietrich Bonhoeffer, and other leading thinkers and writers had multiple opportunities to escape to London or the U.S. In fact, Bonhoeffer came to the U.S, but then went back to Germany because he refused to take the "wide" or the "easy" path.[11] Eventually, he was threatened. He was banned from preaching or teaching. But, he resisted. Secretly and with his own money, he was helping Jews to escape from Germany into Switzerland. Ultimately, he was arrested and imprisoned in Berlin for a year and a half. Then he was sent to several concentration camps. It was at dawn on April 9th of 1945 when he was hanged at Flossenburg. He was 39 years old. Some of his writings have survived and been published. In one place, he wrote: "Cheap grace is grace without discipleship, grace without the cross, grace without Jesus Christ,

8. John 19:39–42.

9. Dunham, "Personal Holiness," 30.

10. "Race" and "fight" are allusions to 2 Tim 4:7.

11. Allusion to Matt 7:13–14.

186   SECTION 5: POST-PENTECOST NON-FESTIVAL TIME BEFORE ADVENT

living and incarnate."[12] He was never more right than when he wrote those words. He was *more* than a spectator. He was *more* than a seeker. He was a *disciple*—a follower of Jesus.

The power for discipleship comes from the presence of God's Spirit within our lives and living. We must be fed and nourished by the presence and power of God. Gathering at the Lord's Table on the first day of the week *reminds* us of that, *enacts* that, and *realizes* it for today and for the coming days. Will you invite God to work in you as you come to the Table? Will you invite the Lord to teach you more about discipleship and about following him? Will you allow the God of grace and help to strengthen you so that you might obediently and sacrificially follow after him in a world that would much prefer you to simply be a spectator?

Amen.

12. Bonhoeffer, *Cost of Discipleship*, 47.

SERMON 38[1]

Little Words, Huge Deal[2]

2 Corinthians 5:11–17

We all know this. We all know that little things can make a huge difference, right? When you get your paycheck for example, it's very important where they put the decimal point. That little dot makes a huge difference. Or when you're punctuating a sentence, that little comma is very important. Some of you may have seen this on a t-shirt or a coffee mug. Here it is on the screen: "Let's eat Grandpa" or "Let's eat, Grandpa"— "Commas: They save lives." That little comma is a *big* deal.

In the passage that we're about to read from 2 Corinthians, there are three words where I want to focus our attention. The words, in English, are very small—two and three letters a piece. They are very small words that make a huge difference.

2 Corinthians 5:11–17

At the beginning of this passage, the apostle Paul is pleading with these Corinthians to give him an honest hearing. He spent a year and a half with them and now he's separated from them. There are some who are being critical of his thoughts and ways. So, from a distance and as gently as he can, Paul is trying to defend himself. It seems as if he's trying to defend himself without appearing to be defensive. That's hard to do, but he gives it a go. He even goes so far as to say, as one translation puts it, "If I acted crazy, I did it

1. Preached at First Church of the Nazarene in Kansas City, Missouri on June 14, 2015 (Third Sunday after Pentecost; Year B).

2. The big theological ideas that were captured in these tiny English words was exciting to think about. The quote from Gordon Smith was so spot on that I couldn't resist quoting it at length. This sermon, I think, was an example of bringing foundational theological convictions and confession into the Sunday morning homiletical experience.

187

188   SECTION 5: POST-PENTECOST NON-FESTIVAL TIME BEFORE ADVENT

for God; if I acted overly serious, I did it for you."[3] In all likelihood, some in Corinth were claiming that Paul was crazy, "beside himself," or out of his mind. For the most part, he couldn't do anything about it. But in verse 14, Paul turns to the love and work of Christ and makes an incredible claim that, in English, involves this very small word with *huge* implications. He says: "We are convinced that one"—meaning Jesus—"died for *all.*" "All"— not the "good," "righteous," "religious," or "spiritual." Not the Jews. Not the Pharisees. Not the "morally upstanding." Not Americans. Not God-fearers. No single group, cluster, ethnicity, demographic, or subset can claim that Jesus died *only* for them—as if to exclude some particular group that, for whatever reason at that moment in history and circumstance, seemed undesirable. No church should say that Jesus died for *this* group to the sad and eternal detriment of *that* group. Nonsense. Unbiblical. Contrary to the plain reading of Scripture. Christ died for all, and "all" means *all.* The word is *pan-tone* in Greek. It's the word from which we get words like "panorama" and "pantheon." It's *all*-encompassing. Don't miss the implication of Christ dying for all which is, of course, that he died for *you.* Christ's death on a Roman cross in the first century was not solely for them, for those, or for the person seated next to you. No, it was for *you.* Don't let any preacher, teacher, or church tell you otherwise.

Now, when Christ died on the cross for you, there was a reason for it. I would dare to say that there were *multiple* reasons for it. Some of those reasons are much more familiar to our vocabulary than others. Some of them have shown up in theological language and images which have been borrowed from the New Testament. That list includes words like justification, pardon, regeneration, and the forgiveness of sins. Most of these would be familiar to many of us and they are important in helping us to understand the meaning or the purpose of Christ's death on the cross. But, those aren't the words or images that Paul uses here in 2 Corinthians. He uses different language and a different image. Look at what he says in verse 15: Christ "died for all, *so that*"—or "for *this* reason" or "to accomplish *this* purpose"— "that those who live should no longer live for themselves but for him who died for them and was raised again." Christ died so that our lives could be centered around him rather than around ourselves.

We are inclined to center life around ourselves. We are prone to make decisions and to situate life in such a way that *our* desires, *our* wishes, and *our* concerns are most important, most cherished, and at the center of life. In other places, the Bible and church has a word for that—we call it sin, and the most prevalent, world-wide, cross-cultural, see-it-everywhere

---

3. Peterson, *Message.*

expression of sin is self-centeredness. Some of you were taught this as a child by using the word "sin" in English. Your teacher drew attention to the fact that right in the middle of the word is the letter "I." Sometimes it was capitalized: "sIn."[4] When Dawn and I were living in Virginia, Margaret Thatcher, the great "Iron Lady" and prime minister, was leaving British politics. At a reception for departing lawmakers, Thatcher was asked what she would miss the most. Her response: "The tremendous feel that you are at the center of things."[5] We are inclined to want to be at the center of things, aren't we? The good news is that Jesus died so that we should no longer live for ourselves, but for him who died and was raised again *for* us. Christ died for *all*. It's a little word, but a huge deal.

The second little word that I want to point out is the word *en* in Greek. It shows up in verse 17 when it refers to Jesus-followers as being "in Christ." You might ask, "What's the big deal?" It's a *huge* deal and let me tell you why. First of all, many scholars now believe that this idea—this phrase—is the key to understanding all of the writings of the apostle Paul. For centuries, the idea of "justification" was the emphasis by those who read and studied Paul. Martin Luther and the Protestant reformers after him right down through scholars in recent years locked in on the idea of "justification" by grace through faith as central to Paul's teaching and thinking. It's very important and there's no doubt about it. Various forms of the word "justify" or "justification" show up in Paul's writings more than twenty times—primarily focused in Romans. Another related word-group is the word "righteous" or "righteousness." It is also very prevalent in Paul's New Testament letters. Again, Romans is the place where it occurs so frequently—more than forty times. When you put these two word-groups together, in Paul's writings in the New Testament, there are as many as *ninety-one* different references. That's a lot, but the little preposition "in" hooked to "Christ," "Jesus," or "the Lord" in the New Testament's writings of Paul *alone* shows up at least *140 times*. Gordon T. Smith writes:

> The phrase "to know, love and serve" is an immensely helpful baseline and aptly captures the call of Matthew, Mark and Luke. But as we probe further into the writings of the New Testament—notably the Gospel of John, the epistles of Paul and the book of Hebrews—what emerges is that the Christian ideal is not so much a life *with* Christ or *for* Christ, but rather a life *in* Christ . . . The Christian is invited not merely into the kingdom

---

4. The image works in English, but not in other languages.

5. Frankel, "British Notables."

of Christ, but specifically into dynamic union with the one who reigns—Christ Jesus himself.[6]

Being a follower of Jesus is not just about going to heaven—like I've got my ticket to the ball game or concert. It's not merely about sins forgiven, although that's important and vital. The *essence* of being a disciple of Jesus is union with Christ. It's about being "in Christ" and him being "in you" by the power of the Spirit. It's a life that is re-oriented entirely around him rather than around yourself.

In an old Broadway musical set in France, two of the main characters are a father and a son. They are arguing about the world and how it's changing. The old man works on a fisherman's wharf in Marseilles and in the midst of the argument, the son accuses his father. He says, "You think that Marseilles is the center of the earth." The old man's response is classic: "It is! That is north. This is south. That—east. That—west. *I* am here at the center!"[7] When we are "in Christ" and Christ is "in us," Jesus is *in* or moving toward the center and we are *out* or moving toward the periphery. *"In"* Christ—it's a little word, but a huge deal.

Next, I would draw your attention to the word "new." It's what happens when we are "in Christ." Look at verse 17. There are some words that show up in the English translations that are not present in the Greek. So, I want to offer a translation that reflects that. When it is translated very literally, here's verse 17: "If anyone—in Christ—*new* creation!"

The apostle Paul had experienced it for himself and he loved the idea of "newness," of transformation. He had left Jerusalem and was headed to Damascus to track down and persecute Christians, but somewhere on the road he came face-to-face with the risen Christ.[8] From that moment, things changed. As he says in Romans, our lives mimic the death and resurrection of Jesus. We're buried with him in baptism and then raised to life. Paul says, "Just as Christ was raised from the dead through the glory of the Father, we too may live a *new* life."[9] In Galatians, Paul writes about his heritage as a Jew and as a Pharisee. He sets it aside in light of being "in Christ." He says, "Neither circumcision nor uncircumcision means anything; what *counts* is a *new* creation!"[10] Ephesians 4, Colossians 3, and in several other places, Paul speaks of the "old self" and the "new self"—the

---

6. Smith, *Called*, 39.

7. *Fanny.*

8. Acts 9:1–19.

9. Rom 6:4, emphasis added.

10. Gal 6:15, emphasis added.

LITTLE WORDS, HUGE DEAL

"old self" being put away, left behind, or crucified and the "new self" being put on and all things becoming new.

Of course, this idea isn't restricted to Paul and his letters. In fact, the book of Revelation is filled with references to the "new heaven," the "new earth," and the "new Jerusalem." Toward the conclusion of the book, at the crucial moment when John is describing the amazing world that God will bring to pass, he writes, God "will wipe every tear from their eyes. There will be no more death or mourning or crying or pain, for the old order of things has passed away. He who was seated on the throne said, 'I am making everything *new!*'"[11] "New" is a little word in English, but it's a huge deal.

As we gather around the Lord's Table to share a little piece of bread dipped in the cup, these little words that have captured huge ideas are here. That Christ died for all is celebrated when we proclaim the Lord's death in our eating together. When we eat and drink, our life *in* Christ and Christ *in* us is portrayed in visible and tangible actions as we take and eat. Then, of course, we're reminded every time we gather that the cup is the *new* covenant in and through the blood—or the atoning death—of Jesus. It's all wrapped up right here in these three little words that are a huge deal: "all," "in," and "new." Christ's death and resurrection is for all. It's for *you* and you are meant to live in him with Jesus at the center of your living. When that happens, you are a new creation—a new creature—and old things pass away. To him be all glory and praise.

Amen.

---

11. Rev 21:4–5, emphasis added.

SERMON 39[1]

Sodas, Seeds, and the Kingdom[2]

Mark 4:26–29

I 've been preaching since I was sixteen years old. Better now than then, I hope. But in about thirty years of preaching and twenty years of preaching every week, I've never preached from this particular passage from the Gospel of Mark. There are, of course, some passages that I have preached from on numerous occasions—John 3, Philippians 2, Genesis 1, and Matthew 28—but *never* from Mark 4:26–29. I don't know really what to do with it and maybe that's the issue. It wants to do something to me. Let's look at these four verses from Mark 4 today.

Mark 4:26–29

This parable is the *only* parable in Mark that doesn't show up in either Matthew or Luke. The rest of Mark shows up in some form in Matthew or Luke and some portions of Mark are found in *both* Matthew and Luke. Most scholars think that Matthew and Luke had read Mark or even had a copy of

1. Preached at First Church of the Nazarene in Kansas City, Missouri on June 17, 2012 (Fourth Sunday after Pentecost; Year B).

2. In this sermon, I intentionally tried to utilize some of the thought and technique of Thomas Troeger. The sermon was intended to be a "movement of images." As described in Allen's *Patterns of Preaching*, "when developing the sermon as a movement of images, the images flow from one to another with a minimum of explanation from the preacher . . . The congregation enters into sights, sounds, touches, smells, tastes, and feelings of the image world." Allen, *Patterns of Preaching*, 104. I tried to string three images together as a way of hinting at the mysterious and elusive meaning of these verses. The first image was the use of a "Big Gulp" cup from 7–11, followed by the contrasting image of tiny seeds scattered in front of the platform, which led into the final image of two babies being dedicated in the place where the seeds were scattered. Typically, in this local setting, we dedicated babies toward the beginning of the service, but this ceremony was planned for the end of the sermon as its culmination and final image.

192

SODAS, SEEDS, AND THE KINGDOM

Mark available to them as they were writing. Most believe that Mark is the earliest of the Gospels that was written and now included in the New Testament. But for whatever reason, *these* verses with *this* teaching from Jesus in *this* parable doesn't get used or copied into Matthew or Luke. Maybe they didn't know what to do with it. Maybe it was a difficult message for even them to hear or understand.

The parables, in general, are quite elusive. For you football fans, they're a bit like Barry Sanders. You think you've got him "cornered" but somehow he slips away. Or, for the state fair folks: The parables are bit like when they turn the kids loose to capture the little, greased pig. One kid grabs it but it slips away and nobody can seem to keep hold of it—at least for very long. The parables are a bit that way, and this one may be particularly so. Part of its elusiveness is because the essence of this parable runs so contrary to the messages of our culture.

Some of you have followed a recent story coming out of New York City. The mayor, Michael Bloomberg, is trying to regulate or restrict the size of sugared sodas that you can purchase.[3] For him, the limit should be sixteen ounces. As you can see this morning, I have here on display a Big Gulp cup from 7-Eleven.[4] All the other competitors to 7-Eleven have similar things as you know, but the Big Gulp was kind of the pioneer. Most of us drank cans of soda or even glass bottles, but in 1980, when I was in junior high school, everything changed when the Big Gulp was introduced. A can had twelve ounces, but a Big Gulp had about thirty ounces. Then came the Super Big Gulp that had forty-four ounces. Now there's the Double Gulp that has about fifty ounces. I hear that they're conducting test-market analysis for the Five Gallon Bucket Gulp. Who knows what's next?

Who knew that *this* would serve as a picture of our culture? You and I live in a world where "bigger is better" in everything except computer micro-chips. Bigger houses, bigger garages, bigger businesses, and bigger churches are all "better." Success, value, and impact are measured by size, amount, or number—and bigger is always better. Sarah Wexler, a writer and historian, wrote a book called *Living Large* and she was interviewed by *Time* magazine. She was asked why Americans are so enamored with big things. She said, "Part of it is based on the history of our country and the idea that we had so much space to spread out across. There was the idea of manifest

---

3. Grynbaum, "New York Plans." Mayor Bloomberg's plan was challenged in court and eventually struck down in 2014.

4. Image number one was a large, plastic cup from a local convenience store. It was not a projected image on a screen but an actual cup.

194 SECTION 5: POST-PENTECOST NON-FESTIVAL TIME BEFORE ADVENT

destiny, that we were destined to expand westward until we hit another ocean . . . We coined the term 'go big or go home.'"[5]

This is simply the environment in which we live. Guinness World Records are being set every other day with the largest stack of pancakes or the biggest flash mob. In just a few weeks, somebody on Coney Island in New York will eat the most hot dogs. If we were fish, this would be the water in which we swim. Yet here comes Mark 4 with this story about seeds that are cast onto the ground and something mysterious and miraculous happens.

I picked up a packet of seeds this week.[6] I can open the package and hold them in my hand. They are tiny and there aren't very many of them. As you can see, they fit easily in the palm of my hand, and the janitors will have to forgive me, but I'm going to cast them right down here in front of the pulpit.[7] This parable says that the kingdom of God is like a man who scatters seeds on the ground. Time passes, and without him knowing how or without explanation, verse 28 says, "all by itself" the soil produces. The word in Greek is *auto-mate*—"automatically"—the seed grows and matures and produces. Wait a minute. If you're anything like me, this just doesn't *sound* right. Something must be wrong with this picture. Are you telling me that Jesus says, "The kingdom is like a farmer throwing out seed, taking a nap, and yet day after day, the seed sprouts and grows"? What about tilling the soil? What about the need for rain and sunshine? What about pulling up the weeds and keeping the critters out? What about the work of fertilizing stuff? What about *all* that? Can all that *work* that the farmer has to do be ignored? Can it be overlooked? I don't *get* this. I don't *like* this. I want to do something. I want to make something happen. Frankly, I don't care much for little seeds. I don't have much of a back yard or a green thumb, but I can tell you one thing: when I go to plant something, I'm not going to plant seeds. I'm going down to Home Depot and buying a tree that's already half-grown. I'm going to dig a big hole and drop it down in there. I don't have time to wait on seeds.

The part of these verses that is so confusing, so counter-cultural, and so hard to grasp is this automatic part—this all by itself part. I mean there were other stories that Jesus told and other comparisons that Jesus made between seeds, planting, the activities of farmers, and different kinds of soil. In some of those places he implied that it doesn't just happen automatically.

---

5. Gibson, "Cars."

6. Image number two was a packet of seeds. Again, it was not a projected image onto a screen, but something that could be held and seen.

7. I tossed the seeds onto the floor of the sanctuary right in front of the platform.

SODAS, SEEDS, AND THE KINGDOM

Why does Jesus use *this* picture in *this* way? Maybe a better question is: Why does the Gospel of Mark preserve *this* story?

There is scholarly debate about a number of issues regarding Mark's Gospel. When was it written? Where? To whom? All kinds of issues arise and, unlike some other parts of the New Testament, Mark isn't filled with many clues. From my study and research, it seems to me that Mark was written from Rome during a time when leaders of the Christian community were being imprisoned, tortured, and killed. It was a time when Jerusalem was being threatened with destruction by the Romans under Vespasian—maybe 67 or 68 AD. Of course, in 70 AD, the Romans destroyed the temple and much of Jerusalem. Things weren't going well for the church. Christians were being killed. Christians were forsaking their faith. Jerusalem, the birthplace of the Church, was being threatened with destruction and the handwriting was on the wall. But Jesus said, "There are these seeds that grow secretly—on their own and automatically—while the farmer goes about his business from day to day." There are these secretly growing seeds.

You and I live in the in-between time. We live between the scattering and the harvesting. We are here between the "already" and the "not yet" of the kingdom. We live in that confusing and difficult place between faithfulness and abundant success. We live between casting the seed and reaping the miraculous crop. Frankly, I don't like living in that place. I would much prefer living with a harvesting sickle in my hand rather than casting tiny seeds onto the ground. But Mark 4 is teaching me that I cannot live in an optimistic arrogance that says that *I* can fix it and that *I* can grow it. Rather, I'm called to live in humble confidence that God is in charge and at work even in ways that elude my vision and grasp. Is that difficult for you? That's hard for me and for us as a congregation, isn't it? We're talented and accomplished in so many ways. We have done some great things as individuals, families, and even as a church. We've come, we've seen, and we've conquered. When others couldn't, we did. When others wouldn't, we did. We've been there and done that before most had ever even *thought* about it.

But, what now? From big sodas to tiny seeds and now to babies.[8] Similarly to "secretly growing seeds," Jesus says that the kingdom belongs to those like little children. In the Gospel of Luke, Jesus uses the word for "babies." This kingdom that Jesus talks so much about and wants to teach his disciples so much about is a kingdom that comes in tiny seeds, in childlike receptivity, in gracious gift, and *not* in grasping achievement. Today at the

---

8. Image number three was a family coming forward to dedicate two children to the Lord. This is a fairly common practice in the Church of the Nazarene. The family stood, essentially, in front of the platform where the seeds had been thrown a few minutes earlier. The baptism of an infant would have been appropriate as well.

196   SECTION 5: POST-PENTECOST NON-FESTIVAL TIME BEFORE ADVENT

conclusion of this sermon, where seeds have been cast, two couples—a part of *one* family—bring little children to be dedicated to the Lord.

> Little children were brought to Jesus for him to place his hands on them and pray for them. But the disciples rebuked those who brought them.

> Jesus said, "Let the little children come to me, and do not hinder them, for the kingdom of heaven belongs to such as these (Matt 19:13–14).

> I tell you the truth, anyone who will not receive the kingdom of God like a little child will never enter it (Luke 18:17).

> Taking a child in his arms, he said to them,

> Whoever welcomes one of these little children in my name welcomes me; and whoever welcomes me does not welcome me but the one who sent me (Mark 9:36–37).

> "I tell you the truth, unless you change and become like little children, you will never enter the kingdom of heaven" (Matt 18:3).[9]

---

9. At this point, the dedication ritual was conducted. Because different churches may have different practices, I have chosen not to include an entire ritual. After the ritual, the service was concluded with a song, prayer, and benediction.

SERMON 40[1]

Amazement, Aesop, and a Faith that Follows[2]

Mark 6:1–6

He died at just thirty-seven years of age and yet he is described as one of the greatest novelists of the twentieth century. William Faulkner even said that he had the best talent of anyone in their generation. His name was Thomas Wolfe. He was born in 1900 in Asheville, North Carolina, and after contracting tuberculosis, he died in Baltimore, Maryland, a little more than two weeks prior to his thirty-eighth birthday. Wolfe pioneered what has come to be called "autobiographical fiction." One of his books was published after his death. The title of the book is important for this morning. The title is *You Can't Go Home Again*. I don't think Thomas Wolfe was thinking about Mark 6 when he wrote that book, but it certainly seems to connect to this story. I invite you to turn to Mark 6.

Mark 6:1–6

Facebook is buzzing with announcements and invitations related to Dawn's twenty-fifth reunion at her alma mater—Southern Nazarene University in Bethany, Oklahoma. People have apparently pulled out their photo albums and have been scanning and posting pictures from the mid and late 1980s. You've never seen so much big hair, mullets, and tie-dyed clothes in all of your life. The reunion is going to take place this fall during the school's

1. Preached at First Church of the Nazarene in Kansas City, Missouri on July 8, 2012 (Seventh Sunday after Pentecost; Year B).

2. The power of this sermon was the interplay of our desire to not be like those in the New Testament who fail and reject, but the realization that, so many times, we are. That thought, coupled with the simple idea of "accompanying Jesus," "living life with Jesus," or "being in the game rather than on the sidelines," was the crux of the message. Like so many sermons, I tried to say the same thing in a few different ways that would connect across the differences of the congregation.

197

homecoming. Every school has one. There are football games, craft displays, barbecue cook-offs, and heavy doses of nostalgia. Who doesn't love homecoming? But, what if things have changed? What if your spouse is no longer at your side because of death or divorce? What if a child has wandered away from the faith and their heritage? What if the dreams that you had have not been realized, but have slowly withered in the face of tragedies and obstacles? What if the reception you receive is not nearly as welcoming and joyous as you anticipated that it would be?

Having left Nazareth at about thirty years of age, having gathered some men around him as his disciples, and having travelled from place to place preaching, teaching, and healing, at *some* point during Jesus' public ministry, he went back for homecoming. He went back to Nazareth. He went *back* to where he had been raised, where he had lived, and where he had worked as a carpenter. He went home. This story of Jesus going home is bookended, in a way, by amazement. Notice in verse 2 that when Jesus comes back to Nazareth, he teaches in the synagogue and the response to his teaching is "amazement." That's how the NIV translates the word. Other translations like the KJV and the RSV say the people were "astonished." "Amazement" or "astonishment"—which ever word is chosen—seems to me like quite a compliment. As a preacher, I can't ever remember *anyone* saying, "Your teaching amazes me or astonishes me." The best I can hope for sometimes is, "At least I didn't fall *completely* asleep." The people of Nazareth—at least the people who went to synagogue that day—were amazed at his teaching. That's how the passage begins, but the passage not only *begins* with amazement, it *ends* with amazement also. Only *this* time, the amazement is on the part of Jesus. Look at verse 6: "He"—Jesus—"was *amazed* at their lack of faith."

I don't think this is how Jesus expected his homecoming to turn out, do you? I mean, if you believe that Jesus knew everything about everybody, all the time, even into the future, then Jesus knew, even before going *back* to Nazareth, that it wasn't going to go well. If Jesus knew everything about everybody all the time, then Jesus knew, even before he began to teach in the synagogue of Nazareth, that these people around whom he had grown up would respond with questions, dismissals, and rejections. But if that's true, *why* would Mark say that Jesus was "amazed at their lack of faith"? Why would Jesus be "amazed" if he already *knew* how his fellow Nazarenes would respond or *not* respond to his teaching? In fact, this passage tells us that the hometown crowd "took offense" or "were offended" at the teaching of Jesus. The word in Greek is actually the word from which we get "scandal." They were "scandalized" by his teaching. They were "amazed" for one reason and Jesus was "amazed" for another. Amazement opens and concludes this passage from Mark.

AMAZEMENT, AESOP, AND A FAITH THAT FOLLOWS   199

But, what *was* it that provoked this kind of response from the people of Nazareth? Why did the Nazarenes react to Jesus this way? This wasn't the reaction that Jesus received in Capernaum or in other places where he travelled. Why this reaction of "offense" or "rejection"? The answer may be found in the thinking and writing of Aesop. You know, Aesop of fable fame. He lived more than 500 years before the birth of Jesus. He was a Greek, story-teller. Several great Greek thinkers like Aristotle, Herodotus, and Plutarch refer to him in their writings. You and I know Aesop from his famous story of the race between tortoise and the hare where the tortoise wins. That's Aesop. But, there's another story from Aesop that goes something like this. It involves a lion and a fox. The fox is terribly frightened of the lion. After all, the lion is bigger and stronger. His teeth are sharp and his claws are long. The first time that the fox met the lion, the fox turned and ran into the woods to hide. The *next* time the fox saw the lion, the fox stopped—at a safe distance—and watched the lion pass by. Aesop's story says that the *third* time, the fox went straight up to the lion and began to talk to him. He passed the day with him and asked when he would have the pleasure of seeing him again. From this story has come a phrase that summarizes the essence of it. It's the moral of the tale. The phrase—which I would imagine that many of you could complete—is this: "familiarity breeds contempt." Jesus says it this way, "A prophet is without honor in his hometown and among his own family." Did you notice the questions that the people asked after Jesus taught in the synagogue? "Isn't this *Mary's* boy?" Can you taste the sarcasm that drips from that question? "Isn't he the *carpenter*?" "This is the guy that fixed my door frame last year. He repaired my wobbly wagon not too long ago." "Well—*that's* his brother James, and *there's* Joseph, and his sisters draw water from the well every day with the rest of us." Jesus was announcing a new world, a new way, and the radical intervention of God in human history in him, and they just couldn't get past the boy they had watched grow up in their midst.

On this side of two thousand years of church history, with multiplied *millions* of people in the world today claiming Jesus as their Savior and Lord, it would be quite easy for us to look at those "original" Nazarenes and think: "How could they be so dense and dull? How could they *miss* it when Jesus was right there among them?" We do that a lot, don't we? How could Peter deny Jesus? How could the disciples be so afraid? How could Judas betray Christ? How could the Nazarenes be so familiar that they dismiss or reject the teaching and power of Jesus among them? Hm. We so desperately don't want to be like them and yet, so many times and in so many ways, we are. We stand back. We look from afar. We listen, but don't hear. We hear, but don't respond. We point out the problems. We explain away the wisdom,

the challenge, or the call. We go to the synagogue and are met by the God of the universe, and we return home with memories of the Jesus who grew up down the street or around the corner, and then we go *back* to the mundane, lifeless routine. There *is* an antidote for that. It's not perfect. It's not without its own challenges. It's not a magic pill or a silver bullet, but it *is* right here in the text. It's one of those phrases that almost gets thrown away. It slips into the background when you first read the passage. It's easy to skim right over it. It's in verse 1. Listen to it again: "Jesus left there and went to his hometown, *accompanied by his disciples.*"

There were these people who were following Jesus around. They were listening to him teach—here and there—in Jerusalem, in Capernaum, along the seashore, and in Nazareth. They were living with him. They walked with him along the roads. They traveled with him at the hospitality of strangers. They sailed with him on the open waters of Galilee. They were sharing life with Jesus and they were *watching* him. They watched how he responded to his critics. They watched how he reacted to the suffering of those around him. They watched how he was moved with compassion for the hurting, the lost, the confused, and the broken. These guys were accompanying Jesus. They were his disciples, and I think the primary difference between *them* and the people of Jesus' hometown was this: their relationship to Jesus was defined, not by familiarity or even by family, but rather by *following*. Theirs was a faith that followed. Their faith was engaged, moving, and active. It wasn't without faults or failures. It wasn't completed or perfect. It wasn't void of misunderstandings or shortcomings, but it was on the road following after and pursuing Jesus.

When I was in the ninth grade, I was on the varsity basketball team at my junior high school. I understand that that may be hard for some of you to believe, but I do have pictures to prove it. That year, we went the entire season undefeated. We won every game. We concluded the year by winning the county championship. We had five terrific starting players—three or four of whom went on to play college basketball. I got to play—*most* of the time— in the fourth quarter after we were winning by at least twenty-five points or more. But there was this one game when Vic Green, one of our starting guards, got into foul trouble in the first half with about three minutes to go. When the coach looked down the bench to find a replacement, he looked and then he pointed at *me*. He put *me* into the game. It was the first half; the game was still on the line. I'll never forget the feeling. I wasn't on the sideline or the bench just observing. I was in the game when it mattered.

If Jesus were to make another appearance among a group of Nazarenes, what would he find? What would he find in your life? Would he find you to be a familiar observer looking on from the sidelines saying, "He's just Mary's

boy"? Or would he find you on the road and in the game when it matters? Would he find you living with a faith that *follows* after him? Today as we gather at our Lord's Table, he invites us to be nourished with his grace and presence for living *with* him and *for* him. He feeds us and nourishes us so that we can truly and resolutely follow him in the world. As you receive the bread and cup—common things—would you welcome them to be vessels of the uncommon—vessels of the power and presence of God among us?

Amen.

SERMON 41[1]

Like Tumbleweed Dipped in Saltwater[2]

John 6:24–35

Maybe this doesn't happen to you or in your family. If not, then just endure for a moment or two. We were on vacation a couple of weeks ago and, of course, one of the burning questions of vacation—every day—is, "Where are we going to eat?" Does that happen to anyone else? There were days when we were eating lunch and the topic of conversation was where we would be eating *dinner*. We had food in our mouths, food on the table in front of us, and our minds were contemplating food for later. In John 6, Jesus has just fed five thousand and walked on water. Before he could even turn around, the crowd has descended upon him again and they want more—*more* bread! The story is found in John 6:24–35.

John 6:24–35

There is this recurring theme in the Gospel of John where Jesus talks about things—about spiritual things and realities—and the people to whom he is speaking just can't seem to get it. They're dull, dense, or distracted. They're blockheaded or confused. In short, they're a lot like us. If you're offended by that, then you're probably in the right place this morning. Earlier in John's Gospel is the story of Nicodemus.[3] He came to Jesus at night, the Bible tells

---

1. Preached at First Church of the Nazarene in Kansas City, Missouri on August 5, 2012 (Eleventh Sunday after Pentecost; Year B).

2. The effectiveness of this sermon rested in the power of a couple of the images that were offered as a rubric for understanding our culture and our compulsions as human beings. The first was the image of the tumbleweed dipped in saltwater and the second was the pelicans searching for food. One was an image of desperation and the other of dullness. Both were so relevant to the human condition.

3. John 3.

202

LIKE TUMBLEWEED DIPPED IN SALTWATER   203

us. He probably came at that time because he was afraid, embarrassed, or thought he had a better chance of talking with Jesus privately. We don't really know for sure. Nicodemus came to Jesus and Jesus wanted to teach him about the kingdom of God. In order to see it or experience it, Jesus said, you have to be born again. Nicodemus was dense. He knew that he had blown out the candles on too many birthday cakes to ever be born again. He was *old*. Birth was for babies and not for old men like himself. Of course, Jesus wasn't talking about birth canals, labor, and delivery. Jesus was talking about being born from above or being born of the Spirit. As the apostle Paul would say it later, it was about "being a new creation in Christ."

There's Nicodemus in John 3. Then there's the woman from Samaria in John 4. Remember what happened? Jesus showed up at the town well. It was kind of a famous spot. It was Jacob's well and had been there for hundreds of years. Jesus showed up at this well about noon. The sun was high and hot. Most people came to the well early or later when it was a bit cooler, but on this day, a woman came to draw water at *noon*. Then, Jesus spoke to her. Culturally and traditionally, this would have been taboo. But Jesus, like with Nicodemus, wanted to talk about spiritual things and realities. He asked her for a drink of the water. She responded with shock and amazement that he would speak to *her*. That exchange opened the way for him to introduce himself and his mission in the world. Jesus said, "Yes, you can draw water from this well, but *I* can give you 'living water.'"[4] She's dense and dull. She said what we would have said, "You don't even have a bucket."[5] Of course, Jesus wasn't talking about H2O and physical hydration. Jesus was talking about life in his presence. He was talking about life filled with God's Spirit.

Nicodemus is in John 3. The Samaritan woman is in John 4. You'd think by the time we get to John 6 Jesus would give up on this confusing, image-laden, metaphorical language that he keeps using with these blockheaded disciples and crowds that keep following him around. They looked on one side of the lake. They found him on the other. They want to know when he got there and Jesus doesn't want to talk about that. Jesus wants to talk about "food that endures to eternal life" not "food that spoils"—not old fish and stale bread from yesterday. But they were hungry again.

You know, a fish dinner only satisfies for a while. It's only so much fuel. That was yesterday and this is today. Jesus can turn water into wine and a boy's lunch into a buffet for thousands and they're hungry again. I mean, those miracles were amazing. Healings, the feeding of the multitude, and walking on water—that's pretty incredible—but my memory seems to

4. My own paraphrase of John 4:10.
5. My own paraphrase of John 4:11.

fade in direct proportion to how loud my stomach growls. "I'm hungry. You're the 'miracle-working' rabbi from Nazareth and I need a sign from heaven or at least from *you*."

When Dawn and I and our kids moved here to Kansas City in September of 2008, the economy was crashing. Markets and emotions were all in an uproar. About that same time, I had picked up a book about the Great Depression and the Dust Bowl era of the 1930s. It was called *The Worst Hard Time*. During that time, and in that area of the country, the drought lingered for years and everything died. Most of the people packed up and moved away. They moved back to relatives somewhere else. A few stayed, endured, and suffered mightily. I remember reading in that book—and it's still hard to imagine—but people were so hungry that they would take *tumbleweed* and soak it in salt-water to soften it up, then they'd eat it. You've got to be *really* hungry to eat tumbleweed.[6]

You and I are living in a world of spiritual tumbleweed; we haven't eaten since yesterday, and our stomachs are growling. Do you understand what I'm saying? Let's try this approach. You've heard the saying, "To a man with a hammer, everything looks like a nail," right? That saying has been updated a bit to reflect the realities of the twenty-first century. It goes something like this: "To someone with a computer, everything looks like data." Here's my take on it for this morning: "To someone with a deep-seated hunger, everything looks like a food source." So we feed ourselves with amusement, stimulation, acquisition, or accomplishment. We dine at the table of fascination with the famous, with the new, or with the spectacular. We crave attention, approval, or exoneration. We run from here to there and around the edge of the lake seeking another sign, another meal, and another experience with the divine. It's as if, spiritually, we're soaking and eating Texas tumbleweed.

I wasn't familiar with the work of Gil Bailie until this past week, but I was captured by a phrase that he has coined. He refers to our "famished craving." We have this desire, need, or compulsion to "fill up" our lives—our inner selves—with whatever we can find or with whatever is available. We are compelled and driven by this "famished craving."[7] We might try to nourish ourselves with sensationalism, sentimentality, or sexual perversion. We might grab fear, false-reality, fantasy, or even Facebook to feed our hunger. We might consume consumerism or masticate materialism until our stomachs are bloated and uncomfortable—the aftertaste like tumbleweed dipped in saltwater. In that context, Jesus says, "You don't need more food that

6. Egan, *Worst Hard Time*.

7. Bailie, *Famished Craving*.

LIKE TUMBLEWEED DIPPED IN SALTWATER

spoils. You need food that *endures* to eternal life. You don't need something else or something new. You need the life that only God can give. You need true bread from heaven." Not a substitute. Not an alternative. Not the latest fad or fetish, but the real, living, presence of Almighty God feeding and nourishing your soul. That happens in a relationship—in an on-going, daily, relationship with Jesus.

You notice from the text, however, that these folks weren't really interested in a *relationship*. They wanted Jesus to perform—to work some miracles and give some signs. "*If* you'll do *that*, then we'll do *this*. We'll examine the evidence and give it some thought. We'll weigh the importance or the clarity of the sign and *then* we'll believe."[8] These folks wanted to strike a deal more than enter into a relationship of commitment, surrender, loyalty, sacrifice, and devotion. That sounds quite familiar in the religious arena in our time, doesn't it?

Now, I understand that in the first century when prophets came along, began to preach, and make claims about things, one of the ways that people tried to get confirmation or tried to authenticate the claims was through the performance or offering of "signs" that what they were saying was true. Yet, Jesus—not twenty-four hours *before*—had taken two fish and five loaves of bread and fed everybody in sight. They had already seen, touched, and tasted a sign from Jesus. Jesus *knew* that. He said in verse 26, "You are looking for me, not because you saw the signs I performed but because you ate the loaves and had your fill." Jesus had already performed some "authenticating signs," but the people were still hungry. Their stomachs were growling and it was time for another fix of the "food that spoils." Jesus wanted to give them "food that endures." C.S. Lewis wrote, "if I find in myself a desire which no experience in this world can satisfy, the more probable explanation is that I was made for another world . . . Earthly pleasures were *never meant* to satisfy it, but only to arouse it, to suggest the real thing."[9] We enter the world hungry and we live every day hungry. Much of our life revolves around addressing the pangs of hunger. This is true physically, but it is also true spiritually. We live in a world, as I said earlier, where when you're hungry, almost anything looks like a food source.

I found an odd story that serves to reiterate that conclusion. It comes from the Associated Press several years ago. In the summer of 2004, a bunch of emaciated, dehydrated, and banged-up pelicans began to show up between Yuma and Phoenix, Arizona. They were brown pelicans. Typically, they live along the coasts near lots of water where they can fish and pester tourists on

8. My paraphrase and interpretation of John 6:30–31.

9. Lewis, *Mere,* III:10, emphasis added.

the boardwalks in the coastal towns of California and Florida. These brown pelicans—about thirty of them—began dropping all over Arizona. What the Game and Fish Department concluded was that there had been a food shortage in California and these pelicans had flown to Arizona looking for fish. As they flew over the shimmering hot air above the Arizona asphalt, the Fish and Game folks concluded that, to the pelicans, it *looked* like water. It looked like a big lake with fish somewhere beneath the surface. When they came down to land in that "water," they discovered that it was not water at all.[10]

There was no possible way that Arizona asphalt was going to satisfy the hunger of food-starved and dehydrated California pelicans. It would have been like trying to eat tumbleweed dipped in saltwater.

Jesus said, "*I am* the bread of life." The presence of God in Christ is the bread for the deepest, the truest, and the most profound hungers of our lives. Before we gather around the Lord's Table, hear the words of a hymn from Charles Wesley:

> Come to the feast, for Christ invites and promises to feed;
>
> 'Tis here his closest love unites the members to their Head.
>
> 'Tis here He nourishes His own with living bread from heav'n,
>
> Or makes himself to mourners known, and shows their sins forgiv'n.[11]

As we come to share communion today, will you allow the Lord to minister his grace and strength to the deepest hungers and needs of *your* life?

Amen.

---

10. Cook, "Some Pelicans."

11. Hildebrandt, *Wesley,* 144.

SERMON 42[1]

The Wise Life[2]

Ephesians 5:15–20

We've been working our way through some sections of Paul's letter to the church at Ephesus. We'll finish up this series next week and then move into the Gospel of Mark through the end of this Christian year which concludes on the Sunday before Thanksgiving near the end of November. I invite you to turn in your Bible, on your iPad, or on your smartphone to Ephesians 5.

Ephesians 5:15–20

The first word that caught my attention was the word "careful." "Be *careful. . . how you live*," Paul says. What comes to mind when you think of a "careful" life? When Dawn and I were young parents, we lived in a basement apartment in Richmond, Virginia. While our firstborn was a baby, everything was fine, but when he became a toddler, we went into full-blown baby-proof mode. All the electrical outlets got those little plastic doohickeys. All the lower cabinets got child-proof doodads. Sharp edges got padded thingamabobs. We wanted to eliminate the risks. Is that how we should imagine a "careful" life? No risk? No chances?

What does Paul mean by "careful"? The word in Greek is *blepo* which is a word related to sight and vision, but it's more than just a physical action

---

1. Preached at First Church of the Nazarene in Kansas City, Missouri on August 16, 2015 (Thirteenth Sunday after Pentecost; Year B).

2. The value of this sermon, I think, was in the way that it took advice and teased out its meaning and implications for living. It read between the lines, which is part of what preaching is about. I'm not sure that I planned it this way, but I like the fact that the key illustrations came from Annie Dillard and Anne Lamont—two writers that challenge the edges of our thought and practices.

207

208   SECTION 5: POST-PENTECOST NON-FESTIVAL TIME BEFORE ADVENT

or capability. It has the connotation of perception and insight. It could be translated as "see with perception," "see with insight and clarity," or even, "pay attention." A "careful" life is an "attentive" life—a life that sees beyond the superficial and temporary.

Paul elaborates on this idea when he refers to this life as a "wise" life. "Be careful and attentive to how you live—not as unwise," he says, "but as wise people." Of course, for Paul, "wisdom" is defined by devotion and service to God. As Proverbs 1 says, "The fear of the Lord is the beginning of knowledge, but fools despise wisdom and discipline." In this context, "fear" does not mean what happens when you jump from an airplane or uncover a spider in the kitchen. Rather, it means "reverence" and "worship." A devoted, diligent Jew like Paul knew well the wisdom literature of Israel, so a concern and commitment to living wisely was in his DNA. Paul wants these new followers of Jesus in Ephesus to embrace the "wise" life—a way of living that reflects and embodies wisdom.

Now, what would that kind of life look like? I think Paul gives us some clues in what he says in the following verses. For example, the "wise" life will be opportunistic. Verse 16 says, "making the most of every opportunity, because the days are evil." Paul, of course, isn't using "opportunistic" in the way that it is often used in our culture and language. In our context, "opportunistic" often has negative connotations. It has the idea of taking unfair advantage because of strange or unusual circumstances. For a criminal, "opportunistic" is when someone leaves the keys in their car and the door unlocked. This is not what Paul means. Paul is urging these followers of Jesus to be "opportunistic" for the Gospel of Christ—for the kingdom of God.

Paul, in some ways, was the exemplar of this practice, right? When he was shipwrecked and floating in the open sea, this became an opportunity to be a witness and to share his faith.[3] When he was jailed or imprisoned, Paul reconceptualized that experience in such a way that it became a tool for understanding his relationship with Christ.[4] When he had a snake latched onto his hand and everyone around was freaked out, even *this*—"opportunistically"—became a testimony of God's protection and care.[5] The "wise" life for Paul was an "opportunistic" life for the gospel.

What would that look like *for you*? Are you paying close attention and looking for opportunities to witness, to share words of encouragement or compassion, and to give cups of cold water in the name of Jesus to someone? Annie Dillard said, "I come down to the water to cool my

3. Acts 27:27–44.
4. Phil 1:13, 21–26, as one example.
5. Acts 28:1–6.

THE WISE LIFE 209

eyes. But everywhere I look I see fire; that which isn't flint is tinder, and the whole world sparks and flames."[6] I think that *most* of the time there are opportunities to partner with the gospel and to spread the influence of Jesus and his kingdom, but we are unaware. We are distracted, insensitive, or numb. We've come to "cool our eyes," as Dillard says, while all around us is "spark and flame."

Would you commit right now to the Lord a desire to be more sensitive, more aware of opportunities to speak words about your life in Christ, more available to offer a prayer for someone who's hurting, or more determined to take advantage of a chance to do some act of kindness for a co-worker or neighbor who's struggling? What would happen if you prayed every morning?: "Lord, help me to be opportunistic for you and for the gospel today. Help me to take advantage of the chances to speak hope, to pray help, and to share hospitality in the name of Jesus to those who come my way." What would happen? Paul says that you would be on the path of the wise life. You would be living "not as unwise," but as "wise." I don't know that it's the first step, like these things necessarily come in a certain order, but it's *part* of the wise life.

Paul goes on to articulate other parts of this life. In verse 17: "Do not be foolish, but understand what the Lord's will is." Now, this can sometimes be a controversial, greatly misunderstood, and confusing topic. It's a question that shows up on college campuses when young people are considering a potential spouse or when they're trying to figure out a career path. What is the Lord's will in this? Should I marry him or not? Should I pursue marine biology like George Constanza,[7] or not? What is the Lord's will?

The wise life understands that at the core of the Lord's will is a life-changing, sin-forgiving, purpose-providing, daily-practiced relationship with God through Christ. With confidence I can say that this is the Lord's will for you, me, and every person on the planet today. I would also go so far as to say that *this* foundational understanding of God's will should be the filter through which other decisions and issues are examined. In regard to marriage, for example: Does this person live in a life-changing relationship with Jesus and will they help to foster the growth of that in me? In regard to an occupation: Can I do this job and live as a follower of Jesus? Through it, can I help to influence others to do the same? The wise life is concerned about and committed to understanding the Lord's will, and pursuing it with all of your strength and energy.

6. Dillard, *Pilgrim*, 14.

7. This is a reference to a character from *Seinfeld*, one of television's most popular situation comedies.

But, then Paul gives us a further indication of what constitutes the Lord's will when he says, "Don't get drunk on wine. Instead, be filled with the Spirit." Human beings were made to be filled. We are vessels—receptacles—for something. We will fill ourselves up with distractions, entertainments, relationships, or pursuits. We will *not* remain empty. We will look and search, and because of sin, we are inclined to look in "all the wrong places" as that great country-singing theologian, Johnny Lee, recorded several years ago.[8] The vessel must be filled, and the go-to solution is to fill it with ourselves. We fill it with our own desires, wants, idols, and passions.

Paul says that the wise life is a life filled with something else. It's filled with the Spirit of God. *This* was what we were created for. Remember Genesis? God formed the human being out of dust. Then what? God *breathed* into him the breath of life. The Hebrew word for "breath" is the same word for "spirit." So, you *could* say, "God *spirited* into him the *spirit* of life and the human became a living being."[9] "This is the wise life, careful life, or the attentive life," Paul says. It's a way of living that is opportunistic for the gospel and the kingdom. It pursues an understanding of the Lord's will. And, it is a life that is filled with the Spirit of God.

Not *all* of our problems would be solved, but a lot of things that weigh us down, sidetrack our living, and bring trouble into our pathway would be resolved if we gave ourselves to the wise life that is reflected in these three straightforward ways. Do you believe that? Well, the wise life *leads* to something. The wise life points in a certain direction. It always points to praise of God, the Father, in the name of Christ, the Son, by the Spirit. The second half of verse 19 and verse 20 says, "Sing and make music in your heart to the Lord, always giving thanks to God the Father for everything, in the name of our Lord Jesus Christ." A wise life leads to a eucharistic life—a life of thanksgiving to God. Part of the reason we gather around the Table of the Lord so frequently is because a life of thanksgiving—a life of praise—is exemplified here and is meant to set the pattern for all that we do. The Greek word in verse 20 for "giving thanks" is a form of the word "eucharist." Thanksgiving is not for a particular moment or a season of the year, but a eucharistic life—a life of praise—is for here and there, for now and always.

Back in 2012, Anne Lamott wrote a book with a subtitle that caught my attention. The subtitle was "The Three Essential Prayers." It was *not* "*Some* Essential Prayers" or "Three *of the* Essential Prayers," but "*The* Three Essential Prayers." The title was "Help. Thanks. Wow." Right in the middle

8 Johnny Lee's "Lookin' for Love" was released in 1980, was a part of the movie soundtrack for *Urban Cowboy*, reached number one on the Country Billboard charts, and sold over a million copies.

9. My paraphrase of Gen 2:7.

THE WISE LIFE   211

of the book and in the middle of the *title* is the prayer, "Thanks." She wrote:
"Gratitude begins in our hearts and then dovetails into behavior. It almost
always makes you willing to be of service, which is where the joy resides."[10]
Eucharist *begins* here, but it's not meant to *end* here. Eucharist is meant to
"dovetail" into our living from moment-to-moment, from day-to-day, and
from year-to-year. So come to the Table of thanksgiving. Embrace the wise
life that points to and directs us toward a eucharistic way of living—a life of
thankfulness, joy, and service.

    Amen.

10. Lamott, *Help*, 56–57.

SERMON 43[1]

Turning Points[2]

John 6:56–69

This is week number five in John 6 and, just so you know, we'll move to
the book of James in the month of September. We'll spend five Sundays
in the book of James. But today, we'll look at another portion of John 6. This
week we'll be in verses 56–69.

John 6:56–69

We've been pushing through John 6 over these last few weeks together. I must
tell you that there were times when I wanted to jump over to some safer, easier,
or softer biblical passage, but here we are again. This week what we see in the
story is the culmination of much that has gone before. Jesus has been preaching and teaching. Jesus has healed and fed. He's been talking about his mission
and ministry in ways that have been difficult to take. All this talk about "eating
his flesh," "drinking his blood," and him being the "bread from heaven" is not
so much hard to understand as it is hard to accept. The issue is not one of
comprehension for these folks who are following Jesus in the first century.
The issue is more about the offensive nature and substance of what Jesus is
preaching. Jesus is confronting the idea and perception among those who are

1. Preached at First Church of the Nazarene in Kansas City, Missouri on August 26,
2012 (Fourteenth Sunday after Pentecost; Year B).

2. This sermon, in its structure, bore the influence of a wonderful Roman Catholic
preacher named Walter J. Burghardt. Multiple collections of Burghardt's sermons have
been published over the years and, for the most part, they all follow a structure of the
introduction concluding with a sentence outlining the coming three sections: section
one drawn from the scriptural passage; section two drawn from the scriptural passage;
and section three directed toward the present moment and audience. As I wrote the last
sentence of the introduction ("one from the Old, one from the New, and one in you"), I
thought, "This is vintage Burghardt."

212

gathered around that his sole mission is to give them what they want—to be the supplier of unlimited food, to heal, to feed, to comfort, and to make easy the way of discipleship. That idea and perception had to be crushed. It was a turning point in the ministry of Jesus.

There are all kinds of turning points and all kinds of literature about turning points. Do a little internet search and you might be surprised by all the "turning points" language. I scanned the first page that appeared and it had all kind of videos, school curriculum, and book titles. Here are just a few that I wrote down:

"Turning Points in the Vietnam War"

"Turning Points in the History of Baptist Associations"

"Turning Points in History"

"Turning Points in *Christian* History"

"Turning Points in American History"

"Turning Points in *Wisconsin* History"

This was just on the *first* screen of possibilities. One of the websites included lectures from a professor at Columbia University. Forty-eight lectures on forty-eight different turning points in Christian history. I want to draw your attention today to three turning points—one from the Old Testament, one from the New, and one in *you.*

First, the Old. There is, in this passage from John 6, a recurring reference to "bread from heaven" or to "manna." This, of course, is a reference to the people of Israel or God's chosen family who were receiving this gift from heaven. God's family—the children of Abraham—had multiplied over the centuries. They had lived most of their years as nomads and shepherds going from place to place grazing their flocks and herds of animals. But there came a severe drought. This was before irrigation systems, assistance from the federal government, and farm aid and subsidy legislation. This was when living off the land meant really living off the land. When *that* wasn't sufficient, it meant begging someone else for help. At one point in their history, God's family ended up begging for help and assistance from Egypt. Big rivers dry up more slowly than little ones, and the Egyptians had the Nile. They had food. They had storehouses of grain. In the providential plan of God, one member of God's chosen family ended up as the manager of all the food supply of Egypt while the rest of God's family was on the verge of starvation. Of course, God found a way to get this strategically-positioned person re-connected to his own family, and, as a result, God's children

ended up living in Egypt. They did so for many years, stretching even into generations.

But then there was a regime change and these children of God were perceived as a threat to the leader of Egypt, so he enslaved them. God's family was now the captive labor force for Egypt and this was the case for hundreds of years. But God, in his mercy, preserved his people. He preserved a miracle-baby named Moses, equipped him for leadership, and after spending forty years in the desert, God sent Moses back into Egypt to lead his people out of their bondage. This event in the life of God's family is called the exodus. The second book of the Bible has this name because it tells that story. When Moses led the people *out* of Egypt, they passed through the Red Sea and escaped from the armies of Egypt. God provided water and food for them in the desert. The food was called "manna"—"bread from heaven." This is a turning point in the life of God's people. It was liberation from an oppressive government, from the oppression of their slavery to the Pharaoh, and it was provision of bread by the miraculous power of God. The story of exodus is *the* defining turning point in the history of Israel.

The people who were following Jesus in John 6 were looking for Jesus to be and to function as a second Moses. They wanted Jesus not only to be their Bread King—their endless and miraculous supplier of food like when he turned a few loaves and fish into meals for thousands—but, they *also* wanted Jesus to deliver them from the oppression of the Roman government at the time. They wanted liberation. They wanted freedom. They wanted out from under the thumb of Rome. They wanted what William Wallace so forcefully and passionately cries for in the movie *Braveheart*. Remember? "Freedom."

These folks in John 6 had preconceived ideas about what a deliverer or a messiah would be and do. When Jesus started down a road that didn't appear to match their assumptions, there was no sense in sticking around. It happens in the other gospel accounts as well. When Jesus begins to talk about his mission, when he says that he's going to Jerusalem to die, and when he says that the culmination of his mission will be his death at the hands of the Romans in Jerusalem, his own disciples are confused at best. They try to dissuade him at worst and the crowds abandon him. This is a turning point in Jesus' ministry.

The miracles were incredible. The teaching and preaching was invigorating. The crowds were exciting, but now that the road to Jerusalem and the reality of the cross had been articulated, the journey took on a different aura—a different feel. Suffering and death loom on the horizon and there's no other way. Jesus will *not* be the "militaristic messiah" that so many were anticipating. His weapons will be turned upside-down. His way will mean

TURNING POINTS 215

the shedding of his *own* blood—the pouring out of his *own* life. Jesus will not be understood by the crowds as a "second Moses" arriving on the scene to liberate them from Rome. Instead, he will die on the Roman's ingenious tool of torture and execution—the cross. When Jesus makes this clear, and begins to speak of his mission in this way as he does in John 6, it has this scattering effect. The crowd dwindles. Jesus wonders if his own inner circle of twelve friends will tag along with the others and leave him all alone. Peter, ever the spokesman for the rest, voices their sentiment: "To whom shall we go? *You* have words of eternal life."

Turning points aren't always what might be expected. They don't happen at times that can be foretold. They aren't predictable. Sometimes they happen when you least expect them. Sometimes they are instigated by people or situations that are utterly surprising. Who would have ever dreamed that the election of a tall, skinny, rail-splitting, perennial election-losing lawyer from Illinois in 1860 to the presidency would be a turning point in the history of the United States? It's amazing how turning points slip up on us. They wrong-foot us and catch us by surprise.

He was on his way to Damascus on an ancient road that is travelled today by tanks and armored cars. On this day, the road was travelled by a man named Saul. His parents had named him after the first king of Israel and he had grown up to be an example and leader among the Jewish people. He described himself as a "Hebrew of Hebrews"[3]—the epitome of Jewish-ness. There had arisen during the recent years a movement—a religious sect of people who called themselves "The Way." They revered and looked to the teachings of a man who claimed to be the Jewish messiah—the long-awaited Savior who would be sent by God. Saul wanted these traitors, heretics, and trouble-makers to be persecuted and even killed. He was willing to lead the charge. In fact, he had already had one of their leaders stoned to death and *now*, he was headed to Damascus to round up some more.[4]

But somewhere between Jerusalem and Damascus, there was a turning point in Saul's life. He was confronted by the risen Christ. He was blinded. He was knocked to the ground, and from that point forward, his life was defined by *that* moment—by *that* encounter with Jesus. There was "before the road to Damascus" and there was "after" meeting Jesus. Saul became Paul and Paul became the greatest missionary that the church has ever known. On the side, he wrote about half of the New Testament. It was a turning point.

3. Phil 3:5.
4. Acts 7:54–60 and Acts 9.

One story from the Old Testament—the story of Moses leading the people out of slavery in Egypt and one from the New Testament—the story of Saul. One from the Old, one from the New, and now, what about you? There have been very important moments in your life. Everyone has them, but I want to speak to you about a turning point—a spiritual moment—a monumental, life-changing turning point. It's really about *discipleship*. It's the same place where "the twelve" found themselves in John 6. Will they follow Jesus on to Jerusalem, or will they scatter with the crowds concluding that this Jesus is not worth following? Dietrich Bonhoeffer, a follower of Jesus, who stood up to and resisted the regime of Adolf Hitler in Nazi Germany eventually paid for his resistance at the end of a rope in the concentration camp at Flossenburg. Bonhoeffer wrote about the cost of discipleship. He wrote:

> When Christ calls a man, He bids him come and die. It may be a death like that of the first disciples who had to leave home and work to follow Him, or it may be a death like Luther's, who had to leave the monastery and go out into the world. But it is the same death every time—death in Jesus Christ, the death of the old man at his call.[5]

In the gracious working of God, we are gathered in this place. We have heard the word read and proclaimed in the presence of the Holy Spirit. The question for us *today* is this: Are we at a spiritual turning point in *our* lives? Is God calling us onto the road of discipleship? Is he calling us to come further down the road of following him or get closer to him on the road? This very moment could be a turning point for you.[6]

---

5. Bonhoeffer, *Cost of Discipleship*, 44.

6. At this point in the service, I invited people to the altar or kneeling rail for a time of prayer and discernment.

SERMON 44[1]

Hygiene, Hypocrisy, and the Heart[2]

Mark 7:1–23

We'll be in the Gospel of Mark for the next several weeks as we make our way toward the end of the Christian year and the beginning of the new Christian year with Advent starting on the last Sunday of November. So, from now until the 22nd of November, we'll be looking together at passages from Mark 7 through Mark 13.

If you didn't know already, there is a strong consensus among biblical scholars that the Gospel of Mark was the earliest or the first-written of the four Gospels that we have in our New Testament. Mark is fast-moving, to-the-point, short, and driven. Matthew and Luke, as they were being written, probably used Mark as a source or reference. It's clear that these three Gospels are similar in a lot of ways. Additionally, they are very different from the Gospel of John. All of that to say, I want us to focus on the passages in Mark and try *not* to look at or refer to parallel passages in Matthew and Luke, if possible. So, let's jump in at Mark 7.

---

1. Preached at First Church of the Nazarene in Kansas City, Missouri on August 30, 2015 (Fifteenth Sunday after Pentecost; Year B).

2. The impact of this message was partly due to the context in which it was preached. Close to the time that I preached this sermon, there were a couple of newsworthy examples of hypocrisy. I made reference to them without mentioning their names (Josh Duggar and Rachel Dolezal). I didn't need to mention their names at the time. Now, readers would probably have to Google them to refresh their memories. I particularly liked portraying John Wesley as a "blockhead" and "dull" because this runs counter to how he is most often portrayed in churches, like this one, that traced its theological heritage through Wesley.

217

218   SECTION 5: POST-PENTECOST NON-FESTIVAL TIME BEFORE ADVENT

Mark 7:1–23

A cursory or superficial reading of this passage from Mark would seem to indicate that this whole "hand-washing" thing is about germs. Of course, this is before anybody knew anything about germs. This is the go-to passage for germaphobes everywhere and it's the chance to say, "See, God knew about bacteria long before humans did. He put these things in place to protect his people from stuff that they weren't even aware of." If we make this story in the life and teaching of Jesus about hygiene, we will be in danger of missing the point. We will be like those religious leaders who, so often, missed the point of Jesus' sayings and stories. Now, don't get me wrong. I'm all for good hygiene. I'm all for washing hands before eating. I'm all for those who cook my food to wash their hands before they do it. Hand sanitizer is our friend. I always use a paper towel to grab the inside handle of the bathroom door when I'm leaving it and I do my best to throw that paper towel in the trash can, no matter how far away from the door they've put it. I don't think I'm a germaphobe, but I can understand why some might be. But this story in Mark is not really about hygiene.

Jesus' target in this story is not hygiene, but hypocrisy. You see, the religious leaders—the Pharisees and teachers of the law—had accused the disciples of Jesus of eating without previously washing their hands in a ceremonial kind of way. Again, it wasn't about germs, but it was about following a certain ritual procedure or tradition. It should have been clear by now, in Jesus' life and ministry, that he was not particularly interested in abiding by or keeping all of the traditions which had grown up around the Law that God had given to his chosen people.

Did you see the story last week about the kid in Taiwan who was in an art museum? He tripped, lost his balance, fell into a $1.5 million painting, and accidentally punched a hole in it?[3] Did anybody see that story? There was no barrier or plexiglass to protect it. He just fell into it. In some ways, the religious leaders and elders had a fear that something like that was going to happen to the Law. Not that someone would literally fall against it and damage it, but that folks would accidentally break the Law and so they set up additional fences around the Law. Then, just to be safe, that fence would need *another* fence. Before long, a whole system of fences and protections had been constructed so that the Law would be preserved.

Part of the problem was that the religious leaders and elders became as concerned about the fences as they were about the Law. They became more interested in the fences for the Law and they became less interested

3. Holmes, "Boy Trips in Museum."

HYGIENE, HYPOCRISY, AND THE HEART

in a relationship with the Law-*giver*. In this context, Jesus points to this as the real problem and he names it as hypocrisy. In verse 6: "Isaiah was right when he prophesied about you hypocrites," Jesus said. Then he proceeded to quote a passage from the scroll of Isaiah. Hear what Jesus said again, "Isaiah was right about you *hypocrites*."

What is hypocrisy? The word is a Greek word that comes from the setting of the theater. A "hypocrite" was an "actor"—a "mask-wearer." A hypocrite was someone who played a part, but it wasn't really who they were. Jesus directs this at the religious leaders who, as verse 1 says, "had come from Jerusalem." These were the people who were perceived to be *most* concerned with the Law, the things of God, and the ways of God and yet, Jesus saw behind the mask, through the façade, and beyond the acting. They weren't what they seemed or claimed to be.

In this digital age, it seems, everyone has or wants 15 minutes of fame. Apparently, many are willing to do anything to get it. In this kind of world, it doesn't take long to form a list of "hypocrites" who aren't what they have claimed to be. Just in the last few days, the internet has been buzzing with news about a person who has been an advocate and example for family values and yet, simultaneously, he has been a client of a website devoted to cheating on your spouse.[4] It's a crazy, mixed-up, hypocritical world in which we live where people will pretend to be a member of a different race so that they can speak to or cast themselves as an expert on particular racial issues.[5] You can't make this stuff up. So, hypocrisy is not limited to a certain group, time, or century. Hypocrisy is an age-old, persistent, enduring problem that happens outside, but also *inside* the religious community and *inside* the church.

As gracious and loving and merciful as Jesus is portrayed in the New Testament, there is something that makes his blood boil and of which he is intolerant and that is hypocrisy. Some of you remember Milli Vanilli.[6] They were a West-German based, singing group. It was two guys and in 1990, they won the Grammy Award for the Best New Artist on the music scene. They were very popular and their debut album was being played on every pop-music radio station across the country. There was just *one* problem. The two guys who were the group hadn't really sung their hit songs on the record. When they went around doing concerts, they were lip-syncing the songs.

4. Tribune Wire reports, "Josh Duggar."
5. Desmond-Harris, "How to Make Sense."
6. Okura, "The Real Voices."

When Jesus identifies the hypocrisy of the religious leaders, he quotes the prophet Isaiah who said, "These people honor me with their lips, but their hearts are far from me" (Isa 29:13). It's lip service. It's lip syncing where they sing the right words, but it's all a façade or game. Jesus, as he does in so many other places and in the midst of so many other circumstances, wants to place the emphasis on the heart. *This* is what truly matters. *This* is where the issue really lies. It's not what goes into the body. It's not what you eat or don't eat, with or without ceremonially cleansed hands. Jesus says, "Don't you see that nothing that enters a person from the outside can make them 'unclean?' Because it doesn't go into their heart but into their stomach, and then out of their body" (Mark 7:18–19). This is a simple, first-century analogy utilizing a basic understanding of how the body works and digests food, but Jesus is drawing attention more generally to the supremacy or the priority of the interior life—of the heart-relationship with God.

Proverbs 4:23 says, "Above all else, guard your heart for it is the wellspring of life." Jesus understood this wisdom from the literature of his family and people. When he used examples of a tree bearing good fruit, it was because the tree was good. If a tree bears bad fruit, it's because the tree is bad. This kind of teaching and thinking was a persistent and regular part of Jesus' life and ministry. But, for whatever reason, even Jesus' own disciples had trouble getting this. Even though they walked with him, observed him, and spent time with him, the disciples had trouble making the connection and understanding. You see that in verse 17 where Jesus leaves the crowd and turns privately to his disciples and asks, "Are you so dull? Don't you get it? Can't you understand what I'm saying?"

Usually when we hear one of these stories from the life of Jesus, we have to choose where we want to be in the story? Most of the time, we don't want to be with the religious leaders. We don't want to be the hypocrites in the story. Well, there's one other choice. We can be the disciples, which means we get to be the dull, blockheaded ones, right? We're slow to grasp and slow to really embrace that God wants our *hearts* first and foremost.

We Nazarenes come from a long line of blockheads—all of whom we love and revere—starting with our theological forefather, John Wesley. As many of you know, Wesley was raised in one of the most religious, godly homes in all of England in the eighteenth century. Wesley's mother, Susanna, was a devoted and diligent follower of Jesus. Wesley's father was a minister serving in a local parish. He was educated and raised with the Bible being studied in the original languages. He put to memory portions of the Scriptures that would be difficult for us to imagine. He went off to college at Oxford and earned a degree. Then, Wesley became a fellow at Lincoln College, which was a part of Oxford. Later he was ordained as a priest in

HYGIENE, HYPOCRISY, AND THE HEART

the Church of England. He was about twenty-five years old at the time. He served in a local church for a while and then returned to Oxford where he helped to form a group that became known as the "holy club." He, his brother, and some others were very interested in serving, fasting, praying, studying the Scripture, and ministering among those who were imprisoned. They were meticulous and diligent. Some called them "methodists" because they were so methodical in their religious practices.

In 1735, when John Wesley was thirty-two years old, he sailed to the new world to become the priest in Savannah, Georgia, and to evangelize the native Americans. He spent two years serving as a priest, preaching the gospel, attempting to lead lost people to Christ, and he was an utter failure. He couldn't get back to England fast enough. After being back for just a little while, he experienced something that would change his life forever. Along with being snatched out of a burning house as a child, this experience would be the thing that he pointed to, wrote about, and remembered as life-changing. It happened in London on a street named "Aldersgate." While someone was reading the introduction to Martin Luther's commentary on the Book of Romans, something happened. Here's what Wesley wrote in his journal: "About a quarter before nine, while he was describing the change which God works in the heart through faith in Christ, I felt my heart strangely warmed. I felt I did trust in Christ, Christ alone for salvation: And an assurance was given me, that he had taken away *my* sins, even *mine*, and saved *me* from the law of sin and death."[7] It took a while for Wesley to get it, didn't it? Even after being raised in it and being ordained as a priest in it and after serving as a missionary in it—*still* Wesley hadn't fully grasped what God wanted for him. But at Aldersgate Street in London when he had this breakthrough, he instinctively knew that it was an issue of the *heart*.

Listen: practices, habits, and rituals are tools to be used by God, enlivened by the Spirit of God to do his work—where?—in our *hearts*. Will you open yourself to the working of God in you today? What kind of "heart" work does God want to do in you?[8]

Amen.

---

7. Wesley, *Works,* 103.

8. This sermon could quite easily conclude with an invitation to prayer or a gathering around the Table.

SERMON 45[1]

Cochlear Implants, Bo Jackson, and Signs[2]

Mark 7:31–37

Today, we continue in the Gospel of Mark. This week we'll be looking together at the last story in Mark 7. It begins at verse 31 and is sometimes entitled, "The Healing of a Deaf and Mute Man." I guess the question is this: Is that all it is? Is it just another healing story? There seem to be so many of those in the New Testament, right? I guess the next question is something like this: "What's the purpose of a healing story?" or "Why did Mark include *this* one and not some *other* story of when Jesus healed someone?"

Let's listen, first, to the story.

Mark 7:31–37

When I read this story again in preparation for today, I allowed my mind to wander. One of the first things that it landed on was something that I had seen on YouTube a couple of years ago. Many of you have probably seen it as well. It's a video of a young woman—maybe in her late twenties—who is deaf. She's sitting in a chair in a doctor's office. She's had, I think, a cochlear implant, and it's the *first* time that she will hear her own voice. The instant that she hears it, she begins to cry tears of joy and amazement. I went looking for that video and I found it almost immediately. While I was searching,

---

1. Preached at First Church of the Nazarene in Kansas City, Missouri on September 6, 2015 (Sixteenth Sunday after Pentecost; Year B).

2. The strength of this sermon was in the push-back against miracles as primarily displays of power. For many, I anticipated, thinking about miracles in another way would be challenging and potentially eye-opening. Talking about signs gave me a chance to do some teaching about the sacraments. Like most things, we learn more by doing than by simply listening, so we participated in the Lord's Supper to respond to the message.

222

COCHLEAR IMPLANTS, BO JACKSON, AND SIGNS   223

I came across another video which is similar in some ways. I want you to take a look at it and listen closely to the comments of the CNN reporter.[3]

[playing of video]

Did you see his reaction? Wasn't that awesome? From not hearing *any-thing* to then hearing his father's voice. Wow. The reporter introduced the story as a "modern day miracle." Did you hear him say that? It's a "miracle," he said.

What is it that makes something a miracle? Is it the amazement that happens as people respond to it? As verse 37 says in this passage: "People were overwhelmed with amazement." Is *that* what makes it a miracle? I don't know about you, but I'm amazed at lots of things that very few people would describe or define as a miracle. I mean, I'm amazed by the table-side magician up at Minsky's Pizza.[4] He does things with playing cards and sleight of hand that amazes me. But it's magic, not a miracle. Or, when somebody sits down at a piano and plays Michael Jackson's song, "Bad." I posted a video of it on my Facebook page this week and I'm just amazed by it. It's incredible. The timing, the talent, and the imagination is wonderful. It's amazing, but no one would say it's a miracle. Does some kind of law of nature have to be broken in order for something to be a miracle, like when Jesus walks on the water or when a lunch is enough to feed five thousand people? We often hear child-birth referred to as a miracle, yet it's been a part of the natural order from the beginning of human history. This idea of the miraculous seems to be somewhat fluid. It's kind of hard to pin down. It seems to vary from culture to culture and from century to century. Undoubtedly, people from previous decades and centuries would have perceived airplane travel, satellite phone calls, or television broadcasts as impossible, outside the natural realm, or things that provoke utter amazement. They would have been seen as miracles.

So, how are we to understand the miracles of Jesus? When Jesus is awakened from sleep by his terrified disciples, he looks around and observes that their little boat is in the middle of a violent storm. Then he stands up, speaks to the storm, commands it to be still, and it obeys. How are we to understand this? When his disciples come to him with anxiety or stress, they urge him to tell the crowds of people to go home because there is no food out here in this desolate place. Then he takes a boy's lunch and feeds the multitudes with it and the disciples get to pick up baskets

3. The video was of a small child who had been deaf, but now could hear. He hears the voice of his parents. His reaction is the epitome of surprise and joy.

4. Minsky's is a local pizza restaurant with which most of the congregation would be familiar.

224   SECTION 5: POST-PENTECOST NON-FESTIVAL TIME BEFORE ADVENT

and baskets of leftovers. What are we to make of this? Or this story when Jesus puts his fingers in a guy's ears, goes through several other strange actions, including spitting and tongue-touching, cries out words in Aramaic that Mark has to translate for his readers and us, and the man's hearing is healed and his tongue is "loosed." How are we to interpret this? How are we to understand this? One way to answer the question is to say that Jesus is calming storms, breaking natural laws, healing the deaf and blind, and resuscitating dead bodies all as a display of his power. "Miracles are about power," some would say.

We're experiencing the resurgence of the Royals here in Kansas City during these last couple of years. I know that it's been a long time coming for those of you who have lived here through all the lean years. Dawn and I lived here when I was a student at Nazarene Theological Seminary, and it was right at the end of the good years—back in the George Brett and Frank White days. They were, of course, incredible ball players, but there was one guy on the team back then who was the epitome of, or specimen of, *power*. His name was Bo Jackson. You never knew what Bo was going to do. The Nike campaign was "Bo Knows," but I don't think even Bo really knew what he was going to do on most nights. Sometimes Bo would strike out two or three times a game. I've seen it happen. He would take the bat and snap it in half over his thigh like it was a toothpick. Recently, I saw a video clip where he took the bat, put it over his helmet, and snapped it like a twig. It served no purpose other than to display his power. Some think that *that* is the purpose of the miracles of Jesus. "The miracles are proof that Jesus is powerful and therefore, divine," some would say. "Only *God* could do something like that," others would add. "This is God's power on display in Jesus," and all you have to do is pay attention. "Look at what Jesus can do," some would conclude. As a result of thoughts like that, there was a growing movement, at one time in Jesus' ministry, to forcibly take Jesus and try to make him into some kind of earthly king who would feed the people, heal the people, and prosper the people with his miraculous and "Midas" touch.[5]

Miraculous power on display—just for the sake of "proving" one's power—was, in fact, one of the temptations that Jesus faced shortly after his baptism by John. Remember? Satan challenged Jesus to leap from the pinnacle of the temple and allow the miraculous power of God in the form of angels to prevent him from being destroyed. Everyone would see it and know that Jesus was "divine." I think we misunderstand the miracles of Jesus when, at their core, they become simply a display of power—even a display of "divine" power.

---

5. John 6:15.

COCHLEAR IMPLANTS, BO JACKSON, AND SIGNS   225

There are a couple of clues in the text that help us better understand the purpose of this miracle of healing in Mark 7. It's really less about what Jesus can do and it's much more about who Jesus was. It's less about power and more about revelation. It's less about "breaking the laws of nature," and more about the "in-breaking kingdom" of God in Christ. The clues come at the end of the passage and are captured in what the people say in response to the miracle. Our Bibles have them inside quotation marks in verse 37. Do you see that? The first one is this: "He"—meaning Jesus—"has done everything well." Most biblical scholars point to this statement and suggest that it is echoing—not quoting—a verse from the book of Genesis. At the conclusion of God creating the world and human beings, God looks on what has been created and concludes that it is "very good."[6] God looks at creation and, to use Mark's phrase, sees that he has "done everything well." That's *one* clue.

The second is right there with what the people say about Jesus and this miracle of healing: "He even makes the deaf hear and the mute speak." Again, scholars are convinced that this is even *more* than an echo, but it is a direct reference to the scroll of Isaiah. As Isaiah is preaching about the coming of the Lord, he says and writes, "Your God will come, he will come with vengeance; with divine retribution he will come to save you. Then will the eyes of the blind be opened and the ears of the deaf unstopped. Then will the lame leap like a deer, and the mute tongue shout for joy. Water will gush forth in the wilderness and streams in the desert."[7]

The miracles of Jesus are not simply displays of power for power's sake, they are signs. They are signals that point us to who Jesus *is* and to the fact that, *in* Jesus, God is moving to redeem and reclaim his broken world. Jesus is not snapping baseball bats to point to his power, but he is revealing the mind, will, and purposes of God in the world. These are signs planted in the ground, here and there, which point us to where God wants us to go and how he wants us to live. They direct us to how he wants us to respond to him, to those around us, and to the hurting, broken, suffering world in which we live. The signs are all around us. The church has identified a couple of signs that are particularly helpful in the process. One is the sacrament of baptism where we celebrate that God has graced us, chosen us, and brought us into his family. It's where the ways of the world and our own selfish desires are drowned under the waters of baptism. The second sign that the church lifts up as peculiarly beneficial and revelatory is the sacrament of communion. Like the miracle of healing that pointed beyond itself, the Lord's Supper is a

6. Gen 1:31.
7. Isa 35:5–6.

sign that points beyond itself to the life, death, and resurrection of Jesus as the pattern of God's engagement with us and with his world. In the taking, the blessing, the breaking, and the giving, we see the revelation of God in Jesus. We see the model for how we are called to live with one another, with our neighbors, and with the other seven billion people inhabiting the planet at the current moment. Not just the life of Jesus, but *our* lives are to be taken into the hands of God to be blessed, broken, and distributed for his purposes of grace, forgiveness, mercy, and healing in the world.

So, come to his Table—not because there is power on display here, but because these are the signs that point us to the life and ways of Jesus. Come, because here is the presence of God's Spirit at work in us to mold us into the image of Christ. As Martin Luther said, God desires to make us "little Christs"[8] in the world who are devoted to sharing his love, reaching to help, stooping to lend a hand, and accompanying others on the road of suffering and grief. So, come—not with clinched fists and expressions of power, but with humility and open hands to receive the grace, life, and help of God to become his people and instruments in the world.

Amen.

8. Luther, *Freedom,* 84.

SERMON 46[1]

The Jesus Way in a World of Selfies[2]

Mark 9:30–37

We have perfected, in our culture, the art of self-promotion and self-absorption like no other. The very fact that we have created a word—the "selfie"—and that we all *know* it and *use* it—is some indication that it pervades our culture and our understanding of reality. Let me simply offer this: self-promotion and self-centered kinds of thinking and living have been around since the beginning of human existence. It certainly was evident in the lives of Jesus' own disciples. We turn to Mark 9 for a story in the first-century that is set in the context of "selfies"—of preoccupation with one's self.

Mark 9:30–37

In the eighth chapter of Mark, Jesus has an interaction with one of his leading disciples, Peter. Jesus had asked his disciples what the people were saying about him. How were they assessing his ministry? What were they comparing it to? The disciples brought back answers like, "John the Baptist," "Elijah," or one of the other great prophets from the history of their people. Then Jesus turned the question to them: "What about *you?* Who do *you* say I am?" In Mark's account, there is no mumbling or stuttering. Peter, without hesitation and without encouragement, says, "You are the Messiah," to use the Hebrew word, or "You are the Christ," to use the Greek word. It's the same concept in two

1. Preached at First Church of the Nazarene in Kansas City, Missouri on September 20, 2015 (Eighteenth Sunday after Pentecost; Year B).

2. This passage from Mark came around in the lectionary when the immigration crisis in Europe was escalating. The last section of the sermon on hospitality was greatly influenced by that current event. I found the cruciform response of communion to be particularly meaningful.

228   SECTION 5: POST-PENTECOST NON-FESTIVAL TIME BEFORE ADVENT

different languages. It's the same declaration: "Jesus, *you* are the 'anointed one' sent from God to save."

Mark says that it was only *then* that Jesus began to teach them—meaning his disciples—that the "Son of Man must suffer many things, be rejected, killed, and after three days rise again." It was as if Jesus took Peter's confession or declaration and, like it was a container of some kind, Jesus began to fill it with his teaching and with his understanding of what being God's "anointed one" meant.

Peter liked the container, but he didn't like what Jesus was filling it with—he told him so. Jesus responds to Peter with a stern rebuke. That's putting it kindly. Jesus calls Peter the devil. How's *that* for the meek and mild Jesus? Anyway, Jesus has begun to teach his inner circle of disciples what being the Christ really will mean. That teaching shows up again in this passage from Mark 9. Jesus summarizes it in verse 31 with "betrayal, death, and resurrection." He doesn't elaborate on the way betrayal will happen, upon the mock trial, the involvement of the religious leaders, or the horrific way in which he will be killed. He simply summarizes: betrayal, killing, and rising.

It's in *that* context of Jesus' teaching about his impending death and resurrection that this story of self-absorption happens. The disciples have been walking with Jesus toward Capernaum which was a favorite place for Jesus. While they've been walking, they've also been talking. The topic of conversation has been who among them will be the greatest. Apparently without them knowing it, Jesus has been eavesdropping on the conversation. Maybe he seemed distracted. Maybe he seemed caught up in his own thoughts and world. Maybe he was so focused or they thought he was praying or some other explanation. While they were arguing about "greatness," Jesus was listening. They were caught up in their own selfishness. They were enraptured in their own self-centered absorption. They didn't have iPhones, but conceptually, they were engaged in a big "selfie." When Jesus asked them about it, they were embarrassed. They "kept quiet," as verse 34 says. They didn't want to verbalize what they had been so interested in verbalizing before.

Like so many other occasions in the Gospels, this setting and context becomes a teaching moment. Jesus wants his disciples to let go of their misconceptions and to receive the reality of what life on the way should look like. If you have had children or helped to care for children, you know that sometimes they'll grab hold of something—a toy, a book, a lock of your hair or theirs—and for whatever reason, they don't want to let it go. Sometimes, the way forward is to give them something else to take hold of, but in order to take hold of it, they have to release their grip on

THE JESUS WAY IN A WORLD OF SELFIES   229

the other thing. Jesus offered to his disciples and he offers to us a way of life to take hold of, but we first have to release the other thing. We have to release the way of the self.

In its place, Jesus points us in *one* direction with *three* expressions. The direction, of course, is the way and lifestyle of Jesus. It is being "conformed to the image"[3] of Jesus. It is "having the mind of Christ."[4] It is thinking, viewing, and living life after the model and example of Jesus. This is the *one* direction. It is the cruciform life—life after the way of Jesus.

To use the image of the cross, let me speak to the three expression of this life that Jesus teaches to his disciples—both then and now. These three expressions are drawn from these verses in Mark 9. The first expression is humility. In verse 35, Jesus says, "If anyone wants to be first, he must be the very last." If you want to understand your life filtered through the life and ways of Jesus; if you desire your life to reflect the life of Jesus; and if you want your life to be more *like* the life of Jesus, then you must seek, embrace, and be shaped by *humility*. The incarnation of Jesus—where Jesus entered our world in human flesh and lived his life as a Jewish man in the first century with all of its limitations and experiences—is an expression of *humility*. Jesus modeled it, but more than that—he *was* it. It was not something he did or tried to do, but rather it was who he was. It was intrinsic to his incarnation. It was intrinsic to him living in the flesh in the world.

The church and her leaders, from the very beginning, have emphasized this fact about the way of Jesus being the way of humility. When the apostle Paul wanted to capture it, he took a song that the church was singing and he included it in his letter to the Philippians as he described what Jesus did in coming into our world. Jesus "did not consider equality with God something to be grasped or held onto, but rather, he made himself nothing . . . and being found in appearance as a man, he"—what?—"he *humbled* himself and became obedient unto death, even death on a cross."[5]

The cruciform life is a life of humility after the pattern of Jesus. It is a life that comes down like the vertical piece of the cross. For Jesus, it meant leaving the throne room of heaven and taking on human flesh. For us, the distance or the difference won't be nearly as dramatic, but the *direction* is the same. The direction is down—from above to among. It is the way of humility. You should be aware that being encouraged or urged to follow after the pattern of Jesus on the path of humility is a counter-cultural direction. This is the age of self-promotion, self-elevation, and self-actualization, but it is

3. Rom 8:29.

4. Phil 2:5.

5. Paraphrase of portions of Phil 2:6–8 with emphasis added.

counter to the ways and model of Jesus. I was thinking this week about how we draw or make the symbol of the cross. Right now, take your finger and on the palm of your hand, draw a cross. Although I'm not a betting person, I would be willing to wager that 100 percent of you drew the vertical piece from the top to the bottom—from up to down or from heaven to earth—in the direction of humility.

Remember that we're talking about one direction—toward conformity to Christ—with three expressions. The first is humility. Now the second expression which is found there in verse 35 is that of *service*—"If anyone wants to be first, he must be the very last, *and the servant of all.*" The way of Jesus is the way of service.

While the disciples were arguing about greatness, Jesus was thinking about service and how this must define what following him will mean. Of course, it wouldn't be long before Jesus gathered with his disciples in an upper room in Jerusalem to share one last meal together and it was then and there that Jesus served in a way that none of his disciples were willing to do. After they had walked through dirty, first-century streets filled with raw sewage and all other manners of filth, Jesus—on hands and knees—took a basin of water, took their feet in his hands, and washed them clean. In service, Jesus did the least desirable job. It was the lowest and most menial task of slaves in that time and culture. In the famous passage from Paul's letter to the Philippians where Paul quoted what the church was singing about Jesus, he wrote that Jesus "made himself nothing, taking the very nature of"—what?—"a servant" or "a slave."[6]

Think again of the cross and imagine that one side of the horizontal piece is the Jesus-way-of-life that reaches out in service. Ask yourself, "Does *my* life reflect the cruciform life of Jesus? Are there expressions of service in *my* living?" Again, this is counter-cultural preaching. The predominant message of our culture is—"Look out for number one." It's a "take-care-of-yourself" kind of world which has little place for service and particularly little place for menial, sacrificial, humble service. But this is what life—perceived through the model and pattern of Jesus—looks like. It's how this life that moves in this one direction takes shape. It's a cruciform shape.

The third expression that Jesus identifies here as a part of a life that follows after Jesus is *hospitality*. In verse 37, Jesus says, "Whoever welcomes one of these little children in my name welcomes me; and whoever welcomes me does not welcome me but the one who sent me." To continue the use of this analogy of a cross-shaped life, hospitality is the other side of the horizontal piece. It, too, reaches out with welcome and care. It's not really

---

6. Phil 2:7.

THE JESUS WAY IN A WORLD OF SELFIES   231

about children per se, but it's about the most vulnerable. It's about people
hurting and in need. In the first century, that meant children and it can still
mean that today, but it's not limited to children. Our world is filled with
people who are vulnerable and in need. The world can be a pretty inhos-
pitable place, can't it? We see it in the headlines of the world's newspapers.
We see it scrolling across the bottom of our televisions screens. We see
stories of inhospitality and rejection.

What about the church? Does the church embody hospitality? What
about *your* life and *mine?* Do our lives have a cruciform shape with humility, service, and hospitality? Our prayer is: "Lord Jesus, in this self-absorbed
culture, make us more like yourself. Feed us with your life and ways. Fashion
us after yourself. Conform us to your image. Plant our way of living in the
cross." When we come to the Table of the Lord, even in this meal we can see
humility, service, and hospitality, for in the breaking of the bread, there is the
brokenness of humility, in the giving of the bread, there is the reaching out
of service, and in the invitation to come and eat, there is the welcome of hospitality. It's a cruciform response for a cruciform life in a world preoccupied
with selfies. With God's help and by his grace, may *we*—Jesus' followers in the
world—be different. May we be shaped by *his* life and *his* ways. May our lives
reflect *his* cruciform life—humble, serving, and hospitable to all.

Amen.

SERMON 47[1]

Jericho, a Cloak, and a Question[2]

Mark 10:46–52

W e've been working our way through portions of the Gospel of Mark over these last few weeks, and we come to a passage today that concludes a particular section of the narrative. After this passage, Jesus enters Jerusalem and the series of events that we typically mark during Holy Week begins. So, I invite you to turn in your Bible or find on your smartphone Mark 10, and we'll read verses 46 through 52.

Mark 10:46–52

This is the second story just since chapter 8 where Jesus heals a blind man. There are some differences in the two stories. For example, in the first story, we don't know the man's name. Jesus spits on the man's eyes and touches him with his hands. Even then, the man's initial response is that his vision is still blurry, so Jesus touches him again. Then the man sees clearly. In this second story revolving around the healing of another blind man, we *do* know his name. Jesus doesn't spit or touch and it doesn't take two tries.

So, why does Mark tell this story? Surely, there's a better reason than to show that Jesus was getting better at this healing thing as he moved along in his ministry.[3] Surely, this is more than like when I give my father a "mulligan"

---

1. Preached at First Church of the Nazarene in Kansas City, Missouri on October 25, 2015 (Twenty-third Sunday after Pentecost; Year B).

2. The impact of this sermon, I think, was in taking a somewhat familiar story and delving more deeply into the details of it. The setting of Jericho, the meaning and importance of a cloak, and the identical question which Jesus asks in two different places—these were the keys that made the message worth hearing.

3. This was a tongue-in-cheek comment that the congregation understood because of my tone, expression, and history with them.

232

JERICHO, A CLOAK, AND A QUESTION

on the golf course—a do-over shot. Part of the reason for Mark's telling of this story at this particular place in the larger narrative hinges on some of the details that we often simply skim over or ignore. One of those details happens right at the very beginning. In verse 46, it says that "they came to Jericho." Now, Jericho is a pretty important place in the story of God's people for one simple reason. Do you remember what happened at Jericho? Jericho was the place that stood between God's people and entrance into the promised land. Jericho was this walled city that the Israelites could not defeat or overpower except by the miraculous moving of God. We used to sing about Jericho when we were kids in Sunday school. But in case you missed out on that, let me review the story for a minute.

God had delivered his people from captivity in Egypt with Moses as the God-appointed leader. They came out of Egypt and through the Red Sea with Egypt's army being destroyed in their wake. Then, instead of going immediately into the land that God had promised them, they hesitated. They became fearful. They were disobedient. As a result, they wandered in the wilderness or the desert for forty years. By the end of those forty years, they had a new leader and they were prepared to do what their predecessors were not. They were ready to enter the promised land. The first major obstacle was Jericho. They marched around the city at the Lord's instruction. They marched a certain number of times for a certain number of days concluding with trumpet blasts and lots of shouting. Miraculously, the walls of Jericho fall down. Notice these three things: Jericho, shouting, and a leader named Joshua.

Here in Mark 10, the setting is Jericho, there's a man shouting, and the leading character in the story is named "Yeshua"—Jesus. This story, in Mark, at this particular place in the timeline is an indication that something great is about to happen. Something miraculous is occurring. Something God-directed is taking place. Someone who brings deliverance and salvation has arrived. As you see in the Gospel of Mark, immediately at the conclusion of this story, Jesus enters Jerusalem and begins the week which culminates in his death and resurrection. This detail about where this healing happens—at Jericho—is important and helps us to see a larger picture, if we pay attention to it.

Another detail in the story that we might easily pass over or ignore is when Mark tells us how the blind man responds when Jesus tells the people to call the man to him. In verse 50, Mark writes, "Throwing his cloak aside, he jumped to his feet and came to Jesus." Even before Bartimaeus is healed, it seems that we already know what's going to happen because this is not just about another blind man receiving his sight. This story is really about becoming a *follower* of Jesus. At the very end of the story, after Bartimaeus

has been healed, Mark adds, "and he followed Jesus along the road." A better translation would be that "he followed Jesus on *the way*." You see, this is the goal of the story. The goal is not *just* that he be healed of his blindness, but that he become a *follower* of Jesus. Some scholars even go so far as to say that this is really a "call story" more so than a "miracle story." It's this aspect of his response to the "call" that catches my attention, even though it may seem like a superfluous detail. Mark says that "throwing his cloak aside," he came to Jesus. You might say, "Well, that's just what happened. Mark saw it. He recorded it. It's no big deal." He could have added that he "kicked off his sandals" or "threw dust in the air" or "'had a smile on his face." But that's not what the story tells us.

Clearly, every detail and every aspect of the story has not been preserved for us, but why does Mark include *this* one about Bartimaeus? Why does he include that Bartimaeus "threw aside his cloak"? In essence, I think, because following Jesus or becoming a disciple of Jesus means abandoning our securities. It means letting go of our plan B and jumping in with both feet. That's what a cloak was in the life of a first-century blind person. It was their safety net. It was their one possession of value, their shield from the cold, and their protection from the sun. It was important, vital, and cherished. But at the call of Jesus, Bartimaeus cast it aside to move toward this one in whom he was trusting for healing, life, and meaning. It was like the apostle Paul's phrase where "old things pass away and all things become new." For Bartimaeus, the "old thing" was a cloak. It symbolized a life of captivity and isolation. The "new thing" was the presence of Jesus and life with him on the way.

On this last Sunday of October, which in many places is called "Reformation Sunday," I'm reminded of the story of Martin Luther. In some ways it looks a bit like the story of Bartimaeus. Luther was a Catholic monk. He had become one in a time of great fear after he was almost struck by lightning. Almost like a foxhole conversion, he vowed to become a monk during a severe thunderstorm. Luther became a good monk. He was scrupulous, meticulous, and devoted. He fasted and prayed. He deprived himself of sleep and stayed out in the cold without covering. He beat himself as a physical expression of his commitment. He earned a doctorate in Scripture and became a Bible professor as a part of his service to the Church. Then, as he studied the Scripture, prayed, and meditated on the Word, Luther wrote, "I began to understand that the righteousness of God is that through which the righteous live by a *gift* of God, namely by faith . . . Here I felt as if I were entirely born again."[4]

---

4. Galli and Olsen, *131 Christians,* 34, emphasis added.

Luther "threw aside his cloak." He let go of his security, like Bartimaeus, when in 1517 on the 31st of October, he publicly challenged some of the teachings and practices of the Church. He had ninety-five things that he wanted to discuss, so he nailed them to the community bulletin board, which at that time was the front door of the Roman Catholic church in Wittenberg, Germany. From that moment forward, Luther's life was cloakless. He had committed his way to Jesus regardless of the consequences. For the rest of his life, Luther lived under pressure, on the run, awaiting trial, and being hidden and protected by his friends. He was public enemy number one. He was accused and threatened at every turn. In two years, it will have been *five hundred years* since Luther, like Bartimaeus, cast aside his cloak and followed after Jesus in a way that he had not done before.

We can't skip over these details in the story that Mark provides us. The place was Jericho. There is the easily-skimmed-over fact that Bartimaeus threw aside his cloak. Then the third thing that we *cannot* miss is this question that Jesus asked the blind man. As verse 51 says, when they called Bartimaeus and they brought him to Jesus: "What do you want me to do for you?" Does that sound familiar? Just last week in the previous passage from the Gospel of Mark, two of the disciples of Jesus came to him and wanted him to do for them "whatever they ask" and Jesus asked in verse 36, "What do you want me to do for you?" *The exact same question.* Remember the answer from last week? The disciples wanted position and power, but Bartimaeus wants to see. We should always understand that as more than just physically being able to see or all the parts of the eye working correctly. We should recognize that this is about seeing and understanding the mission and purpose of Jesus. Bartimaeus sees Jesus' mission more clearly than his own disciples.

In the next chapter, Jesus will enter Jerusalem to be betrayed, arrested, tried, mocked, and crucified. What will the disciples see and understand in this series of events? What do *you* see? Is this the defeat of God's plan? Is this the unjust, unfair, all-that's-wrong-with-the-world victory of violence and death? Is *that* what the disciples see? Or, is sighted Bartimaeus seeing the revelation of the sacrificial, abundant, never-ending love of God in Christ? Does Bartimaeus see what so many others miss? Do you and I see that God's ways are not our ways and that this inbreaking kingdom is defined by surrender, brokenness, and self-giving love? Does the Church see that victory is won through death? Do we see that God's triumph is through a tool of execution? Who would have dreamed of such a thing?

Ernest Shurtleff wrote several songs and hymns, but only one has endured. Interestingly, he was born during the Civil War and died during World War I. In between he went to college and seminary and served as a pastor. It was at his seminary graduation that he wrote his famous song as a

236   SECTION 5: POST-PENTECOST NON-FESTIVAL TIME BEFORE ADVENT

gift to his fellow students, "Lead On, O King Eternal." The verse that captures my attention today is the one that says. "Lead on, O King Eternal, till sin's fierce war shall cease and holiness shall whisper the sweet amen of peace. For not with swords' loud clashing, nor roll of stirring drums; with deeds of *love and mercy*, the heav'nly kingdom comes."[5]

It is to this upside-down, counter-intuitive, mysterious kingdom that you and I are called. To see it, our blindness must be healed, our cloaks of safety and security must be cast aside, and, of course, our walls of isolation, hostility, and idolatry must tumble to the ground like the walls of Jericho. Jesus asks, "What do you want me to do for you?" Today, we respond, "Lord Jesus, help us see that, as we share the bread and the cup, your kingdom has come and is coming among us. Help us see that in your death at the cross, the measure of God's love has been revealed to us. Help us see that in the resurrection of Christ, all things are made new and our lives can be lived for the good of our neighbors and for the glory of God. Help us taste and *see* that the Lord is good."[6]

Amen.

5. Shurtleff, "Lead On," emphasis added.
6. Allusion to Ps 34:8.

SERMON 48[1]

Navigating the 613[2]

Mark 12:28–34

In two days, the citizens—or some percentage of the citizens of this nation of voting age—will elect a president who will serve us for the next four years. Some of you have already voted. Others will go to the ballot box on Tuesday and, hopefully, by Tuesday night it will be decided. I was living in Florida in November 2000 so I'm very familiar with the possibility that it may not be concluded by Tuesday night. Regardless, one of the things that always seems to surface in political campaigns and election cycles is this: "Who has the 'big ideas'? Who is the candidate of 'big ideas' and 'big solutions'?" I thought about "big ideas" as I read and studied another passage from the Gospel of Mark. I invite you to turn to Mark 12.

Mark 12:28–34

613. Is that a busy interstate loop around some major American city? No. 613. Is that the number of political mailings that you've received in the last two months? Probably not. The number's got to be *more* than that. 613. Maybe that's how many political commercials you've watched or how many delegates are part of the electoral college? 6–1–3. Is that the area code from some place where I've lived? What is it? 613. *That's* the number of individual statutes that Jews counted in the first century in the Law of God. *613*. Who can remember them, much less follow them? Surely, there must be some that are more important than others. There must be some that are heavy and some that are light.

---

1. Preached at First Church of the Nazarene in Kansas City, Missouri on November 4, 2012 (Twenty-fourth Sunday after Pentecost; Year B).

2. The power of the sermon, I surmise, was in the simple idea of love as *action*, rather than just a feeling.

A teacher of the law in Mark 12 came to Jesus and wanted to know his answer for how to understand or how to navigate the 613. This wasn't the first time that Jesus had faced difficult questions. In fact, in chapter 11 and into chapter 12 of Mark, there is a sequence of religious leaders who come to Jesus with tricky and sticky questions about a whole host of issues. They start in Mark 11:28. The chief priest and teachers of the law want to know, "By what authority are you doing these things?" Jesus had just made his entry into Jerusalem. All kinds of people were shouting and saying things that set the ears of the religious leaders on edge. Then Jesus curses a fig tree and cleanses the temple and they want to know, "Who gives you the authority to do all this?" He wouldn't answer them directly which probably got under their skin. So, the next thing you know, here come some Pharisees and Herodians who try to "catch him in his words," as 12:13 says. Isn't it interesting that the trickiest, most difficult, and sneakiest question that they can come up with revolves around taxes? "Is it right to pay the imperial tax to Caesar or not?"[3] The Scripture says that Jesus' answer "amazed" them. Somehow Jesus was able to slip out of this tangled net in which they were trying to capture him. In the very next verse, here come some Sadducees—*another* group of religious leaders in the community—and now they want to question him. "If the question about taxes didn't 'stump' him, then we'll get him on marriage in the afterlife. We'll create this hypothetical situation that can't be answered." But again and somehow, Jesus fended it off.

Some of you may remember a movie from a few years ago where Anthony Hopkins plays Zorro. A young protégé of Zorro's wants revenge on someone who has hurt him and his family. Zorro decides to *teach* him the art of sword fighting even though his student doesn't think there's anything for him to learn. In one scene, the student runs at Zorro with his sword swinging wildly and with a little flick of his wrist, Zorro escapes. He lunges at him again and with a subtle, little move, Zorro escapes again. Over and over again, the scene repeats itself. Similarly, Jesus is taking all comers, and with a flick here, a clever answer there, and a subtle move, Jesus deflects or answers all these sticky questions. At the end of this long line of questioners comes the teacher of the law in our passage for today. He asks, "Of *all* the commandments"—not just the Ten, but the 613—"which is the most important?"

This question was not uncommon, but it *was* important. It was a question that other teachers had been asked and had tried to answer. It's possible that this teacher of the law had been a student of a rabbi named Hillel, the Elder. Rabbi Hillel had died about fifteen years before—about

3. Mark 12:14.

10 AD—and he had been asked a similar question. Someone had asked him, "Rabbi Hillel, teach me the whole Law while I stand on one foot." I guess that he *could* have said, "You better be able to stand on one foot for a long time." But, that's not what he did. He simply said, "What is hateful to you, do *not* to your neighbor."[4]

It's kind of a golden rule, but cast in a negative way. It's like the other side of the coin which says, "Whatever you would have done to *you*, do that." Maybe *all* teachers—*all* rabbis—had to answer this kind of question in a context where there were 613 individual statues. When Jesus was faced with it, he pointed to the Scripture. By his answer, he referenced two key portions of what we call the Old Testament or the Hebrew Scriptures. He started by referring to the "Shema"—Deuteronomy 6:4—"Hear, O Israel: the Lord our God, the Lord is one. Love the Lord with *everything!*"[5] This portion of Scripture was quoted *twice* a day by faithful Jews every single day. It was what they said in the morning. It was what they said in the evening. For thousands of years, it is what faithful, religious Jews have said and confessed at the beginning of every synagogue service: "The Lord is one. Love him with your heart, soul, mind, and strength." But then, Jesus quickly adds a verse from Leviticus 19 and says, "Love your neighbor as yourself."[6]

I thought the guy wanted *one* answer. He asked, "What is the most important," right? So, is Jesus' answer *one* or *two*? Is love for God the same as love for neighbor and is love for neighbor the same as love for God? Or, does love for God serve like an umbrella over love for neighbor? Or, is the key *love* which expresses itself in two directions—to God and to neighbor? From Mark 12, what we can conclude is that the one who asked the question of Jesus is pleased or satisfied with Jesus' answer. In fact, he *repeats* Jesus answer in Mark's version of the story and declares Jesus to be "right" in his answer: "You are right," he says.

I don't know if what was happening in the temple courts caught his imagination, whether he could smell the smells, hear the vendors selling animals for sacrifice, or what exactly it was, but the teacher of the law says: "Loving God and loving your neighbor is *more important than all burnt offerings and sacrifices!*"[7]

The first readers of Mark's Gospel were probably people who didn't or couldn't participate in the sacrificing of animals in the temple. They weren't there. The temple in Jerusalem wasn't there or there were any other number

4. Williamson, Jr., *Mark*, 226, emphasis added.

5. My paraphrase.

6. Lev 19:18.

7. Mark 12:33, emphasis added.

240   SECTION 5: POST-PENTECOST NON-FESTIVAL TIME BEFORE ADVENT

of problems, but loving *God* and loving their neighbor was something that they *could* do. It's also something that we can do through the power of God's Spirit within us. But we must understand that it's not just something we *feel* or something we *think* about, but it's something that we *do*. Love takes action. It expresses itself. It finds an outlet—a way of loving.

On this Sunday, when we have emphasized or drawn your attention to the needs of orphans and widows in our world,[8] we do so as a way of saying, "Here's a way to love. Here's a way to do something. Here's a way of being like God because this is what God does." In Deuteronomy, this is how God is described: "The Lord your God shows no partiality and accepts no bribes. He *defends* the cause of the fatherless and the widow, and loves the foreigner residing among you."[9] In Psalm 146: "The Lord *watches over* the foreigner and *sustains* the fatherless and the widow."[10] God doesn't just feel for them and think about them, but he *does* something. He *defends* and *sustains*. These are expressions. These are *actions* of love.

Helen Simmons was eight years old. Her brother, Brandon, was five. Several years ago, on a Saturday, their Dad took them to the mall in Hattiesburg, Mississippi. When they pulled into the parking lot, the kids saw a big truck sitting there with a sign on the side of it that said, "Petting Zoo." "Can we go, Daddy? *Please*." We wouldn't do this with our kids today, but back then and there it was accepted and a common practice. Dad flipped each of them a quarter and said, "I'll meet you back at the car. I'm going to run into Sears for something."

You've been to a petting zoo, right? It's made of some portable fence, some chicken wire, and a little bit of hay thrown down on the parking lot. In the middle of the enclosure, there are a couple of little goats, a duck or two, and maybe a baby pig—if you're lucky. Dave, the dad, says that just a couple of minutes later, he turned around and there's Helen, his eight year old, walking right behind him in Sears. He thought: "Surely she didn't prefer a hardware store to a petting zoo?"

"What's up?" he said. She looked up at her dad and said, "Well, the zoo cost fifty cents. So I gave Brandon my quarter." Then, Dave Simmons says that his little girl said the most beautiful thing that he has ever heard. He said that she repeated to him the family motto. It was something that she had heard said around the house. It was something that Mom and Dad had tried to teach her in those moments of opportunity that would spring up

---

8. The local congregation was encouraged by the district and the denomination to emphasize ministry to orphans and other vulnerable people on this particular Sunday of the year.

9. Deut 10:18, emphasis added.

10. Ps 146:9, emphasis added.

throughout the day. Now it was apparent that she had learned and absorbed it. She had taken it in and she had begun to make it a part of how she lived. He took a few minutes and found the saw blade or the hammer or whatever it was he had gone to Sears to get. Then he and Helen walked back through the parking lot and out to the portable fence of the petting zoo. They stood there while Brandon chased the goats and antagonized a sheep or two. They watched while he kicked up the saw dust. Dave Simmons tells this story and he says, "Helen, my little girl, stood there with her hands and chin resting on the fence and just watched her little brother." He confesses: "I had fifty cents burning a hole in my pocket. But I never offered it to her and she never asked for it because she *knew*—like she had just told me moments ago in the Sears store in Hattiesburg—that the family's motto was this: 'love is sacrificial action.' I didn't want her to lose the lesson that love pays a price. Sacrificial love costs something."[11]

Love *does* something for someone else. The divine pattern of love was revealed to us most clearly in the cross. It was in the death of Jesus *for* us and for our sins that God made a way for our lives and our living to be transformed by his mercy and power. What does a transformed life look like? It looks like a life that receives the grace and love of God and then *shares* it with others—the hurting, the needy, the broken, and the hopeless. It looks like a life that comes to the Table and then goes from the Table into our world to love and serve. In just a moment, we'll come to the Table and then we want to give you the opportunity to go into the corners and sides of the sanctuary to indicate how you can take action and love others—specifically widows and orphans in our congregation and community. After you have received the elements and after you have gone to indicate your willingness to share a part of this ministry effort, you are sent out to enter your world to love God and to love your neighbor.

Amen.

11. Simmons, *Dad,* 123–24.

SERMON 49[1]

Not Out of Obligation[2]

Mark 12:38–44

Next week is our annual Faith Promise weekend with Stephane and Sandra Tibi. If you don't know or haven't met the Tibis, you will not want to miss the opportunities for conversation on Saturday, on Sunday morning, and at the all-church luncheon on Sunday afternoon. I cannot stress enough how pleased we are that the Tibis, who are members of KC First now serving in the French-speaking countries of central and southern Africa, will be with us. Faith Promise is a once-a-year time when we commit, with God's help, to give dollars above and beyond our tithing or regular giving to help fund the work of sharing the gospel around the world. These are dollars that go to fund mission *beyond* this local community. Some can give much. Others may not be able to give as much, but we *all* can commit to giving something *by faith*. So come prepared next week to make your faith promise pledge indicating what you intend to give for this specific purpose over the next year.

The preacher in me wants to point out that this week's passage from the Gospel of Mark is particularly providential since the story revolves around a widow who put in everything or gave a great sacrificial gift to the work of the temple. Who knew when we scheduled our Faith Promise weekend a couple of years ago that *this* would be the lectionary passage for today? Let's look at it together.

---

1. Preached at First Church of the Nazarene in Kansas City, Missouri on November 8, 2015 (Twenty-fifth Sunday after Pentecost; Year B).

2. I chose to leave this locally-specific introduction simply to show how I used it to lead into the scriptural passage. I tried to use a technique of "delay" in the message. I offered a common interpretation and then concluded with, "I don't think that's what this is about." Instead of immediately saying what I thought it was about, I delayed and painted another possible interpretation. This helped maintain interest.

242

NOT OUT OF OBLIGATION

Mark 12:38–44

First of all, we're done a disservice—if your Bible is like mine—by the English translators and the publishers when right after verse 40 they put a break in the text so that they can insert a title for the next story. In mine, they put "The Widow's Offering." Maybe yours has something else. If that is the case, what I want to do is to encourage you to ignore that "break" or interruption in the text and see that these verses are meant to go together. Verses 38–40 are not meant to be separated from verses 41–44. In fact, what happens at the beginning of chapter 13 should not be separated from what happens at the end of chapter 12. There should be no breaks, no titles, and no interruptions. That's a somewhat long and convoluted way of trying to say that these verses must be read in context or in relationship to one another.

Which leads me to say something that I never thought that I would say about this story of the widow's mite or the widow's sacrificial offering: *this* story, as tempting as it is to use in this way, is *not* really a story for a stewardship campaign or a fund-raising effort. In fact, we have to be careful about the assumptions that we bring to the text. We have to be careful that we don't add to the story what isn't there. By that, I mean, Jesus does *not* say—after observing the widow's action—"Go, thou, and do likewise." That's not there. There are some stories where Jesus says something to that effect, but *this* isn't one of them, so we need to be careful about what we add or bring to the story.

The second caution that I would raise is this—and it's something that all of us pay attention to in our daily lives—and it is the issue of *tone.* It's very important the tone in which something is said. When a child responds to a request by their parents to do something and the response is, "I'd be *glad* to, Mom,"[3] that's very different from, "I'd be glad to, Mom."[4] But, how do you get tone out of something that's written on the page? How do you get tone for something that's been written and preserved for almost two thousand years and translated through several languages along the way? It's tough.

What if the tone in which Jesus said what he said about the widow's gift was not a tone of approval or commendation, but rather was a tone of sadness or frustration? What if Jesus said what he said about the teachers of the law and how they "devour widows' houses," and then he watches as a widow puts her last coins into the treasury to support the very work of the teachers of the law and it *bothers* him? Maybe Jesus said that she "put in

---

3. Conveyed with a sense of anger, frustration, or disdain.
4. Conveyed with willingness, delight, and joy.

244   SECTION 5: POST-PENTECOST NON-FESTIVAL TIME BEFORE ADVENT

everything—all she had to live on," and the implication was that she *shouldn't* have done it. How would that change our look at the story?

Like many of you, I've read this story many, many times. I've heard this passage preached by others and I've preached from it myself. I certainly think that there is validity in the view that sees a stark contrast between the external and on-display, pseudo-righteousness of the teachers of the law and the humble, nobody-noticing righteousness of the widow. This kind of contrast shows up in several different places in the New Testament and is consistent with Jesus' ministry where he challenges and condemns the conduct and ways of the religious leaders. They're "white-washed tombs filled with dead men's bones."[5] They "strain out a gnat but swallow a camel."[6] The reality doesn't match the façade and this angers Jesus. It frustrates him. This contrast is evident and clear and it should push us to consider the reality and the integrity of our own spiritual life and walk, but that's not what I think the story is really about.

Another aspect of the story that occasionally gets attention is the fact that Jesus seems to see what others miss or ignore. Apparently, Jesus was very observant. His observation skills were acute and developed. This shows up in all kinds of stories in the New Testament where he sees common things and uses them to teach lessons or to make connections to spiritual and deeper realities. He sees farmers sowing seeds and the condition of the ground in which the seed is sown and this becomes a teaching moment. He sees how women bake bread and how much yeast is necessary and he turns that into a story or parable. Jesus sees the flowing robes of the teachers and it means more than what others observe. He sees the places of honor and the most important seats taken and he knows that there's more to it than what most witness.

Verse 41 says that he "sat down opposite the place where the offerings were put and watched." What did he watch or observe? He watched the crowds. He was able to somehow see who was rich and who was not. He watched what each person did. With lots of people milling around this particular area of the temple grounds, Jesus saw a widow amid all the people. He watched as she brought an offering and put it in the trumpet-like receptacles in the court. Sometimes you will hear this kind of interpretation as a way of assuring people that Jesus sees and knows where you are and what you're going through. Jesus sees what others don't. I believe that to be true and helpful, but it's not what *this* story is about.

5. Paraphrase of Matt 23:27.
6. Matt 23:24.

NOT OUT OF OBLIGATION   245

I do think that when Jesus sees the widow do what she does that what Jesus sees most clearly is a kinship with her. You see, Jesus knows *where* he is and he knows *when* it is. He knows *why* he has come to Jerusalem this one last time. The teachers and religious leaders are circling him like an animal circles its prey. The signs of Roman occupation and oppression are visible at every angle. Jewish pilgrims are gathering in the Holy City fueled by hopes of liberation and deliverance. In this volatile mix, Jesus sees and Jesus knows that very soon *he* will be doing what the widow has done. *He* soon will be putting in everything—all he has to live on. He'll be putting in his *life*.

Now, I do want to draw one very significant distinction in this kinship between Jesus and the widow. In light of the verses that describe the perspective and ways of the teachers of the law, it seems that this widow did what she did under a sense of obligation or pressure. Some might even suggest that there was a measure of manipulation and the piling on of guilt or shame. Although there is a kinship, this is the place where her sacrifice and the sacrifice of Jesus are distinctly different. The whole of Scripture teaches us—and particular portions of Scripture very clearly—that the reason or the motivation for the giving of Jesus' life was *not* obligation but *love*. "For God so *loved* the world that he gave his only Son."[7] This is a portion of the most famous verse in the Gospel of John. But there's another passage in John that also points to this reality. It's not as well known or memorized as often, but it's significant for this point. In John 10, Jesus is in the middle of some teaching where he is repeatedly using the phrase "I am." He says: "I am the gate"[8] for the sheep and "I am the good shepherd."[9] In that passage, Jesus talks about "laying down his life for the sheep" and then he says, "The reason my Father loves me is that I lay down my life—only to take it up again. No one takes it from me, but I lay it down of my own accord."[10] The death of Jesus at the cross is not his obligation—like putting something into the treasury at the temple. No, the death of Jesus at Calvary is the sacrificial, self-giving revelation of God's love towards his wayward world. Hundreds of years of different angles, different perspectives, and competing metaphors of what the atonement means must bow to the over-arching and overwhelming reality that this is *not* a story about obligation or manipulation, but rather a story of God's *love* and *grace*.

Almost three years ago on Valentine's Day, *The Wall Street Journal* ran a story entitled, "How Neuroscience Can Help Us Find True Love." According

7. John 3:16a.
8. John 10:9.
9. John 10:11, 14.
10. John 10:17–18.

to the article, love is just a bunch of chemical reactions in your brain. Here's part of what the article said and I quote:

> Valentine's Day is here so get ready to send and receive heart-shaped chocolates and cards decorated with big red hearts. But wait a minute! Not so fast. Neuroscience has discovered that the heart has very little to do with romance. For accuracy you should send your main squeeze a Valentine's Day card with the image of a squishy gray blob evocative of a rotting cauliflower—the brain—because that's where romance really resides. And instead of saying "I love you," the knowledgeable lover would say, "Darling, dopamine floods my caudate nucleus" every time I look at you.[11]

Other than misunderstanding that "love" and "romance" are the same thing, and other than misunderstanding that the "heart" is simply a symbol for the seat of emotion and affection, neuroscience points to the brain and says, "This is where you find out what love really is." The Scripture on the other hand points to the cross and says, "*This* is God's love revealed and on display. *This* is God's love for all to witness." Today, we point to the cross and to the Table of the Lord where we see, touch, and taste the loving provision of God for us and our lives. Here, we see love. Here we are fed by the presence and power of a gracious and forgiving God. So, come—not out of obligation, pressure, or guilt, but come to be loved, forgiven, and empowered by the grace of our Lord.

Amen.

11. Lowndes, "How Neuroscience."

SERMON 50[1]

Big Stones and Birth Pains[2]

Mark 13:1–8

Today, on this last Sunday of the Christian year, we conclude this series of messages from the Gospel of Mark. Next week—the first Sunday of Advent and therefore, the *first* Sunday of the new Christian year—we will turn our attention to our preparation for Christmas and the coming of the Lord in human flesh into the world. But today, we look to Mark 13.

Mark 13:1–8

I remember the first time that I went to the National Cathedral in Washington, D.C. I had been to the national mall and seen all the monuments. Many of you have been there. The mall with all the monuments is an incredible place. The Washington Monument is impressive. It's tall and straight. It has clean lines and evokes a sense of power and strength. The Jefferson Memorial is beautiful and warm. In the spring, when the cherry blossom trees are in bloom and the water is still next to the Jefferson, there may not be a more beautiful spot. Then, the Lincoln Memorial to me is the most poignant and moving. It's not just an impressive building but it's the portrayal of a man who changed the course of history. After being in D.C. numerous times and taking friends or relatives to see the monuments, the

1. Preached at First Church of the Nazarene in Kansas City, Missouri on November 22, 2015 (Twenty-sixth Sunday after Pentecost; Year B).

2. This sermon was preached in the aftermath of a horrific terrorist attack in Paris, France. It immediately brought back to light the feelings and emotions associated with 9/11. The connection with the "big stones" (signifying indestructibility) of the temple and the World Trade Center towers was in the back of everyone's mind, in my opinion. Simultaneously and not unrelated to Paris, the atmosphere and airwaves were abuzz with the story of displaced persons from Syria and other war-torn places. A feeling of fear was pervasive and needed to be challenged. I waded in.

247

reflecting pool, and the Vietnam Memorial—somewhere along the way—I decided to venture out to other sites. I wanted to see something else and that something else was the National Cathedral.

Have you been there? Words can hardly describe it. It's over a hundred years old and it's been under constant construction during that entire time. They are always adding new carvings. Something is always being restored. They are always making additions to the décor and stained-glass windows. One of the huge windows which is devoted to the glories of creation has a rock from the moon in it. When you walk through the door of the cathedral at the bottom of the cross-shaped sanctuary, it's a *long* way to the top of the cross where the high altar sits. *We* would call it the communion table. From where you enter to there is *six hundred feet*. It's the length of *two* football fields. The Gothic architecture with flying buttresses and high ceilings is unbelievable. The support columns are hard to even describe because they are so huge. It's an incredibly beautiful place. Simultaneously, it is a massive place.

We're enamored with large things like big ships and enormous planes. We love the Big Sky Country of the West. We're impressed by huge churches and large bank accounts. The airwaves are overrun with massive egos. We live in a time and place where "bigger is better" regardless of how you get there. But, this is nothing new. Mark 13 says that Jesus and his disciples were leaving the temple area and one of his disciples—we don't know which one—said, "Jesus. Look at these stones. They're huge. Magnificent." The ancient historian, Josephus, recorded that some of the foundation stones of the temple were thirty-seven feet long, twelve feet high, and eighteen feet wide. Can you imagine?

Jesus responds in a way that blows the disciples' minds. He says, "Not one stone will be left on another." In other words, "This place, this building, and all of this is going to be destroyed one day. It's going to be sooner rather than later because all of this is temporary. It will not stand the test of time." Among a group of disciples who had just recently been arguing about their places in the power structure of the coming kingdom, Jesus wants them to turn their attention from the massive stones, the grandeur of size, and the appearance of substantial things to a faithfulness that suffers, humility that sacrifices, a kingdom where the "first will be last,"[3] and servants are exalted. Jesus wants to re-direct and re-focus their attention.

Sooner than they realized, the servant of all—their teacher—would be exalted onto a Roman tool of execution to suffer and die for the sin and violence of the world. The first hearers or readers of the Gospel of Mark knew *firsthand* the destruction of Jerusalem by the Romans. In 70

3. Mark 10:31.

BIG STONES AND BIRTH PAINS

AD—somewhere around forty years after the death, resurrection and ascension of Jesus—his followers smelled the burning embers and saw the broken down walls of the temple and much of the city. Things would never be the same again. Buildings that were thought to be indestructible proved otherwise. We know that feeling, don't we? Recent violence and tragedy in Paris[4] have only reminded us of the huge, massive towers that were destroyed and collapsed in just a matter of a few hours.[5] As a result, life has never been the same since. We feel that so deeply in these days. We're reminded of the frailty and the fragility of our world and of our own lives, aren't we? This is what "apocalyptic literature" looks like, and this section of Mark falls into that category. It is born in times of pain and conflict, but it always dreams of something better and new. Later in the passage, Jesus says that it's like "birth pains."

How so? Now, some of you have been through that process directly and viscerally. The males in the room who are fathers have been through it, but not in the same way or with the same intensity and sacrifice. How's *that* for a disclaimer? But if Jesus, a male, could talk about it and make a comparison with it, then I guess it's OK for us to do the same. What is it about "birth pains" that is helpful to illuminate or illustrate what Jesus is talking about?

I think the essence is this: when you're expecting a baby, there is anticipation and excitement. There is hope. When the labor begins, there is this strange and intense mixture of hope and pain. There is a combination of excitement and fear. The disciples of Jesus were living in a frightening, dangerous, and violent time. As Jesus said, there would be "kingdoms against kingdoms" and "nations against nations" (Matt 24:7). As they sat on the Mount of Olives and looked across at the temple and the city of Jerusalem, it didn't take them long to see the signs of domination, oppression, and displays of power by the Roman Empire. Shields were glistening in the sun. The feet of soldiers were pounding on the stone. Spears were pointed toward the sky. In a matter of days, Jesus would experience all that the power and violence of Rome had to offer. Yet somehow—mysteriously and miraculously—God turned the tables. God flipped the script and the death of Jesus became the revelation and display of God's love and victory *over* death. Resurrection is exoneration. Resurrection is affirmation. Victory was at the cross. Death is defeated by death.

---

4. A series of coordinated terrorist attacks occurred in Paris on November 13, 2015 in which more than one hundred people were killed and hundreds more injured.

5. This reference to the World Trade Center tragedy on September 11, 2001 needed no explanation.

250   SECTION 5: POST-PENTECOST NON-FESTIVAL TIME BEFORE ADVENT

We are living in the "birth pains." I think the question or the challenge that we face in light of the cross and Auschwitz, Hiroshima, Vietnam, Beirut, 9/11, Paris and any other number of evil and tragic events and places is this: will we live during the "birth pains" with hope and love or with fear and vengeance? The apostle Paul lived in the "birth pains" of the first century. He had been on the giving end of punishment, torture, and death. Before Jesus invaded his life, some people in his world weren't worthy to live, especially if they challenged his own position or thought. The first martyr for the faith, Stephen, was a casualty of Paul's[6] venom. But after Jesus jerked him out of his bubble on the road to Damascus, for the rest of Paul's life, he was on the receiving end of pain, imprisonment, and beatings at the hands of the Romans and others. He knew *both* ends of the stick, you might say. He knew what it was to throw the stone and he knew what it was to catch one off the side of his head. He knew what it was to be left for dead in his own pool of blood. Paul knew the tension of living in the "birth pains" as the kingdom of Jesus was coming, establishing enclaves of followers, and yet, not taking full control. Paul knew the tension. He knew the in-betweenness of it all. He lived in the pain of the present with hope of the new thing that would emerge—the new thing that was on the way. In Philippians, Paul gives voice to that tension. He wrote to the church: "For to me, to live is Christ and to die is gain. . . Yet what shall I choose? I do not know. I am torn between the two. I desire to depart and be with Christ which is better by far, but it is more necessary for you that I remain in the body."[7]

You and I are also living in the "birth pains." We live in a time of violence and fear. We're surrounded by desperation and anxiety. It's an awful feeling. But the good news is that something new is coming. To extend the analogy: as we prepare to enter into the Advent season, something new" is coming. Yes, a baby will be born. Those of you who are parents have watched this happen or experienced it firsthand. The birthing process is difficult, painful, and tense, but when they place that child into the arms of his or her mother, things change dramatically. Immediately, there is joy and peace, but most of all there is *love*. In the "birth pains" surrounded by fear, anxiety, and stress, can you and I live with joy and compassion for each other and for our neighbors, near and far? Can we? The burning question of these recent days is what about the *four million* Syrian refugees?[8] What should the world do? What should the U.S. do? What role

6. I did not take the time to distinguish between Saul/Paul and his change of names.

7. Phil 1:21, 23–24.

8. Jones and Shaheen, "Syrian Refugees."

BIG STONES AND BIRTH PAINS

should the individual states within the U.S. play? What should the Church do? What should *we* do?

I wish that what I want to say would clear up any and all confusion in the news, on Facebook, and in the Twitter-verse, but it won't. I *do* know that in the middle of "birth pains," it's easier to give free reign to fear than it is to move forward with love. It is *not* our natural response to lead with love. That requires the invading, filling presence of God's Spirit to help us live and respond in ways that are not easy or habitual. So, as we do so often, we gather at the Lord's Table because it is a foretaste of the glorious new thing that is coming. We come seeking to be touched by and filled with the Spirit of the Living God so that we might live in the world as people of love and grace rather than people of fear and anxiousness. As the Scripture says, "Perfect loves casts out fear."[9] So we pray, "O Lord, may it be so *in us*. As we give thanks around this Table for the love that you have revealed to us in Christ at the cross, may your love flow through us for each other and for every person in the world. Feed and fill us with your presence, O Lord, so that we may share your compassion with each other, with orphans, with widows, with refugees, and with the least of these in whom we see the face of your Son, Jesus."

Amen.

9. 1 John 4:18.

Bibliography

Achtemeier, Elizabeth. *Preaching as Theology and Art*. Nashville: Abingdon, 1984.

Allen, Ronald J., ed. *Patterns of Preaching: A Sermon Sampler*. St. Louis: Chalice, 1998.

Asimakoupoulos, Greg. "Jesus Is Missing." *Christian Parenting Today* (Nov/Dec 2001).

Augustine. *The Confessions of St. Augustine*. Translated by Rex Warner. New York: Mentor, 1963.

Bailie, Gil. *The Famished Craving: The Attention of Others, the Fascination for the Famous and the Need for Faith*. Minutes of the Meeting; Keeping Faith and Breaking Ground. Read by Gil Bailie. Sonoma, CA: Florilegia Institute, 1995.

Barclay, William. *The Daily Study Bible Series: The Gospel of Matthew, Volume I*. Philadelphia: Westminster, 1975.

Barnes, Brooks, "*Star Wars: The Force Awakens* Breaks Box Office Records," *The New York Times*, December 20, 2015.

Berton, Elena, "State of Paris Streets That's Inspired Its Very Own 'Syndrome,'" *Wall Street Journal*, September 17, 2015.

Bonhoeffer, Dietrich. *The Cost of Discipleship*. New York: Macmillan, 1963.

Brooks, David, "The Moral Bucket List," *The New York Times*, April 11, 2015.

Buechner, Frederick. "Easter." *Blog* (blog), *Frederick Buechner*, October 22, 2016, http://www.frederickbuechner.com/quote-of-the-day/2016/10/22/easter.

Burghardt, Walter J. *Lovely in Eyes Not His: Homilies for an Imaging of Christ*. New York: Paulist, 1988.

———. *Preaching: The Art and the Craft*. New York: Paulist, 1987.

Bush, George W. *41: A Portrait of My Father*. New York: Crown, 2014.

Buttrick, David. *The Mystery and the Passion: A Homiletic Reading of the Gospel Traditions*. Minneapolis: Fortress, 1992.

Calvin, John. *Institutes of the Christian Religion: The Library of Christian Classics*. Philadelphia: Westminster, 1960.

CBS/AP, "Water Crisis in Flint Declared Public Health Emergency," *News* (blog), *CBS News*, October 2, 2015, https://www.cbsnews.com/news/water-crisis-in-flint-michigan-declared-public-health-emergency/.

Christian History editors, "Did You Know?: Our 25 writings 'by the numbers,'" *Christian History*, 2015, https://christianhistoryinstitute.org/magazine/article/did-you-know-great-writings.

Collins, Francis S. *The Language of God: A Scientist Presents Evidence for Belief*. New York: Free, 2006.

BIBLIOGRAPHY

Cook, Blake, "Some Pelicans Mistaking Asphalt for Lakes," *Associated Press*, July 10, 2004.

Cowper, William. "There is a Fountain." In *Sing to the Lord Hymnal*, edited by Ken Bible, #255. Kansas City: Lillenas, 1993.

Craddock, Fred B. *Preaching*. Nashville: Abingdon, 1985.

Desmond-Harris, Jenee, "How to Make Sense of Rachel Dolezal, the NAACP Official Accused of Passing for Black," *Vox*, June 12, 2015.

Dillard, Annie. *Pilgrim at Tinker Creek*. New York: HarperCollins, 1974.

Dunham, Maxie. "The Personal Holiness of the Messenger." In *The Pastor's Guide to Effective Preaching*, 19–32. Kansas City: Beacon, 2003.

Dunning, H. Ray. *Grace, Faith, and Holiness: A Wesleyan Systematic Theology*. Kansas City: Beacon Hill, 1988.

Egan, Timothy. *The Worst Hard Time: The Untold Story of Those Who Survived the Great American Dust Bowl*. New York: Houghton Mifflin, 2006.

Faber, Frederick. "There's a Wideness in God's Mercy." *Sing to the Lord Hymnal*, edited by Ken Bible, #81. Kansas City: Lillenas, 1993.

Fanny, music and lyrics by Harold Rome, dir. Joshua Logan, chor. Helen Tamers, Majestic Theatre, New York, NY, November 4, 1954.

Farmers' Almanac Staff, "The Happy Birthday Song: The Most Sung Song in History," *Blog* (blog), *Farmers' Almanac*, January 1, 2018, https://www.farmersalmanac.com/most-sung-song-in-history-29329.

Faulkner, William. *The Town*. New York: Vintage, 1961.

"Former Atheist Antony Flew Sees God's Design." *Sermon Illustrations* (blog), *Preaching Today*, May 9, 2011, https://www.preachingtoday.com/illustrations/2011/may/2050911.html.

Frankel, Glenn, "British Notables Take Their Leave as Parliament Ends Its Session," *The Washington Post*, March 17, 1992.

Galli, Mark, and Ted Olsen, eds. *131 Christians Everyone Should Know*. Nashville: Broadman, 2000.

Gervais, Ricky, "A Holiday Message from Ricky Gervais: Why I'm an Atheist," *The Wall Street Journal*, December 19, 2010.

Giberson, Karl W., and Francis Collins. *The Language of Science and Faith: Straight Answers to Genuine Questions*. Downers Grove, IL: InterVarsity, 2011.

Gibson, Megan, "Cars, Breasts and Homes: Why America Likes Big," *Time*, November 8, 2010.

Gladwell, Malcom. *The Tipping Point: How Little Things Can Make a Big Difference*. Boston: Little Brown, 2000.

Gori, Graham, "Thrills on the Highway of Death," *Associated Press*, November 24, 2002.

Greer, Peter, and Chris Horst. *Mission Drift: The Unspoken Crisis Facing Leaders, Charities, and Churches*. Bloomington: Bethany House, 2014.

Grimes, William, "The Man Who Rendered Jesus for the Age of Duplication," *The New York Times*, October 12, 1994.

Grynbaum, Michael M, "New York Plans to Ban Sale of Big Sizes of Sugary Drinks," *The New York Times*, May 30, 2012.

Guelich, Robert A. *Mark 1-8:26*. Word Biblical Commentary, vol. 34A. Dallas: Word Books, 1989.

Hall, Elvina. "Jesus Paid it All." *Sing to the Lord Hymnal*, edited by Ken Bible, #218. Kansas City: Lillenas, 1993.

BIBLIOGRAPHY

Hauerwas, Stanley. *Without Apology: Sermons for Christ's Church*. New York: Seabury, 2013.

Hildebrandt, Franz, ed. *Wesley Hymnbook*. Kansas City: Lillenas, 1963.

Hirsch, Alan. *The Forgotten Ways: Reactivating the Missional Church*. Grand Rapids: Brazos, 2006.

Hoffman, Elisha. "Are You Washed in the Blood?" *Sing to the Lord Hymnal*, edited by Ken Bible, #328. Kansas City: Lillenas, 1993.

Holmes, Oliver, "Boy Trips in Museum and Punches Hole in Painting," *The Guardian*, August 25, 2015.

Honor Books. *God's Little Devotional Book*. Tulsa, OK: Honor Books, 1995.

Hussey, Jennie E. "Lead Me to Calvary." *Sing to the Lord Hymnal*, edited by Ken Bible, #232. Kansas City: Lillenas, 1993.

Jones, Sam and Kareem Shaheen, "Syrian Refugees: Four Million People Forced to Flee as Crisis Deepens," *The Guardian*, July 9, 2015.

Keller, Tim. *Counterfeit Gods: The Empty Promises of Money, Sex, and Power and the Only Hope That Matters*. New York: Penguin, 2009.

Kenneally, Christine, "How to Fix 911," *Time*, April 17, 2011.

Klein, Ralph W. *Israel in Exile: A Theological Interpretation*. Mifflintown, PA: Sigler, 2000.

Lamott, Anne. *Help, Thanks, Wow: The Three Essential Prayers*. New York: Penguin, 2012.

Lewis, C.S. *Mere Christianity*. New York: HarperCollins, 2003

Lose, David. "Hoping for More." *Craft of Preaching* (blog), *Dear Working Preacher*, December 2, 2013, https://www.workingpreacher.org/craft.aspx?post=2901.

———. "If It's Not Hard to Believe, You're Probably Not Paying Attention!" *Craft of Preaching* (blog), *Dear Working Preacher*, March 24, 2013, https://www.workingpreacher.org/craft.aspx?post=2498.

Lowndes, Leil, "How Neuroscience Can Help Us Find True Love," *The Wall Street Journal*, February 14, 2013.

Lowry, Eugene L. *The Homiletical Plot: The Sermon as Narrative Art Form*. Atlanta: John Knox, 1980.

Lucado, Max. "The Touch of Christ." *Sermons* (blog), *Preaching Today*, August 2005, https://www.preachingtoday.com/sermons/sermons/2005/august/197.html.

Luther, Martin. *The Freedom of a Christian*. Translated by Mark D. Tranvik. Minneapolis: Fortress, 2008.

Manual of the Church of the Nazarene (2013-17). (Kansas City: Nazarene Publishing House, 2013).

Mariah Carey and Whitney Houston, vocalists, "When You Believe," by Stephen Schwartz, track 1 on *The Prince of Egypt* soundtrack, DreamWorks Records, 1998.

McKenzie, Alyce. "Advice on How Not to Prepare: Reflections on Advent 2, Matthew 3:1-12." *Progressive Christian* (blog), *patheos*, December 2, 2013, https://www.patheos.com/progressive-christian/advice-how-not-prepare-alyce-mckenzie-12-03-2013.

Meyers, Robin R. *With Ears to Hear: Preaching as Self-Persuasion*. Cleveland: Pilgrim, 1993.

Moltmann, Jurgen. *Theology of Hope: On the Ground and the Implications of a Christian Eschatology*. Minneapolis: Fortress, 1993.

Mote, Edward. "The Solid Rock." *Sing to the Lord Hymnal*, edited by Ken Bible, #436. Kansas City: Lillenas, 1993.

BIBLIOGRAPHY

Mumma, Howard, "Conversations with Camus: A Minister and a Seeker," *Christian Century,* June 7, 2000.

Newsweek Staff, "A Life in Books: Garrison Keillor," *Newsweek,* December 15, 2007.

Niebuhr, H. Richard. *The Kingdom of God in America.* Middletown: Wesleyan University, 1988.

Okura, Lynn,"The Real Voices Behind Milli Vanilli Share Their Side of the Lip Syncing Scandal," *OWN* (blog), *HUFFPOST,* February 27, 2014, https://www.huffingtonpost.com/2014/02/27/milli-vanilli_n_4860222.html.

"Ol' Man River," *Show Boat,* music by Jerome Kern, lyrics by Oscar Hammerstein II, 1927.

Olsen, Ted, "There's Still Power in the Blood," *Views* (blog), *CT,* March 31, 2015, https://www.christianitytoday.com/ct/2015/april/theres-still-power-in-blood-of-christ.html.

Ortberg, John. "Anonymous Donor Pays Off Students' Debts." *Sermon Illustrations* (blog), *Preaching Today,* April 2010, https://www.preachingtoday.com/illustrations/2010/april/1041910.html.

————. *The Life You've Always Wanted: Spiritual Disciplines for Ordinary People.* Grand Rapids: Zondervan, 1997.

Osbeck, Kenneth W. *Amazing Grace: 366 Inspiring Hymn Stories for Daily Devotions.* Grand Rapids: Kregel, 1990.

Otto, Rudolph. *The Idea of the Holy.* Translated by John W. Harvey. Oxford: Oxford, 1923.

Payne, Claude, *Reclaiming the Great Commission: A Practical Model for Transforming Denominations and Congregations.* San Francisco: Jossey-Bass, 2000.

Peterson, Eugene. *The Message: The Bible in Contemporary Language.* Colorado Springs: NavPress, 2002.

Porter, Eleanor H. *Pollyanna.* New York: L.C. Page, 1913.

Postman, Neil. *Amusing Ourselves to Death: Public Discourse in the Age of Show Business.* New York: Penguin, 1985.

Ray, Bill, "Doomsday Clock Moved Ahead Two Minutes," *The Arizona Republic,* January 18, 2007.

Seuss, Dr. *How the Grinch Stole Christmas.* New York: Random House, 1957.

Shurtleff, Ernest. "Lead On, O King Eternal." *Sing to the Lord Hymnal,* edited by Ken Bible, #641. Kansas City: Lillenas, 1993.

Simmons, Dave. *Dad the Family Coach: How to Build Teamwork and Team Spirit at Home.* Colorado Springs: Victor, 1991.

Smith, Gordon T. *Called to Be Saints: An Invitation to Christian Maturity.* Downers Grove, IL: InterVarsity, 2014.

Stolberg, Sheryl Gay, Jad Mouawad, and Emma G. Fitzsimmons, "Amtrak Train Derailed Going 106 M.P.H. on Sharp Curve; at Least 7 Killed," *The New York Times,* May 13, 2015.

Sweet, Leonard. *Nudge: Awakening Each Other to the God Who's Already There.* Colorado Springs: David C. Cook, 2010.

"The Westminster Shorter Catechism." *Confessional Standards* (blog), *The Westminster Presbyterian,* http://westminsterconfession.org/confessional-standards/the-westminster-shorter-catechism.php.

Thompson, Francis, "The Hound of Heaven," https://www.poemhunter.com/poem/the-hound-of-heaven/.

BIBLIOGRAPHY

Tolstoy, Leo. *Anna Karenina: A Novel in Eight Parts.* Translated by Richard Pevear and Larissa Volokhonsky. New York: Penguin, 2002.

Tribune Wire reports, "Josh Duggar Admits to Cheating on His Wife After Ashley Madison Hack," *Chicago Tribune,* August 20, 2015.

Troeger, Thomas. *Sermon Sparks: 122 Ideas to Ignite Your Preaching.* Nashville: Abingdon, 2011.

Watling, Marlin. *The Marriage of Heaven and Earth: 50 Pictures to Explain the Rockstar Theologian of Our Day.* Sandhausen, Germany: CreateSpace, 2016.

Wesley, Charles. "And Can It Be?" *Sing to the Lord Hymnal,* edited by Ken Bible, #225. Kansas City: Lillenas, 1993.

Wesley, John. "Catholic Spirit." In *The Works of John Wesley,* vol. 2, edited by Albert Outler, 81–95. Nashville: Abingdon, 1985.

———. *The Works of John Wesley,* vol. 1. Third edition. Edited by Thomas Jackson. Kansas City: Beacon Hill, 1986.

Whitaker, Todd, and Dale Lumpa. *Great Quotes for Great Educators.* New York: Routledge, 2013.

Willard, Dallas, ed. *A Place for Truth: Leading Thinkers Explore Life's Hardest Questions.* Downers Grove, IL: InterVarsity, 2010.

Williams, Colin W. *John Wesley's Theology Today: A Study of the Wesleyan Tradition in the Light of Current Theological Dialogue.* Nashville: Abingdon, 1960.

Williamson, Jr., Lamar. *Mark: Interpretation, A Bible Commentary for Teaching and Preaching.* Louisville: Westminster John Knox, 1983.

Wilson, Paul Scott. *The Four Pages of the Sermon: A Guide to Biblical Preaching.* Nashville: Abingdon, 1999.